HUMAN RESOURCE MANAGEMENT

'The book chapters interweave relevant contemporary and everyday issues, as well as lively current events from the business world, into the study of HRM. The range of research and inclusion of topics from psychology and social sciences enable students to easily make the link between concepts and theories and their application in HR functions. It is very well written, well-resourced and a great book for teaching!'
— Dr Joseph Eyong, *Lecturer in Organizational Behaviour and Human Resource Management, De Montfort University, UK*

'I really appreciate this textbook's ability to combine a high-level and broad perspective while still focusing in on the most important details. This makes the book suitable for anyone, whether you are studying HRM for the very first time, or you know your way around but are looking to improve.'
— Dr Hannes Leroy, *Assistant Professor of Human Resource Management, Rotterdam School of Management, Erasmus University, Netherlands*

'This is an informative and delightful guide, full of the latest information for students, academics and practitioners alike. It also covers an area that has largely been ignored in other textbooks: HRM analytics.'
— Dr Emmanuel Nkomo, *Lecturer in HRM and Strategic Management, Witwatersrand University, South Africa*

'Carbery and Cross have done an incredible job in putting together a wealth of fundamental topics, latest developments and trends in HR management. Whether you are a student, HR practitioner or business owner, you would find this book a concise and essential reference.'
— Dr Siu Yin (Sally) Cheung, *Assistant Professor, Department of Management, Hong Kong Baptist University, Hong Kong, S.A.R., China*

'This is one of the most exciting HRM texts out at the moment that really does bring to life the realities of the HRM profession and its responsibilities in supporting organizational goals. It is one of the most comprehensive textbooks I've seen, which stands out in achieving the right balance of relevant theory with contemporary HRM in practice. An essential text for future HRM professionals, as well as future business leaders in other disciplines!'
— John Watkins, *Head of Department, Management and HR, Coventry University London, UK*

'This new edition provides an excellent text that succinctly captures the pivotal issues in HRM. The chapters marry the traditional areas of HR practice excellently with more contemporary HR issues (e.g. HR analytics and the relationship between HRM and corporate social responsibility) in an impressive manner. The *Spotlight on Skills* resources, reflection points and review questions spread throughout the chapters, along with the *HRM in the News* briefs, make this an exceptional resource for undergraduate and postgraduate students who seek a solid foundation in the principles of HRM.'
— Dr Anthony McDonnell, *Professor of Human Resource Management, Cork University Business School, University College Cork, Ireland and Editor-in-Chief,* Human Resource Management Journal

SECOND
EDITION

HUMAN RESOURCE MANAGEMENT

EDITED BY

RONAN CARBERY &
CHRISTINE CROSS

 macmillan
international
HIGHER EDUCATION

 RED GLOBE
PRESS

First published 2019 by
RED GLOBE PRESS

Red Globe Press in the UK is an imprint of Springer Nature Limited,
registered in England, company number 785998, of 4 Crinan Street,
London, N1 9XW.

Red Globe Press® is a registered trademark in the United States,
the United Kingdom, Europe and other countries.

ISBN: 978–1–352–00402–1 paperback

This book is printed on paper suitable for recycling and made from fully
managed and sustained forest sources. Logging, pulping and manufacturing
processes are expected to conform to the environmental regulations of the
country of origin.

A catalogue record for this book is available from the British Library.

A catalog record for this book is available from the Library of Congress.

Foreword

Work is central to the wellbeing of individuals and societies. One only has to look at the influence that unemployment has on personal wellbeing and morale, and how high levels of unemployment impact at a societal level, to appreciate the implications of a lack of opportunity to work. How we are managed in the organizations we work for has a profound impact on a major part of our adult lives. However, three things which are impacting significantly on our views of work and on its effect at both an individual and societal level are abundantly clear in the current landscape. Firstly, not only have we moved from a world where individuals spend their entire careers in a single organization, to careers unfolding across multiple organizations, but the very nature of jobs and work is shifting. This is reflected in the increasing prevalence of the so-called 'gig economy', where the number of individual contractors in the labour market continues to rise. Individuals often work for multiple employers and more precarious employment becomes the norm for many. The second issue is the continuing globalization of business and work. Technology is a key enabler of accessing talent regardless of where it is located. This brings significant opportunity in terms of tapping into global expertise, while bringing some risks for local employees in terms of insecurity of employment. The final key theme which is evident is the potential impact of artificial intelligence (AI) on the workplace. While a pessimistic view is that this trend will lead to the erosion of millions of jobs worldwide, a more optimistic one is that AI will remove many mundane tasks from the workplace, free up employees to engage in more strategic and creative tasks and ultimately facilitate greater work–life balance.

We have yet to see how these and other trends play out on the future of work. However, what is clear is that the importance of the human resource (HR) function is unlikely to abate in the future. The HR function plays a central role in our experience of work, as the guardian of organizational culture and the owner of the HR systems and processes which set the parameters of an organization's approach towards its employees. Yet while HR governs many of these systems and processes, it is line managers who ultimately implement them. Managing people is challenging and, as the trends outlined above indicate, the role is constantly in flux. Thus, having a comprehensive and evidence-based understanding of current theory and practice in HR is essential not just for HR practitioners, but for anyone with aspirations to be a line manager.

In the second edition of *Human Resource Management*, Ronan Carbery, Christine Cross and colleagues have managed to provide a succinct but authoritative overview of the topography of the key contemporary issues in HRM. In addition to major areas of practice, such as recruitment and selection, reward, and learning and development, they also introduce important contemporary issues, including HR analytics, corporate social responsibility, and diversity and equality. This volume will be a valuable resource for any student looking to get to grips with the key issues in human resource management.

David Collings
Professor of HRM, Dublin City University, Ireland

Brief contents

1 **Introducing Human Resource Management** 1
Christine Cross and Sarah Kieran

2 **Workforce Planning and Talent Management** 21
Ultan Sherman

3 **Recruitment and Selection** 37
Christine Cross

4 **Employee Engagement, Induction, Turnover and Retention** 59
Colette Darcy, Ashley O'Donoghue and Yanqiao Liu

5 **Managing the Employment Relationship** 79
Michelle O'Sullivan

6 **Diversity and Equality in the Workplace** 99
Juliette MacMahon and Mike O'Brien

7 **Performance Management** 121
Steven Kilroy

8 **Managing Rewards** 139
Maureen Maloney and Alma McCarthy

9 **Learning and Development** 163
David McGuire and Thomas N. Garavan

10 **Career Development** 187
Ronan Carbery and David McKevitt

11 **Human Resource Analytics** 207
Caroline Murphy and Jean McCarthy

12 **Health, Safety and Employee Wellbeing** 221
Ronan Carbery and Robert Lynch

13 **International Human Resource Management** 253
Jonathan Lavelle

14 **Corporate Social Responsibility and Human Resource Management** 273
Colm McLaughlin

Contents

Foreword v
List of figures xii
List of tables xiii
About the editors xiv
About the authors xv
Online resources xix
Tour of the book xx
Chapter features and activities xxii
About the Spotlight on Skills contributors xxx
Skills development xxxiii
Preface and acknowledgements xxxvii
Publisher's acknowledgements xxxviii
Abbreviations xl

1 Introducing Human Resource Management 1

Learning Outcomes 1
Introduction 2
Evolution of HRM as an Organizational Function 3
Industrial Welfare 3
Scientific Management 3
Behavioural Science 4
HRM Today 5
Strategic HRM 6
HRM and the Business Context 6
Features of HRM 7
HRM Policies and Practices 8
Linking HR Practices to Organizational Outcomes 9
Who Benefits from HRM? 10
Structure and Role of the HR Function 11
Roles and Competencies of the HR Practitioner 12
The Role of the Line Manager 13
Theoretical Basis of HRM 14
The Michigan Model of HRM 14
'Universal' Approach to HRM 14
Guest Model of HRM 15
Strategic HRM Contingency Approach 16

Strategic HRM Universalist Approach 17
Summary 20
Chapter Review Questions 20
Further Reading 20
Useful Websites 20

2 Workforce Planning and Talent Management 21

Learning Outcomes 21
Introduction 22
Workforce Planning 22
The Human Resource Planning Cycle 23
Stocktaking 23
Forecasting 24
Develop Action Plans, Implementation and Assessment 25
From Workforce Planning to Talent Management 26
What Exactly is Talent Management? 27
Talent Identification 29
Recruiting Talent 31
Talent Management Strategy 31
Summary 36
Chapter Review Questions 36
Further Reading 36
Useful Websites 36

3 Recruitment and Selection 37

Learning Outcomes 37
Introduction 38
Strategic Recruitment and Selection 38
The Recruitment Process 39
Formal and Informal Recruitment Methods 40
Internal Recruitment 41
External Recruitment 42
E-recruitment 43
International Recruitment 43
Role of Employer Brand in Recruitment 44

CONTENTS

The Job Advert 44
Application Forms and CVs/Résumés 45
Shortlisting Stage 45
Online Screening 46
Making the Selection Decision 46
Range of Employee Selection Methods 47
Selection Interviews 49
Structured and Unstructured Interviews 49
Problems with the Selection Interview 51
Psychometric Testing 52
Personality Profiling 52
Assessment Centres 52
Work Sample Tests 53
Graphology 53
Employment Legislation and the
Selection Process 54
Making the Final Selection Decision 54
Post-offer Stage 54
Summary 57
Chapter Review Questions 57
Further Reading 57
Useful Websites 57

4 Employee Engagement, Induction, Turnover and Retention 59

Learning Outcomes 59
Introduction 60
The Role of HR in Engagement, Induction,
Turnover and Retention 60
Work Engagement 61
Employee Engagement 62
Recruitment and Selection 62
Induction 64
What is Induction? 64
Traditional Ineffective Approach
to Employee Induction 65
A New Perspective on Employee
Induction 66
Onboarding 66
What Works in Terms of Induction? 67
Specific Practices to Enhance the
Socialization Process 68
Line Management Involvement in Induction 70
Employee Turnover 71
The Impact of the External Labour Market
Environment on Turnover Levels 72
Should an Organization Seek to Minimize
its Turnover Levels? 73

What is an Appropriate Turnover Level
for a Business? 73
Costs of Labour Turnover 74
What can Organizations do to Limit the
Impact of High-profile Leavers? 74
Measuring Turnover 76
Summary 78
Chapter Review Questions 78
Further Reading 78
Useful Websites 78

5 Managing the Employment Relationship 79

Learning Outcomes 79
Introduction 80
The Nature of the Employment
Relationship 80
Theoretical Perspectives 81
Actors in the Employment Relationship 82
Employee Representation 82
Employer Organizations 84
Employment Rights 84
The Global Economic Crisis 85
Quality of Jobs 86
The 'Gig Economy' 86
Employee Participation and Voice 89
The Nature of Conflict and its Resolution 90
State Agencies for Conflict Resolution 91
Negotiating Skills for Conflict Resolution 92
Summary 96
Chapter Review Questions 96
Further Reading 96
Useful Websites 96

6 Diversity and Equality in the Workplace 99

Learning Outcomes 99
Introduction 100
What is Diversity? 100
Perspectives on Diversity in the
Organizational Context 100
The Benefits and Challenges of a Diverse
Workforce 102
Equality and Discrimination in the
Workplace and Beyond 103
Why is Equality an Important Issue? 104
Human Capital Explanations of Inequality
in the Workplace 105

CONTENTS

Inequality as a Reflection of Social and Cultural Attitudes and Norms   106
Institutional Explanations of Inequality   106
Geographical Variation and the Combined Effects of Inequality   107
National Initiatives to Foster Equality   108
Legislation and Equality   108
Victimization   110
Exceptions to Equality Legislation   110
Inequality in Action: the Case of the LGBT Workforce   110
A Critique of the Equality/Legislative Approach   113
The Positive Discrimination/Positive Action Debates   114
HRM, the Workplace and Equality   115
Summary   119
Chapter Review Questions   119
Further Reading   119
Useful Websites   119

7   Performance Management   **121**

Learning Outcomes   121
Introduction   122
Enhancing Performance through Performance Management   122
Goal-setting Theory   123
Expectancy Theory   123
Equity Theory   124
Den Hartog, Boselie and Paauwe's Model of Performance Management   124
Enhancing Engagement Through Performance Management   125
Performance Management Schemes used in Organizations   126
Rating   126
Ranking   127
The Critical Incident Technique   127
180-degree Feedback   127
360-degree Feedback   128
Competency-based Assessment   128
The Link between Performance Management and Reward   128
Performance Management Pitfalls   129
The Contrast Effect   130
The First Impression Error and the Recency Effect   130
The Halo Effect   130

The Similar-to-me Effect   131
The Central Tendency Bias   131
The Skewing Bias   131
Attributional Bias   131
Stereotyping   131
Overcoming Performance Management Pitfalls   131
How to Manage Underperformance   133
Summary   137
Chapter Review Questions   137
Further Reading   137
Useful Websites   137

8   Managing Rewards   **139**

Learning Outcomes   139
Introduction   140
Reward System Objectives   140
The Reward Package   140
Direct Pay   141
Forms of Performance-related Pay   142
Indirect Pay (Benefits)   144
Nonfinancial Rewards   146
Pay Secrecy   147
Gender and Ethnicity Pay Gaps   148
Determining the Relative Value of Jobs   148
Internal Alignment   148
Non-analytical Methods of Job Evaluation   149
Analytical Methods of Job Evaluation   151
Environmental Factors   152
External Comparisons   154
Determining Competitive Markets   154
Information Sources   155
Pay as a Motivator   156
Summary   162
Chapter Review Questions   162
Further Reading   162
Useful Websites   162

9   Learning and Development   **163**

Learning Outcomes   163
Introduction   164
Key Concepts in Learning and Development   166
How Do People Learn?   168
Cognitivism   168
Behaviourism   168
Experiential Learning   168
Learning Styles   170

CONTENTS

Common Models of Learning and
Development in Organizations 170
   Strategic HRD Model 170
   The Learning Organization Model 172
   The ADDIE Model 173
Exploring the Stages of the ADDIE Model 175
   *Analysis of Learning and Development
   Needs* 175
   Designing Learning and Development 177
   Developing Learning and Development 179
   *Implementation of Learning and
   Development* 179
   *Evaluating Learning and Development
   Activities* 180
Summary 185
Chapter Review Questions 185
Further Reading 185
Useful Websites 185

10   Career Development 187

Learning Outcomes 187
Introduction 188
What is a Career? 188
Traditional Versus Contemporary Career
Perspectives 189
Contemporary Careers 190
   Boundaryless Careers 190
   Protean Careers 191
   Authentic Careers 192
   Kaleidoscope Careers 193
   Off-ramp Careers 193
   Portfolio Careers 195
Graduate Careers 197
Responsibility for Career Development 199
Career Anchor Theory 200
Role of The HRM Function 202
Summary 205
Chapter Review Questions 205
Further Reading 205
Useful Websites 205

11   Human Resource Analytics 207

Learning Outcomes 207
Introduction 208
Defining HR Analytics 208
The Role of HR Analytics in Strategic
Organizational Decision-Making 209

Uses of Data: From Descriptive to
Prescriptive 210
Measurement and Tools 212
   Categorical Variables 212
   Continuous Variables 213
The Internal Consultant: Skill
Requirements for HR Analytics 214
Evidence-based Decision-making:
Analytics in Tandem with Interventions 215
Summary 219
Chapter Review Questions 219
Further Reading 219
Useful Websites 220

12   Health, Safety and Employee Wellbeing 221

Learning Outcomes 221
Introduction 222
Safety Culture 222
Why Accidents Occur 223
   Accidents and Near Misses 224
   Costs of Accidents 225
   Accident Causation Theories 226
Human Factors and Health and Safety 227
   Attitude-based Approach 228
   Behaviour-based Approach 229
Employee Wellbeing 231
   Ergonomics 234
   Job Characteristics 235
   Stress 237
   Job Strain 238
   Bullying 239
   Workaholism 240
   Sickness Absence 241
Employee Wellbeing: Theoretical
Considerations 242
   Mutual Gains 242
   Conflicting Outcomes 242
Key Stakeholders: Where Does the
Responsibility Lie? 243
   The Role of the Employer 243
   The Role of the Employee 244
Health, Safety and Wellbeing and HRM 245
   *Health and Safety Legislative
   Considerations* 248
Summary 251
Chapter Review Questions 251

CONTENTS

Further Reading	251
Useful Websites	251

⑬ International Human Resource Management **253**

Learning Outcomes	253
Introduction	254
International Human Resource Management	254
Globalization and IHRM	258
The Transfer of HRM Practices in MNCs	259
Managing Employees on International Assignments	261
Recruitment and Selection	262
Preparation	263
Adjustment	263
Compensation	264
Performance Management	265
Repatriation	266
Expatriate Failure	267
Alternative International Assignments	268
Summary	271
Chapter Review Questions	271
Further Reading	271
Useful Websites	271

⑭ Corporate Social Responsibility and Human Resource Management **273**

Learning Outcomes	273
Introduction	274
What is Corporate Social Responsibility?	274
Which CSR Issues Should Firms Address?	276
The Controversy of CSR	278
The Shareholder View of the Firm	280
The Stakeholder View of the Firm: the 'Social Contract' Arguments	280
The Stakeholder View of the Firm: the 'Business Case' Arguments	281
The Case Against CSR	284
A Role for Regulation?	288
Summary	291
Chapter Review Questions	291
Further Reading	291
Useful Websites	291
Glossary	293
Bilbliography	300
Index	321

List of figures

1.1 Organizational chart   8
1.2 Employee lifecycle   9
1.3 Linking HR practices to organizational outcomes   10
1.4 HR function   13
1.5 The Michigan model of HRM   15
2.1 The human resource planning cycle   23
2.2 Trend analysis of 'talent management' citations   26
2.3 Potential/performance matrix in talent identification   29
2.4 Analysing the nature of the relationship between performance and the value contributed to the organization   33
3.1 The strategic recruitment and selection process   38
7.1 Example of bell curve distribution for forced ranking   127
8.1 Components and elements of the reward package   141
8.2 Relative value of jobs within an organization   148
8.3 Non-analytical and analytical methods of job evaluation   149
8.4 Example of a paired comparison matrix   150
8.5 Defining the market for employees   155
8.6 Sources of information about pay and benefits   157
9.1 Experiential learning cycle   169
9.2 The ADDIE model   175
12.1 The 1:10:30:600 ratio   225
12.2 The accident cost iceberg   226
12.3 Yerkes-Dodson principle   238
12.4 Employment alignment considerations   243
12.5 SHAPE framework – healthy workplace practices   244
13.1 Factors that influence the transfer of HRM practices   260
13.2 U-shaped curve of cross-cultural adjustment   264
14.1 Carroll's pyramid of CSR   275

List of tables

1.1 Guest model of HRM 16

2.1 Key debates in the literature on talent management 27

3.1 Hair stylist job description 40

3.2 Person specification: hair stylist 40

3.3 Recruitment methods 44

3.4 Example of a shortlisting matrix for a business analyst 45

3.5 Example of an assessment centre day 53

4.1 Example induction schedule for rapid onboarding 69

5.1 Trade union density in selected countries, 1980 and 2014 (%) 83

5.2 Working days lost per 1,000 workers due to strikes and lockouts in selected countries, 1980 and 2015 90

6.1 Sample of factors contributing to labour market inequality 107

6.2 LGBT employment rights: international comparisons 112

7.1 Example of behaviourally anchored rating scale for customer service role 126

8.1 Statutory entitlements in various countries 145

8.2 Advantages and disadvantages of different reward components 146

8.3 Advantages and disadvantages of different job evaluation methods 152

9.1 Characteristic features of the learning organization 173

9.2 Activities engaged in by learning and development specialists during the analysis stage 176

9.3 Learning and development methods: type, characteristics and suitability 180

9.4 Kirkpatrick's four levels of learning and development evaluation: issues and examples 181

10.1 Comparison between traditional careers and contemporary careers 189

10.2 Comparison of contemporary career concepts 196

10.3 Career anchors 201

10.4 Types of career and psychosocial support 201

11.1 Forms of analysis 210

11.2 Sources of data for HR analytics 211

11.3 The five capability enablers for analytical capability 214

12.1 Workplace fatalities (2011–15) 224

12.2 Workplace safety programme guidelines 227

12.3 Categories of human factors 228

12.4 Five domains of wellbeing 232

13.1 Three dimensions of IHRM 255

13.2 Types of employees 256

13.3 Performance criteria for evaluating expatriate performance 266

13.4 Alternative international assignments 268

14.1 ETI Base Code of labour standards 277

About the editors

Dr Ronan Carbery is Senior Lecturer in Management at Cork University Business School, University College Cork (UCC), Ireland. He is co-director of the HR Research Centre in UCC and editor of the *European Journal of Training and Development*. Ronan has co-edited a number of leading international texts, including *Handbook of International HRD: Context, Policy and Practice* (2017), *Organizational Behaviour* (2016), *Human Resource Development: A Concise Introduction* (2015), and *Human Resource Management: A Concise Introduction* (2013).

Dr Christine Cross is Head of the Department of Work and Employment Studies and Senior Lecturer in Organizational Behaviour and Human Resource Management at the Kemmy Business School, University of Limerick (UL), Ireland. Prior to joining UL, she worked for a number of multinational organizations in both management and human resource management roles. This experience has led to a wide range of research, consultancy and publication interests, covering areas such as the 'glass ceiling', the gender pay gap, the lack of women on boards and the workforce experiences of immigrants.

Christine has co-edited a number of leading international texts, including *Organizational Behaviour* (2016), *Human Resource Development: A Concise Introduction* (2015), and *Human Resource Management: A Concise Introduction* (2013).

About the authors

Dr Colette Darcy is Dean of the School of Business at the National College of Ireland. She is a former Government of Ireland Scholar and was awarded the European Foundation for Management Development/ Emerald Outstanding Doctoral Thesis Award for her research examining employee fairness perceptions and claiming behaviour. Her research interests extend to organizational justice, work–life balance and claiming behaviour. She has published in a number of academic journals, including the *European Journal of Industrial Training*, which awarded her the Outstanding Paper Award at the Literati Network Awards for Excellence 2008.

Professor Thomas N. Garavan is Research Professor in Leadership, specializing in leadership development, human resource development and leadership, corporate social responsibility and leadership, and cross-cultural leadership at Edinburgh Napier University. Thomas graduated from the University of Limerick with a Bachelor of Business Studies and completed a Doctorate of Education at the University of Bristol. He is editor of the *European Journal of Training and Development* and associate editor of *Personnel Review*. Thomas is a member of the editorial board of *Human Resource Management Journal*, *Human Resource Development Quarterly*, *Human Resource Development Review*, *Advances in Developing Human Resources* and *Human Resource Development International*. He is the recipient of the Academy of Human Resource Development Outstanding HRD Scholar Award 2013. His research interests include corporate social responsibility and transformational leadership, cross-cultural dimensions of diversity training, tacit knowledge in manufacturing, international human resource management standards and human resource management in multinational corporations.

Dr Sarah Kieran lectures in HRM, strategic HRM and international HRM at the Kemmy Business School, University of Limerick. Prior to joining UL, she worked as a management consultant in strategic and organizational development for a number of multinational organizations. This followed 10 years in the telecoms sector, where she held senior management roles in strategy, CRM and HRM. This experience has led to a wide range of research, consultancy and teaching interests, covering areas such as strategy-as-practice, sensemaking and other discourse-related perspectives on strategy and strategic change. She is also interested in the role of the middle manager, HR analytics, the role of metrics in organizations, the employer value proposition/brand, the HR profession and other such areas which underpin HRM's contribution to organizational performance.

Dr Steven Kilroy is Assistant Professor of Human Resource Studies at Tilburg University. He held previous posts at Dublin City University and Queen's University Belfast. His research interests are at the interface of human resource management and occupational health psychology, focusing on topics such as high performance work practices, leadership, employee wellbeing and performance. In particular, much of his research examines the impact of HR practices on employee wellbeing and performance in the healthcare context. Steven's work appears in outlets including *Human Resource Management* (US), *Human Resource Management Journal*, *European Journal of Work and Organizational Psychology* and the *Journal of Nursing Scholarship*.

ABOUT THE AUTHORS

Dr Jonathan Lavelle is Senior Lecturer in Employment Relations at the Department of Work and Employment Studies, Kemmy Business School, University of Limerick. He is a former postdoctoral fellow with the Irish Research Council for the Humanities and Social Sciences, Government of Ireland Scholar and Marie Curie Scholar. His main research interests are in international and comparative employment relations. He has published in leading international journals, including the *Journal of International Business Studies, Industrial and Labor Relations Review, Human Relations, Human Resource Management, Human Resource Management Journal,* and the *Journal of World Business,* as well as co-authoring a book and a number of book chapters.

Yanqiao Liu lectures and researches in human resource management and performance management in the School of Management at Hebei University. Her research interests include leadership studies, business model innovation, social capital and enterprise performance management, and knowledge management. In the last five years, Yanqiao has published over 10 journal papers, as well as completing ten provincial and departmental research projects. Yanqiao was co-editor of the book *Organizational Behavior* (2015).

Robert Lynch works as a Senior Researcher and EU Project Officer at Cork Institute of Technology, where he also lectures within the National Maritime College of Ireland. He has additionally undertaken several part-time lecturer roles at University College Cork and University of Limerick. His research interests include human resource management, human resource development, marine and transport management, and sport and exercise science. Robert is the holder of the Outstanding Scholar Award for work during his Master's Degree in Human Resource Management at the University of Limerick. Prior to his research career, Robert served in the Defence Forces as a naval officer, where he held various operational, human resource management and learning and development roles.

Dr Juliette MacMahon is Lecturer in Human Resource Management and Industrial Relations at the University of Limerick. She is also a course director. Her research interests include workplace bullying and incivility, workplace climate, zero-hours work, LGBT experiences in the workplace and employment legislation. She has published widely on these topics in academic journals, including *Gender, Work and Organization, Industrial Law Journal, Economic and Industrial Democracy, Employee Relations* and the *Journal of European Industrial Training,* as well as authoring and co-authoring a number of book chapters. She has also worked on a consultancy basis with private and public sector organizations in areas such as performance management, absence management and general employment relations issues.

Maureen Maloney is Management Lecturer at the National University of Ireland, Galway, specializing in HRM, reward management and communications. She is also a part-time PhD student. Her PhD uses a bounded rationality model and investigates the impact of organizational pension communication for defined contribution schemes on employee pension saving behaviour. She is on the executive board of the Pension Policy Research Group (Ireland) and is a member of the European Network for Research on Supplementary Pensions. Maureen's research interests include occupational pension schemes, reward systems and pay communication.

Professor Alma McCarthy is Head of the Department of Management and Professor of Public Sector Management at the National University of Ireland, Galway. Her research interests include human resource development, public sector management and leadership and work–life balance. She has published in peer-reviewed journals, such as the *Public Administration Review, International Journal of Human Resource*

ABOUT THE AUTHORS

Management, Human Resource Management Review, Advances in Developing Human Resources, and the Journal of Managerial Psychology, as well as authoring a range of books and edited books. She recently served as chair of the Irish Academy of Management. She is on the editorial board of *Human Resource Management Journal, Human Resource Development Quarterly, European Journal of Training and Development and the Journal of Managerial Psychology.*

Dr Jean McCarthy is Lecturer in Organizational Behaviour at the Kemmy Business School, University of Limerick. A graduate of the University of Limerick (BBS, 2006; PhD, 2012) and a former Fulbright Scholar at Colorado State University (2012–13), she researches and lectures in the areas of organizational behaviour, human resource development, human resource analytics and research methods within the Department of Work and Employment Studies.

Dr David McGuire is Assistant Head of Department and Reader in Human Resource Development at Glasgow Caledonian University. To date, he has published two textbooks and over 30 journal articles in the fields of HRD, leadership and diversity. David is editor-in-chief *of Industrial and Commercial Training.* He has been the recipient of a number of prestigious research awards, including the Scottish Crucible Award, Fulbright Scholar Award, Government of Ireland Scholarship and a number of Emerald Literati Awards.

Dr David McKevitt currently lectures at University College Cork. He graduated with a PhD from University College Dublin, Smurfit School in 2011 and completed a postdoctoral fellowship in Dublin City University Business School. David's early career research focused on developing competency frameworks for public buyers and examining the role of mentoring relationships in high-potential start-ups. David's current research interest is to better understand the careers of new corporate professions, such as project management and procurement.

Dr Colm McLaughlin is Associate Professor in Human Resource Management and Employment Relations at University College Dublin School of Business. His primary research area is comparative employment relations, with a particular focus on the effectiveness of different systems of regulation in protecting employment standards. He is a graduate of the University of Auckland (BA and MComm) and holds a PhD from the University of Cambridge (Judge Business School and Darwin College). He is co-director of the UCD Centre for Business and Society (CeBaS) and the UN PRME (Principles for Responsible Management Education) Coordinator for the UCD College of Business.

Dr Caroline Murphy is Lecturer in Employment Relations at the Kemmy Business School, University of Limerick. Caroline is a former Industrial Relations Research Trust and Irish Research Council funded scholar. She lectures in employment relations, human resource analytics, human resource management and organizational behaviour. She has worked on a variety of research projects, including Gender Equality in Decision-Making (funded by the European Commission), A Study of Zero Hours Work in Ireland (funded by the Department of Jobs, Enterprise and Innovation) and Reconciling Employment and Eldercare Together (2016, funded by the Irish Research Council). More recently, she has received funding to examine job quality among female entrepreneurs.

Mike O'Brien is Management Development Lecturer at the University of Limerick. As an educator, consultant and course director, he works in collaboration with public, private and voluntary sector organizations to design and deliver bespoke educational interventions that meet the leadership and management development needs of organizations both in Ireland and abroad. He has a specialized interest in the non-traditional career development of management and leaders; understanding and learning from those who have entered management roles from technical backgrounds as to how they acquire the skills and self-efficacy to enable growth and success for their organizations.

Dr Ashley O'Donoghue is Head of Staff Learning and Development at Dublin Institute of Technology. She holds a PhD in Leadership and Organization Behaviour, a Master's in Human Resource Strategies from Dublin City University Business School, and a Bachelor of Arts and H.Dip.Ed. from Maynooth University. Her research investigates the influence of positive and negative leadership styles on follower emotions and their wellbeing (job satisfaction, engagement) and ill-being (workaholism, burnout) at work. Ashley also designs and implements equality strategies and action plans to support a culture of diversity and inclusion. She is a chartered member of the Chartered Institute of Personnel and Development.

Dr Michelle O'Sullivan is Senior Lecturer in Industrial Relations at the University of Limerick. Michelle's expertise is primarily in precarious work and public policy. Her other research interests include trade unions, employee voice, migrant workers, workplace bullying and employment law. She has published widely in international journals, is a co-author of the textbook *Industrial Relations in Ireland*, and co-editor of the book *Are Trade Unions Still Relevant? Union Recognition 100 Years On*. She is co-editor of the *Irish Journal of Management* and is a board member of the Workplace Relations Commission, Ireland's principal dispute resolution body.

Dr Ultan Sherman lectures in organizational behaviour and human resource management at University College Cork. His research interests lie broadly in the relationship between work and psychology, with a specific focus on the psychological contract. His research has been published in leading international journals, such as *Group & Organization Management* and the *International Journal of Human Resource Management*.

Online resources

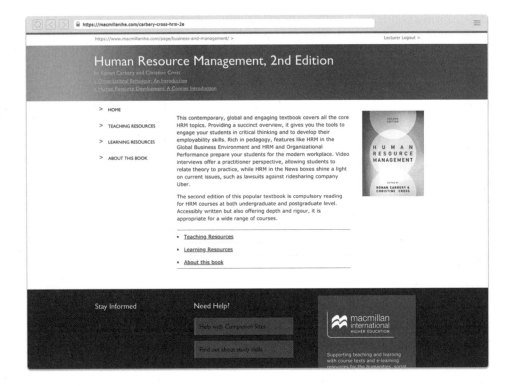

To support the use of this book, the companion website contains a wealth of teaching and learning resources. These can be found at: **www.macmillanihe.com/carbery-cross-hrm-2e**. Our digital ancillaries include:

FOR LECTURERS

- A testbank of multiple choice questions
- Lecture slides to accompany each chapter
- An instructor manual including guideline answers to activities in the book

FOR STUDENTS

- Interactive multiple choice questions to test your knowledge
- Useful weblinks to deepen your learning
- Video interviews to accompany the *Spotlight on Skills* feature

Tour of the book

Learning Outcomes

After you have studied the chapter, completed the activities and answered the review questions, you should be able to achieve each of the objectives stated at the start.

Key Terms

Each chapter contains an on-page explanation of a number of important words, phrases and concepts that you need to know in order to understand HRM, its theoretical basis and related areas.

Making Links

To demonstrate the interconnected nature of topics in the field of HRM, links to related areas in other chapters are clearly identified.

HRM and Organizational Performance

By examining specific company policies and broader trends, and reflecting on the important role played by HR, this feature highlights the relationship between HRM and organizational success.

HRM in the Global Business Environment

To prepare you for work in a globalized and interconnected world, this box compares and contrasts systems and ideas from different regions and countries as well as examining the global pressures that impact on HR.

HRM in the News

These longer case studies examine a topic that has featured in the media. The aim here is to highlight how the constructs and concepts in the chapter are applied to the management of people in the real world. A set of questions accompanies each case to deepen your learning.

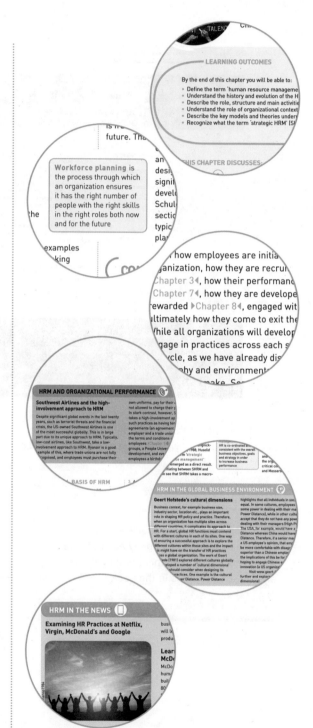

Spotlight on Skills

Learn from the professionals by watching short video interviews on the companion website: www.macmillanihe.com/carbery-cross-hrm-2e. Then, put your learning into practice by responding to a short, fictional scenario.

Consider This

This feature is designed to stimulate your thinking about a specific issue, idea or perspective related to the chapter topic.

Building Your Skills

To develop your skills, you are asked to reflect on key issues that you might face as an HR or line manager or to carry out research into a work-related topic.

HRM in Practice

These longer scenario-based activities ask you to examine your potential actions and responses to a given situation. In doing so, you will develop the skills required by an HR professional. The questions can be answered in class or used as part of an assignment.

Chapter Review Questions

These questions can be used as class exercises or for self-testing and evaluating your knowledge and understanding about the chapter topics.

Further Reading

There are numerous texts on HRM and related topics, but the aim here is to highlight a few specific texts which we believe are the most useful and most relevant to the ideas introduced in the chapter.

Useful Websites

We have identified those websites which we believe you will find most useful in furthering your knowledge and understanding of the discipline. Don't forget to also visit this book's companion website for additional resources: www.macmillanihe.com/carbery-cross-hrm-2e.

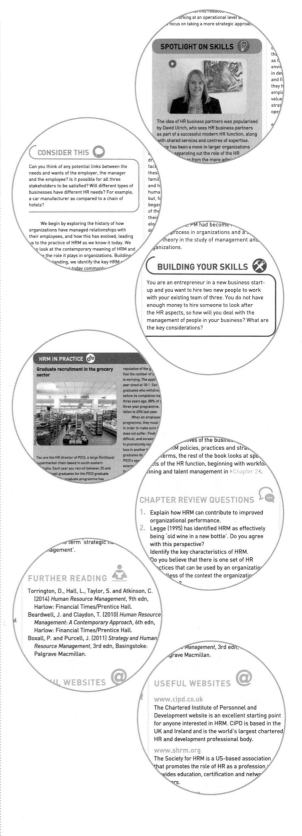

Chapter features and activities

TAKE A CLOSER LOOK AT HRM

Two brand new features have been added to this second edition: *HRM and Organizational Performance* and *HRM in the Global Business Environment*. These have been devised to highlight the relationship between HRM and organizational success, and to demonstrate the impact of a globalized and interconnected world on HRM practice. This edition also includes new *HRM in the News* case studies, which examine relevant topics from the media, as well as new video interviews with HR professionals for the *Spotlight on Skills* boxes.

Feature	Industry/Company	Country	Focus	Page
Chapter 1				
HRM in the Global Business Environment: Geert Hofstede's cultural dimensions	Universal	China; USA	Cultural dimensions: power distance; global transfer of HR practices	6
Spotlight on Skills: Fiona Evans, Human Resources Director	Not-for-profit: Zoological Society of London	UK	Strategic HRM: HR business partner role	12
HRM and Organizational Performance: Southwest Airlines and the high-involvement approach	Airline industry: Southwest Airlines; Ryanair	USA; Ireland; Global	High- and low-involvement approaches to HRM	14
HRM in the News: Examining HR practices at Netflix, Virgin, McDonald's and Google	Media: Netflix; Venture capital: Virgin; Food service: McDonald's; Information technology: Google	Australia; Brazil; China; Germany; Japan; UK; USA; Global	Strategic HRM: vacation entitlements; learning and development; retention	18
Chapter 2				
Spotlight on Skills: David Forkin, EMEA Talent and Learning Manager	Information technology: Hewlett-Packard	Ireland	HR planning; talent management	26
HRM and Organizational Performance: 'Star' employees at Dana-Farber	Clinical research and healthcare: Dana-Farber	USA	Talent management: managing 'star' employees; encouraging collaboration	29
HRM in the Global Business Environment: The transfer of practices from west to east in multinational corporations	Universal	China; Europe; USA	Cultural factors and the perception of employee performance; organizational culture; talent management; global transfer of HR practices	30

Feature	Industry/Company	Country	Focus	Page
HRM in the News: Developing talent at Liverpool Football Club	Professional sports: Liverpool FC	UK	Talent management: cultivating existing talent; retention	32
Chapter 3				
HRM in the Global Business Environment: The *Nitaqat* programme in the Kingdom of Saudi Arabia	Universal	Kingdom of Saudi Arabia	Recruitment: *Nitaqat* requirements in KSA	41
HRM and Organizational Performance: Hiring a diverse workforce	Sporting goods manufacturing: Nike	USA; Global	Recruitment: benefits of diversity	46
HRM in the News: Would you like an employer to check your Facebook page?	Technology: Facebook	Global	Recruitment: searching social media when screening job applications	48
Chapter 4				
Spotlight on Skills: Sabahat Ahmed, HR Consultant	Consulting: PeopleFirst HR Consultancy	UAE	Managing retention	60
HRM and Organizational Performance: Understanding *Googlers*	Information technology: Google	USA; Global	Retention: using a longitudinal study to understand employee motivation and success	61
HRM in the Global Business Environment: Recruitment and retention of doctors in rural areas	Healthcare: rural doctors	Australia; China	Recruitment and retention strategies for 'less desirable' areas	63
HRM in the News: Infosys Global Education Centre	Information technology and consulting: Infosys	India	Strategic HRM: induction and training	70
HRM in the News: The impact of a high-profile leaver	Information technology: Apple	USA	Succession planning; high-profile leavers and organizational performance	75
Chapter 5				
HRM in the Global Business Environment: Trade unions	Furniture and homeware retail: IKEA	Netherlands; Sweden; Global	Employment relations: global differences in trade union acceptance; practices in multinational corporations	82
HRM in the News: Uber and its drivers	Information technology and transportation: Uber	South Africa; UK; USA	'Gig' companies: legal status of 'gig' workers; employment obligations; non-union employee representation	87
HRM and Organizational Performance: Employee voice and participation	Universal	Global	Benefits of employee voice and participation	91

CHAPTER FEATURES AND ACTIVITIES

Feature	Industry/Company	Country	Focus	Page
Spotlight on Skills: Oonagh Buckley, Director General	Public sector: Workplace Relations Commission	Ireland	Negotiation and conflict resolution	92
Chapter 6				
HRM in the News: Every cloud has a silver lining	Recruitment: Silver Human Resource Centres	Japan	Talent acquisition: diversity; valuing age and experience	102
Spotlight on Skills: Lisa Dempsey, Managing Director; Vice President of Learning and Development	Consulting: Leadership Labs International; Professional member organization: Professional Women's Network Amsterdam	Netherlands	Diversity; inclusion	104
HRM in the Global Business Environment: LGBT employment rights	Universal	Global	Equality and diversity: global variations in LGBT employment legislation	112
HRM and Organizational Performance: Bicultural and multicultural employees	Telecommunications: Nokia	Finland; Global	Diversity: value of a multicultural workforce	114
Chapter 7				
HRM and Organizational Performance: Strategic performance management	Universal	Global	Strategic performance management: alignment of performance management and business strategy; creating a high performance culture	124
HRM in the News: Underperformance in Ireland's public health service	Public healthcare: Health Service Executive	Ireland	Managing underperformance; performance criteria; environmental influences on performance; reward	129
Spotlight on Skills: John Counihan, Head of Organizational Design and Development	Food retail and wholesale: Musgrave Retail Partners	Ireland	Performance management; performance appraisals	132
HRM in the Global Business Environment: Performance management and national culture	Universal	Canada; China; Finland; UK; Global	Cultural factors and the perception of performance; expatriate performance; global transfer of HR practices	133
Chapter 8				
HRM in the Global Business Environment: Multinational corporations and reward management	Professional services and consulting: Accenture, Deloitte; Information technology: Microsoft	Global	Influence of multinational corporations on national trends in performance and reward management	142
Spotlight on Skills: Miriam Cushen, HR Professional	Nutrition: Kerry Group	Ireland	The reward package	147

Feature	Industry/Company	Country	Focus	Page
HRM and Organizational Performance: Due diligence	Universal	Global	Local and cross-border acquisitions and the due diligence process; integration of HR systems	152
HRM in the News: The living wage	Universal	USA; New Zealand; UK	Retention; minimum wage legislation; living wage movements	153
Chapter 9				
HRM in the Global Business Environment: Careers at Expedia	Information technology and travel: Expedia	UK; Global	Organizational culture; recruitment; diversity; learning and development; employee engagement; performance management	165
HRM in the News: Training and national competitiveness	Universal	UK	Skills shortages; recruitment; training and development; Brexit	171
HRM and Organizational Performance: Key trends in learning and development	Universal	Global	Use of technology in learning and development; strategic HRM	174
Spotlight on Skills: Aidan Lawrence, Global Talent and Learning Operations Director	Information technology: Hewlett-Packard	Ireland	Learning and development	177
Chapter 10				
HRM in the Global Business Environment: Pursuing a global career	Universal	Global	Expatriates; global careers; staffing strategy	190
HRM and Organizational Performance: Female career development at Google	Information technology: Google	USA; Global	HR analytics; career development; equality	194
HRM in the News: Anthony Bourdain - New York Nomad	Food service industry; media	USA	Career development; contemporary career concepts	203
Chapter 11				
HRM in the Global Business Environment: Show me the money?	Universal	China; UK; USA; Global	HR analytics; reward; cultural factors and global transfer of HR practices	209
HRM in the News: Mind the gap – employers legally obligated to publish the gender pay gap in their organizations	Universal	UK	Equality; gender pay gap	212
HRM and Organizational Performance: Creating a 'data democratic' environment for employees	Consulting: Capventis; retail	Ireland; UK; Global	Enabling access to data to improve performance	215

CHAPTER FEATURES AND ACTIVITIES

Feature	Industry/Company	Country	Focus	Page
Spotlight on Skills: Rob Shanley, People Consultant; Neville Bourke, Organization Change Specialist	Information technology: Google; Consulting: Bourke Human Resources	Ireland	Using HR analytics to solve a problem	216
Chapter 12				
HRM in the News: New approaches to work design	Information technology and retail: Amazon	USA	Organizational culture; work design; wellbeing	236
HRM and Organizational Performance: The 'right to disconnect'	Universal	France	Wellbeing: working hours; managing emails; stress	241
HRM in the Global Business Environment: The working hours debate	Care industry: Gothenburg retirement home; Advertising and public relations: Dentsu; Retail: J.C. Penney	Sweden; Japan; USA; France; South Korea	Wellbeing: working hours	245
Spotlight on Skills: Dr Gonzalo Shoobridge, Head of Action Consultancy	Consulting: Great Place to Work®	UK	Creating a culture of wellbeing	247
Chapter 13				
HRM and Organizational Performance: The benefits of expatriate assignments	Multinational corporation (anonymized case)	Ireland; UK; USA	Expatriate assignments; talent identification and mobility; employee turnover	254
HRM in the News: Brexit: implications for IHRM	Universal	UK; EU	Recruitment; retention; European mobility; expatriate compensation packages; employment regulation; the transfer of HRM practices	257
HRM in the Global Business Environment: Comparing HRM in the USA and Germany	Universal	USA; Germany	Global transfer of HRM practices; employment regulation	258
Spotlight on Skills: Claire Campion, HR Business Partner	Information technology: Google	USA	Transfer of HR practices; expatriate assignments	264
Chapter 14				
HRM in the Global Business Environment: The collapse of Rana Plaza	Clothing manufacturing	Bangladesh; Global	Corporate social responsibility; working conditions in the supply chain	278
HRM and Organizational Performance: Does CSR bring financial benefits?	Universal	Global	Relationship between CSR and financial performance	284
HRM in the News: 7-Eleven Australia wages scandal	Convenience store retail: 7-Eleven	Australia	Corporate social responsibility; underpayment of wages	286

CHAPTER FEATURES AND ACTIVITIES

Feature	Industry/Company	Country	Focus	Page
Spotlight on Skills: Sriram Subramanya, Founder, Managing Director and CEO; Anu Sriram, Co-founder and Joint Managing Director	Publishing services and information technology: Integra; not-for-profit: Sriram Charitable Trust	India	Corporate social responsibility: managing employees; stakeholders; compliance; charitable work	290

DEVELOP YOUR SKILLS

In this book we encourage you to reflect upon your learning and to put your knowledge into practice. This is done in many ways, from the questions that accompany the *HRM in the News* features to the mini scenarios that follow the *Spotlight on Skills* video interviews. For three features, however, reflection and application are the primary focus: *Consider This* boxes have been designed to stimulate your thinking about a specific issue, idea or perspective; *Building Your Skills* boxes ask you to reflect on a variety of issues that you might face as an HR or line manager, or to carry out research into a work-related topic; while the *HRM in Practice* feature provides a longer scenario-based activity where you can examine your potential actions and responses to a given situation.

Feature	Focus	Page
Chapter 1		
Consider This	Balancing stakeholder requirements	3
Building Your Skills	People management in a start-up	4
Consider This	HR practices, strategy and the environmental context	7
Consider This	Links between business strategy and HR strategy in different organizational contexts	11
Chapter 2		
Consider This	Skills planning for the future	22
Consider This	Managing the impact of external recruitment on existing employees	25
Consider This	The underperformance of 'star' employees	28
Building Your Skills	Understanding and recognizing the causes of talent	30
HRM in Practice: Graduate recruitment in the grocery sector	Succession planning; talent management; graduate training; labour turnover	34
Chapter 3		
Consider This	Using competencies in recruitment and selection	39
Consider This	Person specification criteria and competency frameworks	42
Building Your Skills	Choosing recruitment methods	42
Consider This	Person–job fit and person–organization fit	47
HRM in Practice: Understanding recruitment across cultures	Recruitment and selection: choice of recruitment methods; job advertisement; gender diversity; international HRM; employment regulations in Saudi Arabia	55
Chapter 4		
Building Your Skills	Assessing person–organization fit	64
Consider This	Purpose, relevance and promotion of the employee handbook	65
Consider This	The Peter Principle	74

CHAPTER FEATURES AND ACTIVITIES

Feature	Focus	Page
HRM in Practice: Retention issues in a sales team	Reasons for employee turnover; strategies to tackle employee turnover; using information to improve employee retention	77
Chapter 5		
Consider This	Conflicting interests and goals	81
Consider This	Comparing student unions and trade unions	82
Consider This	Decline in unionization	84
Consider This	Non-union employee representation	85
Building Your Skills	Employee voice	89
HRM in Practice: Impact of company culture on employee satisfaction at work	Unionization of the workforce; employee satisfaction; organizational culture	94
Chapter 6		
Consider This	Inclusivity	101
Consider This	Human capital and diversity	106
Building Your Skills	'Retrainability' and 'flexibility' of the workforce	106
Consider This	Sexual orientation, identity and inclusive workplaces	111
Building Your Skills	Equality in the selection process	115
HRM in Practice: A fair day's wage for a fair day's work? The case of supported employment in Australia	Matching diversity management to business objectives; drivers for diversity management; support for diversity management	115
Chapter 7		
Consider This	Expectancy theory	123
Consider This	Equity theory	124
Building Your Skills	Performance management: addressing underperformance	135
HRM in Practice: Performance management at Harvesting Corporation	Analysis of a performance management system specific to an organization; link between performance and motivation	135
Chapter 8		
Consider This	Can a bonus system lead to unintended consequences?	142
Consider This	Paired comparison matrix	150
Building Your Skills	Improving staff morale without increasing pay	156
Consider This	Reward and motivation	157
HRM in Practice: Employee bonus schemes	Evaluating an employee bonus scheme in detail; identifying the costs of failure of a bonus scheme	158
Chapter 9		
Consider This	Reasons for investing in learning and development	167
Building Your Skills	Strategic human resource development	171
Building Your Skills	Digital learning	179
Consider This	Designing a reaction evaluation form	183
HRM in Practice: Upskilling your training team	Creating a learning and development consultant or business partner role in the organization	183
Chapter 10		
Building Your Skills	Boundaryless careers	191
Consider This	Male and female kaleidoscope career patterns	193

CHAPTER FEATURES AND ACTIVITIES

Feature	Focus	Page
Consider This	'Imposter syndrome'	197
Building Your Skills	Graduate career development	199
Consider This	Learning and development and return on investment	200
HRM in Practice: Bad dating service	Coaching and mentoring in the context of career development; formal career planning systems	202
Chapter 11		
Building Your Skills	Aligning performance with organizational objectives	210
Consider This	Establishing an HR analytics team	213
Consider This	Recruiting an HR data analyst	214
HRM in Practice: Measuring morale at Mifloe– perceptions vs reality	Skills required to work in HR analytics; sources of information; value of analytics	216
Chapter 12		
Consider This	Absence of a positive safety culture	223
Building Your Skills	Changing employee attitudes	229
Consider This	Privacy at Rio Tinto, Australia, and Google, USA	231
Consider This	Mental health at university; stress	238
Building Your Skills	Bullying	239
HRM in Practice: Dealing with employee absenteeism	Employee wellbeing; absenteeism; sickness; work design	248
Chapter 13		
Building Your Skills	Dealing with conflict	256
Consider This	Convergence of HRM practices globally	259
Consider This	Preparing for an international assignment	263
Consider This	Reasons for using long-term international assignments	269
HRM in Practice: Global staffing	Global staffing approaches; selecting employees for international assignments; post-assignment considerations	269
Chapter 14		
Consider This	Tescopoly: encouraging large corporations to act responsibly	279
Consider This	Corporate social responsibility and company reputation	283
Building Your Skills	Deciding your CSR principles and practices	285

About the Spotlight on Skills contributors

 Spotlight on Skills boxes are inserted into relevant chapters, which link to a video interview on the companion website: www.macmillanihe.com/carbery-cross-hrm-2e.

There are 14 interviews in total, featuring professionals working across different areas of human resource management, global mobility and corporate social responsibility. Here you can read more about them and the chapters in which they appear. After watching each video, in most chapters you will be asked to use the information you have learned to develop possible solutions to an HR problem.

Chapter 1

 Fiona Evans is Human Resources Director at the Zoological Society of London (ZSL) in the UK, which she joined in 2014, and a fellow of the Chartered Institute of Personnel and Development. Fiona is a creative leader who aims to bring lasting change to the organizations she has worked for. Her introduction of the HR business partner role at ZSL helped her to win HR Director of the Year in 2017 at the HR Excellence Awards, with her team also receiving Best HR team and the HR Excellence Gold Award. With over 30 years' experience in operational and strategic HR, organizational development, learning and development, and also corporate PR and communications, Fiona brings a wide range of knowledge and practice to her role.

Chapter 2

 David Forkin is Talent and Learning Manager for Europe, the Middle East and Africa at Hewlett-Packard. He has over 20 years' experience in HP Human Resources in a wide range of disciplines, including talent acquisition, compensation, business partnering and talent management. David has held worldwide and regional roles across multiple business units and locations, including seven years in corporate headquarters in Palo Alto, USA. In his current role, he works directly with the EMEA leadership in the area of talent management, including succession planning, leadership development and professional skills training. He is based in Dublin, Ireland.

Chapter 4

 Sabahat Ahmed is HR Consultant at PeopleFirst HR Consultancy in Dubai, UAE, a company which achieved Highly Commended at the CIPD People Management Awards in 2017 for the best HR/L&D consultancy. Sabahat is an HR and learning and development specialist with 21 years' experience of working with public and private sector organizations across the UAE and UK. With particular expertise in strategic HR, she has led multiple HR transformation projects covering organization restructuring, HR audit, policies and procedures, talent development, competency frameworks and performance management. As a L&D specialist, she has designed creative and progressive learning interventions, developed a capability building framework and designed a large induction programme with a focus on employee engagement and retention.

Chapter 5

Oonagh Buckley is Director General of the Workplace Relations Commission (WRC) in Ireland. The WRC handles all aspects of individual and collective disputes in the workplace and workplace inspections, as well as dealing with claims of discrimination both in employment and the delivery of services. Prior to her appointment to the WRC in 2016, she was responsible for pay and pensions policy for the Irish public service and led the government team in all the major pay and industrial relations negotiations in recent years. She has also worked in foreign affairs, environment, and wildlife protection. She is a qualified barrister and graduate of both University College Cork School of Law and King's College London. She was appointed as Adjunct Professor in the University College Cork School of Law in 2017.

Chapter 6

Lisa Dempsey is the Managing Director of Leadership Labs International and Vice President of Learning and Development at the Professional Women's Network in Amsterdam, which works to accelerate gender-balanced leadership. Originally from the USA, she has worked for a variety of multinational corporations in the Netherlands, taking her as far afield as Australia, Chile and Singapore. With over 20 years' experience in HR, including roles at Oracle, TNT/FedEx and Liberty Global, Lisa has worked across a range of areas including talent management, engagement, succession planning, global mobility, policy development and organizational design and culture transformation.

Chapter 7

John Counihan is Head of Organizational Design and Development at Musgrave Retail Partners Ireland.

Chapter 8

Miriam Cushen is an experienced business professional with strong HR experience, including generalist and functional expertise such as reward, recruitment, HR systems, HR data management and organization design. Her HR and business experience is with successful global food and drink businesses such as Diageo, Kerry Group, and Glanbia where she has been responsible for the design, implementation and embedding of global strategic HR programmes in dynamic and changing environments. At the time of publishing, Miriam holds the role of Glanbia Global Head of Reward, where she has global responsibility for strategy, policy and implementation relating to Glanbia's reward offering. She has a Bachelor in Commerce from National University of Ireland, Galway, a BSc in HR from Dublin Institute of Technology and an Advanced Diploma from the Charted Institute of Management Accountants.

Chapter 9

Aidan Lawrence is Global Talent and Learning Operations Director for Hewlett-Packard. Managing a worldwide team of L&D professionals, he has direct responsibility for the WW T&L operations function, including global systems and platforms, strategic learning delivery, vendor and partner management, financial and strategy management and acquisition integration.

Chapter 11

Neville Bourke is Founder of Bourke Human Resources and an organization change and leadership specialist. Formerly HR Director of Retail Banking at the Bank of Ireland, he was responsible for leading the people, culture and capability elements during a period of change as the 230-year old organization was transitioning through the digital transformation of financial services. Neville has also held senior HR roles in the medical devices, chemical and metallurgy industries. Neville holds a Business Studies (Human Resources) degree from University of Limerick and an M.Sc. (Management) in Organizational Behaviour from Trinity College Dublin. In 2017 and 2018, he chaired the International LEAP HR Conference 'Radical Change Through People' in New York, focusing on re-evaluating the HR Toolbox in the context of the future of work, as developments such as digital technology and demographic trends challenge historical organizational constructs and people frameworks.

Rob Shanley graduated from the University of Limerick with a degree in Business Studies, majoring in Human Resource Management. He spent a brief time working at Allied Irish Banks as an application support specialist, before leaving to join Google on a temporary contract. After a year as recruitment coordinator, Rob was hired as a full-time employee, working as a recruiter. Rob then joined the engineering team as Programme Manager and worked on a number of projects, including formalizing the hiring process and building the business intelligence for an internal engineering organization; managing the largest rotation programme at Google; and managing an effort to analyse project spend for an engineering organization. During this time, Rob worked in San Francisco, USA for 18 months. Rob now works as a People Consultant (HRBP) in Dublin, Ireland, primarily supporting teams in the Cloud organization.

Chapter 12

Dr Gonzalo Shoobridge is Head of Action Consultancy at Great Place To Work® UK and is also responsible for managing the strategic direction of Great Place to Work® Nigeria. Great Place to Work® is a global organization which undertakes research, consulting and training on the make-up of a great workplace and how this can be achieved. The organization also runs the prestigious Best Workplaces™ Awards. Gonzalo has over 20 years' experience in HR consulting and international business development. In his current role, he oversees all sales initiatives, research programmes, and organizational development and HR consultancy projects, with the ultimate goal of helping companies to transform their workplaces for the better.

Chapter 13

Claire Campion has worked as an HR business partner in a broad range of industries, including hospitality, TV and broadcasting, and most recently in the tech industry. Her background is diverse and includes experience working for large multinationals, such as Viacom International Media Networks, BSkyB, and InterContinental Hotels. Claire is currently working as a HRBP at Google, partnering with the global Site Reliability Engineering teams. Having started her career at Google Dublin in 2012, she is now based at the Head office in Mountain View California. Her areas of HR experience include coaching, change management, international HR, and employee engagement. Claire has an MA in Human Resources from London Metropolitan University. She is an active member of the Chartered Institute of Personnel and Development.

Chapter 14

Sriram Subramanya is founder, Managing Director and CEO of Integra, a digital content services company headquartered in Pondicherry, India, which works with Publishers and Corporates (Learning & Development teams) offering content and eLearning solutions, globally. As well as leading the organization, which is one of India's top 10 digital content services companies, Sriram strongly believes in working for the welfare of the underprivileged. This led him to establish Sriram Charitable Trust in 2006, which works in the areas of healthcare, women's empowerment, education, rehabilitation, rural development and conservation.

Anu Sriram is Co-founder and Joint Managing Director of Integra. She focuses on mentoring the HR and finance functions, as well as working on key customer engagements. A keen advocate for women's empowerment, Anu fosters an inclusive working culture at Integra, promoting her *Sakthi Oli* women's empowerment initiative. Thanks to these efforts, Integra won the NASSCOM Corporate Award for Excellence in Gender Inclusivity in 2006 and was listed as one of the Top 100 Best Companies for Women in India (Working Mother and AVTAR India) for three consecutive years in 2016, 2017 and 2018. Anu is also the chairwoman of the Indian Women Network, Southern Region, a forum which facilitates and promotes women's careers.

Skills development

In this section, we briefly look at four skills that are critical to success both as a student and at work: time management, managing your online communication and your smartphone, presentation skills, and persuading and influencing.

TIME MANAGEMENT SKILLS

People who effectively manage their time are the highest achievers in all walks of life, from business, to sport, to public service. Yet they have only the same number of hours in a day as the rest of us. This is why time management is believed to be a critical skill for success. Many people spend their days in a frenzy of activity, but achieve very little because they are not concentrating on the right things. Mobile phones, laptops and email mean we are virtually contactable 24 hours a day. People often feel unable to even go on vacation without being in reach, and technology means that they are accessible whether on a remote Scottish island or in the Amazon. In the section below, we provide some tips and techniques to help you become more effective at managing your most valuable resource – your time.

Your Workspace

Where you work has a significant impact on your productivity and mental wellbeing. While some people are happy to work surrounded by paper, files, teacups and more, other people seem to be able to work at a clutter-free desk. In reality, the brain can only concentrate fully on one thing at a time. The more 'stuff' on your desk, the more tempted you will be to pick it up. 'Stuff' instantly causes a distraction, so cluttered desks are *not* conducive to clear thinking. You should:

- Clear your desk of *everything* unrelated to what you are specifically working on now; otherwise your attention is constantly being drawn to other issues and tasks.
- Resist the temptation to leave papers, a file or book on your desk once the task is complete.
- Always leave your desk tidy and empty when you have finished for the day.

Work Efficiently

Read email only *once*. The principle behind this is that it forces you to make a decision immediately about every email you read. Avoid reading something and then thinking 'I'll deal with that later'. The rules are:

- Respond straightaway, or
- Decide to postpone a task until later, but set a clear reminder and time frame.
- When in doubt … delete the message!

SMARTPHONES AND ONLINE COMMUNICATION

The phone seems to have taken over our lives. We are no longer able to go anywhere without one. Do you check your smartphone compulsively? Since the more often you check your phone, the more often you feel the need to check it. A Harvard Business School study of 1,600 managers and professionals found that:

- 70% look at their phone within an hour of getting up
- 56% look at their phone within an hour of going to sleep
- 48% look at their phone at the weekend, including Friday and Saturday nights
- 51% look at their phone continuously while on holiday
- 44% would experience 'a great deal of anxiety' if they lost their phone and couldn't replace it for a week (Perlow, 2012).

To avoid this compulsive behaviour, you should:

- Set aside specific time slots for checking your phone.

- Remember that when your phone beeps, you don't have to look straightaway. In fact, you can avoid temptation by turning off the alert signals.

Email, Facebook, Twitter and other social media platforms have become a standard way of communicating at university and work. The biggest problem with this is that they consume large portions of your day, and yet help you achieve relatively little. Email inboxes can be overwhelming. Email can also be the lazy option – distracting you from your real work, especially when you want to avoid making a decision. To deal with these problems and also manage your time better:

- Check your email/Facebook/Twitter pages just two or three times a day, for example in the morning, at lunchtime and in the afternoon. If something is really urgent, someone will call you. Web apps such as Anti-Social for Macs and Cold Turkey for Windows are free productivity programs that you can use to temporarily block yourself off from popular social media sites, addictive websites and games.
- Make a phone call to reply to an email. We spend vast amounts of time composing and replying to emails when one phone call would have dealt with the issue much more quickly.
- Set up email messages with auto-preview as this will allow you to see if the message needs to be opened and actioned straightaway.
- Let people know when you don't want to be copied into emails.
- Use a subject message line each time you send an email, even if it's a reply. This makes emails easier to organize.
- Delete an email once you have read and replied to it, or save it to a personal folder.
- Archive old emails regularly.

PRESENTATION SKILLS

Regardless of the industry sector or the size of organization you work in, you need to have the ability to present your ideas clearly and succinctly. This will often happen in a setting where you use a software program, such as PowerPoint, to provide an overview of a topic, the context and the key points. Increasingly, certain job vacancies require you to make an oral presentation as part of the selection process. In order to present your ideas and arguments cogently, we suggest that you think about your presentation as involving a number of stages, which we outline below. We identify the main points you should consider, which will enable you to improve this important skill.

Planning Your Presentation

These points should be considered prior to giving your presentation:

- *Core message:* Be clear about what your core message is and repeat this at different stages during the presentation in order to increase its impact. Is it to inform? To sell your idea? To defend a position? To present a new idea? Whatever the answer, keep asking yourself this in different ways. What is the objective I want to achieve? What will I accept as evidence that my presentation has succeeded? What do I want the audience to think or feel at the end of the presentation?
- *Audience:* Analyse your audience. What are their expectations of your presentation? Do they expect to be informed? Persuaded? Have their existing ideas challenged? What do they already know? The key to a successful presentation is to know what your audience expects and ensure that you meet or exceed that expectation.
- *Timing:* How much time do you have for your presentation? Be careful not to run over an allocated time slot, as this will detract from its effectiveness.
- *Appearance:* What should you wear? This may seem a little strange to include here, but confidence is an important element in an effective presentation. You need to be comfortable and appropriately dressed to project the 'right' message.

Handling Nerves

Many people find handling their nerves the most difficult part of giving a presentation. Here are a few pointers to help overcome these nerves:

- *Be well prepared and organized:* Most people will feel nervous before a presentation, but knowing what you are going to say will reduce your level of nervousness. The first two minutes of any presentation are the most crucial. If you feel confident and clear about what you are going to say in the early stage of the presentation, this will help alleviate your nerves for the remainder. Once you have passed the first two minutes and have started to believe that the presentation is going well, everything is likely to run more smoothly.

- *Don't read directly from your notes – use visual aids:* This means that the words or images you use on the screen should act as your 'prompt'. Try not to use hard copy notes as they provide a false sense of security. If you lose your place in the notes, or have learned them off by heart and then accidentally mix them up, your level of effectiveness in the eyes of the audience will be diminished.
- *Rehearse in advance:* Trial runs are an excellent method of preparation and allow you to establish how long your presentation will take. This also develops your self-confidence, which will help to reduce nervousness.
- *Pay attention to your 'mannerisms':* Ask a friend or family member to highlight any repeated unconscious behaviours you might have, such as running your hands through your hair, shaking the change in your pocket, swaying from side to side or speaking too fast. These are distracting for the audience, but with an awareness of these mannerisms you can work to overcome them.
- *Practise deep breathing:* Do this before you get to where your presentation is taking place. This will help reduce the overall feeling of nervousness.
- *Arrive early:* This gives you plenty of time to check the equipment and ensure that, if you are using a software program, your presentation is working.
- *Think positively:* This means you are more likely to feel and behave positively.

Structuring Your Presentation

The golden rule is simple:

- Tell the audience what you are going to tell them (introduction)
- Tell the audience (main body)
- Tell the audience what you've told them (conclusion).

The Introduction

- The introduction should comprise approximately 10% of your presentation. It should provide a map for the audience of what is going to come.
- Introduce the topic (and yourself, if necessary).

- Start with an attention-grabbing hook – make a bold claim, present a striking fact or statistic, ask a question, use a quotation. If you have a suitable quote, surprising information or a visual aid, use it to grab the audience's attention.

Delivery and Body Language

- Speak clearly and audibly throughout. Vary the tone of your voice as this will keep the audience interested.
- Don't speak too fast as your message can get lost in translation.
- Project your voice out towards the audience. Do not speak down to your shoes!
- Face the audience, not the screen behind you or your laptop. Speak directly to the audience and make eye contact with people in the room. This demonstrates that you are paying attention to them and encourages them to pay attention to you.
- Show enthusiasm for the topic/issue/idea, as enthusiasm is contagious.
- Regard the presentation as an opportunity to shine.

The Conclusion

- Remind the audience of what you set out to do at the start. This means stressing the main message or aim of your presentation.
- Briefly repeat the main points you made.
- End on an interesting note, as this will assist people in remembering your presentation.
- Thank the audience for listening and invite questions.

PERSUASION AND INFLUENCING SKILLS

Learning how to influence and persuade people to do something they would otherwise not have done is an important life skill. Influencing is essentially getting your own way, unobtrusively. Managers do it most of the time. People are usually not aware that every human interaction involves a complex process of persuasion and influence, and being unaware, they are usually the ones being persuaded to help others rather than the ones who are doing the persuading. The key points to consider in developing this skill are:

- *Know what you want:* If you are not clear about what you want, it will be difficult for you to persuade others around to your way of thinking.
- *Look for points of mutual agreement:* Build on these.
- *Build rapport:* Make a connection with the person you are trying to influence.
- *Ask questions:* The type of question is important; you will need to use a mixture to get the response you are looking for, for example:
  - Find out what the other person is looking to get out of the interaction; ask: 'What do you want to get out of this discussion?' 'What do you want to achieve from this discussion?'
  - Probe to find out why they don't agree with you; ask: 'What is the reason you can't do that?' 'What is stopping you from agreeing with me?'
  - Ask hypothetical questions, as this allows you to gather information without the person actually committing, for example: 'What would happen if you agreed with me?' 'What would happen if we went ahead and did it?'
  - Find out what they need from you in order for them to agree; ask: 'What do you need to get in order for us to agree?' 'What do I need to give you to get you to agree?'
  - Ask challenging questions to test the person's resolve/position. Search for specifics, for example: 'Why don't you agree with this proposal?' 'What specific reason do you have for not wanting to do this?'
- *Listen actively:* This includes being able to paraphrase what the other person has said.
- *Use positive body and verbal language:* This creates the right atmosphere and is more conducive to agreement. For example:
  - Don't use 'flowery language'. Using too many adjectives and adverbs will lose the listener.
  - Use strong not weak words. Which of these two sentences would persuade you? 'I think you might like this new product we have.' 'You're really going to like this new product we are offering.' 'Think' in the first sentence is a weak word. Here is another example: 'I was wondering if you might want to go for a drink with me at the weekend?' A stronger question would be: 'Would you like to go for a drink this weekend?'
  - Focus on using the active voice, not the passive voice. An example of the passive voice would be: 'An account was opened by Mr Smith,' versus the active: 'Mr Smith opened an account.'
- *Stress the benefits for them:* Why should they agree with you?
- *Work towards a decision:* Use all the techniques above to keep building towards their agreement.

Preface and acknowledgements

We were delighted with how the first edition of *Human Resource Management* was received, but the employment landscape rarely stands still. Therefore, this second edition has been written to reflect both societal changes and the latest research in HRM. In acknowledgement of the global nature of many organizations, including our universities, and the range of countries our readers come from, we have adopted an international focus throughout the book. With contemporary examples from across the world, we hope that wherever you live and wherever you may work in the future, you will find this book useful.

While there are a large number of excellent HRM textbooks available, there are very few dealing with HRM in such a concise way. Once again, this book has been written in a succinct style with accessible language. However, this has not been at the expense of depth, rigour or critical analysis. The book delves into the major issues facing HRM practitioners, line managers, organizations and governments today, including topics like the status of 'gig economy' workers, the gender pay gap, ageing populations, and the impact of technology.

The book is suitable for readers at both undergraduate and postgraduate level (including MBA courses). While not all readers will go on to specialize in HRM, the concepts discussed in this book are relevant to any business student and, indeed, to anyone in employment. Whatever you might do in the future, the strong emphasis on career development and building expertise throughout each of the 14 chapters will be of help. We have presented the material in such a way as to highlight the practicality of the issues involved in work and employment, with key features such as up-to-date news pieces (*HRM in the News*), scenario-based activities (*HRM in Practice*), discussion questions and reflective points (*Consider This, Building Your Skills*), interviews with practitioners (*Spotlight on Skills*), an examination of HR practices across the world and in multinational organizations (*HRM in the Global Business Environment*) and of HRM's strategic impact (*HRM and Organizational Performance*). The book's companion website provides extra resources, including videos and self-test questions for students and teaching resources for lecturers.

We would like to acknowledge the help we received with writing this text. Isabel Berwick and Ursula Gavin at Red Globe Press provided tremendous assistance and support throughout the writing. The reviewers of each of the chapters provided excellent feedback for which we are very grateful. In addition to the contributors to the textbook, we would like to thank colleagues at University College Cork and University of Limerick who provided us with support along the way. We are also grateful for the time the participants in the *Spotlight on Skills* video features so readily gave us and for their excellent insights into industry practice. Finally, we would like to thank our families: Michelle and Julie Carbery; and Dave, Oisín and Luíseach Cross.

Ronan Carbery and Christine Cross
October 2018

Publisher's acknowledgements

We are grateful to the following organizations for granting us permission to use their material:

American Psychological Association (APA), for permission to reproduce:

- Figure 12.3, Yerkes-Dodson principle. Adapted from Figure 2, from Hebb, D.O. (1955) 'Drives and the C.N.S. (conceptual nervous system)', *Psychological Review*, 62(4), 243–54. DOI: dx.doi.org/10.1037/h0041823. This article is now in the public domain.
- Figure 12.5, SHAPE framework – healthy workplace practices. Adapted from Figure 2, The SHAPE framework, from Grawitch, M.J., Gottschalk, M. and Munz, D.C. (2006) 'The Path to a Healthy Workplace: A Critical Review Linking Healthy Workplace Practices, Employee Well-being, and Organizational Improvements', *Consulting Psychology Journal: Practice and Research*, 58(3), 129–47. Copyright 2006 by the American Psychological Association and the Society of Consulting Psychology, DOI: dx.doi.org/10.1037/1065-9293.58.3.129.

Chartered Institute of Personnel and Development, London, for permission to reproduce Table 12.4, Five domains of wellbeing. Adapted from CIPD (2016) *Growing the health and well-being agenda: From first steps to full potential*, London: CIPD (www.cipd.co.uk).

Elsevier B. V., for permission to reproduce Figure 2.2, Trend analysis of 'talent management' citations. Reproduced from Scopus®, www.scopus.com. Scopus® is a registered trademark of Elsevier B.V. All rights reserved.

Ethical Trading Initiative (ETI), for permission to reproduce Table 14.1, ETI Base Code of labour standards, from Ethical Trading Initiative (2018a) 'ETI Base Code'. Available at www.ethicaltrade.org/eti-base-code (accessed 26 September 2018). And Ethical Trading Initiative (2018b) 'What members sign up to: ETI corporate membership obligations'. Available at: www.ethicaltrade.org/join-eti/what-members-sign-to (accessed 26 September 2018). Copyright © 2018 Ethical Trading Initiative (ETI).

Gill Education, for permission to reproduce Figure 2.1, The human resource planning cycle. Adapted from Figure 5.1, Human resource planning process, from Gunnigle, P., Heraty, N. and Morley, M. J. (2011) *Human Resource Management in Ireland*, 4th edition, p.103, Dublin: Gill Education. Copyright © Gill Education 2011.

John Wiley & Sons, Inc., for permission to reproduce:

- Figure 1.5, The Michigan model of HRM. Reproduced from Figure 3.2, The human resource cycle, from Devanna, M.A., Fombrun, C.J. and Tichy, N.M. (1984) 'A Framework for Strategic Human Resource Management', in C.J. Fombrun, N.M. Tichy and M.A. Devanna (eds) *Strategic Human Resource Management*, p.41, Hoboken, NJ: John Wiley & Sons, Inc. Copyright ©1984 by John Wiley & Sons, Inc. All rights reserved.
- Figure 2.4, Analysing the nature of the relationship between performance and the value contributed to the organization. Adapted from Figure 2.2, Comparison of ROIP Curves for a Flight Attendant and a Pilot, from Boudreau, J.W. and Jesuthasan, R. (2011) *Transformative HR: How Great Companies Use Evidence-Based Change for Sustainable Advantage*, San Francisco: Jossey-Bass/John Wiley & Sons, Inc. Copyright © 2011 by John Boudreau. All rights reserved.
- Figure 9.1, Experiential learning cycle. Adapted from Figure 2, Basic Learning Processes and the Stages of Problem Management, from Kolb, D.A. (1983) 'Problem Management: Learning from Experience', in S. Srivastva (ed.), *The Executive Mind*, p.120, San Francisco: Jossey-Bass/John Wiley & Sons, Inc. Copyright © 1983 by John Wiley & Sons, Inc. All rights reserved.

PUBLISHER'S ACKNOWLEDGEMENTS

- Table 11.1, Forms of analysis. Adapted from Fitz-enz, J. and Mattox, II, J.R. (2014) *Predictive Analytics for Human Resources*, p.3, Hoboken, NJ: John Wiley & Sons, Inc. Copyright © 2014 by Jac Fitz-enz and John R. Mattox, II. All rights reserved.
- Figure 12.4, Employment alignment considerations. Adapted from Figure 1, Three tests of alignment in employment relationships, from Boxall, P. (2013) 'Mutuality in the management of human resources: assessing the quality of alignment in employment relationships', *Human Resource Management Journal*, 23(1), 3–17. Copyright © 2013 Blackwell Publishing Ltd/John Wiley & Sons, Inc., DOI: doi.org/10.1111/1748-8583.12015.

Monster Worldwide, for permission to reproduce and adapt Table 3.1, Hair stylist job description, and Table 3.2, Person specification: hair stylist. Copyright © 2018 – Monster Worldwide.

Springer Nature, for permission to reproduce:

- Figure 13.2, U-shaped curve of cross-cultural adjustment. Adapted from Figure 1, The U-Curve of Cross-Cultural Adjustment, in Black J.S. and Mendenhall M. (1991) 'The U-Curve Adjustment Hypothesis Revisited: A Review and Theoretical Framework', *Journal of International Business Studies*, 22(2), 225–47. Published by Palgrave Macmillan UK, DOI: doi.org/10.1057/palgrave.jibs.8490301. Copyright © 1991 Academy of International Business.
- Figure 14.1, Carroll's pyramid of CSR. Reproduced from Figure 1, Carroll's pyramid of CSR, from Carroll, A.B. (2016) 'Carroll's pyramid of CSR: taking another look', *International Journal of Corporate Social Responsibility*, 1(3). Published by SpringerOpen, DOI: doi.org/10.1186/s40991-016-0004-6. Copyright © Carroll 2016; reprinted under the CC BY 4.0 licence https://creativecommons.org/licenses/by/4.0.

The Disclaimer of Warranties and Limitation of Liability can be read here: https://creativecommons.org/licenses/by/4.0/legalcode.

Taylor and Francis Group LLC Books, for permission to reproduce Table 13.3, Performance criteria for evaluating expatriate performance. Adapted from Exhibit 12.3, Criteria for Appraisal of International Assignees, from Briscoe, D., Schuler, R. and Tarique, I. (2012) *International Human Resource Management: Policies and Practices for Multinational Enterprises*, 4th edition, p.356, New York, NY: Routledge. Copyright © 2012 Taylor & Francis. Reproduced by permission of Taylor and Francis Group, LLC, a division of Informa plc; permission conveyed through Copyright Clearance Center, Inc.

Taylor & Francis Ltd, for permission to reproduce Table 1.1, Guest model of HRM: demonstrating strategic integration. Reproduced from Figure 2, Linking HRM and performance, in Guest, D.E. (1997) 'Human resource management and performance: a review and research agenda', *The International Journal of Human Resource Management*, 8(3), 263–76. Published by Chapman & Hall in 1997, DOI: 10.1080/095851997341630. Reprinted by permission of the publisher Taylor & Francis Ltd: www.tandf.co.uk, www.informaworld.com.

US Army Public Affairs, for the right to distribute and copy Figure 9.2, The ADDIE model. Adapted from Figure 4.1, The ADDIE Process with Key Management Components, from United States Army Training and Doctrine Command (2017)*TRADOC Regulation 350-70: Army Learning Policy and Systems*, Fort Eustis, Virginia: Department of the Army Headquarters. This figure was derived from original ideas in Branson, R.K., Rayner, G.T., Cox, J.L., Furman, J.P., King, F.J., Hannum, W.H. (1975) *Interservice Procedures for Instructional Systems Development: Executive Summary and Model (Phases I–V)*, Fort Benning, GA: US Army Combat Arms Training Board.

Abbreviations

ATS	applicant tracking system		ILO	International Labour Organization
BARS	behaviourally anchored rating scale		IT	information technology
CIPD	Chartered Institute of Personnel and Development		LGBT	lesbian, gay, bisexual and transgender
			LME	liberal market economy
CME	coordinated market economy		MNC	multinational corporation
CSR	corporate social responsibility		NER	non-union employee representation
ESOP	employee share ownership plan		NGO	nongovernmental organization
ETI	Ethical Trading Initiative		OECD	Organization for Economic Co-operation and Development
EU	European Union			
HCN	host country national		PCN	parent country national
HPWS	high performance work system		PM	personnel management
HR	human resources		PRP	performance-related pay
HRD	human resource development		ROI	return on investment
HRIS	human resource information systems		SHRD	strategic human resource development
HRM	human resource management		SHRM	strategic human resource management
IHRM	international human resource management		SRI	socially responsible investment
			TCN	third country national

iStock.com/Rawpixel

1: Introducing Human Resource Management

Christine Cross and Sarah Kieran

LEARNING OUTCOMES

By the end of this chapter you will be able to:

- Define the term 'human resource management' (HRM)
- Understand the history and evolution of the HRM function
- Describe the role, structure and main activities of the HRM function
- Understand the role of organizational context in HRM
- Describe the key models and theories underpinning the study of HRM
- Recognize what the term 'strategic HRM' (SHRM) means

THIS CHAPTER DISCUSSES:

Introduction (2)

Evolution of HRM as an Organizational Function (3)

HRM Today (5)

Strategic HRM (6)

HRM and the Business Context (6)

Features of HRM (7)

HRM Policies and Practices (8)

Linking HR Practices to Organizational Outcomes (9)

Structure and Role of the HR Function (11)

Theoretical Basis of HRM (14)

INTRODUCTION

Human resource management (HRM) is the term most widely used to describe the activities a business engages in to manage its relationship with employees. Thus, if you are an employer, a manager or an employee, or will be in the future, the issues dealt with in this book are going to be relevant to your working life. Interestingly, your understanding and experiences of HRM will be influenced by your position. You may experience all three roles – employee, manager and employer – as you progress in your career, and your understanding and experiences of HRM might change in the process. This is what makes the study of HRM so interesting. However, it can make the practice of HRM, especially the successful practice of HRM, challenging for businesses.

In every organization the employer needs a successful, profitable business. The manager needs the right people, in the right place, doing the right thing to meet business targets. The employee needs a job they feel capable of, in a fair and safe environment, which pays them appropriately. HRM, therefore, is firstly about understanding and meeting the needs of these three stakeholders. It is also about appreciating that there are potential links between each of these needs but that some stakeholders are quite powerful while others may have very little, if any, power at all.

In order to manage these relationships, organizations choose from a range of policies and practices, which together make up their HRM strategy, such as:

- how to recruit and select employees
  ▶Chapter 3◀
- what terms and conditions employees work under
  ▶Chapter 5◀
- how to ensure that everyone in the organization is treated equally ▶Chapter 6◀
- how to deal with employees who break organizational rules ▶Chapter 7◀
- how to pay and reward employees ▶Chapter 8◀
- what learning and development opportunities the organization should pay for ▶Chapter 9◀.

However, the employer might also want a business that is always innovating and breaking new ground competitively. The manager may want a highly motivated, engaged and flexible team, going beyond the requirements of their day-to-day job. The employee might want new challenges, to develop new skills and have opportunities to advance or earn more money. When we consider HRM from these perspectives, the policies and practices become more complex and the potential links between them more pronounced. For example, how you train someone to build an existing product might be clear. However, how do you develop someone's skills to invent a new product? Should there be a difference in how you reward someone for building an existing product versus inventing a new one? Furthermore, different employees are likely to interpret and react to the same HR policy or practice in different ways. Their prior experiences, their age, their role in the organization etc. are all likely to influence their response.

It is also important to realize that not all businesses operate in the same context. It is likely that McDonald's will make different strategic choices on its HRM policies and practices to the choices the owner of your local convenience store will make or, indeed, the choices you might make if you were starting up your own business. In addition, not all businesses view things the same way. Often, the perspective the owner or CEO has of human resources (HR) will determine the extent to which they recognize the role of the other two stakeholders in the business: the managers and the employees. This is referred to as the **HR philosophy** of the organization.

Does the CEO believe that managers and employees are stakeholders? Are they involved in some of the decisions the business needs to make? These are a few of the questions facing those responsible for HRM. In this first chapter, we explore some of these issues and discuss the process involved in answering these questions, so that organizations make the appropriate HR choices. Given that the focus of this book is on providing an overview of HRM, it would be impossible to include a detailed description of every single issue involved in the strategic choices we are talking about. Instead, we concentrate on identifying some of the key concepts and encourage you to read more about these in order to further your understanding of them. To help you in this endeavour, a further reading list is provided.

> **HR philosophy** – the principles that guide how the organization leads, manages, involves, treats and views all its employees, so that it can successfully achieve its business strategy

CONSIDER THIS

Can you think of any potential links between the needs and wants of the employer, the manager and the employee? Is it possible for all three stakeholders to be satisfied? Will different types of businesses have different HR needs? For example, a car manufacturer as compared to a chain of hotels?

We begin by exploring the history of how organizations have managed relationships with their employees, and how this has evolved, leading us to the practice of HRM as we know it today. We then look at the contemporary meaning of HRM and explore the role it plays in organizations. Building on this understanding, we identify the key HRM practices in which businesses today commonly engage and consider the importance of the environmental context within which these choices occur. Finally, the key models involved in the study of HRM and the concept of 'strategic HRM' are explored. At the end of this chapter, you should be able to understand why HRM is such an important area of study for you as future managers and form your own perspective on its role in business.

EVOLUTION OF HRM AS AN ORGANIZATIONAL FUNCTION

The history of HRM is very interesting and its evolution, it could be said, reflects that of society in general. As we explore its rich history, you will see how HRM today, while evolving in phases over the last 200 years or so, is still very much engaged in practices that originated during each of these phases.

Industrial Welfare

The origins of HRM can be found in the industrial revolution in England in the late nineteenth century. The advent of steam power, iron production and new machine-based manufacturing methods led to the development of the factory system. At this time, the circumstances for men, women and children in these new factories were dreadful. There were, however, some enlightened employers who wanted

to improve working conditions. This was often driven by their religious values, as many of these factories were owned by Quakers. In the 1890s, these employers started providing workplace and family amenities such as lunchrooms, medical care and housing. The impetus for some employers was humanitarian concern and religious principles, but, for others, it was more pragmatic as they began to recognize the link between the welfare of their employees and the level of production in their factories. This led to the creation of stand-alone employment offices where a 'welfare officer' dealt solely with employment issues. This first phase in the evolution of HRM, known as the 'welfare movement', represented a shift in the way management viewed employees and resulted in the creation of some of the HR practices which are often taken for granted at work today, such as compliance with health and safety legislation ▶Chapter 12◀ or the provision of employee benefits like sick pay and pensions. Importantly, however, it established the link between employee welfare and productivity, which is still central to HRM practice today.

Scientific Management

The next phase in the development of HRM, known as the 'scientific management movement', is credited to Frederick Taylor in the early part of the twentieth century. An American managing engineer in a steel factory, he became interested in finding the 'one best way' of working that would increase production (Taylor, 1914). His work led to the development of a systematic approach to the design of jobs and to systems of employment and pay. **Taylorists** aimed to increase productivity through greater efficiency in production practices, selection and training practices and, interestingly, incentivized pay for workers (also known as pay for performance) ▶Chapter 8◀. With the emergence of the production line and large factories in the 1920s, positions such as 'labour manager' and 'employment manager' emerged. Their work involved the centralization and standardization of certain employment-related functions, such as hiring, payroll, record keeping, and dealing with issues such as absences, recruitment and queries over bonuses (CIPD, 2012). The contemporary concepts of lean manufacturing (working on eliminating waste

Taylorist – a factory management system developed in the late nineteenth century to increase efficiency by breaking down production into specialized repetitive tasks from the manufacturing process) and continuous improvement (an ongoing effort to improve products, services or processes), underpinned by HR practices such as job specifications and performance management, have their foundations in the scientific movement. It is also important to note that the recognition of the link between pay and performance in scientific management is still central to HRM practice today ▶Chapter 8◀.

This scientific approach to work led to the tight control of workers. Thus, these practices often met with resistance from workers and are closely associated with the rise of collective action and trade unions. Throughout the 1800s, the employment relationship was recognized as having an imbalance of power between a powerful employer and a relatively powerless employee. To counteract this imbalance, employees throughout the industrial revolution had begun to group together to form or join **trade unions**. Their aim was to exert greater power over the employment relationship and, therefore, have greater influence over their working conditions than would otherwise be the case. In so doing, it gave employees a forum to express solidarity, to have collective protection and to improve their terms and conditions of employment. The scientific management movement led to a significant increase in this already established trade union membership. In the USA, trade union membership doubled between 1896 and 1900 and again between 1900 and 1904. In the UK, a quarter of employees held trade union membership by 1914. Consequently, the HR role at this time largely concentrated on **industrial relations** in the organization. Again, it is important to note that, although the origins and subsequent development of trade unions can be traced back to before scientific management, the role of industrial or employment relations is still very much central to HRM practice today. This aspect of HRM is covered in more detail in ▶Chapter 5◀.

> **Trade unions** – an organized group of workers which represents members' interests in maintaining or improving the conditions of their employment by acting collectively as a way to challenge employer power
>
> **Industrial relations** – the relationship between employers and employees, with a focus on those areas of the employment relationship where employers deal with employee representatives, such as trade unions, rather than individuals

Behavioural Science

The third phase in the evolution of HRM stems from around the time of the Second World War and the work of Elton Mayo and his colleagues in the USA (Mayo, 1949). Known as the 'Hawthorne Effect', as they concerned employees in the Hawthorne plant of the Western Electrical Company, these experiments observed employee performance under a range of different working conditions. The results highlighted new areas of concern for employers and led to an emphasis on personal development, a better understanding of group work, and the importance of working conditions as a means of motivating employees. Yet again, it is important to note that the link between employee behaviours and organizational outcomes, for example the link between motivation and productivity, is still very central to contemporary HRM practice. This shift in focus became known as the 'behavioural science movement', and research in this area has been growing consistently ever since ▶Chapter 12◀.

The 1960s and 70s saw the introduction of a large body of legislation, both in Europe and the USA, which provided rights for employees around dismissals, equal pay, pension rights, and health and safety. In addition to managing the employment relationship through negotiations and interactions with trade unions, this development created additional work as those with responsibility for the employment relationship were now also charged with understanding and applying these pieces of legislation. The emergence of the job title 'personnel officer' and the business discipline of 'personnel management' (PM) can be traced to around this time. By the end of the 1970s, PM had become recognized as a critical process in organizations and a stand-alone theory in the study of management and organizations.

BUILDING YOUR SKILLS

You are an entrepreneur in a new business start-up and you want to hire two new people to work with your existing team of three. You do not have enough money to hire someone to look after the HR aspects, so how will you deal with the management of people in your business? What are the key considerations?

HRM TODAY

This brings us to the most recent phase in the evolution of **human resource management**, starting in the USA in the 1980s, when the concept as we know it today began to emerge. During the 1960s and 70s, personnel management and human resource management largely coexisted as terms and were used interchangeably. However, in the 1980s, there was a move to differentiate traditional PM from HRM. The 'personnel management' of the past was associated with the control and cost-effective operations of employees, adherence to employee legislation, and was dominated by industrial relations and negotiations with trade unions. HRM of the future was becoming more focused on the employee as an asset rather than a cost, and employment relations were becoming increasingly more focused on relationships with the individual rather than the trade union.

There are a number of factors that led to this changing perspective. The recession of the 1980s and the resultant high unemployment levels, coupled with significant competition in the marketplace, especially from Japan, led to a focus on productivity and 'excellence', seen to be associated with leading-edge companies. Rapid technological developments were not just changing the type of industries for which employees were needed, but with the advent of information and communications technology (ICT), the 'job of the employee' versus the 'job of the machine' (or computer) changed forever. There was a decline in traditional manufacturing industries and a significant growth in the service sector and the emergence of the **knowledge worker**. This brought about a decline in trade union membership and the perceived significance of trade unions in managing the employment relationship. Furthermore, with the development of more recent technologies, such as the smartphone and mobile broadband, where and when employees worked changed dramatically. New concepts such as working from home, teleworking and virtual teams emerged. At the same time, shifting demographics, the move towards a 24/7 society and changing workforce values led to employers and employees seeking a more individualized approach to the employment relationship for the benefit of both stakeholders.

> **Human resource management** – the strategic and integrated approach taken by an organization to the management of its most valued assets, namely its people
>
> **Knowledge worker** – an employee whose job involves developing and using knowledge rather than producing goods or services

This gave rise to, for example, tailored personal development, individual performance-related reward and non-standard hours of work ▶Chapters 5, 8 and 10◀. The combination of all these developments necessitated new HR policies and practices to manage these changes effectively. This resulted in the establishment of the HR function in line with other business functions, such as finance and marketing, and a corresponding rise in the position of the HR profession.

However, the differences between PM and HRM are still being debated. For some, HRM is simply a 'relabelling' or 'repackaging' of PM with a new title (Gunnigle and Flood, 1990; Legge, 1995). In many organizations, employees are still considered a labour cost that must be efficiently managed like any other resource, albeit the HR practices through which they manage the employment relationship have become more complex. On the other hand, however, for many other organizations, HRM represents a new paradigm, where employees are considered a unique strategic asset. Barney's VRIO model (1991) suggests that an organization's employees are its single most important strategic differentiator. They are **v**aluable, **r**are, **i**nimitable (not easily copied) and **o**rganized so, though competitors can copy your marketing or service strategy quite quickly, they cannot easily take all your employees and everything they have to offer. In reality, many organizations today engage in a range of HR practices to meet the different needs and roles of employee groups across the business. Some of these practices will be aligned more closely with a PM perspective while others, in the same organization, may reflect a more contemporary HRM approach (Lewin, 2001). In addition, different organizations will have different HR philosophies which might be more consistent with either a PM or HRM perspective. Sometimes this is due to the personal values of the CEO and the style of the senior leadership team. However, the nature and demands of the organization's business context are always a significant factor influencing the approach taken to HRM. Given the global landscape in which businesses have to compete today – the fast pace of technological developments, changing consumer needs and the impact of global economies on local businesses – the focus on HRM as a strategic contributor to the organization is increasing.

STRATEGIC HRM

This contemporary perspective of HRM emphasizes the contribution HRM can make towards business success and identifies HRM as an essential component of business strategy (Schuler and Jackson, 1987; Lengnick-Hall and Lengnick-Hall, 1988; Huselid et al., 1997). The term **strategic human resource management** (SHRM) has emerged as a direct result. In differentiating between SHRM and HRM, we see that SHRM takes a macro-

> **Strategic human resource management** – where HR is coordinated and consistent with the overall business objectives, goals and strategy in order to increase business performance

level approach within the context of organizational performance, whereas HRM operates at the micro-level. The integration between HRM and business strategy is believed to contribute directly to organizational performance (Guest et al., 2003).

The linkages between the context of the organization, the high-level features of the HR approach and the specific practices in which the organization then engage are all critical components of SHRM (Jiang and Messersmith, 2017).

HRM IN THE GLOBAL BUSINESS ENVIRONMENT

Geert Hofstede's cultural dimensions

Business context, for example business size, industry sector, location etc., plays an important role in shaping HR policy and practice. Therefore, when an organization has multiple sites across different countries, it complicates its approach to HR. For a start, global HR functions must contend with different cultures in each of its sites. One way of ensuring a successful approach is to explore the different cultures within these sites and the impact this might have on the transfer of HR practices across a global organization. The work of Geert Hofstede (1980) explored different cultures globally and developed a number of 'cultural dimensions' which HR should consider when designing its policies and practices. One example is the cultural dimension of power distance. Power distance highlights that all individuals in societies are not equal. In some cultures, employees *expect* to have some power in dealing with their managers (low power distance), while in other cultures employees *accept* that they do not have any power when dealing with their managers (high power distance). The USA, for example, would have a low power distance whereas China would have a high power distance. Therefore, if a senior manager seeks a US employee's opinion, that employee might be more comfortable with disagreeing with their superior than a Chinese employee. What might the implications of this be for US senior managers hoping to engage Chinese employees in product innovation (a US organization operating in China)?

Visit www.geert-hofstede.com to read further and explore your country's cultural dimensions.

HRM AND THE BUSINESS CONTEXT

Organizations are effectively all distinctive, each operating in their own business context or internal environment. Even those that produce similar products for similar market segments are essentially different. This distinctiveness is created by many different factors internal to the organization, including:

- *the size and structure of the organization:* for example, small organizations employing small numbers of people tend to have less formal procedures and policies and flatter hierarchical structures than larger organizations

- *the sector the organization operates in:* depending on whether it is a private, public or voluntary body, its approach to HRM may differ
- *organizational lifecycle:* the length of time the organization has been operating, whether or not it is still in a growth phase, has reached maturity, or might be under threat and in decline
- *the financial health of the organization:* often associated with its lifecycle and relating to overall performance and profitability
- *the values and ideology of senior management:* deeply held beliefs and values about the way people should be managed affect issues such as communications, reward systems, management style and equality

- *organizational culture:* 'the way we do things around here'
- *workforce characteristics:* the different education, qualifications, skill sets, demographics and aspirations of its employees, often across different types of jobs, for example knowledge workers, production operatives or customer service personnel
- *established 'custom and practice':* the structure and process of working established in the organization; many practices can become very well embedded and are difficult to change.

However, organizations also operate in an external, environmental context, which presents further opportunities and constraints. The external context comprises many different factors, including:

- *competition:* the economic forces of globalization and consumer behaviour, which impact the organization as their competitors launch new products or services, increase or decrease prices, find new routes to market or enter new markets
- *technology:* the increasing pace of technological advancements such as machine-learning, robotics and big data not only influences *what* the business produces for the market but equally *how* it produces it
- *labour market:* the availability of employees to meet the needs of the organization's workforce characteristics
- *legislation and regulation:* the local and national policies which determine how the business can operate, for example how it must manufacture its products to health and safety guidelines, or whether or not it must recognize trade unions
- *ethics:* how the business must comply with corporate governance and how it responds to expected corporate and social responsibilities and its customers' ethical expectations of them.

CONSIDER THIS

Can you identify three different organizations operating in very different environmental contexts? How might their HR strategy and practices be different? Why? Examples could include a large state-run hospital, a small innovative software development company and an international chain of low-cost retail stores.

FEATURES OF HRM

Having considered their internal and external context, organizations must make some strategic choices about how they configure their HR function, the roles HR practitioners play, the HR policies they adopt, and the HR practices in which they engage. John Storey (1989) identified four critical features that he believes characterize contemporary HRM:

1. HRM is explicitly linked with corporate strategy.
2. HRM focuses on commitment rather than compliance of employees (see Walton, 1985 for a full discussion of this issue).
3. Employee commitment is obtained through an integrated approach to HR policies in the areas of rewards, selection, training and appraisal.
4. HRM is not just the domain of specialists in the HR function; rather HRM is owned by line managers as a means of fostering integration.

Thus, concepts such as 'strategic integration', 'culture management', 'commitment' and 'investing in human capital', together with a unitary philosophy, are considered essential parts of the HRM model. Much has been written on the characteristics associated with contemporary HRM since it first emerged in the 1980s. These are discussed in more detail in the following sections but are summarized here:

- *A strategic approach to the management of people:* a key feature of HRM is the link between HRM strategy and business strategy (Beer, 1984; Schuler and Jackson, 1987; Lengnick-Hall and Lengnick-Hall, 1988). Here, HRM is included in the creation of business strategy, and therefore workforce strategies are designed to support it.
- *A unitarist frame of reference:* a unitarist perspective views the employment relationship as one where both managers and employees have a common purpose and the organization is integrated and harmonious, acting as 'one big happy family' ▶Chapter 5◀.
- *A 'soft' HRM approach:* a distinction has been made in the literature between 'hard' and 'soft' HRM approaches. A 'hard' approach is one in which employees are a resource like any other and should be managed as such, while a 'soft' approach involves treating employees as valued assets and a *source* of competitive advantage, rather than simply *using* people as another resource (Storey, 1989).

- *HR policies and practices are integrated and consistent with the organizational culture:* **vertical integration** refers to the matching of HRM policies and practices with business strategy and is also referred to as 'external alignment'. In addition, **horizontal integration** involves strong consistency and interconnection between HRM policies and practices internally in order to achieve effective performance (Schuler and Jackson, 1987; Huselid et al., 1997). This is also known as 'internal alignment'.

- *Line managers work in partnership with HR:* as Storey (1995: 7) highlights: 'if human resources really are so critical for business managers then HRM is too important to be left to operational personnel specialists' (cited in Sikora and Ferris, 2014).

- *An evidence-based approach:* the design of HR practices is guided by appropriate business information, scientific evidence and critical thinking, and their outcomes are then measured

> **Vertical integration** – the matching of HRM policies and practices with business strategy – also referred to as 'external alignment' or 'external fit'
>
> **Horizontal integration** involves strong consistency and interconnection between HRM policies and practices internally in order to achieve effective performance. This is also known as 'internal alignment' or 'internal fit'

through appropriate business metrics such as the organization's key performance indicators (Rousseau and Barends, 2011; Angrave et al., 2016).

These features and characteristics show how the contemporary HRM function aims to enable organizational growth, productivity and profitability, through the creation of an HRM strategy in line with the overall business strategy. This HRM strategy will then determine the HR policies and practices in which the organization engages, as highlighted in Figure 1.1.

HRM POLICIES AND PRACTICES

Given how organizational context will influence the strategic HR choices the business will make, there are many different types of HR policies and practices in which the organization can engage. One way to examine the range of possible HR policies and practices is to follow the lifecycle of the employee (Figure 1.2). By their lifecycle, we

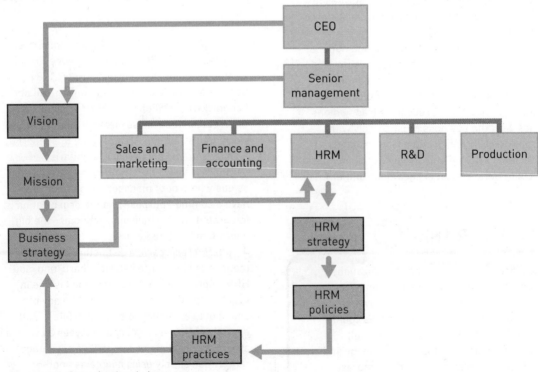

Figure 1.1 Organizational chart

Attract & select
- Employer branding
- Organizational design
- Organizational structure
- Recruitment strategy
- Selection techniques
- Onboarding

Manage & develop
- Organizational culture
- Management style
- Performance management
- Motivation
- Level of employee participation
- Discipline and grievance
- Learning
- Development

Separate
- Exit interviews
- Outsourcing
- Retirement
- Redundancy

Reward & retain
- Pay and benefits
- Recognition
- Employee engagement
- Talent management
- Succession planning
- Career planning
- Employee welfare
- Employment relations

Figure 1.2 Employee lifecycle

mean how employees are initially attracted to the organization, how they are recruited and selected ▶Chapter 3◀, how their performance is managed ▶Chapter 7◀, how they are developed ▶Chapter 9◀, rewarded ▶Chapter 8◀, engaged with over time, and ultimately how they come to exit the organization. While all organizations will develop policies and engage in practices across each stage of the lifecycle, as we have already discussed, the HR philosophy and environmental context will shape the choices they make. Sometimes these choices are more aligned with a more basic PM approach and at other times with a more complex HRM, or even strategic HRM, approach, as discussed later in this chapter.

LINKING HR PRACTICES TO ORGANIZATIONAL OUTCOMES

As mentioned earlier, an HRM approach aims to enable everyone in the organization (leaders, managers, teams and individuals) to contribute fully to meeting the organization's strategic objectives. The strategy will determine the development of a range of HR policies, setting out principles or guidelines for the various practices within HR. Some policies will guide very tangible practices, such as how to recruit, develop and pay employees, while others will guide more intangible practices, such as how to motivate and engage employees. Ultimately, each HR policy should guide an HR practice that creates an organizational behaviour that leads to a desired organizational outcome. The example in Figure 1.3 on the next page looks at how an HR function might enable an organization to become more innovative.

Where organizations develop a suite of HR policies and practices which meet the characteristics outlined above, they are said to have achieved a **high-performance work system (HPWS)** (Guest, 1997). HRM, therefore, is not simply a set of individual practices; rather, it must be viewed as a system, where the elements are integrated and mutually reinforcing in order to produce an effective outcome at an organizational level (Schuler and Jackson, 2014). For an interesting overview of a broad range of high-performance work practices (HPWPs) which are said to comprise the high-performance work system, see Posthuma et al. (2013).

> **High-performance work system (HPWS)** – where the HRM practices are integrated and mutually reinforcing in order to produce an effective outcome at an organizational level

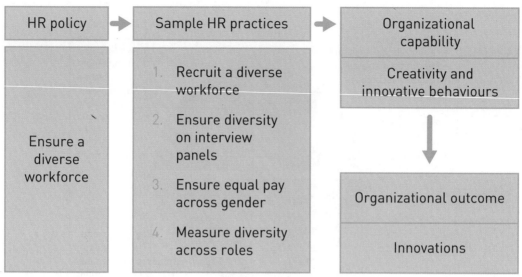

Figure 1.3 Linking HR practices to organizational outcomes

Who Benefits from HRM?

Before we move on, however, it is important to note that the aforementioned debate on the difference between PM and HRM is not about a label; the concerns run much deeper. During the social and economic changes of the 1960s and 70s, there was a belief among employees and trade unions that management did not share the same goals as employees, which led to employees referring to managers as 'them' and to themselves as 'us'. The juxtaposition of 'them and us' highlighted the division between two sides with conflicting interests (Clegg, 1979). Despite significant advances in the theory and practice of HRM, its claims of a unitarist perspective and a decline in the role of trade unions, many would argue that the division between 'them and us' remains and is, in fact, wider than ever. Though contemporary HRM practices espouse notions of 'nurturing' every individual as a 'unique talent' and 'unleashing the potential' of employees, and new HR job titles such as 'head of talent' or 'people director' abound, it has been shown that many employees, including managers (Harding et al., 2014), are experiencing higher levels of control, less ownership of their work and increased work intensification (Boxall and Macky, 2014).

This highlights an inherent conflict in the role played by the HR function, where the question is often expressed as follows: Am I representing the best interests of the employee, or the best interests of the organization? Is the role of HR to act as an organizational guardian or as an employee champion? This is an issue many HR professionals struggle with and there is no simple answer. Ultimately, it must be recognized that, as a business function, HR does not exist to 'serve' the employee but exists to enable a successful and sustainable business for its owners. Therefore, HR is accountable to the employer, and the more closely it is aligned to the employer's business strategy, the more successful the outcome of the HR strategy (Tichy et al., 1982; Guest et al., 2003). However, given its accountabilities around compliance with employee legislation and the known link between employee wellbeing, motivation and productivity, is HR not also accountable to the people who make up that organization? Does this imply HR has a broader role to play then in the 'world of work' and even a role in the impact of corporations on society? This is discussed in more detail in ▶Chapter 14◀. To conclude, the real debate in HRM, therefore, is not the difference between PM and HRM but the role HR plays in ensuring it meets the needs of the business while recognizing the 'human' in human resources. Each organization's HR function, and indeed each HR professional or people manager, must determine whether one can be successfully and sustainably achieved without the other.

As we begin our journey into the world of HRM, it will be up to you to consider this debate. As you progress through this book, you will acquire knowledge on the theory and practice of HRM. It is hoped that this knowledge will allow you to form your own opinions, and develop your own HR philosophy, whether you are an employer, manager or employee. Let us start by looking at the structure of the HR function itself.

STRUCTURE AND ROLE OF THE HR FUNCTION

As it is a key organizational function, in the same way that finance or marketing is, you will see that HR is typically positioned at the same level in the organizational chart (see Figure 1.1 on page 8). However, the size of the organization has an impact on how the HRM function is configured. If, after college or university, you decide to start up your own company, are you likely to have an HR function from the beginning? The answer is probably no. You will make all the decisions yourself about who to hire, what to pay them and how to dismiss them if needs be. Given the significant amount of legislation governing the employment relationship, many business owners use consultants to advise them on specific HR-related issues, or they outsource the main HR functions. This allows them to reduce costs while still ensuring specialist expertise, although it is external to the company. The outsource provider can manage all or part of the HR function, including pay and benefits, administration and the creation of new organization-specific HR policies and practices.

In large organizations, however, such as a multinational corporation (MNC) like Apple or Toyota, the function will be sizeable and highly structured. It is typically led by an HR director, who has a seat on the board of directors, where they have access to and the support of the senior management team. This situation provides a real opportunity for the integration of HR strategy and business strategy. As has been mentioned before, however, the HR philosophy of the owner or CEO will determine the level of involvement HR might have with the business strategy. Fombrun and colleagues (1984), at the Michigan School in the USA, identified the different ways HR strategy can be linked to business strategy. These include:

- *a separation model* where there is no connection between the two
- *a fit model* where the organizational strategy precedes and influences the HR strategy
- *a dialogue model* where the HR strategy has an opportunity to influence the business strategy as it is being developed
- *a holistic model* where they are developed in tandem

- *an HR-driven model* where the HR strategy, and therefore the human resources across the business, drives the development of the business strategy from the bottom up.

Typically, the more engaged an owner or CEO is with the concept of their organization's human resources as a strategic asset, the more likely they are to engage in an HR structure with increased levels of influence over the business strategy.

CONSIDER THIS

Do different organizational contexts require stronger links between the business strategy and HR strategy? Compare the differences between how a factory making cakes and one making medical devices might approach the development of its business and HR strategies.

How the HR function is configured after that often depends on the organization's context, needs and preferences. Some may organize around *specialist* roles. These often follow the lifecycle of the employee as outlined by Beer et al (1984). The different specialisms within the HR function mirror the path of the employee lifecycle as already shown in Figure 1.2.

Other organizations may work with *generalist* roles, where an HR generalist works with a specific group of employees, for example production operators, and handles all the issues related to that group. As the alignment of HR with the business strategy is vital to HR's successful contribution, the role of the HR business partner has emerged in recent years. Developed by David Ulrich and colleagues (2012), the HR business partner is seen as a consultant to the organization, working closely with line managers to ensure that HR practices enable the successful delivery of business strategy. This increased focus on the alignment of HR strategy with business strategy has, in some organizations, led to a separation of the function into operational and strategic teams. The operational team focuses on the day-to-day responsibilities of HR, which could be viewed as the more traditional PM role. This allows the strategic team of business partners to focus on practices more associated with strategic HRM, such as the acquisition and development of 'talent', that is, those employees who are considered to add strategic value to the organization ▸Chapter 2◂. This allows HR to identify and support strategic projects and to focus on long-term business strategies and organizational needs (Gaines Robinson and Robinson, 2005). Interestingly, however, while HR practitioners view strategic partnership as the most important aspect of their roles, Murphy (2010) found that only 15% of HR time is spent on strategic activities.

Many HR practitioners believe the answer to this issue might lie in technology. The creation of a shared services approach is where all the routine 'transactional' HRM services are provided from a central, often remote, location to all parts of the business. These typically include recruitment administration, compensation and benefits administration, answering employee queries related to HR policies, and providing advice to managers on employee issues such as discipline and absenteeism. Many of these services can even be provided in a 'self-service' manner via online solutions. The benefit for the organization is that this reduces the number of HR employees working at an operational level and allows them to focus on taking a more strategic approach.

SPOTLIGHT ON SKILLS

The idea of HR business partners was popularized by David Ulrich, who sees them as part of a successful modern HR function, along with shared services and centres of expertise. There has been a move in larger organizations towards separating out the role of the HR business partner from the more administration and relationship oriented role of HR. As the CEO of a large corporation, how would you structure the HR function? Would your response be the same if you worked for a small business?

To help you consider the issues above, visit **www.macmillanihe.com/carbery-cross-hrm-2e** and watch the video of Fiona Evans from the Zoological Society of London talking about the strategic role of HR.

Roles and Competencies of the HR Practitioner

Ulrich and colleagues, through ongoing, global research with HR practitioners, line managers and HR consultants over the last 20 years, have been exploring the evolution of the HR function (Ulrich et al., 2008, 2012). Their work highlights the increasing complexity of the role. The organizational chart in Figure 1.4 shows the various aspects of the HR function discussed thus far and some examples of the types of practices associated with each area.

Along with the need to focus on specialist areas, Ulrich et al. (2008, 2012) stress the importance of HR practitioners developing the key competencies necessary to deliver a successful and sustainable HR strategy. They believe these competencies are as important as, if not more important than, the configuration of the HR function, as HR practitioners have an impact across four different dimensions:

1. They operate at an individual level, building effective relationships and good reputations across the business.
2. They operate organizationally, as they are responsible for the design and delivery of appropriate HR practices that reach right across the organization.
3. They operate contextually, as their understanding of the internal and external environments specific to their organization are vital in developing the appropriate HR strategy.
4. They operate at a strategic level, as they have a role in developing leader, manager and employee perceptions of the HR function as adding value and enabling them to deliver on the business strategy, rather than just managing the more basic operations of the employment relationship.

In the latest iteration of Ulrich et al.'s (2012) research, the following competencies needed in the mix of the HRM function were identified:

1. *Credible activists* where HR practitioners deliver on their promises, are trusted by the business, and take action in a positive manner as and when needed by the business.
2. *Capability builders* where HR practitioners identify the core processes and capabilities which will positively impact on the business strategy and then deliver the appropriate HR practices to build and sustain these capabilities in the workforce.

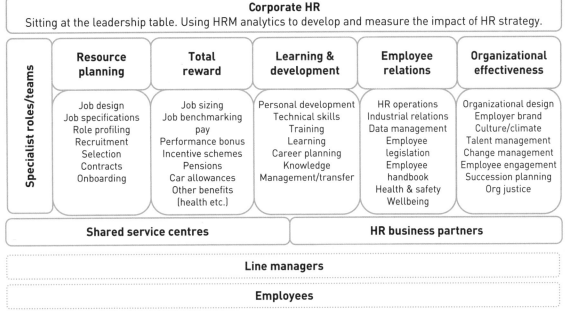

Corporate HR Sitting at the leadership table. Using HRM analytics to develop and measure the impact of HR strategy.					
Specialist roles/teams	**Resource planning**	**Total reward**	**Learning & development**	**Employee relations**	**Organizational effectiveness**
	Job design Job specifications Role profiling Recruitment Selection Contracts Onboarding	Job sizing Job benchmarking pay Performance bonus Incentive schemes Pensions Car allowances Other benefits (health etc.)	Personal development Technical skills Training Learning Career planning Knowledge Management/transfer	HR operations Industrial relations Data management Employee legislation Employee handbook Health & safety Wellbeing	Organizational design Employer brand Culture/climate Talent management Change management Employee engagement Succession planning Org justice

Shared service centres	HR business partners

Line managers

Employees

Figure 1.4 HR function

3. *Change champions* where HR practitioners enable the organization to respond to the external pressures and pace of change, engaging key stakeholders and enabling flexible and adaptable capabilities in the organization.

4. *Innovators and integrators* where HR practitioners use the latest scientific evidence and business insights to continuously develop new HR practices, in a sustainable and integrated manner, as and when they are needed by the business.

5. *Technology proponents* where HR practitioners have the skills to leverage available technologies, which facilitate the effective and efficient delivery of HR practices, but also to use HR analytics to ensure these HR practices are positively impacting the business strategy ▶Chapter 11◀.

The Role of the Line Manager

In reflecting on the different roles in the HR function, it is important to appreciate that simply having a range of HRM policies and practices aligned with the business strategy does not automatically mean that high levels of organizational performance and the realization of that business strategy will follow (Purcell et al., 2003). The role of the line manager, a key stakeholder, in feeding into the

Devolved – the process of moving decision-making downwards, from HR to line managers

Line managers – managers who have employees directly reporting to them and who have a higher level of responsibility than those employees

design of HR practices and their implementation and interpretation locally across the organization is critically important (Purcell et al., 2003). For many years, the literature has identified that the various day-to-day HR practices, once the sole remit of the HR department, need to be **devolved** to **line managers** in order to allow for faster decision-making that is more in tune with business needs. The rationale is that the line manager is the person who works most closely with the employee (Whittaker and Marchington, 2003; Trullen et al., 2016).

The types of activities traditionally devolved to line managers include employee selection, discipline and performance management. HR provides support and guidance to line managers in these activities, which also allows HR the time to move towards aligning the people management agenda with the strategic goals of the organization. However, increasingly, with more evolved strategic HR practices, line managers are being included in the design and development of HR practices at an earlier stage, as it ensures a more successful and sustainable implementation and interpretation of the practice as HR envisaged (Trullen et al., 2016). This move towards a partnership approach between HR and the line manager is central to achieving successful outcomes for the employee and the organization. Of course, this requires a higher

HRM AND ORGANIZATIONAL PERFORMANCE

Southwest Airlines and the high-involvement approach

Despite significant global events in the last 20 years, such as terrorist threats and the financial crisis, the US-owned Southwest Airlines is one of the most successful globally. This is in large part due to its unique approach to HRM. Typically, low-cost airlines, like Southwest, take a low-involvement approach to HRM. Ryanair is a good example of this, where trade unions are not fully recognized, and employees must purchase their own uniforms, pay for their own training and are not allowed to charge their phones on flights. In stark contrast, however, Southwest Airlines takes a high-involvement approach. This includes such practices as having ten separate collective agreements (an agreement made between an employer and a trade union of employees on the terms and conditions of employment >Chapter 5◄) with different employee groups, a People University for all training and development, and even sending each of their employees a birthday card.

---

involvement of HR in developing and supporting line managers to engage in these HR practices locally. This development and support is critical as line managers often believe they are already busy enough with the technical aspects of their role (Whittaker and Marchington, 2003).

THEORETICAL BASIS OF HRM

Having explored the history of HRM and the various elements which go into the design and practice of HRM today, we must now reflect on its theoretical foundations. A number of models are considered particularly influential in understanding the basis of HRM in organizations. Two of the most influential models originated in the USA, and essentially legitimized HRM as a key business process and significantly enhanced its status as an important organizational function.

The Michigan Model of HRM

The first model we will look at is known as the 'fit' or 'contingency' model and was developed in the Michigan Business School by Fombrun, Tichy, Devanna and colleagues in the 1980s (Tichy et al., 1982; Fombrun et al., 1984). This model stresses the importance of that alignment or 'fit' we discussed earlier, firstly between the HR strategy and the business strategy (vertical integration or external alignment) and secondly between the HR practices themselves (horizontal integration or internal alignment). Shown in Figure 1.5, it suggests that this fit can be achieved with a relatively straightforward suite of HR practices and highlights five key areas on which HRM should focus:

1. Selection of the most suitable individuals to meet the needs of the business.
2. Managing performance to achieve corporate objectives.
3. Appraising performance and providing feedback.
4. Providing rewards for appropriate performance that achieve specific goals.
5. Developing employees to meet the needs of the business.

Criticisms of this model include the one-way nature of the HR and business strategy relationship, and the lack of recognition of employee interests and behaviour choice, in that it assumes that all employees are the same. For this reason it is said to be a low-involvement model of HRM or the 'hard' approach which we discussed earlier. Despite these criticisms, this model has been shown to be very effective in many types of organizations and forms the basis of the 'best fit' approach to HRM, discussed later in the chapter.

'Universal' Approach to HRM

The second dominant model was developed by Beer and his colleagues around the same time as the

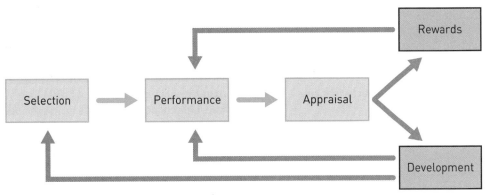

Figure 1.5 The Michigan model of HRM

Source: Figure 3.2, The human resource cycle, from Devanna, M.A., Fombrun, C.J. and Tichy, N.M. (1984) 'A Framework for Strategic Human Resource Management' in C.J. Fombrun, N.M. Tichy and M.A. Devanna (eds) *Strategic Human Resource Management*, p.41, Hoboken, NJ: John Wiley & Sons, Inc. Copyright © 1984 by John Wiley & Sons, Inc. All rights reserved.

Michigan model but at Harvard University (Beer et al., 1984). Referred to by the authors as the HR Territory Map, but now more commonly referred to as the 'universal' or 'soft' approach to HRM, this model recognizes the influence that various stakeholders and situational factors have on the development of HR policies and practices (Beer et al., 1984). Stakeholders have a financial interest in the organization and include shareholders, leaders, managers, employees and other external stakeholders such as the government. Each stakeholder has different interests and the model assumes that these interests are legitimate. Therefore, they should be reflected in the HRM strategy, which is as closely aligned to the business strategy as possible. Situational factors must also be considered in the development of the HR strategy and include aspects of the economic climate, the state of the labour market, the characteristics of the workforce, trade union membership and legislation. The model focuses specifically on how the development of HR practices, incorporating these stakeholder interests and situational factors, will lead to a change in organizational behaviours or the building of organizational capabilities, which in turn lead to specific organizational outcomes (we considered an example of how diverse workforces create innovative behaviours see p. 10).

The main contribution of this model was to highlight the potential benefits of adopting a 'soft' approach to HRM. The inclusion of stakeholders and situational factors in the model was well received; however, some would still argue that manager and employee interests are only being considered in order to meet the needs of the employer. The model has also received criticism for its complexity and high-involvement approach. It suggests there is a formula for building organizational capability but does not provide a list of HR practices for organizations to follow. The search for this 'formula' has been likened to a search for the holy grail (Boselie et al., 2005) or the key to unlocking a 'black box' (Purcell, 2003).

Guest Model of HRM

In the UK, David Guest (1989) considered the benefits of both the low-involvement and high-involvement models. In an effort to balance the 'fit' and 'universal' elements, he built on these models by identifying four key principles that, if followed, would combine to increase organizational effectiveness:

1. *Strategic integration:* HR policies must be aligned to the needs of the business strategy, and the various aspects of HRM must be consistent and mutually supportive.
2. *High commitment:* commitment is sought, in that employees are expected to identify closely with the interests of the organization and behave accordingly.

15

3. *Flexibility:* this involves the ability and willingness of employees to demonstrate flexibility and adaptability to change as business demands change.
4. *High quality:* the quality of management and staff is important in achieving high performance.

Guest believed that these outcomes could best be achieved through appropriate HRM practices in the areas of:

- organizational and job design – job design is the process of arranging work in a way that reduces job dissatisfaction often resulting from repetitive and mechanistic tasks
- change management – the management of change within the organization
- recruitment and selection ▶Chapter 3◀
- appraisal, training and development ▶Chapters 7 and 9◀
- HR movement through, up and out of the organization ▶Chapter 4◀
- reward and communication systems ▶Chapter 8◀.

Ultimately, the three theoretical models discussed here identified the importance of aligning HRM with business strategy. Once again, however, we are dealing with the question of how we identify the HR practices that will enable our organization to achieve optimal organizational performance. In SHRM theory, there are three different perspectives as to how the design and development of such practices can be approached.

Strategic HRM Contingency Approach

The 'contingency' or 'best fit' approach is the belief that organizational context provides the direction as to which HR practices should be chosen. Proponents of this view believe there is no universal answer to the choice of HR practices; the choice is contingent on the context of the organization and its business strategy. So, each organization can choose a different set of practices, depending on their organization-specific context and strategy. External alignment is the key issue (Fombrum et al., 1984; Schuler and Jackson, 1987; Lengnick-Hall and Lengnick-Hall, 1988; Guest, 1997). A number of influential models have been proposed that aim to identify which mix of HR practices is appropriate in

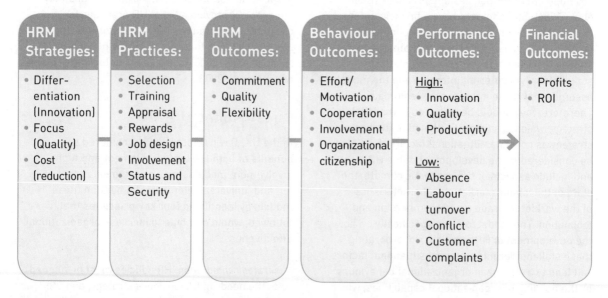

Table 1.1 Guest model of HRM: demonstrating strategic integration
Source: Figure 2, Linking HRM and performance, in Guest, D.E. (1997) 'Human resource management and performance: a review and research agenda', *The International Journal of Human Resource Management*, 8(3), 263–76. Published by Chapman & Hall in 1997, DOI: 10.1080/095851997341630. Reprinted by permission of the publisher Taylor & Francis Ltd: www.tandf.co.uk, www.informaworld.com.

given organizational situations (Miles and Snow, 1978; Schuler and Jackson, 1987; Sisson and Storey, 2000). For example, the work of Schuler and Jackson (1987) suggests that different competitive strategies (Porter, 1985) imply the need for different employee behaviours and thus different sets of HR practices. The most effective way to manage people will therefore depend on issues specific to the organization, such as industry sector, organizational size and economic conditions (see below for more detail on the impact of organizational context on HRM choices). Though considered effective across all business contexts, there is evidence to show that the contingency model is most effective in service environments.

Strategic HRM Universalist Approach

The universalist approach focuses on the existence of one set of HRM 'best practices' aimed at creating and enhancing high levels of employee commitment and performance; these will result in superior levels of organizational performance, regardless of the context in which the organization operates and the competitive strategy of the firm. Pfeffer's (1998) work was influential in this approach. He identified a set of HRM practices, which result in higher performance. His initial work identified thirteen practices, which he later reduced to seven:

- recruiting the right people
- high wages clearly linked to organizational performance
- employment security
- information sharing
- investment in training and skill development
- self-managed teams and decentralized decision-making
- reduced status differentials.

High-involvement HRM – this approach to the employment relationship encourages high levels of employee participation or 'voice' in the decisions that the organization has to make. As such, HR practice and management style seek participation and consultation through a range of formal and informal activities: weekly team meetings, project reviews, employee surveys, etc.

High-commitment HRM – this approach is another way of looking at high-involvement HRM. It refers to an organization's effort to create the right conditions through which employees can be highly involved, but it also stresses the employees' role in fully engaging in this process and working hard to achieve the organization's goals

Low-involvement HRM – this approach to the employment relationship is more control-based, where employees are identified as being core or peripheral in achieving the organization's goals. Peripheral employees are then managed through such HR practices as zero hours contracts, temporary contracts, vendored employment and outsourcing elements of the supply chain

These HR practices are also referred to as **high involvement** (Guthrie, 2001) and **high commitment** (Arthur, 1994). A significant amount of research has focused on testing the existence of these practices. Many studies have indicated a positive relationship between the adoption of a high performance work system and firm-level performance outcomes such as productivity and innovation (for example Appelbaum et al., 2000; Datta et al., 2005; CIPD, 2006; Guthrie et al., 2011), especially in service contexts.

However, critics of the universalist approach would argue that, as mentioned earlier, there is no formula for the most appropriate 'bundle' of HR practices for an organization, and the notion that this high performance work system can ever be realistically achieved is repeatedly questioned (Legge, 1995; Lewin, 2001). Becker and Gerhart, however, provide an interesting overview of the different bundles of HR practices found to be most widely used by organizations (Becker and Gerhart, 1996). There has in fact been much criticism of SHRM overall in terms of this lack of clarity around the appropriate mix of HR practices. Questions over the real levels of integration that can be achieved with business strategy, given that it is constantly evolving, and, most often, SHRM's claim that there is a direct link between HR practice and firm performance, arise continuously in SHRM literature. There is a lack of evidence and consensus as to whether it is the HR practice that has led to performance, or just that high-performing organizations engage more in high-involvement, high-commitment HR practices. In recent years there appears to have been a rise in the use of **low-involvement HRM** with the growing use of zero hours contracts.

HRM IN THE NEWS

Examining HR practices at Netflix, Virgin, McDonald's and Google

Throughout this chapter, we have discussed the different approaches that organizations can take with regard to their human resources: different HR ideologies, business contexts, levels of involvement by HR, and levels of commitment from employees. These approaches determine the strategic choices organizations make around their HR practices. Let us now take a brief look at a range of very different HR practices from around the world and ask the question, 'What does this tell us about this organization?'

Vacation entitlements at Netflix and Virgin

In recent years two big name brands, Netflix in the USA and Virgin in the UK, decided to scrap vacation tracking and entitlements altogether. However, they were not ignoring their legal obligation to provide statutory annual leave to their employees – quite the opposite! These organizations made the bold decision to allow employees to take as much vacation time as they felt they needed, whenever they needed it – as long as it did not compromise their team or the business. It is felt that this more flexible approach will lead to higher creativity, flexibility and productivity among employees.

Getty Images/iStockphoto/Magone

Learning and development at McDonald's

McDonald's takes the development of its human resources so seriously that it has built a state-of-the-art university campus on 80 acres in Illinois and similar campuses in Sydney, Munich, London, Tokyo, São Paulo and Shanghai to provide accredited programmes in management and leadership for all its employees. Employees can attain fully accredited degrees

iStock.com/manop1984

there, giving them access to postgraduate study in other state universities. It has also been noted that McDonald's takes its employee development so seriously that Hamburger University's selection procedure is tougher than that of Harvard!

Retention at Google

The main HRM tool that the company uses for retaining high-quality human resources is its compensation and benefits package ▶Chapter 8◀. In addition to high salaries and wages, employees get a range of benefits which include free meals, dry cleaning, car washing, massages and a company doctor. The typical design of the company's offices emphasizes fun and creativity, which also attracts and retains creative and innovative workers.

Getty Images/Pinghung Chen/EyeEm

Questions

1. What role do you believe the business context plays in relation to each of these HR practices?
2. What different roles might HR and the line manager play in relation to implementing each of these practices?
3. What behaviours and other outcomes do you think each of these HR practices will produce for the organization?

Sources

Netflix Holiday Policy:
Pink, D. (2010) 'Netflix lets its staff take as much holiday as they want, whenever they want – and it works', *Telegraph*, 14 August

Virgin Holiday Policy:
Branson, R. (2014) 'Why we're letting Virgin staff take as much holiday as they want', *Virgin*, 23 September

McDonald's Training Policy:
http://corporate.mcdonalds.com/mcd/corporate_careers2/training_and_development/hamburger_university.html (accessed 11 June 2018)

Walters, N. (2015) 'McDonald's Hamburger University can be harder to get into than Harvard and is even cooler than you'd imagine', *Business Insider* UK, 24 October

SUMMARY

In this chapter we have explored HRM and developed an understanding of the critical role it plays in organizations today. By considering the major characteristics of HRM and looking at who is responsible for HRM, we see where the HRM function should fit into the organizational structure. By understanding the link between business strategy and HRM, we can see how HRM adds value to an organization. The most important thing to recognize is the link between HRM and organizational performance and the extent to which HRM can shape the strategic objectives of the business. Having discussed HRM policies, practices and strategies in general terms, the rest of the book looks at specific aspects of the HR function, beginning with workforce planning and talent management in ▶Chapter 2◀.

FURTHER READING

Boxall, P. and Purcell, J. (2015) *Strategy and Human Resource Management*, 4th edn, Basingstoke: Palgrave.

Robin Kramar (2014) 'Beyond strategic human resource management: is sustainable human resource management the next approach?', *The International Journal of Human Resource Management*, 25:8, 1069–1089, DOI: 10.1080/09585192.2013.816863.

Susan E. Jackson, Randall S. Schuler & Kaifeng Jiang (2014) 'An Aspirational Framework for Strategic Human Resource Management', *The Academy of Management Annals*, 8:1, 1–56, DOI: 10.1080/19416520.2014.872335.

Torrington, D., Hall, L., Taylor, S. and Atkinson, C. (2014) *Human Resource Management*, 9th edn, Harlow: Financial Times/Prentice Hall.

CHAPTER REVIEW QUESTIONS

1. Explain how HRM can contribute to improved organizational performance.
2. Legge (1995) has identified HRM as effectively being 'old wine in a new bottle'. Do you agree with this perspective?
3. Identify the key characteristics of HRM.
4. Do you believe that there is one set of HR practices that can be used by an organization, regardless of the context the organization operates in?
5. Identify five key HRM practices in the employee lifecycle. Describe how each of these would operate in an organization in the manufacturing sector.
6. Explain how devolving HRM practices to line managers has an impact on the role of the HR function.
7. Explain how the seven practices identified by Pfeffer in the best practice approach to HRM can positively impact on organizational performance.
8. Explain the term 'strategic human resource management'.

USEFUL WEBSITES

www.cipd.co.uk
The Chartered Institute of Personnel and Development website is an excellent starting point for anyone interested in HRM. CIPD is based in the UK and Ireland and is the world's largest chartered HR and development professional body.

www.shrm.org
The Society for HRM is a US-based association that promotes the role of HR as a profession and provides education, certification and networking to its members.

www.hrdiv.org
The HR Division of the Academy of Management (www.aomonline.org) looks at how organizations can improve performance through effective management of their human resources. The British Academy of Management (www.bam.ac.uk) also has an HRM Special Interest Group.

www.ahri.com.au
The Australian HR Institute (AHRI) is the national association representing HR and people management professionals in Australia. The website contains lots of useful information, including research and reports.

For extra resources, including videos, multiple choice questions and useful weblinks, go to:
www.macmillanihe.com/carbery-cross-hrm-2e.

2: Workforce Planning and Talent Management

Ultan Sherman

By the end of this chapter you will be able to:

- Understand what is meant by the term 'workforce planning'
- Assess the internal and external factors that shape workforce planning
- Explore each stage of the human resource planning cycle model
- Critically analyse the relationship between workforce planning and talent management
- Critically analyse the key debates in the literature on talent management
- Evaluate the contribution of talent management to the strategic development of organizations

THIS CHAPTER DISCUSSES:

Introduction (22)

Workforce Planning (22)

The Human Resource Planning Cycle (23)

From Workforce Planning to Talent Management (26)

What Exactly is Talent Management? (27)

INTRODUCTION

Do you know where you will be and what you will be doing in five years' time? For many of you, this will be a difficult question to answer. However, this is an issue facing most organizations, and their response will reveal a great deal about how their employees will need to be managed during that period. This is *workforce planning*. While many aspects of HRM attend to the day-to-day running of the organization, there are growing demands on the HR function to plan, predict, develop and adjust staffing needs in order to achieve organizational goals both now and for the future. Accordingly, there is an increasingly strategic focus to the HR function in contemporary organizations.

With this in mind, this chapter explores the key aspects of HR planning and seeks to analyse its strategic dimensions. In relation to this, the central role of 'talent management' in achieving organizational objectives is discussed. Specifically, the emergence of talent management as a significant HR process is outlined and the opportunities and challenges it presents to the organization are analysed. Drawing upon important theory from the HR planning and talent management literatures and using examples from contemporary firms, this chapter aims to provide insight into this critical area of HRM.

WORKFORCE PLANNING

Workforce planning is ensuring the right number of people with the necessary skills are employed in the right place at the right time to help deliver an organization's short- and long-term objectives. In many ways, the HR function is attempting to see into the future to help make decisions in the present day. There are many famous examples down through the years of organizations making bold predictions about the future. From Project Horizon (US military's plan to colonize the moon by the 1960s) to Steve Balmer (former CEO of Microsoft) predicting in 2007 that the iPhone would flop, these cases touch on perhaps the biggest challenge of human resource planning: predicting the unknown. Very few organizations predicted the scale of the global economic upheaval back in 2008. As a consequence, many are still, today, coming to terms

with how dramatic an economic recession it was. In his study on the dynamic work environment, Guest (2004) refers to the 'urgency of change' affecting the employment relationship. He argues that in the last quarter century, societal, economic, political and technological changes have all profoundly shaped how organizations function. The implications of these changes for the HR function are vast.

For example, very few organizations would have forecast Britain voting to leave the EU and Donald Trump being elected as president of the USA. While it remains unclear as to how these seismic events will specifically affect the business landscape, it is likely there will be implications for US multinational corporations (MNCs) in Europe, migration patterns in Britain, and currency rates, as examples. Such developments would represent enormous challenges for the HR function. Let us say you are the HR director of a US MNC in northern England. Trying to plan the HR requirements for the firm over the next five years would be enormously difficult as there could be the possibility of the company pulling out of the region in line with Trump's economic policies. Even if the firm were to remain, there may be issues relating to the supply of labour in the region as a result of increasing numbers of skilled EU nationals returning to their home countries. Similarly, from a day-to-day perspective, there would likely be morale issues amongst staff fearful for their future in the firm. So, workforce planning is fraught with the difficulty of predicting the future. That is not to say, however, that HR should casually ignore the future. Indeed, an HR function following a carefully designed workforce plan will make a significant contribution to the strategic development of the firm (Jackson et al., 2014). The next section discusses how organizations typically approach the workforce planning challenge.

> **Workforce planning** is the process through which an organization ensures it has the right number of people with the right skills in the right roles both now and for the future

CONSIDER THIS

In many ways, workforce planning tries to predict the future. Reflecting on your own career plans, what skills will be needed in your chosen profession in the near future? Are you currently in an employable position or are there areas where you fall short?

THE HUMAN RESOURCE PLANNING CYCLE

Workforce planning is an open-ended process. As long as the organization is still in operation, the HR function will be making workforce plans. To that end, a number of researchers have suggested that the planning process occurs in a continuous cycle (e.g. Hendry, 1995). Figure 2.1 below outlines the key stages of this cycle.

Stocktaking

The first stage in the human resource planning cycle is the identification of the factors likely to shape the operation of the firm, **stocktaking**. Two broad categories of influencers are assessed: external factors and internal factors. There are myriad external factors that affect organizations and, as explained earlier, they can be very difficult to predict. Issues relating to the economic climate, employment legislation and technological advancement are all likely to influence the present and future plans of the firm. These forces, of course, cannot be controlled by the organization. However, the

> **Stocktaking** is the stage of the human resource planning cycle where the organization must identify a range of factors currently impacting its operations

organization can control how they respond to these changes. For example, many countries around the world, such as Sweden, Ireland and Japan, have introduced new employment legislation to increase paternity leave for fathers. Typically, fathers in these countries were legally allowed to take a day or two off following the birth of their child, but recent changes at a societal level have seen fathers assume more responsibility in raising their children. Virgin Group, however, decided to go one step further than simply adhering to this legislation. In a pilot scheme, male managers who have been with the firm for at least four years are entitled to a year's paternity leave on full pay. New fathers who have been with Virgin for two years or less will receive a quarter of their salary. Fully paid paternity leave is obviously a great perk to offer employees, but this proactive step also allows Virgin to assume greater control over employees' leave which puts it in a stronger position when making future workforce plans. It allows Virgin to hire replacements on relatively longer term temporary contracts which can ensure a stronger pool of applicants.

On the other hand, internal factors are those organizational forces that impact the day-to-day running of the firm. The numbers employed, the profile of the workforce (e.g. young or ageing), training provision history, work conditions, performance reviews, team dynamics, and so on, are just some of the organizational factors that shape how employees behave and perform in their roles. The organization can to a large extent control these factors. Early on, it is important to develop an accurate staff profile in terms of age, skills, contract status, and so on. For example, a team leader tasked with managing a large project might find it difficult to make long-term plans if the majority of her team are on temporary contracts. Such employees could be considered 'flight-risks' in that they may seek more secure employment elsewhere. Certainly, the contract status of staff is particularly pertinent when an organization is planning for the future. Assessing the HR profile of the organization is effectively taking a snapshot of current staffing arrangements. It is a necessary step before any strategic change can be implemented.

In general, analysing both the internal and external factors shaping day-to-day operations is an important first step in identifying how HR can contribute to the strategic development of the firm.

Figure 2.1 The human resource planning cycle
Source: adapted from Figure 5.1, Human resource planning process, from Gunnigle, P., Heraty, N. and Morley, M.J. (2011) *Human Resource Management in Ireland*, 4th edition, p.103, Dublin: Gill Education. Copyright © Gill Education 2011.

Forecasting

The second stage of the human resource planning cycle requires **forecasting** both the *supply* of labour and the *demand* for labour. This is arguably the most difficult aspect of workforce planning, as the HR function is tasked with predicting how many employees will be required in the future in line with the strategic development of the firm. However, examining past business trends can help a firm make more sound predictions for the future. For example, a large MNC would reflect on the staffing implications of its last firm acquisition before making decisions about the workforce following its latest acquisition.

If the organization has very clear strategic aims then it is perhaps a little easier to make predictions about the 'demand' for labour. Let us say that a recently established firm with a small marketing function recognizes the need for more advertising in order to continue its growth. To achieve this objective, it may require marketing and advertising specialists to join the marketing team. A job analysis would need to be created, outlining the responsibilities and requirements for each role. So, as the marketing needs of the firm increase, so too does the demand for labour. Of course, for some firms, as one function expands, another may no longer be required. Indeed, a central aspect of workforce planning is understanding the changing need for certain roles and certain skills. For example, the newspaper industry is currently seeing most publications move their content to online platforms. As a result, the demand for labour in these newspapers is particularly focused on IT roles. This development often comes at the expense of the employees working in the print rooms, with thousands of print workers being made redundant in recent years. Of course, a key planning requirement for the HR function is to dispense with workers who are no longer making a strategic contribution to the firm. Other options available to the firm may be implementing reduced working hours, switching to part-time contracts, redeploying staff to other functions in the organization, and so on. Indeed, a change to established working arrangements is a typical consequence of a labour surplus. It is likely that these developments in labour demands in the newspaper industry will continue for some time.

As regards forecasting the 'supply' of labour, the organization examines both 'internal' and 'external' sources. In terms of examining the internal

> **Forecasting** is the stage of the human resource planning cycle where the organization must predict the demand for and supply of labour in order to meet the strategic goals of the firm

supply, the organization assesses the extent to which current staff can help to achieve the strategic objectives of the firm. HR may recognize that there is a labour shortage in certain areas, therefore requiring further recruitment. Or, as is evident in the newspaper example earlier, in line with the future direction of the organization, HR may identify a labour surplus and decide to dispense with certain areas of the workforce. However, forecasting the internal supply of labour is more than a case of simply counting the number of employees in the organization. The HR function must also examine the skills, competencies, motivation, knowledge, and so on of their workforce. For example, a MNC considering setting up a new site in Malaysia would need to know which of the current staff have international experience, are familiar with Malaysian business practices and are interested in an international assignment, before making a decision on staffing the new site. When an organization has completed this type of 'audit', it can start planning the necessary workforce changes for the future.

An important dimension of assessing the internal supply of labour is what the HR function describes as 'succession planning'. This refers to the process through which a successor for a departing staff member can be in found in a way that minimizes any disruption to the organization. Every employee exit presents a challenge to the HR function, but succession planning ensures a smooth transition can occur. Typically, succession planning concerns staff at a more senior level, but it should be in place at all levels, particularly when a poorly planned exit could cause significant difficulties for the organization. Let us say that a junior member of staff identified as an outstanding worker is likely to leave the organization in the near future. If the organization wanted to keep that employee, succession planning may be used to retain them. If, for example, the organization knew that an impending retirement opened up a middle manager position, then presenting this as a promotional opportunity to that employee may help them commit their future to the firm (see Talent Identification on page 29). Of course, not every employee exit can be forecast. However, having a strong internal supply of labour can ensure that any untimely exits can be managed accordingly through effective succession planning.

In terms of examining the external supply of labour, the organization looks outside itself and assesses the extent to which the external labour market can provide suitably qualified personnel. As one might expect, forecasting the external supply of labour is a more difficult task than assessing the internal supply. Labour market trends in recent years have seen huge changes in terms of demographics, migration patterns, work availability, and so on. For example, in Ireland, a number of public sector medical consultant jobs have remained vacant for many years (Wall, 2017). Consultant representative groups argue that Ireland's comparatively low salary levels in the Health Service Executive (the publicly funded state healthcare system) are pushing suitably qualified Irish medics to emigrate and seek better opportunities abroad, and are also discouraging international consultants to apply for the positions. The national wage level is just one of many external factors beyond the organization's control that influences the supply of labour for HR planning. Similarly, using the example of the MNC potentially moving to Malaysia, HR would need to examine the labour market in Malaysia as a means of determining the 'richness' of the supply. An MNC will not set up operations in a location where it believes the supply of labour there is not aligned with strategic corporate plans.

Despite the inherent difficulties of forecasting, it is a necessary step in the strategic development of the organization. When the supply of and demand for labour is understood in line with the future requirements of the firm, the HR function is in a good position to develop and implement subsequent **action planning**.

Develop Action Plans, Implementation and Assessment

When an imbalance occurs between the demand for and supply of labour, the organization is either faced with a labour shortage or labour surplus. Where a shortage exists or is likely to occur, the firm has a number of options open to it. Action plans would typically involve recruitment, retraining or redeployment as appropriate. A labour surplus typically requires the organization to seek redundancies or to reduce the number of hours worked. Whatever course of action is pursued to meet the strategic needs of the organization, there will be significant consequences for the HR function, the workforce and the employment relationship in general. In this sense, it is clear that any plans must be made carefully.

> **Action planning** is the stage in the human resource planning cycle where the organization makes a specific plan regarding how best to use the workforce to help meet the strategic goals of the firm

CONSIDER THIS

Through workforce planning, the HR function might identify a skills shortage amongst its workforce and subsequently decide to hire new staff to address these shortcomings. However, an external appointment often results in an internal candidate being overlooked. Indeed, HR planning often disturbs the status quo in an organization. Is it possible to retain goodwill amongst existing staff when implementing HR plans even if some perceive their career to be stalling as a result? How do you think this can be achieved?

Once the organization has made its decision, the plans are set in motion. Of course, given the turbulent nature of the contemporary business environment, plans need to be constantly monitored and adjusted if required. For example, an organization may recognize that its new training and development plan for staff, designed to strengthen its capacity for succession planning, will not provide any recourse for vacancies in the short term. Therefore, if a vacancy arises and needs to be filled quickly, then the organization may have to recruit from the external labour market. This type of redirection happens frequently in workforce planning as the process itself does not unfold in a linear manner.

The final stage of workforce planning is the assessment stage, where the action plans are evaluated to determine the extent to which they have allowed the organization to achieve strategic goals. Let us say that an organization decided on the back of a labour surplus to let go a large chunk of its middle managers to reduce costs. It may then realize that the economic logic of downsizing often comes at a cost. Research shows that losing middle managers can result in a disconnection between senior and junior managers and that roles and responsibilities are unevenly allocated as a result (Cascio, 2005). In any case, it is important that the organization learns from how the process was implemented so that any successes can be repeated and that any failures can be avoided in the future.

The human resource planning cycle has received much attention from both academics and practitioners alike. The model highlights the key areas of focus and decisions facing the HR function at each of the linked stages. So, from a theoretical

SPOTLIGHT ON SKILLS

Many companies do not appear to engage in formal human resource planning. It can be more reactive than proactive, especially for smaller organizations.

1. What are your views on workforce planning and the approach taken by many large organizations to the use of talent development programmes?
2. Do these programmes mean that not all employees are talented?

To help you consider the issues above, visit **www.macmillanihe.com/carbery-cross-hrm-2e** and watch the video of David Forkin from Hewlett-Packard talking about HR planning and talent management.

perspective, it is somewhat prescriptive. However, as has been explained, the reality of workforce planning in practice is much more complex, with the organization in a constant state of flux. Therefore, the model does not fully capture the difficulties of workforce planning in reality.

FROM WORKFORCE PLANNING TO TALENT MANAGEMENT

As necessitated by the stocktaking and forecasting stages of the human resource planning cycle, organizations are increasingly assessing the capability requirements of their current workforce using a 'future lens' (Collings and Mellahi, 2009). That is, HR, in conjunction with the organization's leaders, is preparing today's employees to address tomorrow's challenges. Contemporary organizations examine their skill, knowledge and ability requirements in the present but more importantly for the future as well, considering the combined scope of the whole organization. As explained earlier, human resource planning is more than just a numbers game. It involves an in-depth assessment of the profile of the workforce as regards skills, experience and expertise. Indeed, in a context where increasing importance is placed on employees' knowledge as a means to organizational success, particularly in knowledge-intensive industries like software design or pharmaceuticals where firms compete against each other to acquire rare, inimitable and valuable intellectual and technical

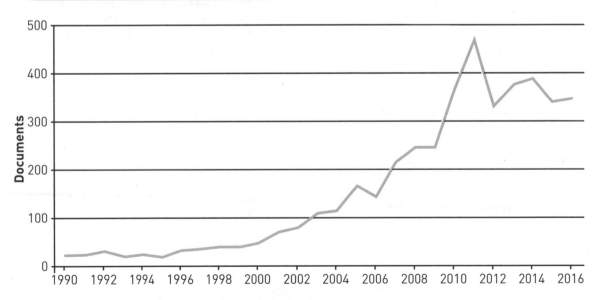

Figure 2.2 Trend analysis of 'talent management' citations
Source: Scopus®, www.scopus.com. Scopus® is a registered trademark of Elsevier B.V. All rights reserved.

skills (Barney, 1991), talent management has emerged as one of the most widely researched topics in the HR literature in the last 20 years. Figure 2.2 on the previous page illustrates the rate at which this concept has received academic interest in terms of citations.

WHAT EXACTLY IS TALENT MANAGEMENT?

The term 'talent management' was first coined in 1997 by a group of McKinsey consultants in their analysis of labour market trends. They explained that the competition between firms to recruit the best employees would be a dominant feature of the HR function in the years ahead. While competing definitions exist, talent management can be broadly defined as the systematic and integrated approach taken within an organization to the attraction, recruitment, engagement and retention of those employees who have been identified to be of particular value to the strategic development of the firm.

Like most 'young' concepts in science, there has been disagreement amongst academics as to what actually constitutes talent management. Table 2.1 below is designed to reflect some of this uncertainty and looks at a number of key questions identified in the literature which require further research.

Question	Debate	Relevant authors
What do we mean by talent?	Talent is a subjective concept in that organizations will differ in their understanding of what it means to be a talented employee (see HRM in the Global Business Environment). However, some researchers argue that the talent management field itself is undermined by what they perceive to be a homogenized conception of what actually constitutes talent (e.g. full-time, male, able-bodied etc.) and that the practice of talent management is often indirectly discriminatory. Some researchers argue that perspectives on talent should focus on skills and behaviours as well as intrinsic traits and characteristics	Iles, Chuai & Preece, 2010 Dries, 2013 Kim & McLean, 2012 Ng & Burke, 2005
Is every employee talented or only certain employees?	This question is at the heart of a central debate in talent management. An 'exclusive' approach differentiates between employees in terms of talent. However, if only certain employees are considered talented, then an organization may need to reassess its approach to staffing. If recruitment and selection are designed to identify the best candidates, then an exclusive approach to talent management would suggest focusing on a very few, outstanding individuals. An 'inclusive' approach sees all employees as talented. But if all employees are considered talented, then how is talent management and all its associated processes different to human resource management? The inclusive/exclusive debate reflects the uncertainty inherent in the practice of talent management	Gelens, Hofmans, Dries & Pepermans, 2014
Should we focus on the person or the position?	In their approach to talent management, some organizations identify specific personnel as talented. That is, they focus on a particular 'person'. As a result, this employee is likely to have a bespoke development plan, additional training and so on. Other organizations differ to this approach in that they focus on a particular 'position'. Certain positions would be considered of strategic significance. This means that the post holder at the time would receive the attention afforded by that particular position. Again, much more research is needed on the strengths and limitations of both approaches	Garavan, Carbery & Rock, 2012

Question	Debate	Relevant authors
Who measures talent?	Another contentious issue for both HR and the workforce is the issue of who measures talent. Typically a line manager or supervisor is best positioned to make judgements about an employee's contribution to the organization. However, within the context of talent, it is important to determine if the line manager has had the requisite training to effectively identify and measure what the organization considers to be talent	Al Ariss, Cascio & Paauwe, 2014
How is talent measured?	This is another contentious issue in trying to establish the distinctiveness of talent management as a unique HR process. Some organizations equate performance ratings to talent. Of course, talented employees often achieve a high level of performance. However, if the organization is simply using performance ratings to determine talent, which often happens, the question remains as to how talent management is distinct from performance management ▶Chapter 7◀. Other organizations attempt to measure potential (see below), but potential is an abstract concept at the best of times. As talent is often subjectively understood, its measurement can be a problematic issue for HR	Lewis & Heckman, 2006
Can we recruit talented employees?	This was the key question in this was the key question in the War for Talent McKinsey report. How can an organization attract talented employees in a competitive labour market? Often, talented employees look beyond financial reasons to join a firm, so HR needs to assess the internal work environment (culture, interesting work, etc.) and determine the extent to which a talented employee can flourish in this workplace	Cappelli & Keller, 2014
How do we develop talent potential in our organization?	Often, talented employees need the right environment for their potential to be reached. Important organizational factors can shape a talented employee's development in this regard, such as the leadership style, work design in terms of opportunities for feedback, autonomous projects and so on. Specifically, organizations need to have a talent development policy for the organization as a whole but also specific talent development plans tailored to meet the needs of each talented employee. This will facilitate the emergence of a talent 'pipeline' providing a continuous supply of star employees to fill any future vacancies (see the discussion on succession planning on page 24)	Claussen, Grohsjean, Luger & Probst, 2014

Table 2.1 Key debates in the literature on talent management

CONSIDER THIS

Sometimes a 'star' – someone identified as an excellent performer who has high potential – does not turn out as expected. Have they lost their talent or were they mistakenly identified as a talented employee? Or are other factors at play? What can an organization do to prevent this happening?

As talent management continues to grow and evolve, organizations are 'waking up' to its potential for bringing about positive organizational outcomes. For example, a study by Ernst and Young in 2010 claimed that over a five-year period, organizations with talent management programmes that are aligned with business strategy deliver a return on investment (measured by return) on common equity on average 20% higher than rival companies where strategies are not aligned (Collings, 2014). Beyond financial benefits, research indicates improved levels of employee engagement in companies with a clear talent management strategy (Bhatnagar, 2007). Certainly, there is a growing body of evidence to support the idea that talent management matters for contemporary organizations. However, it must be stated that talent management does not occur in a vacuum and should not be considered an isolated HR process. As Collings and Mellahi (2009) explain, talent management is most effective when it is supported by a differentiated architecture. That is, rolling out any talent management system only works when it is underpinned by strong recruitment and selection

▶Chapter 3◀, fair reward systems ▶Chapter 8◀ and a clear performance management process ▶Chapter 7◀ for example. Let us say that an organization is looking to create a new approach to talent management that requires a comprehensive measure of employee performance. This new process would not work if supervisors have not been appropriately trained to appraise performance. So, from this example we can see that talent management is dependent on functional *performance appraisal* and appropriate *training* for it to be deemed successful. Indeed, talent management is best understood as a distinct HR process but one that is supported by and relies upon other HR processes for it to be effective.

HRM AND ORGANIZATIONAL PERFORMANCE

'Star' employees at Dana-Farber

In certain industries, 'star' employees expect considerable autonomy and the freedom to pursue individual work goals. This, of course, presents a challenge to organizations when there is a need for these stars to collaborate. Such collaboration can be difficult, especially when stars may be reluctant to relinquish control over projects and have been used to working in 'silos'. At Dana-Farber, a leading cancer research institute, to address this challenge, management introduced a number of key HR changes: star employees received up to 20 times the funding for group projects than for individual projects; collaboration became a key performance metric; and competition between research centres was reduced by making knowledge-sharing a core job requirement. The Dana-Farber approach is a good example of how talent management works most effectively when it is supported by related HR processes (Gardner, 2017).

Talent Identification

The starting point in the development of a talent management process is talent identification. As highlighted in Table 2.1, there is considerable debate as to what actually constitutes talent, which makes it a difficult 'thing' to identify. However, most researchers and practitioners are in agreement that inherent in any conception of talent is the idea of 'potential'. Potential is often judged using previous performance metrics, the individual's abilities and skills, formal qualifications and so on. A talented employee typically is an individual who achieves a high level of performance and has the potential to make a valuable contribution to the firm over time. Or a talented employee may be an individual who may not be achieving high levels of performance at present but may have untapped potential which, in the right circumstances, can be exploited by the organization. Figure 2.3 on the right is an example of

how some organizations categorize their staff when attempting to identify their talented individuals.

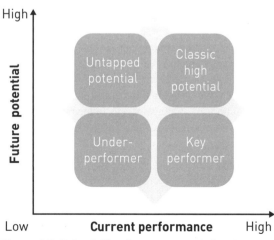

Figure 2.3 Potential/performance matrix in talent identification

BUILDING YOUR SKILLS

Think of three of the most high-achieving members of your group of friends or colleagues. Can you identify what it is about them that makes them a 'high achiever'? Do they share common characteristics, behaviours, abilities? Or is there something similar about each of their environments that is contributing to their 'talent'? Understanding and recognizing the multiple causes of talent is an important skill for HR practitioners to develop.

First, those employees with little potential whose current level of performance is poor are the most obvious candidates to be removed from the firm. When an organization has a labour surplus, these members of staff should be let go first. Of course, the organization may initially decide to address the performance issues as a means of bringing about some improvement, but the consequences of retaining the **underperformers**

> **Underperformers** are those employees who are currently not achieving a high level of performance and have little potential to make a key contribution to the strategic development of the firm

for the strategic development of the firm could be harmful.

The **key performers** are those employees who are highly competent in their present role but are less suited for further development. These workers can present a challenge to HR in that it can be difficult to maintain an effective working relationship with them when they are likely to be overlooked when developmental or promotional opportunities arise. However, the key performers must be reassured of their value to the business. Otherwise they could be a flight-risk.

Those employees in the **untapped potential** category are also a challenging case for the HR function as it is tasked to better understand the reasons why these employees are not realizing their potential. There may be personal difficulties behind their poor performance, and the employee would then need the requisite support. However, there may be knowledge or skills gaps undermining them in the role. In this instance, HR could provide further training, assign a mentor and so on. Interventions like these can help underperforming staff to reach their potential.

HRM IN THE GLOBAL BUSINESS ENVIRONMENT

The transfer of practices from west to east in multinational corporations

Organizations do not always agree on what actually constitutes talent. For example, Google describes a talented employee as 'a challenger who thinks outside the box', whereas PricewaterhouseCoopers considers talented employees as those 'who are willing to take on challenges' (Tansley, 2011). Of course, these firms are MNCs and operate in multiple locations around the globe. Importantly, research demonstrates that cultural factors shape perceptions of employee performance (Hofstede, 1993). For example, in western MNCs there is an emphasis on individual achievement, and talented employees are often viewed first as those who have achieved a high level of individual performance (Dowling et al., 2008). However, in their study of Chinese firms' perspective on talent management, Cooke and colleagues (2014) found that as well as performance, managers considered 'moral

conduct' a key attribute of talented employees. Ethical behaviour is a key virtue of Confucianism, the philosophy underpinning Chinese society, and the influence of Confucian values is evident in this study's findings. But what happens when a western MNC sets up operations in China? Do prevailing Chinese values impact the western approach to talent management? A study of talent management in western MNCs in China by Hartmann and colleagues (2010) found that western MNCs successfully transfer their talent management policies to China without too many changes, focusing specifically on the development of talented employees and establishing an appropriate organizational culture to build an effective employment relationship. This suggests that the organization approach supersedes the national or cultural approach. These and related studies raise important questions about a 'universal' approach to the talent management question.

Finally, those employees identified as having high potential and who are currently achieving excellent performance are often referred to as **HIPOs** (high potentials) or 'stars'. Star employees are rare, so organizations must be delicate in how they manage them so that their 'talent' can be fully exploited by the firm. These employees make up what some organizations refer to as the 'talent pool'. Employees in the pool typically would be appointed to an accelerated development route (which may involve working on special projects). If the company wants to utilize and retain star employees then individual coaching and career management is key.

Identifying talented employees is not an exact science, and developing a typology of employees in terms of performance/potential restricts our understanding of many of the other factors at play such as motivation, life circumstances and so on. However, a talent identification matrix is a useful starting point when assessing the capability requirements of the organization.

Key performers are those employees who are currently achieving a high level of performance but have little potential to make a key contribution to the strategic development of the firm

Untapped potentials are those employees who are currently not achieving a high level of performance but with the necessary changes have the potential to make a key contribution to the strategic development of the firm

HIPOs (high potentials)/ stars are those employees who are currently achieving a high level of performance and have the potential to make a key contribution to the strategic development of the firm

Recruiting Talent

While many organizations prefer promoting talent from within as regards succession planning (see HRM in the News on the next page), at some point in the workforce planning process an organization decides to recruit ▶Chapter 3◀ rather than develop. Having the capacity to attract and recruit talented staff is a key aspect of talent management, particularly where the internal supply of 'talent' is insufficient. However, just because an employee was successful in one firm does not guarantee that they will continue to be a success in the new firm. For instance, there are many examples of sports stars performing at the highest level with one team but then their performance 'flops' following a move to another team. Accordingly, a number of researchers are now focusing on the contextual limitations of talent. An important study on this topic is the work of Groysberg and colleagues in 2004. In their study of the career trajectory of 'star' stock analysts, they found that following a move to a new firm, the star's lustre fades in terms of performance levels. At a group level, the star's new team's performance

slips with an increase in interpersonal conflict. At an organizational level, the firm's valuation suffers following the move (each hiring announcement by Bear Stearns, Merrill Lynch and Salomon Brothers resulted in a fall in their stock prices). The findings of this study have implications for leaders in organizations as they show that recruiting talent is not a guarantee of success and can actually have a detrimental effect at all levels in the firm.

Of course, promoting from within does not always work either. Occasionally, employees identified as star performers or HIPOs do not develop or fulfil their potential as expected. There can be both individual and organizational reasons for this. For example, an employee's motivation in the role might wane and they may lose interest in a particular career path. From an organizational perspective, the individual may have been assigned to the wrong projects and their progress stalled as a result of not being given the opportunity to develop accordingly. In any case, promoting talent from within the organization or sourcing talent externally does not always go to plan ▶Chapter 3◀.

Talent Management Strategy

The airline industry is an interesting context in which to examine how a talent management strategy may be executed. Consider the following question: Which airline has the best pilots? This is a challenging question to answer for many reasons. Firstly, how would you measure the effectiveness of a pilot? Beyond bringing passengers to their destination in a safe way, it is difficult to think of other key performance indicators as perceived by a customer. Also, the safety record of an airline could be attributed to other factors such as the planes used, for example. Now consider this question: Which airline has the best cabin crew? This is perhaps an easier question to answer from the perception of a customer as passengers tend to interact with cabin crew to a greater extent than they do with pilots. So, from a strategic perspective, an increasing number of airlines are focusing on identifying and developing HIPOs amongst cabin crew personnel. Based on the work of Boudreau and

HRM IN THE NEWS

Developing talent at Liverpool Football Club

When Liverpool Football Club recruited Jürgen Klopp as their manager in October 2015, it was generally heralded as a great appointment. Liverpool were struggling but many felt that, with a proven winner like Klopp at the helm, the potential of the young team could be exploited. Klopp had achieved great success in Germany as the manager of Borussia Dortmund with only moderate investment in player recruitment compared to their rivals in the Bundesliga (premier league in Germany). However, most commentators felt Klopp's immediate priority should be to strengthen the squad by buying new players to allow Liverpool to compete with wealthier clubs such as Chelsea, Manchester City and Manchester United.

Early in his tenure, Klopp dismissed this notion. Referring to his success at Dortmund, he argued that player development is sometimes more important than player recruitment: 'My biggest skill is I am patient, so I can wait and we will wait until the [young players] are really ready. It's about timing.' As Liverpool fortunes started to improve, greater attention was focused on the working methods of Klopp and his coaching team and the changes he brought to Liverpool's academy system. Pepjin Lijnders, the club's first-team development coach between 2015 and 2017, illustrates the club's philosophy regarding the development of talent: 'We started the Talent Group so that we have a 15-year-old training with a 19-year-old with the only goal that they know each other. They know the rules of Melwood (Liverpool's training facility), they know the staff, the kitchen, all those things ... but the most important thing is they know each other. They link with each other. Because in the end, and this is our main goal, is that they play together in the first team. And that this is not the first time they have played together. They know each other from 15 years old. There's a saying that talent needs models, it doesn't need criticism. I really believe in that.'

To make it as a professional footballer at the highest level, you have to have a broad range of qualities. However, Lijnders argues that 'talent comes in many different ways ... if you are quick in your mind but not in your legs you can still be a talent'. However, with so few opportunities available to secure a place in the first team, it is perhaps reasonable to expect that individual needs and 'ego' would come at the expense of the collective. Not so, according to Lijnders. While 'character' is important, he believes '70% [of having a career at Liverpool] is feeling for each other and the staff. We believe personal relationships are important.'

When Klopp was asked in his first press conference why he came to Liverpool, his response tapped into his collective philosophy: 'I'm here because Liverpool is a great club but because of the players, because I feel I can help, because we can work together. But we need each other's help.' Liverpool fans are hoping Klopp's approach to talent management pays off.

Questions

1. In what way does a leader influence how talent is managed in an organization?
2. Often, competitive work environments undermine teamwork in an organization. Should being a team player be considered a 'talent' in itself or should it be a basic requirement of every employee?
3. Is it futile for an organization to be patient with an employee identified as having great potential when you consider that they could leave the firm at any stage? What can an organization do to retain potentially great employees?

Sources

Northcroft, J. (2017) 'Football has too much money but you can still be a special player without bling, bling, bling all day', *The Sunday Times*, 8 January, www.thetimes.co.uk/article/football-has-too-much-money-but-you-can-still-be-a-special-player-without-bling-bling-bling-all-day-kjpnw0lj2 (accessed 11 June 2018)

Northcroft, J. (2017) 'Pepijn Lijnders on his role and the stars of Liverpool's academy', Jonathan Northcroft Q&A, *This Is Anfield*, 12 January, www.

thisisanfield.com/2017/01/pepijn-lijnders-role-stars-liverpools-academy-jonathan-northcroft-qa (accessed 11 June 2018)

Jesuthasan (2011), Figure 2.4 below compares the 'value' of talented cabin crew and talented pilots to the strategic development of the airline.

It is clear that that the difference between a high-performing pilot and an average-performing pilot as regards the value to the organization is minimal. However, high-performing cabin crew make a much more valuable contribution than those with average performance levels. Thus, while pilots have traditionally been viewed as core staff and cabin crew positions have been seen as peripheral to the airline's strategy (the positions were relatively low paid and staff were generally seen as easily replaceable), this is starting to change. Airlines are now recognizing that in-flight customer experience is what counts for most passengers (Drescher, 2017), and the cabin crew position is considered of significant strategic consequence.

HIPOs amongst cabin crew are likely to be identified using previous performance measures and other possible valuable skills, such as an ability to speak multiple languages and relevant prior job experience in customer experience roles. Once identified as HIPOs, cabin crew are likely to be appointed a specific development plan. This may involve additional training (e.g. leadership training, first class and business class bespoke training) and being

assigned a mentor. The HIPOs may also be afforded greater autonomy in their role, such as introducing new initiatives to better engage with passengers (of course this may not always be possible in such a regulated work environment). Star employees might be rewarded with bonus pay, flexible work hours, working on more glamorous routes, working on luxury aircraft, ad hoc leadership roles on shorter flights and so on. Managing talented staff in this way facilitates succession planning in that star personnel amongst cabin crew can be promoted to more senior positions without fear of them being ill-equipped to do the job. The HIPOs may be asked to mentor or train the next 'batch' of talented cabin crew, which allows the star employee to share their knowledge and expertise with colleagues. Indeed a central aspect of talent management is to ensure work-related knowledge stays within 'organizational memory' (Wang and Noe, 2010).

There is no agreed-upon way of executing a talent management strategy, in that each industry will typically have its own specific way of managing talented staff. But, as explained earlier, it is universally recognized that the process of strategic talent management is most effective when it is supported by other HR processes, such as performance management, reward management and so on (see HRM in Practice on the next page).

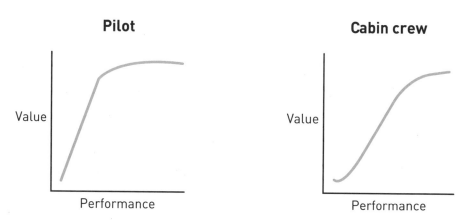

Figure 2.4 Analysing the nature of the relationship between performance and the value contributed to the organization

Source: adapted from Figure 2.2, Comparison of ROIP Curves for a Flight Attendant and a Pilot, from Boudreau, J.W. and Jesuthasan, R. (2011) *Transformative HR: How Great Companies Use Evidence-Based Change for Sustainable Advantage*, San Francisco: Jossey-Bass/John Wiley & Sons, Inc. Copyright © 2011 by John Boudreau. All rights reserved.

HRM IN PRACTICE

Graduate recruitment in the grocery sector

Getty Images/Dario Egidi

You are the HR director of PICO, a large (fictitious) supermarket chain based in south-eastern Australia. Each year you recruit between 25 and 30 third-level graduates for the PICO graduate programme. This graduate programme has been extremely competitive, with an application/selection ratio of 25:1. For the last ten years, PICO was named as one of 'Australia's top 100 graduate employers'. Such an award recognized the valuable training, skills and experience afforded to each employee across a number of different functions in the organization during this programme. Each graduate works for six months in each of the six functions over the course of the three years (procurement, marketing, sales, human resources, finance and planning). At the end of the three years, graduates of the programme are highly sought after by other organizations. However, you are concerned at recent figures presented to you in relation to the programme over the last two years.

Firstly, the number of applications to the programme decreased significantly in the previous two years. You anticipated the recruitment process to be more competitive given the perceived reputation of the graduate programme. To learn that the number of applicants fell so considerably is worrying. The application/selection ratio last year stood at 18:1. Secondly, the number of graduates who withdrew from the programme before its completion has also increased. Up until three years ago, 88% of graduates completed the three-year programme. However, this figure had fallen to 65% last year.

When an employee withdraws from the programme, they must be immediately replaced in order to make sure that their function team does not suffer. Finding a replacement can prove difficult, and occasionally a graduate will have to prematurely leave one function to cover the loss in another function. This means that some graduates do not experience the full range of PICO's operations. If the replacement is recruited externally, they must undergo the compulsory PICO three-week 'Induction and Training Workshop'. In general, untimely exits are a source of great upheaval for the organization.

Thirdly, it has become quite apparent that graduates are choosing to leave the organization upon completion of the programme. While not every graduate can be retained, the organization is structured in such a way that, each year, one or two managerial positions are available in each of the six functions. The best graduates in each function are selected for these managerial roles to ensure an effective 'flow' of employees in the organization. Again, this succession planning was working efficiently. But, in the last two years things seem to have gone awry. The best graduates are not applying for the managerial positions. These roles have been filled by weaker candidates. In October last year, not one single graduate applied for a managerial position in the finance function despite its high salary and flexible arrangement.

You are unsure what has changed in the last two years. The graduate programme salary has not been reduced and remains higher than every other comparable graduate programme in Australia. Unfortunately, both the HR recruitment team and line managers respectively were not particularly revealing when asked to account for the reduced number of applicants and premature departures. Most departures are simply accepted and all efforts are made at finding a replacement. At the Christmas party last year, you overheard one graduate confiding in another that 'she did not spend four years in college just to stack shelves'. She has since left PICO. A few weeks ago, you also happened to run into Mark, a former employee of the graduate programme who had been identified as an 'outstanding marketeer' but who sadly decided to leave the organization. He was not overtly candid when asked why he left but did remark that his experience 'was not as it was sold'. You are reluctant to place too much significance on these two arbitrary instances, but you have precious little information to rely on to explain the increase in voluntary exits.

PICO has made a huge investment in its graduate programme, and you are alarmed at the human resource issues that have arisen in the last two years. You have been unofficially informed that PICO will not be named as one of the top 100 graduate employers in Australia for next year. Should this happen, it will be confirmation of the decline in standards of the graduate programme currently on offer in the organization.

What would you do?

1. What are the barriers to succession planning in PICO? How can they be addressed?
2. What evidence is there to suggest that PICO has a talent management problem? How can it be addressed?
3. Discuss the structure of the graduate programme in PICO. Can you recommend some changes as to how it can be improved?
4. Group discussion: What can organizations do to minimize the number of employees voluntarily leaving the firm?

iStock.com/psisa

SUMMARY

Every effective organization recognizes the central role of workforce planning in its strategic development. Certainly, the process itself does not unfold in a linear manner as the business landscape in which contemporary firms operate is in a constant state of flux. However, there are key principles underpinning HR planning, and adhering to these can allow an organization to develop accordingly in the pursuit of its strategic goals. Of course, a key aspect of HR planning is assessing the profile of the workforce in terms of experience, knowledge, motivation and so on. This assessment is the starting point of talent management, a process through which an organization ensures it can address the staffing challenges that arise as the firm evolves and develops. Nonetheless, talent management is a relatively 'new' concept in the HRM literature, and firms often differ on how talent should be effectively managed. These issues notwithstanding, how an organization harnesses the potential of its staff can go a long way to help achieve its strategic goals.

CHAPTER REVIEW QUESTIONS

1. Why is stocktaking a necessary step in HR planning?
2. What are some of the external factors that can influence an organization's workforce plans?
3. What are some of the criticisms of the HR planning cycle model?
4. What is the best way to deal with a labour surplus?
5. What is the typical profile of a talented employee?
6. How is talent management distinct from other HR processes?
7. Is talent 'contextual'?
8. What is the relationship between workforce planning and talent management?

FURTHER READING

Collings, D.G. and Mellahi, K. (2009) 'Strategic talent management: A review and research agenda', *Human Resource Management Review*, 19(4), 304–13.

Furnham, A. (2012) *The Talented Manager*, Basingstoke: Palgrave Macmillan.

Vaiman, V. (2010) 'Managing Talent of Non-Traditional Knowledge Workers: Opportunities, Challenges, and Trends' in Vaiman, V. (ed.), *Talent Management of Knowledge Workers: Embracing the Non-Traditional Workforce*, 1–22, Basingstoke: Palgrave Macmillan.

USEFUL WEBSITES @

www.pearnkandola.com
Pearn Kandola is a firm of psychologists who work closely with employees and organizations on issues relating to talent management and workforce planning. They have regular blogs and examples of how real-life organizational problems are tackled.

hbr.org
Harvard Business Review is an excellent website for students, with hundreds of articles on talent management and workforce planning written by industry leaders and world-class academics.

johancruyffinstitute.com
The Johan Cruyff Institute aims to educate the next generation of leaders in the sports industry. Its website has many interesting articles on how sports teams all around the world approach the talent management question.

 For extra resources, including videos, multiple choice questions and useful weblinks, go to: www.macmillanihe.com/carbery-cross-hrm-2e.

Getty Images/sturti

3: Recruitment and Selection

Christine Cross

LEARNING OUTCOMES

By the end of this chapter you will be able to:

- Distinguish between the recruitment and selection processes
- Explain the advantages and disadvantages of different recruitment methods
- Identify how the shortlisting process forms a fundamental part of the employee selection decision
- Discuss the range of employee selection methods available and outline how they operate
- Describe the limitations associated with using the interview as a selection tool
- Outline how employment legislation affects the employee selection process

THIS CHAPTER DISCUSSES:

Introduction (38)

Strategic Recruitment and Selection (38)

The Recruitment Process (39)

Shortlisting Stage (45)

Making the Selection Decision (46)

Range of Employee Selection Methods (47)

Employment Legislation and the Selection Process (54)

Making the Final Selection Decision (54)

INTRODUCTION

Employee resourcing is a fundamental component of effective HR practice, and refers to the process of finding the 'right' person for a particular role, in a specific organization. The selection decision is arguably one of the most important issues for any employer, regardless of organization size. Selecting the 'right' employee during the employee resourcing process is critical, as not doing so can be costly for employers. It is therefore vital for an employer to ensure that the resourcing process operates effectively. The purpose of this chapter is to explain how the recruitment and selection processes operate in order to achieve this aim. We begin by outlining the importance of taking a strategic approach to the recruitment and selection decision and then move on to examine the main features of both processes.

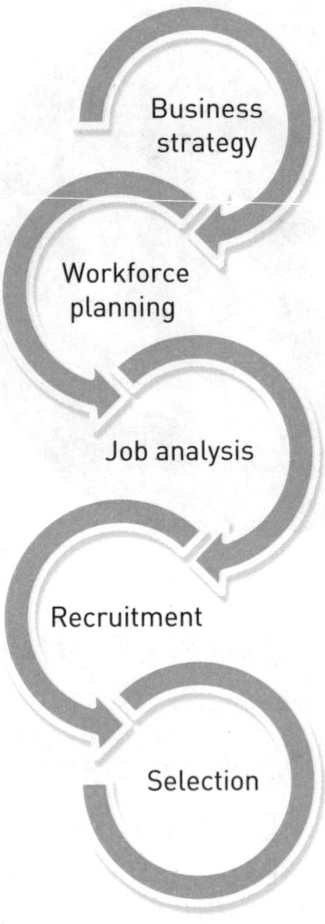

STRATEGIC RECRUITMENT AND SELECTION

It is important to understand that the recruitment and selection process should not operate in isolation. Chapter 1 identified the broader context of managing people in organizations and highlighted the strategic nature of HRM (see Figure 3.1). In order to achieve the competitive advantage that can accrue from having a superior workforce, **selection** has been identified as one of the key elements of the 'best practice' approach ▶Chapter 1◀. This concept is rooted in the philosophy that people are an organization's most valued asset and a key source of strategic competitive advantage (Bartlett and Ghoshal, 2002). As a result, hiring new employees is vital in ensuring the future success of the organization.

Before we begin discussing how recruitment and selection works, it is necessary first to examine the area of competencies that are used by many organizations in the recruitment and selection process. **Competencies** can be defined as the behavioural characteristics of an individual that are causally related to their effective performance in a role (Boyatzis, 1982) ▶Chapter 2◀. Competencies are often compared with knowledge, skills and abilities; they are, however, different, in that while they both indicate an ability to perform in a role, competencies

Figure 3.1 The strategic recruitment and selection process

> **Selection** – a process used to find the candidate who most closely matches the specific requirements of a vacant position
>
> **Competencies** – the behavioural characteristics of an individual that are related to their effective performance in a role

are broader than knowledge, skills and abilities. Competencies are normally worded in a way that identifies specific behavioural aspects of the role (see Consider This on the next page for an example). They are often developed by organizations to represent a set of factors that can assist in achieving success at an organizational level, but they can be implemented either at an organizational level – where one set of competencies is standard for all roles – or at the job level – where specific competencies are needed for a role. Using a competency-based approach to recruitment and selection allows the development of more objective selection criteria, which are focused less on applicants' qualifications and more on their ability to perform in the role. Additionally, competencies can form the basis of the questions asked at the interview stage, providing a consistent, objective approach to the selection decision. We examine competency-based interviewing in more detail later in the chapter.

CONSIDER THIS

Within BankCo (a fictional company), staff members are expected to work cooperatively with others in the achievement of goals while valuing the skills, opinions, roles and diversity of others; deliver on commitments made to others both internally and externally; and develop and foster positive working relationships with individuals both within BankCo and externally in the course of their work.

This is an example of a competency description for *collaboration*. Can you think of another way to express this competency? No doubt you can. What does this tell us about competencies in the recruitment and selection process?

THE RECRUITMENT PROCESS

Following on from the human resource planning process ▶Chapter 2◀, the first stage in the recruitment process is the **job analysis**. You could consider the job analysis to be like an audit of a job, detailing the different tasks the job entails as well as the particular skills and competencies needed to do that job. Detailed information about the role and responsibilities of the vacant position is gathered in this stage, usually by someone in HR. This information can be gathered from the person doing the job, either through observation, interview or questionnaire. The employee's manager can also be asked to indicate the key aspects of the role and how it fits into the overall department or section of the organization. An important concept of the job analysis is that the analysis is conducted about the job, not the person. The key outputs of the job analysis are a **job description** and a **person specification**.

The job description is a detailed inventory of what a particular job entails, while the person specification is essentially the translation of the job description into human terms. The person specification lays out the qualifications, knowledge, skills, personal attributes

Job analysis – the process used to gather detailed information about the various tasks and responsibilities involved in a position. Through this process, the knowledge, skills, abilities, attitudes and behaviours associated with successful performance in the role are also identified

Job description – the detailed breakdown of the purpose of the role and the various tasks and responsibilities involved in a particular job

Person specification – specifies the type of person needed to do a particular job. It essentially translates the job description into human terms

and experience required of an individual in order to match the particular job. When combined, both of these documents produce a set of criteria which are used in making the selection decision.

A trap that organizations can fall into is to create a person specification for the 'ideal' candidate. However, it is important to differentiate between qualities that are essential for the role and those that are desirable. Focusing on too many 'nice to have' qualities is likely to limit the number of people who apply for a role. For instance, a person specification criterion for a particular position may be that it is essential to have an honours degree in Business. In other words, anyone without an honours Business degree would only be considered if the number of applicants in total was disappointingly low, but the organization was unable to wait for more qualified candidates to apply. The person specification should be developed from and accurately match the job description. See the example of a hair stylist job description and person specification in Tables 3.1 and 3.2. You can see that there is a distinction between those requirements that are essential (E) and those that are desirable (D).

As well as, or instead of, the person specification criteria, many organizations formulate competency-based criteria to filter candidates for particular jobs. Competencies can include soft skills such as communication, presentation, leadership and collaborative skills (e.g. teamwork). Whether certain competencies are desirable or essential will depend on the particular job; hence the importance of conducting a job analysis. For instance, if we return to the hair stylist example, the essential competencies for a junior stylist may differ from those for a senior hair stylist.

We now have all the information we need to begin recruiting for the position. Once a position has been identified as being vacant, the organization must decide on the method(s) to use in recruiting for that position. We can identify four broad methods of recruitment: internal, external, online/e-recruitment and overseas/international. You should note that the organization can use one or more (even all) of these methods in any

Hair stylist job description

Purpose of role: A hair stylist serves customers by preparing, conditioning and styling hair.

Hair stylist job duties:

- Maintains supplies by checking stock; anticipating needs; placing orders; verifying receipt.
- Prepares hair for styling by analysing hair condition; shampooing and treating hair.
- Conditions hair and scalp by applying treatments.
- Plans desired effect by studying facial features; examining potential styles; conferring with customer; making recommendations.
- Produces desired effect by arranging, shaping, curling, cutting, trimming, setting, bleaching, dyeing and tinting hair.
- Maintains quality service by following organization standards.
- Maintains safe and healthy conditions by following organization standards and legal regulations.
- Obtains revenue by recording or collecting charges.
- Maintains technical knowledge by attending educational workshops; reviewing publications.
- Contributes to team effort by accomplishing related results as needed.

Table 3.1 Hair stylist job description
Source: copyright © 2018 – Monster Worldwide. Reprinted and adapted with permission.

Person specification: hair stylist

Skills, knowledge and ability	
Ability to analyse information	D
Ability to understand supply chain in hairdressing	D
Ability to handle difficult situations with tact, discretion and assertiveness	E
Ability to handle and accurately account for cash and resources	E
Strong interpersonal skills	E
Personal attributes and attitudes	
Creativity	E
Attention to Detail	E
Confidentiality	E
Professionalism	E

Table 3.2 Person specification: hair stylist
Source: copyright © 2018 – Monster Worldwide. Reprinted and adapted with permission.

one recruitment process. The choice depends on the amount of time and financial resources the organization has at its disposal for the purpose of recruitment. We begin first by examining the difference between the choice of formal and informal methods of recruitment.

Formal and Informal Recruitment Methods

Formal methods are those where the vacancy is officially advertised, for example through different media (print, radio, TV, corporate website, recruitment-specific websites, social media) and/or via employment/recruitment agencies. It would be usual for an organization to use a variety of such methods in its recruitment campaign in order to attract a wide pool of applicants. However, it is also important to keep in mind the suitability of the medium. For instance, if you are looking for a legal expert, you would advertise in legal magazines and websites.

Informal methods are those where candidates find out informally about a potential vacancy. For example, the candidate can be made aware of the vacancy through word of mouth, or via informal social media channels such as Facebook or LinkedIn. Candidates may also send spontaneous (unsolicited) applications to the organization. Interestingly, research suggests that informal recruits often perform better than formal recruits (Barber, 1998). This could be because informal recruits take a more proactive approach since they are interested in the position and/or the organization. Formal recruits, on the other hand, wait until there is a position officially advertised before applying and are more reactive.

HRM IN THE GLOBAL BUSINESS ENVIRONMENT

The *Nitaqat* programme in the Kingdom of Saudi Arabia

If you are working for an organization that has a base in Saudi Arabia, you will see that the way in which people are recruited and selected at work is very different to Australia, Europe or the USA. For example, in Saudi Arabia, the employer will be given a quota for the number of Saudi nationals to be employed. This is called the *Nitaqat* programme.

The number is dependent on the overall number of employees and the sector. The aim of the programme from the Saudi Ministry of Labour is to reduce unemployment among Saudis. Employers with less than ten employees are required to have at least one Saudi national (Proven, 2017). Aside from this government requirement, employers know that it is an advantage to have people working for the company who understand the way business is done in Saudi Arabia.

Internal Recruitment

This is a recruitment method where an open job position is advertised internally within the organization and current employees can apply. There are many advantages of **internal recruitment**. It is cost-effective since the job vacancy advert can be posted on the intranet site (a form of e-recruitment), asking interested candidates to apply directly, rather than taking out expensive print media space. It is also advantageous in that the 'new recruit' is actually an existing employee, who is already familiar with the organizational culture, products and processes. Internal recruitment is important for staff development and staff morale in the organization too. With existing employees motivated by their potential to move to other positions, the probability of staff retention increases.

However, there are some disadvantages to internal recruitment. The primary disadvantage is that it limits the pool of applicants to those already employed within the organization. These employees may not have the skills and competencies required to

> **Internal recruitment –** a vacancy is advertised to potential candidates from within the existing employee base in the organization

perform the job to the highest standard. It also means that an existing employee, deployed through internal recruitment to another position, leaves a skills gap in the position they vacate, which may be more difficult to fill. Another key issue is that it can actually restrict innovation and diversity of mindset in the organization. This is because you are hiring people who are familiar with the organization and indoctrinated in its culture, and so are potentially unable to present novel approaches to performing in the position. Additionally, while internal employees may feel motivated and empowered to apply for a new position in the organization via internal recruitment, these same employees may feel demotivated if their application is unsuccessful. Despite these issues, internal recruitment is considered good practice, as it allows internal candidates the opportunity for lateral and vertical movement through the organization ▶Chapter 10◀. In general, however, it is often the case that organizations use a combination of internal and external methods, as this is likely to produce the best possible candidates. We look at external recruitment in more detail next.

External Recruitment

External recruitment occurs when a vacancy is advertised to potential candidates outside the existing employee base in the organization. External and internal recruitment mirror each other in terms of advantages and disadvantages. The positive elements of one approach are the drawbacks of the other, and vice versa. External recruitment reaches a wider target audience, directly attracting potential candidates with the required person specification or competencies needed for the job. The external recruit should bring fresh blood, new skills and new ideas to the organization, which should improve organizational performance. This approach is also in keeping with promoting diversity in the organization ▶Chapter 6◀. There are a number of disadvantages, however, which involve the costs associated with external recruitment, for instance the use of recruitment consultancies to attract candidates, which is outlined below.

> **External recruitment** – a vacancy is advertised to potential candidates outside the existing employee base in the organization

Recruitment Consultancies

Recruitment consultants find candidates on behalf of their client companies for both temporary and permanent jobs. They are responsible for attracting people to apply for open jobs, placing adverts, interviewing potential candidates and matching candidates to the appropriate roles. They operate in virtually all sectors of the employment market. For specialized positions, recruitment consultancies may have a database of potential candidates on file, which narrows the recruitment search and can save time. This is particularly true in the IT and pharmaceutical industries where the skills required are specific and possibly difficult to find. For senior-level recruits or where skills are in short supply, some recruitment consultancies offer an executive search or 'headhunting' facility, whereby they directly contact individuals with the skills a client

organization is looking for. Recruitment consultants are costly in that they normally charge a percentage of the successful applicant's base salary as their fee for finding the candidate.

Employee Referrals

Many organizations employ this less expensive form of external recruitment. Employee referral schemes work by inviting existing employees to recommend someone from outside the organization for the vacant position. The internal employee receives monetary compensation for their recommendation if the proposed candidate proves successful and remains in the organization for at least a minimum period of time (often six months). It could also be expected that the proposed candidate will fit in with the organization's culture or way of doing business, as people usually associate with others of the same beliefs and values, so are more likely to recommend someone who will fit the organization.

Graduate Recruitment

Graduate recruitment programmes involve specifically targeting graduates to join their organizations. In this way, the organizations go directly to the source for their recruitment purposes. It can involve organizations attending third-level institutions to recruit prospective applicants. Alternatively, graduate recruitment fairs take place in a neutral venue where several employing organizations exhibit and present to graduates. Graduate recruitment is advantageous for an organization in that it allows that organization to cost-effectively target qualified graduates to apply for open positions in the organization. By going directly to graduates in a certain discipline, such as business or IT, organizations seeking to fill positions in those areas have saved time, money and effort in seeking quality candidates for specific roles where such disciplines are essential.

E-recruitment

The third method of recruitment is known as **e-recruitment**. This method can be used as part of both internal and external recruitment, to create the most comprehensive recruitment process. E-recruitment is the use of the internet to help attract candidates to apply for vacancies in the organization. Job adverts can be placed on the organization's intranet page (internal recruitment) or webpage (external recruitment), with details of the job description and person specification, and timelines for receipt of applications. The organizational webpage is often the first place someone looks for a job with a specific organization. The vacancy could also be posted on recruitment websites or through commercial e-recruitment bodies that act as consultants and place the relevant job vacancy notice on different websites for their clients for a fee.

Social networking sites are also used both by employers and candidates. LinkedIn, Facebook and Twitter are the three most commonly used sites. The use of social media as a recruitment tool poses both opportunities and challenges for employers. Social networking sites potentially offer speed, efficiency and the ability to target and attract specific candidates in the recruitment process. For candidates, it potentially offers multiple sources of information about the employer and the possibility of contact with existing employees to gain a more realistic job preview. For example, not only can you apply to work at Accenture and get customized job recommendations directly through its Facebook page, the company also fills the page with information and updates for potential applicants. Its integrated careers calendar shows recruitment events and also details webcast opportunities and other virtual gatherings.

The main advantage of e-recruitment is the size of the target market that can be reached at a relatively low cost when compared to other external recruitment methods, such as print advertisements. The speed of response also tends to be much faster through e-recruitment. The main disadvantage is the sheer number of potential applicants that result from an online job advert, which can then be difficult to filter and shortlist. However, curriculum vitae (CV)/résumé filtering software is available that can help in reducing the numbers of initial applicants to a manageable list. Quite often, applicants need to complete an online application form with standardized questions and information requests. This software can filter the applications using specific keywords based on predetermined criteria. Nonetheless, the growth of e-recruitment has been phenomenal and is not expected to abate in the near future.

International Recruitment

The fourth and final recruitment method to be considered in the search for potential candidates is **international recruitment**. This method is used where the vacant position requires skills and/or competencies which are not readily available in the national context. As a result, organizations engage with international recruitment in order to widen the pool of potential applicants. The main advantage of overseas recruitment is that it increases the probability of finding the specific candidates required for the position. For instance, in the IT sector, organizations may look to India with its large number of IT graduates for skills that may be in scarce supply among graduates in their own country. Organizations could attend graduate recruitment fairs in India in order to find candidates with the IT skills required. International recruitment is often used for senior executive positions, where the best person for the job is sought, regardless of nationality. You can also see this in the international rugby arena, where managers of the national team can be recruited from different countries, provided their track record is positive. However, the costs associated with overseas recruitment can be high. If the candidates are shortlisted, the organization will have to cover transport costs for interviews and relocation. There may also be issues to be dealt with in relation to immigration laws and work visas.

It is important to remember that organizations can use one or all of the recruitment methods discussed. The choice depends on the amount of time and budget they have to fill the vacancy, and which method best suits the particular job description and person specification for the vacant position. This will vary considerably from recruiting someone for a role as a barista in a coffee shop, where employee referrals may be used and prioritized, to recruiting a new chief financial officer for an MNC.

> **E-recruitment** – a vacancy is advertised to potential candidates via the internet. It can target internal and/or external recruits
>
> **International recruitment** – a vacancy is advertised to potential candidates who are currently residing overseas

Recruitment method	Advantages	Disadvantages
Internal recruitment	Cost-effective Form of staff development Motivational tool Increases probability of retention	Limits pool of applicants Not suitable where there are skill shortages Can restrict innovation and diversity Training costs may be high Morale issues for unsuccessful internal applicants
External recruitment	Widens the pool of applicants Advocates diversity Improves employer brand	Expensive to advertise externally Candidates unknown to organization Demotivating for internal employees

Table 3.3 Recruitment methods

Role of Employer Brand in Recruitment

In order to attract the most suitable candidates for a vacant position, it is helpful for an organization to have a positive **employer brand**, which refers to its reputation as an employer (Knox and Freeman, 2006; Mosley, 2007). Being considered an 'employer of choice' is positive for organizations, as it increases labour retention ▶Chapter 4◀ and attracts strong, talented applicants who want to work in such a positive environment. Recently, a variety of awards have gained prominence in this area, such as the Great Place to Work Awards. Organizations such as Google or Microsoft would be considered as having positive employer brands. They have a positive image as an employer, offering competitive financial and nonfinancial rewards, as well as structured internal career paths. In tight labour markets, where there is a shortage of skilled applicants, it is particularly useful for organizations to have a positive employer brand so that they can better entice candidates to apply to join their organization. Having a positive employer brand can often be seen in the amount of unsolicited applications an organization receives from people wanting to join that organization. For example, Google receives 2 million applications each year. It should be noted that an employer can also be associated with having a negative brand, which can then impact negatively on its ability to hire. Being perceived as an unpleasant place to work is not conducive to attracting top talent.

> **Employer brand** – an organization is recognized in its own right as a desirable place to work – positive employer brand – by the internal and external labour market

The Job Advert

As discussed earlier, the job description and person specification are the raw materials used in drafting the job adverts. Once the recruitment method is determined and the type of approach(es) to be used agreed upon, the job advert must be shared with the potential candidates. The job advert will include the relevant information concerning the position, such as:

- name of organization
- job title
- duties
- essential skills/competencies required
- desirable skills/competencies
- the application details (if the candidate needs to send a CV/résumé, cover letter, or if they need to complete an online application form)
- the closing date for applications
- the address/contact details where the application should be sent.

The job advert should be drafted using AIDA criteria – attention, interest, desire and action (Diehl and Terlutter, 2003). In other words, the job advert should gain the attention of potential candidates. It should then generate their interest in finding out more about the vacant role. The job advert should instil desire in the potential candidate to want to fill that vacancy. This leads to the candidate applying for the position.

Application Forms and CVs/Résumés

The organization must decide how it is going to ask candidates to submit their applications for the open position. One option is using an application form. These are designed by the organization and are normally intended to gather specific information on prospective candidates, either electronically or on paper. The information is required in a standard format, which allows for the same job-related information to be gathered from all candidates, making the selection stage easier in terms of comparing like with like. This is difficult when allowing applications by CV/résumé.

> **Shortlisting** – a sifting process where those candidates who most closely match the predetermined job-specific requirements are separated out from all other applicants
>
> **Shortlisting matrix** – a scoring mechanism for placing the candidates who have applied for the position in a ranking order based on their suitability for the role

Information normally required in an application form includes educational qualifications and work history. Recently, employers have also included sections where they ask candidates to answer competency-based questions. For more senior roles, however, it is more common for CVs/résumés to be required. One factor to be considered in the decision is the need to ensure that questions on an application form do not breach any areas of the employment equality legislation (see page 54 for more detail).

SHORTLISTING STAGE

It is unlikely that all applicants will have the necessary skills, abilities, education, experience or competencies required for the vacant position. Additionally, the time, effort and money required to engage all those who have applied for the position

in the full selection process is prohibitive. The aim of the shortlisting stage is, therefore, to reduce the number of applicants and narrow the field by a process of elimination. This process is known as shortlisting. Shortlisting takes place once the advertised closing date has passed and is based on the submitted applications, which are measured against the requirements specified in the selection criteria. A shortlisting matrix is used to evaluate each candidate against these criteria.

The selection criteria used in this matrix are drawn from the job requirements and person specification and should have already been identified prior to the position being advertised. These criteria define the particular skills, knowledge, attributes, qualifications and experience a person needs to successfully carry out the role.

Table 3.4 presents an example of a shortlisting matrix for a business analyst position with the criteria identified in both categories – essential and desirable.

One method of scoring candidates involves the weighting of certain criteria, where particular criteria (normally essential criteria) are viewed as more important than others. For example, if you were recruiting for a sales role, experience may be twice as important as a sales qualification, so you would weight sales experience by two. In terms of scoring, the scoring system includes a '0' for no evidence of the criterion or qualification.

The outcome of using this matrix is to create two groups of applicants – those who are suitable and those who are unsuitable. The decision as to who is suitable or unsuitable will be based on a cut-off score, which

	Business degree (x2)	Work experience (x2)	IT skills (x2)	Collaboration	Totals
Name 1	0	6	10	3	19
Name 2	10	2	6	5	23
Name 3	10	4	2	3	19
Name 4	0	2	10	1	13
Name 5	0	6	6	1	13

Scoring: 0 = no evidence; 1 = little evidence; 3 = moderate evidence; 5 = strong evidence; cut-off score: 15

Table 3.4 Example of a shortlisting matrix for a business analyst

you will need to decide in advance of beginning the scoring process. Candidates who score above the cut-off mark will be called to the next stage of the selection process, and those who do not will be rejected. In Table 3.4, only applicants 1, 2 and 3 would be called to the next stage of the selection process. In countries such as the UK, Australia and the USA, employment legislation highlights the need for a rigorous approach to the shortlisting stage, as those who are not shortlisted can use the discrimination legislation ▶Chapter 6◀ as the basis of a claim for unfair non-selection. In general, using a shortlisting matrix affords those involved in the selection phase some protection against such claims. The completed matrix should be kept with the other selection documents, such as the interviewer's notes, in order to meet the freedom of information requirements in many countries.

Online Screening

As mentioned earlier, a software package, referred to as an applicant tracking system (ATS), which identifies specific keywords on submitted CVs/résumés and application forms, based on the selection criteria, can be used to screen initial applications. If your CV/résumé contains the keywords the employer wants, then the ATS will rank you higher in the search results. This is a useful way for organizations to reduce the number of applicants; however, it may eliminate suitable candidates who actually meet the criteria but have not used the specific words searched for by the ATS. As part of the online screening process, organizations can also use online ability tests and personality questionnaires as an initial method of screening applications. (These types of psychometric tests are dealt with in more detail later in the chapter.) There are, however, difficulties with these tests being taken online. There is the possibility that the person taking the online test is not the person who is actually applying for the position. Additionally, there are 'experienced' applicants who learn how to 'work' the system in order to produce the 'right' answers.

HRM AND ORGANIZATIONAL PERFORMANCE

Hiring a diverse workforce

Hiring a diverse workforce ▶Chapter 6◀ has become a key recruitment and selection strategy for many organizations. Employees from different backgrounds and cultures bring diverse viewpoints and ideas to the organization. If the organization utilizes their different skills and abilities, it will result in higher levels of productivity as each employee 'plays off the strengths and weaknesses of others.' When you have a diverse group of employees, you are also able to offer more value to your customers.

Employees with language skills or knowledge of cultural sensitivities and customs can break down linguistic and cultural barriers, making the organization more attractive to diverse customer groups. This results in a competitive advantage over companies that place less value on diversity than you do. Examples of organizations that successfully recruit a diverse workforce include Nike, who revealed in 2015 that the company had more non-white employees than white employees. https://www.seetec.co.uk/insights/diversity-in-the-workplace-what-are-the-benefits-for-employers

---

MAKING THE SELECTION DECISION

Once the number of applicants has been reduced to a manageable amount, there is a wide range of selection methods an employer can use to decide on the most suitable candidate. The overall aim of the selection process is to predict an applicant's job performance capability, specifically related to the vacant role. This prediction element is seen to be particularly problematic, and so more than one method is often used to assist in the decision-making process. Additionally, person–organization fit and person–job fit are viewed as critical elements in the selection decision for many organizations ▶Chapter 4◀. The realization that 'organizational fit' is as important as individual employee ability has resulted in organizations now considering hiring for attitude, as they believe that new employees can be trained in terms of skills. **Person–organization fit** refers to the extent to which a person and an organization share similar characteristics and/

or meet each other's needs (Kristof, 1996). **Person–job fit** is the degree to which there is a match between the abilities of the person and the demands of the job, or the desires of a person and the attributes of the job (Boon and Biron, 2016). Research has shown that where this fit occurs, employees are more satisfied with their jobs and this is related to higher levels of productivity (Dahling and Librizzi, 2015). Conversely, poor job fit is associated with job dissatisfaction, higher levels of job-related stress and intentions to leave the organization (Lovelace and Rosen, 1996). 'Fit' is viewed by many as an important criterion in the selection decision. Yet, it is difficult to objectively search for these types of 'fit' among applicants. This is often where employers resort to using their 'gut feeling' when making a selection decision, not something recommended in taking a strategic approach to selection.

When choosing the selection methods most suitable for a vacant position, note that different organizational positions require different types. The methods chosen will depend on the particular skills, attributes, knowledge or competencies required for the position. The decision as to which selection method to use is impacted by a number of factors:

- *The ability of the method to predict suitability for the position:* this can depend on the predictive validity of the method, that is, the extent to which the method used can predict successful performance in the role.
- *The appropriateness of the method for the seniority and level of the position:* for example, a retail sales assistant role is likely to require different methods than those used for the chief executive officer (CEO) of a multinational corporation.
- *The specific selection criteria:* for example, if technical competence is required, certain methods are more suitable, for example using a technology test to evaluate fundamental skills.
- *The time and effort required to use the technique:* if a vacancy needs to be filled quickly, some methods are more suitable than others, for example telephone interviewing is quicker than arranging face-to-face interviews. However, the risk factor in making a poor selection decision needs to be considered here. In the example above, time factors should not affect the selection method choice for the CEO position.

> **Person–organization fit** – the extent to which the values, interests and behaviours of the individual match the organizational culture
>
> **Person–job fit** – the extent to which the enthusiasm, knowledge, skills, abilities and motivations of the individual match those required by the job

- *The skills and abilities of those involved in the selection decision:* where psychometric tests are being used, those administering the tests must be appropriately trained and qualified.
- *Costs of each method:* budget restrictions may create a situation where costs dictate that certain methods such as assessment centres are too expensive.
- *Equality issues:* given the volume of employment protection, does the chosen technique directly or indirectly discriminate against any of the groups identified?

CONSIDER THIS

Do you think being in a job you really enjoy and working with colleagues you get along with would affect your job performance?

Have you ever been in a situation where you could not find anything in common with the people you worked with on a daily basis? How did this affect your performance at work? This is person–job fit and person–organization fit in action.

RANGE OF EMPLOYEE SELECTION METHODS

As mentioned earlier, there is a range of methods available to assist with making the selection decision. Normally, more than one method is used in the selection process in order to improve the validity. These include application forms, interviews, psychometric tests, assessment centres, work sample tests and graphology, each of which are described on the following pages. A recent study in the UK highlighted that CVs, references, structured interviews and application forms are the most common selection methods (CIPD, 2015). Zibarras and Woods (2010) also found that public sector and voluntary organizations use formalized techniques, such as application forms rather than CVs, and structured rather than unstructured interviews.

There are two key issues in the choice of selection methods. **Validity** looks at how closely a selection method measures what it is supposed to measure and how successful it is in doing this (Kline, 1998). Here, we are interested in finding out whether the evidence supports the conclusions that are made based on the scores of the selection measure and in what is termed 'predictive validity', which is the extent to which the method used can predict successful performance in the role. If predictive validity scores are high, the method is identified as a good predictor. The closer the score is to 1.0, the better the predictive validity. Research by Smith and Smith (2005) has identified that certain methods have a higher predictive validity than other methods. **Reliability** is also important when deciding which

> **Validity** – the extent to which a selection method measures what it purports to measure and how well it does this
>
> **Reliability** – a method is identified as reliable if it consistently measures what it sets out to measure

selection method to use. A method is identified as reliable if it consistently measures what it sets out to measure (Arvey, 1979). The key issue here is: do we get the same results when we measure the same thing twice?

The selection method chosen should have high validity and high reliability. According to Smith and Smith's research (2005), the highest predictive validity scores are for the combined use of intelligence tests and structured interview at 0.63, with intelligence tests and work samples scoring 0.60. Work sample tests scored 0.54, and structured interviews and intelligence tests each separately scored 0.51. The methods at the lower end of the scoring are personality tests (0.40), assessment centres (0.37), references (0.26) and finally, at the bottom, graphology at 0.02.

HRM IN THE NEWS

Would you like an employer to check your Facebook page?

The controversial practice of searching social media when screening job applications has become more popular in recent years. How would you feel if you did not get called for an interview because a prospective employer had searched Facebook and found some pictures of you that were less than flattering? If you think your information, photos, thoughts and posts are safe just because you are not friends with an employer or anyone in that workplace, think again. Recent news reports actually point out a current loophole in the Facebook privacy settings, linked to your mobile phone number. At some point over the last few months, probably the first time you logged in from a new phone or mobile device, Facebook prompted you to 'claim' or confirm your phone number. When you did that, you also agreed to be searched on the site via that number.

You might not think it matters if a prospective employer looks at your Facebook page. However, aside from the obvious violation of your personal space and privacy, the information that your future employer sees about you on Facebook could adversely impact your chances of getting hired. Around 69% of employers admit to rejecting an applicant after checking them out on Facebook or another social media site; the reasons given for rejection range from inappropriate photographs and posts to misrepresentation of background or abilities. What you post and how you behave on Facebook can create a first impression of the sort of person you might be.

More than half of hiring managers (51%) say that they are looking to see if the candidate will be a good fit with the corporate culture. Your Facebook profile gives a far more accurate portrait of what you are really like than an employer could get from a screening questionnaire. In a questionnaire, you can always give the answers that you think an employer wants to hear. On Facebook, your friends would call you out for 'posing' as something you are not. A person with a lot of Facebook friends who takes a lot of zany photos could be rated as extroverted and friendly, which can be attractive qualities in a candidate, while a person who is overly emotional in their postings might be a less attractive candidate as it may indicate a tendency to mood swings.

Questions

1. How aware were you of the fact that employers are searching Facebook when making a selection decision about you?
2. Do you agree with employers using this method?
3. Is there any legal reason in your country why an employer could not undertake such a search?

Sources

Workopolis (2015) 'The top three things that employers want to see in your social media profiles', 5 April

Hill, K. (2012) 'Facebook Can Tell You If A Person Is Worth Hiring', Forbes, 5 March

Selection Interviews

Selection interviews normally involve an organizational representative meeting the candidates face to face. These remain the most popular method of selection despite their accepted shortcomings. Research over the past 50 years into the effectiveness of the selection interview highlights that they are not particularly successful in predicting future job performance. They have a relatively poor reputation as being overly subjective, prone to interviewer bias and thus unreliable predictors of future performance (Compton et al., 2009). Nevertheless, interviews have been the most popular form of selection for many years and are used in almost every organization for selecting employees at all levels. There are a number of types of selection interview:

- *Telephone interviews:* the interview is conducted by phone. These are relatively popular, particularly for screening purposes, and are useful in that they remove the 'appearance' bias, an accusation often made of face-to-face interviews.
- *Video interviews:* a form of interviewing where technology is used to conduct the interview. This can be in 'real time', where the interview takes place at a prearranged date and time much like a standard interview, but the interviewer and interviewee can be in two different locations, even two different countries. This is viewed as being a cost-effective method of conducting a selection interview. These video interviews can also take the form of asynchronous interviews, where the candidate records the interview at a day, time and place that suits them. Their video is then viewed at a date, time and location that suits the interviewer(s).

The candidate is normally asked to answer a series of pre-prepared questions during the recording.

- *One-to-one interviews:* the candidate is interviewed by just one person (usually from HR) in a face-to-face setting. This has been the standard format for interviews for many years; however, the objectivity of one person making the selection decision has been called into question and this has given rise to the panel interview.
- *Panel interviews:* the candidate is interviewed by more than one person. Panel interviews normally include a representative from HR and the future manager. However, there can be as many as seven or eight panel members depending on the sector and the position in question. More senior positions will usually have more panel members. The roles and contributions of the various panel members need to be managed and this is normally done by a panel chairperson. Once a favourite of public sector organizations, there has been a move towards the use of panel interviewing in many sectors to improve objectivity in the selection decision.

Structured and Unstructured Interviews

Reviews of the selection interview process (see, for example, Dipboye, 2005) have indicated that a structured interview noticeably improves its validity. While it may seem strange for a selection interview to be conducted in an unstructured fashion, this is the case more often than you might think. Unstructured interviews are essentially an informal chat between the interviewer and the prospective candidate and have as much predictive validity as tossing a coin in the air. They involve an interview where different questions may be asked of different applicants. On the other hand, structured interviews can provide an important and valid means of selecting an employee. The interview is structured to ensure that interview questions are based strictly on job-related criteria, and these same questions are asked of all candidates and answers are rated (Arnold et al., 2010). The most common forms of structured interview are the competency-based interview and the situational-based interview. It is also important to ensure that no discriminatory questions are asked during the interview process. (This is dealt with later in the chapter.)

According to the CIPD (2017), different countries take different approaches to which interview type they use. In the UK, it is increasingly common to have a structured interview, and panel interviews are also used, while in the USA, almost all interviews follow a structured process, where all applicants are asked exactly the same questions. In France, they use a more informal, unstructured approach, while in northern Europe, it is common for the HR manager to be one of the interviewers, but this is less likely in other countries in the world. In China, the concept of face defines all business relations, making the in-person interview the most important factor in the selection process. In Asian countries, the interviewer may expect the candidate to avoid direct sustained eye contact as this is perceived as demonstrating respect for the interviewer. Additionally, the interviewer would expect the candidate to take an extended period of time to formulate answers to questions in order to answer in the most thorough and complete manner possible.

Next, we describe three forms of structured interview in more detail, which focus on using objective factors to predict job performance, rather than subjective 'gut feeling' interview approaches: competency-based interviews, situational-based interviews and strength-based interviews.

Competency-based Interviews

Competency-based interviews are conducted by using a series of structured questions designed to gather information on specific behaviours or competencies that

have been identified in the job analysis phase. The competency-based interview is sometimes referred to as a 'behavioural event interview' or a 'behavioural-based interview'. This is because it uses questions that assess candidates on their behaviour in the critical competencies identified for the position. The competency-based interview deals with the analysis of past events and emphasizes facts and examples from real situations to establish the candidate's ability to perform the role. You want to find out how the person behaved in the past in relation to that key competency area. For example, if the competency is a persuasion/influencing skill, your question might be: 'Can you describe an occasion when you were able to persuade your fellow team members to do something that at first they didn't really want to do?' If the competency is problem-solving ability, you might say: 'Tell me about a problem you have solved recently.' In employee selection theory, it has been argued that the best predictor of future behaviour or performance is present or past behaviour or performance of the same type (Wernimont and Campbell, 1968; Janis, 1982).

One of the problems with competency-based interviews is that candidates who frequently encounter them learn to 'fake' answers, as there are many books and websites devoted to learning how to 'perform' in this interview setting. They will have worked on these questions in advance, often delivering answers they believe the interviewer wants to hear.

Situational-based Interview

A situational-based interview (Latham and colleagues, 1980) takes a similar approach but works on the premise that the interviewer wants to establish what the candidate *would do* if presented with a situation. Questions here focus on the future. The candidate is provided with a typical situation and asked how they would respond to it. For example: 'What would you do if your manager presented you with two conflicting deadlines?' These interviews are particularly common in graduate interviewing where the individual is unlikely to have past experience of particular situations. The answers to these questions reveal

> **Competency-based interviews** – these interviews are structured around job-specific competencies that require interviewees to describe specific tasks or situations. They work on the belief that the best indication of future behaviour is past behaviour

how the candidate might handle the situation; however, this is only indicative and should be recognized as such.

Strength-based Interviews

Strength-based interviews are becoming more popular, especially in graduate recruitment. While competency interviews focus on what you can do, strength-based interviews aim to uncover what you enjoy working at. The principle is that if you enjoy doing something then it is more likely that you are also good at it. Companies using this type of approach will look for those who have a natural strength in certain areas as a result of their enjoyment of that task, rather than those who will simply do the task because it is part of the role.

Examples of questions asked in this type of interview are:

- What do you enjoy doing in your spare time?
- What do you feel you are good at?
- Tell me about an achievement you were particularly proud of.
- What kinds of tasks boost your energy?
- What would your closest friend say are your greatest strengths?

One of the main advantages of this type of interview is that recruiters believe they gain a more genuine insight into candidates. And the advantage for the organization is that when an individual uses their strengths, they perform at their best and learn new information quicker.

Problems with the Selection Interview

There are a number of negative issues associated with selection interviewing and these relate mainly to perceptual distortion, subjectivity and lack of interviewing skill on the part of the interviewer:

- *Confirmatory bias:* interviewers are often accused of making their mind up about a candidate within the first 30 seconds of the person entering the room. They then focus on asking questions to confirm their initial impression, either positive or negative. This is referred to as 'confirmatory bias' (Snyder and Swann, 1978) or the 'first impression error'.

A related issue is the effect the perceived attractiveness of the candidate has on the interviewer. Research has highlighted that, in general, more attractive people are identified by interviewers as having more favourable traits (Desrumaux et al., 2009).

- *Horns or halo effect:* a perceptual error, where one single characteristic of the individual creates an overly positive or negative impression of the interviewee and this then carries unbalanced weight in the selection decision. For example, if the person was being interviewed for a customer-facing role and had tattoos on their neck and hands, this might be viewed by the interviewer as a negative characteristic and may have an unduly negative effect on the selection decision. This is the 'horns' or negative effect, while the 'halo' effect is the opposite.
- *Stereotypes:* stereotypes are prejudices or beliefs about the characteristics of people from a particular group of individuals, who are seen as sharing the same attributes (Fiske and Macrae, 2012: 76). When an interviewer stereotypes the interviewee, this can negatively affect the outcome of the decision for the candidate. For example, people who are overweight may be thought of as lazy, or blondes may be viewed as less intelligent than brunettes. The interviewer may alternatively hold a stereotyped image of the 'right' candidate and judge all candidates against this image.
- *Contrast error:* the interviewer compares and contrasts one interviewee with other candidates in a way that artificially inflates or deflates the evaluation of the candidate. Contrast error has the effect of distorting the decision-making process, as each candidate should be judged independently.
- *Projection error:* the interviewer rates candidates with characteristics, experiences or preferences similar to themselves more favourably than other candidates. The reverse is also true.

Despite these issues, it is unusual for an organization to hire a candidate without having conducted an interview, and thus their popularity is unlikely to diminish as there is no other method that allows the prospective employer such flexibility in meeting the candidates in advance of offering the position. This is because the interview is useful for determining if the applicant has the requisite communication and interpersonal skills necessary for the job; it is a flexible method of gathering important information, allowing the interviewer to ask questions that may reveal additional information which can be used in making the selection decision.

Recently, the two-way nature of the selection decision has become even more important, where candidates' impressions of the organizational context and culture become as important a determinant of their decision to accept a job offer as their concern with the job itself. This is particularly true in a tight labour market, and employer branding plays a crucial role in this situation ▶Chapter 2◀.

Psychometric Testing

Psychometric testing is the term most often used to encompass all forms of psychological assessment. 'Psychometric' literally means 'mental measurement'. There has been a rise in the use of these tests recently as the search for more sophisticated selection methods continues. Candidates complete 'pen and paper' tests that are used to measure individual differences in areas such as aptitude, ability, attainment and intelligence (Edenborough, 1999). These are a quantifiable measurement of candidates' cognitive ability and indicate if they have the skills, or the potential to learn new skills, required to perform successfully in a particular role. The premise here is that those who do well in the tests will perform well on the job. Most tests are designed and developed by occupational psychologists. These tests must also be administered and scored by persons qualified in the tests being used. Types of tests include the following:

- *General intelligence tests:* these measure the ability to think about ideas, analyse situations and solve problems. Various types of intelligence test are used.
- *Attainment tests:* these measure levels of knowledge and skills.
- *Cognitive ability tests:* these include:
  - *verbal comprehension:* the ability to understand and use both written and spoken language
  - *numerical ability:* the speed and accuracy with which a candidate can solve arithmetic problems
  - *reasoning ability:* the ability to invent solutions to diverse problems.

Personality Profiling

Personality profiling is based on the fact that personality is viewed by many organizations as an important determinant of behaviour at work. Personality tests are often used as employers search for predictors of success in a role. These personality tests are usually based on the trait-factor analytic model of personality (Arnold et al., 2010). Commonly used profiles include the The Big Five and the Sixteen Personality Factor Questionnaire. The Big Five is based on the five factor model of personality, which proposes that differences in an individual's personality can be measured in terms of openness, conscientiousness, extraversion, agreeableness and neuroticism (to take the test see www.123test.com/big-five-personality-theory). The SHL Occupational Personality Questionnaire (OPQ) is the most widely used measure of behavioural style in the world. The OPQ32 is the most comprehensive version of the OPQ. It provides detailed information on 32 specific personality characteristics which underpin performance on key job competencies critical for graduates, managers and experienced hires. The CIPD (Pilbeam and Corbridge, 2010) and the Australian Institute of Management have cautioned against the use of personality profiles as the sole basis of making the selection decision and suggest they are used in combination with other selection methods. The debate around the use of personality tests centres on a few key issues, namely, the extent to which personality is measurable and remains stable over time and across situations, and the extent to which a questionnaire can provide enough suitable information on which to base a selection decision.

Assessment Centres

Assessment centres were first used in the Second World War to select officers for the Army and the Royal Navy. Today they are used particularly in graduate recruitment. An assessment centre is not actually a place, but describes the process, which normally lasts for one or two full days. In an assessment centre, a group of assessors identify the most suitable candidates by using a series of exercises and tests to assess multiple competencies. The techniques used include:

- *work sample tests* – these are used to test applicants by asking them to complete tasks similar to those involved in the actual job

Candidate timetable						
Time	1	2	3	4	5	6
09.00–10.00	Test	Test	Test	Test	Test	Test
Coffee break						
10.00-12.00	Role play	Role play	Role play	In-basket	In-basket	In-basket
Lunch						
13.00-15.00	In-basket	In-basket	In-basket	Presentation	Presentation	Presentation
Coffee break						
15.00-17.00	Presentation	Presentation	Presentation	Role play	Role play	Role play

Table 3.5 Example of an assessment centre day

- *leaderless group discussions* – a group of applicants discuss an actual job-related problem, and the behaviour of the candidates is observed to establish the leadership and communications skills each person displays
- *psychometric tests* (see previous page)
- *in-tray simulations (in-basket exercises) or the digital 'e-tray' equivalent* – these are a test of your ability to deal with a real work situation, for example email requests, projects and information overload
- *one-to-one interviews*.

Typically, the same competencies are assessed multiple times during the course of the centre. At the end of the assessment centre, the assessors come to an agreed cumulative rating for each individual based on the observations and test scores. Despite their high level of predictive validity, there is one key disadvantage in using assessment centres, which is that they are expensive to operate. The University of Melbourne has an open access video link to a recording of an assessment centre, available at http://vimeo.com/9815762.

Work Sample Tests

Work sample tests are used to test applicants by asking them to complete tasks similar to those involved in the actual job (Thornton and Kedharnath, 2013). This can involve working in the role for a short time, often for one day. They are based on the premise that the best predictor of future behaviour is observed behaviour, and they have a high predictive validity. These tests are common in the service sectors, where an assessment of the candidate's work ability is based around customer service provision and where the outcome of their interaction can be measured immediately. One example of a work sample test is found in a lecturing role. Many universities include a presentation as part of the selection process, as both presenting and lecturing involve similar skills and abilities.

Graphology

Graphology is the study and analysis of a person's handwriting, which is believed to reveal a behavioural profile of the individual. It is regularly used by organizations in Europe, particularly France, where three-quarters of small companies use it in the selection decision. Employers in Belgium and Germany also use graphology (Taylor, 2005). However, popularity should not be confused with validity, as it has a negligible predictive validity score.

Using more than one selection method is advisable as this increases the amount of job-related information available on which to base the selection decision. As noted above, selection methods vary in their reliability, as a predictor of performance in the job, and in their ease and costs to administer. It is becoming more common for particular positions to involve psychometric testing and selection interviews, for example graduate entry positions and public sector positions.

Image Source/John Rowley

EMPLOYMENT LEGISLATION AND THE SELECTION PROCESS

The selection process is expected to operate within a legal framework of fairness and consistency, which removes discrimination and ensures equality of opportunity in the employment process ▶Chapter 6◀. Discrimination means treating one person less favourably than another under specific grounds, either directly or indirectly. These are normally age, gender, sexual orientation, disability and race. Europe, Australia and the USA take a similar approach to protecting individuals affected by the selection process. In Australia, a number of Commonwealth Acts relate to equal opportunity law and these are slightly different depending on the territory. In many countries, data protection and freedom of information have become important areas in relation to the retention of material generated by the selection process. For example, in the UK, the Data Protection Act 1998 applies to personal information used in the selection stage. In Ireland, under the Data Protection Acts 1988 and

2003 and the Freedom of Information Acts 1997 and 2003, persons are allowed access to their own data held respectively by government departments, agencies and other designated bodies in receipt of government funding, and all legal entities in the state. Therefore, candidates who have been unsuccessful in the selection process are entitled to know what information is kept about them and to see that data. Thus, it is of the upmost importance that all interviewers are trained and understand how to take accurate and objective notes during the selection phase to ensure no discrimination takes place.

MAKING THE FINAL SELECTION DECISION

Once all the information is gathered from each of the selection methods used, the selector(s) needs to make a final decision on who is to be offered the position. This means that all the information from each stage of the process must be utilized. There is often a tendency to use the most recent selection method only, which is normally the interview; however, decisions need to be made in advance of the start of the selection process on how to weight the selection methods and how to score candidates where a conflict exists between data gathered from two methods. For example, if a candidate performs well in psychometric testing but poorly in the interview, each element needs to have a weighting to allow for accurate scoring of the candidate overall. The shortlisting matrix is a useful method of recording information from each selection method, as it has identified the key job-related criteria. Once the selection decision is made, the next stage involves taking references, checking qualifications and contacting the candidates.

Post-offer Stage

It is important to note that contacting all candidates is of paramount importance, particularly for positive employer branding. This means ensuring that unsuccessful candidates are contacted in a swift manner. It can be damaging for an employer brand if candidates who attended for tests or interviews are not contacted again by the organization to advise them they were unsuccessful. Some organizations offer feedback to the unsuccessful candidates. For the successful candidate, they should be offered the position, and the details of the appointment should be agreed. They are normally given a period of time within which to accept the offer and agree on a start date. Their acceptance of the offer in writing is normally completed by their signing of the employment contract. They should be informed of how the induction process operates before joining the organization ▸Chapter 4◂.

One area often forgotten about in the selection process is monitoring the success or otherwise of the selection process. It needs to be monitored to ensure the validity of the selection decision. An analysis of the candidates and their performance in the various stages of the process provides feedback about how successful various methods are in making the overall selection decision. More importantly, data should continue to be collected in order to assess the performance of the selected candidates once employed. Information from performance reviews and internal documents can be compared to performance in selection methods, such as psychometric tests. This allows an evaluation of the relationship between selection methods used, selectors and successful role performance.

HRM IN PRACTICE

Understanding recruitment across cultures

You are working in HR for a newish start-up company which has decided to open an office in the Kingdom of Saudi Arabia (KSA) in Riyadh following completion of a successful contract deal with the Saudi Ministry of Labour and Social Development. You are sending one of your existing employees to Riyadh to begin the recruitment of three additional employees to work in the new office there. The aim is to have expats (a person temporarily or permanently residing in a country other than that of their citizenship) working in the office. However, no one in your company seems to know much about recruitment in KSA apart from the fact that, because your company will have less than ten employees, it is required to employ at least one KSA national. A long and detailed search on the internet has revealed the following:

- Employers must advertise roles locally to Saudi nationals though the Human Resource Development Fund for a minimum of two weeks prior to obtaining a visa for an expat.
- Non-nationals can only be employed on a fixed-term contract.
- Probation periods are 180 days.

- Employees are entitled to 21 days annual leave after one year's service, increasing to 30 days on completion of five years' service.
- Expats are entitled to one home flight per year following 12 months of service.
- Women must work in a separate area of the office to men.
- It is the law for all women to wear an abaya when in public.
- The working week is Sunday to Thursday.
- Hajj leave will be granted to Muslim employees once and will not exceed 30 days.
- Financial penalties of up to SAR 100,000 and closure of the business for a period of no more than 30 days can now be imposed for failure to comply with labour law.
- Nitaquat is a Saudization progamme introduced by the Saudi Ministry of Labour aimed at reducing unemployment among Saudis (see HRM in the Global Business Environment on page 41).

- You must have two separate entrances into the workplace for women and men.
- Bribes are a normal feature of doing business in Riyadh.
- The Ministry of Labour and Social Development must approve your employee handbook before it can be given to employees.
- Employment contracts must be issued in both Arabic and English.

What would you do?

1. Identify at least five ways in which recruitment for your new office in Riyadh is different to that in your own country.
2. What will be the most significant challenges facing you in this recruitment effort?
3. Will you hire women in your office? Explain your answer.

Grapheast/Emy Kat

SUMMARY

This chapter has covered some of the key issues involved in sourcing candidates and making the decision about who is the most suitable candidate for a vacant position. The critical role played by the initial shortlisting process cannot be overemphasized. By ensuring that the initial shortlisting criteria are specific to the role and then utilizing these same criteria in all stages of the selection process, the prospect of selecting the most suitable candidate from the applicants is greatly increased. The choice of selection method depends on many factors, and the predictive validity of each method should be a factor in choosing the selection method(s). Using more than one method has the effect of increasing the ability to predict successful performance in the role. Ensuring compliance with employment legislation is important in safeguarding against the possibility of a rejected candidate bringing a case for discrimination.

CHAPTER REVIEW QUESTIONS

1. Differentiate between job analysis, person specification and competency frameworks.
2. Search for a job description and person specification for a job you are interested in as a career. Can you see how the job description and person specification form the basis of a job advert? Can you differentiate between essential and desirable criteria in the job advert?
3. You are recruiting for a graduate to work in the grocery sector. Describe and differentiate between three methods of recruitment that would be suitable for generating interest in this position.
4. When should an organization employ the services of a recruitment agency?
5. Differentiate between validity and reliability in choosing selection methods.
6. Explain the problems associated with using the face-to-face interview as a selection method.
7. Search the internet for three competencies that you believe would be suitable for a role in management. What questions would you ask at an interview to establish if the candidate had these three competencies?
8. Employment equality legislation varies from country to country. Compare the legislation applicable to the recruitment and selection process in your country to that of a country in a different continent.

FURTHER READING

Armstrong, M. and Taylor, S. (2017) *Armstrong's Handbook of Human Resource Management Practice*, 14th edn, London: Kogan Page.

Jeske, D. and Shultz, K. S. (2015) 'Using social media content for screening in recruitment and selection: pros and cons', *Work, Employment and Society* 30 (3), 535–546, https://doi.org/10.1177/0950017015613746

USEFUL WEBSITES

www.hrinasia.com

HR in Asia is an online digital media publication and events platform covering the latest developments in the domains of employer branding, recruitment, retention, employee relations, people development, HR technology and outsourcing.

www.changeboard.ae

Changeboard's website informs professionals across the Gulf Cooperation Council countries.

www.personneltoday.com

Personnel Today is the UK's leading free-access HR website. It provides HR professionals with easy-to-read, timely and relevant content.

www.uniformguidelines.com

This is a US website providing information on all selection procedures used to make employment decisions, including interviews, review of experience or education from application forms, work samples, physical requirements and evaluations of performance.

 For extra resources, including videos, multiple choice questions and useful weblinks, go to: www.macmillanihe.com/carbery-cross-hrm-2e.

Getty Images/BraunS

4: Employee Engagement, Induction, Turnover and Retention

Colette Darcy, Ashley O'Donoghue and Yanqiao Liu

LEARNING OUTCOMES

By the end of this chapter you should be able to:

- Explain the links between employee engagement, induction, turnover and retention and how a strategic approach to their management can increase the overall competitiveness and success of the organization
- Define employee engagement and demonstrate its links to induction, turnover and retention
- Explain what employee induction is, how it is linked to engagement and why organizations invest in these programmes from a strategic perspective
- Understand the term 'onboarding'
- Discuss the impact of employee turnover on an organization and identify specific practices to analyse employee turnover
- Identify what employee retention is, how it is linked to engagement and why it is important from a strategic perspective

THIS CHAPTER DISCUSSES:

Introduction (60)

The Role of HR in Engagement, Induction, Turnover and Retention (60)

Work Engagement (61)

Employee Engagement (62)

Recruitment and Selection (62)

Induction (64)

Employee Turnover (71)

INTRODUCTION

This chapter focuses on employee induction, turnover and retention and how employee engagement is linked to these organizational issues. Within any organization you will find a flow of employees into and out of the organization. People leave jobs; new employees start. Companies are forced to downsize and let people go in bad times and can find themselves expanding rapidly and employing more staff in good times. Managers are tasked with identifying high-performing employees who they want to keep and putting strategies in place to retain them. At the same time, they must monitor the performance of underperformers, with the view to potentially letting go those who, after support, still fail to improve. This flow of employees into and out of organizations is complex and can often be viewed as something that 'happens to' an organization rather than something it actively has control over. The HR function traditionally tracked the movement of employees by monitoring turnover figures or through exit interview transcripts. However, it was not considered a core strategic part of the HR function. The acknowledgement and understanding that people are a source of competitive advantage, combined with the high costs associated with recruiting new staff and inducting them into the organization, has caused the HR function to revisit these areas ▶Chapter 1◀. Employee induction, turnover and retention have become the focus of renewed interest as HR professionals recognize the important contribution that all three areas make to the overall strategic success of the business. Importantly, HR has also recognized the role it has to play in educating senior members of the organization about the impact of employee engagement on these areas and the need for a strategic approach to their management in order to increase the potential overall competitiveness and success of an organization.

It is against this backdrop that we begin our analysis of employee induction, turnover and retention and consider the role of employee engagement. This chapter adopts a different approach to many HR books. Rather than adopting a simple 'how to' approach, the chapter delves a little deeper into the subject to help you to make the link between initiatives aimed at employee induction, turnover and retention and to understand the role of engagement in driving these initiatives so that they contribute to the strategic success of the organization.

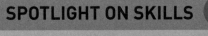

SPOTLIGHT ON SKILLS

To manage retention effectively, HR professionals need to think about retention:

1. before employees are hired
2. while they are working for the organization
3. after they have committed to leave/have left the organization.

You are an HR manager in a large multinational publishing company. You have noticed that although there is no shortage of good candidates for open positions, many employees leave the organization after just one year. For each of the three stages, what initiatives would you seek to implement to address the issue of retention? For each initiative identified, map out how it will work to increase retention rates.

To help you consider the issues above, visit **www.macmillanihe.com/carbery-cross-hrm-2e** and watch the video of Sabahat Ahmed from PeopleFirst HR Consultancy talking about retention policies.

THE ROLE OF HR IN ENGAGEMENT, INDUCTION, TURNOVER AND RETENTION

HR professionals are tasked with understanding the business context or rationale for the introduction of any HR initiative. They must understand the real, tangible benefits that such an initiative will bring to the organization. What does the proposed initiative hope to achieve? How will achieving it help the organization increase its competitive advantage over its rivals? What is the link between this initiative and organizational aims and objectives? Are the links clear to all stakeholders in the organization? HR must constantly think about the organizational benefits of undertaking a new initiative or programme. As a strategic partner to the business, HR must understand the business and be able to demonstrate how its work contributes to the organization's competitiveness and ultimate success.

In addition, HR must understand the associated costs when things are not going well within an organization. For example, it is estimated that the cost of replacing an employee who quits can be as high as 21% of their annual salary (Chamberlain, 2017). Increasingly, organizations are placing more emphasis on adoption of a strategic approach to retention: a key tool for holding on to high performers and thus reducing undesirable turnover. While the direct replacement cost of an employee who leaves the organization

> **Tangible benefits** – benefits for the business that can be measured and reported on; HR must understand the business and be able to demonstrate how its work contributes to the organization's competitiveness and ultimate success
>
> **Longitudinal study** is a research study that involves repeated observations of the same variables (e.g. people) over long periods of time

is fairly evident, there are also many hidden costs within organizations when all is not well. The cost of underperforming or disengaged employees is not as obvious, yet can impact an organization significantly in terms of performance outcomes, including profitability and customer satisfaction. A 2012 report on human capital from McKinsey added to the evidence, noting that organizations with top scores in employee motivation are around 60% more likely to be in the top quartile for overall business profitability. It is important therefore that HR has a good grasp of the activities that promote positive employee engagement but also understands that sometimes it needs to look a little bit closer to fully understand where a problem lies.

HRM AND ORGANIZATIONAL PERFORMANCE

Understanding *Googlers*

Google's People Innovation Lab has developed what it calls 'gDNA' or 'Google DNA', which is Google's first major longitudinal study aimed at understanding Google employees and the way they work. The gDNA study looks to analyse data collected twice a year from a representative sample of over 4,000 *Googlers* to better understand what makes them tick. The data collected will be used by management to gain an awareness of people-related issues, such as the characteristics of employees who excel at Google; what current

staff value in terms of work–life balance; what mix of diverse characteristics a team should ideally possess; how peak performance can be maintained and motivated over the longer term, etc. In doing so, Google hopes to build up an understanding of the kind of people who are likely to be drawn towards the company and those who will excel in this environment. What are the benefits of looking at employee responses over a long period of time? How could an understanding of employee motivation and success benefit the wider company? What other insights could Google obtain from undertaking such a study (Bock, 2014)?

WORK ENGAGEMENT

Work engagement is an issue that is directly related to an organization's competitiveness and success. Work engagement describes how an employee is physically, psychologically and emotionally connected to their work or task (Kahn, 1990). Employees who are engaged work with vigour, dedication and absorption and experience positive emotions, feeling happy, enthusiastic and pleased (Schaufeli et al., 2006).

When employees are engaged, the following are evident:

> **Work engagement** describes the level an individual is prepared to invest of themselves in their work and/or task at hand

- *Vigour* describes how the employee is *physically* connected to their work, demonstrating high levels of energy and mental resilience.
- *Dedication* describes how the employee is *emotionally* connected to their work, demonstrating strong involvement and experiencing a sense of significance, challenge, inspiration, enthusiasm and pride in one's work.
- *Absorption* describes how the employee is *psychologically* connected to their work, demonstrating a state of full concentration; they are so happy and engrossed that time seems to fly by (Breevaart et al., 2012).

Employers strive to have engaged workers, and engagement has now surpassed the concept of employee satisfaction as the 'must-have' for organizations. It is recognized by employers as the ideal employee state, involving high energy accompanied by positive emotions: feeling pleased, happy, enthusiastic, energized and excited. Employee satisfaction, however, is seen as inferior. It is defined as a pleasant but passive state of contentment that is accompanied by low energy and is indicated by emotions such as contentment, relaxation, calmness and tranquillity (Bakker et al., 2012). To drive high performance, employers want engaged employees, not simply ones who are satisfied.

EMPLOYEE ENGAGEMENT

In addition to the benefits brought about by engagement with work, there are also significant advantages to having employees who are engaged with the organization as a whole. **Employee engagement** is a broader concept than work engagement, which involves those initiatives that the organization puts in place to connect the employee with the organization (Truss, 2014). For example, employees may have an emotional attachment to the organization's values, or they may feel connected to the organization because of their manager's support, training and development, the rewards they receive for performance, or the autonomy and challenge they experience from how their work is designed. In simple terms, employee engagement is how the employee is connected to the organization (Truss, 2014).

Both work engagement and employee engagement have a range of positive individual and organizational outcomes. Engagement is linked to higher task performance, higher personal initiative and more innovative behaviour, which benefits the team and the organization. Engagement is also linked to higher organization commitment and retention, and lower absenteeism and turnover rates, which can be quantified in financial terms. HR is therefore committed to finding ways to support employee engagement, to connect employees to their task/role for high performance and to the organization so it can retain engaged employees.

Nita Clarke and David MacLeod have identified four enablers of engagement that they believe can help organizations when looking at ways in which to meaningfully engage with their employees. They specifically talk about having a strong strategic narrative about the organization and its vision and values, which employees can relate to and see those values being actively lived by the leaders in the organization. Secondly, they focus on ensuring that all managers are engaging. By engaging in this context, they simply mean that organizations should recognize and treat employees as individuals working with their strengths and seeking to develop their stretch potential. They also emphasize employee voice as being a fundamental requirement of employee engagement. The ability of employees to contribute to problem-solving, to have a voice and to have that voice heard without being considered troublesome is important to a healthy organization and one where employee engagement can thrive. Finally, the role of organizational integrity is paramount. This encapsulates the idea that organizations, and specifically the leaders within those organizations, should do as they say and that there should be no 'say–do' gap (see http://engageforsuccess.org/ for more information on employee engagement).

RECRUITMENT AND SELECTION

An effective **retention** strategy begins at the earliest stage of the recruitment and selection process.

A company seeking to fill a position within its organization must look beyond the skills required to perform the role effectively, and ensure that the individual demonstrates a good fit with the organizational culture. In other words, in addition to having the necessary competencies to undertake the role, they must also have the right blend of attitude, traits and behaviours to match the core values of the organization. The realization that 'organizational fit' is as important as individual employee ability has resulted in organizations now considering hiring for attitude and then looking to train new employees in terms of skills. It is often easier to provide the necessary training to a new starter with regard to specific skills than it is to change a new starter's attitude or behaviour towards their work (see HRM and Organizational Performance on page 61).

> **Employee engagement** is a broader concept than work engagement insofar as it includes not just the relationship of the employee to their work but also their relationship with the organization itself
>
> **Retention** – a strategic approach adopted by organizations to keep productive employees from seeking alternative employment

In an effort to find individuals who provide a better fit with the organizational values, organizations are increasingly looking towards behavioural-based selection interviewing ▶Chapter 3◀. This can provide insights as to whether an applicant not only has the appropriate experience but also demonstrates values consistent with those of the organization. Scenarios are presented to applicants who must then say how they would react in that particular situation. This type of interview allows an employer to evaluate not only the applicant's use of appropriate judgement, but also to delve into their values and work ethic.

HRM IN THE GLOBAL BUSINESS ENVIRONMENT

Recruitment and retention of doctors in rural areas

The World Health Organization (WHO) estimates that about one-half of the world's population lives in rural and remote areas, but this half is served by only one-quarter of the world's doctors. Any shortage of health workers can prevent good access to health services, which in turn can have a dramatic impact on a patient's quality of life and health outcomes. When such shortages are accompanied by an unequal distribution of healthcare workers, their impact can be even more dramatic. It is a challenge to retain doctors in remote and rural locations irrespective of the perceived wealth of the country. Australia, Scotland and Ireland struggle in the same way as China, Lao People's Democratic Republic and Sri Lanka. The ability to attract and retain doctors in these remote and rural locations has forced local governments to rethink their approach to the attraction and retention of rural doctors. Let us take a look at some examples of how governments are seeking to make rural work more attractive.

Australia

The majority of the population of Australia live in a small number of cities along its coastline. Only 11.3% of the population live outside these urban centres and are spread across the vast continental landmass. The hours tend to be long, the nature of the work is very diverse – often these doctors have to deal with all emergencies and/or medical conditions – and the distances they can be required to travel are immense. It is no wonder that the Australian government has been forced to rethink its approach to the attraction and retention of these rural doctors.

The government has taken a strategic approach to tackling the problem, looking at it from a number of perspectives. Firstly, it has developed and initiated policies aimed at medical education and training, whereby students coming from a rural background are actively targeted and supported through their medical studies. In addition, the government offers specialized grants to medical students willing to commit to spending time as a doctor in a rural location post graduation.

China

China has a population of approximately 1.38 billion people, of which some 850 million live in urban centres. Like Australia, the sheer size of the country means that the distribution of people outside the urban centres is very scattered, and these rural communities tend to be relatively poor in comparison to their urban neighbours.

Similar to the approach adopted by the Australian government, medical students from rural locations are offered waivers on their tuition fees and receive subsidies on condition that students serve in rural areas upon graduation. Interestingly, however, there is a requirement that anyone seeking promotion must first complete a short-term compulsory rural service for health professionals. The duration of the compulsory rural service is not set out but generally is considered to be at least six months in duration (Buchan et al., 2013).

Questions

1. What other policy initiatives could various governments consider to increase the number of rural doctors?
2. If you were tasked with developing initiatives specifically targeting the work–life balance of doctors in rural communities, what factors would you consider?

INDUCTION

Induction is an important organizational initiative which lays the groundwork for employee engagement. It is unlikely that employees will feel connected to the organization or connected to their work, demonstrating vigour, dedication and absorption, if they do not feel a part of the organization from the beginning of their employment and begin the process of understanding and accepting the culture of the organization they have joined.

What is Induction?

Induction as a term is often confused with 'orientation', which is a specific course or training event that new starters attend. The terms are often used interchangeably; however, to do so is to misunderstand the importance of the induction process. The importance of induction and settling new starters into an organization, while gaining more attention these days in the literature, is not a new idea. As far back as 1955, Hill and Trist, in connection with the UK's Tavistock Institute, conducted a number of studies on labour turnover and found that employees are more likely to leave during the early stages of employment, but the longer they remain in employment, the lower the likelihood of them quitting.

Hill and Trist (1955: 276) proposed the **survival curve**, which outlined three distinct phases that employees go through on joining a new organization, each with varying degrees of risk in terms of the likelihood of employees leaving the organization. The first phase they labelled the *induction crisis*, which occurs within weeks of a new starter joining the organization and carries with it the highest likelihood of an employee leaving the organization. Researchers have explored the many different reasons for this induction crisis. For example, it can come as a real shock for employees to realize that in some cases the job they applied for is not quite what they thought. The job may have been oversold at interview by the employer, or the new starter simply thought it would be different from the reality. This notion of unmet expectations is common but could be easily avoided with care and attention at the interview and selection stage. Employers should provide realistic job roles and responsibilities and ensure that they answer

> **Induction** – the whole process whereby new employees in an organization adjust to their new roles and responsibilities within a new working environment
>
> **Survival curve** – a model stating that new starters in an organization are more at risk of leaving in the first six weeks of commencing a new job. The likelihood of leaving decreases as the length of employment increases
>
> **Organizational fit** – the 'fit' or alignment of the personal values and work ethic of the employee with those of the organization's culture and values

candidates' questions as accurately as possible ▶Chapter 3◀.

The literature also points to the idea of **organizational fit**, which may lead to increased numbers of leavers within the first few weeks of employment ▶Chapter 3◀. Employees join an organization and bring with them particular beliefs and attitudes towards work. Where a clash exists between the values or attitude of the new employee and the organization, this can often lead to feelings of unease and doubt. A classic example of poor organizational fit is that of an employee who comes from a bureaucratic organization and joins one that is considered very flat, where employees are empowered and expected to make decisions and take responsibilities for their own actions without the involvement of their line manager. The change in approach to work can be unnerving for the employee and the transition too difficult to bridge, resulting in the employee leaving the organization. They are unable to make the adjustment or settle into the value system of the new organization. This has a direct impact on the dedication dimension of engagement where employees are reluctant to dedicate themselves to an organization they do not believe in or do not feel is the right cultural fit for them.

BUILDING YOUR SKILLS

You are charged with recruiting team members for a new dynamic IT company. How would you go about establishing if a candidate would be a good organizational fit so as to minimize the risk of a new starter leaving?

Interestingly, employees can sometimes find themselves in a position they have applied for and been appointed to, but which is simply beyond their ability. They thought they would be able to rise to the challenge, but the reality is somewhat different. The thrill of seeking a new role and additional responsibilities can often come crashing down as the reality of the situation sinks in. There is nothing worse than being in a role where you know you are unable to perform the duties required of you. The stress of being in such a situation can have a serious medical impact on the individual and lead to **employee burnout** (Schaufeli et al., 2009). This realization can also come within the first few weeks of beginning work in a new organization, leading to high levels of turnover in a short period.

The *differential transit phase* reflects the period when the employee begins to settle into their new work environment and starts to feel more comfortable in their new role. As this settling process continues, the risk of an employee leaving the organization tends to decrease. This phase typically occurs within the first few months of employment. The organization's ability to quickly get a new employee to this phase could be viewed as a potential measure of the effectiveness of the induction programme.

The final stage, *settled connection*, is suggestive of those employees who become fully socialized into the organization. In the words of Hill and Trist (1955), these employees are essentially 'quasi-permanent' and have adjusted to their new role (cited in Zahhly and Tosi, 1989). The quicker an employer can move employees to the settled connection phase, the better, in terms of employee engagement. Employees who are connected to the organization and have adjusted to their new role are more likely to be dedicated to the organization and less likely to leave. Their connection to their work will also encourage them to work with vigour (energy) and absorption (concentration), ensuring that the organization has productive staff members contributing to its competitive success.

Traditional Ineffective Approach to Employee Induction

HR professionals are often criticized for their lack of strategic awareness. There can be a perception within organizations that HR is predominately an administrative function, and the role of HR in developing and rolling out employee induction programmes can often add to this perception if handled in a traditional administrative manner.

The traditional or **informational approach** to induction includes:

- a formal welcome from the new starter's supervisor and introduction to team members
- possibly a general tour of the premises

> **Employee burnout** – this is the opposite to engagement, where the employee disengages and withdraws from work due to emotional and/or physical exhaustion
>
> **Informational approach** – this approach to induction focuses on supplying new starters with basic information regarding the working of procedures within the organization

- an overview, if the new starter is lucky, which might include information on organization-wide trends, key strategies being pursued, key clients and so on
- a presentation on centralized administrative arrangements – expense claims, rules covering absence, discipline, holidays, computer and telephone usage, etc.

After that, the new starter would be free to find their own way in the new world in which they found themselves.

This administrative, informational approach was seen as an opportunity to supply a new starter with standard information regarding the organization and certain core expectations in terms of general employee behaviour. The involvement of line managers in the development or roll out of the induction programme was usually quite limited and it was often a source of irritation to them. Line managers tended to be critical of its effectiveness and frequently questioned its overall purpose. This type of induction programme was often supplemented with the distribution of a weighty and comprehensive employee handbook. If you have had a job, you will know that no one ever reads the employee handbook until a problem arises! The reality is that most new starters put the employee handbook in their desk drawer where it remains until the day they leave.

CONSIDER THIS

In any job you have had, have you ever read the employee handbook? What purpose does an employee handbook serve if it is not read by the majority of employees? Why do organizations spend money on these handbooks? What are the implications of not having an employee handbook?

As an HR professional, how would you go about making the employee handbook more relevant? What media would you use and how would you promote and ensure that employees were familiar with the content of the employee handbook?

This approach to inducting a new employee placed the onus on new starters to seek out and obtain any information they needed in order to be productive in their jobs. It was a case of learning by asking. The difficulty of this approach was that the answer often depended on who was asked, and it may not always have been clear to new starters who the best person was to answer their query. The new starters themselves may be reluctant to admit they do not know something and, instead of seeking help, may opt to remain silent and therefore unproductive. It takes a brave person who has just started in a new position in a company to stand up and admit that they do not know how to do something they have been asked to do, or even how to go about starting it. It is asking a lot of new starters to make them responsible for seeking out the information they need in order to get the job done, especially if an organization fails to provide direction on whom they should approach for help. Research by Ellis et al. (2017) suggests that manager involvement in the onboarding process (see below) is crucial for the successful transition of a newcomer. While there may be a temptation to view employees who actively seek out information as more committed than those new starters who do not, managers need to be careful that they ensure a level playing field where all new starters are supported. An effective way of ensuring this is to actively encourage and measure new starter support as part of the performance management system.

Where organizations promote this type of managerial support for new starters, the results can be quite staggering. Dekas (2013) reported that Google conducted an experiment whereby it gave a sample of managers regular reminders suggesting how they might help a new starter adjust to their work environment. Managers in this sample group were 14% more proactive in helping new starters adjust, and their new employees reported successfully onboarding 10% faster.

With this type of traditional approach to induction, the main risks associated with not offering an induction programme were considered to be limited to the direct costs of replacing a new starter and undertaking a new recruitment drive. There was very little, if any, consideration given to the broader strategic issues, such as ensuring employees understand and accept the mission and values of the organization, that they are settled into the organizational culture, or that they are supported to engage with their work and the organization – the

> **Human capital pool** – the collection of employee skill that exists within a firm at any given time
>
> **Onboarding** – the mechanism through which new employees acquire the necessary knowledge, skills and behaviours to become effective organizational members and insiders

potential benefits of a more robust induction programme. The limited scope of the traditional induction programme, and the absence of a clear business case outlining how this HR initiative contributes to the success of the organization through supporting employee engagement and retention, meant that there was a general lack of interest in induction from both a line management and new starter perspective.

A New Perspective on Employee Induction

New starters should be a source of new focus, new energies and possibly new creativity. The flow of individual employees into and out of the **human capital pool** can bring fresh thinking and new skills and knowledge to an organization. The ability of organizations to quickly tap into this new perspective is fundamental to success. A new employee in a company needs to hit the ground running. Whether it is a small start-up or a large multinational organization, the need to support new hires to be engaged and become productive as soon as possible is critical. In the initial stages, while employees are still acclimatizing to the new environment of the organization, they are a drain on resources without making a contribution. Not only are they a drain but they often take up the valuable time of more experienced staff who are trying to help them navigate their new terrain. It is a steep learning curve for any new starter – on average the time for new hires to achieve full productivity ranges from 8 weeks for clerical jobs to 20 weeks for professionals to more than 26 weeks for executives (Rollag et al., 2005). In the fast-paced competitive environment that organizations now operate in, it is imperative that new starters become productive employees as soon as possible.

Onboarding

Onboarding refers to the mechanism through which new employees acquire the necessary knowledge, skills and behaviours to become effective organizational members and insiders (Bauer and Erdogan, 2011). Onboarding is sometimes referred to as 'organizational socialization'. It is different to induction in terms of its focus. Onboarding is not concerned so much with ensuring that new starters understand, and are familiar with, the company's policies and procedures, but rather with getting new starters to feel like they belong and are a part of their new organization as quickly as possible.

Research has shown that a failure to socialize new starters can have a substantial negative impact on an organization (Cooper-Thomas and Anderson, 2006). These include new starters often showing high levels of unmet expectations, leading to poor attitudes and negative behaviour that, in turn, often result in high levels of turnover (Wanous and Colella, 1989). The recruitment of a new employee is a costly undertaking. The ability of organizations to correctly select employees who are likely to share the organization's values and to socialize them into the organizational culture are key to capitalizing on the investment and ensuring a high calibre of human capital. Onboarding is seen as key to ensuring that new recruits quickly settle into their new role and begin to make a meaningful contribution as soon as possible. The ability of organizations to transform new starters into productive employees is essential (Rollag et al., 2005). A clear linkage between the recruitment drive, the induction process and the organization's culture, that is, its values, norms and politics, is required to ensure that employees are clear in terms of what the organization's strategic goals, mission, vision and values are and what part they can play in achieving them. Organizations should first identify the outcomes that are most important to them, given their strategy and objectives, and then provide the socialization resources that will be most effective in meeting these. The link between the induction process and the overall organizational strategy and objectives is key (Saks and Gruman, 2014).

On joining an organization, new starters quickly get a sense of what is acceptable and unacceptable behaviour within that specific organizational context. First impressions count. The first impressions of an organization for a new starter count in terms of their perception of the organization and their decision to commit or leave, but also, importantly, in terms of their work ethic and the effort they are prepared to put into their role. New starters quickly see what rate others work at and work to this standard. If this standard is high, the new starter will often maintain this level of effort. Unfortunately, if this standard is low, it can often have a permanent negative effect. Take, for example, a new starter who joins an

organization and, on the first day, is eager to please and completes all their tasks within the first half of the day. The new starter approaches their supervisor seeking additional tasks but is told to slow down 'as you are making the rest of us look bad'. So, the new starter, keen to settle in and be accepted, adjusts their work rate to fit in with the information they have received. Conversely, the new starter may find that the pace of work is intense and there are high expectations around delivery of completed tasks. Everyone is responsible for the completion of their own work and this requires the use of initiative and determination to see the task through to completion. Observing their fellow colleagues for a few days, it becomes clear that employees who are not prepared to work at this high level will not survive long in the organization – this sends out a clear message to the new starter regarding expectations of acceptable and unacceptable behaviour and attitudes to work.

What Works in Terms of Induction?

Those organizations that are most successful at quickly getting new starters to the settled connection stage tend to adopt a **relational approach** to induction (Rollag et al., 2005). This approach is based on assisting new employees to quickly build relationships with co-workers so they can access the information they need in order to perform their role. Not only does this approach have the benefit of ensuring that new starters have clear guidance on who to approach with any difficulties they encounter, it also ensures that a new starter quickly feels part of the organization and is socialized into its ways.

Most organizations realize the importance of getting new starters connected quickly to their co-workers; however, they fail to put in place appropriate strategies to make this happen. There is a belief among many managers that if you hire the right person, they will automatically fit right into the organization's way of doing things and will work things out for themselves. 'Good employees' don't need hand-holding. They can adapt to the new situation, make the necessary connections and build their own networks to become productive. Interestingly, the higher up the organization a new starter is, the more truth is placed in this misconception. However, there is an abundance of research showing that for employees to be engaged with their work and the organization, they

> **Relational approach –** this approach to induction focuses on helping new starters rapidly establish a broad network of relationships with co-workers from whom they can access the information they need to be productive members of the team

need support such as training and development (Cullinane et al., 2014), support from supervisors/managers (Bakker et al., 2005) and social and professional support from their co-workers (Cole et al., 2012).

In terms of induction, successful companies are those that strike a balance between information delivery and relationship development. New starters need meaningful information to allow them to make sense of the new world of work in which they find themselves. Such meaningful information might include:

- tailoring the information given to new starters, to show what other departments do and how they interact with the new employee's department and work
- explaining the roles and responsibilities of the key people they will be interacting with during the course of their work
- ensuring that they fully appreciate the strategic goals of the organization and how their work will contribute to the achievement of these goals.

Specific Practices to Enhance the Socialization Process

While a new starter is traditionally taken to a department on their first day and introduced to everyone, or their arrival is announced to a large group at a meeting, research has shown that a strategic approach to introductions is more effective than simply saying 'everyone, this is John'. Thinking about the individual employees who the new starter will interact with and then strategically targeting them for introductions early on in the organizational life of a new starter is likely to be much more effective.

It is not uncommon in organizations for employees to be allocated a formal **mentor**. The **mentoring process** ▶Chapter 10◀ tends to be focused on formal career development and advancement. Mentoring is a process in which the mentor, a more skilled or experienced person, acts as a role model and provides support to the **mentee** to encourage their professional and personal development and help them to reach their full potential (Clutterbuck, 2004; Higgins

> **Mentoring process** – a developmental process focused on the personal and professional development of the mentee
>
> **Mentor** – a more senior or experienced employee who acts as a role model for the employee, supporting their personal and professional development
>
> **Mentee** – the employee who is mentored by a more senior employee within the organization
>
> **Buddy approach** – an informal approach to assisting a new employee to learn about the organization and how things work around or within the organization

and Kram, 2001). The allocation of a mentor is not limited to new starters within an organization and is often used to support career advancement, succession planning and to extend the professional networks and organization perspective of existing employees.

Mentoring provides support to new employees that enables them to connect with the organization. The mentor shares valuable organization knowledge, helping the new employee to understand the organization's culture and history, and giving them access to the key information they need to be effective in their role.

The allocation of a mentor can change over time as an employee's development and career advancement needs change. Mentoring schemes are traditionally formal, with personal and professional development goals in mind, and are often limited to those employees deemed to have promotional potential.

The **buddy approach**, on the other hand, is an informal approach to assisting new employees learn about the organization and how things are done within the new work environment in which they find themselves. While mentors tend to be more formal, buddies are people who can be approached to ask basic questions: 'Where is the paper for the printer kept?' 'Who should I ask about getting a purchase order raised?' Buddies do not necessarily have to be more senior individuals within the firm and, in fact, are more likely to be individuals who are at a similar level in the hierarchy of the organization to the new starter, thereby making it easier to ask for help.

Buddies are often overlooked by organizations, despite the fact that they provide excellent support to new starters and are often the most effective way of socializing new starters into an organizational environment. HR, along with line managers, needs to adopt a proactive approach and identify buddies within each section and department who can assume the role of helping new starters acclimatize to their new environment. They are there to answer any questions, no matter how big or small, and to ensure that the new starter quickly builds a bond with their co-workers, either through formal or informal networks.

Those companies that are successful at rapid onboarding, or quickly getting new starters to make a productive contribution, tend to adopt a combination approach, utilizing an informational and a relational approach (see Table 4.1). The balance between approaches depends on the level of the employee and the number of new starters in the organization. It is likely that general informational training and materials have a role to play, but in order to be truly effective, this must be supported by a conscious effort to combine this with a focused relational approach. The socialization of new starters into any organization ensures that they become engaged with the organization and their

> **Organizational citizenship behaviours** – the behaviour of individual employees that is not directly or explicitly required by an organization as part of the role but which promotes the effective functioning of the organization

work to become productive members of the workforce more quickly and to make a valuable contribution sooner. Not only this, but they are likely to become committed to the organization and demonstrate good **organizational citizenship behaviours** ▶Chapter 14◀. Those new starters who fail to integrate quickly into their new environment are more likely to leave the organization, are slower to become fully productive members of the team, and are less likely to be engaged with the organization and their work.

Stage 1: general induction – informational approach	Stage 2: onboarding – relational approach
Introduction – explain • Mission and strategic objectives of the business • Nature and structure of the business • Roles of key business units within the organizational structure **Employment conditions – explain** • Job description and responsibilities • Work times and meal breaks • Time recording procedures • Leave entitlements • Notification of sick leave or absences **Work environment – show** • Dining facilities • Washing and toilet facilities • Locker and changing rooms • Telephone calls and collecting messages • Out of hours enquiries and emergency procedures **Payroll – explain** • Rates of pay and allowances • Pay arrangements • Taxation (including completion of the required forms) • Superannuation and any other deductions **Health and safety – explain** • Health and safety policy and procedures • Roles and responsibilities for health and safety • Incident reporting procedures	**Orientation – visit and show** • Specific business unit/team objectives and how they relate to the strategic goals of the organization • Clear information on the individual contribution of the role to the achievement of organizational goals and objectives • Roles and responsibilities of key people the individual will be interacting with in order to achieve the set goals and objectives **Meet key people – introduce** • Buddy • Key reports • Members of the direct team • Individuals outside the team within the wider organization and outside the organization who are important relationships/contacts – may require site visits to key clients, customers or suppliers

Table 4.1 Example induction schedule for rapid onboarding

Line Management Involvement in Induction

The failure of line managers to fully engage in the induction process is often viewed as a key problem by HR professionals. Line managers, however, often view induction as the sole responsibility of HR and, from a traditional informational perspective, this was probably a reasonable assumption. This attitude can result in little initial attention being given to new starters who, it is assumed, would go through the induction process and then be in a position to begin work without further input from line managers other than specific day-to-day task allocation. Part of the role of HR is to convince line management of the value of an induction programme and how it can truly add value.

Building a business case to demonstrate the importance of the induction process is more likely to result in support from line managers. If HR can show how a well-balanced and structured induction process can support employee engagement, enhance the human capital pool through knowledge management and retention, and ensure that new starters begin to make a productive contribution as soon as possible, line managers will find it hard to resist. Placing less emphasis on the traditional informational aspect of induction in favour of a more relational approach is also likely to result in more hands-on line management involvement and commitment to the process.

HRM IN THE NEWS

Infosys Global Education Centre

Infosys is an Indian multinational corporation specializing in global business consulting and IT services. Since its foundation in 1981, the company has grown rapidly and currently employs more than 199,000 employees in 32 countries with revenues in excess of US$10.1 billion.

Given the rapid growth of the organization and intense global competition for highly qualified IT engineers, Infosys has taken matters into its own hands when it comes to training and inducting new hires into the company. It has developed the largest corporate training facility in the world at its Mysore Campus. The Infosys Global Education Centre at Mysore is located 140km from India's silicon valley of Bangalore and is capable of training more than 14,000 employees at any one time in various technologies. According to Infosys chairman and chief mentor, M.R. Narayana, the company currently is recruiting approximately 12,000 new employees on average annually. This staggering growth presents challenges in terms of ensuring that these new starters are equipped with the necessary skills and competencies to make a meaningful contribution to the business from the outset. By taking on 4,000 employees at a time onto the Foundation Programme in its Mysore Campus for four months, the organization can meet the organization's demand for 12,000 fully inducted new starters annually.

To provide some sense of the scale of the campus, the Global Education Centre at Mysore has 147 training rooms, 485 faculty rooms, 42 conference rooms, five assessment halls, a cyber café and two state-of-the-art libraries which house over 140,000 books. An induction hall has capacity to seat 400 trainees at any one time, and there are multiple lecture theatres of varying sizes, including 84 100-seater lecture halls. In keeping with the company's philosophy on all-round development, the campus includes an Employee Care Centre, which has a gymnasium, badminton courts, table tennis courts, squash courts, pool tables, an aerobic centre, a swimming pool, jacuzzi, bowling alley, climbing wall and meditation hall, alongside a five-bed medical centre. In addition, there is an international standard cricket ground, a football pitch with an eight-lane athletic track, two basketball courts, a volleyball court and eight tennis courts with synthetic surfaces. The accommodation and facilities at Mysore are considered second to none.

While attending this intensive training programme, all trainees are required to live on campus where they are paid a salary out of which a small deduction is made for accommodation. The training provided is delivered to international benchmark standards and is therefore highly valued by industry. A graduate of the programme can expect the skills learned to be highly transferable; however, such is the esteem in which the programme is held by participants that most graduates of the centre remain loyal to the company over time. It is no surprise to find that the places on the programme are highly sought-after and competition for places is intense, thereby guaranteeing Infosys high-quality applicants and future employees.

Up until June 2015, the Mysore Campus had trained some 125,000 engineering graduates on the Foundation Programme, with approximately 400 'Infoscians' annually completing the Infosys Leadership Institute programme. Take a virtual tour of the Mysore Campus at www.youtube.com/watch?v=DQ5Zn8WFavE.

Questions

1 How does this approach to induction and training assist Infosys in achieving its strategic goals?

2 What is the business case for the level of investment required by Infosys to develop this campus and associated training programmes?

3 What are the likely benefits of having a large in-house training facility like this for an organization?

4 What are the potential disadvantages of such a training initiative in terms of retention and turnover? How might a company such as Infosys mitigate against these potential dangers?

Sources

Infosys (2009) 'Smt. Sonia Gandhi Inaugurates Infosys' Global Education Center - II in Mysore', 15 September

'Infosys has trained 100,000 graduates at Mysuru campus', *Mathrubhumi*, 1 June 2012

'Infosys builds world's biggest training centre in Mysore', *Mysore Samachar*, 9 September 2013

EMPLOYEE TURNOVER

Employees who are engaged with the organization and their work are less likely to leave (Brunetto et al., 2012). HR practices such as training, e.g. induction and onboarding, support employee engagement, helping the new starter to establish a connection with the organization and reducing their likelihood of leaving (Alfes et al., 2013).

Employee turnover, or 'natural wastage' as it is sometimes referred to, is the number of people who will inevitably leave the organization and will need to be replaced in order to maintain production or service (Gunnigle et al., 2011). Employees leaving to travel, spend more time at home, take on new positions in other organizations, who are dismissed, who retire – these are all examples of labour turnover within an organization. Some of these life events can be planned, such as retirement, but others, such as an employee's decision to leave to go travelling, can be difficult to plan for from a management perspective.

> **Employee turnover** – the number of people who leave an organization and need to be replaced in order to maintain production or service
>
> **Pull factors** – those factors beyond the control of the organization that may cause an employee to leave – such as moving to a new location/country, the arrival of children, retirement and so on
>
> **Push factors** – those factors that negatively impact on an employee and may be the trigger to start them thinking about leaving an organization, such as dissatisfaction with their work, their boss or their promotional opportunities, a lack of developmental opportunities and so on

Some of these factors are beyond the control of the organization, such as the employee moving to a new location, a change in family circumstances, retirement and so on. These are known as **pull factors** and there is very little an organization can do to hold on to an employee in this type of situation. Having said that, progressive employers may wish to consider being proactive about a high performer who leaves for these reasons. Being progressive simply means ensuring that the employee is aware that, should they wish to return to employment, the organization would welcome an approach. It is not a promise of a job but more a case of leaving the door open. The employer can also be creative in supporting work–life balance by offering flexible work practices so that an employee can work from home or work reduced hours, etc.

There are also **push factors**, which organizations do have control over. Push factors are those factors that negatively impact on an employee and may be the trigger for them to think about leaving an organization. The main push factors tend to centre on dissatisfaction with work but mainly with a lack of promotional and developmental opportunities. Many employees now look to the companies they work for to provide them with growth and learning opportunities. In particular, high performers often perceive development as a benefit they are entitled to and expect employer-provided opportunities to update and develop their personal skill set. In a fast-paced, competitive environment, the ability to stay current in terms of your skills is considered vitally important to most high-performing employees. This, however, presents organizations with a difficult challenge. Should they invest in their staff to make them more marketable to their competitors? This is a difficult balance between expenditure on training and understandable concerns regarding loss of employees once trained. However, employers can increase the retention of employees they have developed by providing challenging work opportunities for those employees to apply their new learning.

A lack of challenging work and limited opportunity for career progression is damaging to employee engagement. Employee dissatisfaction is often evident but organizations fail to address it adequately until it is too late. Measures seeking to tap into employee attitudes, engagement and satisfaction with their work and environment are essential and a key part of HR's role.

Employee engagement surveys can help an organization determine the level of turnover intention within the organization and identify rewards that are most likely to support the employee to be dedicated to their work and the organization. It is likely, however, that employees do not all place equal value on the rewards offered by the organization ▶Chapter 8◀. In fact, different employees will probably value different things, depending on the stage of their career and where they are in their lifecycle. For example, a younger member of staff who likes to travel may value additional leave as a method of reward, so they could travel for an extended period. On the other hand, a longer serving employee may value additional contributions towards their pension. A new parent may value flexible

> **Employee engagement surveys** – research carried out to assess the feelings of a target group of employees towards various aspects of their work, their team and their organization
>
> **Flexible benefits** – from a defined set of available benefits, employees select the benefits that best meet their needs

working arrangements, while a longer serving employee may value the opportunity to reduce their working week as they approach retirement.

Given that all employees do not place the same value on the rewards on offer, either financial or nonfinancial, the key to success is that organizations know what it is their staff value and target specific groups if necessary. This may involve offering employees the option to choose from a limited selection of reward choices, ranging from additional leave to extra pension contributions. This idea of tailoring benefits to suit the needs of individual employees is known as **flexible benefits**. Offering all employees the same set of rewards is likely to please some but not all employees. Employers and HR also need to educate employees as to the value of the packages they receive. Employees often do not fully understand the benefits offered nor the value of these benefits to them, e.g. disability benefit, death in service, pension, maternity pay and so on. Organizations need to ensure that they communicate effectively with their staff regarding the uniqueness of the package on offer and why the company is a great place to work, supporting their engagement and retention.

The Impact of the External Labour Market Environment on Turnover Levels

In addition to push and pull factors, organizations can often find themselves at the mercy of the external environment. For example, in a booming economy, jobs tend to be in plentiful supply and so the level of turnover experienced by an organization may rocket. High performers may seek out opportunities or, indeed, be headhunted directly by competitors. The upward pressure this can place on salaries can be significant; that is, organizations find that they are having to pay higher and higher levels of salaries to good performers simply to hold on to them and prevent them from leaving for a competitor organization. The focus tends to move towards retention of key performers and putting in place attractive initiatives, which are focused on a healthy level of pay but with significant non-pay elements that bind the employee to the organization. Such non-pay elements might be childcare arrangements, flexible working arrangements, gym membership, parking schemes, training and educational opportunities.

Economics tells us that the boom and bust of economies is cyclical, that is, just as surely as there is a boom, a bust will follow. The time period between the boom and bust is tricky to predict but the cycle generally remains the same. Therefore, organizations will often have to deal with a downturn in the economy and the impact that can have on turnover. In a downturn, attention tends to focus on downsizing employees and the exiting of staff. While difficult decisions have to be made in terms of who stays and who goes, organizations also need to focus on those individuals who remain. The idea of 'survivor guilt' is well documented. Staff who survive a downsizing exercise often feel guilty about their former colleagues losing their jobs, which can have a significant negative impact on productivity. Equally, in a situation where a workforce has been significantly reduced, additional pressures are shouldered by the remaining staff members; that is, less people have to do more in order to get the work done. Again, if not carefully managed, this can create bad feeling or, worse, burnout, which can impact on productivity and morale.

Should an Organization Seek to Minimize its Turnover Levels?

As we have seen, there are many reasons why someone might leave an organization and, despite the negative connotations of the phrase 'turnover', not all turnover is necessarily bad. A certain level of turnover may be considered a good thing and can result in positive benefits for an organization. As new employees enter an organization, they bring with them fresh ideas and perspectives. They may see things differently and ignite new discussions and debate. This idea of bringing new blood into the organization's human capital pool can assist in avoiding the complacency that sometimes arises within organizations. A danger for many organizations is the development of 'groupthink' (Janis, 1982), whereby members of the organization begin to adopt similar thought processes that reinforce each other without question or scrutiny. It is hard to see things differently if, as happens in some organizations, it is the only thing you have ever known. New employees can be a breath of fresh air in terms of their ideas and energy, as well as the new competencies they bring that can add significant

value to the organization. These new competencies can open up opportunities that might otherwise remain unrealized by the organization. They can also enable the organization to adopt new working patterns to maximize its potential.

Turnover may also include those individuals who are underperforming and are forced to leave the organization after being through the performance management and development system, or who leave prior to being forced out when it is clear the situation is unlikely to improve. Again, this type of turnover is not necessarily a negative thing. While organizations do not want to lose their key members of staff, they do not want to have a low turnover rate if that means continuing to employ serial underperformers. Sometimes, organizations boast about their low turnover rate, but we must ask ourselves the question: is the organization holding on to key talent it does not want to lose or is it stuck with a large proportion of underperforming staff whose performance should have been managed more actively? Low turnover rates are not necessarily a sign of a productive workforce.

It is ironic that the employees an organization wants to hold on to are often the very ones most likely to leave. If you think about it, it makes sense. High-performing employees are more likely to be sought after by others, are likely to be ambitious to advance their careers, and are more likely to seek out new opportunities. An underperforming employee, on the other hand, is unlikely to want to leave an organization where their underperformance is not being actively managed. If they are permitted by their supervisors to continue to underperform without any intervention to give performance feedback or agree development targets, it is unlikely they will be motivated to improve their behaviour to reach acceptable levels of performance but, equally, they have no incentive to look for alternative work.

So, if low turnover rates are not necessarily a good thing and high turnover rates are not necessarily a bad thing, what is the appropriate level of turnover?

What is an Appropriate Turnover Level for a Business?

An important issue for any organization is deciding what level of turnover is appropriate for their business model. Most organizations do not give sufficient thought to this matter. Different business models will have different costs associated with turnover. The cost of turnover will be higher, for example, where you have a limited pool of people you can recruit due to their specific qualifications or technical abilities, or if the cost of training those individuals is very high. The cost of turnover will be lower, however, if there is an unlimited supply of individuals who could do the work with little or inexpensive training. Equally, some businesses operate successfully with high turnover and their business model is, in fact, based around a high turnover rate. HRM in the News (page 75) provides an example of how turnover, in this case of a high-profile leaver, can have a negative impact on the business success of the organization.

Costs of Labour Turnover

As we have discussed, the costs of labour turnover vary by sector and organization; however, there are some basic costs common to all, albeit to a greater or lesser degree financially. Every organization has to deal with the costs associated with dismissing an individual from the organization. There are payroll costs and the calculation of outstanding contractual obligations, such as holidays that have to be paid out as they cannot be availed of by the employee. While the replacement recruitment process is ongoing, there is the cost of cover for an employee if additional staff have to be drafted in, or if existing staff need to do overtime in order to take up the excess workload. Then there are the costs associated with the recruitment and selection process ▶Chapter 3◀. This includes everything from advertising the position, to the time taken to arrive at a shortlist of candidates for interview and the interviews themselves, which are all costs to the organization. These costs can be considerable and are, essentially, repeat costs, as you had already spent on hiring in the first place. There are also costs associated with the underperformance of individuals who are working out their notice: upon deciding to leave an organization and handing in their notice, employees can often reduce their input.

Costs tend to be industry specific but, in general, in a tight labour market, organizations can struggle to find a suitable pool of candidates to draw from. This can result in individuals moving quickly through promotional grades without necessarily having gained the equivalent in-depth experience. For example, during the Celtic Tiger years in Ireland between 2003 and 2007, the economy was booming and work was plentiful as organizations were expanding rapidly

to meet increased demand in the market. In this environment it was common for an employee to move five times within three years, with each move receiving, on average, a €5,000 per annum hike in salary. In this rapidly expanding market where it was difficult to attract sufficient staff, it was common to find anomalies of highly paid individuals in organizations who did not necessarily have the skills or competencies required of an employee operating at that level. When the labour market restricted as the economy hit the subsequent recession, organizations were forced to let go of many of their employees as they fought to cut their cost base to reduce their overheads. The result was high employment rates resulting in excess labour with a readjustment in terms of pay levels for many of these individuals.

CONSIDER THIS

Where an individual rises above their level of competency, it is commonly referred to as the **Peter Principle**. Organizations that seek to promote individuals based on performance and achievement and continue to do so will eventually promote an individual beyond their level of ability. For example, you have a great receptionist working for you and you promote them to the role of secretary, in which they do really well. So, you decide to promote them again, this time to personal assistant. Again, they do really well in this role, so much so that you decide they have management potential and you promote them to the position of office manager. Having taken on this role, you find they are a total disaster. They have no people management skills and avoid confrontation, while appearing stubborn with their team. They struggle with the diversity of tasks confronting them and cannot cope with all the people reporting to them seeking answers. This person had been a good receptionist, secretary and PA, but could not make the transition to the next level, that of management, and thus became a victim of the Peter Principle.

What can Organizations do to limit the impact of High profile leavers?

Organizations can adopt a number of strategies to limit the potential damage of high-profile leavers. At a very senior level, it is essential that the organization seeks to have a clear succession plan in place so as to ensure the smooth transition of power, should the leader of the organization leave. Most organizations spend a considerable amount of time assessing and then training and developing potential successors. The cost to an organization of appearing to be 'leaderless' is significant, and, even if a decision is taken to recruit externally, most organizations will put in place a plan to cover any temporary vacancy that may arise.

A major threat to the organization is the loss of critical knowledge as a result of employee turnover. More and more organizations are seeking to encourage a team-based approach to work in order to minimize the effects of one member of the team leaving. If knowledge is shared among a group rather than concentrated in the hands of just one individual, the ability to deal with turnover of individuals becomes manageable.

HRM IN THE NEWS

The impact of a high-profile leaver

We have discussed the cost of turnover for different industries and different business models, but what about the cost to an organization of losing a high-profile leader. The interesting case of Steve Jobs at Apple helps to demonstrate this point.

The news in January 2011 that Steve Jobs was taking a second open-ended leave of medical absence resulted in Apple's share price taking a serious drop. When Steve Jobs took his first leave of absence in 2009, Apple's share price dropped a dramatic 10% before being suspended. Jobs was considered to have such an influence on Apple as an organization, and on its products, that it was often said that the DNA of the company resided with him. When Steve Jobs died of a rare form of pancreatic cancer in October 2011, Apple's share price immediately fell by 5%. In March 2010, financial magazine *Barron's* had attempted to estimate Jobs' value to Apple and came up with a figure of $25 billion.

Since 2011, Apple's share price has increased over 130% following a temporary dip following Job's passing. This may appear to dispel the argument of the influence of a founder of an organization on its success; however, when a comparative analysis was undertaken with similar high-tech organizations, it was interesting to see that these companies had outperformed Apple quite significantly. Google, for example, in the same period returned a 170% increase in share price. Amazon returned a 140% increase in share price over the same period. What is interesting about these organizations is that their founders are still actively involved the business.

Questions

1. In the case of Apple, why did Steve Jobs' death affect Apple's share price and do you believe that it continues to do so? If so, why?
2. What role does succession planning play in ensuring continuity within an organization?
3. How might ensuring clear career advancement opportunities assist an organization with retention?
4. What can organizations do to lessen the effect of high-profile leavers?

Sources

Akers, C., Twitter

Kane, Y. and Lublin, J. (2011) 'Apple chief to take leave: Steve Jobs says he needs to focus on health', *Wall Street Journal*, 18 January, http://online.wsj.com/article/SB100014240527487033966045760876 90312543086.html (accessed 11 June 2018)

Satariano, A., Burrows, P. and Galante, J. (2011) 'Apple's Jobs takes leave as weight loss said to continue; Cook takes over', *Bloomberg*, 18 January, www.bloomberg.com/news/2011-01-17/apple-chief-executive-jobs-granted-medical-leave-of-absence.html (accessed 11 June 2018)

Somaney, J (2015) 'How much is Steve Jobs missed at Apple', *Forbes*, 16 August, www.forbes.com/sites/jaysomaney/2015/08/16/how-much-is-steve-jobs-missed-at-apple/#20b458954100. (accessed 11 June 2018)

Measuring Turnover

Now we turn our attention to how to measure turnover levels in an organization. We can see from the previous discussion that unplanned or unforeseen turnover is often problematic. HR professionals need to be able, as far as possible, to predict and control the rate of turnover within their organization. Different measures of employee turnover are available, and you need to be clear, particularly when it comes to comparing figures across businesses or sectors, which measures are being used ▶Chapter 11◀. As HR professionals, it is essential that there is clarity in terms of what is being measured and what is not. Turnover rate is calculated by taking the number of leavers during a month divided by the average number of employees, multiplied by 100:

> Turnover Rate = Number of Leavers / Average Number of Employees x 100

While this may seem like a straightforward calculation, HR professionals need to be cautious in terms of how they calculate the turnover rate and how they communicate this with the business, so that all the stakeholders in the business are clear on the basis for the calculations. An example where lack of clarity can cause problems may be where there is inconsistency in how average number of employees is calculated. What if one department was including only those in full-time employment in their calculations, while another department included all workers irrespective of the nature of their employment, e.g. part-time employees? What if one department included those employees on maternity leave while another did not? A consistent and clear approach to the calculation of figures allows organizations to ensure that the business decisions made on such data are robust and accurate.

High levels of employee turnover can be an indicator of low levels of employee engagement. The ability to accurately measure labour turnover is an important part of the role of HR, but it is often a crude measure of what is going on more generally within an organization. Correctly identifying problem areas if they exist is essential. Any analysis of turnover should seek not only to measure the rate of turnover but also to analyse where it is happening within the

organization and why. A robust analysis of turnover allows the organization to put in place policies and practices to tackle the retention of key members of staff.

Increasingly, organizations are looking to supplement their turnover analysis with additional information to provide a more rounded picture of what is going on within their organization in relation to turnover. Many organizations conduct exit interviews with departing employees to ascertain their reasons for leaving the organization. This usually takes place during their notice period and is conducted by a member of the HR team. The detailed collection and, crucially, analysis of this information can provide management with useful insights as to where problems are occurring, or may arise in the future, that are causing people to leave the organization. A perceived lack of training or promotional opportunities, a belief that other organizations are paying higher wages, or a negative work environment due to interpersonal difficulties with co-workers or the manager are issues that often arise in exit interviews. Such information should not just be taken at face value, but should form part of a wider analysis of organizational benchmarking against competitors, a review of internal promotions, and a review of the specific work environment and culture within a team or department.

Another useful tool in analysing turnover is cohort analysis. The idea is to analyse the level of turnover in different cohorts, or groups, of employees. These groups may be employees from various departments or grouped by gender or ethnicity. Cohort analysis can be particularly insightful in relation to an analysis of skill sets. If a company finds that it is losing a group of employees with a particular skill set, this may trigger a review of pay or promotion opportunities for that group. The development of individual staff profiles aids this process by easily identifying where turnover rates are high among a particular set of employees with a particular skill set. In undertaking a cohort analysis, the HR function may find that one department in particular is responsible for driving up the overall turnover rate for the organization. The reasons for this high level of turnover among a particular group of employees can then be examined and strategies put in place to reduce the level of turnover.

HRM IN PRACTICE

Retention issues in a sales team

Getty Images/andresr

You have recently been appointed as the director of HR for a Chinese chemical organization. The company has seen rapid expansion over the past three years in particular and prides itself on being innovative and reactive in the fast-changing market. It has been successful since its foundation and there is no reason to think that this success will not continue into the future. The company is well regarded in the industry for its sales network and robust sales systems. It invests heavily in training all sales staff, and all new starters receive two months on-the-job mentoring from a senior salesperson until they are familiar with the sales techniques and systems unique to this organization.

A regional sales director within the company is concerned, however, because of a recent trend which has seen some of the newly employed sales staff leaving the organization for competitors inside a year of starting. The high turnover of sales staff has the sales director questioning if the company is simply providing a free training base for competitor organizations. The company has been described by some in the industry as the 'Whampoa Military Academy'. This academy was founded in 1924 in Guangdong and was considered one of the most important military schools in China for producing so many prestigious commanders and outstanding officers in the twentieth century. While a glowing endorsement of the training received by new starters within the organization, it also means that these individuals are highly sought-after and usually can command more senior positions with better pay in competitor organizations.

Although there is a tradition of internal promotion and a clear career path for employees, the reality is that it is simply not possible to provide promotional opportunities to everyone on the sales team. This, combined with the higher salaries and more prestigious positions on offer in competitor organizations, has resulted in a high number of employees leaving.

The regional sales director is determined to identify the right fit of person for the organization with an emphasis on loyalty, and in doing so hopes to avoid a situation where the company is training people for other competitor companies. The question is where should he start and what specifically should he be examining?

What would you do?

1. As HR director, outline what you see as the problems facing the organization.
2. What initiatives or strategies do you propose in order to tackle the problem(s)?
3. What suggestions do you have in terms of gathering more accurate information for senior management with regard to turnover and retention?
4. How can you use the information gathered to improve overall employee retention?

SUMMARY

We can see that employee engagement, induction, turnover and retention are inextricably linked. A focused and strategic approach to the management of each area, while recognizing the linkages between them, is vitally important. The process begins with a recruitment and selection process to identify a good fit candidate and must be followed through with appropriate induction programmes, which take both an informational and relational approach. This will support employee engagement and enable a more rapid socialization of new starters, while ensuring focused retention policies are in place for high performers. By combining these HR practices, organizations can reduce their exposure to undesirable turnover effects and ensure that high-performing employees are more likely to be engaged and therefore remain productive and happy employees committed to the organization.

CHAPTER REVIEW QUESTIONS

1. What is employee engagement and why is it important for organizations to understand the drivers of engagement?
2. Outline the direct and indirect costs to an organization of turnover.
3. What do we mean by 'good organizational fit' in terms of retention?
4. Outline the different approaches to induction, highlighting the one which you believe would be most effective in ensuring employees are productive as soon as possible.
5. Is all turnover necessarily a 'bad' thing from an organizational perspective? In what circumstances might it not be?
6. Explain what is meant by 'push' and 'pull' factors in relation to turnover. What can an organization do, if anything, to control these factors?
7. What can organizations do to limit the impact of high-profile leavers?

8. What role can employee engagement play in delivering sustained competitive advantage for an organization? Make specific reference to employee induction, turnover and retention in your answer.

FURTHER READING

Wayne F. Cascio (2014) 'Leveraging employer branding, performance management and human resource development to enhance employee retention', *Human Resource Development International*, 17:2, 121–128, DOI: 10.1080/13678868.2014.886443

Elliott, G and Corey, D (2018) *Build It: The Rebel Playbook for World-Class Employee Engagement*, Chichester: John Wiley & Sons.

USEFUL WEBSITES

engageforsuccess.org
A really good resource outlining the latest research on employee engagement, alongside case studies of how organizations are tackling the issue of employee engagement and what they have found works best.

www.ere.net
Useful website with articles about recruitment retention and turnover.

www.cipd.co.uk/search?q=podcasts
This website contains podcasts on many of the issues covered in this chapter.

www.shrm.org/search/pages/default.aspx?k=turnover
SHRM is a useful site for clear definitions and worked-out examples of how to calculate turnover rate within an organization.

 For extra resources, including videos, multiple choice questions and useful weblinks, go to: www.macmillanihe.com/carbery-cross-hrm-2e.

Getty/Moxie Productions

5: Managing the Employment Relationship

Michelle O'Sullivan

LEARNING OUTCOMES

By the end of this chapter you will be able to:

* Explain the nature and theories of the employment relationship
* Outline the role and functions of employee representatives and employer organizations as actors in the employment relationship
* Outline the rationale for, and types of, employee voice mechanisms
* Explain the nature of conflict and the role of the state bodies which help resolve workplace conflict
* Explain contemporary issues including the impact of the economic crisis
* Describe key negotiating skills

THIS CHAPTER DISCUSSES:

Introduction (80)

The Nature of the Employment Relationship (80)

Theoretical Perspectives (81)

Actors in the Employment Relationship (82)

Employment Rights (84)

The Global Economic Crisis (85)

Quality of Jobs (86)

Employee Participation and Voice (89)

The Nature of Conflict and its Resolution (90)

INTRODUCTION

Managers are often placed at the 'intersection' between employees and employers. They have the complex role of delivering the profit and performance expectations of employers, while ensuring that employees are satisfied and engaged in their jobs. How managers undertake this role is influenced by many factors, including their view of the employment relationship and the extent of employment rights and obligations as determined by law and collective agreements. The types of jobs created are also impacted by the wider economic and competitiveness environments. Traditionally, managers hired employees for full-time permanent jobs, but more 'atypical' work is fuelling a debate on the quality of work being created, especially in the aftermath of the global economic crisis. This chapter explores these important issues in the employment relationship. It starts with an overview of the complex nature of the employment relationship, theoretical perspectives and the role of key actors. It explores employment rights, employee voice, the nature of workplace conflict and, importantly, provides insights on negotiation skills to help resolve conflict. The chapter also examines key contemporary issues in employment, including the impact of the global economic crisis and the rise of the 'gig economy'.

THE NATURE OF THE EMPLOYMENT RELATIONSHIP

The manager's role of managing the demands and expectations of their employees and their own senior managers and the employer is a difficult one because of the complexity of the employment relationship. As Brown and Rea (1995: 364) succinctly note: 'the employment contract is rarely in the form of a tidy document. Its content has to be deduced from successive layers of both written and unwritten rules.' In addition to psychological factors such as personalities and human emotions, there are underlying structural reasons why the employment relationship is such a complex one. One reason is that the

exchange that takes place between an employer and employee is difficult to define or 'pin down' when the relationship begins. On commencing employment, a new employee will generally be told what salary and benefits they will receive, but they will not have a clear view of working conditions or other factors, while employers buy 'employees' capacity to work which requires direction' (Sisson, 2008: 14). Companies have different ways of ensuring that employees do what they want them to do. Some companies try to control employees' behaviour through, for example, strict supervision and penalties for not complying with rules. Other companies offer employees good pay and conditions, and decision-making autonomy to encourage them to be committed to their job. This vagueness in the exchange between an employer and employee can lead to disagreements over what constitutes a 'fair day's pay' (D'Art and Turner, 2006: 524).

A second reason for the complexity of the employment relationship is power. It is argued that the differential in power between an employer and an employee is a key feature of the employment relationship (D'Art and Turner, 2006). First, employers' resources are greater than employees'. Secondly, the employment relationship is a hierarchical one, in which managers direct employees to fulfil tasks and enforce employee obligations (Sisson, 2008). Power becomes particularly important when there are differences of interests. Employees generally want higher pay, job security, career progression, development of skills, and employers generally want to maximize their human resources to achieve profit. For much of the employment relationship, employers and employees cooperate with each other. However, Sisson (2008: 19) notes that: 'the potential for specific conflicts of interest is ever present and that the expressions of such conflicts ... is not just a matter of faulty procedures, "bad" management or wilful employees'. When conflict does arise, both sides may exert power to try to force the other party to give in (Lewis et al., 2003). To reduce the potential for conflict to escalate, many companies use mechanisms such as **grievance procedures** and **disciplinary procedures**, collective bargaining and other employee voice mechanisms to address differing interests.

> **Grievance procedure** – a written step-by-step process an employee must follow to voice a complaint in an organization. The formal complaint moves from one level of authority in the organization to the next higher level if unresolved
>
> **Disciplinary procedure** – a written step-by-step process that an organization uses when an employee has broken the organization's rules. Disciplinary procedures can lead to penalties, such as warnings, with the aim of changing an employee's performance/behaviour. In a severe breach of rules, an employee may be dismissed

CONSIDER THIS

Do you think employers and employees have the same interests and goals or are they different? What is the result of this? Is conflict in an organization a good or bad thing?

THEORETICAL PERSPECTIVES

Theoretical perspectives help us to analyse employment relations in an organization, and some of the most influential perspectives were developed by Alan Fox in the 1960s. The first perspective he developed was unitarism. The underlying assumption of unitarism is that employers and employees have the same interests, goals and values and so conflict should not exist in an organization. As employees have the same interests as their employer, there is only one source of authority in the organization (management) and it does not see a need to gain employees' consent to make decisions (Salamon, 2000). As employees should have the same interests as management, there is no need for trade unions – they are seen as troublemakers. If conflict does occur, the unitarist perspective does not view the reasons for this as being related to the nature of employment, such as an imbalance of power. Instead, conflict is believed to occur because of personality clashes and poor communications. While at first glance unitarism might seem utopian and unrealistic, Storey (1992) notes that many elements of HRM are unitarist in nature. According to Wallace et al. (2013), unitarist management can manifest itself through two management styles – paternalistic and authoritarian:

1. *Paternalistic management:* managers look after employees and use 'soft' HRM practices such as good salaries, benefits to employees, direct communications and teamworking. The purpose of these is to keep employees satisfied, emphasize management as the source of authority, reduce the potential for conflict and prevent unionization.
2. *Authoritarian management:* a more dogmatic management approach, whereby there may be little concern for employees and suppression of

> **Collective bargaining –** negotiations between an employer/group of employers and one or more workers' organizations to determine terms and conditions of employment and to regulate relations between employers and workers
>
> **Capitalist system** – an economic system of private enterprise for profit

any attempts by employees to introduce a trade union into the workplace (Wallace et al., 2013).

Pluralism is a framework with an entirely different perspective of employment relations. Pluralism assumes that the organization is made up of groups with different interests and goals. As there are differing interests, conflict is inevitable and pluralism accepts the legitimacy of trade unions as representatives of employees. It is management's role to balance the interests of different groups in the organization, and it is legitimate to establish mechanisms to address conflict, such as dispute resolution procedures and **collective bargaining**. These differing interests and any ensuing conflict must not be so great as to be irreparable (Lewis et al., 2003). Those organizations that negotiate with trade unions are based on a pluralist perspective of employment relations. Similarly, governments in many countries have established bodies to help organizations resolve conflict – again reflective of a pluralist perspective.

A more radical perspective on the employment relationship is Marxism, which has been one of the most influential theories in employment relations, sociology, politics and economics over the past 100 years. Karl Marx's ideas have been the subject of extensive analysis in a great many fields, but can only be briefly sketched here. Marx argued that conflict in organizations merely reflected conflict between classes in society – between a minority who are employers (capitalists or bourgeoisie), who own the means of production (companies, assets), and a majority who are workers (proletariat), who only own their labour (Grint, 1991; Salamon, 2000). Marx viewed the **capitalist system** as having negative and alienating effects on workers, because they did not control what they produced, work involved mindless repetition, and workers competed against one another (Grint, 1991). While pluralism views mechanisms for managing conflict, such as dispute resolution procedures, as legitimate and necessary, the Marxist perspective views these mechanisms as advancing the interests of management (Salamon, 2000). The value of the Marxist perspective lies in its sophisticated understanding of the employment relationship by relating it to conflict in the wider society – something unitarism and pluralism do not do.

ACTORS IN THE EMPLOYMENT RELATIONSHIP

The regulation of the employment relationship, in terms of how pay and conditions are set, varies across organizations, industries and countries. In some organizations, pay and conditions are unilaterally set by the employer, and in others there is some scope for negotiation between an employer and an individual employee. In other organizations, employees are represented by a trade union, and the employer may be a member of an employer organization, and both sides negotiate and agree pay and conditions on a collective basis so, for example, employees doing comparable work would get similar pay increases or benefits. Unions remain a key source of independent employee representation in many countries, but there can also be non-union representatives in organizations. We now outline the roles and functions of employee representatives and employer organizations.

Employee Representation

Historically, the primary representative of employees has been trade unions. Trade unions are organizations whose aim is to protect and defend the interests of their members. They do so by acting collectively to challenge employer power (Kelly, 1998). For example, if one employee has a dispute with an employer and decides to take some form of industrial action, it may not have much effect. If a large number of employees take industrial action together, this will interrupt business and be costly to the employer, and so it may persuade the employer to negotiate with employees or concede to their demands. However, taking industrial action is often a last resort for unions. The most common ways in which they try to protect members' interests are through collective bargaining with employers, lobbying the government for worker-friendly policies, representing members in grievance and disciplinary procedures and providing employment rights advice to members. Unions are financed by their members' fees and are staffed by full-time or part-time officials. Workplaces with a union usually also have workplace representatives or shop stewards. They are employees of the organization who act voluntarily as a union representative, effectively acting as the link between the union and the members.

A common feature of employment relations in many countries is the formation of one or more confederations of trade unions. These confederations do not generally represent members in the workplace but act as the voice of the union movement at the national level. Examples include the Trade Union Congress in the UK, the Irish Congress of Trade Unions in Ireland, the American Federation of Labor–Congress of Industrial Organizations and the Change to Win Federation in the USA, Landsorganizationen i Sverige in Sweden, the Australian Council of Trade Unions and the African Regional Organization of the International Trade Union Confederation.

CONSIDER THIS

What do you think might be the similarities between student unions and trade unions? Draw on your experience of college/university and work.

HRM IN THE GLOBAL BUSINESS ENVIRONMENT

Trade unions

In recent years, an alliance of global trade unions has called on IKEA, the Dutch-owned retail company of Swedish origin, to end what it claimed were anti-union activities in its stores in a number of countries including the USA and Ireland. Trade unions claimed that IKEA was openly opposed to unions in those countries. This contrasts with the company's employment relations approach in Sweden, whereby it recognizes unions, and union representatives sit on the company board. These differences indicate that a company's approach to trade unions can be influenced by the employment relations environment within a country. The extent to which unions are an accepted part of society differs across countries. We can roughly categorize countries into three groups, though these should be seen as indicative rather than authoritative. The first group are countries where trade unions are an accepted part of society, have historically been supported by governments, and are negotiated with extensively by government and/or employer organizations. Such countries include France,

Germany, Austria and Scandinavian countries. The second group are countries where unions are an accepted part of the historical development of industry and society, but governments and employer organizations negotiate less than the first group, and there may be a less supportive employer or political environment, ranging from benign to hostile. This group can include the UK, USA, Ireland and Australia. Amongst African nations, South Africa lies somewhere between the first and second group by having the most advanced institutional support for trade unions (Horwitz, 2006). The third group are countries with political environments that make it difficult for independent unions to represent members' interests, and often the state keeps significant control over industrial relations. This group includes Russia, China, Vietnam, some African countries such as Ethiopia and Zimbabwe, some East Asian countries such as Malaysia and, in more extreme cases, some Middle Eastern countries (Clarke, 2005; Cammet and Posusney, 2010). For example, trade unions are not allowed to exist in Saudi Arabia and United Arab Emirates.

Declining Unionization

The fortunes of trade unions internationally have changed substantially since the 1980s and many are facing significant challenges. A 2011 study of **union density** found that it had declined in 23 out of 24 countries in the previous 30 years (Schnabel, 2013). Table 5.1 provides an indication of the declines in selected countries. However, there is still substantial variation across the world, for example union density in Scandinavian countries remains high at over 65%. Trade union density is only a partial indicator of union strength, and in some European countries such as France, Austria and the Netherlands, collective agreements negotiated between trade unions and employer organizations can be extended by government across an industry. This means that workers can be covered by a collective agreement whether or not they are in a trade union. Research in Europe suggests that there is strong support for trade unions (Turner and D'Art, 2012), so declines in union density have been largely attributed to the growing ability of employers to resist unionization in their organizations. This power has been influenced by globalization and the increasing ability of companies to move locations, as well as less union-friendly political environments. For example, in the USA, a number of states passed laws in 2011 which weakened or abolished the collective bargaining rights of public sector employees (Freeman and Han, 2012). The impact of a decline in unionization is significant because fewer workers have an independent representative voice that defends their interests, and falling unionization is also linked to a rise in income inequality. Trade unions are trying to reverse declines in unionization through a variety of methods such as internal restructuring, allocating more resources to organizing members, cooperating with trade unions internationally and encouraging citizens to vote for union-friendly political parties.

> **Union density** – the proportion of a country's employees who are union members

Country	1980	2014
Ireland	57.1	27.4
United Kingdom	51.7	25.1
United States	22.1	10.7
Australia	48.5	15.5
Sweden	78	67.3
Japan	31.1	17.6
OECD countries	34.1	16.7

Table 5.1 Trade union density in selected countries, 1980 and 2014 (%)
Source: data from OECD (2017) 'Trade Unions: Trade union density', *OECD Employment and Labour Market Statistics* (database). Available at http://doi.org/10.1787/data-00371-en (accessed February 2017).

The second type of representation is non-union employee representation (NER), in which one or more employees act in a representative capacity for other employees in their organization, such as through committees, forums and works councils (Taras and Kaufman, 2006: 515). Many forms of NER are not involved in bargaining on pay and conditions and, from an employee perspective, may be unsuitable to do so because they are resourced by the employer and are therefore not independent (Gollan, 2000). From a management perspective, NER may be introduced to improve communication with employees and enhance employee 'voice' (Taras and Kaufman, 2006) (see page 89 for a discussion of voice).

Employer Organizations

Employer organizations are effectively a union of employers which represent employer interests nationally and internationally, advise members on HRM, undertake research, represent members in negotiations with employees, and lobby governments for employer-friendly policies. Employers voluntary decide whether to join an employer organization or not (an exception is Austria where employers are legally required to join an employer organization), and employers' subscription fees fund employer organizations' activities. Some employer organizations represent employers in certain sectors only or certain types of employers, such as small businesses. Employer organizations are well developed across Europe and Australia and may engage in collective bargaining with unions, but the extent of bargaining differs depending on the country, sector and strength of unions. In the USA, there is a much less developed system of employer organizations and less collective bargaining with trade unions. Indeed, it has been argued that union avoidance is one of the objectives of some US employer groups (Bamber and Lansbury, 1998; Block, 2006). Examples of national employer organizations are the Confederation of British Industry, the Irish Business and Employers Confederation, the Confederation of Swedish Enterprise and the Australian Industry Group. In Europe, 41 central industrial and employers' federations from 35 countries are affiliated to BusinessEurope, which acts as the voice of business and employers in European policy-making.

CONSIDER THIS

What do you think are the consequences of the decline in unionization for organizations and employees?

EMPLOYMENT RIGHTS

Workers have employment rights which are generally determined by employment law, set by government, or decided through collective agreements between unions and employers. The growth in employment legislation was one of the most significant developments in employment relations during the twentieth century. In Europe, many countries have introduced employment rights as a result of EU Directives, which EU countries are required to transpose. There have been Directives on working time, health and safety, parental leave, maternity and adoptive leave, part-time, fixed-term and agency work, and equality ▶Chapter 6◀. An interesting issue in the UK concerns the potential impact of Brexit on employment legislation introduced as a result of EU Directives. It is possible that the British government could seek to dismantle employment legislation, but this would involve a complicated process so it is difficult to predict what the impact might be. There are still a number of areas of employment not governed by the EU which individual countries decide on, such as minimum wages. In 2017, 22 out of 28 EU countries had a statutory minimum wage. In Austria, Denmark, Finland, Italy, Sweden and Cyprus, there is no statutory minimum wage and minimum wages are set in collective agreements. The USA introduced a series of employment laws in the 1980s and 90s in the areas of minimum wages, termination of employment, discrimination, and health and safety. In Australia, employment rights are laid down by legislation, registered agreements between employers and employees and 'awards' covering different industries and occupations.

Employment law is a significant policy area for governments, and they are often lobbied by trade unions to have stricter employment regulation and by employer organizations which seek less of it. Employers often argue that more legislation means increased costs for them and makes labour markets too restrictive and unable to adapt to changing economic conditions. Conversely, unions argue that legislation is needed to prevent workers from being exploited by organizations, to ensure fairness and improve living standards. The strictness of employment legislation differs greatly across countries. However, the OECD has noted a trend over the past decade of a reduction in the strictness of employment protection in relation to dismissals. Between 2008 and 2013, over a third of OECD countries relaxed their dismissals regulations to some extent (OECD, 2013).

As line managers are increasingly responsible for HRM or act as partners with HR practitioners, they should be informed about employment laws. This is even more important in countries with stricter employment laws, as line managers in such countries are more likely to be responsible for HR decision-making (Gooderham et al., 2015). Yet research shows that line managers' knowledge of employment law can vary significantly and that the effectiveness of law can be obstructed by managers' limited knowledge (Bond and Wise, 2003). HR practitioners can advise or command line management on the implementation of policies on employee rights and obligations (Armstrong, 2006a). Employees might have a grievance if they feel an employment right has been breached, and this might escalate to the employee feeling disengaged, leaving the organization or taking a case against their employer to a tribunal or court. It should be noted that employment laws lay down minimum standards, and collective agreements generally include more generous terms and conditions. Indeed, a key reason people join unions is so that they can improve their pay and conditions through collective bargaining. Research suggests that unionized workers earn approximately 6–10% more than non-unionized workers (Turner and Flannery, 2016). In addition, employers can choose to provide more benefits than workers might be legally entitled to, such as additional holidays or sick pay. This can have the benefit of improving morale and productivity, adequately rewarding performance, and preventing employees from moving to other firms. The extent to which organizations can offer enhanced pay and conditions can depend on the health of the industry or economy.

CONSIDER THIS

From a manager's perspective, what would be the possible advantages and disadvantages of having non-union employee representation (NER) in an organization?

THE GLOBAL ECONOMIC CRISIS

The global economic and financial crisis, also referred to as the 'Great Recession', was the most severe economic downturn experienced by the USA, and countries in Europe, Asia, Russia, Latin America and Africa since the early twentieth century. The global economic crisis which began in 2007/08 had numerous causes, including financial institutions engaging in risky investments leading to a financial crisis starting in the USA, inadequate financial regulation, income inequality and consumption fuelled by debt, followed by declines in countries' income, trade and output levels (UN, 2011). There is ongoing debate about the consequences of the crisis for work, with some arguing that it triggered a deep transformation of employment and others arguing that it resulted in incremental, pragmatic changes in employment (Roche and Teague, 2014). Effects of the crisis on employees have included increases in job insecurity and work intensity and decreases in working time, absenteeism and employee wellbeing. The most significant impact has been increased unemployment. Unemployment rose in the EU28 from under 7% in 2008 to 11% in 2013, before falling back to 8% in 2017 (OECD, 2017). In South Africa, unemployment rose from 21% to almost 28% between 2008 and 2017 (OECD, 2017). In the USA, unemployment rose sharply initially and then fell quickly to under 5% in 2017 (OECD, 2017).

A key feature of the economic crisis in the EU has been the intervention of supranational institutions in national policies on wages and collective bargaining. During the crisis, the EU sought for national governments to undertake austerity policies such as reductions in public sector wages and expenditures. A number of countries such as Ireland, Greece, Hungary and Portugal needed financial support from the so-called 'Troika' (European Commission, European Central Bank and International Monetary Fund) and, in return for finance, the Troika demanded significant changes. These included cuts and freezes in public sector wages, cuts or freezes in national minimum wages and changes in collective bargaining, such as restricting collective agreements from being extended to wider groups of workers (Schulten and Müller, 2013). The EU and the Troika pursued these goals, arguing that that they would lead to economic recovery and greater competitiveness, but the measures have been widely criticized for compounding the negative impact of the economic crisis on the incomes of citizens and the role of trade unions.

QUALITY OF JOBS

The quality of jobs being created in modern economies has become an issue of significant debate and concern. International organizations such as the EU, OECD and International Labour Organization (ILO) have called for jobs of high quality which foster sustainable growth. This worry has arisen due to concerns about the global economic crisis, the growth of atypical jobs and growing income inequality. There is also some concern about the impact of job quality and atypical jobs on the psychological contract, that is, the implicit employee beliefs about their obligations to an employer in return for incentives such as pay and security (Rousseau, 1990). The psychological contract is important because it is linked to employees' levels of organizational commitment and motivation. It has been argued that whether workers choose a particular type of contract or not is an important consideration in examining their beliefs about the employment relationship (Guest, 2004). Atypical or 'non-standard' contracts include part-time, fixed-term, agency work, zero-hours, 'gig' jobs and self-employment. Employers hire people on atypical arrangements to reduce costs and to easily adapt workforce numbers to their business needs. In the EU, 'standard' full-time permanent contracts are still the most common type of working arrangement, accounting for 59% of employment in 2014, but they are declining while atypical jobs are growing, especially part-time work (Broughton et al., 2016).

Atypical jobs are not automatically of poor quality, but research has found that they are more likely than standard jobs to be precarious. Precarious employment is 'characterized by uncertainty, low income, and limited social benefits and statutory entitlements' (Vosko, 2010: 2). International studies show that precarious jobs are particularly prevalent in certain sectors such as hospitality and retail. Zero-hours work has been described as extremely precarious because it involves employers giving no guaranteed hours of work and has received much public attention in recent years in Ireland, the UK, Finland and New Zealand (O'Sullivan et al., 2015). A wide variety of factors have been identified as facilitating organizations to increase flexibility and offer more precarious jobs, including globalization, corporate restructuring, technological advances, labour migration, the growth of the services sector, falling unionization and financialization, which involves the increasing role of financial markets, financial actors and financial motives in organizational life. Trade unions are particularly concerned about precarious jobs because, they argue, they can lead to job and income insecurity for workers and contribute to income inequality. It should be noted, however, that job quality and the extent of precarious employment vary across countries. For example, Scandinavian countries have high job quality in the EU and this has been attributed to their strong trade unions and political environments favourable to workers.

Many people in developed labour markets are not in precarious jobs. In theory, as economies modernize, it would be expected that their labour markets would progress from mostly low-level, low-paid jobs to higher level, higher paid jobs. A key question is how have occupations actually changed over time? A global study examining occupations since the 1990s has found that in Australia, China, Russia and South Korea, the greatest employment growth has been in well-paid jobs and the lowest employment growth in low-paid jobs (Eurofound, 2015). This change is known as 'upgrading'. In the EU, Japan and the USA, the greatest employment growth has been in well-paid jobs, with modest relative growth in low-paid jobs and a relative contraction of mid-paid jobs (Eurofound, 2015). This occupational shift is known as 'polarization', involving the expansion of higher and lower occupations.

The 'Gig Economy'

Discussions on freelance work have arisen most prominently in the context of the so-called 'gig economy' in recent years. The gig economy can be broken down into 'crowdworking' and 'work on demand via apps'. Crowdworking refers to online platforms through which workers complete tasks for organizations (De Stefano, 2016). Examples of crowdworking platforms are Amazon Mechanical Turk and Crowdsource,

> **Agency worker** – a worker with a contract of employment or an employment relationship with a temporary work agency with a view to being assigned to another organization to work under its supervision
>
> **Zero-hours contract** – when a worker is not given any guaranteed hours of work by an employer
>
> **'Gig' jobs** – where someone is paid to complete a task, also called a 'gig', for an organization which has outsourced work and does not want to create a long-term employment relationship. An online platform acts as the intermediary between the worker and the organization

which are online marketplaces for small tasks such as translations and data cleaning. 'Work on demand via apps' refers to apps which connect people for the purpose of undertaking traditional types of work such as transport and cleaning (De Stefano, 2016). Examples of these types of apps are Uber and Ola, transport services, TaskRabbit and Airtasker, home improvement services in the USA and Australia respectively, and Deliveroo and Foodora, food delivery companies. There is no reliable national-level data available on the number of people who work in the gig economy. In the USA, one study concluded that 0.5% of all workers engaged in gig working in 2015 (Katz and Krueger, 2016) while another study, using wider definitions, put the figure at 11% (Robles and McGee, 2016). Some suggest that gig working is extensive while others argue that its extent has been exaggerated. In any case, it is a growing phenomenon.

There are contrasting views on the implications of gig working. One argument is that gig working is good for workers because it allows them to be 'entrepreneurs' who control the type and timing of work, thereby increasing flexibility. An opposing argument is that gig working is exploitative, with workers having little income security and few employment rights. Indeed, there have been significant disputes in recent years on this issue, including multiple legal cases brought against Uber (see HRM in the News) and strikes and protests by Deliveroo cyclists in the UK, Germany and Spain. At the core of these disputes is the employment status of the workers which is a critical issue in the employment relationship. Establishing employment status is very important across countries because it determines not only employment rights but also tax and social insurance obligations. The online platforms do not see themselves as employers but as intermediaries between clients and independent contractors. These independent contractors can work for multiple clients on the platform, can accept or reject work offered and have no employment rights. Workers in the disputes argue that, in reality, they are not independent contractors but are employees who are controlled by the platform and should have rights under employment law. Case law is developing in this area, so it is important for managers to carefully consider the nature of the employment relationship when they hire someone and to have a contract with them that reflects the reality of the employment relationship.

HRM IN THE NEWS

Uber and its drivers

When did you last order an Uber? There is a good chance that you were one of the 40 million monthly riders across North, Central and South America, Europe, the Middle East, Asia, Africa, Australia and New Zealand where Uber operates. Uber was only formed in 2009, but the brand has already achieved international recognition and the company is valued at approximately $60 billion. Uber is synonymous with the 'gig economy' phenomenon: the rise of short-term, freelance positions and 'on demand' work.

Uber offers an online platform that allows car drivers and customers to connect with each other. Uber sets the fares that customers pay and retains a percentage fee for each ride made. It attracts drivers by advertising that they can work their own hours, providing flexibility, a message that has been used to recruit successfully: in 2015, Uber had 327,000 active drivers in the USA and 40,000 in the UK. However, the business model employed by 'gig' companies has come under significant pressure and the issues involved have played out in legal cases taken against Uber.

In the USA, class action lawsuits were taken by drivers against Uber in a number of states, including California and Massachusetts, and the New York Taxi Alliance filed a federal lawsuit against the company on behalf of drivers. In the UK, drivers took a case against the company to an employment tribunal while drivers in South Africa took a case to the Commission for Conciliation, Mediation and Arbitration (CCMA). All have claimed that Uber misclassified the drivers as independent contractors instead of employees. Indeed, this is the business model of most 'gig' companies, whereby the people undertaking the work through their platforms are employed as contractors, so that the 'gig' company does not have the same employment obligations towards them as an employer and generally does not have to pay tax or social insurance on their behalf.

In California, a lawsuit resulted in a $100 million settlement between Uber and the drivers in 2016, but critically this did not include the drivers being reclassified as employees. However, a federal judge has since rejected the agreement as being unfair to the drivers, leaving the case as yet unresolved. In another turn of events, in 2016 the company, which is non-unionized, agreed to allow drivers to have a representative body in New York which is affiliated to a trade union (the International Association of Machinists and Aerospace Workers Union). The body, known as the Independent Drivers Guild, will have monthly meetings with Uber about driver issues but will not have collective bargaining rights over fares or benefits. In return for giving the drivers an employee voice mechanism, the trade union agreed that it would not try to unionize the drivers or encourage them to seek 'employee' status with the company.

In South Africa, the CCMA decided in 2017 that eight drivers who took a case should have been classified as employees because Uber exerted significant control over their performance, and drivers were economically dependant on Uber for income. Uber has indicated it will appeal the decision. In the UK, the employment tribunal decided in 2016 that Uber drivers are not independent contractors but 'workers' (in the UK a 'worker' is a legal category between 'employee' and 'self-employed' whereby the person has some limited employment rights, such as to the minimum wage). Like in South Africa, the UK tribunal examined the reality of the relationship between Uber and its drivers and concluded that the company had more control over drivers than it had argued. Uber appealed the decision but the appeal was rejected by the employment appeal tribunal in 2017. The company has said it will launch a further appeal to higher courts. Employment-related issues also featured in a decision by the Transport for London regulator in 2017 not to renew Uber's licence to operate in the city. It noted that Uber was not fit for purpose and demonstrated a lack

of corporate responsibility on a number of issues, including the reporting of serious criminal offences and background checks on drivers. Uber has initiated an appeal of the decision.

Questions

1. What are your views on the decision of the trade union in the USA not to unionize Uber drivers and to allow an employee representative forum instead?
2. The Independent Drivers Guild is an example of non-union employee representation discussed earlier. What are the benefits and disadvantages to drivers of the NER?
3. What factors would influence your decision on whether or not to undertake work through an online platform like Uber?

Sources

Kokalitcheva, K. (2016) 'Uber now has 40 million monthly riders worldwide', *Fortune*, fortune.com/2016/10/20/uber-app-riders (accessed 11 June 2018)

Mabuza, E. (2017) 'CCMA says SA's Uber drivers are employees, but Uber still disagrees', www.businesslive.co.za/bd/companies/transport-and-tourism/2017-07-25-ccma-says-sas-uber-drivers-are-employees-but-uber-still-disagrees (accessed 11 June 2018)

Osborne, H. (2016) 'Uber loses right to classify UK drivers as self-employed', *The Guardian*, www.theguardian.com/technology/2016/oct/28/uber-uk-tribunal-self-employed-status (accessed 11 June 2018)

Reuters (2016) 'New York City Uber drivers sue over employment status', *Fortune*, fortune.com/2016/06/02/uber-new-york-taxi-drivers (accessed 11 June 2018)

Scheiber, N. and Isaac, M. (2016) 'Uber recognizes New York drivers' group, short of a union', *The New York Times*, www.nytimes.com/2016/05/11/technology/uber-agrees-to-union-deal-in-new-york.html?_r=0 (accessed 11 June 2018)

Transport for London (2017) 'Licensing decision on Uber London Limited', tfl.gov.uk/info-for/media/press-releases/2017/september/licensing-decision-on-uber-london-limited (accessed 11 June 2018)

Uber Technologies Inc (2017) 'Find a City', www.uber.com/en-GB/cities (accessed 11 June 2018)

Uber Technologies Inc (2017) 'Finding the way: Creating possibilities for riders, drivers, and cities'.

https://www.uber.com/en-GB/about/ (accessed 11 June 2018)

Wong, J.C. (2016) 'Uber v drivers: judge rejects "unfair" settlement in US class action lawsuit. *The Guardian*, www.theguardian.com/technology/2016/aug/18/uber-drivers-class-action-lawsuit-settlement-rejected (accessed 11 June 2018)

EMPLOYEE PARTICIPATION AND VOICE

Some organizations try to encourage their employees to be more committed to their jobs by seeking their views and including them in decision-making. Indeed the Davignon Group (1997), an EU high-level expert group on workers' participation and involvement, concluded that if companies want skilled, committed, mobile employees, they should be involved in decision-making at all levels in a company and not just follow management instructions. Employee participation occurs when employees have influence over decisions in an organization (Busck et al., 2010). Participation can be direct, through individual employees or teams, or indirect through employee representatives. Busck et al. (2010) argue that direct participation often involves employees having an influence over operational issues such as job performance, whereas indirect participation suggests more strategic-level influence. In Germany, for example, employee representatives on **works councils** have significant influence on company decisions, and employee representatives have a legal right to sit on the supervisory boards of large companies. In order for employee participation to take place, employee voice mechanisms must be in place (Wilkinson and Fay, 2011). Employee voice has been defined as 'an opportunity to have "a say" but this does not necessarily mean that employees will have influence or participation' (Wilkinson and Fay, 2011: 66). Voice is important for employees, enabling them to express their opinions and grievances and act as 'industrial citizens' (Dundon et al., 2005). Employers have introduced voice mechanisms for a range of reasons, such as wanting to improve the employment relations

> **Works councils –** bodies which provide employee representation in a workplace. They are not trade union bodies but trade unions can be influential in them. Works councils can mean employees have significant powers of decision-making within a workplace

environment, and preventing employees from joining a union (Dundon et al., 2004).

Organizations' choice of voice mechanism can be influenced by the country of origin of the company, the size of organization and the industry (Lavelle et al., 2010). Laws can also influence voice. A number of EU Directives have favoured indirect forms of voice. The 1994 Works Council Directive (94/45/EC) requires large multinational companies to have a works council, in which management consult with employee representatives across countries. Similarly, under the 2006 Information and Consultation of Employee Directive (202/14/EC), all organizations except small firms must inform and consult employee representatives about certain company decisions such as restructuring.

Studies in Anglo-Saxon countries show the growing incidence of organizations using direct voice, where individual employees are involved in decisions affecting their jobs and immediate work environment (Lavelle et al., 2010). In the UK, the incidence of union-only voice dropped from 18% of workplaces to 4% between 1984 and 2004, while direct voice mechanisms increased (Gomez et al., 2009). Equally, a study of multinational companies in Ireland found that many preferred to use direct voice mechanisms to distribute information, for example through team briefings (Lavelle et al., 2010). In Australia, it was found that 28% of employees are in workplaces with direct voice only, 12% are in workplaces with union-only voice and 12% have both union and direct voice channels (Pyman et al., 2010).

BUILDING YOUR SKILLS

As a manager, what kind of mechanisms would you put in place to enable employees to express their opinions?

THE NATURE OF CONFLICT AND ITS RESOLUTION

Conflict in the employment relationship can take many guises. Individual employees can express conflict by raising a grievance with their manager, being frequently absent from work, leaving the organization, or taking a legal case against an employer. Collective forms of conflict, involving groups of employees or trade unions, include strikes, refusal to work overtime, sit-ins and work-to-rules, where employees work strictly to the letter of their contract. Employers can also engage in conflict through, for example, lockouts, where they prevent employees from entering a workplace (Wallace et al., 2013). The most visible form of conflict expressed by employees is strikes, which involve an organized cessation of work. Employees use strikes as leverage in negotiation, hoping to persuade employers to undertake a course of action such as increasing pay or stopping redundancies. A pattern evident across developed and developing countries since the early 1980s has been a fall in the number of **strikes** and **working days lost** (Wallace and O'Sullivan, 2006). Table 5.2 shows reductions in working days lost in selected countries over a 35-year period. While some might suggest that the fall in strikes is reflective

> **Strike** – a work stoppage caused by the refusal of employees to work, in order to persuade an employer to concede to their demands
>
> **General strike** – a strike by workers across many industries usually in protest against a government policy or action
>
> **Working days lost** – a measure of strike activity, calculated by multiplying the number of persons involved by the number of normal working days during which they were involved in the dispute

of a better employment relations environment, Wallace and O'Sullivan (2006) argue that other factors explain the decline, pointing to globalization and a more neoliberal political environment, which favours minimal state intervention in the employment relationship and is opposed to unions. Research on strikes in Western Europe has found that there has been a decline in strikes against employers but an increase in the number of **general strikes** (Johnston et al., 2016). A significant number of general strikes have taken place in Western Europe, especially Greece, since the global economic crisis as workers protest against government austerity measures.

Many organizations recognize that mechanisms are needed to be able to address and resolve conflict in the workplace. It is generally good employment relations practice for companies to introduce policies and procedures, and many countries have employment laws which require organizations to have procedures on issues such as dismissals and equality issues ▶Chapter 6◀. This is to ensure that all workers are treated fairly and consistently through due process and natural justice. In a disciplinary procedure, this means that:

- employees would be informed of company rules and what would happen if they are breached

Country	1980	2015
India	11537.5	4940.3
Ireland	13346.2	873
United Kingdom	14350.5	6
United States	26208.9	1
Australia	2831.1	7.9
South Africa	2903.1	28.5*
Sweden	5997.9	0.1

*2014 figure

Table 5.2 Working days lost per 1,000 workers due to strikes and lockouts in selected countries, 1980 and 2015
Source: data from International Labour Organization (ILO) (2017) 'Days not worked per 1000 workers due to strikes and lockouts by economic activity', *ILOSTAT*. Available at www.ilo.org/ilostat.

- employees must be allowed to defend themselves
- employees must be allowed representation
- there must be an appeals mechanism if an employee is dissatisfied with a management decision.

Similarly, if employees believe they have a grievance about a workplace issue, the grievance procedures should inform them of the steps they can take to have their complaint brought to management's attention. These types of rules on grievance and disciplinary issues are common in the EU and Australia. Managers should ensure that they familiarize themselves with company procedures to help them deal with employment problems.

US employers do not have the same level of obligations as those in EU countries or Australia in relation to dismissals procedures. In the USA, the principle of 'employment-at-will' exists, whereby employers can dismiss an employee without reason except in certain situations such as discrimination. In the equality area, the US Equal Employment Opportunity Commission offers guidance to employers. In the USA, if a company does include grievance and disciplinary procedures in a collective agreement, the outcome of the procedure is legally enforceable in court (Block, 2006).

HRM AND ORGANIZATIONAL PERFORMANCE

Employee voice and participation

Employee voice and participation are beneficial for organizations because, by involving employees in decision-making, they can offer ideas and information which can improve teamworking, work organization, efficiency, quality and productivity.
By giving employees the opportunity to contribute to decision-making, their commitment to the organization can be strengthened. Employee voice mechanisms allow employees to air their concerns, which can prevent an escalation of conflict and can prevent absenteeism and higher employee turnover, i.e. the percentage of employees who leave an organization in a period.

State Agencies for Conflict Resolution

Over half of OECD countries have special courts or tribunals to hear employment disputes, while ordinary civil courts are used in the remaining countries (OECD, 2013). In many places these tribunals or other state bodies also offer free conciliation and mediation services, in which an independent third party seeks to encourage a settlement between employers and employees without the need for adjudication. If mediation or conciliation is unsuccessful, then cases will likely proceed to arbitration or adjudication in which an independent third party makes a decision as to how a dispute should be resolved. Usually if a breach of employment rights is found in adjudication, the employee will be awarded compensation and the employer may be liable for fines and/or imprisonment depending on the country and issue. In most countries, the onus is on the employee to pursue an employment rights claim against their employer but in others, such as in Sweden, cases can only be directly referred to the Labour Court by

a trade union or employers' association. In the UK, ACAS (Advisory, Conciliation and Arbitration Service) is the state body which offers conciliation, mediation and arbitration services. If a dispute remains unresolved after ACAS intervention, employment rights cases can be investigated by employment tribunals and taken to the employment appeal tribunal.

In Ireland, the Workplace Relations Commission provides conciliation and mediation services and also adjudicates on employment rights cases. Appeals of adjudication decisions are heard by the Labour Court. In Australia, the Fair Work Commission (FWC) is the national workplace relations tribunal which provides conciliation, mediation and adjudication services to resolve disputes. Unlike its Irish and UK equivalents, the FWC also regulates how industrial action is taken by workers. In the USA, the National Labor Relations Board supervises employee elections on union representation and investigates claims by employers or employees of unfair labour practices. The Federal Mediation and Conciliation Service provides mediation, conciliation and voluntary arbitration to assist in employment disputes and negotiations. There are also state bodies that aid employment relations in specific sectors, such as public sector employment (the Federal Labor Relations Authority) and railway and airline industries (the National Mediation Board).

In addition to providing conciliation, mediation and adjudication services, countries may also have a labour inspectorate service to enforce employment laws. Labour inspectors employed by governments may investigate workplaces and examine documents to ensure compliance. Some are charged with targeting certain sectors which have a history of noncompliance or which employ more 'vulnerable workers,' such as migrants, who may be at risk of not receiving employment rights (Ebisui, 2016). Countries with labour inspectorates include Ireland, Australia, the USA, Japan, Spain and Canada.

SPOTLIGHT ON SKILLS

You are a manager in a fast-food organization in a busy location. There are 70 employees working a variety of shifts. Over 60% of the employees are college students who often only stay in the organization for a few years before leaving. As manager, you oversee operations, while supervisors are responsible for the scheduling of employees' hours and managing staff. On a busy Saturday during lunchtime, a small number of disgruntled employees have come to you complaining that a supervisor has been scheduling hours in an unfair manner.

1 What is your immediate response to the employees about their complaint?
2 If you are to meet the employees again, what research and preparation should you undertake beforehand?
3 What questions would you ask the employees and supervisor about the issue to find out their needs?

To help you consider the issues above, visit **www.macmillanihe.com/carbery-cross-hrm-2e** and watch the video of Oonagh Buckley from the Irish Workplace Relations Commission talking about conflict resolution.

Negotiating Skills for Conflict Resolution

Managers often have to carry out performance management reviews, deal with grievance and disciplinary issues, bargain with trade unions and, particularly since the economic crisis, implement difficult measures such as redundancies, increased workloads and pay reductions. All these tasks require managers to have effective negotiation skills. Negotiation is about solving a problem and resolving a conflict between parties. Managers and employees negotiate with each other because there is a level of interdependence, i.e. they need each other. In addition, a key reason why management involve employees in decision-making is to increase employees' commitment to implementing a decision and to meeting the needs of the organization (Salamon, 2000). Here we provide a brief summary of negotiation skills that can be used to resolve workplace conflicts.

Effective Negotiation Involves Character and Integrity

Negotiations between management and employees can be short and simple, but they can also be complex, lengthy and involve heightened emotion. Management can fear the implications of not reaching performance targets and meeting their employers' demands, while employees can worry about job and income security and workload. Negotiations can be contentious and it can be easy for people to let their emotions guide their behaviours. In such circumstances, people can engage in personalized attacks and blaming. A key difference between negotiations in organizations and other negotiations, such as buying a car, is that the former involve long-term relationships. When emotions dominate a negotiation and things are said 'in the heat of the moment', it can damage the relationship and sometimes this can be difficult to repair. Effective negotiators, therefore, ensure that they control emotions and assess a situation through preparation and information.

Managers and employees can be under pressure in negotiations to achieve certain objectives and there can be temptations to breach ethical standards. In some countries, it is normal practice in negotiations to exaggerate demands, for example, employees asking for a 5% pay rise when they might settle for 2%. However, negotiators must be careful not to use tactics which could be considered culturally unethical, such as lying or making promises they do not have the authority to make or cannot meet.

The goal of negotiation is to reach an agreement between parties. In organizations, such agreements often involve commitments by management and employees to undertake a course of action in the future. It is therefore important that any commitments made are adhered to and implemented. Frequently, disputes between management and employees arise because of a perception that the other party did not stick to their side of the bargain. People will remember if past commitments were not followed through and this can lead some negotiators to adopt a much tougher stance in future negotiations. Effective negotiators should have integrity and consider ethical standards before negotiating, and ensure that they stick to any commitments made.

Effective Negotiation Involves Understanding

An error that people make in negotiating is that they frequently use the same style of negotiation without considering the nature of the problem, what their goals should be and the other party's goals. Indeed, there are a number of styles we can use in a negotiation, as developed by Pruitt and Rubin (1986). When we think of negotiating, the image of a customer haggling with a salesperson over the price of a car or new television often comes to mind. In this type of negotiation, the buyer uses tactics such as bluffing and pretending that they might walk away to convince the seller to sell for the lowest price possible. However, these tactics

are associated with just one style of negotiating, known as the 'competitive style', where the buyer is purely concerned with getting the best outcome for themselves and not about the relationship. As we often want to maintain amicable relationships in organizations, a competitive style might not be appropriate for the workplace. An alternative style is collaboration, where parties work together to problem-solve and produce a solution which satisfies each party's needs. Other styles include compromising, often associated with 'meeting in the middle', and accommodating, where one side meets the other party's needs at their own expense. Sometimes it can also be a rational strategy to avoid a negotiation, but managers should be aware that a conflict may escalate if avoidance is used.

Before a manager or employee even enters a negotiation, they should undertake significant preparation. They should determine what the problem is and what their goals are. They should also consider what the likely goals of the other party might be, but they will not know these for sure until they talk to each other. Indeed, a key error people make in negotiating is assuming they know what the other wants and needs, and therefore they do not ask enough questions to determine the reality. Preparation should also involve research on the other parties, especially if they are from other countries or if the negotiation will take place in another country. Cross-cultural awareness is important so that negotiators do not cause offence and antagonize another party through ignorance.

Negotiators will have to undertake research. For example, in a pay dispute, a manager should gather contracts, pay slips, company policies, collective agreements and employment legislation, as well as external information such as pay benchmarks in other companies and relevant decisions from state dispute resolution bodies such as employment tribunals. Before negotiations, managers might seek the advice of an employer organization and an employee might seek the advice of a trade union.

Once a negotiator has identified their goals, they should develop arguments to support their position, for example using evidence that a company cannot afford a pay rise. They should also think of the questions that they will ask the other party to challenge their arguments, and they should consider the outcomes that they would be prepared to accept. For example, most people would not buy a car from one dealer without checking similar cars from other dealers first, and the same principle applies in workplace negotiations. If a manager thinks that an employee might threaten to leave an organization if they do not get a pay rise, what are their options? They could try to find the additional money to give the pay rise because they really need the employee (accommodating style) or refuse the demand and prepare how work will be undertaken if the employee does leave (competitive style) or discuss with the employee their needs and try to find alternative ways of satisfying them (collaborating style). This last option is important because it suggests that there can be differences between what someone demands and what their needs are. An employee may demand a pay rise, but the reason for this may be to satisfy their underlying need to feel valued and recognized in the organization or to address worries about financial security.

Effective Negotiation Involves Communicating

In order for agreements to be reached, parties must communicate with each other. Doing so effectively is not easy and requires preparation and practice. Good communication skills include active listening for what is said and not said and checking that one party understands the other. Negotiators should communicate their ideas clearly because people often overestimate the extent to which the other party understands them. Effective questioning is critical. Not all questions are good questions, for example the question, 'is that your best offer?', is likely to illicit the response 'yes'! Questions have different functions in a negotiation, including finding out factual information, checking for understanding, exploring the needs of the other party and presenting hypothetical situations as a way of solution-building. Generally, open questions are useful in the early parts of a negotiation. These are questions that invite someone to speak openly about an issue. For example, 'can you tell me about your career progression plans in the company?' Closed questions are useful in the later stages of a negotiation when you want to check for accuracy and understanding. These are questions that may illicit a restricted answer such as 'yes' or 'no'.

An agreement reached should be written down precisely to avoid misinterpretation. Sometimes this might be done by email, or, in more formal and complex negotiations, the agreement will be in a written document. The agreement should be clear as to the terms reached and include who it applies to, the length of time it applies and how the parties might address future disputes about the agreement. For example, disputes might be settled with the assistance of a conciliation or mediation service of a state conflict resolution body. Managers and employees should be aware of the legal status of agreements. In some countries, agreements do not have legal force behind them, while in others they can be legally enforced.

HRM IN PRACTICE

Impact of company culture on employee satisfaction at work

iStock.com/SolStock

You were successful in getting a job as HR manager of a multinational software company six months ago in Silicon Valley. You were delighted because the company is internationally well known and a brand leader. This is the most prestigious job on your CV/résumé. Your previous HR roles were in traditional manufacturing companies which negotiated with trade unions, so there were many policies and procedures and you spent a lot of time negotiating on pay and conditions. The software company is non-unionized and employs a young and highly educated workforce, many of whom are from other countries. You have experienced a slight culture shock; there are bean bags in the workplace and hot desks (a system where employees are not given allocated seats, but instead choose where to work each day), as well as free food and games rooms.

From an HR point of view, there are also fewer rules and policies in this company, for example on promotion. There are no collective negotiations on pay and conditions, and pay is determined by the company, although some employees with scarce skills can negotiate higher pay.

As HR manager, you first thought that the 'fun' and innovative culture would cut down on bureaucracy. However, you have also developed serious concerns about the company's relationship with employees. When you asked for HR analytics when you joined the company, you noticed that employee turnover is quite high, which surprised you given that the jobs are generally high paying, especially after performance bonuses. In addition, you noticed that many employees who resign go on long-term sick leave beforehand. The analytics suggested that a low number of employees make formal complaints about the company, and you would have thought that the significant amount of teamworking in the company would address employee issues. You are careful not to be seen publicly to investigate the issue within the company but walk around the workplace, having informal conversations with employees. Many say they have no time to talk and you notice that they seem stressed, working very long hours with few breaks. You decide to check social media and find a number of websites on which ex-employees complain about working conditions, and some mention that a local trade union is strategizing on how to unionize workers. You are now very concerned that the company culture is contributing to employee dissatisfaction which could escalate into further conflict. You know the CEO will be furious if the employees unionize because his business model is based on a belief that unions are an interference in the employment relationship and will create inflexibility, preventing employees from pursuing excellence. As HR manager, you know you are in a difficult position, caught between the wishes of the CEO and the needs of the workforce.

What would you do?

1. What suggestions could you as HR manager make to improve employee satisfaction?
2. What are the dilemmas you face as HR manager if you make suggestions and if you do not make suggestions?

iStock.com/PeopleImages

SUMMARY

This chapter has outlined the complexity of the employment relationship and the many factors that influence it, both in terms of the theoretical perspectives and the external organizations, such as trade unions and employer organizations, that play an active role. These factors impact on the rules governing the employment relationship, notably employee rights and employee voice and participation. Organizations often have internal procedures to prevent and address workplace conflict, and many countries offer external services to help companies and employees settle disputes. We also reviewed some of the key issues in the debates on the modern employment relationship. The global economic crisis has had a major impact on employment, pay and conditions. There is a concern internationally about the quality of jobs being created in the aftermath of the crisis, and we outlined the growth in atypical work and its association with precarious jobs. Atypical work through the 'gig economy' has become very topical because of concerns about its implications for workers. As labour markets are changing, it is even more important for managers to develop their competencies in negotiating so as to effectively manage employers' and employees' needs.

CHAPTER REVIEW QUESTIONS

1. How do the unitarism, pluralism and Marxist perspectives view the employment relationship?
2. What are the different services generally offered by state dispute resolution bodies?
3. What is the difference between the functions of employee representatives and employer organizations?
4. What are the common reasons for increasing employee voice and participation in an organization?
5. Outline the trends in unionization and offer some possible explanations for them.
6. Explain the effects of the global economic crisis on employment.
7. Outline the meaning of a 'precarious job'.
8. What are the implications for workers of a growth in the 'gig economy'?

FURTHER READING

Broughton, A., Green, M., Rickard, C. et al. (2016) *Precarious Employment in Europe. Part 1: Patterns, Trends and Policy Strategy*, Brussels: European Union. Available at www.europarl.europa.eu/RegData/etudes/STUD/2016/587285/IPOL_STU(2016)587285_EN.pdf.

Fisher, R., Ury, W. and Patton, B. (2012) *Getting to Yes: Negotiating an Agreement without Giving In*, New York: Penguin Books.

Lyons, D. (2016) *Disrupted: My Misadventure in the Start-Up Bubble*, New York: Hachette Books.

Weil, D. (2014) *The Fissured Workplace*, Cambridge, MA: Harvard University Press.

USEFUL WEBSITES

www.ilo.org
The website of the International Labour Organization, a tripartite United Nations agency which sets labour standards; the website includes research on employment.

www.eurofound.europa.eu
The European Foundation for the Improvement of Living and Working Conditions is an EU agency which designs better living and working conditions. Eurofound undertakes significant research.

www.oecd-ilibrary.org
The Organization for Economic Co-operation and Development promotes policies on economic and social wellbeing, and it undertakes research reports on employment and labour market issues.

www.worker-participation.eu
A website provided by the European Trade Union Institute which provides information on industrial relations and employee participation across the EU.

www.dol.gov

The US Department of Labor website has information and guidance on labour laws.

www.theconversation.com/au/business

An independent news website on Australian business issues based on academic research and expertise.

For further information on managing the employment relationship in an Irish context (including trade unions, employer organizations, the nature of employment relations, and conflict and its resolution), go to the companion website listed below.

For extra resources, including videos, multiple choice questions and useful weblinks, go to: www.macmillanihe.com/carbery-cross-hrm-2e.

© Royalty-Free/Corbis

6: Diversity and Equality in the Workplace

Juliette MacMahon and
Mike O'Brien

LEARNING OUTCOMES

By the end of this chapter you will be able to:

- Explain the concepts of diversity, social exclusion, equality and discrimination
- Understand the various perspectives on diversity in the organizational context
- Reflect on the benefits and challenges of a diverse workforce
- Explain the reasons why inequality exists in the labour market and in workplaces
- Discuss the controversy relating to positive discrimination and the difference between this and positive action
- Identify key differences between equality regulation in different countries
- Explain the role of HRM in promoting equality, ensuring that the workplace is free from discrimination and dealing with complaints
- Identify and explain the key processes and procedures utilized by organizations, namely, equality and dignity at work policies

THIS CHAPTER DISCUSSES:

Introduction (100)

What is Diversity? (100)

The Benefits and Challenges of a Diverse Workforce (102)

Equality and Discrimination in the Workplace and Beyond (103)

Why is Equality an Important Issue? (104)

CHAPTER 6

Geographical Variation and the Combined Effects of Inequality (107)

National Initiatives to Foster Equality (108)

Legislation and Equality (108)

The Positive Discrimination/Positive Action Debates (114)

HRM, the Workplace and Equality (115)

INTRODUCTION

This chapter deals with three related areas: diversity, inequality and fair treatment at work. Diversity within organizations and labour markets is becoming more and more the norm. Examples of trends in this area include: an increasingly ageing population in developed countries; higher labour market participation by women; a growth in population in Africa in contrast to a falling population in developed areas such as Western Europe; a generation of 'millennials' who expect to work internationally (PWC, 2015). Trends such as these present both opportunities and challenges for society and organizations. Furthermore, organizations are increasingly operating in global markets and often find that norms may exist in some countries of operation that may not be acceptable in their home country, for example attitudes to women in the workplace, attitudes to minority groups, etc. This poses challenges for the HRM function in these organizations regarding their responsibilities to promote equality and justice. This chapter aims to critically examine such issues. Firstly, we examine the overarching concept of diversity in the workplace: how do we define diversity, perspectives on diversity, and the advantages and challenges that a diverse workforce brings. Following this, we turn to a discussion of the broad issue of inequality in society and how this can translate into the workplace. What can be done to counteract it? We examine why discrimination occurs, who is most at risk, and the key aspects of the legislation that exists to counter discrimination. We then consider the legal obligations of employers in this regard and discuss the measures that organizations can take to ensure fair treatment of employees. We also briefly look at the variations across different countries in their approaches to this issue. Next, we examine the critiques of the legislative approach to protecting diverse groups/individuals. Finally, we look at the role of HR professionals in promoting and ensuring equal treatment in the workplace.

WHAT IS DIVERSITY?

Diversity as a concept refers to the 'difference' between people. Kirton and Greene (2016) differentiate between collective diversity, mostly associated with social groups (e.g. gender, race, ethnicity, religion, disability, sexual orientation, etc.), and individual or 'deep level' diversity (such as education, personality, lifestyle, personal interests, etc.). The latter has also been termed 'invisible diversity' because it encapsulates qualities or attributes that are more subtle and not immediately explicit (Bell, 2007). O'Leary and Sandberg (2016), for instance, found evidence in their study of diversity management that some managers ignored socio-demographic groups and focused on the individual attributes of employees. Thomson (2016) argues that we need to look at both dimensions, that is, to consider each unique individual in the context of the broad collective groupings when examining the concept of diversity.

Perspectives on Diversity in the Organizational Context

According to Mor Barak (2016), the management of diverse workforces is one of the biggest challenges facing organizations today, and it is a challenge that is here to stay. There is a burgeoning literature surrounding the concept of diversity in the organizational context (Bendl et al., 2016; Mor Barak, 2016), and a key area of debate is whether employees should be treated equally regardless of their differences or whether organizations should recognize diversity and adapt to take account of difference. These perspectives are summed up by the **social justice approach** to workplace equality, and the **diversity management perspective**, both of which are outlined below.

The Social Justice Perspective

Social justice, as the term suggests, involves viewing diversity within the broader context of morality and fairness. The key principle here is that organizations exist as part of a wider society or community, are embedded within it and, as such, have a duty to contribute to the creation of a more equitable and inclusive society. The social justice perspective is largely associated with the introduction of equality legislation to counter discrimination against those social groups that are recognized as suffering from disadvantage or discrimination in the labour market. Such legislation varies across countries and regions and is often context specific. For instance, there is specific legislation in India to counter discrimination based on caste, which would not be relevant in all countries. Equality legislation will be discussed in more detail later in the chapter. The social justice approach is viewed as being an equal opportunities approach to diversity. In this respect, it has been criticized in that of itself it is a norm-based approach. For instance, a selection process based on an equality of opportunity approach will allow applications from all candidates. Candidates will be equally judged across strict criteria relating to the job in question. This appears fair at first glance. However, if we then apply this process to people with autism, who may find such a selection process problematic and stressful, then we see that this approach may not facilitate 'difference'. The diversity approach is one which takes difference into account.

The Diversity Management Perspective

Kandola and Fullerton (1998: 8) were among the first authors to highlight this perspective, defining it as follows:

> [Diversity management] accepts that the workforce consist of visible and non visible differences which will include factors such as sex, age, background, disability and work style. It is founded on the premise that

> **Social justice approach** – the social justice case for equality holds that organizations have a moral and legal obligation, regardless of profit, to recognize diversity and to develop policies and procedures to ensure that people are treated in a fair and equitable manner in all facets of the business
>
> **Diversity management perspective** – the diversity management perspective holds that organizations should recognize difference as a positive organizational factor and should foster, value and utilize this difference for the benefit of the organization

harnessing these differences will create a productive environment in which everybody feels valued, where their talents are being fully utilized and in which organization goals are being met.

The central tenet of the diversity management approach is the belief that difference should be recognized as positive, difference should be nurtured, and that this should be achieved through a cultural transformation of the organization rather than a reliance on legal regulation (Pitts et al., 2010). Advocates of this view would argue that the social justice perspective is flawed in that it brings about a system of sameness whereby difference is diluted or even denied. Organizations should strive to achieve a culture whereby difference and diversity are viewed positively and actively promoted and supported since this is good for business. In other words, diversity brings about a 'special contribution effect' (Kirton and Greene, 2016) which adds value to the bottom line (see The Benefits and Challenges of a Diverse Workforce on page 102). The problem with such an approach is that if fostering difference is contingent on its financial contribution to the organization, it can be rationally argued that in times of recession, or where it is perceived that such diversity initiatives no longer contribute to profit, these policies can validly be set aside (Noon, 2007; Tomlinson and Schwabenland, 2010).

CONSIDER THIS

According to Mor Barak (2000, 2016), an inclusive workplace is one which:

1. recognizes the value of difference between individuals and groups within the work environment and will modify policies to accommodate this difference
2. acknowledges its role in the wider community by engaging in activities to tackle disadvantage and to contribute to the community (regardless of whether it derives a profit from this local environment)
3. works with individuals, groups and organizations across national and cultural boundaries.

Do you think that this approach to diversity is feasible?

THE BENEFITS AND CHALLENGES OF A DIVERSE WORKFORCE

There is considerable research exploring the possible benefits of diversity to the organization (Bell, 2007). For instance, having a more diverse workforce can have a positive effect on financial performance (Opstrup and Villadsen, 2015), group performance (Roberge and van Dick, 2010), innovation (Østergaard et al., 2011), ways of viewing problems, turnover (Armstrong et al., 2010) and productivity (Herring, 2009). A very good example of this is recent research, which highlights the benefits to organizations of employing people who are on the autism spectrum (Cockayne and Warburton, 2016). Employees with Asperger's can bring unique traits to an organization, such as ability to solve complex data issues, attention to detail and high levels of focus. In recognition of this, some of the world's leading IT companies, such as Microsoft and SAP, now have specific recruitment programmes in place that target candidates with autism (Warburton, 2018). A perception of an organization as welcoming diversity can also generate a more positive public image of the company, which in turn can impact on its appeal to the most talented potential employees. Having a more diverse workforce may also enable organizations to stay in touch with what appeals to a broad customer base (Herring, 2009), provide goods and services that meet these needs, and thus be more profitable.

Some of the challenges of having a diverse workforce include possible increases in training and development costs, the potential for increased conflict between employees, and claims of reverse discrimination. Farndale et al. (2015), for instance, highlight language and cultural differences in globally staffed multinational corporations as a potential area for conflict as well as a potential source of innovative thinking.

HRM IN THE NEWS

Every cloud has a silver lining

Research worldwide finds that populations in many countries are 'ageing' while birth rates are falling (ILO, 2015). Workers over the traditionally 'accepted' retirement age of 65 may thus be a valuable pool of talent to organizations. However, in many countries, attitudes to older workers are not necessarily positive. According to McCarthy and Heraty (2017), there is emerging evidence across the globe that organizations frequently have reservations about employing 'older' workers and that there is widespread evidence of negative attitudes to this cohort.

In Japan, however, an innovative approach to talent acquisition is leading the way. It is estimated that 27% of Japan's population will be aged 65 and over by 2017. Reflecting its strong cultural commitment in valuing age and experience, the Japanese government established the first 'Silver Human Resource Centre' (SHRC) in 1974, in Tokyo. Today, more than 1,300 centres operate throughout Japan and service in excess of 700,000 members.

Recognizing and valuing the highly diverse, educated, experienced and skilled 'silver' human resources, these centres form part of a national government programme to both leverage skills and provide employment for retired citizens. Any individual over 60 years of age can register and begin working.

Clients of SHRCs do not generally find positions that they had previously occupied, but they do benefit from guidance and support in redeploying their skills into new roles. Small businesses in Japan, which struggle to compete with larger organizations, are particularly keen to recruit older workers (Higo, 2006).

This unique HRM service hinges on the SHRCs acting as brokers; they develop profiles of their clients' skills and experience and then match them with what businesses require. It is considered a win for the businesses who gain a diverse, skilled addition to their workforce; a win for the retiree who re-enters the workforce; and a win for the public purse with the expansion of the taxpaying base.

Questions

1. What are the possible challenges and benefits to organizations of recruiting older workers?

2. Age discrimination in recruiting is often driven by a common perception bias that younger workers are more productive, creative, trainable and cheaper. What do you think?

3. The concept of hiring retirees or older workers is a very honourable notion. In reality, most employers worry that older workers may not contribute to increased productivity or to cost savings. Is such a concept a realistic position?

4. Silver Human Resource Centres could only work in Japan; they would not function in other countries or cultures. Comment/discuss.

Sources

Flynn, M. (2014) 'Lessons from Japan: helping the older unemployed back into work', *The Careers Blog*, 17 July, www.theguardian.com/careers/careers-blog/retirement-ageing-workforce-japan-jobs (accessed 1 March 2017)

Flynn, M., Schroder, H., Higo, M. and Yanada, A. (2014) 'Government as institutional entrepreneur: extending working life in the UK and Japan', *Journal of Social Policy*, 43(3), 535–53.

Higo, M. (2006) 'Aging workforce in Japan: an overview of three policy dilemmas', *Hallym International Journal of Aging*, 8(2), 149–73.

International Longevity Center Japan (2017) 'Japan's Silver Human Resources Centers: undertaking an increasingly diverse range of work', longevity.ilcjapan.org/f_issues/0702.html (accessed 19 February 2017)

Ministry of Labour and Welfare (2005) *Annual Report on Health and Welfare: Social Security and National Life'*, Tokyo: Japanese Ministry of Labour.

Shiroi, K., Iso, H., Hideki, F. et al. (2006) 'Factors associated with "Ikigai" among members of a public temporary employment agency for seniors: Silver Human Resource Centre in Japan', *Health & Quality of Life Outcomes*, 4(12), 53–66.

Regardless of whether we perceive diversity in a positive or negative light, it is an accepted fact that labour markets are becoming more diverse. For instance, there is evidence of demographic changes worldwide and thus in the labour market. Decreasing birth rates in many countries are predicted to lead to labour shortages that could be filled by an increasing number of older workers (Parry and McCarthy, 2017). However, this potential may be hindered by inequality and discrimination and may not translate into employment or career advancement. It is to this which we now turn.

> **Equality** – the state of being equal, especially in status, rights or opportunities
>
> **Discrimination** – treating a person or group differently and unfairly on the basis of certain traits or characteristics, such as sexuality, gender, race, religion or disability

inequalities continue to persist in the workplace and that individuals continue to experience discriminatory practices and attitudes.

What do we mean by equality and discrimination? These are terms we often utilize but rarely define; indeed, it is difficult to find accepted definitions. In broad terms, equality can be viewed as the state of being equal, particularly in relation to status, rights or opportunities; while discrimination focuses on treating a person or group differently, or unfairly, on the basis of certain traits or characteristics, such as sexuality, gender, race, religion or disability. From these definitions, we can see that equality and discrimination are broad terms encompassing far more than a person's experience or treatment at work. This is important, as research has shown that unequal treatment in the workplace often stems from discrimination in wider society (Le Grand, 2003) and can take many forms. Consider, for instance, a woman who may not be offered a job because an employer worries

EQUALITY AND DISCRIMINATION IN THE WORKPLACE AND BEYOND

Despite the stated advantages of diversity in the workplace, there is ample evidence to show that

about her commitment to the organization as she has a number of children to care for, or someone experiencing harassment or bullying in the workplace because they have a particular sexual orientation. Consider also someone who cannot accept a job offer because they use a wheelchair and the workplace cannot accommodate them, or someone with literacy problems who cannot meet the minimum requirements for many jobs. Another question is: why is there a persistent wage gap between men and women in most countries, which cannot be explained away by skill and experience differences alone (Eurofound, 2014). We can relate these and other instances of workplace disadvantage to wider social issues.

SPOTLIGHT ON SKILLS

Cristina Stoian Portraits

You are an HR manager in a large firm providing services to both private and public sector clients. You have noticed that while there is a gender balance at the entry and middle levels of the organization, there are very few women in senior positions. There is also very little racial diversity among staff at any level, and you are unaware of anyone with a disability on the payroll. You want to bring this up at the next senior management team meeting, but you think you will need to have some persuasive arguments to convince the firm that this is an important issue that should be actioned. Prepare and present your plan of action for the meeting.

To help you consider the issues above, visit **www.macmillanihe.com/carbery-cross-hrm-2e** and watch the video of Lisa Dempsey from the Professional Women's Network talking about diversity and inclusion.

WHY IS EQUALITY AN IMPORTANT ISSUE?

The ability to participate in and to progress within employment is extremely important for many individuals. Much research demonstrates that the ability and opportunity to gain access to employment are key factors in what we term **social inclusion**, and inequality in employment is often indicative and reflective of inequality in the wider society. According to a European Commission report (2005), employment is a key factor for wider social inclusion, not only because it generates income, but also because it can promote social participation and personal development and contributes to maintaining adequate living standards in old age. Current statistics indicate that every fourth person remained at risk of poverty in the EU between 2010 and 2014 (Eurostat, 2016). Moving from unemployment to employment considerably lowers the likelihood of being exposed to the risk of poverty in general. Gaining access to employment is, however, problematic for many people, and it has been shown that this is not necessarily due to people 'not wanting to work', 'doing better on welfare' or 'being lazy'. For many people, barriers to accessing employment and obtaining equality at work are due to deep-rooted factors in society, which will be examined below.

There are many groups of people who are disproportionately marginalized with respect to access to employment and the ability to retain employment in times of recession. Who these groups are can vary across countries, but research identifies women, young unskilled workers, low-skilled workers in general, older workers, people with a disability, ethnic minorities, lone parents, and people living in marginalized communities as those suffering most from difficulties in gaining employment, confinement to low-paid jobs, unequal treatment in the workplace and so on (Le Grand, 2003; European Commission, 2009). For example, recent research found that just 26% of blind and visually impaired people of working age in the UK were employed (RNIB, 2016).

We can all relate to discrimination and unequal treatment caused by people's attitudes to others, but if we take the example of someone not being successful in the job market because of a lack of qualifications, is this simply the 'fault' of that person? Should they not just increase their qualifications to become more competitive? However, the situation for many people is not as straightforward as this, as you will see in the following sections.

Equality and equal treatment in the work situation cannot be viewed in isolation. Equal access to work and subsequent career success are influenced by many factors, such as a person's social background, access to education, gender, race and disability. Key questions are: why do certain groups find themselves disproportionately disadvantaged in the labour market? Who are these groups? What can be done to change the situation? There are three key explanations, based on existing research, as discussed below.

> **Social inclusion** – a measure of the extent to which a person or groups can participate in aspects of society to the same level as (or relative to) the average population. Key measures of social inclusion are access to work, adequate housing, education levels and access to education, healthcare and so on

Human Capital Explanations of Inequality in the Workplace

Human capital explanations of a person's competiveness in the labour market are based on an analysis of the combination of qualifications, skills, competencies and relevant work experience a person possesses. Possessing a third-level qualification, for instance, has been identified as a key factor in human capital terms, conferring significant advantages in competing for jobs and promotion within jobs (Russell et al., 2005; Eurostat, 2016). People with a higher level of human capital would be expected to compete more successfully in the labour market than those with a lower level. For instance, if two people apply for a job and one has more relevant experience for the position and also an applicable higher qualification, we would expect that person to have a greater chance of securing the job. This seems perfectly rational and fair. However, we need to examine why some people possess less human capital than others. Some research contends that this is based on the choices people make. Using the example of women in the labour market, it has been argued by some that the difference between women's and men's experiences is because women choose to prioritize family commitments over work. Thus, women will, for instance, take maternity leave or take leave to care for children, thereby reducing their work experience relative to men (Anker, 2001; Baron and Cobb-Clark, 2010; Turner and McMahon, 2011). However, we must consider if this choice is one that is freely made. To take another example, studies internationally have shown that migrant workers suffer disadvantage in their 'host' labour markets, as their qualifications may not be recognized and they therefore find themselves working in jobs with lower status and/or pay (Reyneri and Fullin, 2011). In some situations, even where their qualifications are recognized, a language barrier may have a negative effect on migrant workers' ability to compete in the labour market (Chiswick and Miller, 2009). Conversely, as before, it could also be argued that such workers make choices in terms of their ability to speak different languages.

The OECD (2016) has identified a particular problem with 'early school leavers'. This is a situation whereby young people leave school as soon as they are legally entitled, but before they have the necessary qualifications to enable them to access third-level or higher education. These young people may struggle to find employment, leading them to be described as 'NEETs' (not in education, employment or training). They come primarily from socially disadvantaged areas, and race and ethnicity are also predictors; thus these young people can often face multiple levels of disadvantage in the labour market. For instance, in the USA, Native American young people are twice as likely to fall into the NEET category as white American youth (OECD, 2016). Recent figures from EU member states (Eurostat, 2016) identify that currently more than 11% of 18- to 24-year-olds have left school with lower secondary education or less (this ranges from a high of 19% in Spain to a low of 2.8% in Croatia). In the USA, the figure is 14% (OECD, 2016).

We can also look at the stark evidence of the significant disadvantages that face young people from black and other ethnic minorities in Britain today. A report by the UK Equality and Human Rights Commission (2016) found that there was a 49% increase in unemployment among young people from ethnic minorities between 2010 and 2015; that black workers with degrees earned on average 23% less than their white counterparts; and that black and Asian workers were moving into more insecure forms of employment at a much faster rate than white workers: they were twice as likely to be in involuntary temporary employment. Overall, the unemployment rate in 2013 for white workers was 6.3% as opposed to 15% for black workers. The report also found that in 2014 the executive teams of FTSE 100 companies in Britain were 69% white.

CONSIDER THIS

Do you agree with the concept that if women choose to withdraw from the workplace to care for children, they are themselves responsible for possessing less human capital? Think about other groups of people who might possess less human capital than others and why this might happen.

Inequality as a Reflection of Social and Cultural Attitudes and Norms

Human capital factors cannot be considered in isolation from the social, cultural and institutional context of any labour market (Blau and Kahn, 2006). Taking gender, for instance, the human capital explanation that women may 'choose' to opt out or take breaks from the labour market because they prioritize childcare is contested by many commentators (Petrongolo, 2004; England, 2005; Tomlinson et al., 2009). The ability of women to participate in the labour market, it is argued, is affected by deeply rooted social norms that serve to limit their choices and oblige them to withdraw from the labour market. In many Western European countries, women are overwhelmingly viewed in societal terms as the primary carer and are naturally assumed to be the parent who will take time off when needed to care for children. For instance, a study of men and women in Ireland found that only 2% of people surveyed who listed their primary activity as looking after home/family were male (Central Statistics Office, 2013).

Thus, this second perspective on inequality takes into account social attitudes and norms. According to this view, unfairness in the allocation of jobs and promotions occurs as a consequence of the way opportunity has been embedded in societal norms (Anker, 2001; Noon 2004; Price, 2004). By that, we mean that inequality is viewed as *socially constructed* rather than based on objective criteria (Gardiner, 1998). In other words, as society develops over time, we accept certain perceptions of groups in society as 'normal' and 'acceptable'. For instance, until the 1920s, it was considered 'normal' that women did not have the opportunity to vote in Britain. Equally, racial segregation in parts of the USA earlier in the twentieth century severely restricted the ability of African Americans to gain access to 'good' jobs, which had wider implications for this societal group in terms of wealth and social standing. The reasons these accepted 'norms' develop are complex and a combination of many historical, cultural, legal and other factors. Have you ever considered why, for instance, racial segregation was once considered 'normal' in South Africa and the USA; why the ethnic Roma population of Europe were not accepted as members of 'normal' society; or why it has traditionally been accepted that women are viewed as the primary carer in families and men as the main breadwinner? Why is homosexuality punishable by death in some countries?

Dominant or accepted beliefs in society with respect to various groups of people may then be translated into the workplace. For example, the view that older people may not be open to learning new skills or may not be able to cope with new technology has been shown to affect access to employment and promotion for older workers. In one US case in 2008, a company that was selecting people for layoff instructed managers to rate employees based on how 'flexible' and 'retrainable' they were. Of the 31 people selected for redundancy, 30 were over the age of forty. The workers subsequently won a Supreme Court case on the basis of age discrimination (*Meacham* v. *Knolls Atomic Power Lab*, No. 06-1505, 2008). A key challenge for the HRM function within organizations is to ensure that all employees right up to senior managers behave in a way that supports equality and diversity regardless of deep-rooted social norms.

BUILDING YOUR SKILLS

Why do you think the employees selected for redundancy in the *Atomic Power Lab* case above were considered less 'retrainable' and 'flexible'? If you were a line manager in a company, what criteria could you identify that your company might use to objectively measure a person's 'retrainability' or 'flexibility'? Compare this case to the example earlier in the chapter on the employment of 'older' workers in Japan.

Institutional Explanations of Inequality

The third explanation for inequality emphasizes the effect of institutional factors on work outcomes. **Institutional barriers** to employment result from dominant structures, systems and rules that can act to limit access and opportunity for certain people in the workplace. For instance, a 'long-hours' culture, often used as a measure of commitment by organizations, can act as a barrier to promotion for parents with family and childcare responsibilities (Collinson and Hearn, 1994; Kirton and Greene, 2005). Generally speaking, women work shorter hours than men and are more likely to work part time (Presser et al., 2008; OECD, 2010).

Indeed, the accepted unwritten norm that a committed worker is one for whom temporal barriers do not exist has been shown to disadvantage women in many professions in terms of advancement and pay. It also discourages men from availing themselves of flexible work practices for fear of being overlooked for promotion or, conversely, being selected for redundancy (Hamel et al., 2006; Harrington et al., 2008; Rudman and Mescher, 2013). Other institutional barriers that have been identified are the traditional ways of doing business, and making an impression on the boss by association with the 'old boys' network'. This 'boys' club' involves activities such as golf outings and sessions in the pub, which can often exclude female employees and those from non-drinking cultures. Given these institutional barriers, it might be predicted that women will subsequently be overrepresented at lower levels in organizations, underrepresented at more senior levels and also be paid less, and this is indeed borne out by statistics (World Economic Forum, 2016). As an example, the average gender pay gap across the European Union in 2015 was over 16% (Eurostat, 2017a). In the USA the average gender pay gap is 21% (US Census Bureau,

> **Institutional barriers** – those barriers to employment or progression within employment posed by existing structures, systems and rules, which act to exclude certain groups of people, for example a lack of childcare facilities

2016). In India it has been reported as 67% (Accenture, 2017)

If we take people with disabilities as another example, this cohort of the workforce have often suffered from a lack of institutionalized support to enable access to education and work (Eurostat, 2015). Such facilities range from physical assistance, like wheelchair access, to extra support for people with disabilities such as sight loss, dyslexia and intellectual disabilities. Thus, people with disabilities may be prevented from gaining the appropriate qualifications necessary to have sufficient human capital to compete in the workplace. Consider for a moment what difficulties you would face in your current course if you suffered from one of the following: sight loss, hearing loss, being confined to a wheelchair or mental health issues. If people with disabilities do gain qualifications, they often face further obstacles in gaining access to employment due to a lack of suitable workplace facilities and transport to workplaces.

GEOGRAPHICAL VARIATION AND THE COMBINED EFFECTS OF INEQUALITY

Table 6.1 provides a summary of the three explanations for inequality discussed earlier. While the three perspectives give us a useful framework

Human capital factors	Socially constructed factors	Institutional factors
• Formal qualifications • Acquired skills • Work experience • Formal and informal training and development, e.g. workshops, on-the-job training, coaching, mentoring	• Accepted social and cultural norms, e.g. women as carers • Prejudice and attitudes, e.g. racism, ageism • Self-perception as 'inferior', e.g. a member of a traditionally excluded minority ethnic group may have low expectations • Prevailing political ideology	• Rules and legislation, e.g. prohibiting refugees from working • Lack of relevant support, such as childcare, funded training, transport for disabled people • Membership of professional associations with restricted entry • Informal 'customs' that facilitate progression, e.g. 'old boys' network', golf club outings • Lack of protective legislation

Table 6.1 Sample of factors contributing to labour market inequality

with which to analyse the reasons for inequality in the labour market and the workplace, it must be acknowledged that the effects of the various factors on equality vary across countries. Significant contemporary barriers affecting female and lone-parent participation in the labour market, for instance, include the availability of childcare support. Taking Ireland as an example, there is an absence of state support for childcare in comparison to most other European countries. Childcare costs in Ireland rank among the highest in Europe (Immervoll and Barber, 2005; OECD, 2016); a significant contrast to many of the Scandinavian countries, which have state-supported childcare and paid leave opportunities for parents.

Furthermore, the three explanations of inequality should not be viewed in isolation, as they are, in fact, interrelated and interwoven. With respect to lone parents, this cohort often face multiple barriers to work and social inclusion (Evans, 2003). Studies in the UK (Millar and Evans, 2003; Bradshaw, 2016) have shown that most lone parents are women, and over a half of all lone parents have neither technical nor academic qualifications. Lone parents also tend to be concentrated in more socially disadvantaged communities. Thus they may face multiple challenges to work inclusion, such as potential negative attitudes and the lack of a third-level qualification. Lone parents are also disproportionately affected by the cost of childcare which in turn can impact on their ability to access work. In the USA, for instance, it is estimated that 52% of a lone parent's net income will be swallowed up by childcare, as opposed to 25.6% of the net income of a couple (OECD, 2016).

NATIONAL INITIATIVES TO FOSTER EQUALITY

In many countries, it is recognized that certain groups of people are disproportionately disadvantaged in the labour market. Governments have recognized that measures need to be taken to try and 'level the playing field', that is, create equality of opportunity for people trying to access jobs and minimize any discrimination with respect to

> **Protected grounds** – those identified by national institutions as relating to areas where discrimination has or is likely to occur, such as race, sex, sexual orientation, religion, age and disability, and which are subsequently covered by equality legislation

all aspects of employment. This is not just restricted to access and applying for jobs but includes promotion, access to training, freedom from bullying and harassment, selection for redundancy and unfair dismissal. In countries such as Sweden, Belgium and Austria, companies are required to conduct pay surveys/audits which make transparent any pay differences between men and women (European Commission, 2014).

Generally speaking, governments tend to promote and support equality through funded information and awareness measures and the enactment of protective legislation. In many countries, such as the UK and Ireland, South Africa, the USA and Japan among others, legislation forbids discrimination on the basis of **protected grounds**. A protected ground is a trait or condition identified by legal jurisdictions that cannot be used as the basis for employment decisions. Such characteristics can include race, gender, age, family status, disability, being a member of an ethnic minority and so on. Depending on the country, governments will focus initiatives and legislation on characteristics that have been identified as being associated with social and work disadvantage.

LEGISLATION AND EQUALITY

Governments utilize legislative measures that confer obligations on employers with respect to equal treatment of employees and prospective employees. This varies from country to country. Differences between countries' approaches to legislation are influenced by the prevailing political ideology, and historical, cultural and social factors. Suk (2012), for instance, highlights a key difference in legislative provision between US and European equality legislation. In the USA, mandatory maternity leave is considered discriminatory, while, in Europe, mandatory maternity leave is upheld by legislation. According to Suk, these divergent approaches are underpinned by a highly individualistic US society that values individual autonomy, while the European approach is underpinned by a more collectivist approach. Having said that, if we examine the existing legal provision for equality and non-discrimination across different countries, we find a generally accepted idea that a violation of the principle of non-discrimination would be said to occur in the following circumstances: a person is subject to different treatment from a comparator and the difference in treatment does not have an objective and reasonable justification, or if there is no proportionality between the aim sought and the means employed.

Overall, the laws governing equality in Britain, the Republic of Ireland, other EU member states and the USA are similar in terms of their principles, prohibited actions and modes of redress. However, there are significant differences between the policies of 'westernized' countries and those of some countries in Africa, the Middle East and Asia. In Saudi Arabia, for example, it is permitted to openly advertise for jobs whereby applicants belonging to certain religious groups are excluded (ILO, 2007). A report by the OECD on Middle East and North African countries shows that in many countries, such as Kuwait, Morocco and Yemen, there are built-in legal restrictions that limit the hours and type of work open to women (OECD, 2016), while a World Bank report (2015) found that women are specifically legally excluded from working in over 450 specified jobs.

A key difference between the USA and the EU is that the USA draws mainly on its own civil rights legislation and has also introduced an Act prohibiting the use of genetic information to discriminate against potential employees. Interestingly though, small companies employing less than 15 people are exempt from much of the equality legislation in the USA. One of the reasons put forward for this exemption is the cost associated with complying with the legislation. This is not the case in Ireland and other EU member states. In general terms, in the USA, the UK and other European countries, employers are not allowed to discriminate against people who fall under protected grounds, namely race, religion, disability, sex, sexual orientation, ethnic origin, national origin, religion or belief, and age (European Union Agency for Fundamental Rights, 2011). However, because of the federal structure in the USA, there are variations in depth and breadth

> **Comparator** – a person or group that someone making a claim of discrimination will compare themselves to, with the purpose of demonstrating that they have been treated differently/unfairly using that comparator as a standard
>
> **Direct discrimination** – discrimination that is obviously contrary to the terms of equality legislation, such as explicitly excluding people over 50 from applying for a job
>
> **Indirect discrimination** – this occurs when a seemingly neutral provision attached to a job acts to exclude a person or group protected under equality legislation; for example, a requirement for people to be over 2m tall for a job in a shop would effectively exclude more women than men

of legislation. A good example of this is legislation protecting people on the basis of sexual orientation (see HRM in the Global Business Environment) which will be examined in more detail later in this chapter.

Most EU member states adopt legislation in line with Directives issued by the EU. These Directives are based on the underpinning principles of various EU treaties, most notably the Treaty of Rome (1957) and, more recently, the EU Charter of Fundamental Rights (enacted in the Treaty of Lisbon on 1 December 2009). As a result, most EU member countries have broadly similar laws governing workplace equality, with small variations. For instance, in many countries such as Germany, India, China, France, Austria, Poland and Japan, there is a legal obligation on employers whereby they must set aside a certain percentage of jobs for people with a disability. If they fail to achieve this then the normal penalty is a levy. This is not the case in other countries such as the UK, the USA and Canada.

Discriminatory advertising is also prohibited. This is advertising that acts to discourage or exclude applications from people protected by equality legislation. For instance, an upper age limit on a recruitment advertisement would be considered contrary to equality legislation. Distinctions are made between direct discrimination and indirect discrimination under EU legislation. Direct discrimination is obvious discrimination, for example explicitly limiting access to a job to people of one gender in an advertisement. Indirect discrimination is a more subtle form of discrimination. This is said to occur where there is a seemingly neutral condition attached to a job or access to a job, but it can be shown that this provision materially disadvantages a person who has rights under equality legislation. For instance, it has been held that requiring a part-time employee to switch to full-time work, due to restructuring of a company and a change in personnel need, while not an explicit contravention of equality legislation in most countries, can materially affect the ability of women (as primary carers) and parents to continue working in a job, and this has been held to be indirect discrimination on the grounds of gender and family status (see, for example, *Downie* v. *Coherent Scotland* (2017)).

Where legislation exists, there are also institutions through which employees and job seekers can pursue complaints and cases, and which provide information on rights and employer obligations ▶Chapter 5◀. The following example demonstrates how this works in practice. In 2007 in Northern Ireland, a 58-year-old man won an equality case under the Employment Equality (Age) Regulations (Northern Ireland) 2006, in which it was found that he had been discriminated against on the grounds of age when applying for a job as a salesperson with a timber firm. The tribunal found that he had been asked age-related questions and also pointed to the advertising of the position, which stated that the successful applicant would display 'youthful enthusiasm'. It concluded that but for his age he would probably have been successful in getting the position. The claimant subsequently said that the experience made him feel as if he had 'been flung on the scrapheap' (*McCoy* v. *James McGregor and Sons*, 00237/07IT).

Victimization

In many countries, employers are prohibited from **victimizing** people who make a complaint or take an equality case against an employer in good faith. For instance, if an employee makes a formal complaint for discrimination in a promotions process and they are subsequently fired, they would have a clear case for victimization. To give an example: a worker attends an interview for promotion. He does not get the job but feels he has been unfairly treated due to his sexual orientation. He makes a formal complaint to his employer, and thereafter his life at work is made difficult as he is given extra work that other people do not get, he is constantly reprimanded by his employer in front of colleagues, and he is eventually demoted. This could be viewed as victimization. The concept of victimization should not be overlooked by employers, as tribunals and courts can add a significant amount to a basic discrimination award on the basis of stress and trauma caused by victimization. In a decision in the UK, where £4.5 million was awarded to a female doctor on the grounds of discrimination, approximately £56,000 of this was awarded for psychological stress (*Michalak* v. *Mid Yorkshire Hospitals NHS Trust*, ET/1810815/2008).

> **Victimizing** – an act that treats someone unfairly

Exceptions to Equality Legislation

There are certain exceptions to equality legislation in most countries. In general, exceptions to the rule rely on a test of objective justification, which means that an employer is required to show that the treatment or provision corresponds to a real business need, and is appropriate, balanced and necessary to achieve that particular need. For example, in a German case concerning the firefighting service in Frankfurt, a Mr Wolf objected to being turned down for a job as a firefighter as he was over 30 years of age. The case came before the Court of Justice of the European Union (CJEU) which ruled against Mr Wolf. The authorities submitted evidence that the physical nature of a firefighter's work meant that employees older than 45 had to be assigned less demanding duties. Thus if too many older workers were recruited, the capacity of the service to carry out its activities would be reduced. The CJEU decided that it was an 'occupational requirement' to have 'especially high physical capacities' and that the under-30 rule was 'proportionate' in trying to meet that requirement. This was adjudged an allowable discrimination under European equality law (*Wolf* v. *Stadt Frankfurt am Main* [2010] 2 CMLR 849). It is important to insert a note of caution here, as the bar for objective justification is a high one for employers to prove.

In another German case, a nurse on a temporary contract was unsuccessful in her application for a permanent job. The respondents' justification was that a requirement of the job was that a large proportion of the work would take place in an operating theatre and that the claimant would be exposed to substances that could be harmful to her unborn child. However, the claimant's case was upheld on the basis that the condition of pregnancy was only temporary and the job was a permanent one. The CJEU found that while it was acceptable to impose temporary limits on the work of pregnant women based on the results of risk assessments, it was disproportionate to impose a permanent ban on their access to a job on the basis of a pregnancy. Such a ban constituted discrimination (*Mahlburg* v. *Land Mecklenburg-Vorpommern* [2000] ECR 1-549).

Inequality in Action: the Case of the LGBT Workforce

It is difficult to get accurate data on the proportion of people in any country who are LGBT, (lesbian,

CONSIDER THIS

In 2007 Lord John Browne resigned as CEO of BP after a 38-year career. His resignation followed the publication of an article in a British tabloid newspaper which 'outed' him. In his book, *The Glass Closet* (Browne, 2014), Browne details how he kept his sexuality a secret at work. He felt that he did not have a choice and that if he was open about being gay his career would be over. After his mother died in 2002, he embarked on his first relationship. The relationship ended after three years and his ex-boyfriend sold the story to a tabloid.

Throughout his career, Browne felt that he was doing BP a service by remaining in the closet, but in hindsight he realized that in reality he had wasted a 'colossal' amount of energy covering his tracks that he could have invested in the company. Thus he argues that inclusive workplaces will be more profitable by being open and allowing employees to work to their full capacity without fear of negative consequences. In an interview with *The Guardian* newspaper (Aitkenhead, 2014), he said that he wrote the book because 'I wouldn't want anyone to go through what I went through.'

1. Have you ever given any thought as to how sexual orientation or sexual identity might limit someone's career? Reflect on the experience of Lord Browne.
2. Do you think things are different now (given Lord Browne started his career in 1969)?

gay, bisexual and transgender) but research in the USA would indicate that 8 million people or 4% of the workforce identify themselves as part of this group (Gates, 2011). McFadden (2015) and Badgett et al. (2013) highlight a comprehensive amount of empirical research that shows that there is a strong economic rationale for fostering a diverse and open workplace with respect to LGBT employees. However, there are clear indications from research that people do suffer from discrimination with respect to sexual orientation and/or gender identity in the labour market (Pizer at al., 2011). In studies globally, a high proportion of LGBT workers report experiencing discrimination in respect of hiring (Tilcsik, 2011), job promotion, dismissal (Sears and Mallory, 2011), harassment, and levels of pay relative to heterosexual counterparts (Hollis and McCalla, 2013). For example, in 2011, during an unfair dismissal case in South Africa, it emerged that only homosexual employees were required to fill out a 'personal particulars form'. This form asked questions about a number of personal issues, including health status. The claimant declared that he was HIV positive and he was subsequently dismissed. Discrimination against people with HIV/Aids is prohibited in South Africa. The claimant was awarded compensation amounting to 12 months' remuneration (*Allpass v. Mooikloof Estate (Pty) t/a Mooikloof Equestrian Centre* (2011)).

Many LGBT employees still choose not to be 'out' in the workplace (34% in the UK and over 40% in the USA, for example) as they fear homophobia or that they will be overlooked for promotion. Transgender workers would appear to be particularly vulnerable to discrimination and there is a consistently high level of unemployment among members of the transgender community (Sears and Mallory, 2011; Ozturk and Tatli, 2016). Furthermore, efforts to conform (Hewlin, 2009) and/or fear of negative consequences as a result of revealing sexual orientation have been found to impact on mental health and wellbeing (Sears and Mallory, 2011; Ruggs et al., 2013). Research internationally has also indicated that even in workplaces with strong policies on equal treatment, many LGBT employees still experience negative reactions from fellow employees due to a deep-rooted culture of 'heteronormativity', i.e. heterosexuality is so deeply embedded as the norm that, regardless of organization policies, LGBT employees are still subjected to negative attitudes by their colleagues and consequently internalize the view that they are abnormal and deviant. As a result, LGBT employees remain silent at work even in situations where they should be reporting negative actions towards them (Reingarde, 2010; Priola et al., 2014). This fear of being 'out' at work from a career point of view has given rise to what is termed the 'glass closet' (Browne, 2014).

HRM IN THE GLOBAL BUSINESS ENVIRONMENT

LGBT employment rights

Unequal treatment of people based on sexual orientation or sexual identity varies across countries, as we can see from the sample presented in Table 6.2. This ranges from extreme and explicit negative attitudes

Country	LGBT employment protection against discrimination:		Same-sex marriage	Homosexuality	Service in the military
	Sexual orientation	Sexual identity			
USA	Varies in different states*	Varies in different states **	Legal	Legal	Legal
UK	Yes	Yes	Yes	Legal	Yes
Australia	Yes	Yes	Varies by region†	Legal	Yes
Saudi Arabia	No protection	No protection	Not recognized	Illegal (death penalty)	No
Russia	No protection	No protection	Not recognized	Legal	Yes
Turkey	No protection	No protection	Not recognized	Legal	Yes
Spain	Yes	No	Yes	Yes	Yes
Ireland	Yes	Not specifically but can get protection under equality legislation.	Yes	Legal	Yes
South Africa	Yes	Yes	Yes	Legal	Yes
Kuwait	No	No	not recognized	Illegal (imprisonment as penalty)	No
Italy	Yes	No	Civil unions	Legal	Yes
China	No protection	No protection	Not recognized	Legal	No
Uganda	No protection	No protection	Illegal	Anti-homosexuality Act 2014 annulled by constitutional court in 2014. However, engaging in homosexual 'acts' remains illegal	No
Greece	Yes	Yes	Civil unions	Yes	Yes

* Twenty-two States have statutory employment protection in both the public and private sector. Sixteen States have no protection. Other states have protection for public sector employees only.

** Twenty States have statutory employment protection. Twenty States have no protection. Other states have protection for public sector employees only.

† Civil unions in Queensland, partnerships in Victoria and NSW, unrecognized in other regions.

Table 6.2 LGBT employment rights: international comparisons

and laws, both in societal terms and at work, such as in Saudi Arabia, to more supportive country contexts such as in the UK where the rights of the LGBT community are upheld both in employment legislation and in other civil rights-based legislation, such as that recognizing marriage.

Questions

① Reflect on different laws relating to LGBT both in the workplace and society in the global context: how would these impact on careers and opportunities?

② Think about multinational organizations that may operate in countries with repressive attitudes and laws regarding the LGBT community. What responsibilities do you think

such organizations should have: should they abide by these attitudes/laws or challenge them?

③ You are an HR director of a global multinational organization. Your operations within host countries are run by people from that country. How can you ensure that your equality and diversity policies are being complied with and promoted?

Equality legislation continues to evolve across the world. For instance, in many European countries, 65 was accepted as a mandatory retirement age and this was upheld by the courts. However, in recent times and following cases in the Court of Justice of the European Union (CJEU), organizations in Europe can no longer assume that employees are required to retire at 65. Indeed, employers must now objectively justify such a rule.

A Critique of the Equality/ Legislative Approach

Employment equality legislation is associated with a social justice perspective to diversity. This perspective has been criticized for fostering a compliance culture within organizations, whereby organizations only introduce minimal diversity policies to comply with legal regulations (Foster and Harris, 2005; Kirton and Greene, 2016). Elson (1999) noted that institutional arrangements, such as laws and policies designed to combat segregation and inequality within workplaces, often do not work, due to the countervailing forces of accepted structures, unwritten rules and norms. The accepted metric for access to employment and advancement continues to be based on the notion that workers should be well educated (with qualifications that are recognized in the country), able to work long or irregular hours (and thus have few domestic responsibilities)

and, in some cases, be physically fit. Thus, by (objectively) assessing people against this metric, organizations are requiring diverse individuals and groups to conform to a norm. It is argued that this in effect denies or neutralizes difference, rather than accepting it, and engenders 'sameness' in the workplace. The ultimate consequence of this is that individuals or groups in society who cannot conform to the accepted norm continue to be excluded from accessing jobs or progressing within organizations regardless of legislative provision designed to help them. As outlined in the section on social exclusion, there are many groups who for one or multiple reasons remain at a disadvantage in the labour market, and thus it could be argued that a focus on equality legislation is not an ideal solution to achieving fairness in the workplace and opportunities for marginalized groups to progress.

Some researchers would argue that, in some instances, the effect of legislation with respect to work has had an impact, albeit a modest one in some instances. Dickens (2007) recognizes the positive aspects of employment equality legislation (for instance in narrowing pay gaps between men and women) but argues that this needs to be part of a wider mainstreaming of an equality agenda in general, whereby there is a recognition of the impact of broader inequalities in society and the need to incorporate measures to address these in any initiatives on equality in the workplace.

HRM AND ORGANIZATIONAL PERFORMANCE

Bicultural and multicultural employees

Research by Brannen et al (2010, 2013) examines bicultural and multicultural employees. Bicultural/multicultural employees are those who can identify with or have internalized two or more cultures due to reasons such as cultural background of parents, having lived in other countries etc. This research shows that bicultural or multicultural employees can add significant value to organizations in terms of team and organization performance (Brannen and Lee, 2014). They found that such people can act as 'bridgers' for helping multinationals navigate language issues as well as cultural and business norms in new markets. For instance, a Chinese American employee might be able to advise on a new venture into China. She cites the example of Nokia, which was able to leverage the knowledge of a multicultural workforce and learned that many parts of the world did not have landlines. This knowledge spurred Nokia to develop mobile phone technology and enter these markets, thus establishing itself as an early and dominant entrant into the mobile phone market. Brannen's research illustrates the importance of HRM in leveraging the value that multicultural and bicultural employees offer.

THE POSITIVE DISCRIMINATION/ POSITIVE ACTION DEBATES

A long-running, controversial debate surrounds the issue of **positive discrimination**. Supporters of positive discrimination hold that certain groups of people have suffered such levels of disadvantage over a protracted period of time that employers need to positively discriminate in their favour if we are ever to have equality in the workplace. This would mean that an employer could, effectively, discriminate against other applicants in order to recruit people who are disproportionately underrepresented in the workplace. In other words, employers could use discriminatory practices to ensure that the workplace population reflects the wider population, such as discriminating against people below 40 to ensure that a representative cohort of over-40-year-olds are present in a company's workforce.

Positive action differs from positive discrimination in that it does not seek to discriminate in favour of disadvantaged groups at the expense of others, but seeks to enhance the employability and labour market competitiveness of certain groups in particular national contexts; for example, young black males in the UK, North African migrants in France, members of the Roma population in Europe, people with disabilities in the workplace and so on.

> **Positive discrimination** – preferential discriminatory treatment of a minority group over a majority group to try and counter disadvantage in the labour market
>
> **Positive action** – measures undertaken with the aim of achieving full and effective equality for members of groups that are socially or economically disadvantaged

One form of positive action would involve governments, employers and other influential bodies identifying groups of people who, whether by race, gender, age or family status, are underrepresented in the workplace, and through positive action schemes create more opportunities for these groups. Examples of this are language training programmes funded by government or organizations, advertising that actively encourages applications from underrepresented groups, and funding for various types of training to enable underrepresented groups to compete on a more equal basis. Cohen (2007) refers to this as 'positive action' as opposed to 'negative action' or 'negative inaction'. She provides the example of how the Household Cavalry (a senior part of the British Army) sought to address a serious underrepresentation of black and Asian recruits. An outreach programme was devised, whereby current members of the Household Cavalry joined sports centres used by black and Asian young men, visits were arranged to schools and communities to meet potential recruits and their parents to persuade them that the Army was a good career, and black and Asian young people were invited to visit the Household Cavalry to see what it involves and the training it offers. Following these initiatives, within four years, ethnic minority recruitment had jumped from 0%

to about 14% (Cohen, 2007). This form of positive action is generally accepted and welcomed. More controversial, however, is where positive action becomes part of the legal obligations of employers. Section 159 of the UK Equality Act 2010 introduced a provision for positive action in relation to recruitment and promotion. Section 159, which came into force in April 2011, permits but does not require an employer to take a protected characteristic into consideration when deciding who to recruit or promote, where people having the protected characteristic are at a disadvantage or are underrepresented. This positive action can be taken only where the candidates are 'as qualified as' each other. In 2010 there was much debate in the British media that employers may leave themselves exposed to legal claims of discrimination if they do exercise this option to favour one candidate over another because they have a protected characteristic. However, it seems that the positive action provision has had little impact.

BUILDING YOUR SKILLS

You have been asked to give a training session to new supervisors on their obligations with respect to equality in the selection process. Outline the key issues you would address in such a training session and why you would include these.

HRM, THE WORKPLACE AND EQUALITY

Organizations have to be cognizant of the equality legislation and implement policies, procedures and practices to ensure compliance with the relevant laws. HR has an integral role to play in ensuring that all employees and prospective employees are treated fairly and treat their co-workers in a fair and equitable manner. This can be achieved through the creation and dissemination of development and awareness programmes and clear statements and policies regarding equal treatment of employees. It is also important that HR ensures that all organization members, from senior management down, are aware of the consequences of discriminatory behaviour towards employees and prospective employees. Methods of dissemination include employee handbooks, training seminars and induction programmes for new employees. In many countries, it is also obligatory, or at least advisable, to make sure that handbooks and other documentation are available in various languages, especially where a sizeable proportion of the workforce may normally speak a different language. For instance, in some US states, many companies would provide employees with handbooks in Spanish. Case law in various countries has established that policies should not be treated as 'window dressing' but must be acted on by organizations, and they must be seen to be acting in a fair and consistent manner.

HRM IN PRACTICE

A fair day's wage for a fair day's work? The case of supported employment in Australia

PhotoDisc/Getty Images

Research globally shows that people with disabilities experience difficulties accessing employment (Shur et al., 2009; ILO, 2015). In Australia the situation is similar; a 2015 report from the Australian Bureau of Statistics indicated that, in 2012, the labour force participation rate of people with a disability was 52.8%, as opposed to 82.5% of those without a disability. Thus, nearly half of people registered with a disability (47.2%) were not participating in the labour force, i.e. they were not employed and were not looking for work; 19.3% of people with a disability (201,500) reported that it was not their disability that prevented them from working.

The report also indicated that for many people with a disability, support in employment is essential; nearly a quarter of those with an intellectual or psychological disability were likely to require special working arrangements and assistance, such as a support person to assist or train them on the job, whereas 11.2% of people with a physical disability said that they required special working arrangements, mainly in the form of special equipment.

Providing a solution

One method by which many Australians with a disability access employment is through enterprises known as Australian Disability Enterprises (ADEs). These enterprises provide supported employment to people with disabilities. Such companies receive financial support from the Australian government, and it is estimated that up to 20,000 people with intellectual disabilities work in ADEs.

The problem

Whilst ADEs receive financial support from government, they are expected to operate as economically viable entities. There is a recognition that the productivity of a person with a disability may not equal that of a non-disabled person, even with support. This in turn could possibly impact on the ability of a company to remain solvent. Thus

the rates pay of disabled workers in ADEs are determined by benchmarking their productivity against non-disabled workers on the lowest rate of pay in their particular area of work. Once the 'gap' is established, the disabled worker is paid on a pro rata basis. So, for instance, a worker might be paid 50% of the normal rate for a particular job. Companies are required to use an approved assessment tool to measure the workers' productivity.

Up until recently, a commonly used assessment tool for the purpose of measuring productivity of workers with a disability was the Business Supported Wages Assessment Tool or BSWAT. This tool was developed by the Australian government and assessed two components: firstly, it tested a worker's productivity (a measurement of actual work done), and, secondly, it tested a worker's competency. Competencies in general examine a worker's level of aptitude and knowledge. The competency and productivity elements of BSWAT counted for 50% of the assessment respectively.

However, in 2012, a challenge to BSWAT was heard by the High Court of Australia. The case was taken by representatives of two plaintiffs (Michale Nojin and Gordon Prior), who argued that the effects of the outcome of BSWAT effectively discriminated against both men contrary to their rights under the relevant Australian equality legislation (the Disability Discrimination Act).

Michael Nojin has cerebral palsy. He was employed by an ADE called Coffs Harbour Challenge Inc. and was paid A$1.85 per hour for destroying documents. Gordon Prior, who is legally blind and has a mild/moderate intellectual disability, was paid A$3 per hour to maintain gardens. The national minimum wage in Australia at that time was around A$16.37 per hour.

The decision

Three judges heard the case: Judge Buchanan, Justice Katzmann and Justice Flick. None of the judges had a problem with the productivity tests. Michael Nojin worked mainly in secure document destruction. For the productivity element of his test, he was required to complete tests measuring his productivity rate in activities such as inserting flyers into pamphlets and feeding one crate of pre-sorted documents through a mechanical shredder. Gordon Prior worked at mowing lawns and raking leaves. He normally worked under direct supervision. His productivity test involved timing him mowing an area of lawn. This was then compared to the length of time his supervisor took to mow the same area. For example, Mr Prior took 14 minutes and 10 seconds on his first assessment to mow a 5m x 10m area of lawn. The comparator, his supervisor, took 9 minutes to mow a similar area.

The key problems in the opinion of two of the judges lay with the competency element of the test. As part of the BSWAT competency assessment, workers were asked four questions measuring 'core' competencies and four measuring 'industry' competencies. A score was allocated to each question.

> The basic defect in the use of BSWAT is that it reduces wages to which intellectually disabled workers would otherwise be entitled by reference to considerations which do not bear upon the work that they actually do. In my view, that approach is not reasonable. (*Nojin* v. *Commonwealth of Australia* [2012] FCAFC 192, per Justice Buchanan at [148])

The conclusion of the judges in this appeal was that use of the test was not reasonable to determine the wages of people with intellectual disability, and in fact it served to discriminate against this cohort of the community. This hinged mainly on the competency elements of the BSWAT, which the judges felt tested concepts which people with intellectual disabilities could never fully articulate because of their particular disability (as opposed to people with a physical disability who very often could satisfy

the competency tests). The court found for the plaintiffs, declared the test to be discriminatory, made an award of compensation and called for a review of such tests.

The outcome

The decision was appealed by the Commonwealth but the appeal was rejected. However, BSWAT continued to be used, and the Commonwealth refused to compensate employees for underpayments. Finally, in 2016, a class action was taken by Tyson Duval Comrie, a worker with an intellectual disability, and this was settled in late 2016. As a result of this case and the case cited on the previous page, a one-off payment was approved for those employees with intellectual disabilities who had been assessed using BSWAT. ADEs were instructed to cease using BSWAT by 2016 and must transition to another tool.

The situation has generated some debate. Many ADEs have asserted that they would not be able to remain in business unless they were allowed to utilize a tool to judge workers' productivity and to allocate a pro rata wage that is below the industry norm.

What would you do?

1. What are your thoughts on this situation and case? Are there justifications for the payment of lower wages to people with a disability?
2. You are an HR generalist in an organization, and you are starting to examine the company's diversity. You want to begin with the issue of disability.
   (a) Prepare a report for the senior management team on the labour market participation and employment rates of people with disabilities in your own country. Do people with different disabilities fare worse than others? Are there any supports/initiatives available

in your country to support people with disabilities in accessing jobs?

(b) Prepare a convincing argument for having a more inclusive workplace in this regard.

3 People with disabilities are said to often possess less human capital than people who do not have disabilities. What do we mean by human capital? Why do you think people with disabilities might have less human capital? What can be done by governments to change this situation?

4 Compare the equality legislation governing disability in your country with that in two other countries (one in a different continent).

IMAGE SOURCE

SUMMARY

This chapter has examined the concepts of diversity, equality and discrimination in the workplace, and the positive returns from having a diverse workforce have been highlighted. However, inequality is deeply rooted in society and the workplace, and certain groups of people continue to face greater barriers than others in accessing employment and in progressing within employment. In recognition of the disproportionate disadvantages experienced by certain groups, countries across the world have introduced legislation in a bid to counter discrimination and level the playing field with respect to employment. Broadly speaking, the legislative measures in various countries prohibit discrimination on the basis of defined 'grounds', which can include sex, race, disability, age and religion, with some exceptions allowable. The HR function plays a critical role in developing policies and procedures, communication, developing and providing relevant training and development, supporting employees and investigating and processing complaints and cases in relation to equality and diversity. The next step for governments and organizations is how to move beyond legislative, procedural approaches to equality and find alternative approaches that work. The key question remains: unless this is profitable for organizations, will they be interested in pursuing this agenda?

CHAPTER REVIEW QUESTIONS

1. Compare and contrast the diversity management and social justice perspectives of diversity. Which perspective do you agree with and why?
2. What are the main benefits and challenges of a diverse workforce? In what ways do both organizations and workers benefit from this diversity, if at all?
3. What do you understand the principal differences between equality and discrimination to be? Provide examples in support of your understanding.
4. Outline and explain the key reasons why inequality continues to persist in the workplace and why individuals continue to experience discriminatory practices and attitudes.
5. Discuss the often deep-rooted barriers that prevent individuals from accessing employment and obtaining equality at work. How, in your opinion, could these barriers be overcome?
6. Consider the worth of your current and potential human capital. Think about some of the issues raised in this chapter and how they might affect your human capital, for instance gender, age, disability, race, sexuality.
7. Do you agree with positive discrimination and positive action? How do they differ?
8. Prepare an argument addressing the following statement: 'equality legislation is effective in terms of tackling inequality in the workplace'. You could look at one or more of the groups of people covered by legislation in your country. Also consider and examine nationally published statistics and any published relevant research you can source.

FURTHER READING

Kirton, G. and Greene, A.M. (2016) *The Dynamics of Managing Diversity: A Critical Approach*, 4th edn, New York: Routledge.

Mor Barak, M.E. (2016) *Managing Diversity: Toward a Globally Inclusive Workplace*, 4th edn, London: Sage.

Wilkinson, R. and Pickett, K. (2010) *The Spirit Level: Why Equality is Better for Everyone*, London: Penguin.

USEFUL WEBSITES

European Union

ec.europa.eu/eurostat

Eurostat provides a wealth of statistical information at European level. It also publishes reports that will be useful to anyone researching labour markets, diversity and equality issues.

United Kingdom

www.acas.org.uk

The Advisory, Conciliation and Arbitration Service website provides useful and detailed information on statutory rights and obligations in the workplace, as well as information on relevant documentation that would be needed when processing a claim. It is also the investigating body for claims.

www.achieveability.org.uk

This organization works for the promotion of educational, employment and training opportunities for people who are neurodivergent (autistic, dyspraxic, dyslexic, ADHD)

Republic of Ireland

www.workplacerelations.ie

Workplace Relations is an Irish government website that provides information on legislation and rights, publications on equality and information for employers and employees.

Australia

www.humanrights.gov.au

The Australian Human Rights Commission is responsible for promoting and protecting human rights in Australia. You can read about their campaigns and work with different groups, such as Aboriginal and Torres Strait Islander peoples, on their website. They also investigate complaints about discrimination and breaches of human rights.

India

labour.gov.in

The Ministry of Labour and Employment is responsible for protecting and safeguarding workers' interests in India, and particularly for those who are poor or disadvantaged.

USA

www.eeoc.gov

The Equal Employment Opportunity Commission website has information on equality issues, research, news, access to information on rights and obligations, and access to information on processing claims and cases.

For extra resources, including videos, multiple choice questions and useful weblinks, go to: www.macmillanihe.com/carbery-cross-hrm-2e.

iStock.com/faithiecannoise

7: Performance Management

Steven Kilroy

THIS CHAPTER DISCUSSES:

Introduction (122)

Enhancing Performance through Performance Management (122)

Enhancing Engagement through Performance Management (125)

Performance Management Schemes used in Organizations (126)

The Link between Performance Management and Reward (128)

Performance Management Pitfalls (129)

Overcoming Performance Management Pitfalls (131)

How to Manage Underperformance (133)

INTRODUCTION

Performance management is important for the organization in order to track its progress and ensure it achieves its objectives. However, performance management is also important for employees as it provides them with a platform to monitor their progress and it can enhance their engagement at work. In light of the benefits derived from performance management and because of the severe difficulty in 'getting it right' in organizations, it continues to be a topic of major interest for academics and practitioners alike. This chapter will discuss the role of performance management in promoting higher levels of employee engagement and performance. Then it will describe some of the main techniques or schemes used to assess performance and identify how performance management and reward are inextricably linked. Next, the challenges associated with performance management will be critically evaluated, with a particular emphasis given to the annual performance appraisal interview. Finally, the key strategies that can be used to manage underperformance are highlighted.

ENHANCING PERFORMANCE THROUGH PERFORMANCE MANAGEMENT

Performance management has been defined as a 'process for establishing shared understanding about what is to be achieved, and an approach to managing and developing people in a way which increases the probability that it will be achieved in the short and long term' (Armstrong, 2003: 479). Most employees in a work setting experience performance management in some capacity, and in practice this becomes apparent during the **performance appraisal**.

Over the last two decades, performance management has been synonymous with, and has grown in popularity as part of the emerging research on, strategic human resource management (SHRM) ▶Chapter 1◀. This stream of

> **Advanced HR practices** – people management practices which are strategic or progressive in nature
>
> **Performance appraisal** usually consists of an interview that takes place between employees and their managers to review the employees' performance, and set future goals which can be used to make reward, promotion and development decisions

> **Performance management** is concerned with establishing and measuring employee goals in order to improve individual and organizational performance

literature suggests that **advanced HR practices**, also referred to as high performance work practices (HPWPs), e.g. pay for performance, information sharing, teamwork and performance management, can increase organizational performance (Huselid, 1995).

One of the dominant models in the HRM literature which explains how HPWPs impact performance is the ability–motivation–opportunity (AMO) model (Appelbaum et al., 2000). The premise of this model is that HR practices play a significant role in increasing employees' *ability* (A), *motivation* (M) and *opportunity to participate* (O), which in turn enables them to perform better on the job. Thus, performance (P) = A + M + O. Practices such as pay and performance management ▶Chapter 8◀ are important in motivating employees to better perform their jobs. Practices such as teamwork and information sharing ▶Chapter 9◀ can provide employees with the opportunity to use their skills and motivation to deliver superior performance. Finally, training which can be used as part of a performance management intervention can enhance employees' ability to effectively perform their job ▶Chapter 9◀. Managing performance is important for both managers and employees alike. For managers, it enables them to clarify key organizational goals and priorities, measure subordinates' work performance and motivate them by recognizing achievements. For employees, performance management enables them to learn what is valued by the organization, communicate their views about the job and identify career and training development needs ▶Chapters 9 and 10◀.

According to Strebler and colleagues (2001), there are a number of principles which are necessary for performance management to work effectively. The performance management system must:

- have clear aims and measurable success criteria
- be designed and implemented with appropriate employee involvement
- be simple to understand and operate

- have its effective use core to all management goals
- allow employees to see clearly how their performance goals are linked with the goals of the organization as a whole
- focus on role clarity and performance improvement
- be closely aligned to a clear and adequately resourced training and development infrastructure
- make clear the purpose of any direct link to reward, and build in proper equity and transparency safeguards
- be regularly and openly reviewed against its success criteria.

At its core, performance management is about improving individual and organizational performance. A number of theoretical perspectives and models have emerged to explain how this might be done (Den Hartog et al., 2004). We now examine three of these theories and a conceptual model of how performance management works, respectively goal-setting theory, expectancy theory, equity theory and Den Hartog, Boselie and Paauwe's performance management model.

Goal-setting Theory

According to goal-setting theory (Locke and Latham, 1990), setting goals which are specific and challenging yet attainable can result in motivation to increase performance. After all, if we do not have goals that we aspire to achieve, we are unlikely to be motivated to exert significant effort in the workplace. It is believed that goal commitment, goal importance, **self-efficacy** and receiving **feedback** are important factors which can strengthen the relationship between goal setting and performance. Therefore, setting important and attainable goals to which employees are committed and providing feedback are pivotal to performance management. A good way to think about the suitability of goals is the SMART framework – are goals *specific*, *measurable*, *attainable*, *realistic* and *timed*? Despite the usefulness of goal-setting theory, actually setting goals which can be effectively measured proves extremely difficult for organizations time and time again.

> **Self-efficacy** – self-confidence in one's ability to perform
>
> **Feedback** – information (positive and negative) on how an employee performs

Expectancy Theory

Expectancy theory (Vroom, 1964) also demonstrates the role of performance management in enhancing employee motivation and performance. This theory helps to explain why a lot of workers lack motivation in their jobs and merely do the minimum necessary to get by. Specifically, expectancy theory suggests that employees' motivation to perform is based on a combination of three factors: (E) *expectancy*, (I) *instrumentality* and (V) *valence*. Expectancy refers to the probability that work effort will be followed by a given level of task performance. For example, if I study hard for my exam, is it likely that I will perform well in the exam and obtain a good grade? Instrumentality refers to the probability that a given level of achieved task performance will lead to various work outcomes. For example, if I perform well and reach my targets, do I trust that I will receive the associated reward, e.g. a good grade, recognition, a promotion? Valence refers to the value attached by the individual to various work outcomes. For example, do I value the reward enough, e.g. a good grade, to work hard for its attainment? Thus, expectancy theory argues that the strength of a tendency to act in a certain way depends on the strength of an expectation that the act will be followed by a given outcome and on the attractiveness of the outcome to the individual. Therefore, as individuals base their decisions about behaviour on the expectation that a certain action will lead to needed or desired outcomes, there should exist some system of performance management in organizations which recognizes and rewards achievements to stimulate motivation. Although expectancy theory provides a useful and practical understanding of motivation, the theory does somewhat assume a rationality with respect to how the individual thinks and behaves, which does not always materialize in reality. Moreover, what is valued may vary significantly from one person to another. This is difficult for organizations, which must therefore strive to motivate people in different ways and by paying attention to their individual needs.

 CONSIDER THIS

Consider that you are being offered €100,000 by your lecturer to successfully memorize this textbook by tomorrow morning. With reference to expectancy theory, will you be motivated to perform this task?

Equity Theory

Another prominent theory underpinning the rationale for performance management is equity theory. Equity theory (Adams, 1963) refers to the comparison between inputs (what an individual brings to employment, such as effort and performance) and outputs (factors received in return for inputs, such as reward and recognition). Equity theory also focuses on how fairly employees have been treated in comparison to others. When there is a perceived inequity in the employment relationship, the individual tries to restore equity by either distorting their inputs (e.g. reducing effort and performance levels), disregarding the comparable other (i.e. a fellow employee) and referring to a new one, or terminating the relationship (Adams, 1963). Likewise, outputs on the basis of poor performance can be changed by the organization through offering lower reward and recognition and potentially terminating the employee's contract. This theory highlights the importance of having a transparent performance management system in place to ensure that employees are being adequately

rewarded for their inputs and fairly treated in comparison to others. Although this theory is intuitive and simple, like expectancy theory, it is difficult to understand how employees might actually define inputs and outputs in the first instance.

Den Hartog, Boselie and Paauwe's Model of Performance Management

Often formulated on the basis of the aforementioned theoretical perspectives, there exists a wide range of performance management models in the literature which delineate how performance management can translate into improved performance. Den Hartog, Boselie and Paauwe (2004) offer a simplistic yet effective model of performance management which suggests that performance management which is aligned with other HR practices impacts employees' perceptions and attitudes (e.g. commitment, trust and motivation). Perceptions and attitudes in turn are expected to affect employee performance and ultimately organizational performance. The alignment of performance management with other HRM practices is necessary in order to ensure that consistent messages are communicated to employees. The model also emphasizes the central role of line managers as, although performance management and related HR policies are defined by the HR department, it is line managers who are responsible for their implementation, i.e. conducting the appraisal, providing regular feedback, and training and coaching employees. The fact that HRM responsibility is increasingly devolving from HR professionals to line managers (Bos-Nehles et al., 2013) is reflective of the evolution of HR from an administrative function to a strategic one (Guest,

> **Strategic performance management** – focuses on aligning individual goals with the goals of the organization to achieve a competitive advantage in the marketplace

CONSIDER THIS

Consider that you are being paid an annual salary of €40,000 for working as a bank official. You learn during lunch in the canteen that your friend, who is also a bank official and started working at the bank at the same time as you, is earning an annual salary of €45,000. According to equity theory, what feelings will this revelation evoke and what are your likely responses?

HRM AND ORGANIZATIONAL PERFORMANCE

Strategic performance management

Strategic performance management is considered to be instrumental in delivering higher levels of individual performance and ultimately organizational performance. It can do this through creating a high-performance culture and by aligning the performance management strategy with the business strategy (Armstrong and Taylor, 2017). This ensures that employees act in ways

that are beneficial to the organization as the behaviours required to deliver on the strategy are encouraged and reinforced (Schuler and Jackson, 1987). Performance management enables organizations to identify talented employees so that they can be effectively rewarded and thus retained (Armstrong, 2006b). Likewise, it enables underperformers to be identified so that corrective action, i.e. additional support and training, can be taken to increase performance.

1987). Indeed, when operational activities are transferred to line managers, the HR professional can concentrate to a greater extent on their strategic and change management roles (Teo and Rodwell, 2007).

Although a full discussion of the theoretical perspectives and conceptual models underpinning performance management is beyond the scope of this chapter, it is clear that to elevate motivation and performance, employees need to perceive that their efforts are measured and rewarded, that performance goals are challenging but achievable, and that they are treated fairly with regard to their contributions and in comparison with others. Performance management should also be aligned with other HR practices so that they work in harmony and the messages conveyed are consistent.

ENHANCING ENGAGEMENT THROUGH PERFORMANCE MANAGEMENT

We have seen how performance management might increase performance, but this may be achieved either independently or indirectly through its role in enhancing employee engagement. Formally defined, engagement refers to 'a positive fulfilling, work-related state of mind that is characterized by vigor, dedication and absorption' (Schaufeli et al., 2002: 74). Therefore, engagement reflects the extent to which employees demonstrate energy, dedication and immersion in their work. Engagement is a particularly important concept in the HR field. Research has revealed that when employees are engaged at work, they perform much better (Harter et al., 2002) and thus the organization can gain a competitive advantage (Macey et al., 2009). There are many reasons to expect that a well-designed performance management system can enhance employee engagement. Indeed, performance management can create meaning and interest for employees in performing their work as it focuses on intrinsic motivating factors, such as taking responsibility for job outcomes and achievement and fulfilment of personal goals and objectives (Armstrong, 2006b). The classic job characteristics model (Hackman and Oldham, 1980) has long acknowledged the important role of feedback amongst other job characteristics in creating meaning for workers and providing them with knowledge of results achieved – both important predictors of work engagement (Kahn, 1990). Empirical research has also supported

> **Engagement** – the energy, enjoyment and enthusiasm that employees exhibit towards their work

the notion that feedback, as part of performance management, constitutes a valuable resource for employees which enhances their engagement through opportunities for growth and development and by fostering self-efficacy (Xanthopoulou et al., 2009). In other words, when we learn about what we are good at and what we can improve upon, this can build confidence in our abilities and enable us to set goals to further improve performance.

In a similar way to equity theory, discussed earlier, Gruman and Saks (2011) argued that for performance management to be effective in increasing engagement and performance, it must be carried out in a way which adheres to the principles of trust and fairness. If the appraiser is not trusted by the appraisee, or if the performance review is not conducted in a fair manner, the assessment of performance is unlikely to be viewed as credible, thus causing disengagement. Prior research has acknowledged that trust is an important precondition of engagement (Ugwu et al., 2014). Moreover, Latham and colleagues (2005) argued that, to be effective, performance management must be perceived as fair in the sense that it adheres to the principles of procedural, distributive and interactional justice. Procedural justice ensures that the process through which performance management is carried out is transparent and fair, and that employees have input into the process, e.g. employees are involved in setting performance goals. Distributive justice refers to the fairness of the actual outcomes decided upon during performance management. For example, based on a particular performance rating, did employees receive extra support and training, and did they get recognized for their achievements? Interactional justice refers to the manner in which employees are treated and communicated with throughout the performance management process. For example, during the appraisal interview, is the manager respectful in their interactions?

The HR professional will have an important role to play in advising line managers and monitoring the performance management process to ensure it adheres to the principles of trust and fairness. A well-thought-out performance management system should also be effectively aligned with other HR practices to foster engagement, and getting this alignment correct forms a central part of the HR professional's role. Gruman and Sacs (2011) argue that job design, leadership, coaching, supervisor support and training are all important factors that should accompany performance management in facilitating employee engagement. When the organization provides employees with good coaching, training and support, and designs their jobs in an interesting way, enhanced engagement is often a means by which employees reciprocate the benefits provided to them (Farndale and Kelliher, 2013). Therefore, it is evident that engagement is a critical outcome that can be enhanced via effective performance management, a finding which is also supported by empirical research (e.g. Risher, 2005).

PERFORMANCE MANAGEMENT SCHEMES USED IN ORGANIZATIONS

The performance appraisal interview is at the heart of performance management. It consists of, usually, a discussion between an employee and their line manager about the employee's performance and any concerns that both parties may have. While the performance appraisal interview was traditionally an annual process, intervals for employees have significantly shortened, ensuring that reviews every six months or quarterly are more common. Decisions surrounding training, promotion, payment and termination often follow the performance appraisal interview. Some of the most commonly used metrics or techniques include rating, ranking, the critical incident technique, 180-degree feedback, 360-degree feedback and competency-based assessment. Each of these are now examined.

Rating

Rating involves the appraiser rating an employee's performance on a predetermined scale. Employee performance can be judged on a range of criteria using, for example, a scale of (1) poor to (5) excellent. A typical example of a rating scale which is widely adopted by organizations is the behaviourally anchored rating scale (BARS), which is a specific method of linking ratings to behaviour at work. Indeed, the scale assesses the relative amount of activity on a certain behaviour, examples of activity related to this behaviour, and a numeric scale is used to judge this. The example in Table 7.1 highlights a BARS for a customer service role. An advantage of rating is that it is relatively simplistic and aims to focus on individual objective performance where possible. However, there is a high degree of subjectivity to the rating process as managers can often be either harsh or lax when rating employees, and this could vary significantly between managers, thus undermining objectivity and consistency (Luffarelli et al., 2016). It can be difficult to achieve procedural justice with a rating system of this nature.

Performance Category	Points	Examples of Activities for Customer Service
Outstanding performance	1	Suggests and implements valuable approaches for improved sales and builds enduring positive relationships with staff, customers and senior management around all stores
Good performance	2	Initiates creative ideas for improved sales and is highly effective at building relationships with customers and staff
Fairly good performance	3	Regularly takes into consideration stock requirements/makes orders on time and attempts to make small talk and build relationships with customers
Acceptable performance	4	Often positively interacts with customers and ensures stock is delivered when required
Fairly poor performance	5	Can manage but finds it difficult to deliver stock on time and interact with customers
Poor performance	6	Only greets some customers positively and is often unwilling to directly approach and assist
Extremely poor performance	7	Takes regular breaks inside normal working hours and is often impolite with customers

Table 7.1 Example of behaviourally anchored rating scale for customer service role

Ranking

Another performance assessment technique is ranking, of which forced ranking is the most well-known example. Ranking involves managers ranking workers from best to worst, based on specific characteristics or overall job performance (Armstrong, 2006b). For example, employees might be categorized as A, B or C players in an organization. Figure 7.1 depicts an example of a forced ranking system on the basis of a bell curve distribution. Ranking is usually simple to implement and enables easy comparisons between individuals in an organization. Such a system is usually seen in large financial sector organizations, such as banks, who tend to rate workers in relative (compare workers against each other) rather than in absolute (objective performance criteria) terms. Although popular, the ranking technique has been criticized on ethical grounds. Enron, a former American energy company, famously adopted a forced ranking approach which was colloquially referred to as 'rank and yank'. Under this performance management system, the company terminated the employment of bottom 10% of performers in the company each year. This system promoted an aggressive culture, internal competition and the adoption of creative but unethical accounting practices, which contributed to the financial crisis and ultimately the demise of the firm. Bazerman and Tenbrunsel (2011) argue that rewarding unethical decisions which have positive outcomes for individuals and organizations in the short term is a recipe for disaster in the longer term. Another problem associated with ranking, much like rating, discussed earlier, is that the notion of performance may not be adequately defined and therefore not measurable (Armstrong and Taylor, 2017).

The Critical Incident Technique

The critical incident technique is widely adopted in organizations. This technique focuses on collecting and analysing reports of incidents of actual behaviour which constitute job performance (Anderson and Wilson, 1997). In this approach, the appraiser or supervisor will often observe incidents of good or bad performance, and these are then used as a basis for assessing or discussing performance. While this approach might be considered objective as the behaviours assessed are job-related, such an approach to performance measurement is also cumbersome as it can be costly, timely and requires managers to have excellent observation skills.

180-degree Feedback

Recognizing the multidimensionality of performance and the complexity of effectively assessing it, a host of new, more comprehensive approaches have been developed over the years. For example, 180-degree feedback, a form of upward appraisal, has gained popularity and involves employees rating their manager's performance via, for example, an anonymous questionnaire. Managers may also rate employees. It is important that the questionnaire is anonymous in order to limit the potential for managerial retribution, e.g. treating the employee unfavourably as a result of the rating provided.

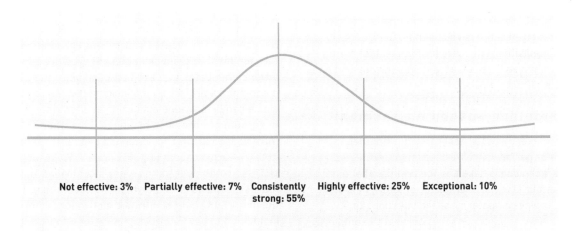

Not effective: 3%   Partially effective: 7%   Consistently strong: 55%   Highly effective: 25%   Exceptional: 10%

Figure 7.1 Example of bell curve distribution for forced ranking

The main benefits of an upward appraisal are that it can improve managerial effectiveness and leadership as well as give employees more voice and empowerment in the organization (Armstrong, 2006b). Indeed, counselling or expert coaching are often provided to managers as a result of the feedback (Armstrong and Taylor, 2017). On the other hand, managers might perceive upward appraisal as a threat to their own career.

360-degree Feedback

An inclusive approach to performance assessment which is becoming established in many organizations is the use of 360-degree feedback. 360-degree feedback is derived from a composite rating from peers, subordinates, supervisors and superiors, and occasionally customers and clients. Such feedback is usually provided using a questionnaire and can be done anonymously or not, depending on how open the organizational culture is. 360-degree feedback is particularly useful and pervasive in the modern world of work. This is because work is now less hierarchical, more team-based and more customer-focused, and, because of the flexibility in work arrangements, managers alone might not always be the best persons to observe and subsequently rate employees' performance (Adler et al., 2016). The main advantages of 360-degree feedback are that it enables employees to obtain a broader perspective of how they are perceived by others; it supports a climate of continuous improvement; and because the feedback is wide-ranging, it is considered to be more reliable (Armstrong, 2006b). On the other hand, some potential problems are that people do not always provide honest feedback; there is often inaction following the feedback provided; and it can be a bureaucratic process to implement given the variety of sources relied upon. Careful design, communication, adequate training and follow-up can minimize these disadvantages (Armstrong and Taylor, 2017).

Competency-based Assessment

A competency-based assessment is another popular performance measurement technique. This technique is based on the premise that past behaviour is the best predictor of future behaviour. This is why competency-based questions to interviews ▶Chapter 3◀ focus on what the employee has done in the past and attempt to capture the behaviours displayed while performing on the job. A competency-based approach to performance management aims to establish the skills and behaviours needed to be successful in employees' current roles and for future development in the organization (Martone, 2003). Behavioural expectations are usually set out by managers regarding different competencies, e.g. teamwork and communication skills, which are then converted into specific examples of desirable and undesirable behaviours that are used as a means to evaluate performance (Armstrong, 2006b). A particular strength of the competency-based approach is that it uses a 'how well it's done' measure in addition to the traditional 'what is achieved' measure, although defining all competencies in terms of specific behaviour is not always easy. A competency-based approach is believed to help organizations manage their talent pool and assist with succession planning (Martone, 2003).

THE LINK BETWEEN PERFORMANCE MANAGEMENT AND REWARD

The purpose of the aforementioned performance management schemes is to assess employees' performance against some criteria, and, if satisfied or exceeded, reward and recognition usually follow. An example of this in practice is performance-related pay (PRP), where an employee's pay is variable in respect to their performance. Such reward or payment could come in the form of, for example, bonuses or stock/share option plans. However, the real benefits of an effective performance management system lie in its potential to act as a reward mechanism in itself. Recognizing achievements, providing recognition through feedback, opportunities for growth and advancement and increased responsibility and meaningful work are all intrinsic motivating factors which can be provided as part of an effectively integrated performance management system (Armstrong, 2015). The continued popularity of the 'total reward' concept (e.g. Fuehrer, 1994), which seeks to combine traditional pay incentives with the intrinsic aspects of employment, is a testament to the important value of intrinsic motivating factors in addition to pay. See ▶Chapter 8◀ for a full discussion on rewards.

HRM IN THE NEWS

Underperformance in Ireland's public health service

The minister for health in Ireland, Simon Harris, has written to the Health Service Executive (HSE) director general to report back on the performance of senior managers in Ireland's public health service. This comes amidst an RTE television documentary which highlighted that there were thousands of patients on waiting lists and a record number left on trolleys in hospitals due to lack of capacity. The minister for health is attempting to 'shine a light on HSE management', and claims that if they do not 'measure up', he will demand legislation that will see them removed from their roles. Currently, HSE managers' performance is rated on the basis of four criteria: financial, access to services for patients, quality of service and safety of service. Despite the public criticism, some hospital chief executives have argued that the crisis is not the fault of management. They claim that management is working extremely hard to reach their targets but that the issues have been caused by a growing and ageing population. At the same time, critics have suggested that the reality is that there is little that can be done to discipline underperforming managers in the HSE, which has a history of job security. They note that when serious incidents have happened in the past, managers have not been dismissed. Although HSE managers get paid relatively well, it is only a fraction of what they could be earning in the private sector where the costs of failure are much less. The prevailing view is that there are no rewards (financial or otherwise) for good performance among HSE managers and this is perhaps expected in a system which values caution rather than innovation.

Questions

1. Do you think HSE managers should be held accountable for the enormous waiting lists?
2. Do you think the performance criteria that HSE managers are rated on is justifiable and achievable? Explain why.
3. What role can the external environment play in the health minister's decision to measure employees' performance and subsequently remove them from their roles?
4. What aspects of the performance management system would you focus on to motivate senior management in the HSE?

Sources

Raleigh, D. (2017) 'Hospital managers "not to blame" for trolley crisis', *Irish Times*, 5 January

Cullen, P. (2017) 'Why it is hard to punish poor-performing HSE managers', *Irish Times*, 11 February

Ryan, P. and Begley, I. (2017) 'Remove managers who fail to fix trolley crisis – Harris', *Irish Times*, 5 January

PERFORMANCE MANAGEMENT PITFALLS

As we have seen in this chapter, there are many benefits derived from performance management, including its potential to motivate employees, reward them fairly and transparently, and more objectively make decisions with regard to training, promotion and termination. In fact, the practice of performance management has been glorified in much of the literature, largely emanating from a positive stance advocated by strategic HRM scholars. However, performance management has also attracted a considerable amount of criticism as a practice and in particular in how it is implemented. The nature of performance management is contentious as it involves monitoring and controlling employees, and making decisions (often based on subjective information) that can profoundly impact their careers. A more radical and critical analysis of performance management questions management's preoccupation with controlling, directing and shaping employee behaviour (Taylor, 2013). The prevailing ideology is that managers are simply implementing regimes of surveillance to control employees and therefore employees and their representatives i.e. unions, should resist. The view is sometimes advanced that the performance expectations communicated by HR practices, including performance management, have the potential to induce pressure and strain on workers (Jensen and van de Voorde, 2016). In fact, Taylor and colleagues (2003) found that performance monitoring is directly related to employee stress, mental fatigue and physical tiredness. Although the aims of performance management are to create a high-performance culture conducive to individual and organizational growth, over time employees may feel that the constant targets and pressures are too much to cope with, thus leaving them fed up, stressed and even burned out ▶Chapter 12◀.

The feedback which is provided to employees can also cause more harm than good. While feedback is generally perceived as a constructive tool, some feedback will not always be accepted and embraced. The traditional focus of performance management on deficits or weaknesses can be frustrating, demoralizing and demeaning for employees, as it essentially implies asking them to be something that they are not (Kaiser and Overfield, 2011). Receiving destructive or negative feedback as part of the performance management process can have a debilitating effect on employees as it can threaten their self-esteem (Kluger and DeNisi, 1996).

Another potential problem with performance management is the central focus given to rating employees. Ratings can often be irrelevant and employees sometimes have little control over the performance targets, which can be highly discouraging (Dobbins et al., 1993). We also know that what is intended in the strategy designed by senior managers and the HR department is not always what is actually enacted by the line managers (Farndale and Kelliher, 2013). Sometimes, line managers have a significant degree of discretion in terms of whether employees are assessed in a lenient or strict manner (Luffarelli et al., 2016). Therefore, in the context of the performance appraisal in particular, we can see that many human errors, especially by line managers, can make performance management a subjective and contentious process. W. Edwards Deming, an influential management thinker, even went as far as to describe performance appraisal as one of the most 'deadly diseases' in modern management (Deming, 1986). He argued that it

can create fear, inhibit teamwork, build rivalry and politics, and curb long-term planning.

Grote (1996) pointed out numerous human biases among raters which can plague the performance appraisal interview. Specifically, he suggested that the most common appraisal errors are as follows: the contrast effect, the first impression error and the recency effect, the halo effect, the similar-to-me effect, central tendency bias, negative and positive skew, attribution bias, and stereotyping. We will now look at each of these.

The Contrast Effect

The contrast effect occurs when an appraiser makes exaggerations about an employee's performance based on the prior candidates assessed. For example, an appraiser might rate someone superbly on the basis that the previous candidate performed very poorly and vice versa. The contrast effect can be highly demotivating for employees because if they are constantly being compared to an unrealistic target, e.g. exceptionally performing, experienced peers, their true potential may never be realized (Battaglio, 2015).

The First Impression Error and the Recency Effect

The first impression error occurs when an initial judgement is made about someone (either positive or negative) and subsequent performance is ignored. For example, an employee could have demonstrated excellent performance at the beginning of the review period, and the appraiser will base their overall assessment on this first impression even though subsequent performance could have been below par. This is obviously problematic as the entire review period is not taken into account. The recency effect is the term given to the opposite problem: it occurs when the appraiser only remembers the end of the appraisal, thereby ignoring what happened at the beginning of the review period.

The Halo Effect

The halo effect occurs when a rater lets their overall opinion of an employee influence the rating of specific performance-related aspects of the employee's work (Thorndike, 1920). A supervisor who observes an employee arriving late to work on certain occasions or dressed inappropriately might form a negative perception of their performance even though being late and wearing unsuitable clothing might have had no objective bearing on their performance.

The Similar-to-me Effect

The similar-to-me effect occurs when an employee receives a favourable rating because they exhibit similar characteristics or qualities as the rater (Battaglio, 2015). For example, an employee might have an interest in football and this positively influences the appraiser's assessment of the person and their performance because they also like football.

The Central Tendency Bias

The central tendency bias occurs when an appraiser gives employees a score in the middle of the rating scale, thus rating all employees as average. In doing so, the rater avoids making tough decisions about poor performance or even good performance. Supervisors have a responsibility to give fair ratings so that those who are high achievers get rewarded and those who are underperforming get the support and training they need. However, evidence suggests that managers find it extremely difficult to criticize people and risk confrontational situations (Armstrong and Taylor, 2017), particularly when they have close relationships with the employees (Bol, 2011).

The Skewing Bias

The skewing bias (positive or negative skew) occurs when performance results are scored largely to the left or the right of the scale, i.e. the appraiser is overly positive or overly negative in their ratings, which distorts the accurate assessment of performance. Giving overly positive ratings, for example, often occurs because empathy and affection are involved and this obviously overrides objective performance assessment (Cardy and Dobbins, 1986).

Attributional Bias

Attributional bias is a cognitive bias that refers to the systematic errors people make when evaluating or trying to find reasons for their own and others' behaviours. An appraiser might assume that an employee's performance is below par because the person is 'lazy', thereby providing them with a low score. However, there may be other underlying reasons for poor performance, for example the employee is lacking the appropriate knowledge and skills to adequately perform the job or other situational factors.

Stereotyping

Stereotyping refers to our tendency to make generalizations about particular types of people, which distorts our overall perception. For example, on the basis of somebody's nationality, an appraiser might make distorted assumptions about the employee's performance.

OVERCOMING PERFORMANCE MANAGEMENT PITFALLS

The HR professional plays a pivotal role in ensuring that training is provided to line managers in recognizing the aforementioned biases and how to overcome them. For the line managers themselves, the problems associated with the performance appraisal interview emphasize the importance of managerial skill in building rapport and trust (Farndale and Kelliher, 2013) as well as conducting the appraisal in a consistent and fair manner (Den Hartog et al., 2004). Line managers also need to recognize that performance management is their responsibility and their implementation of it will ultimately affect its success or otherwise. Thus, recognizing performance management delivery in line managers' own performance plans is a worthwhile endeavour. To overcome some of the problems with the appraisal interview and the performance management process more generally, Armstrong (2006b) offers the following advice to ensure success:

- Ensure that the appraiser is adequately trained.
- Ensure that line managers and employees are involved in the design.
- Ensure performance management is an open system visibly owned by senior management.
- Ensure performance management has an ease of administration associated with it.
- Ensure there is always a follow-up on the appraisal actions.

Nevertheless, given the abundant problems associated with the performance appraisal, recent research has called for abandoning performance ratings and the appraisal method altogether (e.g. Adler et al., 2016). This is because performance reviews of this nature are believed to be backward-looking rather than looking to the future to establish development needs (Armstrong and Taylor, 2017).

Google is one such organization that has paved the way in abolishing the traditional performance review. Google, well known to be an innovative and creative enterprise, has adopted a system referred to as objectives and key results (OKRs), which is a technique for setting and communicating goals whereby multilevel and ongoing feedback is built in. The consequences of the review are decided upon not solely by management but by other members of the organization who act as a 'peer reviewer'. It is believed that this performance management system is a central ingredient in the company's success. However, Google's highly advanced recruitment and selection process and its continuous improvement culture underpin the success of this approach, and maintaining these features is likely a prerequisite for the system's sustainability. Such a performance management system may not translate well into some organizations, where tasks are more narrowly defined and the education/knowledge and skills of the workforce are lower.

An additional innovative approach to performance management which has surfaced in recent times is feedforward interviews. Feedforward interviews are a strengths-based approach to performance evaluation, whereby employees are invited to reveal the positive experiences they had at work, experiences they felt excited and energized about, before obtaining knowledge of the results of their actions (Van Woerkom and De Bruijn, 2016). Then the idea is to reflect on the conditions that made this experience possible within the individual and organization and compare this to current conditions and behaviour. An approach like this enables employees to identify their own strengths and areas for improvement without an externally imposed standard. Such an approach is also credited with recognizing the diversity that individual employees bring to their respective roles. Nevertheless, despite the many innovations in recent years and the host of biases with performance appraisal, like the traditional selection interview which is also contaminated with errors and biases ▶Chapter 3◀, it is hard to see the traditional performance appraisal interview disappearing anytime soon.

SPOTLIGHT ON SKILLS

John Redmond is an employee at a clothing store. He has been working there for the past two years and considers most of the employees there not only as colleagues but also as good friends. Recently, John received a promotion to sales manager based on his consistent demonstration of excellent customer service skills, his ability to exceed sales targets and his long-term employment in and commitment to the organization. As part of the sales manager role, John has been informed that he is required to administer a performance appraisal for all sales staff in the coming weeks, which will be based on established store performance criteria including sales targets, customer service and punctuality. On the basis of these criteria, John is expected to make decisions about employees' bonuses, training and possible disciplinary action. To make matters more complicated for John, many employees have failed to achieve their sales targets and punctuality standards leave a lot to be desired. John is anxious about conducting the performance appraisals as he has not received any formal training in how to conduct them, and he worries about potential confrontational situations emerging between himself and co-workers.

❶ Why do you think John is so nervous about conducting the appraisals?

❷ As the HR manager for the company, what could you do when designing the performance management system to avoid some of the problems associated with conducting the performance appraisal interview?

To help you consider the issues above, visit **www.macmillanihe.com/carbery-cross-hrm-2e** and watch the video of John Counihan from Musgrave Retail Partners Ireland talking about performance appraisals.

HRM IN THE GLOBAL BUSINESS ENVIRONMENT

Performance management and national culture

Multinational corporations (MNCs) face a daunting task in managing the performance of employees across national boundaries. Dowling and colleagues (2008) point out that cultural adjustment, the level of headquarter support received, the environment and the type of assignment are all important factors which influence an expatriate's performance, and these should therefore be recognized when undergoing performance management. The transportation of HR practices from one country to another is not always possible due to cultural and institutional barriers. In addition, there may be variations between countries, e.g. eastern versus western, with respect to the attributions employees make about their performance. A study by Chiang and Birtch (2007) found that Western countries (UK, Canada and Finland) report personal factors (individual effort/achievement/ability) to be

the most important predictors of performance. However, in Eastern countries (Hong Kong, S.A.R., China), external factors (luck/cooperation/group effort) in addition to internal factors were considered to be the important drivers of performance. In countries with collectivist values such as in Africa and China, managing performance may also be drastically different as firing employees on the basis of underperformance, for example, is much less common. Such findings demonstrate the salience of national culture in the workplace (Hofestede et al., 2010) as it can influence how employees think and behave with respect to performance and its measurement at work. Importantly, it becomes clear that 'managing performance in the multinational context necessitates examining differences in employees' cognitive processes' (Chiang and Birtch, 2007: 233) as only then can organizations understand how employees will regulate their behaviour during the performance management process and motivate them accordingly.

HOW TO MANAGE UNDERPERFORMANCE

Managing performance is critical for organizations as, without addressing performance issues, the good people will leave (Sujansky, 2007) and the poor performers will continue to undermine the success of the entire organization. Research has revealed that high-performing individuals generally outperform average performers by 100–200% (Spencer, 2001). Hunter and colleagues (2001) found that the top 1% of workers were anywhere from 50% to 127% more productive than average workers, and this was particularly the case for more complex jobs. The impact of a single underperformer is devastating for individual productivity, team productivity and line manager productivity. Indeed, team productivity could suffer directly by not maximizing the purported synergy gains associated with teamwork and also indirectly through other members reducing their contributions due to feelings of inequity (Armstrong and Baron, 2005). Line manager productivity can also deteriorate as they now have to spend substantially more time dealing with performance problems. A key question

facing line managers and HR managers is how to effectively manage underperformance.

Charles Handy famously said that managing underperformance should be about 'applauding success and forgiving failure' (Handy, 1989). We might be quick to suggest that an employee is 'lazy', for example. However, performance problems sometimes have little to do with motivation or ability (Gruman and Saks, 2011). Therefore, it is imperative from a strategic, moral and legal perspective to investigate the performance issue thoroughly in order to get to its 'root cause' and devise an appropriate solution. Many options are available to rectify performance problems before entering the formal disciplinary process. Indeed, disciplinary procedures ▶Chapter 5◀ should be considered as an option of last resort. Armstrong (2009) advances five basic steps to manage underperformance: identify and agree the problem; establish the reason(s) for the shortfall; decide and agree on the action required; resource the action; and monitor and provide feedback. In managing underperformance, identifying and correctly diagnosing the problem is imperative. This can be done more objectively by evaluating targets or by observing, researching and assessing performance on a range of criteria. Then, line managers can more accurately address the underperformance issue through appropriate strategies. These might include goal setting, coaching, training, redesigning the role and job rotation, to name but a few.

Most performance management models generally involve setting goals, monitoring performance, performance appraisal and feedback, and ultimately improved performance (Gruman and Saks, 2011). Identifying performance problems early involves asking questions about how SMART (specific, measurable, attainable, realistic and timed) the goals were; whether the objectives gained the commitment of the employee; whether specific measures that would facilitate the identification of performance problems were included; and whether managers frequently engaged with employees to review progress and provide feedback. Although goals which are set as part of the performance management process often use the SMART framework, research has revealed that in Microsoft, a company renowned for its goal-setting activities, less than 40% of the goals were actually measurable (Shaw, 2004). Organizations often think they have clear and measurable goals but in reality tend to set goals which are vague and constructed in a way which makes their measurement either difficult or impossible. In providing feedback on performance, it is important for managers to ensure that goals are clear in the first instance and that they focus their feedback specifically on the gap between the actual and desired performance on each goal (Brown et al., 2016). Setting genuinely SMART goals and revisiting them where necessary is a critical step in ensuring that performance problems are addressed from the outset.

One strategy managers can adopt to address underperformance issues is coaching. As a manager, a central prerogative is to act as a coach, responsible for supporting other people and attempting to develop their careers ▶Chapter 10◀. For underperforming employees, a coach can assist and provide valuable feedback to raise performance. Coaching is also useful for instilling confidence or self-efficacy in employees which can ultimately help them improve (Gruman and Saks, 2011). One coaching model that is widely used to address underperformance issues is the GROW model. The GROW model was developed in the

1980s by Graham Alexander, Alex Fine and Sir John Whitmore. It involves setting a *goal* (G), assessing the current situation or *reality* (R), assessing the available *options* (O) and deciding what you *will* do (W). The key point about the GROW model is that it does not assume that the coach is necessarily an expert in the client's, i.e. underperformer's, situation. It is advised that the coach take on the role of a facilitator, whereby they help the employee choose the best solution for themselves. Indeed, it is more powerful for people to draw conclusions for themselves rather than having them thrust upon them. Coaches can have a significant role to play at the *will* stage of the GROW model by acting as a reality check on the employee's thinking by asking very specific questions about planned actions to address underperformance.

Another widely adopted strategy for addressing underperformance issues among employees is to provide training and development ▶Chapter 9◀. Underperformance can often be caused by a skills or abilities deficit and, in this case, providing training and development may be a worthwhile endeavour. Such training can also be useful for increasing employees' self-efficacy as well as enabling them to more effectively perform their tasks and deal with their job demands (Gruman and Saks, 2011). When organizations invest in their employees, employees may also feel supported and reciprocate with more positive attitudes and behaviours as well as higher performance (Blau, 1964).

A further strategy that can be used to rectify underperformance issues is to redesign the employee's role or assign them to a new one. Such a strategy may be particularly useful, for example, when the underperformer in question is highly qualified and possesses specialized knowledge that the organization does not wish to lose. In this regard, job redesign or relocation recognizes that certain employees may add value in different aspects or functions of the organization, and putting them in a role which capitalizes on their strengths may be more sensible than losing the employee altogether (van Woerkom and De Bruijn, 2016). This also recognizes the fact that in the modern world of work, employees are constantly 'job crafting' or redesigning their role in a way which not only increases their own engagement but also adds value for the organization (Gruman and Saks, 2011).

When managing underperformance, HR departments have a particularly important role to play. Firstly, they have a responsibility to provide support and guidance to line managers who are involved with identifying and resolving underperformance issues (Farndale and Kelliher, 2013). For example, they can advise managers on which strategies might be useful in attempting to improve employee performance and, should performance not improve, provide advice on alternative courses of action. Secondly, before and during the formal process of a disciplinary interview ▶Chapter 5◀, HR is likely to be directly involved and assisting with legal advice where relevant in order to avoid a potential lawsuit. Thirdly, HR has a role to play in terms of documenting all stages of the process in an independent manner. This may be useful in the context of disagreements or ambiguities which could emanate from the employee's or manager's perspective.

BUILDING YOUR SKILLS

Consider that you are an HR manager working for a large financial services organization. Tom Bradley, a local full-time sales employee, has been working at the organization for the past eight months. He is responsible for selling all property commodities including mortgages, car loans and business loans. At the beginning of the job, Tom was reaching all his sales targets. However, over the past four months, Tom has not achieved his targets and does not demonstrate the same enthusiasm in his role now as he did eight months ago. Following best practice guidelines, what advice would you give to Tom's line manager to address his underperformance?

HRM IN PRACTICE

Performance management at Harvesting Corporation

Getty Images/_ultraforma_Mark Lakomcsik

Harvesting Corporation is a large (fictitious) bank located in London, UK. The organization employs 350 employees at its London office. The bank provides corporate and institutional banking, treasury and security services to its clients around the world.

The bank operates a performance management or appraisal system which covers all financial staff in the company. Every year, an annual performance appraisal interview is conducted whereby line managers, using a rating scale, are required to judge the performance of their subordinates. Developed by a group of HR consultants when the business initially began trading in 2013, the performance management system uses a points scale with the following ratings: (a) = excellent, (b) = good, (c) = satisfactory and (d) = unsatisfactory. The following criteria form the basis upon which performance evaluations are to be made: sales, introduction of new business, client satisfaction, cross-referral of business within the firm, and financial miscalculation errors/service complaints. Employees' monetary rewards are decided based on the ratings that they receive.

Those employees who receive an (a) receive a financial bonus of 15% of their annual salary. Those who receive a (b) receive a financial bonus of 10% of their annual salary. Those who receive a (c) receive a financial bonus of 5% of their annual salary. In addition, these employees are also called into a performance meeting attended by the line manager and the HR manager for the purpose of discussing the employee's performance and developing an improvement plan to accelerate performance. Those who receive a (d) have their contract automatically terminated by the bank. Therefore, in effect, the so-called 'D players' are unwanted in Harvesting Corporation. It was envisaged by the team of consultants charged with implementing this performance management system that it would promote a performance culture, recognize the achievements of those who excel in their jobs, offer developmental opportunities for average performers and weed out underperformers.

Despite the merits of the performance management system at Harvesting Corporation, many employees have become disillusioned with it. Many believe that the performance targets are unrealistic, out of their control and do not take into account the key performance criteria set by the bank. Getting ranked into the category (a) and (b) seems extremely difficult. Although a performance culture prevails, many employees feel that the existing system is subjective, unfair and not very transparent. Many employees believe that the performance management system promotes aggressive internal competition and promotes risks which are detrimental to the long-term viability of the business deals. Many personnel have complained that the division into categories (a), (b), (c) and (d) is conducted in an arbitrary manner, and the relationship employees have with their line managers seems to be of greater importance when it comes to bonus decisions. The constant threat of job losses at the end of year also creates a culture of fear and stress for workers.

Many of these problems have led to a major turnover crisis for the bank, a situation likely exacerbated by terminating the category (d) employees and because of the stress and fear induced by the forced ranking system. Turnover is a costly outcome for Harvesting Corporation because many employees are joining rival banks in the city who can capitalize on their developed expertise. For line managers who are charged with conducting the performance appraisal, many are reluctant to provide honest feedback and make the tough decisions because of the consequences involved.

Since the bank has substantially grown since its inception in 2013, and because of the problems being experienced, the senior management team recognize that tackling the problems with the performance management system is a major priority.

What would you do?

1. In your capacity as HR manager, you have been asked by the senior management team to identify the key problems with the existing performance management system in the bank.
2. Advise on the best approach to rejuvenate it in order to ensure that motivation is enhanced and staff turnover minimized.

iStock.com/alice-photo

SUMMARY

This chapter has highlighted the role of performance management in fostering higher levels of employee performance and engagement. The problems of implementing performance management continue to haunt managers, and issues associated with feedback and biases ensure that well-established theoretical models of performance management rarely translate smoothly into practice. There is a wide range of performance assessment techniques adopted by organizations and each have their advantages and disadvantages. The process through which performance is rated usually takes the form of an appraisal interview. While useful if carried out with skill, fairness and transparency by line managers, it is distorted with countless biases which call into question its validity in driving performance. To make matters more complex, linking performance management with other HR practices is a prerequisite for success. Moreover, the international nature of business ensures that the transportation of HR practices across countries will not always be successful because of unique cultural and institutional contexts. Nevertheless, managing performance and rectifying underperformance issues is and will remain an important activity of HR professionals and line managers in the pursuit of sustainable competitive advantage. After all, if we do not have goal posts, how will we know who won.

CHAPTER REVIEW QUESTIONS

1. What are the main performance management schemes adopted in organizations? Discuss the benefits and drawbacks of each.
2. Your company director is seeking to enhance the engagement of the workforce. She wants your advice as HR manager on which aspects of the performance management system will achieve this aim and how. What would you recommend?
3. Identify and discuss the key reasons why performance management can fail to deliver for both individuals and organizations.
4. The annual performance appraisal interview is viewed negatively in your organization and perceived by many workers to be subjective and unfair. In your capacity as HR manager for the organization, what actions would you recommend for redesigning the performance management system?
5. You are the HR manager in a large fitness organization. An employee in the sales team has failed to achieve their performance targets for the third month in a row. What advice would you give to the line manager to deal with this issue?
6. You have been asked to address your organization's executive board about the possibility of introducing a new performance management system. Decide what your performance management system would include and outline the key points you would make in support of its introduction.

FURTHER READING

Aguinis, H. (2013) *Performance Management*, 3rd edn, Upper Saddle River, NJ: Pearson/Prentice Hall.

Aguinis, H., Joo, H. and Gottfredson, R.K. (2011) 'Why we hate performance management – and why we should love it', *Business Horizons*, 54(6), 503–7.

Armstrong, M. (2017) *Armstrong's Handbook of Performance Management: An Evidence-based Guide to Delivering High Performance*, London: Kogan Page.

Armstrong, M. (2017) *Armstrong on Reinventing Performance Management*, London: Kogan Page.

Buckingham, M. and Goodall, A. (2015) 'Reinventing performance management', *Harvard Business Review*, 93(4), 1–10.

Culbert, S.A. and Rout, L. (2010) *Get Rid of the Performance Review: How Companies Can Stop Intimidating, Start Managing – and Focus on What Really Matters*, New York: Business Plus.

Posthuma, R.A. and Campion, M.A. (2008) 'Twenty best practices for just employee performance reviews', *Compensation & Benefits Review*, 40(1), 47–55.

Shields, J. (2016) *Managing Employee Performance and Reward: Concepts, Practices, Strategies*, 2nd edn, Cambridge: Cambridge University Press.

USEFUL WEBSITES

www.mckinsey.com

This is the website of global consulting firm McKinsey & Company which offers its services to businesses, governments and non-profit organizations around the world. On its website, the company shares some of its cutting-edge practical articles which contain advice from many global leaders and HR directors about effective performance management.

dupress.deloitte.com

This website is called Deloitte University Press and provides insights, analysis and advice for businesses on many HR topics including performance management.

www.ahri.com.au/assist/performance-management

This is the website of the Australian HR Institute (AHRI) which is the national association representing HR and people management professionals in Australia. This website contains many practical, easy-to-read and fun articles on performance management.

For extra resources, including videos, multiple choice questions and useful weblinks, go to: www.macmillanihe.com/carbery-cross-hrm-2e.

Image Source/Alexander Porter C

8: Managing Rewards

Maureen Maloney and
Alma McCarthy

LEARNING OUTCOMES

By the end of this chapter you will be able to:

- Outline the key aims and objectives of an organization's reward package
- Distinguish between the different elements of the reward package, that is, direct and performance-related pay, benefits, and nonfinancial rewards
- Explain the factors influencing an organization's pay and reward decisions and understand the advantages and disadvantages of different types of pay and reward
- List and explain the factors that affect how an organization determines the relative value of jobs
- Outline the different approaches to job evaluation
- Describe the options available to employers who implement performance-based reward schemes and their impact on employee motivation

THIS CHAPTER DISCUSSES:

Introduction (140)

Reward System Objectives (140)

The Reward Package (140)

Pay Secrecy (147)

Gender and Ethnicity Pay Gaps (148)

Determining the Relative Value of Jobs (148)

Internal Alignment (148)

Environmental Factors (152)

External Comparisons (154)

Pay as a Motivator (156)

INTRODUCTION

A critical part of the employment relationship involves the management of rewards. Rewards are used to attract the quality of applicants required to drive organizational performance and retain those employees who contribute to that objective. Reward management is an important aspect of HRM ▸Chapter 8◂. An organization's business strategy and culture influence reward management, and the reward package impacts employee attraction, motivation and retention, which in turn is linked to employee and organizational outcomes, including performance. It is also used to motivate employees to behave in ways that promote organizational strategy. Historically, the concept of a fair day's work for a fair day's pay was a guiding principle on how employees were rewarded for the efforts they expended while at work. Although reward management is now significantly more strategic and complex, the fairness of reward policies and practices based on internal and external comparisons remains important.

We begin by explaining the objectives of a reward system and some of the challenges that this presents to employers. Next, we explore the different options and choices for a reward package, examining their advantages and disadvantages. We then discuss the methods and information sources used by employers to determine the relative worth of jobs in their organization. Finally, the role of pay as a motivator is discussed.

REWARD SYSTEM OBJECTIVES

The **reward system** refers to the combination of financial and nonfinancial elements used by an organization to compensate employees for their time, effort and commitment at work. The reward system is shaped by the organization's philosophy, strategy, competition, ability to pay and legal responsibilities.

The objectives of the reward system are to:

- support the organization by designing policies aligned with organizational strategies and goals
- attract and retain employees who add value to the organization by offering an attractive reward package

- motivate employees to perform effectively to achieve valued organizational outcomes by applying policies in a fair and consistent way
- integrate with other HR policies, including career development and work–life balance
- comply with legislation.

Organizations are increasingly focused on rewarding the jobs and employees who add the most value. This places considerable pressure on HR departments to align pay policies to the behaviours required to execute organizational strategy. However, motivating and retaining employees requires that they understand that these pay policies are applied fairly and consistently. Managers may find themselves in the uncomfortable position of justifying decisions that pay one employee more than another. HR departments must therefore support managers in making reasoned decisions regarding payment based on employee contribution.

Because potential and current employees can compare the pay they receive with pay offered by other similar organizations, competition impacts on the financial and nonfinancial elements with which an employer chooses to reward employees. However, reward management is an active process. Savvy employers manipulate the elements of their reward system to attract, motivate and retain the best possible employees. Reward management systems and the choices companies make about how they reward their employees are impacted by a range of subjective values and decisions. For example, some companies decide to be a salary leader in their sector and that influences the reward management system decisions they make.

Reward management does not operate in isolation. Strategic organizations connect it with other HR policies, including workforce planning ▸Chapter 2◂, recruitment and selection ▸Chapter 3◂, training ▸Chapter 9◂, performance management ▸Chapter 7◂, career development ▸Chapter 10◂ and work–life balance ▸Chapter 12◂. It is the effective combination of reward and other HR policies that contributes to an organization's strategic advantage.

> **Reward system** – the combination of financial and nonfinancial elements used by an organization to compensate employees for their time, effort and commitment at work
>
> **Reward package** – the financial and nonfinancial elements offered to an employee in return for labour

THE REWARD PACKAGE

The **reward package** refers to the specific financial and nonfinancial elements which are offered to an employee in return for labour. There are many options available to organizations when rewarding employees for their performance in the workplace. However, because labour costs are a significant part of the total costs for most organizations, reward packages are coming under greater scrutiny to ensure that they match employee expectations while also suiting the changing needs of the business.

Figure 8.1 presents the components and elements of a reward package. The organization will decide on the most appropriate elements in order to attract, retain and motivate the quality of employees they require. The reward packages offered may also vary within the same organization, recognizing that certain categories of workers are motivated by different reward packages. For example, the sales representatives for manufacturing companies may be paid differently from the people who are producing the goods. Each of the components and elements of the reward package will now be discussed.

Direct Pay

The largest component of the reward package is **direct pay**. The main element of direct pay, and the most costly part for the employer, is **base pay**, defined as the hourly, weekly or monthly amount paid to an employee if they conform to the terms of their contract. Later, on page 148, we discuss how jobs are valued to determine their worth. Employees paid by the hour often

> **Direct pay** – the financial element of the reward package received by the employee in the form of cash, cheque or direct deposit
>
> **Base pay** – hourly, weekly or monthly amount paid to an employee if they conform to the terms of their contract
>
> **Performance-related pay (PRP)** – a form of direct pay linked to the performance of an individual, team or all employees when predefined objectives are achieved

receive overtime if they work more than the number of hours legally designated as full time. Premium pay may also be added to base pay. For example, many manufacturing organizations that operate a 24/7 schedule pay a shift premium for weekends, evenings and night shifts to recognize the hardship caused by working antisocial hours.

Performance-related pay (PRP) is another component of direct pay. It is linked to the performance of an individual, team or employees throughout the organization and paid when predefined objectives are achieved (Nyberg et al., 2016). In some cases, PRP is consolidated into base pay, leading to a permanent increase of an employee's salary when the objectives are met. More often though, PRP is variable, meaning that the payment is additional to base pay and received if, and only if, the employee achieves the goals and objectives established for each particular pay period. While base pay is financial recognition for past achievements, education, years of service and competence, PRP is aimed at motivating future actions. It is an incentive to employees to behave in ways that will promote organizational goals.

A key objective of PRP is to allow the reward package to be responsive to the needs of the organization and its workforce. PRP is frequently used to support a high performance work system ▶Chapter 1◀, and its popularity

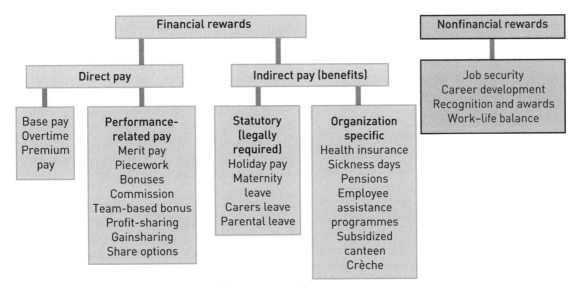

Figure 8.1 Components and elements of the reward package

can be attributed to a belief that it can focus attention on the behaviours valued by the organization and recognize high performance through pay (Armstrong, 2015). According to Satterfield (2011: 43), an incentive plan that is properly designed and communicated is 'one of the best tools we have for linking pay and performance'. On the other hand, there is considerable debate about the ability of PRP to achieve these objectives in practice. Pink (2012: 77), for example, suggests that while PRP may work well for routine tasks, it is 'far less effective for complex, creative, conceptual endeavors'. This suggests that PRP works better for some jobs than others. Kohn (1993) goes much further, suggesting that PRP works like a bribe. It may achieve results, but often there are unintended consequences that undermine organizational values and relationships. Therefore, Kohn (1993) suggests that PRP should rarely, if ever, form part of a reward package. We know that

CONSIDER THIS

Before the global financial crisis, banks offered a modest basic salary with a large percentage bonus based on the individual's contribution to revenue. One of the main ways of contributing to revenue was through granting personal and commercial loans. Banks argue that a bonus is one of the main ways to attract and retain staff, but can it lead to unintended consequences?

PRP is commonly used in practice. However, its effectiveness is constantly debated.

Forms of Performance-related Pay

Merit Pay

Merit pay rewards higher performing employees with additional pay and is normally linked to a performance appraisal conducted by a supervisor or line manager. When this term 'merit pay' is used, it generally means that the pay increase is consolidated into base pay, meaning that it is permanent addition to the employee's pay. The criterion used for merit pay varies. In some organizations, the payment is related to the achievement of goals and objectives established at the beginning of the appraisal period. Desired behaviours such as cooperation and leadership may also be included. Merit pay is considered to be fair if the performance appraisal system is fair. A survey by Eurofound (2016) reported that pay related to a performance appraisal is the most common type of performance-related pay, practised by 43% of the companies surveyed that operate in the EU. In a global survey of companies operating in 29 countries, Willis Towers Watson (2016) reported that less than half of the employers surveyed believed that increases to base pay were driving improvements to individual performance. Further, less than half of their employees believed that high performance was rewarded at their organization. This highlights the difficulty of linking pay with performance appraisal.

HRM IN THE GLOBAL BUSINESS ENVIRONMENT

Multinational corporations and reward management

Multinational corporations (MNCs) are generally large organizations that offer generous reward packages. National trends in reward management often begin with changes to MNCs' practices. Rock and Jones (2015a) discussed the reasons why some MNCs, including Accenture, Microsoft and Deloitte, are abandoning the annual performance evaluation linked to a merit increase. First, the changing nature of work means that 12 months is not always the right timespan for goal setting. Secondly, competition

among workers for top ratings negatively impacts on the collaboration needed between team members. Thirdly, attracting and retaining employees, particularly millennials, requires more frequent engagement with their manager. Finally, the administrative burden and costs of the performance evaluation system are not offset by performance improvements. Rock and Jones (2015b: 4) suggest that PRP remains but 'companies are encouraging managers to get to know their people better through having better quality conversations about performance, then to differentiate compensation based on their own judgement'.

Piecework

Piecework is a payment given for each unit of production or 'piece' produced. It is based on a standard developed to reflect the units of output a worker can complete per period of time. While pay increases with output, most piecework schemes guarantee a base pay, particularly in jurisdictions where there is minimum wage legislation. There are special allowances for downtime due to equipment maintenance or failure. Piecework schemes are appropriate to those organizations where:

* work is repetitive and unskilled
* workers can influence the pace of production without jeopardizing quality standards
* they are easy to operate and monitor.

Commission

Commission is usually paid to sales representatives or the sales staff in retail stores. Payments are made as a percentage of sales and are generally paid in addition to the base wage. The percentage may vary with volume, rewarding top performers at a higher rate when sales increase beyond an agreed threshold. Commission attracts people who are mainly motivated by financial rewards and works best for employees who can work with minimal supervision.

Bonuses

Bonuses can be paid to individuals, teams or divisions in return for the achievement of predetermined performance targets. Bonus schemes can be designed for any classification of employees. In manufacturing settings, workers are often paid for increased productivity or quality improvements, while executive directors receive bonuses for improved profits. Usually, bonuses are a form of variable pay and must be re-earned each year. It is challenging to develop bonus schemes that are affordable, understandable and motivational, promoting behaviours that lead to organizational competitive advantage.

Team-based Pay

Team-based pay, usually in the form of a bonus, is a payment given to members of a formally established team that is linked to their performance. For example, a research and development team may receive a bonus when a new product completes the regulatory process. The intention is to motivate members to cooperate to enhance team performance. Team-based pay is suited to many organizations, provided that the team is clearly defined, the goals are explicitly established and performance can be measured.

Profit-sharing Schemes

Profit-sharing schemes are based on organizational performance and enable employees to share in the prosperity and success of the business (Joo Hun et al., 2015). A proportion of the company's profits are paid to staff across the organization in the form of a bonus payment. This is a variable form of PRP paid out when profits exceed a threshold. In some cases, profit-sharing takes the form of shares rather than cash, where employees can buy shares in the company at preferential rates. Employees then become shareholders in their own company or a parent company. A proportion of the company's profits in any one year can be used by employees to increase their shareholding.

Employee Share Ownership Plans

Employee share ownership plans (ESOPs) are legally established and used by companies to distribute shares to employees. The idea behind this is simple. If employees are shareholders, their behaviour will be aligned to shareholders' interests, improving business profitability. ESOPs are a long-term incentive because employees cannot gain the full benefits from their investment for a number of years.

ESOPs are governed by national legislation, so there are large variations in the way they operate in different countries. Also, company practices differ. While some companies distribute shares relatively evenly among employees, others award a disproportionate number to top executives.

The European Federation of Employee Share Ownership is an international not-for-profit organization with a mission to promote employee share ownership in Europe. It believes that share ownership combined with participative management practices can lead to organizational competitive advantage. Its 2016 annual survey found that 94% of large European companies had employee ownership plans and 53% of the plans were broad based including all employees (European Federation of Employee Share Ownership, 2017).

Gainsharing Schemes

Gainsharing schemes operate where companies attempt to accrue savings by changing work practices. They usually involve all employees at a single location and work best under collaborative working conditions. It is a 'bottom-up' initiative – to be effective, there must be a participation structure to generate ideas and to determine the 'best' ideas to implement.

Typically, a small number of measures are chosen because they are important to the business. Operational measures (productivity, rejects, on-time shipment, safety) are preferred to financial measures (profit, revenue, earnings per share) because employees have greater influence. Any improvements from a baseline operational measure, calculated using a pre-agreed formula, are a 'gain' that is 'shared' between employees and the organization. For example, an improvement based on a reduction in rejects over a one-year period, resulting in savings for the company, may go into a pool that is split evenly between employees (50%) and the organization (50%). Each employee typically receives an equal share, regardless of their position. The organization's share is often reinvested to improve organizational competitiveness.

Indirect Pay (Benefits)

Benefits are sometimes called **indirect pay** because they are received by employees in forms other than cash, for example health insurance, childcare, provision of a company car. They have a financial value but this is not always transparent to employees, who use them when and if they are needed. Small companies may not provide any benefits beyond those that are statutory or required by law. For large companies, however, benefits can comprise a significant percentage of total labour costs and may include benefits that are specific to the organization. Communicated properly, information about benefits sends a powerful message about the organization's concern for the present and future security of their employees and can be used to develop a reputation as an 'employer of choice'.

> **Indirect pay or benefits** – these have a financial value but are rewarded to employees in forms other than cash

Statutory Benefits

In many countries, both employees and employers pay into a social insurance fund. For employees, these contributions are deducted each pay period. These funds are used to provide statutory benefits to people in employment, including, for example, maternity leave. Employers 'hold' the job of employees availing themselves of these benefits who are entitled to a social welfare payment. In the case of injury or layoffs, people who paid social insurance are entitled to disability or redundancy benefits. By law, in some countries, employers are also required to pay employees for a minimum number of holidays. Employers may 'top up' statutory entitlements. They may increase the number of paid holidays or pay additional salaries to women on maternity leave.

Table 8.1 demonstrates the great differences between countries in relation to statutory benefits. Sweden and the USA are both wealthy countries; however, Sweden has very generous statutory benefits while the USA is much less generous.

Organization-specific Benefits

The list of organization-specific benefits is long and growing. Not only is there an array of choices, the way in which benefits are managed differs significantly between organizations. For example, some organizations choose a small number of benefits and fully pay for them. Other employers offer flexible benefit plans: employees are allowed to divide an amount of money, usually a percentage of their salary, on a limited menu of benefits. While providing choice to employees, flexible benefit plans also help employers to limit their contribution to benefits with escalating costs, such as healthcare. Other benefits are not funded by employers at all. For example, an HR department may negotiate discounts for services like gym memberships and arrange for payments to be made by payroll deduction.

Some of the most popular additional organization-specific benefits are shown in Figure 8.1 on page 141. Private health insurance is a common benefit. Some organizations negotiate corporate rates and then fully or partially pay for this benefit. Sometimes, the insurance is extended to the employee's family. Another popular benefit is

Statutory benefit	Australia	Colombia	India	South Africa	Sweden	USA
Maternity leave	12 months unpaid	2 weeks before and 12 weeks after birth at full salary	12 weeks at full salary	4 months unpaid	At least 7 weeks before and 7 weeks after birth at 80% of salary	Up to 12 weeks unpaid
Paternity leave	Same as mother if father is primary carer	8 working days paid	Not available	3 days paid	10 working days at 80% of salary	Up to 12 weeks unpaid
Parental leave	12 months split between parents unpaid	Not available	Not available	Not available	480 days per child split between parents at 80% of salary	Not available
Holiday entitlements	4 weeks + 8 public holidays paid	15 days + 18 public holidays; pay is not mandatory	12–21 days per year (local laws apply) + 11 public holidays paid	21 days + 12 public holidays paid	25 days + 12 public holidays paid	No legal requirements for holidays or public holidays

Table 8.1 Statutory entitlements in various countries
Sources: data from Skene et al., 2017; Santos Angarita, 2017; Nooreyezdan et al., 2017; Neiuwoudt et al., 2017; Nordlof and Berterud, 2017; Susser et al., 2017.

sickness days. In some organizations, the number of paid sick days increases with the years of service.

The legal requirements governing employer contributions to occupational pensions vary across the world. Some employers contribute more than is required by law. A popular method to promote pension savings is for employers to contribute to their employees' pension funds on a matching basis. For example, if the employee pays up to 5% of their income, their employer will match percentage for percentage up to 5%.

Stressful life circumstances can negatively impact on work performance. An employee assistance programme (EAP) is an important benefit that can be provided to an organization's workers who are experiencing problems in their professional and personal life. The company pays for EAP services, provided in confidence by experts outside the organization. They are most commonly used for depression, stress, anxiety, conflict in the workplace, substance abuse (alcohol or drugs), family and marital problems, and grief and loss.

Subsidized canteens are another important benefit to employees, particularly in manufacturing settings located far from stores and restaurants. Finally, subsidized, on-site crèche facilities are provided by some large employers to help employees manage childcare.

Component	Advantages	Disadvantages
Basic salary/pay	Straightforward to administer	Viewed as an entitlement
	Less complex in terms of fairness and equity across employees	Limited in terms of motivating employees to higher levels of performance
	Costs are known, assisting budgeting	
Individual PRP	Focuses employee attention on the performance objectives in the organization's competitive environment	Difficult to determine appropriate measures
		Costs may be higher than predicted
	Incentivizes those employees motivated by money	Perceived as unfair if inconsistently applied
		Incentivizing individual behaviour can detract from teamwork and corporate citizenship
Team-based PRP	Promotes cooperation and flexibility within teams	Difficult to determine appropriate measures
	Provides an incentive for a collective improvement in performance	Risk of 'free-riders' who do little but earn the same as other team members
	Functions as an effective lever for cultural change, promoting, for example, quality and customer focus	Disliked by some employees who prefer individual incentives
Profit-sharing, share options, ESOPs and gainsharing	Promotes corporate citizenship and cooperation at all levels, while also focusing attention on organization-wide performance measures	Line of sight difficult for profit- and share-based schemes, especially in large companies
	Forms part of a wider employee participation programme, encouraging more open and trusting relations with management and promoting better communication throughout the organization	In unfavourable economic circumstances, some companies may not be able to contribute in spite of employee efforts
		Not suitable for companies in a start-up phase, when companies tend not to make profit or have gains to share
		Share-based schemes are subject to large variations in price, so affecting their value
Benefits	Demonstrates employer concern for employee welfare	Additional expense to employers that may not be appreciated or understood by employees
	Particularly helpful to employees during periods of stress and illness	Labour intensive for HR departments to explain and administrate
	Differentiates an employer's reward package from others	

Table 8.2 Advantages and disadvantages of different reward components

Nonfinancial Rewards

Some organizations take a 'total rewards' perspective. This means that their reward system includes **nonfinancial rewards** in addition to direct and indirect pay. These organizations attempt to package all the financial and nonfinancial elements of the employment relationship that are perceived to have value to employees.

The most common choices are shown in Figure 8.1 on page 141. In an increasingly volatile global market, job security is especially prized by some employees. When a job is made 'permanent', an employer recognizes the long-term potential contribution of the employee. It makes it much easier for employees to start families, buy houses and plan for their future in an orderly way.

Career development ▶Chapter 10◀ is another important policy that is added to the reward package. Employees concerned with their employability are always looking for their next job either within or outside their current employment. Career development discussions are normally linked to performance appraisals ▶Chapter 7◀. By planning training or arranging different types of work experience within their current role, employees' future job prospects and earning power are improved.

Work–life balance policies are particularly valued during parts of employees' lives when they face intense family responsibilities. They complement statutory benefits, allowing employees to remain working when maternity or carers leave entitlements end. A number of different policies fall into this category, including flexible working hours and e-working from home. Employees facilitated with these policies often remain loyal and committed to their organization.

Finally, recognition policies and practices are a type of reward that can be formal or informal. Both can be promoted through manager training. Informal recognition involves a word of thanks or acknowledgement for work well done. It can be the cheapest and most effective form of reward. Carefully used, it can steer employee behaviour towards achieving organizational goals. Formal recognition programmes vary from individual awards for outstanding behaviour to division events celebrating an important achievement.

> **Nonfinancial rewards –** a wide array of HR policies and practices designed to support employees both in their lives and in their careers

PAY SECRECY

In most private sector organizations, employees do not tend to openly discuss the financial elements of their reward package with colleagues. In many public sector organizations, there is more transparency as public sector salaries and pay scales are published and available to citizens. In many private sector organizations, there are pay secrecy policies in place to prevent workers from discussing wages and salaries. A recent study by Rosenfeld (2017) in the USA found that pay secrecy policies are commonplace despite being illegal. Even where there is not a formal pay secrecy policy in place, the culture dictates that discussion of wages and salaries is strongly discouraged in many organizations. Pay secrecy is a factor leading to gender and ethnicity pay gaps and can inhibit dealing with pay discrimination (Ferguson, 2015). Pay secrecy can also lead to employees questioning the fairness of wage and salary decisions, especially if there is not openness about how these decisions are made. Day (2014) argues that pay transparency or openness where salaries are published can lead to greater innovation, higher performance and help address gender and ethnicity pay gaps. However, pay secrecy remains prevalent in the majority of private sector organizations.

SPOTLIGHT ON SKILLS

You have been asked to assist a friend who has started their own business selling cosmetics. They are about to employ three salespeople, and want your advice on how best to pay these individuals, saying: 'I want to make sure I offer the right package so that I get the best salespeople, but I have limited resources.' To advise your friend, consider the following questions:

1. What is the best way to pay salespeople?

2. What will make salespeople work harder?

3. What benefits apart from basic pay and commission would be attractive for them?

4. How should your friend evaluate how effective their reward system is?

To help you consider the issues above, visit **www.macmillanihe.com/carbery-cross-hrm-2e** and watch the video of Miriam Cushen talking about pay and reward.

GENDER AND ETHNICITY PAY GAPS

The gender pay gap refers to the difference in pay and reward packages between male and female workers. Despite legislation in many countries to prevent pay differences on the grounds of gender, there is a persistent gap that remains between men's and women's wages and salaries for the same work undertaken where men are paid more than women. In the European Union (EU), Eurostat (2017a) reports that, in 2015, women's gross hourly earnings were on average 16.3% below those of men in the EU28, ranging from 5.5% in Italy and Luxembourg to 26.9% in Estonia, with Ireland reported at 13.9% and the UK reported at 20.8%. In the USA, the United States Census Bureau (2016) reports that women earned 80% of what their male counterparts earned in 2015. There are numerous reasons for the existence and size of a gender pay gap, including consequences of breaks in career or part-time work due to childbearing, decisions female workers make in favour of family life, and gender differences in ability to negotiate pay.

A number of policies are being introduced at national government level to address gender pay gaps, which include the requirement for organizations to report pay for men versus women. For example, in the UK, by April 2018, all private sector companies and public sector organizations employing 250 or more people had to, for the first time, report the difference between what they pay their female and male staff. This information must be published on the company's website and on the UK government website. The publication of gender pay differences is seen as an important step in addressing the gender pay gap, making pay difference data transparent and readily available.

Similar to the gender pay gap, recent research draws attention to the prevalence of an ethnicity pay gap whereby members of minority ethnic groups receive lower wages comparative to white employees. Brynin and Güveli (2012) found that the gap can result from discrimination that occurs at two points: (1) at entry to the job where non-white employees find it more difficult to work in well-paid occupations; and (2) within-job gaps where minority ethnic employees obtain the same types of jobs as white employees but receive less pay. Similar issues are reported in the USA by Asante-Muhammad et al. (2016, 2017).

Gender and ethnicity pay gaps are important issues for government, organizations and society. Through national statutory or regulatory policies and voluntary/discretionary practices at organizational level, there is much work being done to reduce or eliminate gender and ethnicity pay gaps. Assessing the progress will be somewhat easier in the future through mandatory reporting and the availability of data which, in turn, can be used to determine what policies are needed to ensure sufficient progress is made.

DETERMINING THE RELATIVE VALUE OF JOBS

An organization's pay structure is developed using two processes: **internal alignment** and **external comparisons**, both shown in Figure 8.2. The amount that is paid for jobs within an organization can be determined using both internal and external sources of information.

Internal alignment refers to the relative value of different jobs within an organization. External comparisons are used to determine the amount or range of pay for each job based on an examination of the pay practices of competitors. There are many formal and informal methods used by organizations to gather the required information.

> **Internal alignment** – the hierarchy of the relative value of jobs within an organization
> **External comparison** – the amount or range of pay for each job based on an examination of the pay practices of competitors
> **Job evaluation** – a technique used by organizations to establish the relative worth of jobs

INTERNAL ALIGNMENT

Job evaluation refers to the techniques used to establish the internal alignment of jobs within an organization. The analysis is carried out on the job itself, as opposed to looking at the person who holds the job.

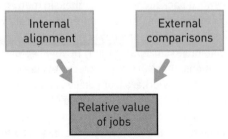

Figure 8.2 Relative value of jobs within an organization

There are at least three reasons why organizations would decide to implement a job evaluation system:

1. To provide a strong defence against legal challenges to pay practices through a well-conceived and consistently applied job evaluation system.

2. To ensure that they make consistent decisions on rates of pay that are related to the value added by the position. Although an employee may do excellent work, the amount they are paid must be related to the importance of the job to achieving organizational competitive advantage.

3. To establish an equitable hierarchy or structure of jobs that is **felt-fair**. This concept was identified by Canadian Elliott Jaques (2002), who suggested that trust-inducing pay systems are based on differentiating between levels of responsibility and complexity of tasks associated with each job within an organization. If successful, the job evaluation process ends with an intuitive acceptance by employees that the difference in pay between jobs is based on a fair assessment of the characteristics of the job. This means that employees should be able to look at other positions within the organization and understand why those jobs are paid more or less than their job. According to Willis Towers Watson (2016), base pay is the top driver for attracting and retaining employees in emerging and mature economies. They state, 'in addition, the perception of fairness in base pay is linked to an employee's engagement, which, in turn, drives productivity and financial performance' (p. 14).

All forms of job evaluation require job descriptions. For large organizations, the job descriptions are developed using job analysis, a process that examines jobs systematically to identify similarities and differences between them ▶Chapter 3◀. Job analysis requires information about job content and the characteristics required of the jobholder. A job analysis would reflect, for example, that an office manager's job requires more diverse tasks, greater responsibility, more conflicting demands, greater education, more years' experience, supervisory responsibilities, greater control over financial resources, and more complex external

> **Felt-fair** – trust-inducing pay systems that are accepted by employees because differences in pay are based on a fair assessment of job characteristics
>
> **Non-analytical methods** – whole jobs are compared to determine the organization's internal pay structure
>
> **Analytical methods** – they identify characteristics of the job that are valued by the organization and assess the degree to which they are present in the job

contacts than the receptionist's job. A job description summarizes this information.

There are different types of job evaluation that range from very simple to very complex. **Non-analytical methods** are relatively simple. Comparisons are made between whole jobs without analysing them into constituent parts or elements. **Analytical methods** are more complex. Important characteristics of jobs that promote organizational competitive advantage are identified and the degrees to which they are present in the job are assessed. Figure 8.3 shows different methods of job evaluation.

An organization can develop its own analytical job evaluation method. In practice, most large organizations adopt systems developed by large consulting firms such as the Hay Group, Mercer and Willis Towers Watson.

Non-analytical Methods of Job Evaluation

Most organizations are small. For example, in 2016, almost 90% of EU businesses were classified as micro-sized, meaning they employ less than 10 employees (Eurostat, 2017b). They also comprise a large percentage of all enterprises in other parts of the world such as Brazil (85%), Israel (92%), Korea (93%) and the Russian Federation (81%) (OECD, 2016). Generally, new positions are added one at a time. The employer compares the new

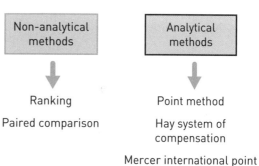

Figure 8.3 Non-analytical and analytical methods of job evaluation

job with existing jobs and decides where it fits by determining the value it adds to the organization. This comparison is the basis of non-analytical job evaluation.

Ranking and Paired Comparisons

Ranking is the simplest non-analytical form of job evaluation. Whole jobs are compared to others and placed in order of importance to the enterprise. Paired comparison is a slightly more complicated variation. It involves a matrix used to compare all possible pairs of jobs before placing them in order of importance.

Consider a self-employed accountant, who hires a bookkeeper to assist them and then a junior accountant. Both jobholders work in the office and neither interact regularly with clients. Later, a senior accountant is hired to find new clients and manage the junior accountant and bookkeeper. Finally, a receptionist is hired. Figure 8.4 shows an example of a paired comparison for the four employees hired by the business owner.

Start with the bookkeeper (left of matrix) and compare the job with the junior accountant (top of first column). 'Junior accountant' is placed in the box because this job ranks higher than the bookkeeper. The senior accountant's job is compared to the bookkeeper and junior accountant. It ranks higher than both and therefore appears in both boxes. Finally, while the receptionist's job requires interacting with customers and the public, it is an entry-level position that does not require any specific knowledge or experience. The jobs of bookkeeper, junior accountant and senior accountant rank higher than the receptionist and these jobs appear in the boxes in the third column. A score is tallied, counting the number of times a job receives the highest rating. Placing the jobs in order from highest to lowest

indicates their importance to the business (shown to the right of the matrix).

When there is a small number of jobs and the decision-maker is familiar with all aspects of them, ranking or paired comparisons are quick and easy ways to place the jobs in order. The advantages and disadvantages of ranking and paired comparisons are described in Table 8.3 on the next page 152.

CONSIDER THIS

Place yourself in the role of the business owner (and senior accountant). Because the business is growing, you decide to hire an office manager. Add this role to the paired comparison matrix illustrated in Figure 8.4. Describe any difficulties you encounter in completing this task.

Classification Systems

Classification systems begin with a set of similar jobs called a 'class' or 'job family', described using a common set of characteristics. The classification should be broad enough to encompass several jobs that are significantly different from jobs in other classifications. Classifications are then divided into grades that are differentiated using characteristics such as impact, knowledge and experience. The characteristics are described, rather than quantified as they are for the point method (discussed pages 150-151).

In the small but growing organization we considered above, there are two classifications. The 'accounting' classification administers, supervises and/or performs professional, technical or related clerical activities related to account preparation for clients. The jobs of senior accountant, junior

	Junior accountant	Senior accountant	Receptionist	Final ranking
Bookkeeper	Junior accountant	Senior accountant	Bookkeeper	Senior accountant (3)
	Junior accountant	Senior accountant	Junior accountant	Junior accountant (2)
		Senior accountant	Senior accountant	Bookkeeper (1)
				Receptionist (0)

Figure 8.4 Example of a paired comparison matrix

accountant and bookkeeper would represent separate grades based on differences in impact, knowledge and experience. The 'administrative support' classification administers, supervises or performs all the activities required to support the business. Currently, only the receptionist's job fits into this classification, probably at the lowest grade.

The US government, one of the world's largest employers, uses a classification system to determine the internal alignment of the civil service. There are 23 classifications for the 'white collar occupational group'. The 'trade, craft and labour group' comprises 36 job families that range from painting and paperhanging to ammunition, explosives and toxic materials handling (US Office of Personnel Management, n.d.). The advantages and disadvantages of classification systems are described in Table 8.3 on the next page 152.

Analytical Methods of Job Evaluation

Point Methods

The point method is an analytical form of job evaluation based on identifying factors relevant to all jobs within the organization, numerically scaling those factors to reflect their relative importance, and then developing a hierarchy of jobs based on the accumulated points for each role. All point methods, whether tailor-made or purchased from consultants, follow this general system. These methods are more complex to develop and implement than the non-analytical methods. However, they help ensure that equal work receives equal pay. This is important in relation to establishing internal alignment. It is also a strong defence for legal challenges based on claims of unfair pay practices.

To develop and implement a point method of job evaluation:

- First, identify factors relevant to all jobs such as impact, knowledge and problem-solving. The factors should be aligned to the organization's strategy and values. They should also be acceptable to stakeholders.
- Next, assign a range of numeric values to each factor to allow you to distinguish the degree to which it is present in different jobs. When assigning the numeric values, you should also weight the factors to reflect their relative importance to the organization. For example,

an employer may weight the factor 'impact' more than 'knowledge', believing that it is more important to achieve competitive advantage.
- Before implementation, prepare manuals and train everyone involved in applying the point method. Explain the procedures to all employees. The appeal system should also be decided and explained. Transparency promotes both the consistent application and acceptance of the point method.
- Begin implementation by calculating the points for each job based on the extent to which each factor is required to adequately perform the role. Then place all jobs in order according to their scores from highest to lowest. Higher scores reflect the greater importance of the job to the organization. Recheck for fairness. Examine the order of the jobs to ensure that it is 'felt-fair' and that differences between scores do reflect the relative importance of the jobs to the organization.

Rather than creating their own method, many large organizations use 'off-the-shelf' systems developed by large consulting firms. The most frequently used point method is the Hay System of Compensation developed in the 1950s. This method gained prominence because it identified a small number of factors that can be compared across a large number of jobs. The factors used for the Hay System include accountability, problem-solving and know-how. Other consulting firms such as Mercer and Towers Watson developed similar systems. There are several reasons why these systems are used:

1. Developing a job evaluation system internally takes months, if not years, so it is more efficient to buy an existing system.
2. Consulting firms train employees and provide computerized systems that make the implementation process easier.
3. Hay, Mercer and Willis Towers Watson conduct salary surveys. Organizations that use their job evaluation system can avail themselves of this additional service and easily compare their jobs with other companies, often those competing in the same sector.

There are advantages and disadvantages to each method of job evaluation. They are summarized in Table 8.3. The choice made by organizations is based on the size of the company, complexity of jobs, availability of resources to buy or develop a system, and the likelihood of legal challenge.

Method	Advantages	Disadvantages
Ranking/paired comparison	Easy to understand	Unclear basis of comparison between jobs
	Quick to implement	
	Inexpensive	Unwieldy as the numbers and types of jobs increase
		Relative difference between jobs is unclear
Classification system	Easy to understand and develop	Unusual jobs not classified
	Differences between jobs based on characteristics	Relative position of classification is inflexible even if job content changes
	Expands for growing organizations	Relative difference between jobs is unclear
Point method	Accommodates any number of jobs	Costly to develop or to buy
	Establishes order and relative differences between jobs based on systematic analysis	Off-the-shelf methods use general rather than organization-specific factors
	Decisions are based on factors that are important to organizational competitiveness	
		Time-consuming to implement
	Defensible against legal challenges	Difficult to explain to employees

Table 8.3 Advantages and disadvantages of different job evaluation methods

HRM AND ORGANIZATIONAL PERFORMANCE

Due diligence

Some organizations grow inorganically through local or cross-border acquisitions. Carrying out a 'due diligence' is a key element of the decision-making process and includes an examination of financial information, HR-related data, assessment of talent, supplier and competitor analysis. Due diligence should determine if there is a good management and cultural fit between the target and acquirer organizations. Full integration of the target's HR and payroll systems assists the movement of employees around the organization. This requires consistency that can be achieved by conducting the same analytical job evaluation process across both organizations and harmonizing compensation and benefits policies.

ENVIRONMENTAL FACTORS

Organizations make decisions about their reward system in a complex external environment where many factors are outside their control. These factors need to be managed for an organization to remain competitive.

Globalization impacts on businesses in the traded sector. These organizations sell goods and services that compete with imports and exports from other countries. This competition places pressure on organizations to keep labour costs as low as possible. If an organization's labour costs are higher than competing businesses in other countries, jobs can be lost. Multinationals operating within a country are 'footloose'. They can easily close in one jurisdiction and open in another to reduce labour costs. All the environmental factors associated with globalization therefore encourage organizations to keep their labour costs low.

As the world's largest trading block, the EU provides an interesting example regarding the effect of external environmental factors. Organizations competing in the EU face conflicting pressures. Some of these pressures promote lower labour costs while others cause them to increase. Labour costs for organizations competing in the eurozone are transparent. It is easy to see if national or organizational wages are out of line with other eurozone countries. This places pressure on organizations to keep labour costs low. However, trade unions place upward pressure on wages. Trade union membership varies considerably between EU countries. Even in countries with low trade union membership, trade unions negotiate wage agreements at the national, industry or enterprise level. Also, EU labour market Directives are translated by national governments into legislation. These laws help to protect labour but tend to increase labour costs for organizations operating in the EU.

At the national level, there are also conflicting pressures on labour costs. Periods of recession place downward pressure on wages because the supply of labour is greater than the demand. The opposite is true during periods of expansion. National labour market legislation can also add to labour costs. For example, minimum wage legislation is enacted to help low-paid workers. However, it places a floor under all wages. Countries with a minimum wage that is high relative to other countries will have higher labour costs that can threaten organizational competitiveness. Taxation policy can also impact on labour costs. The tax rates charged to businesses to pay for social insurance, for example, add to labour costs.

Organizations also compete within industries. There are large differences in wages between organizations in the accommodation and food sector when compared with the information and communications (ICT) sector. A business competing in the ICT sector will have to pay more to attract and retain competent employees. In some industries, like construction, an organization's wage bill is a significant percentage of total costs. Employers in these sectors will be more sensitive to granting a wage increase than employers in high-tech manufacturing, where labour costs comprise a relatively small percentage of total costs.

Finally, there can be competing pressures on pay at the local level. Labour shortages within localities can lead to wage increases across industries, especially for unskilled or semi-skilled workers, as supermarkets, for example, compete with manufacturers for employees. Labour surpluses have the opposite effect. Further, the higher cost of living in urban areas can lead to a premium being paid to urban workers relative to employees doing the same job in towns or rural localities.

These environmental factors are outside an organization's control. While some exert pressure on the organization to reduce labour costs, other factors cause labour costs to increase. They form the context in which pay decisions are made. Some of these factors are reflected in the salary surveys used by employers making external comparisons with competitors.

HRM IN THE NEWS

The living wage

In March 2017, two UK professors revealed that most football clubs in the English Premier League pay millions to players and managers but less than the 'living wage' to other employees. According to Dobbins and Prowse (2017), the exceptions are Everton and Chelsea, who pay all of their employees, as well as workers hired through agencies and contractors, the living wage.

Most of our discussion so far has focused on the employers' handling of the strategic reward system and the implications for attracting, motivating and rewarding employees. However, for employees, pay is much more. It is their livelihood, their ability to buy a house, start a family, educate children and participate in social and community life. Of growing concern in countries with high living standards but unequal income distributions, is the number of people who are in work but living in poverty.

In many countries, for example the USA, the UK and New Zealand, there is minimum wage legislation, intended to keep people out of poverty. The minimum wage provides a 'floor', meaning that wages should be at or above this level. Generally, there is one rate for adult workers and lower rates for other workers defined differently in each country. In the three countries listed here, lower rates can be paid to younger workers and those undergoing training. However, the minimum wage is not always seen as sufficient for an acceptable standard of living. Therefore, many countries also have living wage movements.

The living wage is generally higher than the minimum wage and is calculated to provide a decent living standard (Living Wage Foundation, 2017) enabling 'workers to live with dignity and to participate as active citizens in society' (Wait, 2013: 33). In the USA, the federal minimum wage in 2017 is $7.25, less than one-half of the living wage. Fight for $15 (2017) is an international movement that started with fast-food workers in New York. Now, it organizes protests, including strikes, because it states, 'we can't feed our families, pay our bills or even keep a roof over our heads on minimum wage pay'. This movement influenced states, including California, to increase the hourly minimum wage to $15 per hour.

The organizations promoting the living wage attempt to persuade governments, business owners and individuals that paying a living wage is helpful for individuals, families and their children, but also for businesses and society in general. The Living Wage Foundation (2017) provides case studies indicating that companies that adopt the living wage experience lower absenteeism, less turnover, quality advances and improve their corporate reputations.

Research conducted by Linneker and Wills (2016) reports findings that are mixed for both employers and employees. They found that workplaces adopting the living wage in London improved their employee retention rates, and,

in some cases, productivity increases covered the increased labour costs. In other companies, however, profits were reduced. Full-time workers whose hours of employment remained unchanged were the main beneficiaries. Some workers' incomes also decreased because of working hour reductions. Linneker and Wills (2016: 774) conclude that the living wage 'was no "magic bullet" for reducing in-work poverty' but is a useful intervention combined with other anti-poverty policies.

Questions

1. Do you think that the living wage is a good idea for employees and employers?
2. Can all employers afford to pay a living wage?
3. If two members of a family with children are working but living in poverty, does this impact on society?

Sources

Dobbins, T. and Prowse, P. (2017) 'How football's richest clubs fail to pay staff a real living wage', *The Conversation*, 30 March, http://theconversation.com/how-footballs-richest-clubs-fail-to-pay-staff-a-real-living-wage-74347 (accessed 3 April 2017)

Fight for $15 (2017) *About Us*, http://fightfor15.org/about-us/ (accessed 3 April 2017)

Linneker, B. and Wills, J. (2016) 'The London living wage and in-work poverty reduction: Impacts on employers and workers', *Environment and Planning C: Government and Policy*, 34(5), 759–76.

Living Wage Foundation (n.d.) *Who are we?*, www.livingwage.org.uk/who-are-the-living-wage-foundation (accessed 3 April 2017)

Wait, D. (2013) 'Working for a living wage', *Kai Taiki Nursing New Zealand*, 19(4), 33.

EXTERNAL COMPARISONS

All organizations make choices about how much to pay employees and the composition of that pay. There are competing objectives at play here. First, organizations want their reward system to attract and retain competent employees. Secondly, organizations need to manage their labour costs. Both objectives

are achieved by gathering information about the pay packages of competitors.

Determining Competitive Markets

The first task is to determine the organization's competitors for employees. For a small corner shop, this is easy. They are competing for employees with

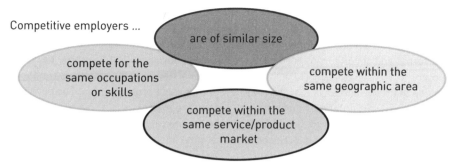

Figure 8.5 Defining the market for employees

other shops in the area. However, a large business with several classes of employees may compete with organizations in several industries or geographic locations for their employees. The different markets for employees are shown in Figure 8.5.

Organizations often hire graduates from degree courses from third-level institutes. However, a graduate may be qualified to enter many different industries. For example, graduate process engineers can find employment in the biotechnology, food, petrochemical, manufacturing or pharmaceutical sectors. Therefore, if a business in the pharmaceutical industry is hiring process engineer graduates, it will be competing with businesses from several other industries. For senior or specialized positions, organizations often look for candidates with experience in their own product or service market. For example, if Abbott Laboratories is hiring a senior process engineer, it competes with other companies in the pharmaceutical industry such as Pfizer and GlaxoSmithKline.

Depending on the position within the organization, the relevant geographic market may differ. For example, if Abbott Laboratories in Omaha, Nebraska is hiring an administrative assistant and a senior process engineer, they will compete in different geographic markets. For the administrative assistant, the competitors are local, while competitors for the senior process engineer are state-wide or regional. The size of an organization is also important. On average, large US-based organizations (employing more than 250 people) pay between $1,200–$1,700 per week, while small companies pay between $800–$900 per week (US Bureau of Labor Statistics, 2016). Abbott Laboratories will therefore compare itself against businesses of similar size rather than against small businesses that pay considerably less.

To summarize, before looking for information about competitors' reward systems, the organization must define the relevant markets for competent employees and determine its competitors in those markets. The relevant markets are defined by skills and occupations, products and services, geography and size. A business may compete with different organizations depending on the job.

Information Sources

Organizations can obtain information about competitors' pay policies from many different sources that range from informal to research based, and from free to very expensive. The goal of the organization is to gather information that is sufficiently reliable to make good decisions at the lowest possible cost. There are three basic strategies used by organizations to find relevant pay information – they can access information, buy survey data, or collect survey data.

Access Information

Organizations can access free information from internal or external sources. Often, this information is gathered for a different reason but is useful for determining the market value of a job. Most countries gather labour market statistics on earnings and labour costs for business sectors on a regular basis to identify competitiveness and inflation trends. Industrial relations and business periodicals publish occasional surveys and articles on wages and benefits. Sometimes, these relate to jobs across a variety of sectors. Alternatively, they may report on a wage deal made within a particular organization. HR professionals belong to informal and professional networks, and they can often be helpful in providing ad hoc information. Job advertisements in the national press or specialist journals sometimes include information about salaries and benefits. During their exit interviews, departing employees may disclose the terms and conditions offered by their new employer.

The advantage of these sources is that they are free. However, there are disadvantages. Information that is collected on a regular basis by government offices is often out of date by the time it is published. When reported at the sector level, there is often no specific information about jobs within the sector. Articles and surveys in journals and newspapers appear on an irregular basis. Information from colleagues, job advertisements and exit interviews, although specific, are not consistently available. In general, these sources are not reliable because they do not provide consistent information about similar jobs in competitor organizations on a regular basis.

Buy Survey Data

Organizations can buy information that is industry specific, occupation specific or related to their job evaluation system. Industry-specific information is gathered by the industry itself or employer organizations ▶Chapter 5◀. Occupational surveys are published by professional associations for groups such as engineers, accountants or HR professionals. The information is often based on tenure and professional qualifications rather than jobs. Consulting firms like Hay, PricewaterhouseCoopers and Mercer also conduct surveys for large occupational groups, often gathering information from organizations using their job evaluation methods. One advantage of these sources is that consistent information is regularly collected. In relation to disadvantages, these surveys are expensive and may not encompass a wide variety of jobs. Also, the participating organizations may not be competitors within the relevant markets. Finally, the organization may require specific information that is not gathered for these off-the-shelf surveys.

Collect Survey Data

Organizations can make their own surveys or pay a consultant to gather information from competitors. Third-party bespoke surveys are conducted by consultants who gather information from a number of competitors within the same industry. Although this survey may be repeated regularly, the participants in the survey may change. Pay

club surveys are an arrangement between industry competitors to exchange information about pay and benefits on a regular basis. The advantage of these sources is that the same pay information is consistently gathered about similar jobs from comparable organizations. The disadvantage is that they are expensive.

The range of information sources that organizations can use is shown in Figure 8.6. At the bottom of the arrow are sources that are free but not reliable. Moving up the arrow, the sources become more reliable and expensive.

In practice, large organizations participate in several surveys and use a variety of sources in order to obtain reliable information. This is because they hire employees for a large number of jobs, with competitors in many different markets. Although the costs are high, the costs of uncompetitive pay practices are higher. If pay and benefits are too low, organizations will not be able to attract and retain productive employees. If pay and benefits are too high, organizations will lose competitiveness within their industries. The hierarchy of jobs in an organization is determined using a job evaluation method, as discussed earlier in the chapter. The information from competitors is then used to determine the salary range for each job within an organization. Combined, the two information sources are used to determine the relative value of jobs within an organization.

BUILDING YOUR SKILLS

You are working in a retail store as supervisor. You have noticed that there is poor morale in the shop. Most of the staff are part time and are paid low wages. Given difficult economic conditions, increasing pay rates is not an option. What recommendations can you make to your general manager to improve morale without increasing labour costs?

PAY AS A MOTIVATOR

One of the key debates in the HRM field and particularly the reward management area is the link between pay and motivation. The assumption is that the higher the employees' motivation levels,

Pay club
Third-party bespoke surveys
Occupational surveys conducted by consulting firms
Occupational surveys conducted by professional bodies
Industry surveys
Exit interviews
Social and professional networks
Job advertisements
Articles in IR and business periodicals
Government statistics

Reliable and expensive

Not reliable and free

Figure 8.6 Sources of information about pay and benefits

the higher their performance. Since Maslow's contribution to the motivation debate, there is much discussion about the impact of pay on motivation levels (Milkovich et al., 2010). Maslow suggested that there are five levels of need that motivate human behaviour: (1) physiological needs; (2) safety needs; (3) love and belongingness needs; (4) esteem needs; and (5) self-actualization needs. The first, lower or 'basic' needs are physiological needs that have to be met to survive (e.g. air, food, water) and safety needs (e.g. physical and economic security and stability). Maslow argued that people are motivated to behave in ways that meet these needs. When applied to reward management, having a basic salary that allows people to cover basic living needs motivates their behaviour. Once that level of need is met, Maslow argues that people are then motivated by needs at the next level including, for example, security of employment or access to a pension in addition to having a basic wage or salary. Once these second-order needs are met, people are motivated by needs at the third and fourth levels which include love/belonging and esteem needs (e.g. achievement, respect, personal growth). In the context of work, this can include promotion and being part of a team. The highest level of needs is called self-actualization, occurring if an individual reaches their full potential and can reflect high levels of job satisfaction. Each need, beginning with physiological, must be satisfied before a person is motivated by needs at the next level. Maslow argued that pay is a physiological or safety need. Once satisfied, pay does not motivate higher levels of performance as elements such as self-esteem and self-actualization become motivators of people's behaviour at work.

Rynes et al. (2004) conducted a meta-analysis (review of many published studies) to explore the importance of pay in determining employee motivation. They found that 'money is not the only motivator and it is not the primary motivator for everyone. However, there is overwhelming evidence that money is an important motivator for most people' (p. 391). They also found that there is a discrepancy between what people self-report about the impact of pay on their motivation levels and performance versus their actual choices and behaviours. Rynes et al. note that people tend to say that pay is not important for their motivation, yet their behaviour indicates that, in reality, pay is important in understanding motivation. Studies of actual behaviours in response to motivation initiatives show pay to be the most effective, though not the only motivator in most cases.

Rynes et al. (2004) found that pay is an important motivator if:

- there is some form of PRP
- PRP is paid to people on low wages because a small change can make a significant difference
- employees assess that they are being fairly paid in comparison to their colleagues.

CONSIDER THIS ⊙

Think about a time when you were working (summer job, part-time work and so on). Do you feel you were fairly rewarded? Why? Why not? What change to the reward system would have motivated you to work harder? If your suggestion was implemented, do you think it would motivate other employees to work harder?

HRM IN PRACTICE

Employee bonus schemes

iStock.com/sergeyskleznev

You are the HR manager of a (fictional) Adventure & Recreation Centre, located near Christchurch, New Zealand. It is a private business that employs about 100 people in peak season. The centre provides activity-based holiday packages for individuals and families. In June 2017, you design a bonus scheme for all staff after liaising with other department heads (administration and front office, catering, housekeeping, park development and adventures). In August 2017, you present the scheme to all the employees through a series of meetings. The scheme was officially launched in September 2017. Exhibit 1 below details the elements of the bonus scheme.

This was the first time that you ever developed a bonus scheme and you are delighted when the 'roll-out' is complete. The points awarded by supervisors are entered each week onto a master spreadsheet by your clerical assistant. You become busy with other projects.

During the first week of December, you look at the attendance figures and see that there has not been a significant improvement since the beginning of the scheme. You decide to take a closer look at how the scheme is operating, beginning with the information that your assistant recently entered into the master spreadsheet (see Exhibit 2 below). You are concerned, after looking at the point awards, and decide to conduct a survey to gather feedback from staff about the bonus scheme (Exhibit 3). The results of that questionnaire are shown in Exhibit 4. Having reviewed the results of the survey, you are trying to decide the next step.

Exhibit 1 The bonus scheme

Elements	Detail
Participants	Staff
Method of payment	Westfield Gift Cards that can be used in multiple shops and entertainment venues at the Westfield Riccarton Shopping Centre, a popular destination for employees in nearby Christchurch.
Frequency of payment	The amounts earned each month are small. Employees on temporary contracts can collect their vouchers at the end of their contract. Full-time employees can collect their vouchers in June and December.
Criteria for bonus	Bonus points are awarded per week for each of the following measures: • *Attendance:* full attendance (10 points) • *Punctuality:* arriving on time each day, returning on time from scheduled breaks and completing entire shift (10 points) • *Appearance:* staff member conforms to the procedures for appearance outlined in the employee handbook given during induction training which includes wearing the uniform with the company logo (10 points) • *Teamwork:* outstanding contribution to the employee's work team (30 points maximum) • *Customer comments:* written comments by a customer concerning a staff member, or verbal comments made to another member of staff (20 points maximum)

Elements	Detail
Translating points to payment	Employees receive NZD$1 (New Zealand dollar) for each 10 points accrued on a weekly basis
Points awarded	The employee's immediate supervisor decides the number of points awarded each week and returns the results to the HR department
Notification of points	The points received by each employee are displayed each month on the department bulletin board
Termination/ Change of scheme	Management reserves the right to change or discontinue the scheme after three months' notice

Exhibit 2 Award points allocation for three departments, Week 1, December 2017

		Attendance	Punctuality	Appearance	Team	Customer comments	Total
Department: Catering							
Hoani	Pip	10	8	10	30		58
Wilson	Denis	10	10	9	30		59
Williams	John	10	10	10	30		60
Tahuri	Jude	10	10	9	30		59
Brown	Wendy	10	7	10	30		57
Kumar	Joseph	10	10	10	30		60
Harris	Anna	10	8	10	30		58
King	Michelle	10	10	10	30		60
Taylor	Andrew	7	10	10	30		57
Martin	Priscilla	10	9	10	30		59
Department: Adventures							
Paratene	Benita	10	10	10	30	15	75
Zhang	Jo	10	10	10	20		50
Singh	Sandeep	10	0	10	15		35
Jones	Arana	10	10	10	30		60
Patal	Ananya	0	10	10	20	10	50
Ratana	Moana	10	0	10	15		35
Anderson	Mike	10	0	10	25		45
Ngaga	Nanaia	10	10	10	15	20	65
Li	Jack	10	0	0	20		30
Department: Administration & Front of House							
Thompson	Drina	10	10	10	25		55
Walker	James	10	10	10	15		45
Crean	Lucy	10	10	10	30	20	80

Exhibit 3 Evaluating the award scheme: survey questions

This questionnaire/survey contains a number of questions you are asked to comment on by circling a number that best corresponds to your opinion. If you think it is impossible to form an opinion, just skip the question.

	I strongly disagree	I disagree	I neither agree nor disagree	I agree	I strongly agree
1. I understand how the incentive scheme operates	1	2	3	4	5
2. In order to get more points, I make a special effort to work well with others within my department	1	2	3	4	5
3. The way my manager distributes points to each member of staff in my department is fair	1	2	3	4	5
4. The managers of other departments distribute points in the same way as my manager	1	2	3	4	5
5. I am satisfied with the size of the bonus I received	1	2	3	4	5
6. The criteria measured under the incentive scheme are important to my job performance	1	2	3	4	5
7. In order to get more points, I am careful to arrive on time every day	1	2	3	4	5

Exhibit 4 Evaluating the award scheme: survey response analysis

The following graphs show the responses of staff to the survey.

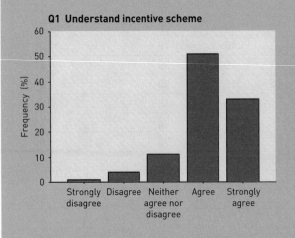

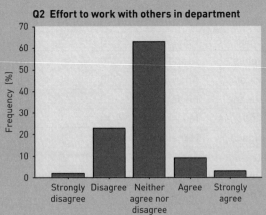

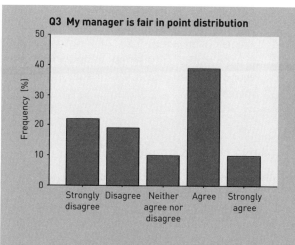

Q3 My manager is fair in point distribution

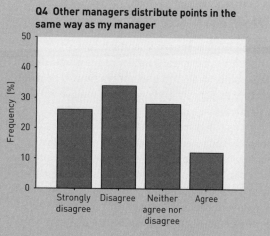

Q4 Other managers distribute points in the same way as my manager

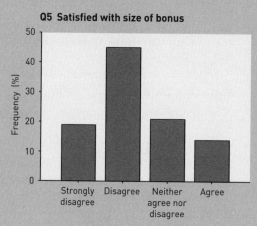

Q5 Satisfied with size of bonus

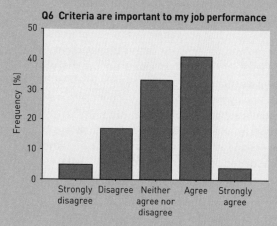

Q6 Criteria are important to my job performance

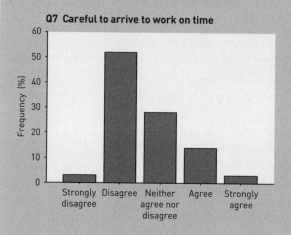

Q7 Careful to arrive to work on time

What would you do?

Evaluate the scheme at the Adventure & Recreation Centre.

1. What could you have done differently in designing and implementing this scheme?
2. What features of the scheme work well and what features are problematic?
3. What should you do next?

SUMMARY

While all HR policies are important, reward management can greatly influence the employment relationship. Ideally, all parts of the reward package are fairly and consistently applied. Employers, particularly large ones, expend considerable resources to ensure that their pay structure is internally consistent and externally competitive. Organizations choose from a wide array of financial elements. While all reward packages include base pay and statutory benefits, organizations differentiate their reward package using performance-related pay and benefits. Employers who use a total reward approach also include nonfinancial elements in an effort to capture all the aspects of the employment relationship that are valued by their employees. Recognition, job security, career development and work–life balance policies are presented with financial rewards to capture the total worth of the employment relationship. Labour costs are a significant proportion of total costs for many industries. Reward management must always balance the need to attract, retain and motivate employees with the requirement to control labour costs.

CHAPTER REVIEW QUESTIONS

1. What is meant by reward management and what are the typical objectives of a reward system?
2. What are the differences between nonfinancial and financial rewards? In your opinion, which are the most important for delivering higher levels of performance?
3. Describe the various PRP options available to organizations.
4. Describe the reasons why organizations conduct job evaluation. Under what circumstances are non-analytical methods effective?
5. How does the minimum wage differ from the living wage?
6. Describe the environmental factors that impact on the labour costs of a multinational call centre operating in a rural location.
7. Describe the methods a small retail store owner with five employees may use to determine the relative value of their jobs.
8. Is pay a motivator? Discuss, using examples from your own experience or from friends and family members.

FURTHER READING

Armstrong, M. (2015) *Armstrong's Handbook of Reward Management Practice*, 5th edn, London: Kogan Page.

Newman, J., Gerhart, B. and Milkovich, G. (2016) *Compensation*, 12th edn, Boston: McGraw-Hill Irwin.

Perkins, S., White, G. and Jones, S. (2016) *Reward Management: Alternatives, Consequences and Contexts*, London: CIPD.

Rose, M. (2018) *Reward Management: A Practical Introduction*, 2nd edn, London: Kogan Page.

USEFUL WEBSITES

www.kornferry.com/solutions/rewards-and-benefits/work-measurement/job-evaluation
A website offering guidance to companies keen to improve their methods of job evaluation.

youtu.be/u6XAPnuFjJc
Highlights from an interview with Dan Pink about motivation.

www.ted.com/talks/david_burkus_why_you_should_know_how_much_your_coworkers_get_paid
Discussion by management researcher David Burkus about pay transparency.

www.eurofound.europa.eu/topic/pay-and-income
EU website covering topics related to pay including wage inequities, statutory minimum wage legislation and collective bargaining arrangements.

For extra resources, including videos, multiple choice questions and useful weblinks, go to: www.macmillanihe.com/carbery-cross-hrm-2e.

Gettylmages/iStockphoto/monkeybusinessimages

9: Learning and Development

David McGuire and Thomas N. Garavan

LEARNING OUTCOMES

By the end of this chapter you will be able to:

- Examine the differences in the provision of learning and development at the individual, team, organizational and societal levels
- Explain the differences between learning and development and other terms used to describe these activities in organizations
- Explain how individuals can learn in organizations and how individual learning styles vary
- Explore common models of learning and development in organizations
- Review the stages of the ADDIE model
- Examine the process of analysing and identifying learning and development needs
- Understand the key issues to be considered when designing learning and development interventions
- Outline the key steps to be considered when evaluating learning and development and measuring return on investment

THIS CHAPTER DISCUSSES:

Introduction (164)

Key Concepts in Learning and Development (166)

How Do People Learn? (168)

Common Models of Learning and Development in Organizations (170)

Exploring the Stages of the ADDIE Model (175)

INTRODUCTION

Learning and development activities are integral to the growth and prosperity of individuals, teams, organizations and society. At the individual level, learning and development is concerned with equipping people with the knowledge, skills, abilities and other attributes needed to make a valuable contribution to their teams, organizations, communities and society. In today's fast-paced world, learning and development processes help individuals to stay abreast of changes occurring in the work environment and to adapt to evolving regulatory requirements and new technological practices. They can also boost an individual's motivation and confidence in their ability to perform the job effectively and can prepare individuals to work competently in groups and teams. When properly structured, learning and development activities often fit within larger career development plans, as discussed in ▶Chapter 10◀.

At the team level, a focus on learning and development should result in the acquisition, sharing and enhancement of new knowledge and skills, the building of group confidence and cohesion in relation to task performance, and the setting of group standards and performance levels. Through the power of learning and development activities, individuals may be able to perform tasks with greater speed and accuracy and to utilize resources more effectively. Learning and development activities can also enhance team communication, the skills to handle team conflicts and team decision-making, and can build greater resilience in managing setbacks and failures.

At the organizational level, learning and development is vital in delivering improved performance through identifying efficiencies and raising productivity levels. Learning and development is often linked to issues of competitiveness and informed by approaches that seek to leverage human capital in building organizational value. As organizations seek to compete in the global economy, they increasingly focus on strengthening employee capacity to absorb and process new information, acquire new skills and adapt effectively to new realities. Learning and development professionals are tasked with the goals of fostering a learning culture within organizations and ensuring that the organization has an appropriate knowledge-skills mix to meet future needs and respond flexibly to external environmental changes. For further information on planning learning and development, see ▶Chapter 9◀. Research has consistently demonstrated that learning and development

activities can impact organizational performance (Clardy, 2008; Vidal-Salazar et al., 2012), including profitability, quality, customer service, customer satisfaction, workforce productivity and reduced costs. Learning and development activities can be used to retain employees, boost customer and employee engagement levels and enhance social capital and relationship-building with suppliers and customers.

At the community and societal level, a focus on developing talent through education and vocational training is prevalent. The goal of such initiatives is to grow national prosperity through upskilling citizens to make a productive contribution to the economy. Alignment of learning and development activities to employer needs is imperative to ensuring that educational and training institutions are offering appropriate programmes which meet both student and organization requirements. Investments in human capital at the community and societal level are also made to enhance the attractiveness of regions and countries to overseas investors and to enable countries to attain comparative advantages over their neighbours. Incoming employers will often use learning and development to induct local employees to organizational norms as well as to help expatriates on overseas assignments adjust to local cultural norms. Learning and development activities can be used to gain the involvement of stakeholders, such as trade unions, professional bodies, community groups and employer groups, in enhancing society as a whole. To this end, learning and development initiatives at the community and societal level may seek to achieve a multitude of goals, including attracting inward investment, alleviating poverty, strengthening community engagement, empowering women and minority groups and improving literacy and quality of life.

In essence, learning and development activities are focused on maximizing human potential at the individual, organizational, community and societal levels. In this chapter, we begin by defining key terms that underpin learning and development as a field of study. Then we explore how individuals learn, examining the approaches of cognitivism, behaviourism and experiential learning. We consider common models of learning and development to gain an understanding of the scope of learning and development and how it is practised in organizations. Finally, we undertake a comprehensive examination of the ADDIE model, looking at the five stages in depth, to provide a template for designing learning and development interventions.

HRM IN THE GLOBAL BUSINESS ENVIRONMENT

Careers at Expedia

Named as the No. 1 'Best Place to Work in the UK' in 2016 and 2017, Expedia has been rated by its own employees as an outstanding organization to work for (Wadlow, 2016). Established as a small division within Microsoft in 1996, Expedia set out to provide customers with a revolutionary new way of researching and booking travel. The past two decades have seen the company grow rapidly and adopt brands such as Hotels.com, Orbitz, Hotwire, Trivago and Travelocity (Expedia, 2018a). The company prides itself on adhering to six cultural norms:

- *We Believe in Being Different*: Expedia is keen to explore new ideas, perspectives and ways of doing things. It is welcoming of a diverse workforce and extols the virtues of being different in its approach.
- *We Lead Humbly*: Expedia adopts a servant leadership approach and is keen for leaders to work closely with teams to improve learning and knowledge.
- *We are Transparent*: Expedia emphasizes the importance of open and honest communications at all levels of the organization.
- *We Organize for Speed*: Expedia underlines the necessity of analysing data quickly and making decisions effectively.
- *We Believe in the Scientific Method*: Expedia uses hard data to justify decisions and actions taken.
- *We Act as One Team*: Expedia invests in its teams and looks to improve the quality of life of its employees (Expedia, 2018b).

With more than 22,000 employees in over 30 countries, Expedia has long recognized the importance of having a sophisticated approach to HRM and career development (Expedia, 2018a). Johan Svanstrom, president of Expedia Affiliate Network, has spoken about the importance of employees in the following terms: 'We continue to invest in attracting and retaining a fantastic team of employees from very diverse backgrounds. They really drive ideation and execution of great services to partners and customers and enable our company to stay ahead in the ever-changing travel tech landscape. The combination of our talent with an outspoken culture of fun, openness and true ambition makes Expedia such a great place to work' (Wadlow, 2016). In order to motivate, develop and incentivize employees, Expedia provide perks such as free breakfast once a month, lunchtime masterclasses, gym membership and medical and travel benefits (Glassdoor, 2018).

Expedia focuses on hiring internally to fill positions, where this is possible, and developing its own employees. This provides opportunities for staff to build longer term careers in the organization. An essential aspect of the recruitment process is ensuring that staff possess the right technical qualifications, as well as, more importantly, an ability to collaborate and work in an organization built around continuous change (Jee, 2017). To this end, Expedia has heavily invested in leadership development and mentoring programmes, helping staff to learn and grow with the company. Key to ensuring that Expedia attracts the right people has been the worldwide university internship programme, which allows Expedia to attract fresh talent into the organization. Expedia has also worked hard to ensure gender pay parity, so that men and women are paid equally across equivalent roles (Expedia, 2018c) ▶Chapter 6◀.

Key to the success of Expedia has been the importance of flexibility and trust. The organization is a fast-moving company and sometimes requires employees to take early or late calls – but works to give employees a positive work–life balance by allowing staff to come to work late, drop their children off at nursery before work or work from home ▶Chapter 12◀. This necessitates a high degree of trust between Expedia and its employees – something that has been integral to building a high-performing, engaged workforce (Jee, 2017). Such a culture led to the scrapping of performance ratings, with performance management now focused on providing employees with ongoing feedback (Pocha, 2016) ▶Chapter 7◀.

CHAPTER 9

Questions

1. What impact do Expedia's learning and development activities have at the individual, organizational, community and societal levels?
2. How might mentoring and leadership development help improve organizational performance?
3. How important is fun in the workplace? How might this be carried through to Expedia's learning and development activities?
4. Why is talent diversity important to the success of Expedia? How might its learning and development activities assist with recruiting a diverse workforce?
5. What effect do you think the workplace culture at Expedia has on learning and development in the company?

KEY CONCEPTS IN LEARNING AND DEVELOPMENT

A variety of terms are used to describe learning and development activities in organizations, including 'training', 'education', 'learning', 'development' and 'human resource development'. In this section, we will define these terms and examine key differences that distinguish each of these concepts.

Training can be considered the traditional way to describe learning activities in organizations. It is largely concerned with the process of acquiring the knowledge, skills and attitudes required to perform an organizational role effectively. Training is considered a narrow term that focuses on employees achieving an improved work standard within a short time period. It can take place in a formal (classroom or training room) or informal (on-the-job) setting and can be highly structured, semi-structured or less structured in its approach. The focus of training may be general (preparing individuals for a range of situations) or specific (focused on a particular set of knowledge, skills and behaviours) and often requires satisfactory performance in relation to a prescribed set of goals. Aguinis and Kraiger (2009) summarize the benefits of training for individuals and organizations as being skill enhancement, competence development and improved organizational performance.

Education relates to the acquisition of knowledge, skills and experience through a period of sustained study, often leading to a qualification. By its nature, education is broad-based, preparing individuals for a range of jobs and roles. It is delivered over a longer period of time than training, and the objectives of education are often framed in wider, general terms. While the education received during an individual's early years can be considered formative and helps individuals acquire a bedrock of knowledge and skills, education received in later years is often self-directed and linked to specific career goals. Education is often characterized by a prescribed curriculum and delivered by means of lectures, tutorials, seminars, readings and debate. Governments are often heavily invested in the structure of national education and qualification systems, and educational programme offerings are frequently linked to national economic priorities.

Learning is a foundational concept underpinning notions of training, education, development and human resource development. There are numerous goals associated with learning, and they may include the acquisition of knowledge, skills and experiences to enhance personal, organizational and societal growth, the development of greater self-awareness and insight and the changing of behaviour arising from exposure to new experiences. According to Marsick and Watkins (2001), learning may be formal, informal or incidental in nature. Formal learning is typically characterized as highly structured, classroom-based learning that is often instructor-led and institutionally supported. In contrast, informal learning is learning that is not highly conscious or structured, but is integrated into daily routines and influenced by chance. It can include self-directed learning, networking,

> **Training** – the process of acquiring the knowledge, skills and attitudes required to perform a role effectively
>
> **Education** – the acquisition of knowledge, skills and experience through a period of sustained study, often leading to a qualification
>
> **Learning** – a range of formal, informal or incidental activities leading to a semi-permanent or permanent change in behaviour which can contribute to individual, team, organizational and societal effectiveness

coaching and mentoring and revolves around processes of reflection and action. Finally, incidental learning arises from a particular context, situation or critical event and is unplanned. It can occur through observation, repetition and social interaction without much external facilitation or structure. Examples of incidental learning include observation of colleagues at work, mistakes in the performance of tasks and the use of problem-solving approaches to deal with unexpected situations.

Development refers to a gradual unfolding or growth of an individual, whereby they grasp work and life opportunities as they arise. In contrast with training, which takes place over the short term, development is considered a long-term process where the individual largely takes responsibility for its direction. Development involves a series of personal choices, and it is through these choices that individuals make decisions about their careers and understand the contribution they wish to make to society. It may encompass both formal and informal opportunities, but the development journey is largely constructed by the individual themselves. The term 'employee development' was in vogue during the 1980s and 90s; however, it fell out of favour with new perspectives on how to describe an employee. It is considered a hierarchical term that does not account for current representations of employees, with terms such as 'partner' and 'associate' now being commonplace in organizations.

Human resource development (HRD) exists as a field of practice and involves helping individuals to achieve their potential through boosting knowledge, skills and capabilities. While the field of human resource development exists at the individual, organizational and societal level, the dominant focus has been on organizations. It draws upon training and development, career development and organizational development to improve the effectiveness of organizations and achieve strategic alignment to the external environment. In so doing, human resource development is intended to build a learning capacity and culture throughout organizations and to help shape and influence corporate strategy. Some commentators have criticized human resource development for overemphasizing organizational approaches and reducing employees to the level of a resource, which can be leveraged and maximized (Nair et al., 2007).

> **Development** – a range of activities leading to the gradual unfolding or growth of an individual and the enhancement of knowledge, skills and experiences over the long term
>
> **Human resource development (HRD)** – the provision of learning, development and training opportunities to improve individual, team, organizational and societal effectiveness

In summary, the wider field of 'learning and development' encompasses several foundational concepts which describe a variety of activities designed to support individual and group learning. The Chartered Institute of Personnel and Development (CIPD) and the Australian Human Resource Institute recognize this broad term to capture the complexity of such activities in organizations. First, it is considered a democratic term that can apply to people irrespective of their contractual position: it could include contractors, suppliers, volunteers, consultants and customers, or anyone who contributes to the success of the organization. Secondly, it is a term that captures the wide diversity of learning and development processes and incorporates the formal, informal and incidental learning that is found in organizations. For a business, the most powerful outcomes of learning and development are to do with enhanced organizational effectiveness and sustainability. For an individual, they relate to improved personal competence, adaptability and employability. It is therefore a critical business process, whether in for-profit or not-for-profit organizations.

CONSIDER THIS

Many organizations invest in learning and development activities for the wrong reasons, and thus they represent a waste of money. Organizations frequently invest in learning and development activities because they are viewed as an easy answer to solve a problem that in reality does not have a learning and development solution. They may also invest in learning activities in the hope that they will contribute to competitiveness without any systematic evaluation of learning needs and what learning activities can contribute to the bottom line. Some organizations view learning and development as a luxury, part of employees' benefits, rather than something that will generate value for the organization. So, it is important for organizations to be clear about why they invest in learning and development activities. When should organizations invest in such activities?

HOW DO PEOPLE LEARN?

The process of individual learning lies at the heart of learning and development. Learning is defined as a process of acquiring knowledge, skills and developing attitudes. It is a process of change that comes about as a result of instruction, experience, self-directed learning activities, reflection, and trial and error. People are motivated to learn by the desire to learn something new, to perform a task or role more effectively, and to avail themselves of incentives or rewards. Motivation is central to the learning process, and organizations can do a number of things to enhance this motivation, including encouragement to participate in learning, rewarding learning behaviours, and providing employees with the resources to learn. In this section, we review three common schools of learning: cognitivism, behaviourism and experiential learning.

Cognitivism

Cognitivism focuses on the mind and the process of how learning is absorbed, stored and retrieved in the brain. Learning is viewed as a process causing a semi-permanent change in mental processes and creating associations between different aspects of knowledge. Learning is initially absorbed through the senses (sight, sound, taste, smell, touch), and individuals create a mental schema involving actions, events and perspectives. Mental schemas represent internal structures which may be combined, extended or altered to accommodate new knowledge and information. These structures represent an efficient storage mechanism which helps the recall and retrieval of knowledge. An important figure from the cognitivist school of learning is Jean Piaget (1886–1980), who developed a theory of cognitive development which showed how children absorb and process information as they grow up. He argued that children pass through evolutionary stages from basic sensory absorption of information (sensorimotor stage from birth to 24 months) through to abstract reasoning and complex problem-solving (formal operational stage from age 11 through adulthood).

Within a learning and development context, trainers applying cognitivist principles who are introducing new topics will first stimulate and draw upon previous knowledge in order to bring existing schemas to the fore. Trainers should take care in the sequencing of learning to ensure learners can process and organize information effectively. Examples such as demonstrations, mnemonics, metaphors and concept mapping are useful mechanisms which aid in the processing of information and make use of existing schemas.

> **Cognitivism** – the process of absorbing, storing and retrieving learning in the brain through the creation, amendment and structuring of mental schemas
>
> **Behaviourism** – semi-permanent change in behaviour resulting from the application of positive and negative reinforcements
>
> **Experiential learning** – the cyclical process of making meaning through reflection and experience

Behaviourism

Behaviourism examines the rewards and punishments associated with learning and how learning effects changes in behaviour. It recognizes that learners respond to stimuli in the external environment and are conditioned to behave in particular ways due to feedback received in relation to responses to stimuli. Reward reinforcements will strengthen particular behaviours and increase the likelihood of their reoccurrence, while punishment reinforcements will weaken specific behaviours and decrease the likelihood of their reoccurrence. A key figure in the behaviourist school is Ivan Pavlov (1849–1936) who conducted research into the conditioning process. Pavlov is best known for his experiments with dogs, whereby behaviour could be controlled and influenced by reward and punishment.

Within a learning and development context, trainers applying behaviourist principles will focus on trying to achieve behaviour change through the application of positive feedback, encouragement and reinforcement. Practice opportunities should be linked to feedback which constructively seeks to correct mistakes, and learners should be provided with clear guidance and rules associated with learning. Trainers should also pay attention to the layout and set-up of the training room to guide and promote positive behaviours. For example, to encourage group discussions, a circular room layout may be adopted.

Experiential Learning

An important issue concerns how individuals learn from experiences. The **experiential learning** cycle (Kolb, 1984) proposes four key stages in the learning cycle (Figure 9.1). On the next page is a brief overview of each stage.

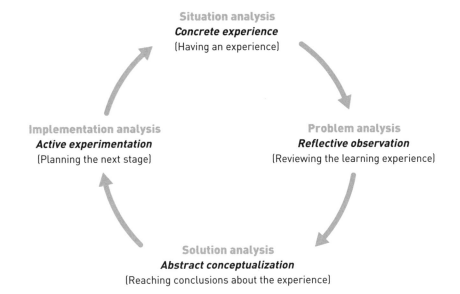

Figure 9.1 Experiential learning cycle
Source: adapted from Figure 2, Basic Learning Processes and the Stages of Problem Management, from Kolb, D.A. (1983) 'Problem Management: Learning from Experience', in S. Srivastva (ed.), *The Executive Mind*, p. 120, San Francisco: Jossey-Bass/John Wiley & Sons, Inc.

Stage 1: Having an Experience

Learners can pursue experiences in both a reactive or proactive way, though increasingly they are expected to be productive and seek out learning opportunities themselves. These opportunities may occur in a work or non-work setting. Learning experiences may involve performing a task for the first time, participating in complex projects or activities, and seeking feedback from a manager, coach or mentor.

Stage 2: Reviewing the Learning Experience

Reflection is a vital part of the experiential learning process. Thus, in order to maximize the process of reflection, learners should think about what has been learned:

- Think about other ways in which the task or activity could have been undertaken.
- Make comparisons between set targets and realized targets.
- Engage in guided reading and discussion with others.

Stage 3: Reaching Conclusions about the Experience

Experiential learning requires that learners reach conclusions about what has been learned from the experience. Learners should seek out the lessons learned and reach conclusions. The learner should ask these questions:

- What have I learned from the experience?
- How does the experience differ from previous experiences?
- How will I handle similar experiences in the future?
- What could I have done differently?

Stage 4: Planning the Next Stage

Experiential learning theory argues that having reached a conclusion about what was learned, it is important to plan how to do things better the next time. To do this effectively, a learner needs to be clear about what needs to be done differently and translate this learning into subsequent action.

Learning Styles

Adult learners are usually keen to get involved in the learning process, but it is well established that different learners have a preference for different ways of learning. While there have been many approaches taken to identifying learning styles, Honey and Mumford (1992) and Kolb (1984) suggest that there are four learning styles that link with the four stages of the learning cycle:

- *Activists:* They like to get fully involved in the action. They continually seek out new experiences and are enthusiastic about new ideas and techniques. Activists are open-minded and may be overenthusiastic about novelty. They have a tendency to act first and reflect on the consequences later.
- *Reflectors:* They like to stand back and observe experiences from different perspectives. They like data collection and analysis and are slow to reach definite conclusions. Reflectors tend to be shy and not necessarily involved in discussions or debate. They will always focus on the big picture when they act and will factor in the observations of others.
- *Theorists:* They continually focus on analysis and the development of theories based on multiple observations. They like to think in a logical, step-by-step way. Theorists have a great capacity to integrate many different facts and observations into coherent explanations.
- *Pragmatists:* They are focused on trying out new ideas, theories and techniques to see how they will work in practice. Pragmatists continually search for new ideas and will avail themselves of every opportunity to try out new applications. They dislike long drawn-out discussions.

It is critical that learning and development specialists consider learning styles when designing activities since they are important when selecting learning methods. An effective learning experience will provide space for all four learning styles, including opportunities for doing things.

> **The learning organization** – an organization focused on building a learning culture and integrating learning across all levels, systems and employees of the organization
>
> **Strategic human resource development (SHRD)** – learning activities focused on individuals, teams and organizations and aimed at enhancing the alignment of human resources with the strategic goals of the organization

COMMON MODELS OF LEARNING AND DEVELOPMENT IN ORGANIZATIONS

Organizations have a number of choices when it comes to how they approach learning and development activities. Three models are frequently used: the strategic HRD model, **the learning organization** model and the ADDIE model. Each of these models will be discussed, outlining their key features, advantages and limitations.

Strategic HRD Model

There is an increasing requirement for people to be a source of competitive advantage. Therefore, learning and development activities need to be organized to ensure that they make a strategic contribution. **The strategic human resource development (SHRD)** model focuses on articulating the characteristics of learning and development activities that are imperative to this. It seeks to foster a learning culture and to help organizations build agility and flexibility amongst employees so that organizations can respond effectively to changes in the external environment. An SHRD model (Garavan, 1991, 2007, 2012) emphasizes the following important features:

1. *Strategic integration*: This suggests that SHRD will both support the implementation of business goals and help shape the formulation of corporate strategy and goals. SHRD supports and is supported by other strategic human resource management activities (see ▶Chapter 1◀) and it will contribute to strategic change.
2. *Multi-stakeholder perspective*: An SHRD model recommends engagement with a variety of stakeholders in order to deliver value to the organization. These stakeholders will include senior management, line managers, employees and the HRM function. Millmore et al. (2007) argue that engagement with senior management is essential because they reflect the strategic agenda and the desired organizational culture and they are the key decision-makers within an organization.

3. *Dynamic capabilities:* The provision of SHRD will help organizations build flexibility in employee knowledge and skills – such that employees and teams will engage in sensing, seizing and reconfiguring internal processes to meet external realities.

4. *Centrality of knowledge management systems:* The ability to access information, process it and generate new knowledge is critical to creating sustainable organizational value. There is increasing awareness of the need to engage in boundary scanning of the external environment and recognition of the need to access external knowledge and integrate it within internal organizational systems. Knowledge management systems play an important role in storing, sharing and communicating knowledge to different units across the organization.

5. *Creation of a learning culture*: An important component of the SHRD model concerns the creation of a learning culture that promotes learning and development for all individuals. A particular dimension of this culture concerns organizational support for development. Organizations implementing SHRD approaches are likely to foster organizational learning as a mechanism for identifying and responding to high levels of environmental uncertainty.

In summary, an SHRD model suggests that learning and development should be concerned with shaping the strategic agenda rather than simply responding to it. However, it is clear from the available evidence that SHRD can often experience difficulties in aligning its activities with strategy and other HRM practices (Pett and Wolff, 2007). Organizations that implement an SHRD model include Dell, Microsoft, Hewlett-Packard and Kerry Group.

BUILDING YOUR SKILLS

SHRD is frequently considered to have a major role in shaping the context in which it operates. It suggests that learning and development practitioners should become organizational change consultants who possess the skills to influence corporate culture, form strategic partnerships with line managers, participate in top management discussions of strategy and advocate the SHRD agenda. Interview a senior learning and development specialist in a large organization, such as your university. Find out the challenges involved in working at senior levels in the organization and investigate the skills required to perform at such a senior level.

HRM IN THE NEWS

Training and national competitiveness

With the advent of Brexit looming on the horizon, many UK businesses are becoming increasingly anxious about its effects on national competitiveness and the ability of UK businesses to source highly trained and qualified staff to fill job vacancies. Coming on the back of a global recession, Brexit poses important challenges for UK businesses as UK government ministers seek to conclude trade deals with overseas nations and reassure a nervous population that all will be okay after the UK leaves the European Union. In recent times, three reports have set out some of the challenges facing UK businesses.

A white paper issued by the Chartered Management Institute in May 2017 entitled *Skills First: Connecting Employers, Further Education and Training Providers* found that UK businesses were struggling to find new recruits for existing vacancies and then were failing to train them adequately. The report indicated that 70% of employers were failing to train new managers sufficiently to allow them to succeed in their roles, with the Department of Business, Innovation and Skills reporting that poor management and leadership was costing the UK economy upwards of £19 billion per year in lost productivity.

A May 2017 report by the OECD also identified a need for increased training in UK companies to maintain managerial effectiveness in an era of intense global competition. It found that a lack of training and skills has resulted in an underdeveloped workforce and cautioned that the UK could lose its edge in high-tech sectors to neighbouring European countries. It reported that 27% of British adults struggle with literacy or numeracy or both and underlined the importance of boosting employee skills to meet the requirements of technologically advanced organizations.

A third report by training platform Course Library, and reported on by the CIPD in June 2017, found that 81% of workers had experienced a 'career slump' at some point in their working career. A lack of career progression and training and development opportunities were the most common factors cited by respondents in relation to this career slowdown. Around 41% of employees surveyed indicated that they had left their jobs in response to the career slump, with boredom and a lack of enthusiasm and motivation cited as key factors underpinning the need to seek out a new employment opportunity.

All in all, the three reports underscore the need for businesses to invest in training and development to ensure productivity levels do not suffer and employees feel that they are valued and respected in the workplace.

Questions

1. How can organizations help employees expand their skill sets and grow alongside the business?

2. What actions do national governments need to take to boost national competitiveness and productivity?

3. How can the benefits of investing in training and development be explained to employers?

4. What role can vocational training play in helping workers who experience a career slump?

5. Should vocational programmes exclusively target specific employability skills or adopt a wider developmental approach?

Sources

Calnan, M. (2017) 'Four out of five workers have experienced a "career slump" – and almost half quit over it', *People Management*, www2.cipd.co.uk/pm/peoplemanagement/b/weblog/archive/2017/06/06/four-out-of-five-workers-have-experienced-a-career-slump-and-almost-half-quit-over-it.aspx (accessed 11 June 2018)

Haughton, J. (2017) 'The trouble with training: why good managers are being refused the training they need', Chartered Management Institute, www.managers.org.uk/insights/news/2017/april/the-trouble-with-training-why-good-managers-are-being-refused-the-training-they-need (accessed 11 June 2018)

Wallace, T. (2017) 'UK could lose jobs overseas because workers lack skills and literacy is stagnating', *The Telegraph*, www.telegraph.co.uk/business/2017/05/04/uk-could-lose-jobs-overseas-workers-lack-skills-literacy-stagnating/ (accessed 11 June 2018)

The Learning Organization Model

The second model that may inform learning and development in organizations is the learning organization model. Central to the concept of the learning organization is the idea that learning is a key source of competitive advantage (Sloman, 2010). The learning organization model focuses on learning how to learn, enabling employees' learning to generate outcomes such as creativity, innovation, change and transformation, facilitating learning that focuses on changing organizational behaviour, and viewing learning as an end in itself. Table 9.1 summarizes the characteristic features of the learning organization as a model or approach to learning and development in organizations.

A highly influential figure in facilitating thinking about learning organizations is Peter Senge. In his work, Senge identifies five disciplines which he believes lie at the heart of the learning organization. The first discipline, *Systems Thinking*, recognizes that underpinning the effectiveness of organizations lie a myriad of processes, structures and strategies

- Learning is derived from a multiplicity of experiences: planned/unplanned, deliberate/accidental, successes/failures and is used to shape future behaviour

- Learning has significance in itself and learning how to learn is a critical aspect of the learning organization

- Organizations learn from the external and internal environment and this occurs at all times within the organization

- A learning organization encourages collaboration and teamworking amongst its employees

- Learning is continuous, habitual and internalized

- Learning is utilized by an organization to enable change and transformation

- Organizational leaders play a key part in role-modelling and supporting learning within and across the organization

- Enquiry, dialogue and the creation of new learning opportunities lie at the heart of the learning organization

- Learning occurs because it is facilitated by managers and employees and occurs naturally within an organization

Table 9.1 Characteristic features of the learning organization
Sources: inspired by information in Garavan, 1997; Sun and Scott, 2006; Felstead et al., 2007; Marsick and Watkins, 1999.

which must work together in harmony. The second discipline of *Personal Mastery* recognizes that organizations can only learn through their people and, thus, it encourages employees to achieve a high level of competence and expertise in their chosen field. The third discipline of *Mental Models* recognizes that mental schemas play an important role in shaping behaviour in organizations and inhibiting creative and 'outside the box' thinking. He asserts that existing mental models may need to be challenged in order to drive innovation and creativity. The fourth discipline of *Building a Shared Vision* identifies the importance of ensuring that there is alignment across departments and business units in relation to the goals, values and mission of the organization. Finally, the fifth discipline of *Team Learning* underscores the importance for individuals to work together and collaborate effectively.

The learning organization model is a difficult one to realize in organizations. Important learning activities that may help in the creation of a learning organization include those that facilitate the emergence of a learning culture, such as recognition and rewards for learning, the allocation of resources to learning and development, and role-modelling by senior leaders of openness to learning. A variety of processes can also be implemented, such as

structures and routines for knowledge-sharing and redesigning organizational structures to facilitate collaboration and teamwork. Evaluation is viewed as a vital continuous process to ensure that decisions about learning and development are informed by evidence.

In summary, the learning organization model represents an idealized way in which to think about learning and development activities in organizations. However, there is doubt concerning its practical application. At best, it represents a progressive process because the conditions necessary for it to flourish are difficult to find in many organizations. It visualizes an organization that is continually transforming itself and, in reality, few organizations meet this condition. It is difficult to identify examples of organizations that identify themselves as learning organizations, but those that have features of a learning organization include Apple, Samsung and Merck.

The ADDIE Model

The ADDIE model is a well-established and popular instructional design approach used to develop training programmes in organizations. The model offers a robust, logical, linear methodology for producing training in organizations. As a model,

HRM AND ORGANIZATIONAL PERFORMANCE

Key trends in learning and development

With organizations increasingly seeking to maximize the contribution of key employees, learning and development has become an important tool in growing, empowering and retaining key talent. Learning and development professionals are being tasked with ensuring the organization's talent pipeline possesses sufficient strength and depth to meet current and future needs. Companies are becoming more strategic in how they allocate learning and development expenditure and are looking to innovative technological solutions to improve learning and development provision. Wentworth and Lombardi (2014) identify five key trends in the field of learning and development:

1 *Going mobile:* Organizations are increasingly looking to mobile learning solutions to help meet the needs of busy executives who are regularly on the go in order to provide easily accessible, engaging, bite-sized learning that improves productivity and performance. While current adoption rates of mobile learning amongst leading organizations remain low, uptake of mobile learning solutions is expected to steadily increase.

2 *Social collaboration:* Social learning tools such as blogs, discussion forums, file-sharing sites and interactive platforms are increasingly used by companies to encourage employee collaboration and to foster a strong learning culture within organizations. With the widespread appeal of social media, organizations increasingly recognize the value of social learning and interaction and are examining ways of fostering greater mobile and online collaboration.

3 *Adaptive learning:* Organizations are increasingly seeking ways of customizing and individualizing the learning experience. This marks a strong shift away from 'sheep-dip' (i.e. where all employees receive the exact same training) approaches and recognizes the value of offering learning that meets the needs of specific employees.

4 *Strategic alignment:* As companies prioritize competitiveness, there is a strong drive to link learning to business goals and objectives. This ensures that learning is closely linked to issues related to organizational performance, engagement and productivity. It also avoids the possibility of departmental silos and ensures a cohesive learning identity across the organization.

5 *Establishing effectiveness:* Examining the effect of learning on company metrics has become a key trend. While many organizations have moved away from 'return on investment' to 'return on expectations', organizations are still strongly interested in ensuring that investment in learning and development delivers real-time organizational value.

its relative longevity and widespread acceptance amongst training professionals attests to its effectiveness as a standardized approach for producing training programmes. The origins of the ADDIE model lie in efforts by the US military to develop more effective training solutions in the aftermath of the Second World War. The model is extremely simple to understand, which is a significant strength and also its weakness. While it is a useful starting point, providing organizations with a basic framework for how learning and development activities are formulated, the model's weaknesses include the following:

- It does not consider organizational strategy, learning and development strategy and HRM strategy as key components of the cycle.
- The model ignores the political realities that exist in organizations: namely, the competition for resources; the lack of support for training; and shifting organizational priorities.
- In its earliest conceptions, evaluation was considered the final stage in the model. Increasingly, it is recognized that learning facilitators should embark upon continuous evaluation as they progress through the stages of the ADDIE model. Leaving assessment and

evaluation until the end of the training can do little to help improve the instruction.

- Harrison and Kessels (2004) have criticized its lack of attention to key stakeholders within and external to the organization. The model is silent on how stakeholders should be included in key decisions related to all stages of the instructional design process.
- The model assumes that instructional designers are aware of all the relevant training requirements prior to developing the training content, which is not always realistic.
- While the ADDIE model proposes a step-by-step systematic approach, this may not be cost-effective and may be impractical in today's fast-paced organizations.

The ADDIE model, presented in Figure 9.2, depicts a cycle of activities comprising:

- **A**nalysis of learning and development needs
- **D**esign of learning objectives and assessment instruments
- **D**evelopment of learning content and activities, and the embedding of content within technological platforms
- **I**mplementation of learning, including plans for training the learner and teacher
- **E**valuation of the outcomes of the learning interventions.

We now explore each of the stages of the ADDIE model in more depth.

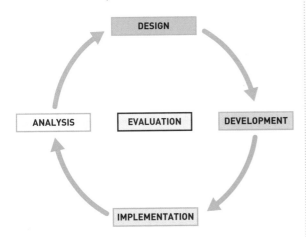

Figure 9.2 The ADDIE model
Source: adapted from Figure 4.1, The ADDIE Process with Key Management Components, from United States Army Training and Doctrine Command (2017) *TRADOC Regulation 350-70: Army Learning Policy and Systems*, Fort Eustis, Virginia: Department of the Army Headquarters.

EXPLORING THE STAGES OF THE ADDIE MODEL

Analysis of Learning and Development Needs

The analysis of learning and development needs represents the first important step in ensuring effective alignment of learning and development with organizational goals. Bee and Bee (2003) have suggested that the process of learning needs analysis operates from the assumption that learning and development will contribute to organizational performance when learning needs are clearly identified and matched with appropriate learning interventions. Harrison (2009) suggested that the needs identification process consists of three key stages:

1. *Data collection:* This involves finding out the nature of the need and whether it is an individual, team or organizational need. A learning and development specialist can consult a variety of information sources to find out about current capability and performance levels. These information sources include:
   - self-assessment information such as the opinions of jobholders and personal development plans
   - feedback information from appraisal and competency assessments
   - the assessments of supervisors and managers
   - customer survey data and data derived from benchmark studies and objective measures such as productivity, quality data and exit behaviour data such as absenteeism.

   In the case of organizational needs analysis and where the focus is on future capability and performance issues, the learning and development specialist will consider information sources such as strategic targets, planned organizational change initiatives, customer and market data, and issues related to the expansion or contraction of the business.

2. *Identification of the capability/performance gap:* Learning and development interventions are frequently wasted in organizations. They are often not the most appropriate solution or may not be a solution at all. Therefore, the purpose of this stage is to determine the nature and extent of the performance/capability gap and make an assessment as to whether the gap can

be addressed using an appropriate learning and development intervention. The type of analysis undertaken to determine the performance/ capability gap will be decided by the trigger for the needs analysis process. In situations where some form of learning intervention is the expected outcome, a trainer-led approach may be appropriate. An organization-wide intervention is appropriate where the needs of all employees are the focus of the analysis.

3. *Recommendations and prioritization of learning needs:* A key outcome of the needs analysis process focuses on making recommendations on training activities that are relevant to the context, feasible within organizational and budgetary constraints, and are capable of being delivered within the capabilities of the learning and development function. When recommendations are made concerning prioritizing learning and development needs, the following issues should be taken into account:

– the importance and urgency of the learning need
– whether the learning need is related to the strategic objectives of the organization
– whether non-learning and development actions are more appropriate to address the problem
– the feelings of jobholders and their managers
– that the supporting information is evidence-based rather than opinion-based
– that the business case is supported by a clear indication of the investment involved
– the level at which the need exists in the organization
– whether the learning need requires a decision on whether to purchase a training course from an external provider or design it internally.

The analysis stage also requires learning and development specialists to engage with a number of important activities. Table 9.2 sets out some of these.

Activities	Actions
Take responsibility for the development of learning and development strategy	• Create a learning and development strategy development group • Involve key stakeholders such as line managers, HRM specialists and employees
Clarify the organizational mission and strategy	• Read formal strategy documents to gain insights on current strategic priorities • Gather and interpret information from key individuals in the organization
Conduct an internal and external stakeholder analysis	• Specify the key performance issues from the perspective of each stakeholder • Identify how each stakeholder contributes to learning and development and their expectations of learning and development • Analyse the key barriers and enablers to strategic alignment and the emergence of a learning culture and climate
Specify the strategic challenges and opportunities facing the organization	• Differentiate strategic from operational effectiveness issues • Identify issues that have learning and development implications • Differentiate between those issues that have learning and development implications and those that do not
Generate strategic alternatives for learning and development and gain commitment from stakeholders	• Prioritize learning and development goals that add value to the organization's strategic imperatives • Focus on issues that can achieve quick wins as well as long-term successes • Focus on issues where there are clear learning and development applications • Identify benefits for individuals as well as the organization

Activities	Actions
Agree a strategic learning and development strategy and plan	• Specify clear learning and development goals to be achieved within a specified time frame • Specify the resources required to achieve the goals • Allocate accountabilities and responsibilities to achieve learning and development goals

Table 9.2 Activities engaged in by learning and development specialists during the analysis stage

SPOTLIGHT ON SKILLS

As a learning and development specialist, you have received a request from a line manager who needs you to supply a learning and development solution to address a problem within a team. The line manager is not sure what the precise problem is but is convinced that some form of learning intervention would be of help.

1. How will you initially approach this request?
2. What types of questions will you ask to find out whether it is a problem with a learning solution?
3. What types of data would you like to obtain concerning the functioning of the team?
4. How will you sell the proposed learning solution, assuming it is appropriate, to the team?
5. What criteria will you use to assess the effectiveness of any learning solution you propose?

To help you answer the questions above, visit www.macmillanihe.com/carbery-cross-hrm-2e and watch the video of Aidan Lawrence from Hewlett-Packard talking about learning and development.

Designing Learning and Development

The design stage of the ADDIE model concerns itself with defining an overall approach to the learning and development content. It involves using the information collected during the analysis stage to build a course or programme that meets the learners' needs. A key consideration is the logical and orderly organization of planned content so that it meets instructional goals. A number of important decisions need to be made by the learning and development specialist at this stage, including:

• the formulation of learning objectives or outcomes
• the planning of the assessment strategy
• the determining of the levels, types and difficulty of the activities within the module or course
• the selection of the delivery method for learning.

Formulation of Learning Objectives/Outcomes

In the formulation stage, learning needs should be translated into specific learning objectives/outcomes. These should be measurable and consist of statements of specific outcomes that will form the basis for the design of the learning intervention. Learning outcomes will focus on knowledge, skill and/or attitudes. Once learning objectives/outcomes have been defined, it is appropriate to consider the selection of learning and development strategies.

Planning of the Assessment Strategy

The planning of the assessment strategy is critical to ensuring that participant learning remains on track. Assessment should be decided upon prior to the development of learning content to ensure that instructional goals are well covered by the assessment strategy. Learning and development specialists should pay attention to learner characteristics when formulating the assessment strategy to ensure there is a good fit with the experience, background and aptitudes of learners. Examples of assessment instruments can include written tests, reflections and performance tests.

Determining the Levels, Types and Difficulty of the Activities within the Module or Course

One of the essential tasks within the design stage of the ADDIE model is to determine the structure and sequence of learning. Ensuring that there is a logical flow to the learning activities will help learners process and store learning efficiently. Learning and development specialists will ensure appropriate task progression from the easiest to the most difficult so that learners can build confidence in their own abilities.

The Selection of Delivery Methods for Learning

A learning and development specialist will have a wide variety of options when selecting learning and development strategies. Learning and development strategies include bite-sized and blended learning, formal classroom courses, digital learning, coaching, mentoring, job instruction, planned work experience, projects and assignments. Detailed discussion of these is beyond the scope of this chapter, but a brief description of each is provided below.

Bite-sized and Blended Learning Strategies

Bite-sized learning strategies have become increasingly popular in organizations. They are typically designed to help employees who have limited time to attend learning and development activities to participate in short, quick training events. They provide employees with an opportunity to dip into learning (Pett and Wolff, 2007) and to keep up to date with developments in technical and professional areas. Blended learning is also a popular learning and development strategy, because it can be customized to suit the needs of individuals. It typically includes technology-based strategies combined with more individual learning strategies such as coaching, mentoring, guided reading and learning logs. The key challenge is to achieve a blend of approaches appropriate to the learning needs of the individual.

Classroom Courses

These are structured learning interventions undertaken in a classroom setting. They will vary on whether they are instructional or facilitative, and whether they take place within or outside the organization. They are a frequently used learning and development strategy. They have several advantages related to their cost-effectiveness and capacity to deliver common sets of knowledge and skill to a large group of learners. They do, however, encounter transfer of learning problems as classroom settings may be quite different from actual workplace settings.

Digital Learning, or Technology-delivered Instruction

Digital learning, or technology-delivered instruction, has become increasingly popular as a learning and development strategy. Digital learning can be used as a blended learning strategy and combined with more traditional classroom-based learning. Its major advantage is that it allows learners to choose when, where and what to learn. However, a significant drawback is that it transfers responsibility to the learner to make the decision to participate in learning and development activities. Digital learning as a learning and development strategy has expanded to include online tutoring, chat rooms, discussion groups, social networking sites, audiovisual conferencing, virtual classrooms and two-way live satellite broadcasts.

Coaching and Mentoring

Coaching and mentoring (see ▶Chapter 10◀ for more information) are commonly used learning and development strategies to develop managers and leaders. Coaching focuses on helping individuals or groups to perform more effectively, while mentoring involves guiding and suggesting appropriate learning experiences for the mentee. Coaching and mentoring place a strong emphasis on the role of a more experienced employee as a facilitator of learning. Both strategies are designed to encourage individuals to learn, and to learn in different ways according to their development needs.

Job Instruction and Planned Work Experience

Job instruction focuses on one-to-one or group instruction that is carried out at the workplace and delivered while the learner is engaged in performing work tasks and activities. It is typically conducted between an experienced trainer and a learner. Planned work experience involves the learner performing a variety of roles throughout the organization for specific periods of time in order to sample different tasks, often as part of a graduate development programme. Both strategies take place on the job and therefore maximize the opportunities for the transfer of learning.

Projects and Assignments

Projects are a commonly used learning and development strategy to develop technical and/or managerial skills. Projects can be undertaken individually or as part of a team. Projects are frequently used in organizations to develop teamworking and collaboration skills, and skills in the implementation of major change or transformation initiatives. Job assignments are commonly used to prepare managers for promotion and advancement within an organization. The assignment may involve an international component, and it may also involve either a team-building challenge or a volunteering component. For example, a manager may be given an assignment to close down a loss-making business unit or to develop cross-cultural awareness and skills. Both strategies can be extremely powerful, provided they are well planned and effectively structured, supported and monitored.

BUILDING YOUR SKILLS

Digital learning is increasingly popular as a learning strategy. However, it is not a strategy that everyone enjoys. Undertake some research on digital learning in an organization (perhaps your university). Then answer the following questions:

❶ What do employees or students think of digital learning?
❷ Is it an effective learning strategy?
❸ For what types of learning needs is digital learning more and less appropriate?
❹ What steps can be taken to encourage employees or students to participate in digital learning activities?

Developing Learning and Development

The development stage in the ADDIE model involves the building of content and materials following the plans and blueprints produced in the design stage. In constructing content, instructional designers need to keep in mind the profile of learners, the mix of learning methods, the level of interactivity within individual sessions and the opportunities to receive feedback and practise the learning. Such considerations are necessary to ensure that participants transfer as much of the learning as possible back to the workplace. In essence, the development stage involves the drafting, production and testing of learning materials. At times, this may involve running a pilot of the training activity to ensure that the intended goals are realized. Table 9.3 on the next page outlines some of the most common learning and development methods and indicates some criteria for establishing their suitability for a proposed learning and development programme.

Implementation of Learning and Development

The implementation stage of the ADDIE model is where the course or instruction is delivered to learners. Trainers need to make appropriate preparations for the course delivery, including setting up the training room; managing learner registration; organizing catering, equipment and software; and distributing schedules, handouts and course booklets. The effective implementation of learning and development activities requires that trainers are aware of:

- the different ways in which people learn (see page 168)
- the needs of adult learners, giving them significant control over how and when they learn
- the motivation of learners
- the environment in which the learning occurs.

Trainers need to provide:

- opportunities for learners to learn by utilizing practice, trial and error
- feedback during the learning process
- the opportunity for learners to make sense of what they have learned.

Learning method	Trainer or learner centred	Suitability
Lecture: a structured, planned talk usually accompanied by visual aids	Trainer centred	Ideal for large training groups and when large amounts of information need to be communicated. Does not allow for a high degree of participation by learners
Group discussion: allows the free exchange of knowledge, ideas and opinions on a particular issue/theme	Learner centred	Appropriate when the learning objective is to share viewpoints or analyse complex organizational issues. Requires the trainer to manage the process and keep the discussion focused
Role play: the enactment of a role in a protected environment. Learner suspends reality and adopts a particular persona	Learner centred	Learners have an opportunity to act as if they were in real-life situations. Learners can practise their responses and receive feedback from a trainer on key learnings. Can provide learners with enhanced self-awareness, self-confidence and the ability to learn from mistakes
Case study: the examination of a situation or events. Learning takes place through the analysis of detailed material and the identification of potential solutions	Learner centred	Provides learners with the opportunity to examine a situation in detail and generate solutions. Allows a group of learners to exchange ideas and discuss complex organizational issues. Key challenge is to select a case study that matches the skills of participants but also stretches their knowledge and skill
In-tray exercise: learners are given a series of documents, files, letters and memos and are asked to select appropriate actions	Learner centred	Learners are exposed to a simulation of real life. Provides learners with an opportunity to experience the kinds of issues that will arise in their work
Video or film: used to show a real-life situation and different ways of dealing with it or to provide key information to a large audience	Trainer centred	Suitable to deliver information to large groups of learners and demonstrate examples of effective and less effective behaviours. Demands little in the way of participation by an audience but can be used as a springboard for discussion and questions

Table 9.3 Learning and development methods: type, characteristics and suitability

For larger groups, the implementation stage may involve train-the-trainer activities. The course designer needs to make sure that those who will facilitate the course have sufficient mastery of the material and have an opportunity to address any queries.

> **Evaluation** – establishing the intended and unintended outcomes of learning and development activities and assessing whether the benefits justify the investment

Evaluating Learning and Development Activities

Evaluation is a key feature of the ADDIE model and seeks to answer the following questions:

- How effectively did the organization undertake the learning needs analysis?

- Were the learning and development strategies and methods effective in addressing the identified learning needs?
- Did learners enjoy the learning intervention and did they perceive it as relevant to their current or future roles?
- What did participants learn as a result of participation in the learning intervention?
- What changes in work performance can be attributed to the learning intervention?
- To what extent has the learning intervention contributed to the achievement of organizational objectives?

These questions are asked in order to meet four important purposes:

1. To *prove* that the learning investment added value to the organization and to understand whether the learning intervention worked and achieved what it was supposed to achieve. Earlier, we highlighted that investment in learning and development can lead to performance improvements for individuals and organizations. Therefore, one of the tasks of evaluation is to prove these outcomes.
2. To *control* learning and development activities to ensure they are of an appropriate standard, delivered within budget and fit in with organizational priorities.
3. To *improve* the quality of learning and development activities.
4. To *reinforce* the learning that took place during the learning intervention.

The most widely used training evaluation model among practitioners is Kirkpatrick's four-level evaluation model (Kirkpatrick and Kirkpatrick, 2006). However, despite its popularity, the four-level model is widely contested – not least because the four levels are not correlated. The four levels are reaction, learning, behaviour and results evaluation, with the key issues to be considered at each level summarized in Table 9.4.

Evaluation level and type	Evaluation description and characteristics	Examples of evaluation tools and methods	Relevance and practicability
1 **Reaction**	Reaction evaluation focuses on the personal reactions of participants to the learning and development experience: • Did participants enjoy the training? • Did participants consider the training relevant? • Was the training a good use of participants' time? • Did participants like the administrative arrangements and learning setting?	• 'Happy sheets' – feedback forms based on subjective personal reaction to the training experience • Verbal feedback at the end of the programme either individually or as part of the group • Post-training surveys or questionnaires	• Completed immediately after the training ends • Easy to obtain reaction feedback • Feedback is not expensive to gather or to analyse for groups • Important to know if participants were not positive about the training
2 **Learning**	Learning evaluation is concerned with the measurement of learning before and after a learning and development event: • Did participants learn what was specified in the learning objectives? • Did participants enhance their skills as a result of the training?	• Learning is typically assessed using structured assessments or tests that are administered before and after the training • Interviews or observation can also be used before and after the training	• Organizations typically undertake post-training assessment; however, pre-training learning assessments are less common and may elicit unfavourable reactions from participants • It is important to design valid and reliable learning assessment methods to assess knowledge

Evaluation level and type	Evaluation description and characteristics	Examples of evaluation tools and methods	Relevance and practicability
	• Did the training result in a change in participants' attitudes and values?	• Methods of assessment need to be closely related to the learning objectives specified for the training	• The assessment of attitude change is complex and the assessment of a change in skills can be subjective
3 **Behaviour**	Behaviour evaluation focuses on how the learning and development activity impacted on job-related behaviours: • Did participants transfer their learning to the workplace? • Did participants develop the relevant skills and knowledge? • Were there observable and measurable changes in trainees' performance when back in their role? • Did trainees sustain the behaviour and performance changes? • Are trainees aware of changes in their behaviour, knowledge, skill level?	• Observation and interviews carried out over time are required to assess changes in behaviour, and the relevance and sustainability of the change • One-off assessments are not reliable because people change in different ways, at different paces and at different times • Assessments need to be subtle and ongoing, and then transferred to a suitable analysis tool • Assessments should be designed to reduce the subjective judgements of the observer or interviewer	• Measurement of behaviour change is complex, and more difficult to quantify and interpret than reaction and learning evaluation • Surface-level questions and tick box approaches will not generate strong evidence • Line managers may not be willing to participate in the evaluation process • The analysis of job behaviour evaluation data is complex and there is the problem of being certain that the behaviour change can be directly related to the training
4 **Results**	Results evaluation focuses on the measurement of return on investment (ROI) and organizational performance as a result of investment in training: • Lag measures will be used because the impact of training and performance may take some time to manifest itself • Typical measures include volumes, values, percentages, timescales, ROI, and other quantifiable aspects of organizational performance, for example numbers of complaints, staff turnover, attrition, failures, wastage, noncompliance, quality ratings, achievement of standards and accreditations, growth, retention and so on	• Many of these measures will already be in place via normal management systems and reporting • The challenge is to identify which measures are relevant and how they relate to the training • ROI evaluation requires a clear quantification of the costs and benefits involved in the learning and development intervention	• ROI evaluations are typically undertaken for single training programmes rather than for a suite of learning and development activities • ROI evaluations are expensive to conduct as they require a large amount of data collection and sophisticated statistical analysis techniques • In the final analysis, it may be difficult to prove that a particular set of benefits can be related to a particular learning and development activity

Table 9.4 Kirkpatrick's four levels of learning and development evaluation: issues and examples
Sources: inspired by information in Garavan et al., 2003; Kirkpatrick and Kirkpatrick, 2006.

CONSIDER THIS

You have been asked to design a reaction evaluation form to evaluate participants' reactions to a leadership development programme. What questions would you include in the form? How would you sequence them? How many questions would you include? Explain the reasoning behind your decisions.

HRM IN PRACTICE

Upskilling your training team

CORBIS

You are the learning and development specialist in a financial services organization located in Denmark employing 950 people. You joined the organization nearly five years ago as head of learning and development. However, during that time, the nature of the role has changed. The core team is relatively small, with two direct trainers delivering standard curriculum-based financial training courses. The third member of the team focuses on learning processes and performs a range of administrative tasks. You now realize that you need a member of your team who is not just proficient in delivering standardized training courses but can perform a range of duties that correspond to a learning and development consultant or business partner role. Increasingly, you receive requests from business unit managers to provide more individualized and customized solutions. They expect the learning and development team to deliver tailored learning interventions rather than simply focusing on short courses.

The core skills of a learning and development consultant or business partner consist of a combination of systematic training skills, such as learning needs identification, learning design, delivery and evaluation, as well as a variety of business and consultancy competencies, including a broad understanding of the business, an understanding of organizational processes and advanced problem-solving skills. The learning and development consultant will also be expected to possess good interpersonal skills and the ability to build strong relationships with managers and clients at all levels within the organization. It is important that the role is performed with credibility, professionalism and confidence. Stakeholder management is a key requirement of the role, and the learning and development specialist will be required to demonstrate value and convince business unit managers that learning interventions add value to their business operations.

You do not have the option to recruit a new member to the team, as a recruitment freeze is in operation and only core business roles will be filled. This freeze will last for at least one more year. As a result, you have to consider your two direct trainers for the role. Both are highly committed but are very comfortable and skilled in performing the direct trainer role. This presents you with a significant dilemma with two possible options: should you select one of your direct trainers and develop that individual into the role, or should you hold off until the recruitment freeze is lifted? You are keen to continue to work in a strategic role within the organization and to provide consultancy and strategic business partner services to three of the most important business units. You would like the two additional business units to come within the remit of one of your existing direct trainers. You are now at a crossroads because the managing director is putting pressure on you to have someone trained up and performing the role within three months.

What would you do?

1 Write a memorandum to your general manager outlining how you propose to address this situation. What options will you propose?

2 Assuming you decide to select one of your existing direct trainers for the role, set out a development plan to bring that individual up to speed. What particular development strategies do you propose in order to develop their confidence and skill to perform a learning consultancy or strategic partner role?

© Royalty-Free/Corbis

SUMMARY

Learning and development has emerged as a significant strategic issue, and this chapter has examined how training supports the effectiveness of individuals, teams, organizations and society. Key concepts related to learning and development were defined, highlighting key distinctions between training, education, learning, development and human resource development. Understanding how people learn is critical to understanding how individuals acquire new knowledge, skills and behaviours. The principles of cognitivism, behaviourism and experiential learning were explored in order to develop an insight into how training can be most effectively delivered. Three common models of learning and development were then reviewed, including the strategic HRD model, the learning organization model and the ADDIE model. To conclude, the five stages of the ADDIE model were examined in depth to provide a template for how to design learning and development interventions in an effective manner.

CHAPTER REVIEW QUESTIONS

1. What do you understand by the term 'learning and development'?
2. How do the terms 'training', 'development', 'learning' and 'education' differ?
3. Outline the key differences between how people learn.
4. How is SHRD different from learning and development?
5. What are the key characteristics of a learning organization?
6. What are the stages in designing learning and development programmes?
7. How should learning and development be evaluated?
8. Discuss the four stages in Kirkpatrick's evaluation model.

FURTHER READING

Carbery, R. and Cross, C. (2015) *Human Resource Development: A Concise Introduction*, London: Palgrave.

Gibb, S. (2011) *Human Resource Development: Foundations, Process, Contexts*, 3rd edn, Basingstoke: Palgrave.

McGuire, D. (2014) *Human Resource Development*, 2nd edn, London: Sage.

USEFUL WEBSITES

www.iipuk.co.uk

Investors in People UK is a business improvement tool that provides an accredited framework for organizations wishing to achieve business goals and performance through people.

www.eurydice.org

Eurydice, the information network on education in Europe, provides information on and analyses of European education systems and policies and is coordinated and managed by the EU Education, Audiovisual and Culture Executive Agency in Brussels.

www.ahrd.org

Academy of Human Resource Development is a global organization comprising a scholarly community of academics and reflective practitioners. It studies HRD theories, processes and practices and disseminates information about HRD through four affiliated peer-reviewed journals.

www.cedefop.europa.eu

Cedefop is the European Centre for the Development of Vocational Training. It works closely with the European Commission, governments, representatives of employers and trade unions, vocational training researchers and practitioners to strengthen European cooperation.

CHAPTER 9

For extra resources, including videos, multiple choice questions and useful weblinks, go to: www.macmillanihe.com/carbery-cross-hrm-2e.

Getty Images/iStockphoto/pawel_p

10: Career Development

Ronan Carbery and David McKevitt

LEARNING OUTCOMES

By the end of this chapter you will be able to:

- Define the concept of a career
- Identify the changing contexts of work and career
- Discuss how traditional understandings of careers differ from contemporary career types
- Understand the context of graduate careers
- Discuss the role of career anchors in facilitating career progression
- Outline the role of the HRM function in facilitating career development

THIS CHAPTER DISCUSSES:

Introduction (188)

What is a Career? (188)

Traditional Versus Contemporary Career Perspectives (189)

Contemporary Careers (190)

Graduate Careers (197)

Responsibility for Career Development (199)

Career Anchor Theory (200)

Role of the HRM Function (202)

INTRODUCTION

In this chapter we look at the concept of contemporary career development. Over the past three decades, there have been significant changes in the way work is organized and career paths have developed (Chudzikowski, 2012). The ability to predict careers has decreased, flexibility has increased, and if individuals are willing to follow opportunities as they arise, then it has been argued that greater career success is the outcome (Gunz et al., 2000). As we have seen from ▶Chapter 8◀, individuals' expectations as to what they want from employment have changed, making it necessary for employers to accommodate more flexible working patterns. The effect of this change in the way jobs are organized has resulted in a shifting of the employability risk from organizations to individuals (Bridges, 1994; Lips-Wiersma and Hall, 2007). There has been exploration of the impact of the work situation and the risks on professional wellbeing as a consequence of job insecurity (Bakker et al., 2003) and precarious employment ▶Chapter 5◀. Further, there have been implications on person–organization fit (Maslach and Leiter, 1997), explained as being 'the congruity between the person and the workplace in key aspects, such as workload, control, rewards, community feelings, fairness, and values' (Sortheix et al., 2013: 468). Many of these elements are demonstrated through the approach taken to ensuring continued employability and career development. A short-term focus is likely to inhibit the uptake of longer term development opportunities, and it raises questions over organizational investment in careers when the return on that investment may be unlikely to be revealed within the organization (Maurer and Chapman, 2013) or, worse, might result in advantage for a competitor. Development to enhance employability is often portrayed as being someone else's problem; with popular press reporting of an ill-prepared workforce providing an example (Gough, 2013).

A number of new career types have been proposed to describe contemporary careers, such as boundaryless, protean, authentic, portfolio and kaleidoscope careers, which we explore later in the chapter. One commonality shared by these concepts is that of self-directedness. The career is directed by the individual rather than the organization. It is likely to involve a number of shifts in employment,

between organizations, industries and, perhaps, cultures. The purpose of this chapter is to look at careers today and understand different career types that people can choose to pursue. We contrast these with a traditional understanding of careers and ask: who should be responsible for career development? We also consider the role of the HRM function in managing careers. We begin first by considering what a career actually is.

WHAT IS A CAREER?

The term **career** was initially used to indicate a designation of privilege. Only a small number of individuals, predominately males, had careers in stereotypical professional jobs, for example law, medicine and education. The terms 'occupation' or 'job' were used to describe most situations where individuals exchanged their labour or skills for monetary reward. Now, however, the term 'career' has significantly broadened to include the entirety of work experiences that a person engages in, rather than focusing solely on employment in one industry or profession. Arthur et al. (1989: 8) describe a career as 'the evolving sequence of a person's work experiences over time'. The distinguishing characteristics of this definition are:

> **Career** – a person's work experiences over the course of their life
>
> **Career development** – how a person manages their life, learning and work to achieve career goals

- its emphasis on the 'evolving sequence', which recognizes that careers are not stationary, but change over time
- 'work experiences' include paid employment, but also denote homemaking and other productive efforts such as sitting on boards or doing voluntary work that provide important career skills
- 'over time' suggests that a career lasts a lifetime.

Perhaps the most important part of this definition is that it indicates that each person has only one career. Even if individuals have worked in three or four different occupations or industries, these experiences form part of the same career. The definition therefore encourages individuals to look at ways in which their different experiences all relate to one another.

Career development is a lifelong process where individuals look at the occupational options available to them, select an option, and continue to make choices from the vast possibilities available to them. It is a developmental process that occurs over the life of an individual and this series of decisions constitute an integrated career path. The word 'path' in this context is important, as most careers are described in terms that suggest a journey; for example 'career path', 'career ladder' and 'getting to the top' all suggest that a career is characterized by the continual movement of the individual. However, the notion of a journey also indicates a destination or end point. As we will see, new careers may be more accurately described in more open-ended metaphors, such as 'travelling' rather than 'journeys'.

TRADITIONAL VERSUS CONTEMPORARY CAREER PERSPECTIVES

Traditionally, a person's career was expected to involve employment with one or two organizations over the course of their lives, and, by working hard, they would gradually take on more responsibility when the organization considered them ready for advancement or promotion (Super, 1957; Levinson, 1978). Success was defined by the organization and measured in objective terms such as promotions and salary (Hall, 1996). Wilensky (1961: 523) defined a traditional career as 'a succession of related jobs arranged in a hierarchy of prestige through which people

> **Traditional career** – a direct line of career progression where seniority and length of service are rewarded with progression from one specific job to a more senior job

move in ordered (more or less predictable) sequence'. This type of career can be considered the conventional public sector career path in a large number of European countries for example, where employment is generally characterized by job security and lifelong employment. This way of thinking about careers was standard until the 1990s.

The usual starting point for understanding traditional career development theory is Donald Super's life span theory (1953, 1980), which suggested that people's careers unfold in a linear manner where they have only a small number of employers. This perspective on careers is very much a product of its time in the 1950s; today it is generally not applicable to women or men who may have extended periods of absence from the workforce for family-related reasons.

The work of Arthur and Rousseau (1996) has significantly influenced current career thinking, and their definition, outlined at the beginning of this chapter, highlights that any occupation can be considered the basis for a career. The distinction between traditional and contemporary careers lies in the emphasis that Arthur and Rousseau place on the subjective interpretation of what constitutes a career, which can only be answered by the individual. Contemporary careers are thought to be more flexible and mobile, with goals defined by individuals themselves. Table 10.1 summarizes the differences between traditional and contemporary careers.

	Traditional career	Contemporary career
Employment relationship	Job security for loyalty	Employability for performance and flexibility
Transitions	Within the firm	Within and between firms, in and out of the labour market
Skills	Firm specific	Transferable
Determinants of success	More objective factors such as pay, promotion	More subjective factors such as job satisfaction and autonomy
Responsibility for career management	Organization	Individual

Table 10.1 Comparison between traditional careers and contemporary careers

CONTEMPORARY CAREERS

A number of career conceptualizations have emerged in the past decade that have influenced career theory and research and become part of the new career vocabulary. These new concepts have emerged as organizations have sought to restructure and downsize to compete on a global scale. In addition, as individuals attempt to develop flexibility in their work arrangements, they frequently depart from traditional career paths and seek alternative routes for career success.

Current careers tend to be dynamic, less predictable and boundaryless (Lips-Wiersma and Hall, 2007), with the individual at least as equally in charge of career development as organizations. The essence of careers has changed, and under this revised conceptualization, individuals bear primary responsibility for planning and managing their own careers (Grimland et al., 2012). In particular, two career concepts, boundaryless and protean careers, have dominated the thinking of academics and career practitioners in recent debates. Authentic, kaleidoscope and off-ramp careers have also been proposed as being relevant to contemporary careers. The ability to pursue these career types is, however, challenged by the prevailing economic climate. During the period of consistent economic growth from 2002 to 2008, employees had increased job mobility because of a tight labour market. Those with high educational qualifications and enhanced capabilities increased the value of their human capital to organizations, which led to more promotions and higher compensation (Wayne et al., 1999; Stumpf, 2010). This wave of mobility slowed with the beginning of the recession in 2008. An open marketplace where professionals had been experiencing advancement changed to a labour market that threatened their employment and slowed their career progression (Briscoe et al., 2012). While much of the initial research on these contemporary career types was carried out in stable and predictable economic circumstances, recent research looking at their applicability in an economic recession suggests that protean and boundaryless attitudes may help employees develop career skills and ultimately cope with uncertain career environments (Briscoe et al., 2012). We now look at each of these career concepts in turn.

HRM IN THE GLOBAL BUSINESS ENVIRONMENT

Pursuing a global career

The idea of expatriate assignments as a form of career development is changing. Expatriates are increasingly rejecting the 'one assignment' concept of expatriation and are instead adopting a 'career' approach, joining together multiple reassignments into meaningful sequences that fulfil their long-term personal and professional aspirations for building career capital (McNulty and Vance, 2017). These global careers are pursued across national and organizational boundaries in different forms of multinational corporations (MNCs), including private, public, non-profit and domestic organizations, and are on the rise. Expatriates pursuing global careers represent an emerging and potentially critical component of MNCs' overall talent pool and global staffing strategy. Organizations have recognized this by using the opportunity to pursue a global career as part of their recruitment and employer branding strategies ▶Chapter 3◀. A glance at the careers pages of organizations such as PWC, EY, KPMG and IBM shows references to 'global careers' and the opportunities that lie therein. With globalization changing the types of jobs that are available, pursuing a global career highlights the importance of learning and development in the workplace.

In a dynamic economy, workers are expected to adapt and pick up new skills when necessary. That requires successful learning and development programmes, which are addressed in more detail in ▶Chapter 9◀.

Boundaryless Careers

The concept of the **boundaryless career** moves away from the traditional notion of a career sustained within one physical organization. It

> **Boundaryless career** – sequences of jobs that can cross occupational, organizational and geographic boundaries

widens our perspective of a career to incorporate a range of possible role changes both within and across organizations or even industries. A boundaryless career is not determined by the prevailing career system of one employer (Tams and Arthur, 2006) nor represented by an orderly sequence of hierarchical upwards movement. As the employment landscape becomes less stable and less structured, normal career boundaries and structures become more permeable, enticing individuals to cross them, for example by changing employer, sector or profession.

Boundaryless careers can exist in a variety of forms and it can be difficult to capture all the different types. Though the term most often refers to voluntary movements across organizations, it can also incorporate situations where individuals are forced to leave an organization or take voluntary redundancy, ending career advancement therein. Not all boundaryless careers are confined to physical changes of employment: the notion also applies to movement across psychological boundaries. In this context, psychological boundarylessness refers to an individual's propensity and attitude towards initiating and pursuing work-related relationships outside their own workplace. For example, the career success of both consultants and academics depends upon their ability to create and sustain relationships across organizational boundaries (Arthur and Rousseau, 1996).

Boundaryless careers have particular relevance to organizations operating in unpredictable, opportunistic markets characterized by discontinuous change, such as the IT sector, research and development functions, and financial services. Individuals are exposed to a high degree of employment uncertainty because employers seek to pass on the financial, regulatory or technological risks that are created by unstable external markets. Consequently, these organizations offer the incentive of wider employability in terms of the marketability of the skills and competencies which the individual will gain instead of promising long-term employment within the organization (Arthur and Rousseau, 1996). At the same time, individuals continuously evaluate how well their employers are meeting their stated and implied contractual obligations, along with the perceived availability of alternative employment opportunities in the external labour market.

Employees often seek to manage their own careers by taking advantage of opportunities to maximize their success and realize higher levels of salary, bonus and status (Judge et al., 1994; Eby et al., 2003). For example, Cheramie et al. (2007) conducted a longitudinal analysis of executive managers from a boundaryless career perspective, using extrinsic rewards such as pay rises or bonuses as determinants of career

success. They found that in managing their careers, these individuals sought to maximize their extrinsic rewards ▶Chapter 8◀.

A perceived decline in the 'health' of the organization also increased the likelihood of changing employer.

From a boundaryless career perspective, career development requires the strengthening of self-direction and adaptability within a more transactional employment relationship. Through the development of social networks, relevant competencies and career-related knowledge, an individual can gain the confidence necessary to master current and future jobs, as well as career-relevant networks in which they can generate knowledge, learn, and develop a reputation. An understanding of career competencies also allows employees to evaluate which skills, competencies or networks can facilitate mobility in the future. Thus,

BUILDING YOUR SKILLS

In a constrained labour market, how easy is it to pursue a boundaryless career? If you were a line manager and an employee came to you seeking to pursue this type of career, what choices do you have to facilitate this? Are there certain industries where people are more likely to be able to pursue a boundaryless career?

employees may have multiple job movements during their lifetime (Sullivan and Arthur, 2006).

Protean Careers

Derived from Proteus, a mythical Greek sea creature who could change shape at will, the literal interpretation of protean indicates something that is versatile, variable and capable of taking many forms. Like the boundaryless career, a **protean career** offers a self-directed approach to career management, though in this case driven primarily by the values of the individual (Briscoe and Hall, 2002).

In an early study of managerial careers, Hall (1976: 201) noted the tendency of organizations to take control of employees' careers for them. He suggested the protean career concept as a contrast, defining it as 'one in which the person, not the organization is managing. It consists of all the person's varied work experiences

> **Protean career** – a career defined by uniquely individual psychological success which can mean personal accomplishment, feelings of pride, achievement or family happiness

in education, training, work in several organizations, changes in occupational field, etc.' The protean career is driven by the individual rather than the organization, based on individually defined goals, such as satisfaction, achievement and work–life balance; it encompasses the whole life space and is directed by psychological success rather than objective measures, such as monetary rewards, power and position within the organization. For example, a particularly strong form of protean career orientation occurs when the individual's attitude towards their career reflects a sense of calling in their work or an awareness of purpose that gives deep meaning to the career (Hall and Chandler, 2005).

Briscoe and Hall (2002) posit that a protean career orientation represents a self-directed perspective for an individual to evaluate their career and provide a guide to action. So, it bears similarities to an attitude, in that it has a cognitive component (a set of beliefs about the career), an affective component (beliefs as to what constitutes a 'good' or 'bad' career for the individual), and a behavioural element (a predisposition to react in certain ways). The protean career is therefore a mindset about careers, an attitude towards careers that reflects autonomy, self-direction and making choices based on personal values.

A person pursuing a protean career moves quickly to improvise new ways of working, making the most of the empowerment it provides them. The challenge with an individual practising ongoing self-direction and adaptability in their career is that while they may become skilled at adapting to change, they may also lose a sense of overall direction. The protean career can therefore act as a compass in providing that direction (Hall, 2002). The compass comes from the person's sense of identity: understanding who they are and knowing their values, needs, goals and interests. It moves beyond simple adaptability; it also requires self-knowledge and self-identity. One commonly cited example of a protean career is that of Mary Robinson, former president of Ireland (1990–97), and UN High Commissioner for Human Rights (1997–2002). Robinson constantly adapted to new challenges based on her consistent set of values and identity as a lawyer, politician and activist, and in 2004 she received Amnesty International's Ambassador of Conscience Award for her work in promoting human rights.

Hall (2004) identified two competencies that help individuals become more protean. These are adaptability and self-awareness. Self-awareness and understanding are pivotal to the values-driven nature of a protean career, ensuring a secure personal base from which to foster career success and interact with changing external conditions. Adaptability involves the capacity to change career and work behaviours in a way that allows the individual to succeed in a number of contexts. The capacity for reflection on the part of the individual is central to the ability to drive these two competencies. The greater the ability to harness these attributes, the greater the likelihood of promoting protean attitudes and identity.

Authentic Careers

The **authentic career** concept (Baker and Aldrich, 1996; Ibarra, 1999; Svejenova, 2005) defines an authentic individual as one who makes career choices that are consistent with the past or with an imagined future about who they would like to become. The key characteristic is that there is a consistent set of beliefs guiding the career.

> **Authentic career** – a career characterized by consistency between an individual's public and private beliefs

Being truthful in authentic terms relates to the notion of consistency between how a person expresses themselves in public and what they feel in private. Much of the research on authentic careers has been carried out in a creative context by considering the careers of musicians, film directors and actors. For example, an authentic musician is variously considered to be one who does not 'sell out' by allowing their music to appear in commercial advertisements, writes their own lyrics, demonstrates social concern, and maintains a sense of consistency between their music and their personality. Claiming authenticity in music has long been a controversial area, with the absence of it igniting heated debate. For example, in 2011, Lana del Ray, a then 25-year-old US singer/songwriter released her first single 'Video Games' and became an internet viral sensation, with her apparently home-produced video for the song viewed over 20 million times on YouTube in a matter of weeks. Del Ray was praised for her perceived authenticity and becoming successful on her own terms. Yet it quickly emerged that she was the carefully planned creation of a powerful record label. Indeed, even her name was chosen by her management team. In real life, 'Lana del Ray' was actually Lizzy Grant, and she had previously released an album in 2009 that was funded by her millionaire father. Attempts were made to remove traces of the album, along with videos and interviews of Grant from the internet prior to the appearance of del Ray in 2011. Music blogs and other media outlets turned on del Ray in spectacular fashion with sustained attacks on her lack of credibility and authenticity. Interestingly, few of these attacks were based on her perceived talent, suggesting that genuine authenticity in terms of musical ability is very difficult to achieve.

In career terms, this perspective suggests that an authentic career-oriented individual is one willing to take the initiative and responsibility for their career and able to achieve consistency between past and current, and private and public expressions of themselves (Svejenova, 2005).

Kaleidoscope Careers

Mainiero and Sullivan (2006) offer another perspective on current careers with the kaleidoscope career concept. Similar to boundaryless and protean careers, a **kaleidoscope career** is created and evolved on the individual's own terms, defined by their own values, life choices and parameters, rather than by the organization. As an individual's life changes and evolves, their career path may adjust to these changes rather than surrendering control and allowing an organization to dictate time and energy demands imposed by work. This particular concept has a predominantly female-oriented focus. Individuals amend, adjust and modify this kaleidoscope or career pattern, by rotating the various aspects of their lives to arrange roles and relationships in new ways.

Like the mechanics of a kaleidoscope, where the movement of one part causes another part to move, changing patterns as new arrangements fall into place, individuals shift the patterns of their careers by changing different aspects of their lives to realign roles and relationships. Mainiero and Sullivan's (2006) longitudinal study of over 3,000 individuals suggests that people continually evaluate the choices and options available to them through this kaleidoscopic lens to determine the most beneficial fit between a myriad of relationships, work constraints and opportunities. Making a new decision regarding the career path affects the outcome of the kaleidoscope career pattern.

Building on the authentic career concept, Mainiero and Sullivan

(2006) suggest that the kaleidoscope career model incorporates a sense of authenticity in terms of being genuine and allowing personal and work behaviours to be closely aligned with personal values; that individuals strive for challenging work that facilitates career advancement and increases self-worth; and that a need for balance exists with regard to work, relationships and personal concerns.

CONSIDER THIS

Mainiero and Sullivan (2006) found that men and women tend to follow different kaleidoscope career patterns. Women tend to focus on challenge in early career, with balance becoming more important in mid-career, and authenticity becoming the primary focus in late career. Men, on the other hand, focus on challenge in early career, authenticity in mid-career, and balance in late career. Discuss the reasons why you think male and female careers unfold differently.

Kirk (2016) highlights the inherent tensions between individuals and organizations in pursuing a kaleidoscope career due to the fact that individuals' career requirements come in cycles aligned to lifecycle stages, whereas organizational needs change in response to perceived threats and opportunities to the organization. This presents opportunities and challenges for individuals in the acquisition and use of **career capital** to balance work- and non-work-related demands in their careers.

Kaleidoscope career – a career that adjusts to changes in an individual's circumstances and motivation

Career capital – the skills that differentiate a person's portfolio of job, industry and networking knowledge and abilities

Off-ramp career – a non-traditional career path that recognizes that individuals, usually women, will take some time out from their careers

Off-ramp Careers

A predominantly gender-specific career concept has emerged recently in response to the 'male competitive model' of careers (Hewlett, 2007: 13). Hewlett (2007) presents the idea of the **off-ramp career** that provides an arc of career flexibility, which allows women to 'ramp-down' or take time off from their career and then 'ramp-up' or re-enter the labour market without losing career traction. Women may need to take extended periods of time off from work to have children, raise children, or care for their own parents.

HRM AND ORGANIZATIONAL PERFORMANCE

Female career development at Google

In Google, engineers are allowed to put themselves forward for promotions when they feel that they are ready. They write a self-assessment of their own accomplishments, ask their peers and manager for written feedback, and then an independent committee of senior engineers reviews the material and makes a final decision. The People Analytics team, which collects and uses data to bolster the company's own management practices, looked into the data and found that, on average, male employees were applying for promotion a year before they were actually ready, and that female engineers were applying a year after they should have been. Google could not understand why women were not going for more advanced roles and higher pay when it had a system whereby anyone could apply for promotion.

Based on studies of gender equality indicating that girls do not raise their hands as often as boys when answering mathematics problems at school, even though they have a higher rate of accuracy when they do so, and that females do not offer up their ideas as often as men in business meetings, Google tried an experiment. One of the heads of engineering sent an email to his staff describing the two studies and then reminding them it was time to apply for promotions. Immediately, the application rate for females soared, and the rate of women who received promotions rose higher than that for male engineers. Each time the engineering manager sent the same email reminder, female promotion rates climbed. When he once forgot to send that email, the number of female applicants dropped sharply. Simply presenting the evidence to individuals was enough to change their behaviour and significantly impact upon female career development (Kang, 2014).

Based on the premise that over 60% of women have nonlinear careers (Hewlett, 2007: 29), by taking off-ramps and diverse career paths, it makes it difficult for women to engage in the continuous, cumulative employment that is deemed necessary for success within predominantly male-oriented competitive career models. The end result is that a vast number of talented women either leave their careers or remain on the sidelines. This research has had a significant impact on the discourse around female careers, with the author behind the concept of off-ramp careers, Sylvia Ann Hewlett, being recognized in 2014 as the Most Influential International Thinker by *HR Magazine* and winning the Google Global Diversity award the same year.

It is argued that the male competitive model of careers evolved to meet the needs of middle-class white men in the 1950s and 60s when access to well-paid jobs was primarily limited to this demographic group. It developed around a traditional division of labour between men and women, with men acting as primary earners and women playing the role of wife, mother and homemaker (Shelton and John, 1996). The male competitive model is characterized by:

- a strong preference for full-time, continuous, linear employment history
- an emphasis on being physically present in an office for up to ten hours a day
- an assumption that professionals are motivated by money
- a belief that the steepest gradient of a career curve occurs in one's thirties – the individual either achieves objective career success in this period or does not at all; there are no second chances.

While broadly suitable for men, this career path presents numerous difficulties for women, to the extent that most women cannot or choose not to attempt to pursue it (Gilligan, 1982: 149). A preference for a continuous employment history penalizes women who need to take time out of their careers for the reasons identified earlier. Furthermore, the notion that career success is achieved in the thirties occurs at the ages when childbearing and child-rearing demands are likely to be most pertinent and can be particularly time-consuming. A framework that indicates the need for individuals' careers to take off in their thirties is largely incompatible from a work–life balance perspective for most women. Hewlett (2007: 29) found that 37% of female managers take what she terms an 'off-ramp' at some point in their careers, that is, voluntarily leaving their job for a short period of time, and another 30% take a 'scenic route', for example working reduced hours, working from home, or using flexible working arrangements.

The difficulty women face is when they decide to return to employment, be it for financial, sense of identity or satisfaction reasons. Data suggests that only 40% of professional women return to full-time employment after an off-ramp pause in their career, with a quarter engaging in part-time work, while women at managerial levels find it particularly difficult to return at the same level, citing suspicion that either their skills are outdated or they no longer have the commitment deemed necessary for the job. Facilitating ease of access in returning to careers has led to organizations introducing a variety of career flexibility and flexible working arrangements, such as reduced hour options, flexible working times, job sharing, telecommuting and seasonal flexibility. This implies a fundamental reimagining of when, where and how work is carried out. Jobs are being delineated and delayered, duties shared and work teams deployed in ways that allow responsibilities to be seamlessly handed over. This allows high-value professionals and managers to carry out work in clearly delineated portions of time. Indeed, rather than label such working initiatives as 'women-specific' accommodations, organizations are beginning to position these arrangements as a key business strategy in the hope of attracting and retaining talented individuals.

The concept of off-ramping is not, however, the sole preserve of women. Almost a quarter of men in professional careers voluntarily leave their jobs at some stage, although they do so for markedly different reasons from women. Men cite switching careers and undergoing additional training and development as the most important factors in taking a break in their career path, whereas women name childcare and family responsibilities as the determining factors. This suggests that off-ramping from a male managerial perspective is concerned with the strategic repositioning of their career rather than family-related concerns.

Portfolio Careers

One consequence of globalization is the emergence of constantly changing organizations offering a wide range of opportunities outside the traditional model of full-time employment with a single employer. The growth of employment options such as freelance work, consultancy work, fixed-term work, contract work, project-based work and self-employment has led to individuals pursuing what Handy (1989) terms **portfolio careers**. Rather than pursuing a single full-time job, the individual balances a portfolio of different and changing employment opportunities. For example,

> **Portfolio career** – a career that involves doing two or more different jobs for different employers

in the UK alone, there are over 1 million people who have two or more jobs, and 65% of them work this way out of choice (Clinton et al., 2006). The relatively small amount of literature on portfolio careers suggests that they are pursued by professionals and managers rather than operative and semi-skilled employees (Mallon, 1998).

The portfolio career concept envisages that individuals build careers around a collection of skills and interests and places a strong emphasis on self-management. Career development is thus based on a different set of assumptions to the traditional perspective of careers and the relationship between the organization and the employee. Instead of entering a sequence of hierarchically arranged positions, employees are hired to accomplish specific tasks and become contractors. Under the portfolio-centred model:

- the contract output is identified
- the matching portfolio of skills needed to complete the contract is specified
- individuals with those skills are then located in the HR information system
- the contract is offered and then managed.

This shift of focus requires a parallel shift in career development roles and activities. At the risk of oversimplification, career development professionals will need to recognize some significant differences in the organizational and individual needs of different types of organizations and employees.

With traditional careers, because employees are a long-term investment, success in identifying learning and development needs leads to longer term effectiveness for the organization. Under portfolio-centred HRM, however, the HRM function takes on new roles. For example, consideration must be given to determining which aspects of the firm's activities could be contracted out or dealt with on a contract basis and which employee groups are considered core ▶Chapter 2◀ (Handy, 1989). Instead of dealing with the pattern of positions in the organization, under the portfolio-centred model, the HRM function concentrates on understanding the skill requirements needed to accomplish a contract. Rather than identifying the best individuals with long-term potential, the focus is on locating individuals with the precise skill sets needed for accomplishing that specific task or contract. As a result, instead of creating progressive learning and development programmes such as second-level training and management training, the focus and resources are shifted to identifying individuals with the needed skill sets. Learning and development become the individual's responsibility rather than the organization's. Orientation activities also change from having a socialization focus, providing new long-term employees with an understanding of the organization's culture and expectations, to a specific focus on contract and performance definition. This includes an introduction to only those specific individuals and policies needed for the accomplishment of the contract. Performance management and career planning activities become short term in orientation. Table 10.2 presents a comparison of the six contemporary career concepts we have discussed.

Career concept	Characteristics
Boundaryless	<ul><li>Consists of infinite trajectories and possibilities</li><li>Not tied to a single organization</li><li>Not an orderly sequence of jobs</li><li>Focuses on opportunities across organizational boundaries</li><li>Transcends physical, psychological and subjective boundaries</li></ul>
Protean	<ul><li>Focuses on the subjective perspective of the individual career actor</li><li>Career actor defines individual goals, which encompass the whole life space</li><li>Driven by psychological success rather than objective success</li><li>Has a cognitive and a behavioural component</li><li>A mindset about a career; an attitude towards a career</li></ul>
Authentic	<ul><li>Individuals have ownership of their careers</li><li>Individuals can enact their careers in different ways</li><li>Individuals adopt 'true-to-self' strategies in their career roles</li><li>Individuals search for ways of integrating the present, previous and future self</li><li>Individuals seek to be truthful to themselves</li><li>Individuals adapt and grow and are shaped by context</li><li>Individuals explore a range of roles and identify which is most satisfactory as an expression of their talents</li><li>Careers are embedded structurally and historically</li></ul>
Kaleidoscope	<ul><li>Created on the individual's own terms</li><li>Career path adjusts to changes in values, life choices and parameters</li><li>Individuals modify career pattern by rotating the various aspects of their lives to arrange roles and relationships in new ways</li><li>Individuals evaluate the choices and options available to them to determine the most beneficial fit</li></ul>
Off-ramp	<ul><li>Nonlinear</li><li>Came about as it is difficult for women to engage in continuous, cumulative employment</li><li>Need for career flexibility and flexible working arrangements</li><li>From a male perspective, off-ramping is generally concerned with strategic repositioning of the career</li><li>Women tend to off-ramp for more family-related concerns</li></ul>
Portfolio	<ul><li>Career built around a collection of skills and interests</li><li>Multiple part-time jobs with a number of different employers</li><li>Multiple jobs and employers within one or more professions</li><li>Dominant theme is one of self-management and self-direction</li></ul>

Table 10.2 Comparison of contemporary career concepts
Sources: inspired by information in Arthur and Rousseau, 1996; Craig et al., 2002; Hall, 2002; Svejenova, 2005; Hewlett, 2007.

CONSIDER THIS

Have you ever thought that you are a fraud and do not deserve the success you have achieved? Have you ever worried that you are not really as good at your job as everyone says you are or that you do not deserve the grades you get in your studies? Do you dismiss your successes as being down to luck, the work of others or timing? Are you worried that you might be found out as incapable? If so, you may suffer from 'impostor syndrome'.

Increased attention to the imposter phenomenon, described as persistent thoughts of inadequacy and an inability to internalize successes despite evidence to the contrary, suggests that many professionals experience imposter thoughts at some point in time (Kets de Vries, 2005). Most research exploring imposter tendencies has been carried out on early career professionals, particularly graduate students and medical residents, as they embark on the challenging

experience of developing early career identities. Research among such professionals has primarily focused on identifying the prevalence of imposter thoughts and significant correlates such as increased depression and anxiety (McGregor et al., 2008), burnout (Legassie et al., 2008) and psychological distress (Henning et al., 1998).

An estimated 70% of people will experience at least one episode of impostor phenomenon in their lives, according to Sakulku and Alexander (2011). Indeed, moments after winning the Oscar for Best Performance by an Actress in a Supporting Role (for *Fences*) at the 2017 Academy Awards, Viola Davis told ABC News (2017) that she battles with doubt despite her career success: 'It feels like my hard work has paid off, but at the same time I still have the impostor, you know, syndrome. I still feel like I'm going to wake up and everybody's going to see me for the hack I am.'

GRADUATE CAREERS

The recent economic climate post-2007 has had a profound impact on graduate careers. Prior to 2007, third-level graduates enjoyed near full employment after graduation in the majority of EU countries, including the UK, and the USA, but research from these areas indicates that substantial numbers now re-enter formal education in the years after graduation as high unemployment and increased competition in the wider labour market take their toll (Coates and Edwards, 2011). Between 2008 and 2014 in Australia, for example, the proportion of new university graduates in full-time employment dropped from 56.4% to 41.7% (National Institute of Labour Studies, 2016). In China, approximately 15% of new graduates were unemployed six months after graduation (BBC, 2014), but this figure hides the more nuanced issue of 'underemployment', where many graduates end up working part-time, low-paid jobs (MyCOS, 2015). More than half of UK graduates had undertaken some form of additional education or training, within three or four years of graduation, and 40% of US graduates had enrolled in another university-level qualification within ten years of graduation. In addition, based on 2011 patterns, the OECD expects that 15- to 29-year-olds in the UK will spend 2.3 years on average either unemployed or outside the workforce (slightly higher

than the EU average of 2.2 years for 15- to 24-year-olds). In 2013, the rate of unemployment in the eurozone reached an all-time high of 12.2%, but youth unemployment (those aged 15–24) was far higher. In 2013 youth unemployment showed figures of 41% in Italy, 56% in Spain and 62.5% in Greece (Eurostat, 2013). These are not uneducated youths; 40% of those unemployed Spanish youths were educated to third-level standard; the corresponding figure for unemployed Greek youths was 30%.

In such difficult labour markets, the competition for graduate jobs has intensified (Taylor, 2011). Consequently, when graduates do find employment, it is not always at a skill level or pay rate commensurate with their education. Figures from the UK Office of National Statistics point to 47% of graduates employed within six months of graduation not being in jobs that require a degree (Kesvani, 2014). Additionally, research in the UK has shown that the starting salaries for graduate jobs have decreased by 11% over five years (BBC News, 2014). It can be seen therefore that the 2008 economic recession and subsequent period of austerity and gradual recovery, as indicated by GDP growth statistics (Office for National Statistics, 2015), have had a notable impact on the graduate labour market in the UK.

Given the challenging economic climate, it is important that graduates are well prepared for the labour market. In a comparison of graduate and employer perceptions of the skills required to get ahead in the workplace, Rosenberg et al. (2012) highlight that leadership skills, management skills, interpersonal skills, critical thinking skills and a strong work ethic are among the most essential for employment. Additionally, leadership skills and IT skills have been identified as the strongest predictors of the career advancement potential of employees (Heimler et al., 2012), while employers themselves consider leadership skills to be most important when assessing the potential for progression.

With such skills becoming increasingly important in a competitive labour market, educational institutions have come under intense pressure to equip their students with more than just academic knowledge. Universities and colleges are now frequently giving employability greater priority at central or strategic level and are increasing their efforts to promote the employability of their graduates. Within the UK, many universities and colleges in the third-level sector have a central careers service, whose role is to review the employability skills of future graduates, suggest what particular skills individual students require and identify how students can develop them, and signpost new work and employment opportunities (Hinchliffe and Jolly, 2011; Lowden et al., 2011). **Employability** has been defined as a set of skills, knowledge and personal attributes that make an individual more likely to secure and be successful in their chosen

> **Employability** – being capable of getting and keeping fulfilling work

occupation to the benefit of themselves, the workforce, the community and the economy (Moreland, 2006). This can be enhanced through the creation of employability programmes and awards, with allocated personnel championing and coordinating employability initiatives (Lowden et al., 2011). Knight and Yorke (2004: 38) suggest using a model of graduate employability that draws upon the deeper learning and broader student experience that go beyond a narrow skills agenda. They suggest that graduate employability encompasses the combination of four aspects of higher education:

1. *understanding of subject matter* – propositional knowledge in the form of mastery of the subject matter of the degree
2. *skilful practices* – characterized as procedural knowledge
3. *efficacy beliefs* – belief that one generally can make some impact on situations and events
4. *metacognition* – awareness of what one knows and can do, and of how one learns more.

Initial entry into the labour market is important, but the nature of contemporary knowledge work means that the foundations of many careers take years to develop. Research in the UK suggests that graduates' career progression can be relatively slow for three to four years following graduation. For many, the benefits of university study on labour market outcomes only become noticeable a few years after leaving university (Purcell et al., 2005).

Getty Images

Kaplan (2008) indicates that in order to advance their careers, individuals need to take ownership of and responsibility for their careers by:

- assessing their career, skills and performance
- seeking coaches and mentors
- having the modesty to confront personal weaknesses
- having an intrapreneurial attitude – demonstrating entrepreneurial behaviour within their own organization
- seeking opportunities without putting their own self-interests ahead of the organization
- being willing to voice dissenting views.

BUILDING YOUR SKILLS

You are an HR manager recruiting graduate employees from university. What skills and competencies will you look for in these graduates? What responsibility does the organization have for graduate career development?

RESPONSIBILITY FOR CAREER DEVELOPMENT

Changes in organizations as a result of globalization and advancements in technology have led to a revised notion of the traditional 'career contract', resulting in a decrease in employers' commitment and willingness to retain individuals (Robinson and Rousseau, 1994). In the knowledge-intensive economies of today, lifetime employment is not guaranteed and individuals need to be resigned to change jobs at least once in their career.

This lack of job security places the onus on the individual to take control of their future employability, take responsibility for their own personal development, and view their career in terms of wider employability across industries and sectors. Organizations are now adopting greater flexibility in terms of business risks to employees through the introduction of share ownership, profit-sharing and profit-related pay schemes ▶Chapter 8◀ and differentiate between core and

> **Psychological contract** – the unwritten rules and expectations that exist between the employee and employer
>
> **Transactional psychological contract** – a situation where extra money and learning and development opportunities are provided in exchange for commitment and loyalty to the organization
>
> **Relational psychological contract** – a situation where job security is provided in exchange for commitment and loyalty to the organization

peripheral employees ▶Chapter 1◀. Employees are increasingly negotiating individualized work opportunities that fit their career and work–family relationships and so expect greater flexibility on the part of their employer to provide options that support this. For example, one employee might have more flexible hours than their peers but otherwise share their same reward structure, job duties, and other conditions of employment.

In discussing responsibility for career development, we must consider the nature of the psychological contract. **Psychological contracts** are the individual belief systems held by employees and employers regarding their mutual obligations to and agreements with each other (Rousseau, 1995). Since employment relationships are subjectively interpreted and experienced by each party, these perceptions that constitute the psychological contract are important. The psychological contract develops and evolves constantly based on communication, or lack thereof, between the employee and the employer. Promises over promotion or salary increases, for example, may form part of the psychological contract. Equally, investment in learning and development has been found to have positive effects on individuals' psychological contracts and, significantly, employees transferring what they learn on training programmes to the workplace (Pate et al., 2000). There are two kinds of psychological contract (Rousseau, 1995):

1. **Transactional psychological contracts**: the focus is on specific monetary exchanges that are short term in focus and include working longer hours and accepting new job roles and responsibilities in exchange for increased pay and training benefits (Herriot and Pemberton, 1997).

2. **Relational psychological contracts**: the focus is on loyalty and discretionary behaviour in exchange for job security, financial rewards and training and development opportunities. Discretionary behaviours are those performed by the employee as a result of personal choice, and go above and beyond what is written in the job description, e.g. the choice

to stay late or come in to work at weekends. Individuals tend to identify with the organization, promoting support for the organization's efforts to improve performance (Rousseau and Tijoriwala, 1999). These contracts are positively related to employee beliefs that their employer supports them personally.

It should be noted that transactional and relational psychological contracts are not mutually exclusive; all contracts contain elements of both, but the contract may lean more towards one or the other. Organizations have a choice to engender loyalty or commitment via transactional or relational means.

Transactional psychological contracts tend to be related to lower levels of employee flexibility and contribution and are less elastic than relational psychological contracts in times of change (Dabos and Rousseau, 2004). While these arrangements may be characteristic of workers in more peripheral roles in organizations (Dabos and Rousseau, 2004), individuals with high bargaining power, such as managers or highly valued employees, or those pursuing a portfolio or boundaryless career path (see pages 190–196) can also develop transactional contracts.

Transactional psychological contracts have given rise to 'i-deals' (Rousseau, 2005) – idiosyncratic deals that individuals negotiate with their employer regarding terms that mutually benefit both parties. They are voluntary, personalized agreements of a non-standardized nature that vary in scope from a single feature to the entire employment relationship. For example, an employee studying part time for a degree programme may negotiate fewer travel demands than other employees, but otherwise share the same job duties, pay scales and so on. The market power of individuals and/or the value the employer places on them enables employees to engage in individualized bargaining. When the work offered is neither highly standardized nor easily monitored or where it is scarce, individuals are in a position to exert considerable bargaining power. This level of power allows the individual to decide when, how and for whom to be productive.

Job security is being replaced with security based on the individual's value in the marketplace. While individuals may no longer have a job with a single employer, they may maintain employment with a number of organizations for the duration of their working career. This lack of job security places an onus on individuals to take control of their own employability and adopt independent and assertive career behaviours.

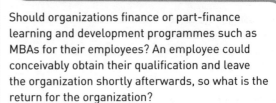

CONSIDER THIS

Should organizations finance or part-finance learning and development programmes such as MBAs for their employees? An employee could conceivably obtain their qualification and leave the organization shortly afterwards, so what is the return for the organization?

CAREER ANCHOR THEORY

A key issue with careers in the twenty-first century is the need to link organizational career systems to individual career progression. Progression may no longer be defined narrowly as upward mobility or indeed advancement in the context of one organization. The theory of career anchors (Schein, 1975) provides a useful lens for organizations and individuals to manage career progression, especially in the establishment phase of an individual's career. Career anchors describe self-perceived attitudes, values, needs and talents that develop over time and, which when developed, shape and guide career choices and directions (Schein, 1975).

Schein and Van Maanen (2013) argue that individuals with sufficient work experience (approximately 35 years +) can easily identify one dominant career anchor out of a total of eight (Table 10.3). Employees are asked to examine the list of eight anchors and decide, 'Which one of these would I *not* give up?' Whilst identifying a dominant anchor is straightforward, there are important implications of doing so for both the individual and the organization. Each anchor in fact attaches different meaning to 'progression' and predicts why employees value the same aspects of their job differently. For example, take the general management career anchor. This is perhaps the anchor that organizations assume to be held by middle management and prioritizes climbing the organization's hierarchy. However, a software developer may instead value functional expertise above other anchors; that is, they are likely to value personal mastery of technical competence and external professional recognition. They may have little interest in assuming responsibility for managing people that often comes with hierarchical advancement.

The career system of an organization typically has many policies and processes to assist with

	Career anchor	Description
1	**General management**	Rise to a high level in the organization
2	**Functional expertise**	Seek high levels of challenge in expertise
3	**Autonomy**	Want working life to be under your control
4	**Security and stability**	Need to feel economically secure and stable
5	**Sense of service**	Job must fulfil the values you hold
6	**Pure challenge**	Enjoy overcoming impossible barriers
7	**Creativity**	Want to create a product/service of your own
8	**Lifestyle**	Want work to integrate with other areas of your life

Table 10.3 Career anchors
Source: inspired by information in Schein and Van Maanen, 2013.

individual progression, including succession planning and talent management processes ▶Chapter 2◀. In order to identify and reward exemplary performance, a small proportion of employees in large organizations earn the title of 'high-potential employee'. These employees are encouraged to avail themselves of a number of opportunities, including temporary secondments to a different department or function, managing strategic projects, expatriation to a subsidiary in another country, to name but a few. However, it is important for the HRM function to avoid a cookie-cutter approach. Employees may well deserve 'high-potential' designation yet value autonomy or perhaps security and stability more, and therefore they may resist such prospects. It is important that the individual and the organization understand and accept career anchors.

One 'soft support' that all employees can avail themselves of is **mentoring**. Traditionally a one-to-one relationship between a mentor and mentee ('protégé'), mentoring involves the exchange of career and psychosocial support (Kram, 1983). Career support includes sponsorship by a senior figure, exposure and visibility, whereas psychosocial support involves validation and friendship. A sponsor in this context is someone who acts as an advocate for an individual when it comes to career opportunities, promotions, and who has the power to effect change. The more senior the sponsor, the more power they have to advance the career of the person they are sponsoring.

The literature (cf. Higgins and Kram, 2001) now encourages less dependency upon one mentor in favour of cultivating multiple developmental relationships. It is acknowledged that, in the contemporary workplace, it may be unreasonable to expect one individual to discharge both career and psychosocial support simultaneously. Nevertheless, there are different combinations of career and psychosocial support that coexist alongside the traditional mentoring concept (Table 10.4).

> **Mentoring** is the voluntary and informal exchange of career and psychosocial support

	High career assistance	Low career assistance
High psychosocial assistance	Mentor	Friend
Low psychosocial assistance	Sponsor	Ally

Table 10.4 Types of career and psychosocial support

HRM IN PRACTICE ⚙

Bad dating service

Olivier, a business and legal studies major from a French university, joined Viola, a (fictitious) Paris-based software company, and began working in its finance function as a graduate trainee. A year later he sought to specialize in IT and pursue a technical career path within Viola. This decision saw him return to education to complete an MSc in Software Engineering on a part-time basis.

Lacking contacts within Viola's software division and facing a 'career-limiting manager', Olivier began to investigate mentoring. An internal careers website recommended that a mentee needs to have a defined goal in order to establish a mentoring relationship. Olivier's goal was to find a 'technical mentor' in order to assist him to scope out a dissertation topic. He scanned through an online employee directory for potential mentors and came across Mikel, a senior technical leader in Viola's software division. Mikel had an impressive range of technical competencies and experience of being a mentor.

Olivier and Mikel initially discussed ideas for the dissertation over email and then by phone. Mikel subsequently invited Olivier to visit the software division in person. Olivier's manager initially blocked this face-to-face meeting ('he discouraged it, was anxious about it, didn't support career change'), which then led Mikel to intervene on Olivier's behalf. According to Olivier:

'It's fair to say but it's true I guess that maybe I was using the [MSc] as my shield, my cover to meet with Mikel, the real reason was ... I had my own ideas as to how this project was to go and I used the MSc project as something that we could very clearly talk about. That for me was the springboard to have "extra-curricular" chats with Mikel, so I'd talk to him

about my project and then I remember discussing, when the opportunity came up, how do I move ...'

For Olivier, the focus on career rather than job tasks meant that the mentoring was more open and frank about new opportunities relative to conversations that he could ever have with his own manager: 'There were never any repercussions when discussing with Mikel how I was really feeling, whatever I said would not leave the room.'

Indeed Mikel's motivation to mentor was based on his own experience of 'selfish business constraints' imposed by managers. It was his view that employees should expect something different from mentors. Mikel was not a fan of Viola's formal mentoring programme, which attempted to match mentees with mentors. He also identified with Olivier's goal and how he set about building the relationship:

'You really need, you know, people like Olivier and myself, if you really want to help yourself out, you should target people and not just settle for someone that's blindly matched to you in a bad dating service.'

What would you do?

1. What does Olivier and Mikel's mentoring relationship suggest about the value of formal career planning systems?
2. How do you think Olivier's actions conflict or support contemporary career concepts?
3. Some employees regard Olivier's actions as unethical whilst others regard it as selfish. Can both views be right?
4. Why do you think organizations attempt to match mentors and mentees?
5. If you were tasked with developing Viola's formal mentoring programme, how would you want to run it? What steps would you take?

ROLE OF THE HRM FUNCTION

Significant shifts in the relationships between employers and workers are also motivating companies to rethink career development. Research has found that workers tend to be more engaged when given opportunities for development, growth,

and career progression. Organizational career systems are 'the collections of policies, priorities, and actions that organizations use to manage the flow of their members into, through and out of the organizations over time' (Sonnenfeld and Peiperl, 1988: 588). Essentially, they relate to the set of HRM policies and practices and management actions that are used to direct employees during their employment. The majority of research on career systems has focused on the practices contained within organizational career systems (Bowen and Ostroff, 2004). However, changes in the external environment and an organization's strategy often cause employers to change the supposedly objective nature of the employment relationship and the subsequent composition of career systems (Slay and Taylor, 2007).

Cappelli (1999: 1) describes these changes as follows:

> What ended the traditional employment relationship is a variety of new management practices, driven by a changing environment, that essentially brings the market – both the market for a company's products and the labour market for its employees – directly inside the firms ... pushing out of its way the behavioural principles of reciprocity and long-term commitment, the internal promotion and development practices and the concerns about equity that underlie the more traditional employment contract.

Individual-level career perspectives such as boundaryless (Arthur and Rousseau, 1996) or protean (Hall, 1996) careers that transcend organizations (Peiperl and Baruch, 1997) have a strong appeal among academics and individual employees (Baruch, 1999); however, organizations face the practical task of actually managing people in a turbulent business environment. They require guidelines to help them manage individuals, to indicate what practices can be useful, and under which circumstances. A large number of traditional organizational career management systems are based on archaic approaches that assume old-style hierarchical frameworks. The 1990s and 2000s have fostered a new organizational way of thinking, which includes more flexibility, an evolving culture, and the impact of technology and information systems (Baruch and Peirperl, 2003).

The traditional hierarchical management framework, within which long-term career planning was possible, is gradually being abandoned by organizations and individuals. While we have emphasized the role of the individual in career management, it is important to note that organizations should not be excluded from the process. It may not be necessary for organizations to abandon career management, but to adjust the career system to the new patterns of employment (Peiperl et al., 2000). The engagement of employees is important in this respect. Employees who report being engaged at work demonstrate greater workplace performance, and engaged workers possess personal resources, including optimism, self-efficacy, self-esteem,

HRM IN THE NEWS

Anthony Bourdain – New York nomad

Alexander Tamargo/Getty Images

Anthony Bourdain, who sadly died in June 2018 at the age of 61, described his work as a 'fantasy profession'. He was an international celebrity with a difference; the first half of his career was spent as a chef in New York, having graduated from the Culinary Institute of America in 1978. His long-term friend Joel Rose once described Anthony as, '[not] a great chef, but organized', a combination that would allow him to save many an ailing restaurant from bankruptcy. The decade up to 1990 saw Bourdain develop and subsequently beat chronic drug and alcohol addiction but his experimentation with writing continued. He attended writing workshops in order to 'write his way out of the kitchen' despite being appointed in 1998 executive chef of *Les Halles* in New York City.

Following two unsuccessful novels in the 1990s, international acclaim followed his publication of *Kitchen Confidential* in 2000. 'Every day, he rose before dawn and banged out a new passage at his computer, chain-smoking, then worked a twelve-hour restaurant shift' (*New Yorker*, 2017). Bourdain would spend the next half of his career on television, not as a celebrity chef, but as a connoisseur who travelled the world in search of good food, particularly good street food. 'I'm in the business of finding great places.'

Although an interest in food was a constant, the value of travelling to find it was rooted in early childhood. A young Anthony visited family in France and was an avid reader of *The Adventures of Tintin*. The comic book based on a Belgian adventurer 'took me places I was quite sure I would never go'. Two hundred and forty-eight episodes later, the New York nomad had visited 80 countries to write and present a unique TV show that blended food and culture. His TV career began on the Food Network, followed by the Travel Channel (2005–12) and finally CNN (2013–18). Each 60-minute episode took a week to produce.

Although he still identified as a chef, unlike many of his peers he did not 'cash in' his celebrity to a restaurant chain. Instead, he tried stand-up comedy in local clubs in New York, and in the summer of 2015 he embarked on a 10-city tour. In 2016, Bourdain's *Hunger* tour visited 15 different cities across North America. He agreed to lend his name to a $60 million open-air food project on New York City's Pier 57, designed to recreate the exotic open-air food courts he had shared with viewers, but the plan was eventually abandoned

Fellow chef Éric Ripert muses that Bourdain may have been driven, in part, by a fear of what he might get up to if he ever stopped working. 'I'm a guy who needs a lot of projects,' Bourdain acknowledged. Indeed there was no shortage of accolades for Bourdain's TV work either. Between 2013 and 2015 he collected three Emmy Awards, plus a Peabody Award. Other projects included earning a blue belt in Brazilian jujitsu in 2015. Despite having a 'pathological' obsession with being on time, finding and maintaining friendship became difficult. 'I'm not there. I'm not going to remember your birthday. I'm not going to be there for the important moments in your life. We are not going to reliably hang out, no matter how I feel about you.'

Indeed, for the past 15 years, Bourdain had been travelling for 200 days a year. He would likely have made a good friend, however. Whether you were a farm labourer in Vietnam or president of the USA, Bourdain treated all hosts and guests with the same respect and dignity. 'You eat what's offered wherever you are. That's why the show works the way it does, because not just me but my whole crew take that attitude, that we're happy and grateful to be there and we're willing to try anything that's offered in good faith.'

Questions

1. What evidence is there of a protean attitude on the part of Anthony Bourdain?
2. How would you describe the career of Anthony Bourdain using contemporary career concepts?
3. Boundaryless careers are really about changing identities. Discuss.

Sources

Keefe, P.R. (2017) 'Anthony Bourdain's moveable feast', www.newyorker.com/magazine/2017/02/13/anthony-bourdains-moveable-feast (accessed 11 June 2018)

resilience and an active coping style, that help them control and impact on their work environment successfully, and achieve career success (Luthans et al., 2008). Both managers and the HRM function are in a critical position to increase or decrease engagement because they deal with issues such as accountability, work processes, compensation, recognition and career opportunities. From a career development perspective, there is often a mismatch between employees' expectations and the roles offered by the organization. So, processes should be put in place to check that employees' career goals are clearly understood and that job roles are defined with as close an alignment to career aspirations as possible.

Organizations with effective career development strategies tend to focus less on particularly innovative ideas or leading practices and more on alignment with organizational goals and needs. Companies that align the way they move people through the organization and support career management as an organizational priority often have more effective career development strategies.

SUMMARY

This chapter highlights the importance of individuals taking responsibility for their own careers. This brings with it significant responsibilities. Careers no longer follow a traditional career model. Instead, individuals are expected to be self-directed and pursue careers that are increasingly fragmented, nonlinear and which involve numerous career changes. Employees will find themselves becoming less competitive unless they are open-minded and make career choices that reflect their personal values and career trajectories. They may have to finance some of their development and participate in more career development activities outside work. For HR practitioners, a key challenge is to support career development by creating programmes and activities to provide skill development, such as job rotation, mentoring, internships, coaching and career strategy groups, and by making supervisors and managers accountable for supporting employee development efforts.

CHAPTER REVIEW QUESTIONS

1. What do you understand by the term 'career'?
2. How do contemporary career development concepts differ from Super's model of career development?
3. Contrast the protean career construct and the boundaryless career construct. In what ways are they similar and different?
4. How has the nature of contemporary careers changed? What are the implications of this for HR practitioners?
5. Should an organization provide career development opportunities?
6. What are the career challenges facing graduates today?
7. How can career anchor theory help individuals manage their career progression?
8. What role does the HR function play in facilitating career development?

FURTHER READING

Arthur, M.B. and Rousseau, D. (1996) *The Boundaryless Career: A New Employment Principle for a New Organizational Era*, Oxford: Oxford University Press.

Baruch, Y. (2004) *Managing Careers: Theory and Practice*, Harlow: Pearson Education.

Greenhaus, J.H. and Callanan, G.A. (2006) *Encyclopedia of Career Development*, Thousand Oaks, CA: Sage.

Hall, D.T. (2002) *Careers In and Out of Organizations*, Thousand Oaks, CA: Sage.

Hewlett, S.A. (2013) *(Forget a Mentor) Find a Sponsor: The New Way to Fast-Track Your Career*, Boston, MA: Harvard Business Review Press.

Inkson, K. (2007) *Understanding Careers: The Metaphors of Working Lives*, Thousand Oaks, CA: Sage.

USEFUL WEBSITES

www.cipd.co.uk/hr-careers

CIPD's HR Careers site provides an excellent overview of the various career options available to those interested in a career in HR, in addition to a 'careers clinic' and various resources that should be of interest to anyone looking for assistance in seeking employment.

collegegrad.com

College Grad is one of the most popular sites in the USA for college students and recent graduates. The site provides entry-level job listings, internship listings, as well as advice for those who are looking for a job or have an offer lined up.

www.glassdoor.com

Glassdoor is a website where employees and former employees anonymously review companies and their management

 For extra resources, including videos, multiple choice questions and useful weblinks, go to: www.macmillanihe.com/carbery-cross-hrm-2e.

Getty Images/Netta/Clerkenwell

11: Human Resource Analytics

Caroline Murphy and Jean McCarthy

LEARNING OUTCOMES

By the end of this chapter, you will be able to:

- Define what is meant by human resource (HR) analytics
- Identify factors driving the utilization of HR analytics in organizations
- Discuss the role of HR analytics in organizational decision-making
- Differentiate between descriptive, predictive and prescriptive data uses
- Understand various forms and sources of data in organizations
- Differentiate between categorical and continuous data sets, or variables
- Identify common software tools used in HR data analysis
- Discuss the skill requirements for HR analytics

THIS CHAPTER DISCUSSES:

Introduction (208)

Defining HR Analytics (208)

The Role of HR Analytics in Strategic Organizational Decision-making (209)

Uses of Data: From Descriptive to Prescriptive (210)

Measurement and Tools (212)

The Internal Consultant: Skill Requirements for HR Analytics (214)

Evidence-based Decision-making: Analytics in

Tandem with Interventions (215)

INTRODUCTION

The old adage of *'what gets measured gets managed'* has long been a mantra in many organizations. While the phrase may be described as a cliché, the message is clear: measuring work and, indeed, behaviours at work provides us with the information needed to confirm whether or not organizational goals and/ or targets have actually been achieved. If they have not, the measurement data can be used as a basis for future decision–making to address these goals and targets. While measurement and metrics feature strongly in business areas like production, sales and marketing, not all organizations gather sufficient data around HR issues, systems and employee performance ▶Chapter 7◀. In fact, where organizations do gather data through their **human resource information systems (HRIS)**, the data is often not utilized within the organization to support strategic decision-making. **Human resource (HR) analytics** is an emerging phenomenon in the HR field which aims to facilitate improved organizational decision-making by applying sophisticated analysis to existing HR metrics and data pertaining to both human resource (employee) performance and HR systems. HR analytics has been hailed as 'a "must have" capability that will ensure HR's future as a strategic management function while transforming organizational performance for the better' (Angrave et al., 2016).

> **Human resource information system (HRIS)** – a software system for data entry, tracking and information needs of the HR function
>
> **Human resource (HR) analytics** – the use of people-related data in analytical processes to address business issues
>
> **Inferential statistics** make predictions about a population (e.g. employees within an organization) based on a sample of that population (e.g. a cross-section of employees in an organization); whereas descriptive statistics provide descriptions of a population
>
> **Causal factors** are determinants. For example, education is a causal factor in employability, such that higher levels of education are determinants of greater job opportunities for individuals

DEFINING HR ANALYTICS

HR analytics, sometimes referred to as 'human capital analytics' and 'people analytics' (see Waber, 2013; Huus, 2015), is a relatively new term. Marler and Boudreau's (2017: 14) review of major research databases found that the term 'HR analytics' first began to appear in HR literature in 2003–04. In the years since, it has received significant levels of attention, both in industry and in academic research. Perhaps unsurprisingly though, given the nascence of the term, Marler and Boudreau note that there is still some ambiguity regarding its definition.

Fitz-Enz and Mattox (2014: 3) define HR analytics as 'primarily a communication device, bringing together data from disparate sources such as surveys, records and operations to paint a cohesive, actionable picture of current conditions and likely futures'. They argue that a conceptualization of HR analytics as just 'statistics' is incorrect. While they recognize that statistical analysis is a fundamental part of HR analytics, they emphasize that an understanding of interactions and relationships also constitutes a significant part. In contrast, Edwards and Edwards (2016: 2) offer a narrower definition, describing predictive HR analytics as 'the systematic application of predictive modelling using **inferential statistics** to existing HR people-related data in order to inform judgements about possible **causal factors** driving key HR related performance indicators'. At the other end of the scale, the very broadest definition of HR analytics is provided by Mondare et al. (2011); they state that HR analytics is simply a process which demonstrates the direct impact of people on important business outcomes. Throughout the remainder of this chapter, in the activities and links which we direct learners towards, it is worth keeping this definition in mind.

Lawler et al. (2004) distinguish HR analytics from HR metrics. They argue that HR metrics are *measures* of specific HR outcomes such as efficiency, effectiveness and impact. However, they claim that analytics are not measures but rather *techniques* used to show the impact of HR activities through the *analysis* of HR metrics. Despite this definition, Marler and Boudreau (2017) state that ambiguity still exists; however, they also concur that HR analytics and HR metrics are not one and the same.

Marler and Boudreau's (2017) review of definitions of HR analytics found that authors tended to categorize HR analytics as either an analysis process or a decision-making process (discussed later in the chapter). In this chapter, however, we adopt their (2017: 15) all-encompassing definition of HR analytics as:

> a HR practice enabled by information technology that uses descriptive, visual and statistical analyses of data related to HR processes, human capital, organizational

performance, and external economic benchmarks to establish business impact and enable data driven decision-making.

It is important to note that, often, both researchers and practitioners may use the terms HR metrics and people analytics to refer to HR analytics. We caution against the use of these terms as synonymous with HR analytics, as they fail to acknowledge the complex set of factors used in data analysis as it relates to the HR function.

HRM IN THE GLOBAL BUSINESS ENVIRONMENT

Show me the money?

Most multinational organizations have sophisticated pay and reward systems, many of which emphasize performance-related pay. However, employee attitudes towards performance-related pay vary, depending not only on personal characteristics but also in line with national culture. Therefore an American multinational may find that employees respond positively to individual performance-based bonuses in one subsidiary of the business in the UK, while in another subsidiary in China the same reward system is not viewed favourably. Through appropriate data collection and analysis, organizations can use HR analytics to determine what HR systems, in this case reward systems, work well in a given part of the world and which programmes do not.

THE ROLE OF HR ANALYTICS IN STRATEGIC ORGANIZATIONAL DECISION-MAKING

Research demonstrates that organizations continually fail to provide quantitative evidence for the relationship between HRM and performance, known as the 'black box' in the HRM literature (Banks and Kepes, 2015; Thunissen, 2016); the CIPD (2017) claims that HR analytics is the emerging 'must-have' HR capability for organizations in order to open this 'black box' and document the HRM–performance relationship.

Despite the relatively recent emergence of the term, Marler and Boudreau (2017) argue that analytics in the field of HRM is nothing new; they point out that Kaufman (2014) has traced the notion of measurement in HR back to the early 1900s. Waber (2013) purports that analytics is simultaneously an extremely old and yet also new phenomenon. He argues that the recent catalyst for HR analytics is the explosion of hard data about human behaviour at work coming from a variety of sources, e.g. digital traces of activity from email records, web browsing history, and data stored in IT systems regarding the time, place and pace at which people work. While Waber points to the importance of these sources of information from the digital domain, he also emphasizes the role of data derived from the physical world through, for instance, developments in wearable sensing technology including mobile phones, ID badges, motion detectors and speaking patterns.

Having an HR analytics strategy is key to ensuring that this data plays a role in organizational decision-making. The CIPD (2016) outlines that an HR analytics strategy should meet three aims:

* to connect HR data with business data in order to explore how the HR function influences outcomes at the organizational level
* to enable HR leaders to design and implement HR management activity in an efficient and effective manner
* to allow the organization to measure the effectiveness of HR in delivering against its objectives.

The emergence of inferential (predictive) analytics holds great potential for organizational management according to Fitz-Enz and Mattox (2014). While they acknowledge that analytics is a practical tool, they describe it as a meeting of art and science; analytics, as they see it, not only reveal how to look at some phenomenon (art) but also how to do something about it (science). While a practitioner focus on HR analytics is growing, with organizations such as Google, Sysco and Tesco stating that they use HR analytics in an effort to improve HR processes and to show HR strategic impact on firm performance (Davenport et al., 2010; Harris et al., 2011; Rasmussen and Ulrich, 2015; Angrave et al., 2016; Marler and Boudreau, 2017), empirical research on HR analytics has been slow to develop. Indeed, the rise in popularity of HR analytics has been accompanied by scepticism about the ability of HR professionals to effectively utilize HR data to reap organizational benefits (Harris et al., 2011; King, 2016). The remainder of this chapter explores how HR professionals can use HR data and HR analytics to both prove and improve the strategic importance of the HR function.

BUILDING YOUR SKILLS

Ultimately, HR's role is to ensure that employee performance aligns with organizational objectives. For many organizations, this means ensuring that customer needs are met. Yet the design, distribution and results of customer satisfaction surveys often remain the remit of sales and marketing departments. Assume you are an HR manager: what information would you like to capture or analyze from a customer satisfaction survey that would be valuable to you in designing policies or training materials to maximize employee performance?

USES OF DATA: FROM DESCRIPTIVE TO PRESCRIPTIVE

Fitz-Enz and Mattox (2014) contend that the data used in HR analytics can be analyzed in three ways: descriptive, predictive and prescriptive. Table 11.1 below provides an overview of these levels of data. Fitz-Enz and Mattox (2014) state that HR analytics begins with basic reporting of HR metrics (descriptive) and from there has the potential to proceed up to prescriptive modelling of business practices. They argue that the purpose of HR analytics is to find the 'best path through a mass of data to uncover hidden value' (Fitz-Enz and Mattox, 2014: 4).

Data can be obtained from a variety of sources, both internal and external, and span a wide variety of functional areas. Bersin (2012) identified three categories of source: people, process and performance. People data includes basic demographic information, such as age, gender and nationality, as well as the specific qualifications and skills of the employee. Data pertaining to individual reward and remuneration also falls within this category. Next is programme level data

Forms of analysis	Description	Examples
Descriptive	The primary focus at the descriptive level is on cost reduction and process improvement. Efficiency-based HR metrics provide the basis of investigation at this level. The aim of descriptive analytics is to describe relationships and current and historical data patterns through data mining and periodic reports	Employee turnover rate, the cost of new hires, training costs
Predictive	Predictive analysis includes techniques such as statistics, modelling and data mining that use current and historical facts to make predictions about the future through the use of probability	The probability of selecting the right employees for promotion
Prescriptive	Prescriptive analytics moves beyond prediction by providing decision options for workforce optimization. It is used to analyze complex data to predict outcomes and show potential impacts where various alternative scenarios are presented	Return on investment from different learning and development programmes resulting in changes to the bottom line

Table 11.1 Forms of analysis
Source: adapted from Fitz-enz, J. and Mattox, II, J.R. (2014) *Predictive Analytics for Human Resources*, p. 3, Hoboken, New Jersey: John Wiley & Sons, Inc. Copyright © 2014 by Jac Fitz-enz and John R. Mattox, II. All rights reserved.

which includes information on aspects such as employee attendance, participation in training and development activities, leadership development and key projects. Finally, performance data encapsulates performance ratings from supervisors and even peers or customers captured via 360-degree feedback ▶Chapter 7◀, together with data regarding goal attainment, talent and succession plans, and assessments. Table 11.2 below identifies a variety of sources of data that HR teams can draw on.

Form	Source of data	Content
HR planning	Labour market data, big data and national survey data	Economic forecasts, sectoral trends, demographic trends
Demographic data from employee records	HR administration	Age, gender, nationality, family status, start date with organization, qualifications
Pay and benefits	Compensation and benefits	Annual salary, hourly rate, overtime rates, bonuses, share allocations, healthcare package, company car
Skills and competencies	Learning and development	Training courses completed, training pending, attendance at learning and development events, leadership development
Employee elevator pitches	HR administration	Geographic mobility, career aspirations
Performance reviews and evaluations	Line managers/HR administration	Employee goal achievement, future targets, developmental objectives
Customer/client feedback	Sales and marketing	Customer service, job ability
Peer reviews	HR administration	Teamwork ability, collegiality, agreeableness
Organizational climate survey	HR administration/learning and development	Job commitment, job satisfaction, motivation levels
Critical incident/accident reports	Health and safety	Causal factors in accidents, outcomes of critical incidents
Exit interviews	Recruitment and selection	Job commitment, job satisfaction, motivation levels, career moves
Assessments test	Learning and development	Aptitude or outcome of training
Time and attendance	HR administration	Absenteeism, punctuality

Table 11.2 Sources of data for HR analytics

Bersin (2012) recommends a four-level process in the development of HR analytics capabilities in organizations, allowing a gradual build-up of analytical skill and capacity. The first level develops junior analysts' capability in defining metrics and ensuring that the key data is collected, reported and stored in a usable manner. The second level is the creation of a reporting function that links HR information to business objectives and relevant external data in a visually interesting and understandable format. This enables the data to be used to persuade senior management of the need for action on strategic matters. The third stage is strategic analytics which focuses on aspects such as the segmentation and optimization of talent by modelling with statistical tools. Finally, by the fourth stage, predictive skills allow organizations to forecast risks through the design of algorithms.

Mind the gap – employers legally obligated to publish the gender pay gap in their organizations

In 2015, then British prime minister, David Cameron, announced plans that would compel large companies (over 250 employees) to publish the difference in earnings between male and female staff in a bid to ensure equal pay. The average gender pay gap in the UK stood at nearly 20% at the time of the announcement. The prime minister, argued that forcing companies to publish details of pay 'will cast sunlight on the discrepancies and create the pressure we need for change, driving women's wages up'. The Confederation of British Industry (CBI), however, was critical of the announcement, claiming that the publishing of such information 'should not be used to name and shame firms, as data will only be able to present a partial picture, particularly given factors such as the mix of part-time and full working and sectoral differences'. The director of the CBI argued that 'where reporting can be useful is as a prompt for companies to ask the right questions about how they can eradicate the gender pay gap'. These regulations came into effect in 2018, meaning that organizations must now gather and analyze and publish their pay data.

Prior to this announcement, even organizations which did focus on examining their pay data for gender pay gaps largely only compared average hourly earnings of men with average hourly earnings of females; however, this does not tell the whole story. Bonuses, performance-related pay awards and company share allocations all contribute to the gender pay gap. Therefore, meaningful information is only achieved when the pay data is examined by job level within organizations.

Consider that you work in the HR management department of an organization with 2,000 employees in the UK financial services sector. You are part of a team which has been tasked with identifying why a 19% gender pay gap exists in your organization.

Questions

1. What data do you think you would need to analyze to help identify the root causes of the gender pay gap?
2. What challenges do you foresee in introducing changes to close the gender pay gap?
3. Based on previous chapters, how would you communicate the data to staff?

Sources

Rigby, E. (2015) 'UK companies told to publish gender pay audits', *Financial Times*, 14 July

Prime Minister's Office (2015) 'My one nation government will close the gender pay gap', 14 July

Mason, R (2016) 'Gender pay gap reporting for big firms to start in 2018', *Guardian*, 12 February

MEASUREMENT AND TOOLS

> **Variable** – a thing (a phenomenon or element) that is liable to vary, or change

The data items (or sets of data) that are collected in an organization (see Table 11.2 on page 211) are called **variables**. A variable is any phenomenon measured that can *vary* or *change* – characteristics, numbers and quantities (e.g. employee gender; productivity output; sales). Based on what they are measuring, variables are categorized along two dimensions: categorical and continuous. As such, they can also be referred to as 'measures' in the context of HR analytics.

Categorical Variables

Categorical variables are variables that comprise a number of categories. For example, when considering job type, employees can be categorized based on their role or position in the organization (e.g. engineer, administrator, sales executive), and each employee can only be in one category. Another example of a categorical variable is employee job level (e.g. junior/senior administrator or manager/non-manager). There are three distinct types of categorical variables (measures):

1. *Binary variables:* these are variables that only comprise two categories, for example a driving licence – employees either have or do not have a driving licence.
2. *Nominal variables:* these variables comprise three or more categories, for example nationality – employees' nationality can vary across 196 countries.
3. *Ordinal variables:* these are categorical variables that can be ordered, in other words the possible data values can be ranked in order. For example, you can rank employees based on their educational level according to lower or higher levels of educational attainment.

Continuous Variables

Continuous variables are variables that can be measured on a numerical scale or those that have a numerical value. For example, employee salary, productivity output and sales output would all be considered continuous variables. Other examples of variables that can be measured on a numerical scale include employee performance and employee job satisfaction. These types of variables are usually measured along what is known as a 'Likert-type scale'. Employee job satisfaction, for example, would usually be measured on a scale ranging from 1 (very dissatisfied) through 2 (dissatisfied), 3 (neutral), 4 (satisfied) to 5 (very satisfied). Likert-type scaling (Likert, 1932) is usually used to measure the strength of employee attitudes in organizations.

Variables measured via various forms (see Table 11.2), e.g. through organizational climate surveys, performance appraisals, or stored in employee databases, can be analyzed using a number of sophisticated software programs. Some common ones used in organizations include Advanced Excel, SPSS and the R Project.

Advanced Excel

Many organizations analyze their data using advanced techniques within the Microsoft Excel software program. Microsoft Excel is a spreadsheet tool which features calculation, graphing and macro programming functions. Advanced techniques can be used within this tool to analyze complex data and relationships between specific variables. For more information, visit: www.office.com/.

SPSS

The Statistical Package for Social Sciences (SPSS) is a widely used software program, produced by IBM, which features statistical analysis, data management and data documentation functions. SPSS is considered a 'user-friendly' software program which allows for complex analyses of data. We consider this particular package as the most useful to analyse data descriptively, predictively and prescriptively. For more information, visit: www.ibm.com/analytics/us/en/technology/spss/.

The R Project

The R Project is a computer language and a computing environment for statistical analysis and graphic presentation of data. It comprises a set of tools for a wide array of data manipulation tasks. The R Project is free, and researchers all over the world are continually adding new features, packages and programs to its environment. For more information, visit: www.r-project.org/.

CONSIDER THIS

We have discussed the measurements and tools that form part of HR analytics. A wide array of software is on offer, which organizations can purchase to support the analysis of staff and performance-related data. While many organizations may consider developing their HR analytics capabilities, doing so is not always possible without specific training for existing staff or, in some instances, without incorporating different talents into the HR department directly or by aligning with other departments such as statistics or information technology. Read an account by the chief operating officer of DBS Bank on her experience of establishing an HR analytics team at www.humanresourcesonline.net/dbs-coos-5-tips-setting-human-capital-analytics-team/ (accessed 11 June 2018).

Based on discussions in ▶Chapter 3◀ (Recruitment and Selection), what factors do you need to consider when establishing an HR analytics team?

THE INTERNAL CONSULTANT: SKILL REQUIREMENTS FOR HR ANALYTICS

Organizations commonly spend significant amounts of money each year on consultants and advisers when they need guidance on, or insights into, particular aspects of their business. HR is one such area where organizational consulting has become extremely common, for example, in assisting the organization with the design and delivery of organizational climate surveys, identifying staff turnover issues or even identifying productivity or performance gaps. However, HR analytics provides most organizations with a means to interrogate their own data and key performance indicators so as to identify solutions to these problems internally, i.e. by having an HR professional act as an internal consultant. However, there are challenges for most organizations in making this a reality.

CONSIDER THIS

What do you think are the advantages and disadvantages of hiring a computer science graduate with less than three years' experience to perform in the role of HR data analyst?

According to Deloitte's Global Human Capital Trends 2015 study, 75% of organizations believe that using analytics in HR is 'important'; however, only 8% believe that their organization is 'strong' in this area. Forbes (2015) emphasizes the need to develop expertise and knowledge to effectively implement HR analytics. But what sort of talent are organizations looking for in this area? The CIPD (2013) acknowledges that 'HR people generally prefer solving big picture problems and working on relationships and context. They are comfortable with ambiguity but less comfortable with analysis.' Bersin (2015) revealed findings of companies drawing on the expertise of individuals with PhD level qualifications in occupational psychology, engineering and statistics to support their analytics projects. Edwards and Edwards (2016: 5) contend that the vast majority of people who enter the HR profession do not have the specific skills required to conduct sophisticated HR analytics, since the third-level courses do not involve that form of statistics training. Indeed, Edwards and Edwards also point out that, in the UK at least, the professional qualifications awarded by the CIPD to accredit HR professionals have very limited requirements in regard to developing numerical capability. Therefore they argue that a competence gap currently exists in the field of HR which must be addressed if the HR function is to move beyond intuitive decision-making to making decisions based on trends and patterns of behaviour. They argue that learning how to carry out predictive HR analytics will fundamentally strengthen the skill set of the HR profession. See Table 11.3 below for an overview of capability enablers for HR analytics.

Enabler	Description
People	Although powerful, the advantages and value of analytical tools can only be fully delivered when people make use of the data to take action by thinking analytically about business problems. Deloitte has described the process of building analytical capability as a 'journey', which calls for the 'reassessment and realignment' of business-focused analytical skills among staff, as the field of analytics matures
Processes	Through analytics, factors which have an effect on how business is conducted can be identified; however, this data is only useful if changes can be implemented. Organizations may need to adapt their 'decision-support processes' in order to effectively implement changes
Technology	New IT solutions are available to support HR analytics but organizations can also consider utilizing existing HRIS
Data	Data identified for use in analysis, either from internal or external sources, should first be examined to establish if it is timely, accurate and secure
Governance	An HR analytical system should operate within a system of governance where a person/group is accountable for facilitating the analytics and obtaining insights from data

Table 11.3 The five capability enablers for analytical capability
Source: inspired by information in Deloitte Development LLC (2011).

HRM AND ORGANIZATIONAL PERFORMANCE

Creating a 'data democratic' environment for employees

In 2017, Capventis, a specialist business and technology consultancy company based in Ireland and the UK, launched an online survey to examine the extent to which employees have easy access to the data required to perform their duties to their full potential. It refers to the term 'data democratic' – the extent to which all stakeholders, including employees, can access the data they need to do the best job possible. The link to the survey featured in one of the national papers, along with an account of how a major retailer with 70,000 staff uses analytics to allow employees more knowledge and understanding of performance.

This global retail leader provides access regarding key performance data and metrics to its entire workforce, both full- and part-time staff, and suppliers. This means that 'a shop worker in Dublin can compare and contrast performance in her store with stores worldwide, and get ideas on how best to improve sales and customer care' (Capventis, 2017). By becoming 'data democratic', this global retailer has empowered its workers and suppliers to make better decisions for the business and consequently add greater value (Fitz-Enz and Mattox, 2014).

In groups, assume that you work in a retail environment. What data do you think would facilitate you improving your performance at work?

EVIDENCE-BASED DECISION-MAKING: ANALYTICS IN TANDEM WITH INTERVENTIONS

Bassi (2011) stresses the need to take an evidence-based approach to people management decisions. While HR metrics in relation to key performance indicators such as productivity, and attendant aspects, for example attendance and turnover, have long been utilized by HR practitioners, more recently the emphasis has moved towards more sophisticated analysis and modelling for predictive purposes. However, Rasmussen and Ulrich (2015) caution that without embedding the analytics process within strategic decision-making aspects, the analytics process risks becoming another HR 'fad'. They make the point that HR analytics is not 'new' at all, but rather comprises measures and processes that organizations have been doing for years. The difference now is that analytics promises evidence-based initiatives, data-based decision-making and the introduction of efforts to bridge management, academia and practice that bring rigour to the HR function.

Finally, there is an ethical dimension to HR analytics that must be considered. Lupushor (2017) points out that, while having the ability to use data to influence dynamics in the workplace can be very positive for HR leaders, there is a flipside that must be considered for employees. She emphasizes that analytics can trigger 'mixed emotions' for employees who, on the one hand, can see the positive impact that can be achieved in the organization but, on the other, can be fearful of how decisions could have a negative impact on their lives. Lupushor refers to an example whereby an algorithm designed to examine turnover and attrition trends identified that those living further away from the office were more likely to leave the organization. However, the group identified as living further away were also more likely to be from less advantaged backgrounds. Therefore, the company risked discriminating against people in its hiring practices on the basis of the algorithm. An example like this indicates the importance of both local and tacit knowledge that can only be considered through the human interpretation of the results of any data analysis, thus emphasizing the need to maintain the involvement of local HR and people managers in decision-making based on predictive analytics. Indeed Froud (2017) points out that employers should be mindful in how they use particular data since it could give way to legal claims from employees. For example, he argues that where an employee refuses to give their consent to process their data, and they are subsequently not promoted but others are, they could potentially claim that they are being discriminated against.

SPOTLIGHT ON SKILLS

You are an HR manager in a large manufacturing organization in the UK. Productivity level per worker on one of the production lines is lower than on the two other production lines. There are no major differences between any of the work groups in terms of job tenure or turnover rates. You have been asked by the production manager to help them identify possible reasons for the disparity in productivity. In terms of data, you have access to information for:

1. time, attendance and 'clocking-in' for all employees
2. training and development uptake
3. accident reports
4. defect reports
5. organizational satisfaction results
6. supervisor engagement scores.

Identify three ways in which you could use HR analytics to try to identify reasons for this disparity in productivity levels. Prepare and present your plan of action for the meeting.

To help you answer the questions above, visit **www.macmillanihe.com/carbery-cross-hrm-2e** and watch the videos of Rob Shanley from Google and Neville Bourke, Founder of Bourke Human Resources, talking about the applications of HR analytics.

HRM IN PRACTICE

Measuring morale at Mifloe – perceptions vs reality

Getty Images/iStockphoto/fizkes, Станислав Уваров

You have been fortunate to obtain the position of HR director for Europe, Middle East and Asia (EMEA) at Mifloe Ltd, a large (fictitious) Canadian multinational software development company, employing approximately 8,000 people internationally. The company, which was founded in 2006, specializes in the development of online sales and security technologies for large and small retailers. The company's European headquarters are in Toulouse, France, where it employs 2,000 people in a range of technological, corporate and administrative roles. Mifloe is widely recognized as a progressive employer, offering a modern workplace with competitive salaries and attractive employee benefits. As a result, the company has a low employee turnover rate of just 5% annually at junior management levels and above. Indeed, many of those who join the organization as graduates continue their employment there for many years.

However, the low turnover rate has some drawbacks; it means that natural promotional opportunities are scarce, as turnover is very low in senior roles. Therefore, promotional opportunities emerge only from business growth, which has led to some employees claiming that Mifloe can be a pressurized environment to work in. Furthermore, with limited promotional opportunities, employees are very reliant on achieving positive performance reviews in order to secure incremental pay increases since Mifloe operates a performance-related pay system.

On the other hand, among entry-level roles, particularly call centre-based employees, a high level of turnover exists. The customer contact centre employs over 1,000 staff in total in a range of IT, finance and support functions. The largest single cohort of staff (over 700) are the customer engagement agents, whose call centre-based role is to manage immediate queries and redirect issues onwards to the appropriate IT or technical advisory experts. Each team has a customer engagement manager, with 12 individual customer engagement team leaders who in turn have a team of agents of between 30 and 40 members. The contact centre operates seven days a week from 7.30am to 11.30pm with two different shifts: 7.30am to 4pm and 3pm to 11.30pm.

Mifloe operates a pay-related performance management system (outlined in Exhibit 1 below). Employees at all levels are included in the review process. In the customer contact centre, performance reviews are conducted annually, each April, by the customer engagement team leaders and customer engagement manager. Employees are asked to complete a self-report assessment of their own performance in advance of the meeting. At the meeting, the team leaders and customer engagement leaders complete a performance review form, outlining goals for the coming year, and a review of performance over the previous year. One of the wider current goals for the contact centre is to improve (i.e. reduce) the average duration of calls from 8.5 minutes to 6.5 minutes.

Exhibit 1 Pay-related performance management system

Performance rating	Description	Salary increment
Exceptional	Exceeds expectations in own role and consistently makes an outstanding contribution to the organization which extends the impact and influence of the role	5%
Very effective	Achieves all objectives, exceeds standards and performs tasks in a proficient manner	3%
Effective	Achieves required objectives and meets the normal expectations of the role consistently well	2%
Developing	Achievements are stronger in some objectives than others, most objectives are met but there is room for improvement in others	1%
Improvable	Achievements generally do not meet the expectations set. Room for improvement in several areas	0%
Unacceptable performance	Failed to meet critical objectives, shows little commitment to improving performance to an acceptable standard	0%

A number of issues were identified by your predecessor as priority areas in need of solutions, including the following:

- There is a perception among some junior management that the promotion track is 'too slow' in Mifloe; this previously was not an issue when the company was expanding rapidly, but recent year-on-year growth has slowed.
- The customer contact centre call times are currently too long relative to other call centres, and this could potentially impact on attracting and maintaining the client base.

- Turnover among the customer engagement agents is currently 17% annually, which is much higher than the industry average but is also costing the organization in terms of recruitment, training and productivity.
- Linked with this, the customer engagement manager (CEM) is concerned that this high employee turnover rate is having a significant impact on morale among the agents. The CEM explicitly stated that 'all these changes in staff mean there is no time for the agents to develop working relationships with one another; people are frustrated with having to constantly deal with newcomers and we need to do something now'.

Having recently attended a Chartered Institute of Personnel Development event in London on the topic of HR analytics, you believe that the organization should make more effort to make evidence-based decisions around staff. Moreover, at your previous organization, you found the responses contained in the annual organizational climate surveys with staff very enlightening. You were surprised to find that Mifloe does not currently conduct such a survey. In building your new team, you identify the need for an HR analytics specialist. This new role will be responsible for introducing a new organizational climate survey, 'MiView at Mifloe'.

What would you do?

❶ What core competencies do you think the new HR analytics specialist would require?

❷ Assuming you fill the role, what sources of information do you think the HR analyst could draw upon to begin to explore the underlying issues identified by both your predecessor and the CEM?

❸ Outline what measures you would include in the 'MiView at Mifloe' survey.

Getty Images/Image Source

SUMMARY

In this chapter, you have developed an understanding of what HR analytics is, explored its development and learned how organizations can use various HR analytics techniques to better utilize their data for strategic decision-making. Throughout the chapter, we have focused on how HR analytics can impact on organizational performance through making improvements in processes which facilitate gains in human performance. However, one thing we have not discussed is the impact of HR analytics on those working in or employed by organizations. Waber (2013: 192) takes the view that people analytics takes place in the background and will continue to do so as technology develops. He argues that, from an employee perspective, 'work will look pretty much the same'. However, he contends that a key difference will be that the work environment will have been engineered in such a way that it will naturally bring out the best in workers and facilitate greater enjoyment in the roles they carry out. In ▶Chapter 4◀, you learned about employee engagement. If Waber's (2013) contention is true, then job design and engagement are areas where organizations should in time see significant improvement where they have successfully deployed HR analytics tools. Of course, it must be acknowledged that a dark side to the use of HR analytics can also exist, where organizations use data to identify further efficiencies in work practices which could have negative effects on working conditions or lead to the replacement of some roles altogether, either through technology, off-shoring to another location or redesigning work to absorb tasks into other existing roles. Indeed, King (2016) cites a lack of usable data, a lack of skills and knowledge within HR departments to use the data available, and the inability of HR practitioners to obtain support for analytical efforts as drawbacks of HR analytics. Van den Heuvel and Bondaruck (2016) in fact argue that the 'HR analytics function may very well be subsumed in a central analytics function – transcending individual disciplines such as marketing, finance, and human resource management, which could imply that HR analytics, as a separate function, department, or team, may very well cease to exist, even before it reaches maturity'.

Whilst many scholars and practitioners argue that HR analytics enables managers to make objective decisions, there has been limited investigation of the risk of biased decision-making due to over reliance on HR analytics. While research has shown that intuition/experience-based decisions can be very effective (Khatri and Ng, 2000), recent trends continue to demonstrate that managers rely almost exclusively on data. If this trend persists, some HR roles will be in jeopardy of being substituted by artificial intelligence (Frey and Osborne, 2017). Therefore, it is important that HR practice focuses on human interaction with HR data, including an understanding of how line managers interact with and use the outputs of HR analytics data in their day-to-day roles, to ensure high-quality decision-making which is critical for organizational success.

CHAPTER REVIEW QUESTIONS

1. Define HR analytics.
2. Contrast HR metrics with HR analytics.
3. What is the advantage of predictive data over descriptive data?
4. Identify five sources of data that could be used in HR analytics.
5. How are variables, or data items, categorized?
6. What are the three most common software packages used in HR analytics?
7. What challenges do you think an organization might face in aiming to be data democratic?
8. What ethical issues do HR practitioners need to consider when gathering data for HR analytics purposes?

FURTHER READING

Angrave, D., Charlwood, A., Kirkpatrick, I. et al. (2016) 'HR and analytics: why HR is set to fail the big data challenge', *Human Resource Management Journal*, 26(1), 1–11.

Fields, D.L. (2002) *Taking the Measure of Work: A Guide to Validated Scales for Organizational Research and Diagnosis*, Thousand Oaks, CA: Sage.

Higginbottom, K. (2015) 'Portrait of an HR data analyst', *Forbes*. Available at www.forbes.com/sites/karenhigginbottom/2015/04/13/portrait-of-a-hr-data-analyst/#702b98946d38.

Marler, J.H. and Boudreau, J.W. (2016) 'An evidence-based review of HR analytics', *International Journal of Human Resource Management*, 28(1), 3–26.

Rasmussen, T. and Ulrich, D. (2015) 'Learning from practice: how HR analytics avoids being a management fad', *Organizational Dynamics*, 44(3), 236–42.

USEFUL WEBSITES

**www.cipd.co.uk/knowledge/strategy/
analytics/factsheet**
The CIPD is a professional body for HR and people
development – experts on the world of work and
career partner to over 140,000 members around the
world. This website contains a number of interesting
factsheets, articles and reports centred on HR
analytics.

www.youtube.com/watch?v=Ft04PactXos
The website of the Society for Industrial and
Organizational Psychology (SIOP) is the premier
membership organization for those practising
and teaching industrial and organizational

psychology. While an independent organization
with its own governance, SIOP is also a division
within the American Psychological Association
and an organizational affiliate of the Association
for Psychological Science. There has been an
increasing awareness among psychologists of the
usefulness of data analytics in making HR-related
decisions.

**insidebigdata.com/2017/03/30/
government-use-data-analytics-case-
studies**
insideBIGDATA is a news outlet that distills news,
strategies, products and services in the world of big
data for data scientists as well as IT and business
professionals. The focus is on big data, data science,
artificial intelligence, machine learning and deep
learning.

For extra resources, including videos, multiple choice questions and useful weblinks, go to:
www.macmillanihe.com/carbery-cross-hrm-2e.

Getty Images/Image Source/Frisco

12: Health, Safety and Employee Wellbeing

Ronan Carbery and Robert Lynch

LEARNING OUTCOMES

By the end of this chapter you will be able to:

- Understand the concept of safety at work
- Know why accidents occur and differentiate between theories of accident causation
- Identify how relevant human factors affect health and safety behaviour
- Differentiate between the behaviour-based and attitude-based approaches to health and safety
- Understand the issues that can affect employee wellbeing and their implications in the workplace
- Differentiate between the mutual gains and conflicting outcomes perspectives on HRM and wellbeing
- Identify the stakeholders responsible for wellbeing in the workplace
- Establish the role of the HRM function in promoting health, safety and wellbeing at work

THIS CHAPTER DISCUSSES:

Introduction (222)

Safety Culture (222)

Why Accidents Occur (223)

Human Factors and Health and Safety (227)

Employee Wellbeing (231)

Employee Wellbeing: Theoretical Considerations (242)

Key Stakeholders: Where Does the Responsibility Lie? (243)

Health, Safety and Wellbeing and HRM (245)

INTRODUCTION

In this chapter we look at a number of important aspects of managing health, safety and employee wellbeing in organizations. Developments in the field indicate an increased concern for the quality of working life. For example, in Europe the number of health, safety and wellbeing-related EU Directives highlights a growing concern for safety in the workplace. In China, strong economic growth has seen GDP grow significantly with a concomitant increase in health and safety risks; in 2011 over 200 million workers in China suffered occupational hazards that existed across 16 million organizations (Hui et al., 2013), and the Chinese National Center for Disease Control reported 27,240 cases of occupational diseases in 2010, which was over twice the number of cases reported in 2001.

It is commonly acknowledged that the establishment and maintenance of a safe and healthy working environment is a central feature of good business and modern-day HRM. Over the past 35 years, the subject has become an increasing priority for the HRM function in organizations. Employers are now expected to provide a range of safety, health and wellbeing provisions and proactively manage this important element of the employment relationship. There is a body of research evidence indicating that good safety, health and wellbeing practices contribute to enhanced employee morale, lower levels of stress and foster greater commitment to an organization's goals and objectives. The increasing awareness of the need for safe working practices has also been driven by recognition of the considerable costs associated with accidents and unsafe working behaviours. Through an appreciation of these costs and the prospect of further reduced costs through safer and healthier workplaces, it is apparent that more proactive safety management practices are now emerging in organizations.

The nature of work has changed considerably too, with the traditional 8-hour working day and 40-hour working week giving way to a range of different working time arrangements ▶Chapter 5◀. Long working hours consume employees' resources and create stress for individuals (Ilies et al., 2009). The number of work hours is one of the primary demands that work places on individuals (Voydanoff, 2004). In the USA, for example, this is especially pertinent as most employers impose overtime hours on employees rather than allowing their employees to have control over the amount of overtime they work (Berg et al., 2014). Lack of control over work hours has been linked to a variety of negative physical and psychological health outcomes (Kramer and Son, 2016).

To understand how organizations manage health, safety and employee wellbeing, we consider key behavioural and psychological concepts and contemporary research. The chapter begins with an examination of safety culture, followed by an analysis of why accidents occur and theories of accident causation. We then look at how to manage the human factors that impact on health and safety and the behavioural science approach is explored. Next, the discussion turns to employee wellbeing, with a consideration of the different issues that can affect wellbeing at work and an analysis of the theory. We raise the question: who is responsible? Finally, we look at the role of HRM in relation to health, safety and wellbeing at work.

SAFETY CULTURE

Safety culture is a subset of organizational culture ▶Chapter 1◀, which is thought to affect employee attitudes and behaviour in relation to an organization's ongoing health and safety performance. An analysis of safety culture captures concepts such as explicit management commitment to health and safety, employee empowerment for safety, reward systems that reinforce health and safety, and efficient reporting mechanisms.

The organization's senior management has a crucial role in promoting a positive organizational safety culture and should demonstrate the extent to which safety is seen as a core value or guiding principle. A commitment to safety is, therefore, reflected in senior management's ability to demonstrate a long-term, positive attitude towards safety, even in times of economic uncertainty, and to actively promote safety in a consistent manner across the organization. Managerial commitment to safety is also reflected by managers' presence and contribution to safety seminars and training, taking responsibility for safety critical operations, and the extent to which there is regular communication regarding safety issues.

Organizations with a positive safety culture often seek to empower their employees and ensure that they

> **Safety culture** – the attitudes, beliefs, perceptions and values that employees share in relation to safety

understand their critical role in promoting safety. **Empowerment** refers to an employee's attitude and perception that they have control and influence over their situation, which arises from being entrusted with authority or responsibility by management. Within the context of health and safety, employee empowerment means that employees have a substantial voice in safety decisions, the power to initiate and achieve safety improvements, hold themselves and others accountable for their actions, and take pride in the safety record of their organization. Cheyne et al. (1998) suggest that employee attitudes are one of the most important measures of safety culture because they are often influenced by other features of the working environment, and attitudes towards safety are a basic element of safety culture.

Reward systems ▶Chapter 8◀ are also an important aspect of safety culture as they indicate the manner in which safe and unsafe behaviour is evaluated and the consistency with which rewards or penalties are provided. A transparent evaluation and reward system can promote safe behaviour and discourage or correct unsafe behaviour. Safety culture, therefore, is reflected by the extent to which an organization uses a fair system for reinforcing safe behaviours, for example through monetary incentives or public praise and recognition by management and peers, as well as through systems that discourage or punish unnecessary risk-taking and unsafe practices.

Reporting systems are useful in identifying a weakness or vulnerability in safety management before an accident occurs. The willingness and ability of an organization to proactively learn and adapt its work processes based on events and near misses before an accident takes place are fundamental to improving safety. Reporting systems should also encourage the free and uninhibited reporting of safety issues that come to the attention of employees during the course of their work, and of any accidents that do occur so that they can be avoided in future. It is important to ensure that employees do not experience punishments or negative outcomes as a result of using the reporting system, and to have a structured feedback system to inform employees that their suggestions or concerns have been reviewed and what action will be taken to solve the problem.

> **Empowerment** – entrusting employees to take responsibility for their health, safety and wellbeing by giving them the right skills, and encouraging them to get involved in making decisions
>
> **Accident** – an unplanned or unforeseen event that could lead to injury to people, damage to plant or machinery, or some other loss

CONSIDER THIS

Management at the Chernobyl nuclear power plant in the former Ukrainian Soviet Socialist Republic and the relevant government officials assumed that a safe culture existed in their nuclear plants because they had never had any accidents. Only after the accident on 26 April 1986 at Chernobyl involving a nuclear reactor, which exposed 20 million people to radiation and resulted in at least 9,000 deaths from cancer as a result of radiation exposure, did it become apparent that the safety culture was completely inadequate. This lack of a safety culture was evident in management's confusion as to how to respond to hazards, but also in the design, engineering, construction, manufacture and regulation of the nuclear plant. Does the absence of a positive safety culture only become apparent after a major accident?

WHY ACCIDENTS OCCUR

One of the primary aims of health, safety and wellbeing at work is to reduce **accidents** and ensure that employees act in a safe manner. Apart from the moral obligation to provide a safe workplace for employees, there is also an economic incentive to minimize the likelihood of accidents occurring. For example, in the UK in 2014, there were over 475,000 occurrences of employees taking up to six days off work as a result of a workplace accident – and a further 154,000 occurrences of workers taking even longer (Health and Safety Executive, 2015). Workplace injuries and ill health (excluding cancer) cost UK society an estimated £14.1 billion (Health and Safety Executive, 2016). According to the International Labour Organization (2003), on a worldwide scale, workplace accidents and work-related illnesses annually result in 2.3 million fatalities and cost the global economy an estimated $1.25 trillion. To put this into context, it means that every 15 seconds, a worker dies from a work-related accident or disease, and that every 15 seconds, 153 workers have a work-related accident.

Country	2011	2012	2013	2014	2015
USA	4,693	4,628	4,585	4,818	4,500
Canada	Not available	977	902	919	852
UK	175	171	148	136	147
Australia	224	229	201	194	195
Korea	1,271	1,292	1,245	1,123	1,069
Japan	1,024	1,093	1,030	1,057	972
China	79,552	75,500	Not available	68,061	Not available
Mexico	1,578	1,534	1,314	1,330	1,444

Table 12.1 Workplace fatalities (2011–15)
Sources: data from the International Labour Organization (ILO) databases, *ILOSTAT*. Available at www.ilo.org/ilostat.

Table 12.1 presents a comparison of workplace fatalities between 2011 and 2015. In China in 2010, 79,552 people died in work-related accidents, an average of 218 people a day, official figures show. It should be noted that this is a significant improvement since its worst year for workplace deaths in 2002, when 240,000 people died in 1.07 million workplace accidents. However, it is more than 21 times the rate of workplace fatalities in the UK, which has one of the lowest rates of workplace fatalities on a per capita basis (Eurostat, 2017c). Before the Occupational Safety and Health Administration (OSHA) was created in 1971, an estimated 14,000 workers were killed in the USA on the job every year. Today, workplaces are much safer and healthier, going from 38 fatal injuries a day to 12, but this still means that approximately 4,500 workers die each year in America.

Suchman (1961) suggested that there are three indicators of an accident: a high degree of unexpectedness, a low degree of avoidability, and a low degree of intent. This interpretation defines accidents only as events that result in physical injury to persons or property. Interestingly, many safety practitioners prefer to use the term 'incident' rather than accident, in the belief that the word 'accident' suggests something unavoidable and that whatever happened was simply due to chance or bad luck. Many organizations that adopt a best practice approach to health, safety and wellbeing use the term 'incident' because they want their employees to understand that most accidents can be avoided through safe working practices.

Accidents and Near Misses

As performance indicators, accidents are a post-hoc measure; they measure the failure of accident prevention activities. To prevent accidents, the preferred approach is to identify deficiencies before accidents occur. In 1969, a study of industrial accidents was undertaken by Frank Bird of the Insurance Company of North America to investigate the suggestion that for every workplace accident that resulted in 1 major injury, there were 29 minor injuries and 300 near misses. This ratio had first been discussed by Herbert William Heinrich in his 1931 book, *Industrial Accident Prevention*.

Bird's analysis of 1,753,498 accidents reported by 297 companies revealed the following statistics and ratios in the accidents reported (see Roughton and Mercurio, 2002):

- For every reported major injury, resulting in fatality, disability, lost time or medical treatment, there were 9.8 reported minor injuries requiring only first aid.
- 47% of the companies said that they investigated all property damage accidents and 84% stated that they investigated major property damage accidents, and 30.2 property damage accidents were reported for each major injury.
- Part of the study involved 4,000 hours of confidential interviews by trained supervisors on the occurrence of events that, under slightly different circumstances, could have resulted in injury or property damage. Analysis of these interviews indicated a ratio of approximately 600 such events for every 1 reported major injury.

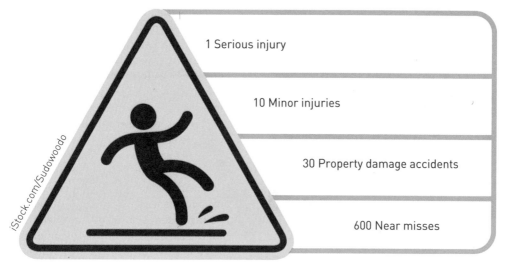

1 Serious injury

10 Minor injuries

30 Property damage accidents

600 Near misses

iStock.com/Sudowoodo

Figure 12.1 The 1:10:30:600 ratio
Source: inspired by information in Bird and Germain, 1996.

The data gathered by this survey resulted in what is commonly referred to as the 1:10:30:600 ratio (see Figure 12.1). This ratio indicates how misguided it is for organizations to only concentrate on the relatively few events resulting in serious or disabling injury, when there are so many significant opportunities that provide a much larger basis for more effective control of total accident losses. While the exact ratios have been questioned by Manuele (2002), they demonstrate the importance of recording and documenting near misses. A near miss resembles an accident in almost every other respect. It has the same direct cause and similar if not identical contributory factors. If organizations can determine what went wrong and correct the problems, it can minimize the likelihood of accidents occurring.

Incidentally, if we consider the 30 property damage accidents that occur for each serious or disabling injury, these incidents cost hundreds of thousands of euros/pounds/dollars annually and yet they are frequently misnamed and referred to as near misses.

Costs of Accidents

There is often a tendency to underestimate the cost of workplace accidents. It is easy to look at the direct costs to an organization in terms of compensation payments for injuries sustained on the job, which cover medical costs and indemnity payments for the injured worker, but relatively few organizations consider the indirect costs of an accident. These include:

- safety administration costs that occur as a result of time spent investigating and documenting accidents
- legal costs
- cost of time to other employees assisting the injured employee
- the cost of replacing the injured employee
- training replacement workers
- damage to plant and machinery
- increase in insurance premiums
- low morale among employees
- increased absenteeism.

This has given rise to the iceberg theory of accident costs (Bird, 1974), which looks at the relationship between direct and indirect costs. It suggests that accident and ill health costs can be likened to an iceberg: costs that are recoverable are visible but those that are unrecoverable are hidden below the waterline and are many times greater (see Figure 12.2 on the next page). It is often assumed that most accident and incident costs are recoverable through insurance. This is a dangerous misconception. In Australia, work-related injuries cost the Australian economy $28 billion, representing 2% of GDP (Safe Work Australia, 2015). In the UK, the Health and Safety Executive estimates that the ratio between insured and uninsured costs lies in the range of £1:8 to £1:36. In other words, for every £1 recovered from insurers, at least £8 is lost entirely. Therefore, the real costs of accidents will not be recognized if an organization only considers accidents that result in time off work.

Macmillan Australia Primary Library.

Figure 12.2 The accident cost iceberg
Source: inspired by information in Bird, 1974.

Accident Causation Theories

A number of different theories exist that seek to explain why accidents occur. The majority of these theories look at human error, in the belief that most accidents can be traced to an erroneous human act. **Human error** is any deviation from a required standard of human performance that results in an unwanted state of events – delay, malfunction, difficulty, accident and so on. The human decision or behaviour does not necessarily have to cause damage to be classified as an error.

> **Human error** – a human decision or behaviour that has undesirable effects

Heinrich (1931) developed a theory of unsafe acts and conditions, which he labelled the 'domino theory'. This influential theory dominated thinking about industrial safety and accidents for decades. Heinrich analysed 75,000 accident reports and concluded that 88% of all accidents are caused by the unsafe acts of people, 10% by unsafe physical conditions and 2% by acts of god. Domino theory states that accidents result from a chain of sequential events, like a line of dominoes falling over. When one domino falls, it triggers the next one and so on, but removing a key factor, such as an unsafe condition or an unsafe act, prevents the start of the chain reaction. Five factors were identified in this chain:

1. *Social environment and ancestry:* This deals with worker personality. Heinrich explains that undesirable personality traits, such as stubbornness or recklessness, can be passed along through inheritance or develop from a person's social environment, and both inheritance and environment contribute to undesirable behaviour or acts.

2. *Fault of person:* This also deals with worker personality traits. Heinrich believed that obtained character flaws such as bad temper, inconsiderateness and ignorance contribute at one remove to accident causation. Natural or environmental flaws in the worker's family or life cause these secondary personal deficiencies, which are themselves contributors to unsafe acts.

3. *Unsafe act and/or unsafe condition:* This addresses the direct cause of incidents. Heinrich (1931) suggested that these factors included acts such as using machinery without warning and the absence of rail guards. Heinrich felt that unsafe acts and unsafe conditions were the central factor in preventing incidents and the easiest of the five factors to correct, a process which he likened to lifting one of the dominoes out of the line. Heinrich (1931) defined four reasons why people commit unsafe acts: improper attitude, lack of knowledge or skill, physical unsuitability, and improper mechanical or physical environment. For example, an employee who is asked by his supervisor to urgently (social environment) move boxes of files from one room to another, may do so without using a trolley (fault of person) and carry multiple boxes (unsafe act) causing him to injure his back (accident).

4. *Accident:* Accidents are the occurrence of a preventable injury that is the natural result of a series of events or circumstances, which invariably occur in a fixed and logical order. In other words, accidents result from a combination of steps 1–3.

5. *Injury:* Injury results from accidents, and includes muscle sprains, cuts and broken bones, etc.

Heinrich's theory has two central points: injuries do not occur in isolation and are caused by the action of preceding factors; removal of the central factor (unsafe act/hazardous condition) negates the action of the preceding factors and so prevents accidents and injuries. Most accidents are caused by unsafe acts of people, and a person who gets injured at work is likely to have had many near misses prior to the accident. As presented in Table 12.2, Heinrich (1931) proposed a set of guidelines to form the basis of any workplace safety programme.

While Heinrich's ideas remain popular, most recent theories of accident causation have

1. Injuries result from a complete series of factors, one of which is the accident itself. Therefore, the accident is directly caused by an unsafe act and/or a physical or mechanical hazard

2. Most accidents occur as a result of unsafe acts committed by people

3. An employee who has had an injury caused by an unsafe act is likely to have had over 300 narrow escapes from serious injury as a result of committing the very same unsafe act. Likewise, people are exposed to mechanical hazards hundreds of times before they suffer injury

4. The severity of an injury is largely fortuitous and the occurrence of the accident that results in the injury is largely preventable

5. If we can understand the reasons why people do unsafe acts, it can help in taking corrective action

6. Four basic methods are available for preventing accidents – engineering revision, persuasion and appeal, personnel adjustment, and discipline

7. Accident prevention techniques are related to best quality and production techniques

8. Management should assume responsibility for safety as it is in the best position to get results

9. Supervisors play a key role in accident prevention. A supervisor's control of worker performance is the factor of greatest influence in successful accident prevention

10. Every accident has direct and indirect costs. The direct cost to the organization of compensation claims and medical treatment for industrial injuries is only one-fifth of the total cost the employer must pay

Table 12.2 Workplace safety programme guidelines
Source: inspired by information in Heinrich, 1931.

labelled his ideas too simplistic. They say safety performance measurement must also account for the behaviour of management and supervisors. Barrie and Paulson (1991) suggest that while unsafe acts of workers are the leading cause of accidents and injuries, they are only indicative of other safety management system problems or dysfunctions. They propose that to improve safety in the workplace, the organization must first address the context within which they occur. In other words, an organization-wide approach that includes management and supervisors, and an analysis of all the organizational factors that influence health and safety in addition to human behaviour, is the only way meaningful changes in safety standards can be addressed. This leads us to consider the relationship between human factors and health and safety.

HUMAN FACTORS AND HEALTH AND SAFETY

Traditional approaches to health and safety in the workplace tended to focus on the engineering design approach, whereby the physical design of the workplace took precedence in making environments, technology and processes safer. This essentially centred on the **ergonomics** domain, where responsibility for health and safety lay in the hands of engineers and those who were responsible for designing the layout of workplaces and work processes. Organizations also focused on employees' cognitive errors and looked at accidents that occurred as a result of mental lapses or forgetfulness.

The interaction between individuals and the physical dimensions of the workplace is known as **human factors**. Human factors focus on human beings and their interaction with products, equipment, facilities, procedures and the surrounding environment. A simple way to look at human factors is to think about three aspects – the employee, the job and the organization – and how they impact on employees' health and safety-related behaviour. Each employee's personal attitudes, skills, habits and personalities can be strengths or weaknesses depending on the task demands. Individual characteristics

> **Ergonomics** – the relationship between employees, physical work equipment and the environment; it focuses on matching people capabilities to their work environment and includes such things as correct working height and correct viewing distance
>
> **Human factors** – how characteristics of the organization affect employee behaviour

influence behaviour in significant ways. Their effects on job performance may be negative and may not always be lessened by job design. Characteristics such as personality are fixed and difficult to change. Others, such as motivation and attitude towards risk, can be modified.

From the job perspective, tasks should be designed in accordance with ergonomic principles that take into account the physical and mental characteristics of employees. Matching the job to the person will ensure that they are not overloaded and can make the most effective contribution to organizational performance. Physical fit includes the design of the whole workplace and working environment. Mental fit involves the individual's information and decision-making requirements, as well as their perception of the tasks and risks. Mismatches between job requirements and people's capabilities increase the potential for human error and accidents occurring.

Organizational factors have the biggest influence on individual and group behaviour, yet they are often overlooked during the design of work and during investigation of accidents and incidents. Organizations need to establish their own positive health and safety culture. The culture needs to promote employee involvement and commitment at all levels, emphasizing that ignoring established health and safety standards is not acceptable. Table 12.3 provides a list of the most relevant human factors for HR practitioners.

Sanders and McCormick (1993) suggest that the human factor perspective is unique, in that it recognizes that:

1. Machines, procedures and systems are built to serve employees and must be designed with the end user in mind.
2. The design of machines, procedures and systems influences the safety behaviour of employees.
3. Employees, machines, procedures and the work environment do not exist independently of each other.
4. Objective data should be gathered by organizations on a regular basis to generate information about human behaviour that can allow organizations to minimize the likelihood of accidents occurring.

While the previous approaches played an important role in improving organizational health and safety, many organizations hit a glass ceiling in terms of ongoing improvements. The need to take a more proactive role and consider other factors and how they contribute to accidents, and the assessment of the likelihood of accidents occurring, has led to organizations adopting a **behavioural science approach** to health and safety. This approach suggests that for health and safety programmes to be effective, they must address the agent most responsible for health and safety, the employee. Therefore, organizations need to understand the psychological factors influencing health and safety before they can take steps to improve safety performance. Research suggests that behavioural science allows safety specialists to address:

> **Behavioural science approach** – how to describe, explain and predict human behaviour in a work context
>
> **Attitude-based approach** – focuses on changing a person's feelings and inner thoughts towards safety

- the types of hazards people can spot easily and those they are likely to miss
- the time of day and sorts of jobs in which people are likely to create hazards
- the extent to which we can predict the people who will have accidents and in what circumstances
- why certain people ignore safety rules, or fail to use protective equipment
- the role and value of training in fostering safety awareness.

Two broad approaches to the behavioural science perspective exist: the attitude-based approach and the behaviour-based approach. We will consider both in turn.

Attitude-based Approach

The **attitude-based approach** adopts the belief that attitudes influence behaviour. While there is a link between attitudes and behaviour, they are not

Personal	Job	Organizational
• Attitude	• Equipment design	• Size
• Attributions		• Technology
• Motivation	• Machine systems	• Culture
• Perception	• Working height	• Goals and strategies
• Memory		
• Information processing	• Job tasks	

Table 12.3 Categories of human factors

the same thing. Behaviours are everything a person does or says and are usually an outward expression of attitude. Attitudes reflect how we feel about something, either positive or negative. It is not a guarantee that a person will act in the same way every time.

Cox et al. (1998) suggested that the main influence on employee attitudes to safety was how committed they perceived the management of the organization to be towards safety. This includes the quality of near miss reporting, whether the focus was on accident prevention rather than blame, the encouragement of safety ideas, the effectiveness of safety committees, and how safety is prioritized in relation to other issues. Cheyne et al. (1999) found the factors underlying employee attitudes to safety were dependent on the industry in which they worked. For example, within the manufacturing sector, employee attitudes to safety were linked to how their managers acted. In the transport sector, however, management had no influence on attitudes towards safety, perhaps due to the autonomy in the working practices of transport workers. Nevertheless, management actions for safety should be a key area for influencing employee attitudes in most sectors. Central to the creation of a culture where management values health and safety is the perception that safety is a top priority and employee welfare is more important than quotas, deadlines or orders. Lee and Harrison (2000) found that team briefings that included discussion of safety were correlated with positive attitudes towards safety by staff. Training is also important ▶Chapter 9◀. Employees, especially long-term employees, often take a relaxed approach to health and safety as they become more familiar with their jobs. Training serves as a reminder that no amount of time on the job will keep employees immune from an injury.

The concept of **risk** is often addressed when examining attitudes towards safety. People tend to be either risk averse or risk takers. The concept of 'risk homeostasis' suggests that individuals have a fixed level of acceptable risk that they are prepared to take. When the level of risk in one part of the individual's life changes, there will be a corresponding rise or fall in risk elsewhere to bring the overall risk back to that individual's equilibrium. For example, research carried out in Germany on taxi drivers looked at cars fitted with an anti-lock braking system (ABS) and compared them with cars fitted with conventional braking systems (Aschenbrenner and Biehl,

1994). The crash rate was the same for both types of cars, indicating that drivers of ABS-equipped cars took more risks in the belief that the ABS system would take care of them, while the non-ABS drivers drove more carefully since the ABS system would not assist them in the event of a dangerous situation. Further research carried out in Sweden on the use of studded and non-studded car tyres looked at driver speed (Rumar et al., 1976). Studded tyres offer greater resistance in icy conditions in order to make driving in these conditions safer. When faced with icy roads, drivers with studded tyres actually drove faster than drivers who did not have studded tyres, believing that the increased safety afforded to them meant they could increase their level of risk.

BUILDING YOUR SKILLS

Consider any road safety campaigns or advertisements you have seen. Do they tend to focus on changing behaviours or changing attitudes? What techniques are often used in these campaigns to communicate their message?

If you wanted to change employees' attitudes towards health and safety in an organization, what steps would you take?

Behaviour-based Approach

The **behaviour-based approach** to safety looks at how people actually behave rather than their attitudes to safety. Many safety campaigns try to change people's attitudes in the hope that this will then change their behaviour, believing that attitudes cause behaviour. However, research from the psychology field suggests that this is misguided and that attitudes have a tenuous link to behaviour (Wicker, 1969). Attitudes often express how we would like to see ourselves behave, rather than how we actually behave. Crucially, a person may have a positive attitude towards safety in the workplace, but this does not always translate into safe working behaviours; for example, if a person is under pressure to complete a task, they may avoid wearing the correct protective clothing as it may slow them down.

Based on the work of Heinrich in the 1930s, who stated that approximately 90% of all accidents

> **Risk** – a situation involving exposure to danger
>
> **Behaviour-based approach** – focuses on what people do, analyses why they do it, and then applies a research-supported intervention strategy to improve what people do

are caused by human error, the behaviour-based approach advocates that getting people to behave safely reduces accidents. As discussed earlier, Heinrich (1931) claimed that accidents result from undesirable traits of a person's character that are passed along through inheritance and are the fault of employees who commit unsafe acts. However, he did not believe that it was worth trying to change people's attitudes. Instead, he believed that behaviour can potentially influence the formation and change of attitudes. This approach emphasizes the encouragement of desirable behaviour, rather than the punishment of undesirable behaviour. For example, employees should be encouraged to wear personal protective equipment when handling dangerous materials or wear hard hats on a construction site. In many organizations, though, the emphasis on safety is still communicated by disciplining employees for noncompliance instead of rewarding them for compliance. Another fairly simple way of encouraging desired behaviour is to praise people for behaving safely in order to bring about the required changes. This essentially links the desired safe behaviour to the praise received.

> **Hazards** – any source of potential damage, harm or adverse health effects on something or someone under certain conditions at work

Four factors influence behaviour in the presence of potential danger:

1. *Perception:* in order to react to danger and do something about it, it must be perceived by the individual.
2. *Psychological:* once the individual perceives danger, they psychologically evaluate and assess the level of danger, who is responsible for it, the most appropriate action to take, and the practical outcomes of that action.
3. *Action:* the individual takes a specific course of action, which will depend on their reflexes, abilities, experience, dexterity and physical condition.
4. *Outcome:* if the action taken is sufficient, the danger is averted; if the action taken is insufficient, the danger remains or increases.

Thus, behavioural-based safety programmes use a variety of people-focused techniques aimed at modifying employee behaviour via the involvement of employees and management:

- setting clear definitions of the desired safety behaviours expected at all levels
- observing existing workplace behaviours
- focusing on specific behaviours identified from safety assessments, incident data, near miss data and observations
- providing feedback for employees, supervisors, managers and executives on these behaviours in order to improve them
- setting up a process to identify and correct unsafe conditions as well as improving the consistency of safe behaviours.

This approach is popular with many organizations as it shifts responsibility for health and safety to employees and does not require significant change in the work process, engineering design or management system. One frequent criticism of the approach is that it ignores injuries and illnesses that are caused by exposure to hazards. **Hazards** include any aspect of technology or activity that produces some degree of risk. A best practice HRM approach to behaviour-based safety, however, should never attribute blame to the employee. It should seek to understand the causes of accidents and near misses and correct them through appropriate behaviour. The avoidance of hazards often requires behaviour change from supervisors and managers; and equipment redesign requires behaviour change of engineers (Garavan, 2002).

As discussed earlier, an important feature of health, safety and wellbeing in any organization is that employees are encouraged to report and document any accidents that occur, as well as near misses. The focus should be on rewarding and recognizing improvements in behaviour, not focusing on the lack of accidents. In an effort to involve employees in workplace safety, many organizations use incentive schemes that promise employees rewards for a reduction in accident rates or an increase in near miss reporting. The danger with this approach is that such reward schemes can encourage underreporting of accidents and allow workplace hazards to go unchecked. While incentive schemes can appear to produce reductions in workplace accidents, employees may essentially be rewarded for not reporting accidents. Effective behaviour-based safety programmes should not include incentives for long periods without an accident precisely because it is understood that this may lead to underreporting. Instead, positive reinforcement is delivered after safe behaviours and improvements in safe behaviours over time.

EMPLOYEE WELLBEING

Employee wellbeing has been described as a multifaceted concept, which includes a diverse array of considerations including mental health, emotional exhaustion, and psychological and emotional wellbeing (Wright and Doherty, 1998). One of the greatest challenges that HR practitioners, line managers and employees themselves face is the 'subjective' nature of the diverse array of components associated with wellbeing (Zizek et al., 2013). What causes one employee to become adversely affected in terms of wellbeing may have little or no adverse effects on another. Given the subjective and indeed complex nature of these concepts, the need for not only an understanding of employee wellbeing, but also that of the roles and responsibilities of key stakeholders, e.g. employers and employees, is essential in order to achieve positive wellbeing and an environment which is conducive for work.

> **Employee wellbeing** – the overall quality of an employee's experience at work

The CIPD (2007) developed an employee wellbeing model, which in essence outlines a change in perspective on employee wellbeing, in which industry has shifted to having a more 'holistic' approach to health and wellbeing, as opposed to the classic perspective which focused mainly on health and safety within the workplace. It is proposed that employee wellbeing (EWB) can be categorized into five domains: physical health; emotional health; values; personal development; and organization and work, as outlined in Table 12.4 on the next page. The purpose of this model was to provide employers with the necessary knowledge to reflect on what a healthy organization should look like. Later work conducted by the CIPD (2016) further expanded on the original five domains, providing key stakeholders with not only additional knowledge, but also practical real-life examples of how best to address the wellbeing needs of a workforce. While there is a great deal for employers and employees to consider and address within this model, the significant interdependence between the domains suggested by the CIPD (2016) provides stakeholders with the opportunities to address a multitude of considerations with a single initiative. For example, as suggested by the Irish Business and Employers Confederation (IBEC, 2016), ensuring that line managers are appropriately trained and competent to fulfil their roles has the potential to address both directly and indirectly additional considerations and domains within this model, such as mental health, work demands, change management, values/principles, collective/social and personal growth. It can also be argued that failing to ensure that line managers are trained/competent can have an adverse effect on the outlined additional domains/considerations. This is therefore an effective model and guide which employers and employees can refer to in order to ensure that employee wellbeing needs are being addressed within the workplace.

CONSIDER THIS

Just how much privacy are you entitled to at work? Rio Tinto is a British-Australian multinational and, with an operating income of $6.8 billion in 2016, is one of the world's largest metals and mining corporations. The organization has long mined the Pilbara region of Western Australia for iron ore, but it became embroiled in controversy when *The Guardian* reported in December 2016 that it planned to use drones to monitor workers' private lives. Due to the remote location of the mine, thousands of employees live in company-run mining camps. In March 2016 the organization awarded a 10-year facilities management contract, covering operations and accommodation, to Sodexo, a French company, 'to get to the point where we capture individual insights on where employees are spending their time and money' (Oprey, 2016). In the same month, a lawsuit was filed in the California Superior Court in San Francisco, alleging that Google operates what amounts to an internal 'spying program' on its own employees. The suit alleges that employees are prevented from putting in writing concerns over perceived 'illegal' activity, posting opinions about the company, and even writing novels 'about someone working at a tech company in Silicon Valley' without first giving their employer sign-off on the final draft. How are initiatives such as this likely to affect employee wellbeing at work?

EWB domain	Considerations and initiatives

Health	**Physical health/wellness:**
	• Health promotion initiatives
	• Health/wellness consultations
	• Effective rehabilitation
	• Wellness/wellbeing rewards
	• Employee health insurance
	• Disability management
	• Occupational health support
	• Employee assistance programmes
	
	Mental health/wellness:
	• Stress management
	• Effective risk assessment and management
	• Targeted continuous professional development:
	  • Dispute resolution training
	  • Line management training
	• Managing mental ill health
	• Occupational health support
	• Employee assistance programmes
	
	Physical health and safety:
	• Safe working practices
	• Providing a safe working environment and equipment
	• Employee safety training

Work	**Working environment:** • Work spaces which are ergonomically designed • Organizational cultures which are open and inclusive **Effective line management:** • People management policies which are effective and in line with organizational ethos and values • Customized management and leadership development programmes • Fair and transparent sickness absence management procedures **Work–life balance:** • Job design • Job roles • Work demands • Working hours • Job satisfaction **Self-control/autonomy:** • Individual control/input with task and role management • A work environment which promotes innovation and entrepreneurship • Fair and transparent whistleblowing practices **Organizational change:** • Effective leadership strategies which align with change initiatives. • Communication between all stakeholders and levels of employment • Inclusion of relevant stakeholders **Pay and reward:** • Remuneration packages which are fair and transparent • Flexible reward packages which include nonfinancial reward

EWB domain	Considerations and initiatives
Ethos and values	**Organizational leadership:** • Leadership strategies which are value-based, and in line with organizational objectives • Organizational strategies and objectives which are clear • Employee wellbeing strategies • Corporate governance • Organizational trust **Ethical standards:** • Dignity at work • Corporate social responsibility • Investing in local communities **Diversity:** • Diversity and inclusion • Cultural engagement • Learning and development initiatives • Placing a value on diversity
Collective/social	**Employee voice:** • Organizational communication which allows employees to be heard • Involvement and inclusion in organizational decision-making **Positive relationships:** • Leadership and management styles • Collaboration/teamwork • Positive relationships between employees and managers • Dignity and respect
Growth opportunities	**Career development:** • Coaching and mentoring programmes • Performance management practices • Performance development planning • Effective skill utilization • Succession planning **Emotional considerations:** • Positive healthy relationships with co-workers and managers • Personal resilience development • Financial wellbeing **Learning and development:** • Performance development planning • Learning and development opportunities • Mid-career reviews • Work which overloads and challenges the workforce appropriately **Creativity:** • An open and collaborative workplace • Opportunities which develop and promote innovation and entrepreneurship

Table 12.4 Five domains of wellbeing

Source: adapted from CIPD (2016) *Growing the health and well-being agenda: From first steps to full potential*, London: CIPD, with the permission of the publisher, the Chartered Institute of Personnel and Development, London (www.cipd.co.uk).

We will now consider a number of specific issues that affect employee wellbeing, the first of which is ergonomics.

Ergonomics

The design of workplaces in most organizations creates conditions that expose employees to numerous hazards, for example poorly designed floor layouts, excessive noise, exposure to chemicals, and improperly designed seats and workstations. Ergonomics is a science concerned with the fit between people and their work. It puts people first, taking account of their physical and mental capabilities and limitations. It aims to ensure that tasks, equipment, information and the environment suit each worker.

To assess the fit between a person and their work, it is important to consider a number of factors:

- the job being done and the demands on the worker
- the type of equipment used
- the information used, for example machine displays and controls
- the physical environment, for example temperature, humidity, lighting, noise, ventilation, vibration
- the social environment, such as teamwork and supportive management.

The physical aspects of an employee that we need to consider include:

- their body size and shape
- fitness and strength levels
- posture
- the senses, particularly vision, hearing and touch
- the stresses and strains on muscles, joints, nerves.

The psychological aspects of employees must also be considered, including their mental abilities, personality, learning, and level of experience. Improper design of the work environment and job activities can cause significant psychological stress and health problems for employees (Smith and Sainfort, 1989). Poor ergonomic characteristics of work can cause visual, muscular and psychological disorders, including visual fatigue, eye strain, sore eyes, headaches, fatigue, muscle soreness, back disorders, tension, anxiety and depression, and repetitive strain injury (RSI). These effects may

be temporary and may fade when the employee is removed from the workplace or given an opportunity to rest at work, or when the design of the work environment is improved. When exposure to poor ergonomic conditions is prolonged, the effects can become permanent.

The application of basic ergonomic principles to the workplace not only reduces the likelihood of ill health and the occurrence of accidents, it can also increase productivity and efficiency. For example, if we look at the layout of controls and equipment, these should be located in relation to how they are used by employees. Those used most often should be placed where they are easy to reach without the need for bending or stretching.

Common ergonomic issues in workplaces include:

- *Manual handling:* too much physical demand placed on the employee when lifting heavy or bulky loads; frequent repetitive lifting without sufficient rest periods; lifting loads above shoulder height; lifting on uneven or wet surfaces.
- *Display screens:* poorly positioned screens that are too high/low/close/far from the worker, or offset to one side; too much glare from lights or sunshine that increases the risk of eye strain; staring at a screen for eight hours a day without changes of activity also increases the risk of eye strain.
- *Work-related stress:* if work demands are too high and the employee is under constant pressure to meet targets and deadlines, it can result in work-related stress and increase the likelihood of ill health and reduced performance and productivity.
- *Work design:* chairs that are too high or too low for the employee, desks that are not height adjustable, and telephones that are situated too far away from the employee can all cause muscular fatigue and back strain.

HR practitioners can identify possible ergonomic issues by involving employees in assessing the design of their workplaces, analysing the way work is done in the organization, examining the circumstances surrounding frequent accidents and near misses where mistakes have occurred and people have been injured, and monitoring sickness and absenteeism records. In many instances, a relatively small adjustment is all that is needed to make jobs easier to perform.

Some of the most common ergonomic solutions are to:

- provide height-adjustable chairs and desks so individual employees can work at their preferred work height
- ensure that people working on computers take regular breaks from looking at displays
- provide guidance on correct posture to avoid RSI
- remove obstacles from under desks to create sufficient leg room
- arrange items stored on shelving so those used most frequently and those that are the heaviest are between waist and shoulder height
- raise platforms to help operators reach badly located controls
- introduce job rotation between different tasks to reduce physical and mental fatigue.

Job Characteristics

▶Chapter 3◀ looked at the recruitment and selection of employees to fill jobs and roles within organizations. What, however, is a 'good' job? There are two considerations here: individual expectations of what an employee wants from a job; and their perception of work as a central component of their lives. Eklund (1998) developed a set of characteristics of a 'good' job that combines best practice human factors and ergonomic principles:

> Mental workload – the mental demands placed on humans at work
> Work capacity – how much physical work an individual can do

- *Variation:* employees should be allowed to perform a variety of tasks in their jobs.
- *Overview of process:* if employees are allowed to see an overview of the whole production process, it will make their own job more meaningful.
- *Freedom to move:* employees should have physical freedom to move around.
- *Long cycle time:* employees should have sufficient time between work tasks to allow them enough time to do their jobs correctly.
- *Self-paced work:* employees should be allowed to carry out their job at a pace that best suits them.
- *Influence on choice of working methods:* employees should have some degree of autonomy or freedom to choose how they carry out their job on a daily basis.
- *Influence on production quality:* employees should have a say in ensuring that quality standards are met.

- *Involvement in problem-solving:* employees should feel that their opinion is valued and that they can contribute to solving any problems that arise.
- *Lack of time pressure:* employees should not be put under constant pressure to achieve deadlines.
- *Continuous development of skills:* all employees should be allowed to engage in learning and development to ensure that their skills do not become obsolete ▶Chapter 9◀.
- *Positive work management climate:* ideally, the organizational culture should advocate a supportive climate where employees interact with colleagues and managers.

There are two particular characteristics that must be considered when designing jobs: mental workload and work capacity.

The concept of **mental workload** has recently become important. The use of many modern semi-automated and computerized technologies can impose a severe burden in terms of the mental or information-processing requirements placed on employees. Mental workload looks at the input aspects of tasks, essentially the requirements and demands made by the job on the employee. The mental aspects of workload are conceptualized in terms of information processing and the cognitive and emotional demands placed on employees at work. Air traffic controllers, pilots and anaesthetists are examples of jobs with high mental workloads. If employees find that the mental requirements of their jobs are too complex or that time pressures and mental requirements are too frequent, they are likely to suffer from mental fatigue and become frustrated and anxious. On the other hand, if the mental requirements are too seldom, or frequent but too simplistic, the employee is likely to suffer from boredom on the job. The challenge with mental workload is not to minimize but optimize it.

Work capacity refers to an employee's capacity to carry out physical work. A number of personal and environmental factors affect work capacity. Personal factors include body weight, age, height, gender, and whether the individual is a smoker or non-smoker. Environmental factors include workplace temperature, level of humidity, noise levels, levels of ventilation and availability of the correct protective equipment.

HRM IN THE NEWS

New approaches to work design

In August 2015, the *New York Times* published an article detailing Amazon's somewhat secretive corporate culture. What it described was anything but pretty. Based on interviews with 100 current and former 'Amazonians,' as Amazon employees are called, the article described an autocratic workplace filled with 'a pattern of burn and churn', 'unfair' performance evaluations, and impossible demands.

Amazon has surpassed Walmart as the most valuable retailer in the USA so the fallout from the story was significant, damaging the perception of the organization among customers and potential employees, at a time when competition for talented workers in technology is strong.

The story depicted a taxing workplace environment, where the hours are long, where a worker's every move is monitored, and where the internal politics are ruthless and the company's 360-degree feedback system is 'frequently used' by employees 'to sabotage others'. One of the most regularly highlighted quotes was from an employee who said, 'Nearly every person I worked with, I saw cry at their desk.'

The feature illustrated the alleged poor welfare with anecdotes from employees. One woman with breast cancer was allegedly put on a 'performance improvement plan', while another was sent on a business trip the day after having a miscarriage. A staff member with thyroid cancer was also allegedly marked with a low performance score on returning to work and told that the organization was more productive without her.

The interviews suggested that Amazon's atmosphere was one where employees actively competed against one another; where only those that were perceived to be fully committed and prepared to make sacrifices thrived, while others were treated harshly.

According to the interviewees, Amazon employees' working and personal lives were tracked and quantified, with their movements, productivity and successes or failures being constantly measured. The results of these measurements were used by managers who were forced to rate their employees and fire their lowest-scoring workers.

Amazon's CEO, the usually guarded Jeff Bezos, felt the need to address the report in a memo to staff, saying, 'The article doesn't describe the Amazon I know or the caring Amazonians I work with every day.'

Interestingly, a year after the *New York Times* article was published, Amazon launched a programme to test a 30-hour working week in order 'to create a work environment that is tailored to a reduced schedule and still fosters success and career growth'. While plenty of employees at Amazon are part time, the novelty of this project is that it will be targeted at teams who are entirely made up of workers on a reduced schedule, including managers.

Questions

1. Is this type of work culture necessary for success?
2. Do you think Amazon can continue to attract the talent needed to sustain such a highly competitive and innovative organization?

Sources

Kantor, J. and Streitfeld, D. (2015) 'Inside Amazon: Wrestling Big Ideas in a Bruising Workplace', *New York Times*, 15 August

Gibbs, S. (2015) 'Jeff Bezos defends Amazon after NYT exposé of working practices', *Guardian*, 17 August

AFP (2016) 'Amazon dabbling with 30-hour work weeks: report', 27 August

Cook, J. (2015) 'Full memo: Jeff Bezos responds to brutal NYT story, says it doesn't represent the Amazon he leads', *GeekWire*, 16 August

Morris, D. (2016) 'Amazon Tests 30-Hour Work Week', *Fortune*, 28 August

Stress

Research suggests that the workplace can be one of the greatest sources of **stress** in people's lives, with numerous sources proposing that a stress-filled workplace can have detrimental effects on an organization (Carr et al., 2011; CIPD, 2016; IBEC, 2016). While contemporary work practices have provided employees with the opportunity to approach their work in a more 'flexible' manner, such practices have resulted in work becoming more mobile, resulting in employees becoming more contactable. The prevalence of smartphones means that employees cannot 'switch off' from work even outside office hours during the evening or at weekends; they are constantly connected. This blurring of work and home boundaries has led to increased incidences of work stress. In the UK, the Health and Safety Executive (2016) found that 43% of days lost to illness were stress related. Australian employees are absent for an average of 3.2 working days each year through stress, costing the Australian economy approximately $14.2 billion. The American Psychological Association (2015) found that the two most common stressors were work and money, and the incidence of stress often results in irritability, anger, nervousness and anxiousness – all behaviours that can cause tension when brought home after work. Stress can also contribute to accidents and injuries by causing people to sleep badly, overmedicate themselves or drink excessively, or by causing them to feel depressed, nervous and anxious, or angry and reckless. Organizations are aware of this issue, with 79% of European managers concerned about stress in their workplaces; however, less than 30% of organizations in Europe have procedures for dealing with workplace stress (ESENER, 2010). Stress is the demand made on the adaptive capacities of the mind

> **Stress** – the demands of the work environment and the ability of the employee to meet these demands

and body. Carr et al. (2011) suggest that there are two main types of stress:

1. *Acute stress:* short-term stress resulting from unexpected stressors. It occurs in response to a terrifying or traumatic event, or witnessing a traumatic event that induces a strong emotional response from the individual. Symptoms include a sense of numbing or detachment from emotional reactions, anxiety, including restlessness, difficulty sleeping and concentrating, and the avoidance of stimuli that act as reminders of the event, such as feelings, thoughts, places, individuals and activities.
2. *Chronic stress:* longer term stress associated with prolonged physiological agitation which has not been resolved. Symptoms include depression or general unhappiness, anxiety and agitation, irritability or anger, feeling overwhelmed, and loneliness and isolation.

One of the greatest challenges for employers when considering stress management is the subjective nature of stress. It has been well documented that the effect of stress on an individual is based on the following factors (Halkos and Bousinakis, 2010; Carr et al., 2011; CIPD, 2016):

1. Stress levels depend on the individual's perception of the stressor – the stimulus, condition or event that causes stress – and can be a positive and a negative factor in life.
2. It is the reaction to the events, rather than the actual events, that determines whether the outcome is positive or negative.
3. An individual's ability to handle the demands/overload determines the results. When the capacity for handling stress is strong and healthy, the outcome is positive. With a lack of ability to handle the demands, the outcome is negative.

It is important to note that a certain amount of stress can be stimulating and helpful. Life changes and challenges can motivate individuals and provide the drive for accomplishing specific goals in life. The challenge is in finding the right balance. Too little stress leads to boredom and monotony, while too much stress leads to physical and mental breakdown. The Yerkes-Dodson principle (Yerkes and Dodson, 1908) is useful in this respect, suggesting that a specific amount of stress is healthy and even beneficial. For example, consider sporting events, or studying for your exams. As stress levels increase, so too can performance. However, this relationship between increased stress and increased performance does not continue indefinitely. As shown in Figure 12.3, the Yerkes-Dodson principle (or law) illustrates that a lack of stress can cause underperformance. If stress or arousal is increased, it can also increase performance, but only up to a point. Thereafter, when stress exceeds an individual's ability to cope, this overload contributes to diminished performance, inefficiency and, potentially, health problems caused by excessive pressure and anxiety.

Research by Halkos and Bousinakis (2010) suggests that when experienced at the appropriate level, stress can have a positive influence on an employee's approach to a difficult task, motivating them to overcome a particular obstacle. The challenge for employees, and indeed employers, is to ensure that the appropriate level of overload is applied in order to provide opportunity for growth as opposed to deterioration, as we have seen with

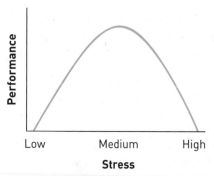

Figure 12.3 Yerkes-Dodson principle
Source: adapted from Figure 2, from Hebb, D.O. (1955) 'Drives and the C.N.S. (conceptual nervous system)', *Psychological Review*, 62(4), 243–54. dx.doi.org/10.1037/h0041823. This article is now in the public domain.

the Yerkes-Dodson principle. When attempting to address this, Carr et al. (2011) suggest that employers should consider the following:

- Is the workload distributed evenly among employees?
- Can temporary workers be hired in periods of excessive workload?
- What were the reasons for employees leaving the organization and have they been resolved?
- Are there roles which involve excessive hours and is it really necessary for them to do so?

CONSIDER THIS

Stress is obviously not confined to workplaces. The Institute for Public Policy Research (2017) published a report highlighting that, in the UK, the number of first-year university students who disclose a mental health problem has risen fivefold in the past decade. A record number of students with mental health problems dropped out of university in 2015, and the number of students in the UK seeking counselling increased by 50% between 2012 and 2017, to more than 37,000.

What do you think the reasons are for the significant increase in student stress? What do universities need to do to alleviate these issues?

Job Strain

Job strain is distinct from job stress, but the two are related. Job strain refers to the negative physical and psychological toll that is placed on employees when jobs involve high demands and workers feel they have little control over decision-making (Kuper and Marmot, 2003). Employees who have both low decision-making ability and high demands cannot manage the stress caused by the high demands through time management or learning because of their limited power to influence the situation. It is this combination of constraints on decision-making together with high demands that produce the unhealthy condition of job strain. For example, doctors who have a lot of decision-making ability in their jobs are less likely to have job strain than someone working on a busy factory production line with limited control. Job strain has been shown to have a number of adverse health effects, and a recent study looking at over 200,000 employees found that job strain was linked to a 23% increased risk of heart attacks and deaths from coronary heart disease (Kivimäki et al., 2012). The same study also found that job strain was more common among lower skilled employees, due to their reduced autonomy to make decisions on the job.

While experiencing job strain may be unavoidable in some cases, how employees deal with this strain has a significant impact on their likelihood of developing heart disease. Employees who smoke may smoke more when they experience job strain; active employees with job strain tend to become less active; and employees with job strain often eat more. It is important that organizations attempt to minimize the risks of job strain by encouraging employees to eat healthily, take regular exercise, and quit smoking. Also, where possible, jobs should be designed or redesigned to give employees more decision-making control. This has been shown to reduce job strain without changing the level of work completed (Kuper and Marmot, 2003).

Bullying

Another issue that needs to be considered from a health, safety and wellbeing perspective is **bullying** at work. It can take many forms, including:

> **Bullying** – inappropriate behaviour at work that repeatedly undermines an employee's right to dignity and causes that employee to become subject to high stress

- ignoring or excluding someone
- spreading malicious rumours or gossip
- humiliating someone in public
- giving someone unachievable or meaningless tasks
- constantly undervaluing someone's work performance.

While not all countries have a legal definition of workplace bullying, the Irish Health and Safety Authority (2007: 5) defines it as:

> repeated inappropriate behaviour, direct or indirect, whether verbal, physical or otherwise, conducted by one or more persons against another or others, at the place of work and/or in the course of employment, which could reasonably be regarded as undermining the individual's right to dignity at work.

BUILDING YOUR SKILLS

Research suggests that only 50% of organizations have a policy for dealing with bullies. On top of that, just 7% of employees know of someone who has used that policy and 6% say that it did not work to stop the bully. Instead of punishing the bullies, many workplaces reward them. Treadway et al. (2013) found that bullies tend to be very good at office politics and using gossip through office social networks to attack those they consider rivals.

Either as a student or an HR practitioner, what techniques would you propose for dealing with bullies?

An isolated one-off incident of the behaviour described in this definition would be considered an insult to dignity at work but must occur repeatedly to be considered bullying.

Since bullying can occur in any organization, it is important for HR practitioners to understand what constitutes bullying and what the consequences can be. Bullying can have significant negative effects for employees and organizations. Individual responses to bullying are varied, but include:

- stress, anxiety or sleep disturbance
- panic attacks or impaired ability to make decisions
- loss of self-confidence and self-esteem or reduced output and performance
- depression or a sense of isolation
- physical injury
- reduced quality of home and family life
- suicide.

The costs to the organization include reduced efficiency and productivity for the victims and their colleagues, poor morale, an unsafe work environment and the costs of sickness absence, increased absenteeism and staff turnover, in addition to the costs of investigation, litigation, compensation claims and industrial unrest. The Advisory, Conciliation and Arbitration Service (ACAS, 2015) estimates that bullying costs the UK economy £18 billion a year and that it accounts for half the reported occurrences of work stress. Unfortunately, bullying appears to be common. Research from VitalSmarts (2014) found that 96% of respondents experienced workplace bullying, so it is critical that HR takes it seriously.

The legal situation varies, but many countries or regions do have laws regarding workplace bullying; for example, in the USA between 2003 and 2017, 30 states introduced Happy Workplace bills to make bullying at work illegal. Unfortunately, none of those laws have yet been enacted. However, regardless of the legal situation, an organization's goal should be to develop a culture in which harassment is known to be unacceptable and where individuals are confident enough to bring complaints without fear of ridicule. Organizations should deal promptly, seriously and discreetly with any issues that are raised.

The first step in minimizing workplace bullying is for organizations to develop an anti-bullying policy. This should summarize the organization's approach to tackling bullying and include:

- a statement from senior management endorsing the policy
- specific definitions of what constitutes unacceptable behaviour
- details as to how employees can raise their concerns about bullying
- any procedures the organization will follow for the complainant and the alleged bully
- information about the potential outcomes and assistance provided.

It is important that this policy is widely publicized and that all employees are familiar with it.

Workaholism

The term 'workaholic' is used in everyday language to describe individuals who are addicted to work. Workaholics are defined as task-oriented, compulsive, perfectionist, neurotic, rigid, highly motivated, resourceful, impatient and self-centred individuals (Andreassen et al., 2007). They tend to work overtime on a regular basis, identify themselves with work, and often lack the ability to relax. The main feature is the high investment in work, with those who work more than 50 hours a week often characterized as workaholics. Machlowitz (1980) defined 'workaholics' as individuals who always devote more time and energy to work than the work situation demands. Griffiths (2011) identifies a number of characteristics of workaholics:

- Work is the single most important activity in the workaholic's life.
- Working gives workaholics positive emotions.
- Workaholics need to 'up the dose' by increasing the hours they work each day.
- When unable to work, workaholics experience withdrawal symptoms such as irritability.
- Working long hours brings workaholics into conflict with others, including colleagues, partners and friends.
- 'Reformed' workaholics easily slip back into their old behaviour patterns.

Workaholism is viewed in a different light to other dependencies such as alcohol or drug addiction, in the sense that it is almost a respectable addiction. However, recent research demonstrates the adverse health effects of workaholism. According to Gibb et al. (2011), people who work at least 50 hours a week are up to three times more likely to face alcohol problems. Virtanen et al. (2012) conducted a study of over 22,000 participants showing that overworkers are 40–80% more likely to suffer heart disease than others.

The culture of the organization plays an important role in prompting and reinforcing workaholism. Behaviours become repeated when they are rewarded. Since people tend to abandon behaviours that do not result in some sort of payoff, it is possible that organizations, perhaps unwittingly, reward workaholics as a result of their excessive working. A number of companies have recently created policies instructing employees that they are not to read or answer work emails after normal work hours. However, these policies are the exceptions to the rule, as many companies today are happy to see employees handling work tasks in the evenings, over the weekends and during vacations. Attempts to address workaholism must begin by looking at the culture of the organization to ensure that addictive behaviours are not reinforced by financial or social rewards.

HRM AND ORGANIZATIONAL PERFORMANCE

The 'right to disconnect'

On 1 January 2017, a new law in France came in place protecting workers' 'right to disconnect'. The law mandates organizations with more than 50 employees to establish hours when their employees should not send or reply to emails. The main objective of the law is to try and prevent burnout by protecting private time.

The French minister for labour, Myriam El Khomri, highlighted in 2016, when explaining the need for the new legislation, that burnout was becoming more common as the boundaries between personal and work life were getting blurred.

The new legislation does not completely ban work-related emails, but does obligate affected organizations to put in place new protocols to prevent work from spilling over into employees' free time.

Some consultants have suggested avoiding the 'reply all' option in group emails to prevent 'half the office' receiving messages unnecessarily.

Another proposal involves setting a time in the evening beyond which employees should not respond to emails. Many businesses have chosen the hours between 9pm and 7am, or 7pm and 7am for this (Rubin, 2017).

Those who support the new law highlight that when there is an expectation to check and respond to emails outside working hours, employees are not being paid properly for their overtime. It can also result in relationship problems, difficulties sleeping, stress and burnout (BBC News, 2016).

The email restrictions could potentially benefit both workers and businesses, by making employees more relaxed and effective. Recent research shows that people who checked their email only three times a day were found to be less stressed than those who could check their emails continuously (Kushlev and Dunn, 2015). Another study found that even the anticipated stress of expecting after-hours emails might have a negative effect on our wellbeing (Belkin et al., 2016). It will be interesting to see if other countries follow in France's footsteps.

Sickness Absence

Employee absence from work is a major cost to organizations. For example, the UK lost approximately 190 million working days to absence in 2015, with each employee taking, on average, 5.8 days off sick. This cost the economy approximately £16 billion, including more than £2.7 billion from 30.4 million days of non-genuine sickness absence (XpertHR, 2015). In Australia, 92 million days are lost annually due to employee absence. In Ireland, 8 million work days are lost each year due to absenteeism, with a direct cost of sickness absence of €1.1 billion (Edwards and Greasley, 2010). Sickness absences can be either short or long term. The main causes of employee sickness absence are minor illnesses, such as colds and flu, back pain, stress, musculoskeletal injuries, family issues, recurring medical conditions, and depression. For HR practitioners, effective absence management involves finding a balance between providing support to help employees with health problems stay in and

return to work, and taking consistent and firm action against employees who try to take advantage of organizations' sick pay schemes.

Options for managing short-term sickness absence can take the form of return to work interviews, providing sickness absence information to line managers, establishing disciplinary procedures for unacceptable absence levels, establishing formalized leave policies for family circumstances, and offering flexible working. Return to work interviews can help identify short-term absence problems at an early stage. They also provide managers with an opportunity to start a dialogue with staff about any underlying issues that might be causing the absence. Disciplinary procedures for unacceptable absence may be used to make it clear to employees that unjustified absence will not be tolerated and that absence policies will be enforced. Managing long-term sickness absence requires careful consideration of a formal return to work strategy for those returning after a long absence by keeping in touch with sick employees, adjusting workplace design elements if necessary, offering professional guidance and designing a return to work plan. Line managers have a particularly important role to play in the management of sickness absence. It is important that they have good communication skills to encourage employees to discuss any problems they may have at an early stage so that they can be given the necessary support or advice before more serious problems arise.

An issue related to sickness absence is employee presenteeism. Simply put, this is the act of attending work while ill. Like sickness absence, presenteesim can be costly to organizations. McGregor et al. (2016) propose that the costs associated with presenteeism are significant, but difficult to quantify since they are less obvious than those associated with absenteeism. However, it has been shown that a combination of 'lost productivity' from employee absenteeism and presenteeism costs the US economy $227 billion a year (Integrated Benefits Institute, 2012). Numerous sources suggest that presenteeism is associated with jobs which have high demands, and that it is one of the leading causes of later long-term absence (Gustafson and Marklund, 2011; Aaronsson et al., 2011; CIPD, 2016; McGregor et al., 2016). Research conducted by McGregor et al. (2016) argues that indirect links exist between job demands, resources and presenteeism, suggesting that increased job demands and a lack of resources resulted in employees experiencing fatigue, burnout, and an increased prevalence of illness, but that they were far more likely to attend work even though they were experiencing such negative effects.

EMPLOYEE WELLBEING: THEORETICAL CONSIDERATIONS

Numerous authors have attempted to develop frameworks in relation to employee wellbeing, with very few delivering models that are both reliable and valid (DeVoorde et al., 2012; Valizade et al., 2016; Guest, 2017). Two areas which have received extensive focus, however, are those of 'mutual gains' and 'conflicting outcomes'.

Mutual Gains

The 'mutual gains' school of thought suggests that HRM provides benefits for employees in terms of wellbeing, while also providing benefits for employers in the form of increased organizational performance (DeVoorde et al., 2012). In effect, HRM practices which foster employee wellbeing will, in

turn, result in improved operational and financial outcomes for the organization, since employees who share a mutual gains relationship with their employers tend to deliver improved performances (Taneja et al., 2015). Guest (2017) highlights the prevalence of this approach, suggesting that HR practices which promote positive employee relationships and offer opportunities to develop relationships and partnerships can in turn provide mutual gains for employers and employees.

One of the main challenges for academics and HR practitioners is that of aligning efforts and advantages in order to ensure that the benefits of a practice are indeed 'mutual'. Boxall (2013) attempts to address this, suggesting that there are three dimensions of alignment which must be considered in order to determine the extent of the 'mutuality' between the employer and employee: capability match; commitment match; and contribution match (see Figure 12.4). While there is evidence to suggest that such employer and employee partnerships generally result in an imbalance in favour of the employer, there is a wide body of literature which proposes that an organization which has a positive employment relations culture is far more likely to develop partnerships which are mutually beneficial for all stakeholders (Valizade et al., 2016).

Conflicting Outcomes

The second theoretical framework, 'conflicting outcomes', has been described by some researchers as the 'sceptical' or 'pessimistic' view, in that it can lead to the proposition that HRM has no effect on employee wellbeing, and can in some cases have a negative impact (Paauwe and Boselie, 2005; DeVoorde et al., 2012). Earlier work by Boxall et al. (2003) suggests that employee wellbeing and organizational performance are two goals which cannot be achieved in parallel, as they are influenced by different HR practices. Research presented by Jensen et al. (2013) supports this view, outlining that HRM practices linked with increased job performance, job satisfaction and commitment tend to be associated with increased levels of stress, with outcomes relating to health and wellbeing being difficult to determine and quantify.

In response to the issues raised by the conflicting outcomes perspective, Applebaum and Batt (1994) propose that an approach based on the AMO model, that is, improving an employee's *abilities*, increasing *motivation*, and providing the employee with the *opportunity* to contribute ▶Chapter 7◀,

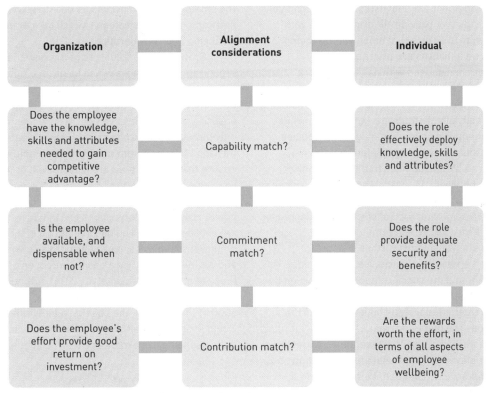

Figure 12.4 Employment alignment considerations
Source: adapted from Figure 1, Three tests of alignment in employment relationships, from Boxall, P. (2013) 'Mutuality in the management of human resources: assessing the quality of alignment in employment relationships', *Human Resource Management Journal*, 23(1), 3–17. Copyright © 2013 Blackwell Publishing Ltd/John Wiley & Sons, Inc., DOI: doi.org/10.1111/1748-8583.12015.

has the potential to enhance both organizational performance and employee wellbeing. Subsequent research has lent support to this concept, suggesting that employees respond positively to HR approaches based on this model. However, later work completed by Boxall (2013) highlights that as this model was designed for the purpose of improving organizational performance, with improved employee wellbeing a 'by-product', the model leans more towards the employer's interests. Boxall and Macky (2009) therefore suggest a need to further review and develop work practices which not only involve higher performance, but increase employee involvement and decrease stress. The authors suggest the need to focus more on longitudinal data in order to determine the long-term effects on organizational performance over time, and perhaps the same case can be made for employee wellbeing. As opposed to focusing on cross-sectional data which outlines the current state of play, an analysis of the effect on employee wellbeing over time may provide a more reliable, valid and indeed global perspective.

KEY STAKEHOLDERS: WHERE DOES THE RESPONSIBILITY LIE?

The Role of the Employer

A significant amount of research tends to discuss employee wellbeing from the perspective of the employer, highlighting the importance of awareness of employee wellbeing within the workplace, while also outlining the need to develop and introduce positive preventive strategies for the workforce (Grant et al., 2007; IBEC, 2016; CIPD, 2016). Renwick (2003) goes as far as to label HR practitioners as the 'guardians' of employee wellbeing, suggesting that the strategic change agent functions of their roles places them in an ideal position to champion and promote such a cause. More recent industry-based sources lend further support to this perspective, suggesting that HR practitioners are in a key position to manage the wellbeing agenda within the workplace due to the interactions they have with both employees and senior management (CIPD, 2016). The interactions with senior management are suggested to be of significant importance, as they provide HR practitioners with an opportunity to ensure that employee wellbeing practices and initiatives are prioritized by key stakeholders and aligned with day-to-day work practices. Line managers are also deemed to be an essential component in managing employee wellbeing as they directly affect employee experiences, while also operationalizing people management policies. Further to this, research completed by Rahmnia and Sharifrad (2015) suggests that there is a direct correlation between managers who adopt an authentic leadership approach and positive employee wellbeing effects, such as greater job satisfaction and decreased perceived stress and stress symptoms.

Baptiste (2008) lends further support to this under the heading of social exchange theory, suggesting that if the social relationship between line managers and their employees is positive, it directly influences their attitudes and beliefs towards the organization. The theory proposes that these attitudes and beliefs influence employee wellbeing variables such as employee commitment, job satisfaction and work–life balance satisfaction. With this in mind, industry sources highlight the need for employers to ensure that line managers have the necessary knowledge, skills and attitudes to effectively consider employee wellbeing when managing the workforce (IBEC, 2016). It is recommended that line managers adopt methods such as regular work planning sessions, appraisals and informal discussions in order to provide neutral and 'non-stigmatizing' opportunities to discuss the employee's wellbeing.

The Role of the Employee

The focus so far has been on the key role that the employer plays in promoting and maintaining employee wellbeing when implementing management practices, but consider for a moment the role of the employee. It has been proposed that people cannot fulfil their full health potential unless they take ownership of the factors which influence their health. Consequently, the WHO (1986) suggests that empowerment is one of the most essential principles of health promotion. Taneja et al. (2015) outline research from the financial services sector in which it is suggested that the use of empowerment by employers through open communication and business alignment was essential for achieving effective employee engagement. One can therefore assume that within an 'open communication' environment, the responsibilities do not just lie with the employer, but also with the employee to ensure that

the employer has the necessary data to plan, develop and implement HR strategies which take employee wellbeing into consideration.

Grawitch et al. (2006) share the view that organizational practices which focus on employee 'participation' through empowerment and various other methods (see Figure 12.5) are essential for ensuring employee involvement. It is suggested that only through such involvement and participation, through effective communication, can employers ensure that HR practices are aligned with employee wellbeing considerations. More recent research lends further support to this concept, suggesting that health promotion interventions and initiatives which are self-directed and guided in nature, i.e. that involve employees taking responsibility for their own health and wellbeing, have had a positive effect on participants (Page et al., 2013; Kaplan et al., 2014). Although there is an apparent lack of empirical evidence to fully support this concept, the positive, albeit limited, results would suggest that employees that take ownership of their wellbeing can experience beneficial outcomes.

Figure 12.5 SHAPE framework – healthy workplace practices
Source: Figure 2, The SHAPE framework, from Grawitch, M.J., Gottschalk, M. and Munz, D.C. (2006) 'The Path to a Healthy Workplace: A Critical Review Linking Healthy Workplace Practices, Employee Well-being, and Organizational Improvements', *Consulting Psychology Journal: Practice and Research*, 58(3), 129–47. Copyright 2006 by the American Psychological Association and the Society of Consulting Psychology, DOI: dx.doi.org/10.1037/1065-9293.58.3.129, adapted with permission.

HRM IN THE GLOBAL BUSINESS ENVIRONMENT

The working hours debate

Could reducing the amount of hours employees work actually improve organizational performance? Just because people are present at work does not mean that they spend their time in the most productive ways – in 2012, J.C. Penney, an American retailer, reported that around a third of its headquarters' bandwidth was taken up by employees watching YouTube videos (Huffington Post, 2013).

Under 40-hour work weeks are relatively common throughout Europe but far from the norm worldwide. In South Korea, it was reported that 35% of people work over 49 hours a week (McCurry, 2015). The 2017 presidential election in France saw the debate over working hours take centre stage, with conservative candidate Francois Fillon vowing to scrap the 35-hour work week, which he claimed had 'done a lot of damage' (Bloomberg News, 2017). Fillon proposed returning to a legal 39-hour working week in both the public and private sectors, up from the 35-hour week which had been in place since 2000. This law has required employers to pay extra or allocate time off in lieu for any additional work over the 35 hours (Reuters, 2017). The eventual winner, Emmanuel Macron, has indicated that he wants to introduce flexibility around overtime in a bid to move away from the sacred 35-hour working week (Bamat, 2017). Almost a year after the election took place, little progress has been made in this regard, however.

This is in stark contrast to the gruelingly long hours many Japanese employees are expected to work. In February 2017, the Japanese government introduced an optional scheme to allow employees to leave at 3pm on the last Friday of every month. The aim of the scheme, known as Premium Fridays, is to encourage individuals to use the extra hours of freedom to shop or make an early start on their weekend plans (McCurry, 2017). Leaving at 3pm might not seem like much, but in Japan over 20% of full-time employees work an average of at least 49 or more hours a week — far above the 11% and 16% rates reported in France and the USA respectively, though below South Korea mentioned earlier (McCurry, 2015). The Premium Fridays initiative was prompted by the suicide of a 24-year-old employee at the advertising company, Dentsu, who had been working over 100 hours' overtime in the months leading up to her death (McCurry, 2017). This also comes 30 years after Japan legally recognized the concept of death by overwork (*karoshi*).

At the other extreme, as part of a government study, a select group of retirement home workers in Gothenburg, Sweden worked just 30 hours each week for two years between February 2015 and February 2017. The results showed that the employees felt healthier, took less sick leave, and that there was less absenteeism and patients were better cared for. To cover the reduced hours for the 68 nurses, the home had to hire 17 extra staff at a cost of about 12 million kronor ($1.3 million) – a 22% increase in gross costs (Bloomberg News, 2017). However, results found the benefits of the trial were considerable. Reduced working hours led to a 10% drop in sick leave, meaning that the employer had to spend less to hire cover (CareerBliss, 2017). Compared with care home workers with normal working hours, the perceived health of the carers at the retirement home improved by about 50% (Oltermann, 2017).

One key issue with transferring the six-hour work day to other workplaces in Sweden and elsewhere is a possible reduction in salaries. While Sweden's trial did not reduce salaries, this was one of the major problems with the cost of the project. Income and stability are two major factors that affect employees' health and work life, so it remains to be seen if employees would be willing to work less hours if their pay were similarly reduced.

HEALTH, SAFETY AND WELLBEING AND HRM

It can be argued that health, safety and wellbeing require more involvement from employees, unions, supervisors and management than any other area of HRM and that they impact on the majority of HRM activities. Recruitment ▶Chapter 3◀, training ▶Chapter 9◀ and performance management procedures ▶Chapter 7◀ include consideration of issues such as manual handling, general health status and stress-coping mechanisms; job and work design systems incorporate ergonomic concerns; and reward management systems ▶Chapter 8◀ can include incentives for achieving specific safety targets.

With regard to health, safety and wellbeing, HR practitioners have to:

- develop health, safety and wellbeing policies and modify existing policies as necessary, in conjunction with workplace representatives, unions and management
- keep up to date with health and safety issues and the relevant legislation
- communicate these to employees
- analyse accident rates
- promote safe working behaviours
- consider the impact of new technology or work processes on employee health, safety and wellbeing.

A best practice approach to health, safety and wellbeing in an HRM context should be situated within a strategic HRM approach ▶Chapter 1◀. A strategic HRM approach to health, safety and wellbeing advocates the need for autonomy, individual responsibility, flexibility and adaptability. This is most apparent when we consider the change that has taken place across EU countries in terms of the approach to safety legislation. The focus has shifted from simple compliance with basic, minimum legal requirements to the adoption of a proactive approach to health, safety and wellbeing that advocates the involvement of employees and managers in developing safety management systems, implementing them and evaluating their effectiveness. The picture is somewhat different in the USA where the Occupational Safety and Health Act was passed in 1970 to govern health and safety in the private sector and federal government. The Act created the Occupational Safety and Health Administration (OSHA). The powers of OSHA have been hampered by political inference, however. For example, OSHA expended considerable efforts in the 1990s working on a standard designed to reduce debilitating musculoskeletal injuries from repetitive-motion work, such as meatpacking and sewing. Known as the 'ergonomics rule' it was issued in final form in November 2000 and would have offered protection to more than 100 million workers, according to OSHA. The Republican Congress at the time voted to repeal it. George W. Bush called the rule 'burdensome and overly broad' and said it could

cost organizations billions of dollars. In the time since the ergonomics rule was thrown out, OSHA has issued only two health standards, leaving employees at risk of potentially outdated health and safety guidelines.

Garavan (2002) characterizes the professional HRM approach to health and safety as follows:

- The creation of a culture where health, safety and wellbeing are considered important to the organization. Regularly updated policies and procedures must reflect the importance of a safe and healthy work environment. The safety policy statement contributes to this if it is appropriately constructed, understood, revised and acted upon. The legal requirements must be complied with and risk assessments conducted. Campaigns and publicity materials should be used to promote a culture of health, safety and wellbeing and this should be driven by the HRM function with top management support. This requires the gathering of information about health and safety matters and the conduct of a cost–benefit analysis to determine the contribution that health and safety management practices make to the organization's overall effectiveness.
- Commitment from senior management to the ongoing achievement of increasingly higher standards of health and safety via the implementation of safe working systems and the monitoring of their effectiveness.
- Organization-wide commitment to health, safety and wellbeing. This means that all parties must understand their responsibilities for health and safety, their targets in the area and their contribution to the organization's effectiveness. It is recommended that safety should be considered part of performance management systems ▶Chapter 7◀. If employees themselves are encouraged to take responsibility for health, safety and wellbeing and made accountable for their own actions, this increases the likelihood that they will be committed to fostering a safe working culture.
- Managers should lead by example in demonstrating their commitment to health, safety and wellbeing. This can be done by motivating employees to make a contribution to health and safety improvements and providing feedback or communicating results on health and safety initiatives.
- Policies and procedures should be designed to encourage the prioritization of a safer and healthier working environment. Systems should

also be put in place to evaluate the effectiveness of these policies and procedures.

- Sufficient resources should be allocated to health and safety equipment and training and education to reinforce the priority given to health, safety and wellbeing in the workplace. While the provision of these resources can be costly, the absence of investment in this area usually ends up costing more money. Research evidence confirms that those organizations with superior health and safety records allocate greater resources to this area.

A best practice HRM approach to health and safety advocates that all organizations should have safety statements. The safety statement has a central role to play in the management of safety, health and welfare. Ideally, all workplaces should have written safety statements based on the hazards identified and the risk assessment, setting out how the safety, health and wellbeing of employees will be protected and managed.

Safety statements must be specific to the workplace and must set out:

- the hazards identified and the risks assessed
- the protective and preventive measures taken and the resources allocated to safety, health and welfare
- the plans and procedures for dealing with emergencies or serious and imminent danger
- the duties of employees as regards safety, health and welfare at work, and the requirement for them to cooperate with their employer in these matters
- the names and, where applicable, job titles of persons assigned to perform tasks relevant to the safety statement
- the arrangements for the appointment of safety representatives. A safety representative is an employee chosen by other workers to represent them in consultations with the employer on matters of safety, health and wellbeing in the workplace. A safety representative should have the right to inspect the workplace at a frequency or on a schedule agreed between them and the employer, based on the nature and extent of the hazards in the workplace.

The aims of the safety statement are to:

- involve management up to the highest level by assigning clear responsibilities in the control of safety, health and welfare at the workplace

- ensure that appropriate steps are taken to comply with the relevant statutory provisions and that those measures are monitored and reviewed on a regular basis
- identify hazards and prioritize risks
- ensure that sufficient resources are allocated to safety management
- ensure that every person in the workplace is informed and involved in the control of safety, health and welfare
- ensure the systematic follow-up of problems as they arise.

The employer must bring the safety statement to all employees' attention, and in a form, manner and language that is easily understood. This should be done at least annually, or when it is amended. It should also be brought to the attention of newly recruited employees at the induction stage.

SPOTLIGHT ON SKILLS

One of your first tasks as a newly appointed HR manager in a large IT firm based in London is to introduce an employee wellbeing initiative. As a result of discussions with the CEO, two things stand out to you:

1. Employees are expected to work long hours.
2. Supervisors and managers regularly have to dial in to conference calls to the US headquarters late at night and early in the morning for the Japanese office.

Describe how you would design this initiative.

To help you answer the question above, visit **www.macmillanihe.com/carbery-cross-hrm-2e** and watch the video of Dr Gonzalo Shoobridge from Great Place To Work® talking about wellbeing in the workplace.

Health and Safety Legislative Considerations

Common law has a major role to play in health, safety and wellbeing. A third of the world's population live in common law jurisdictions. The UK, the Republic of Ireland, America, Australia and Canada are common law countries. Over the centuries, as judges have heard cases, they have issued judgments. The body of law that has been developed by these judgments is known as 'common law'. Common law develops and expands to meet newly emerging situations.

> **Common law** – law developed by judges through decisions made in courts and similar tribunals

The significance of common law to health and safety practitioners, and to employers, lies in the fact that most actions for personal injuries, be they employer liability claims or public liability claims, are brought at common law. The claimant (injured person) sues their employer or the owner/occupier of the premises where the accident occurred. The claimant alleges that the employer or owner/occupier has been negligent and in breach of the duty of care owed to the employee or visitor to the premises. When taking an action, the claimant may also allege that the employer is in breach of a statutory duty, so an action may be grounded on the tort (wrong) of negligence and the breach of the provisions of legislative acts.

There is a general obligation under common law requiring employers to take care of employees' safety. This common law duty of care requires that employers:

- provide a reasonably safe workplace
- provide reasonably safe plant and equipment
- operate reasonably safe systems of work
- ensure that staff are competent and safety conscious.

An employer may be held negligent by the courts if it failed to take such care and an employee subsequently suffers an injury and sues. However, the duty is not absolute. Negligence is assessed against two tests:

1. Has the employer taken reasonable care to protect its employees?
2. Was it reasonably practicable for the employer to take the measures necessary to protect its employees?

HRM IN PRACTICE

Dealing with employee absenteeism

Getty Images/Wavebreakmedia Ltd

You are an HR manager for a (fictitious) medium-sized UK enterprise, SeaMils.com, employing a workforce of 50–60 people that consists of office staff, production workers and delivery drivers. The office staff work regular 9–5 hours completing administrative and general management functions, while the production staff work shift hours involving prolonged periods of time at fixed production points. The delivery drivers work flexible, part-time hours which vary greatly depending on production levels and customer demand. When it comes to employee wellbeing, SeaMils.com offers subsidized healthcare policies to employees, while also having an active and proactive health and safety committee/management team.

While reviewing HR metrics for the previous 12 months, you notice that there has been a steady increase in annual sick days per employee, rising from an average rate of 3.25 days per employee, to 5.75 days per employee (a 77% increase).

Taking a closer look at the data, you notice that a number of trends have begun to emerge within the various sections of the workforce. Firstly, the office workers make up the largest proportion of the increase, with their annual sick days increasing by 1.75 days throughout the year. The production workers have the next highest increase, experiencing a rise of 0.75 days, while the delivery drivers saw no increase. You check the records to try and find out some of the reasons why employees went on sick leave, and again notice some trends within the various groups. The reasons that the majority of the office staff gave for going off sick were due to short-term illnesses related to acute and chronic conditions such as high blood pressure, diabetes and severe fatigue. As regards the production workers, as the business has a healthy and proactive approach to health and safety, there were very few sickness absence days relating to workplace injuries recorded. There was, however, a significant spike in sickness absence after periods of peak production in which the workers were required to do their jobs at a much higher rate of pressure.

You approach one of the business directors, Melissa, highlighting your concerns about the increases, suggesting that time and resources need to be spent addressing this for the sake of the workforce and the business. Melissa is very receptive to your concerns and observations and offers to allocate support, provided that any suggested courses of action are beneficial to the workforce, the organization and provide a return on investment for the business.

You contact a former colleague, Nathaniel, an HR business partner with a leading multinational company, in order to gain some insights into how other organizations approach employee wellbeing. Nathaniel outlines that the company had experienced similar increases in sick days and consequently developed an in-house employee wellness programme designed to address physical and mental wellness. This consists of health assessments, gym membership schemes, healthy eating initiatives in the staff canteen, health walks during break times and financed corporate team-building sessions. It also trained up its shift managers as mental health first aiders and provides each employee with a personal 'wellness' budget of £250 per year to spend as they see fit for their own wellness needs. Nathaniel suggests that these initiatives had extremely positive outcomes during the first 12 months, with annual sickness days per employee reducing from 7.25 days to 3 days. There were also additional indirect positive outcomes such as improved levels of employee engagement, increased work outputs, and in general there was a much more positive and healthy atmosphere around the office.

This gives you a lot to consider. However, given that SeaMils.com is a medium-sized enterprise, financial constraints play a major role in determining the options available to you. Schemes which would be heavy on financial resources, such as fully funded gym memberships, life coaching, corporate team building and training up all shift managers, would probably not be an option. Also, Melissa, the business director, although supportive, is very clear on the need for any proposed schemes to provide a return on investment.

As your first step, you examine the food in the canteen. Although you feel that there is no scope to spend additional money here, you do notice that 'healthy' snacks, such as fruit and yoghurts, are at a similar price to the 'not so healthy' options of chocolate and crisps. There are similar observations to be made with the drinks. As regards the gym membership, a fully financed scheme may not be an option, but you do remember reading a recent ad from a local gym offering group/corporate discounts on membership and classes. Finally, in terms of mental health, although there is no evidence to suggest that this is an issue, you are keen to be proactive. However, an already stretched learning and development budget would not facilitate relevant training for all shift managers. You do note, though, that the floor foreman and office manager have direct contact and interactions with almost all employees within the production and office staff.

What would you do?

❶ Considering the increases in annual sick days, what aspects of the five domains of health and wellbeing could have directly and indirectly contributed to the rise?

❷ Is there a chance that the nature of the work completed by employees contributed to their sickness absence?

❸ What steps will you take next at SeaMils.com? Why?

Getty Images/iStockphoto/zhudifeng

HEALTH, SAFETY AND EMPLOYEE WELLBEING

SUMMARY

This chapter has demonstrated the often-overlooked importance for HR practitioners to understand the significance of ensuring the health, safety and wellbeing of all employees. Developing an organizational culture that truly believes in the value of safe working behaviours is particularly important. If we take the time and effort to understand why accidents occur, and document the causes and factors contributing to accidents, we can lessen the likelihood of future occurrences. By understanding the effect of ergonomic and job design characteristics, we can make work safer and more enjoyable. Organizations have a moral obligation and an economic incentive to provide a safe workplace.

CHAPTER REVIEW QUESTIONS

1. Outline the concept of safety culture in organizations.
2. In which two ways is the behavioural science approach to health and safety different from the traditional engineering design approach?
3. What is the difference between a behaviour-based approach to health and safety and an attitude-based approach?
4. What is the significance of the accident cost iceberg?
5. Can you give two indirect costs of an accident?
6. Suggest and justify two occupations where mental workload capacity is an important element of safe work behaviour.
7. What are the main features of a person-centred approach to ergonomics?
8. Suggest two examples of how one domain or consideration of employee wellbeing can influence others in a positive or negative manner.

FURTHER READING

Hughes, P. and Ferrett, E. (2016) *Introduction to Health and Safety at Work,* 6th edn, New York: Routledge.

Robertson, I. and Cooper, C. (2011) *Well-being: Productivity and Happiness at Work*, Basingstoke: Palgrave Macmillan.

USEFUL WEBSITES

www.hse.gov.uk
The UK Health and Safety Executive provides a wealth of information on health and safety matters for individuals and organizations.

www.ergonomics.org.uk
The Institute of Ergonomics and Human Factors provides regularly updated news regarding ergonomics in the workplace and has a large library of useful books and journals.

www.hsa.ie
The Irish Health and Safety Authority provides specific guidance for Irish organizations and has a dedicated section for small to medium-sized enterprises.

osha.europa.eu/en
The European Agency for Safety and Health at Work looks at risks at work and how to integrate health and safety into other policy areas, such as education, public health and research at a European level.

ec.europa.eu/eurostat/web/health/health-safety-work
Eurostat is the statistical office of the EU and its task is to provide the EU with statistics at European level that enable comparisons between countries and regions, in this case comparisons on health and safety statistics across European countries.

 For extra resources, including videos, multiple choice questions and useful weblinks, go to: www.macmillanihe.com/carbery-cross-hrm-2e

13: International Human Resource Management

Jonathan Lavelle

LEARNING OUTCOMES

By the end of this chapter you will be able to:

- Outline the differences between domestic and international human resource management
- Discuss the impact of globalization on international human resource management (IHRM)
- Examine the influences on the transfer of HRM practices within multinational companies
- Identify the key issues in the recruitment, selection and preparation of employees undertaking international assignments
- Describe the complexities in compensating and managing the performance of employees on international assignments
- Explain the importance of the repatriation stage in the management of employees on international assignments

THIS CHAPTER DISCUSSES:

Introduction (254)

International Human Resource Management (254)

Globalization and IHRM (258)

Managing Employees on International Assignments (261)

Expatriate Failure (267)

INTRODUCTION

This chapter focuses on international human resource management (IHRM), which broadly translates into looking at the human resource management policies, processes and practices in multinational companies (MNCs). The chapter explores both the academic and practical elements of IHRM. The first section provides a definition of IHRM and a useful model to help explain what we understand IHRM to be all about. For example, how does IHRM differ to what we may term domestic HRM – i.e. HRM practices in local/domestic companies? The second section then focuses on one

of the key debates within IHRM, namely, what are the issues that impact on the transfer of HRM practices in MNCs? Here we explore the different factors that may influence an MNC's decision to transfer its HRM practices across its foreign subsidiaries. The third section focuses on one of the key practical issues for IHRM, which is the management of employees who relocate from one operation to another operation in a foreign country. This section discusses the complexities in managing employees on long-term assignments and explores alternative options that MNCs may pursue. Finally, we look at expatriate failure.

HRM AND ORGANIZATIONAL PERFORMANCE

The benefits of expatriate assignments

Multinational companies (MNCs) can draw on a significant pool of talented people from across their global operations. This can help them to locate the right person to solve a challenge in another part of the business. A subsidiary of a US-owned MNC in Ireland was having a significant problem in relation to employee turnover – its

turnover rate was running at 150%. To deal with this issue, corporate headquarters in the USA identified a person in the UK with particular expertise in dealing with employee turnover and seconded him to the subsidiary in Ireland for a two-year assignment. Through a range of training initiatives based around employee engagement, the subsidiary significantly reduced its turnover rate to 26%.

INTERNATIONAL HUMAN RESOURCE MANAGEMENT

IHRM is a relatively new field, emerging largely due to the pressures of globalization and the growth of companies operating internationally. For the purposes of this chapter, the focus is on HRM within MNCs. While there are many ways of defining what an MNC is, it generally refers to a company that has operations across different countries, often called 'foreign subsidiaries', but is managed centrally by a corporate headquarters (HQ) or parent company located in the country from which the company originated. Some of the largest and most well-known MNCs include IBM, Google, Samsung Electronics, Toyota, Axa, Facebook and General Electric. Traditionally, the field of study of IHRM largely focused on

> **Expatriation** – the process of transferring an employee to other international operations of the MNC to carry out a particular assignment
>
> **Expatriates** – also known as 'international assignees', they are employees who undertake international assignments

the issue of **expatriation**, concentrating on the management of **expatriates** on international assignments. The field of study has developed, however, and now encompasses a greater variety of HR issues. A commonly used definition identifies IHRM as 'the HRM issues and problems arising from the internationalisation of business and the HRM strategies, policies and practices which firms pursue in response to the internationalisation process' (Scullion, 1995: 352).

Morgan (1986) provides a useful model to gain a broader understanding of IHRM. According to Morgan (1986: 44), IHRM involves the interaction of three dimensions the HR activities of procurement, allocation and utilization; the national or country categories involved in HRM tasks; and the categories of employees that exist in MNCs. These are illustrated in Table 13.1 on the next page.

1. The three broad HR activities of procurement, allocation and utilization. These include:
   - *employee resourcing*: HR planning, recruitment and selection, induction, retention ▶Chapters 2, 3 and 4◀
   - *performance management*: performance management systems, performance appraisal ▶Chapter 7◀
   - *reward management*: reward packages, performance-based pay ▶Chapter 8◀
   - *training and development*: learning and development for employees and the organization, learning styles ▶Chapters 9 and 10◀
   - *employment relations*: the employment relationship, key employment relations actors, employment legislation ▶Chapter 5◀

2. The three national or country categories involved in HRM tasks:
   - *host country:* where a foreign subsidiary of the MNC is located
   - *home country (or country of origin):* where the MNC originated from or is headquartered
   - *third countries:* may be a source of labour, finance and other inputs

3. The three categories of employees that exist in MNCs:
   - host country nationals – HCNs
   - parent country nationals – PCNs
   - third country nationals – TCNs

Table 13.1 Three dimensions of IHRM
Source: inspired by information in Morgan, 1986: 44.

A key question at this point is: how does IHRM differ from domestic HRM? The broad answer is that the functions are quite similar but the issues are more complex. Dowling et al. (2013: 4–5) identify a number of examples as to how IHRM differs from domestic HRM (see Dowling et al. (2008) for a more comprehensive discussion):

1. *More HR activities:* IHRM deals with HR issues that have a strong international aspect, which domestic HRM generally does not have to deal with, for example international relocation.
2. *A need for a broader perspective:* Generally, domestic HR involves developing and implementing HR policies and practices for a single national group of employees, although this is changing as workforces become more diverse ▶Chapter 6◀. IHRM involves developing and implementing HR policies and practices for more than one national group of employees, for example PCNs, HCNs and TCNs.
3. *Greater involvement in employees' lives:* In IHRM, there is a greater need for involvement in employees' lives. For example, in supporting expatriates on international assignments, it is often necessary to deal with issues around housing, visas, taxation, healthcare, cost of living and the expatriate's family circumstances.
4. *Managing different employees:* The need to manage different categories of employees and how this changes as the mix of these categories – PCNs, TCNs and HCNs – varies.
5. *Risk exposure:* The human and financial consequences of failure in the international arena are more severe than in domestic business.
6. *Broader external influences:* Major external factors that can influence IHRM are the type of government, the state of the economy, and the generally accepted practices of doing business in all the host countries in which the MNC operates. Again, these external issues are confined to one country when looking at domestic HRM.

Having understood what IHRM is, we now explore some of the HRM issues and problems that MNCs face within international business – the impact of globalization on IHRM and the transfer of HRM practices within MNCs.

Host country nationals (HCNs)	• HCNs are employees from the country the foreign subsidiary is located in; for example, an Australian national working in a US-owned MNC in Australia • HCNs are most likely to fill mid-level and lower level jobs, but may fill more senior positions • Advantages of filling more senior positions with HCNs include their extensive knowledge of the local business environment, the career opportunities provided for local employees, and that it is cheaper than using PCNs or TCNs • Disadvantages include difficulties for the MNC headquarters to coordinate, control and communicate with subsidiaries as HCNs may be unfamiliar with HQ, and HCNs may lack the required technical and managerial competence for the job
Parent country nationals (PCNs)	• PCNs are employees from the country where the MNC originated from or is headquartered; for example, a US national working in a US-owned MNC • PCNs are generally used to fill upper level and technical positions • Advantages of using PCNs include their ability to help control the MNC's foreign subsidiaries and transfer corporate philosophy/culture and expertise • Disadvantages include the high cost of sending PCNs to international assignments, issues around inequality, such as restricting career opportunities for local employees, and pay, as PCNs are often paid more than local employees
Third country nationals (TCNs)	• TCNs are employees who come from neither the host nor the parent country, that is, they come from third countries; for example, a New Zealand national working in a US-owned MNC in Australia • TCNs are often used for upper level and technical positions • Advantages include that they may have a better understanding of the local environment due to geographical proximity and they may possess important technical and managerial competencies • Disadvantages include difficulties in returning TCNs back to their country as there may not be an appropriate position for them, they may often be viewed as substitutes for PCNs, and the country from which they originate may not have a good relationship with the host country, for example India and Pakistan

Table 13.2 Types of employees
Source: inspired by information in Collings and Scullion, 2006: 24–27.

BUILDING YOUR SKILLS

The vice president for human resource management at corporate headquarters has communicated that a new performance appraisal system must be implemented in all foreign subsidiaries. However, you know that the local trade union is not going to be happy with the system and it is likely to lead to conflict. How would you go about dealing with this type of situation?

HRM IN THE NEWS

Brexit: implications for IHRM

One of the biggest issues to hit the news in relation to IHRM in 2016 was Brexit. Brexit refers to the decision by the United Kingdom (UK) to leave membership of the European Union (EU). Whilst the terms of this exit are still subject to negotiations between the UK and the EU, the decision has created huge uncertainty for MNCs operating in the UK, particularly in relation to issues around access to the European market and immigration. These concerns have a number of implications for IHRM.

First, what is going to happen to all of those EU citizens currently working in the UK? Some commentators have suggested that one option may be that EU citizens could remain in the UK for a specified period of time, after which they would need to obtain a visa or residency on the same basis as people from outside the EU (Brazier, 2016). Another suggestion is that Britain may grant EU citizens currently in the UK the right to stay as part of its negotiation strategy with the EU. There are also suggestions that MNCs are considering leaving or transferring employees from the UK – rumours have suggested that financial institutions, such as JP Morgan, Goldman Sachs and HSBC, are considering relocating (Crawley, 2017).

Secondly, it is clear that attracting talent into the UK is now going to be much more difficult, bureaucratic, complex and time-consuming. For example, the Boston Global Relocation Service has noted that immigration issues pose an additional challenge for MNCs' talent strategy, with the effect that they may have to recruit locally or opt against deepening their roots in Britain (BGRS, 2017). Not only is it going to make the hiring process more complex, but the opportunity to attract talent in the first place may be constrained: some commentators have remarked that the negative discussion in relation to foreigners during the debate on Brexit means that people may not feel so welcome in the UK anymore. Also, for MNCs that have employees on international assignments in their UK operations, it has made the calculation of compensation packages much more difficult given the currency fluctuations that go with this uncertainty around Brexit.

Thirdly, it also has implications for the UK as a source of expatriates within MNCs. UK nationals are attractive as third country nationals, particularly for assignments in EU countries. But given that UK nationals may not be able to freely move around the EU, their attraction in this regard will be diminished, thereby reducing the talent pool that an MNC can choose from. Some commentators have suggested that we are likely to see a rise in self-initiated assignments though.

The final issue that arises for IHRM is the likely impact on the UK HRM/industrial relations (IR) system. Of course there are differences across EU countries in relation to HRM/IR, but there are many common employment standards set by the EU through European Directives. Leaving the EU means that the UK will no longer be bound by such Directives and will be free to amend or repeal such legislation as it wishes. Changes to the HRM/IR system in the UK have implications for the transfer of HRM practices in MNCs; thus they will be keen to keep an eye out for any future amendments.

Many of the issues caused by Brexit involve HRM, which means that this is an opportunity for the HRM function to play a strategic role in how MNCs respond to these challenges (Goldberg, 2016).

Questions

1. Discuss the implications for attracting talent to the UK as a result of Brexit.
2. Discuss the implications for HRM in the UK if EU Directives on employment rights are amended or repealed.
3. Discuss how the HRM function might play a strategic role in addressing the challenges of Brexit.

Sources

BGRS (2017) 'Brexit: impact on mobility', www.bgrs.com/insights-articles/brexit-wait-see/ (accessed 11 June 2018)

Brazier, M. (2016) 'Will Brexit impact on global mobility?', www.k2corporatemobility.com/Will-Brexit-Impact-on-Global-Mobility (accessed 11 June 2018)

Crawley, E. (2017) 'Brexit and the City: Will firms jump ship?', www.hrmagazine.co.uk/article-details/brex-and-the-city-will-firms-jump-ship (accessed 11 June 2018)

Goldberg, A. (2016) 'Brexit and global mobility: what you and your employees need to know', www.lexiconrelocation.com/blog/brexit-and-global-mobility-what-you-and-your-employees-need-to-know (accessed 11 June 2018)

Shield GEO (2017) 'Four consequences of Brexit on global mobility', http://shieldgeo.com/four-consequences-brexit-global-mobility/ (accessed 11 June 2018)

Wilkins, B. (2016) 'Brexit and global mobility: keeping abreast of the changes', http://pwc.blogs.com/global_mobility/2016/07/brexit-and-global-mobility-keeping-abreast-of-the-changes-.html (accessed 11 June 2018)

GLOBALIZATION AND IHRM

'Globalization' is an often used term but, as Sparrow et al. (2004) noted, a phenomenon that is not easily or well defined. Briscoe et al. (2012: 15) state that globalization generally refers 'to the ever-increasing interaction, interconnectedness, and integration of people, companies and cultures and countries'. MNCs are seen as the key drivers of globalization (Ferner and Hyman, 1998). According to Javidan and Bowen (2013), the number of MNCs has increased from 3,000 in 1990 to over 100,000 in 2012. These 100,000 MNCs have over 900,000 affiliates and assets valued at $57 trillon (10 times more than in 1990) (Javidan and Bowen, 2013: 145). A glance at the statistics illustrates the role of MNCs in the internationalization of business. For example, in 2007, foreign direct investment (FDI) inflows reached a record of over $1.8 trillion, surpassing the previous peak in 2000. The global financial crisis (2008–09) negatively impacted global FDI flows, but since 2009 global FDI has steadily increased and is expected to hit $1.8 trillion in 2018 – slightly below the 2007 peak (United Nations Conference on Trade and Development, 2017).

> **Globalization** – the opening up of national markets and the creation of a global economy through the deregulation of trade, growth in foreign direct investment (FDI), movement of people and capital, and advances in information technology

HRM IN THE GLOBAL BUSINESS ENVIRONMENT

Comparing HRM in the USA and Germany

The management of human resources in a global business environment is complicated by differences in HRM across countries. This has implications for the types of HRM practices MNCs can employ in their operations. In the USA, managers enjoy significant freedom and autonomy to manage human resources due to weak trade unions and low levels of employment regulation.

Thus a key characteristic of HRM in the USA is the concept of 'employment at will', which means that managers can easily hire and fire employees as they feel the need to. In contrast, in Germany, due to strong trade unions and high levels of employment regulation, managers are more constrained in how they manage human resources. For example, issues such as breaks, how wages are paid and group work must be agreed jointly by management and employees.

Globalization has had a significant impact on HRM, most notably on the development of IHRM as a field of study. One particular area where globalization impacts on HRM is in relation to the debate about the convergence or divergence of management practice. Scholars have debated whether HRM is becoming similar across all countries, the convergence thesis, or whether it will continue to differ across countries, the divergence thesis. The evidence to date regarding this debate is largely inconclusive in terms of support for either side (Katz and Darbishire, 2000; Brewster et al., 2004, 2008; Pudelko and Harzing, 2007). Proponents of the convergence thesis (Harbison and Myers, 1959; Kerr et al., 1960) point to the increasing pressures of globalization on companies, particularly those that operate in an international context. These common pressures, it is claimed, will lead to companies adopting similar responses, leading to similarity in management practice across companies. According to this school of thought, we are likely to see a set of dominant or 'best practice' ▶Chapter 1◀ HRM policies emerge to deal with these pressures. It is suggested that these best practices are likely to reflect a US model of HRM, given the significance of the US way of doing business. For example, Pudelko and Harzing (2007, 2008) found evidence that the HRM practices of Japanese and German MNCs were converging towards dominant US practice.

Proponents of the divergence thesis (Hofstede, 1980; DiMaggio and Powell, 1991; Scott, 1995; Whitley, 2000; Hall and Soskice, 2001) disagree with the notion of convergence and argue that, far from converging, HRM policies and practices are likely to become more different across countries because of institutional and cultural reasons. For example, each country has its own unique mix of institutions – such as educational and training institutions, financial institutions, industrial relations actors, government agencies – which put pressure on inward-investing MNCs to localize or adopt local HRM practices in the host country. The most popular framework for understanding differences in HRM across countries is the varieties of capitalism framework (Hall and Soskice, 2001). This framework identifies two ideal types of capitalist political economy – a liberal market economy (LME) (e.g. USA) and a coordinated market economy (CME) (e.g. Germany) – which have implications on how HRM is practised in those countries. For example, in LMEs, characteristics of HRM include strong managerial autonomy, flexible employment arrangements, performance-related pay and a short-term perspective on the employment

relationship. In contrast, HRM characteristics within a CME include strong channels of worker voice, constraints on management decision-making, high levels of job security, extensive training programmes and a more long-term perspective on the employment relationship.

Similarly, differences in terms of culture – people's values, beliefs, attitudes and behaviours – across countries affect HRM. Hofstede's (1980) seminal research on culture focused on identifying and categorizing different dimensions of national culture. These are:

1. *Power distance* – the extent to which individuals accept differences in power in society.
2. *Individualism versus collectivism* – the extent to which individuals are focused on themselves or a group.
3. *Masculinity versus femininity* – the extent to which individuals are interested in material values versus welfare values.
4. *Uncertainty avoidance* – the extent to which individuals are willing to tolerate/accept risk and uncertainty.

The implications of national culture for HRM within a country are wide-ranging, for example the extent to which people are willing to accept hierarchical structures in organizations; whether pay is determined at an individual or collective level; the extent of employment regulation; and maternity, paternity and childcare policies.

CONSIDER THIS ⚬

Many scholars have suggested that HRM policies and practices are likely to converge globally to a US style of HRM. This largely means that the practice of HRM will be the same, regardless of the country context. Do you think that HRM will ever look the same in China as it does in the US? Why/why not?

The Transfer of HRM Practices in MNCs

A key strategic HRM question for MNCs is whether to attempt to standardize or localize HRM practices in their foreign subsidiaries (Rosenzweig and Nohria, 1994). MNCs have the ability to transfer practices to all or some of their operations globally, meaning that HRM practices developed in operations in one country (usually at the corporate HQ) may be transferred to operations in other countries. Not all MNCs look to transfer their HRM practices, however, and even where they do, this transfer of practices can be contested or disrupted by foreign operations (Edwards, 2011). Edwards and Ferner (2002) and Edwards (2011) identify four factors that influence the transfer of HRM practices across national borders within MNCs – country of origin effects, dominance effects, international integration, and host country effects (Figure 13.1), which we now briefly discuss.

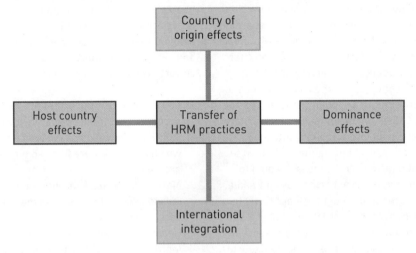

Figure 13.1 Factors that influence the transfer of HRM practices
Source: inspired by information in Edwards and Ferner, 2002 and Edwards, 2011.

Country of Origin Effects

The country from which the MNC originates exerts a distinct effect on the way labour is managed (Ferner, 1997), giving rise to **country of origin effects**. A range of sources indicate that even the largest MNCs retain strong roots in their home country. For example, the majority of sales, assets, employment, financial resources, and research and development activity are likely to be located within the country of origin. Furthermore, individuals from the country of origin are likely to hold the most senior managerial positions within the company. These strong roots in the home country mean that senior managers at the company HQ may seek to transfer HRM practices to their foreign subsidiaries (Ferner, 1997). In other words, many foreign subsidiaries' HRM practices resemble those of the parent company back in the country of origin. For example, in Ireland, a large-scale survey of MNCs found evidence of strong country of origin effects, particularly among US MNCs (Lavelle et al., 2009). Similarly, strong country of origin effects were noted among South African MNCs operating in

> **Country of origin effects** – the influence the country from which the MNC originates has on HRM in its foreign subsidiaries
>
> **Dominance effects** – the influence that dominant economies, like the USA, have on HRM in MNCs, regardless of where they are from or located

African countries whereby headquarters sought to transfer HRM practices to their subsidiaries (Woods, 2015; Adams et al., 2017). As time goes on and the MNC evolves and becomes more international, the country of origin effect may weaken. For example, it may be the case that there is no apparent benefit to transferring home country practices and it is more beneficial to look outside the country of origin for best practices.

Dominance Effects

Dominance effects relate to the dominance of the economy where the practices originate. This notion of dominance effects largely originates from the work of Smith and Meiskins (1995), who argue that there is a clear hierarchy of economies within the international system, with economies at the top of this hierarchy enjoying an influential position. Traditionally, the US economy was seen as the dominant player and thus many countries looked to it as the source of best practices. Managers within MNCs, both at the parent company and in foreign subsidiaries, may look to implement HRM practices from these dominant economies.

Edwards (2011: 276) identifies a number of problems with the dominance idea. These include:

- its reliance on the assumption that there is a hierarchy of economies
- that differences between economies can be explained by superior organizational and management practices
- the assumption that there are practices common to all firms within a country and that other countries can identify and imitate them.

Notwithstanding these criticisms, the dominance effect retains value in explaining the transfer of HRM practices (Pudelko and Harzing, 2007; Edwards et al., 2016).

International Integration

MNCs have operations across a number of different countries, and it is the **international integration** of these operations that is of interest when considering the transfer of HRM practices. MNCs that are internationally integrated are defined as those that generate inter-unit linkages between their operations across countries (Edwards, 2011). This integration may take many forms (Edwards, 2011: 278):

- *Outsourcing:* operations in one country provide products or services to operations in another country.
- *Segmentation:* operations in different countries perform different activities from one another.
- *Standardization:* operations in different countries perform similar activities.

Edwards (2011) postulates that the scope for the transfer of HRM practices is limited in MNCs that outsource or segment their international operations as there is no benefit to having standardized practices. However, operations that are standardized are much more likely to benefit from standardized practices and therefore more likely to transfer HRM practices.

Host Country Effects

The host country, the country in which the foreign subsidiary operates, can have a significant influence on the transfer of HRM practices, so-called **host**

country effects. There are a number of aspects of the host country's national business system that can limit the scope of MNCs to transfer HRM practices. These include labour market institutions, such as employment legislation, trade unions and works councils ▶Chapter 5◀, cultural barriers, and lack of specific skills or aptitudes. For example, the transfer of HRM practices to Germany, with its strong trade unions, high levels of collective bargaining and strong employment legislation, may be more difficult. It must be noted, however, that, in some cases, the limitations provided by the national business system may only be partial; for example, it may be that HRM practices need to be tweaked or adapted so that they can be successfully implemented. It is also worth noting that even where there appear to be institutional and/or cultural constraints to the transfer of HRM practices, these constraints may often be malleable to the influence of large MNCs, particularly MNCs from dominant economies (Edwards et al., 2016). Collings et al. (2008), for example, note the ability of US MNCs in Ireland to implement HRM practices that are at odds with the host country's institutional environment. MNCs can also pressurize governments to relax regulations and pressurize unions; again Ireland is a case in point here, with MNCs particularly vocal and influential in the drafting of employment legislation implementing EU Directives (*Industrial Relations News*, 2005).

> **International integration** – how strongly integrated all the MNC's international operations are with each other
>
> **Host country effects** – the influence the country in which a foreign subsidiary is located has on HRM in that subsidiary

MANAGING EMPLOYEES ON INTERNATIONAL ASSIGNMENTS

Having explored some of the HRM issues, problems and challenges that MNCs face, we now move to the HRM strategies, policies and practices that MNCs employ. Specifically, we focus on a major function within IHRM – the management of people undertaking international assignments, often referred to as 'expatriation'. Indeed, much of the interest in IHRM focuses on this particular aspect. This process of expatriation involves relocating an employee – referred to as an 'expatriate' – from the MNC's operations in one country to another operation in another country to perform a particular assignment. Generally, much of the focus on international assignments has been on the movement of employees to and from the MNC's company HQ; that is, employees from the company HQ relocating to a foreign subsidiary or employees from a foreign subsidiary relocating to the company HQ, but it also includes employees who move between different foreign subsidiaries.

Edstrom and Galbraith's (1977: 253) work is the most cited research when it comes to identifying reasons for relocating employees across operations. They identify three particular reasons for the transfer of employees across operations:

1. *To fill a position:* A particular job may require specific skills, competencies or experiences, which are not available locally, and therefore an MNC will send an expatriate to carry out the job. This is the most common reason for relocating employees.
2. *Management development:* The use of expatriates is seen as having a positive impact on the development of an employee. Employees can gain valuable international experience, which can assist them in their own career development.
3. *Organizational development:* Expatriates can help facilitate transfer of knowledge across operations and assist in the control and coordination of foreign subsidiaries.

Managing the expatriation process is complex and there are many issues that need to be considered. These include how to recruit and select people to undertake an international assignment, how to prepare people for, and help them adjust to, the assignment, how to reward and manage their performance, and finally how to bring these people back when their assignment is finished. We now discuss each of these issues.

Recruitment and Selection

The first step in managing expatriates is to recruit and select the individual ▶Chapter 3◀. Selecting individuals to go on an international assignment is a difficult task as a proven track record in a domestic context is no guarantee of success in an international context (Caligiuri and Bucker, 2015). There are many issues that are important when recruiting and selecting a candidate to undertake an international assignment (Brewster et al., 2007; Briscoe et al., 2012; Dowling et al., 2013). These include:

- *Job suitability:* This is about matching the requirements of the job with the person. It is important to identify the required professional and technical skills and abilities the person will need in order to successfully perform the assignment. Other useful characteristics when undertaking international assignments include motivation, leadership, communication, problem-solving and relational abilities.
- *Language skills:* Where the assignment is in a country with a different language, it may be important for the person to be proficient, or at least conversational, in this language. However, language skills are not always necessary to be successful in the role, particularly where the assignment involves a strong technical aspect.
- *Ability to adapt to the foreign culture:* There may be strong cultural differences between the home and host country, so an ability to adapt to the new culture will be important.
- *An awareness of issues in international management:* Individuals who are more aware of international management issues may be better prepared to deal with the many challenges they may encounter when on an international assignment.
- *Previous international experience:* Past performances on international assignments can be a useful predictor of a person's ability to carry out another assignment successfully.
- *The family situation:* While being mindful of legislation covering family status ▶Chapter 6◀, a candidate's family situation can have a strong influence in determining whether they are suitable for undertaking an international assignment. One important point is the dual career issue, whereby the trailing spouse may have to give up a career or put it on hold. Furthermore, having a spouse and children may also make adjusting to the foreign location more difficult.
- *Desire for international assignment:* Undertaking an international assignment can be a difficult and daunting task, and the decision to undertake such an assignment should not be taken lightly. It helps if the individual has a strong desire for such a task.

There are a number of different selection methods that may be used when choosing a person to go on an international assignment (Briscoe et al., 2012: 232–3). These include:

- *Interviews:* often carried out by a mix of representatives from the home and host country.
- *Formal assessment:* instruments designed by psychologists to evaluate a candidate's personal traits and competencies ▶Chapter 3◀.

- *Committee decision:* many MNCs have committees made up of HR representatives at the company HQ and managers from the home and host countries who select individuals to carry out international assignments.
- *Career planning:* many assignments undertaken by expatriates form part of a larger career or succession plan ▶Chapters 2 and 10◀.
- *Self-selection:* individuals themselves assess whether they are ready and prepared to undertake an international assignment.
- *Internal job posting:* usually combined with other methods such as interviews.
- *Recommendations:* candidates are selected on the back of recommendations by people in the MNC, often senior executives.
- *Assessment centres:* some MNCs use assessment centres but usually in conjunction with other selection methods ▶Chapter 3◀.

One particularly popular selection method noted in the literature is that which Harris and Brewster (1999) refer to as the 'coffee machine' system of selection. This method involves informal discussions over coffee about an international assignment, which then leads to selection.

Preparation

Once the individual has been selected, the next stage in the process is preparing them to undertake the assignment. This is seen as a critical step in ensuring that the international assignment is a success from both the individual's and the MNC's point of view.

In preparing an individual to undertake the international assignment, a number of methods can be used. As well as cross-cultural awareness training, these include preliminary visits, language training, and assistance with practical matters (Brewster et al., 2007; Dowling et al., 2013):

- *Cross-cultural awareness training:* involves providing individuals with an understanding of and appreciation for the prevailing culture in the foreign location. Ideally, such training should be provided to trailing spouses/partners and families.
- *Preliminary visits:* the advantages of preliminary visits to the foreign location are that they allow the individual, and families where applicable, to get a feel for the foreign location, including the local culture and business environment, and to assess their suitability and interest in the location.

- *Language training:* often viewed as a lower priority in pre-departure training, because MNCs from English-speaking countries do not feel the need to provide training in other languages, as English is seen as the business language. This can, however, restrict an individual on international assignment, as they may not be able to fully understand and monitor what is happening in the local environment and so will have to rely on locals to provide them with the necessary information. Being able to speak the language will not only help the individual in work situations, such as negotiations, but also in adjusting to the local environment.
- *Practical matters:* involves providing assistance with matters such as schooling, housing, social clubs and security, which are all important to travelling individuals, and families.

CONSIDER THIS

You work for a large MNC and have been chosen to carry out a long-term international assignment at its foreign subsidiary in Japan. You have never visited Japan and, aside from a knowledge of anime, you know nothing about the country. What kind of issues would you consider important in your preparation for this assignment?

Adjustment

A key concern for all involved in the process is the successful adjustment of the employee, and their family if applicable, to the local environment. One of the most common models for understanding expatriate adjustment is provided by Black et al. (1999). According to the Black et al. (1999) model, adjustment can be broken down into three dimensions:

1. *Work adjustment:* how the employee adjusts to the new work environment.
2. *Interaction adjustment:* how the employee adjusts to interacting with people from the host country.
3. *General adjustment:* how the employee adjusts, in general, to the new (non-work) environment, including housing, food, shopping, schooling and so on.

According to Brewster et al. (2007: 250–1), a number of factors can influence adjustment:

- *individual factors:* interpersonal skills and self-confidence, cultural empathy, emotional stability, language ability and previous international experience
- *non-work factors:* family situation and cultural distance
- *organizational factors:* organizational culture novelty, social support and logistical help
- *job factors:* role novelty, role clarity, role discretion, role conflict and role overload.

An adjustment cycle or curve is helpful in understanding the typical stages that expatriates may encounter when getting used to their new surroundings (Black and Mendenhall, 1991) (see Figure 13.2). Black and Mendenhall (1991) identify four stages that an expatriate may encounter when they go on international assignments:

1. *Honeymoon stage:* when the expatriate first arrives, they may be full of excitement about the novelty of their surroundings and role.
2. *Culture shock:* this can be a critical time, as this is when the expatriate may feel disillusioned and frustrated and may decide to return home.
3. *Adjustment:* the expatriate gradually begins to adapt to their new environment.
4. *Mastery:* the expatriate is now at a healthy level of adjustment.

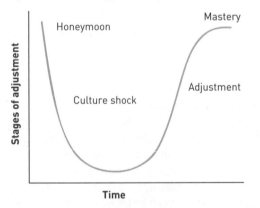

Figure 13.2 U-shaped curve of cross-cultural adjustment
Source: adapted by permission from Springer Nature, Palgrave Macmillan UK, Journal of International Business Studies. Reference: Black J.S. and Mendenhall M. (1991) 'The U-Curve Adjustment Hypothesis Revisited: A Review and Theoretical Framework', *Journal of International Business Studies*, 22(2), 225–47. Copyright © 1991 Academy of International Business, DOI: doi.org/10.1057/palgrave.jibs.8490301.

SPOTLIGHT ON SKILLS

The corporate headquarters of a US-owned MNC is keen to introduce a new induction system to its foreign operation in Brazil. Identify the advantages and disadvantages of sending an expatriate to manage this process.

An important issue for an expatriate going on an international assignment is the quality of life at the foreign location. Evaluate quality of life issues for an American expatriate travelling to Brazil for a long-term international assignment. What issues are likely to be of concern?

To help you consider the issues above, visit **www.macmillanihe.com/carbery-cross-hrm-2e** and watch the video of Claire Campion from Google talking about expatriate issues.

Compensation

Another issue in managing employees on international assignments is how to compensate them. What do you pay an employee on an international assignment? Do they receive the same payment as they receive at home? If they do, you are not providing any incentives for the employee to take up the international assignment, apart from gaining useful international experience. On the other hand, if the expatriate receives higher pay than local employees but is doing a similar job, this may cause problems at the foreign subsidiary. Do you pay the employee the local rate? But what if the local rate is lower than that in their home country, which means they may actually earn less money? Add in issues around different laws and regulations in relation to compensation, different currencies, different taxation systems, different inflation rates, cost of living adjustments and lifestyle issues and it soon becomes clear that compensating expatriates is a complex and costly process.

International compensation packages may include all or some of the following elements – a base salary, a foreign service inducement/hardship premium, allowances, and other benefits (Dowling et al., 2008). There are many approaches to international compensation that companies can take – these include the going rate approach, the balance sheet approach, a one-off lump sum payment, a global pay approach, a local pay approach and a cafeteria approach whereby expatriates can choose benefits up to a specified amount. However, the two most well-known approaches are the going rate approach and the balance sheet approach.

The going rate approach favours a compensation package based on local market rates. Local market rates are usually determined by survey comparisons with local countries, expatriates of the same nationality or expatriates of all nationalities. Once a suitable comparison is found, compensation is based on that. Generally, base pay and benefits are supplemented by additional payments, particularly for expatriates operating in low-pay countries. The benefits of the going rate approach are:

* it is simple to administer
* it encourages the individual to identify with the host location
* it ensures equality in terms of pay with local employees and employees of other nationalities (Dowling et al., 2013: 221).

The negatives associated with such an approach include:

* the variation in compensation between assignments for the same individual
* the variation between individuals of the same nationality in different countries
* the potential for re-entry problems (Dowling et al., 2013: 222).

The balanced sheet approach, which tends to be the most popular approach to compensating expatriates, is designed to maintain expatriates' living standards irrespective of their assignment location. The objective is to maintain the expatriates' home country living standard, and to provide some additional financial incentives for undertaking the assignment. Thus, expatriates are kept on their home pay, while allowances and differentials are used to maintain home equity for items such as goods and services, housing and income tax. The idea is that the expatriate should neither gain nor lose, thus encouraging mobility. The benefits associated with the balanced sheet approach are that:

* it provides equity between assignments
* it provides equity between expatriates of the same nationality
* it can facilitate expatriate re-entry
* it can easily be communicated to employees (Dowling et al., 2013: 223).

The negatives associated with such an approach are that:

* it is difficult to administer
* it can result in great disparities between expatriates of different nationalities and between expatriates and local nationals
* it can be quite intrusive in employees' lives (Dowling et al., 2013: 224).

Performance Management

Performance management is another issue of concern when managing an employee on an international assignment. Managing and effectively conducting performance management for expatriates is a complex task.

When it comes to evaluating performance, issues such as what should be evaluated, who should do the evaluation and how to carry out the evaluation are important (Briscoe et al., 2012). What should be evaluated relates to the criterion used to evaluate performance. Identifying these criteria is problematic as there may be differences between expectations held at the parent company compared to those at the local level. Briscoe et al. (2012: 356), drawing on a range of sources, identify the following performance criteria in Table 13.3.

Another issue is who should carry out the performance evaluation. Generally, it is carried out by superiors, but, in relation to expatriates, this is complicated by the fact that their own superiors are located in the home country and may not be in the best position to evaluate their performance. On the other hand, host country superiors may be in a better position to evaluate their performance, but this will generally only relate to goals and objectives at the local level and they may not be in a position to evaluate the expatriate's broader goals and objectives. Many MNCs use multiple raters, for example 360-degree evaluations, which

Qualifications	Training, experience, technical skills, social and language skills, education
Targets	Derived from the parent company's objectives, the subsidiary objectives, or local objectives and targets individually dictated
Attitudes	Flexibility, interpersonal understanding and communication skills, dealing with stress, openness to change
Job performance	Results, development of locals, communication and decision-making, individual growth and development, application of new expertise

Table 13.3 Performance criteria for evaluating expatriate performance
Source: copyright © 2012 Taylor & Francis. Adapted from *International Human Resource Management: Policies and Practices for Multinational Enterprises*, 4th edition, by Dennis Briscoe, Randall Schuler and Ibraiz Tarique. Reproduced by permission of Taylor and Francis Group, LLC, a division of Informa plc; permission conveyed through Copyright Clearance Center, Inc.

include superiors, peers, subordinates, customers and clients ▶Chapter 7◀. However, trying to involve so many raters across different countries makes 360-degree evaluations difficult when evaluating an expatriate's performance.

How the evaluation should be carried out relates to the form the evaluation will take, the frequency of evaluation, and feedback. The dilemma facing MNCs is whether to use a standardized evaluation form or a customized form, specific to the expatriate. Most companies develop standardized evaluation forms, and while they work fine in domestic settings, when you move to the international level it becomes more problematic; for example, some questions may not be appropriate or effective in another country. The frequency of evaluations can differ enormously – they can be monthly, quarterly, biannual or annual, and even more ad hoc, such as at the end of the assignment or whenever the opportunity arises. Generally, most companies aim to carry out evaluations once a year, which usually extends to expatriates. Providing feedback is an important part of evaluations but is more complex when it comes to expatriates. For example, issues like time and distance hamper effective feedback to the expatriate on performance.

A key practice of a performance management system is performance appraisal ▶Chapter 7◀. But for expatriates on assignment, what type of appraisal system do you use? Is it the local appraisal system that exists in the foreign subsidiary? This might not capture the expatriates' work accurately. Do you develop a global appraisal system? But how do

you do this? What criteria do you use to evaluate their performance? Is it related to the success of the foreign subsidiary? This may not always be accurate, as the expatriate may be performing very well but the foreign subsidiary, for reasons outside the control of the expatriate, is not. MNCs tend to use a variety of methods to appraise performance. They may combine formal performance appraisal with visits from HQ, visits back to HQ, an assessment of results in the area under the expatriate's command, reports, emails – generally adopting an approach of gathering as much information as possible. Evidence suggests that a majority of companies prefer to use host country performance reviews to evaluate expatriate performance, with a surprisingly significant number of companies not measuring assignment performance against pre-agreed metrics (BGRS, 2016).

Repatriation

The final concern in managing employees on international assignments is to successfully bring them back to their original location – the process of **repatriation**. This is an important activity as a major problem for MNCs is employees leaving the company on their return. A number of reasons for this have been identified (Brewster et al., 2007; Briscoe et al., 2012; Dowling et al., 2013), including:

> **Repatriation** – the process that involves bringing the expatriate back to their home country after completing their international assignment

- *No position available in the company:* when the expatriate returns, the least they will expect is their previous job back, but they will more than likely expect a newer role, reflecting their new level of international experience.

- *Loss of status:* when on assignment, the expatriate often enjoys a high(er) level of status. But when they return, they often simply fit back in again to their old role and do not maintain the level of status they enjoyed when on assignment.
- *Loss of autonomy:* similar to status, expatriates often enjoy quite a significant level of autonomy when on assignment. However, when they return home, this autonomy is often no longer available and returning expatriates can feel aggrieved.
- *Loss of career direction:* employees who undertake an international assignment often do so as part of a structured career path. However, where the assignment is not part of a career path, the returning expatriate may often feel a loss of direction. Having completed an international assignment, the returning expatriate often expects that this experience will lead to some kind of career progression.
- *A feeling of being undervalued:* expatriates often report that they feel their work is undervalued. It is often a case of 'out of sight, out of mind'. The good work and skills developed by the expatriate are not acknowledged and this can leave the employee feeling aggrieved.
- *Loss of income:* depending on the type of compensation package the expatriate enjoys while on assignment, they can suffer a loss of income when they return to their original location.
- *Lifestyle:* the expatriate may have become accustomed to a particular standard of lifestyle, and if this lifestyle is not matched when they return, this can have a negative impact on the returning expatriate.
- *Family readjustment:* the family's readjustment to their home location is not always straightforward. This is particularly the case when the family has been away from their home country for a long period of time. The home country may have changed and the family may simply not be able to readjust to their original location.

Many MNCs do not provide post-assignment guarantees – that is, promotion or the return of the expatriate's previous job – but a majority do hold repatriation discussions (BGRS, 2016). Briscoe et al. (2012: 248–9) note that MNCs can provide support for repatriation at different stages:

- *Before the assignment:* the MNC may provide expatriates with career planning prior to the assignment, so that expatriates have an idea of what to expect when they return home. Also, an MNC may appoint a mentor in the home country to act as a point of contact and look after expatriates' interests when they are away.
- *During the assignment:* MNCs should look to provide clear, constant and regular communication with expatriates, regular travel trips home, a mentor in the home country, and any intra-office communication should include expatriates (Briscoe et al., 2012).
- *After the assignment:* managers in the home country must be aware that expatriates and their families may experience readjustment problems and that they may therefore need to put in place plans to reintegrate them back into the home country.

EXPATRIATE FAILURE

Having outlined the issues in managing expatriates on international assignments, it is clear that it is complex and there are significant opportunities for something to go wrong. Hence, IHRM also focuses on expatriate failure. Expatriate failure is generally referred to as the early return of an expatriate to their home country. As noted earlier, the cost of a failed international assignment is extremely high. Failure rates are estimated to run between 16% and 50% (Harzing, 1995). However, the real cost is much higher; for example, one needs to factor in not only the cost of recruitment and selection, training, preparation and moving, but also the consequences of poor performance in lower revenues, lost business opportunities, and damage to the company's reputation, which may undermine future ventures in the host country. There are a number of reasons as to why expatriate failure might occur. Briscoe et al. (2012: 236), in a review of the existing literature, list some of the main reasons for failure:

- inability of the expatriate and/or the expatriate's family to adjust
- mistake in selecting the expatriate to undertake the assignment
- the international assignment did not live up to expectations
- personality traits of the expatriate
- expatriate not able to match expectations of the assignment
- expatriate's lack of technical competence

- expatriate's lack of motivation for the assignment
- expatriate's dissatisfaction with the quality of life in the foreign location
- expatriate's dissatisfaction with compensation and benefits
- inadequate pre-departure training
- inadequate support for the expatriate and family while on the assignment.

Alternative International Assignments

Given the complexity, failure rates and high costs involved in long-term expatriate assignments, there are now questions over the utility and viability of such assignments. Collings et al. (2007) identify a number of reasons for this debate:

- *Supply side issues:* The shortage of international managers to undertake long-term international assignments.
- *Cost issues:* It is estimated that it costs, on average, three to five times more to employ an expatriate compared to employing a host country national (Selmer, 2001).
- *Demand side issues:* The demand for such managers has increased due to the rapid growth of emerging markets in places such as Asia and Eastern Europe and because a greater number of organizations are looking to use expatriates, for example small and medium-sized enterprises and international joint ventures.
- *Failure issues:* Problems of expatriate failure in terms of direct costs, that is, salary, training

costs, travel and relocation expenses, and indirect costs – damaged relations with foreign subsidiaries and potential loss of market share.
- *Management issues:* Complexities around the management of expatriate performance.
- *Career issues:* Collings et al. (2007) note two trends here:

  - Employees are focusing more on career mobility and becoming less committed to organizations ▸Chapter 10◂. Thus, companies may invest in an employee through an expatriation programme but lose them when they return.
  - The growth in self-initiated international assignments or assignments initiated by employees without company support or assistance means that companies may look to use these people to fill positions at a lower cost than a traditional expatriate.

Despite these problems, there is little evidence of a significant decline in the use of long-term assignments. However, alternative forms of international assignments are beginning to emerge, including short-term international assignments, frequent flyer assignments, commuter and rotational assignments, and global virtual teams. Table 13.4 provides a brief review of each of these assignments (cf. Collings et al., 2007). While the traditional expatriate assignment is likely to continue, we are also likely to see a continuation in the strong growth of these alternative forms of international assignment (Collings et al., 2007: 204–7).

Short-term international assignments	• 'A temporary internal transfer to a foreign subsidiary of between one and twelve months duration' (Collings et al., 2007: 205)
	• Family generally remains at home
	• Useful for the transfer of problem-solving skills, as a means of control, for managerial development, training of local workforce and to work on specific project-based tasks (Tahvanainen et al., 2005)
Frequent flyer assignments	• Involve short international business trips; employees who undertake such assignments are often referred to as 'international business travellers'
	• Family remains at home
	• Suitable for irregular specialized tasks, such as annual budget meetings, production scheduling, networking and to maintain personal contact with subsidiary without needing to permanently relocate (Collings et al., 2007)
	• Particularly useful in developing markets or volatile countries where people may be reluctant to relocate (Welch and Worm, 2006)

Commuter and rotational assignments	• Commuter assignments: employees commute from their home base to their post in another country
	• Rotational assignments: employees commute from their home base to their post in another country for a short period followed by a period of time off in their home country
	• Family generally remains at home
	• Rotational assignments are commonly used on oil rigs
	• Seen as viable alternatives to expatriate transfers, particularly in places like Europe where travel is shorter and easier (Mayrhofer and Brewster, 1996)
Global virtual teams	• Employees remain geographically dispersed but coordinate their work through electronic information and communication technologies
	• Family and employee remain at home
	• Particularly useful for relatively routine activities (Collings et al., 2007). Evidence suggests that companies have not quite maximized the potential of global virtual teams (Collings et al., 2007)

Table 13.4 Alternative international assignments

CONSIDER THIS

It is clear from the literature that managing international assignments is a very difficult and complex process, with many opportunities for the assignment to end up in failure. Indeed, we have witnessed a growth in alternative forms of international assignments as a way of mitigating these problems. So, why do multinational companies continue to use long-term international assignments?

HRM IN PRACTICE ⚙

Global staffing

It is almost two years since Peter Murphy left his position in the corporate headquarters in Texas to go on an international assignment that involved setting up the latest foreign subsidiary of Woodhouse Medical Ltd (a fictitious company) in China. The Chinese operation is the fifth foreign subsidiary opened by Woodhouse Medical Ltd in the last three years as it continues a major internationalization strategy. The company now has operations across ten countries in Europe, Asia and North America. A key part of the internationalization process is having someone from corporate headquarters manage the foreign subsidiary. This is something that Woodhouse Medical Ltd is extremely committed to – each foreign subsidiary must be managed by someone from corporate headquarters.

Peter was initially reluctant to go on the international assignment for a number of reasons. First, he felt that his family circumstances were not suitable for an international assignment at that particular time – he had a partner with a very promising career in the banking sector and two young children aged three and seven. Secondly, Peter had never been to Asia, nor did he know anything about that part of the world. But Peter was approached one morning during a coffee break by a senior manager about the assignment to China and he felt he had no choice but to agree to take on the trip. What also bothered Peter was that he was only given four weeks' notice before having to relocate himself and his whole family to China. The company did provide a lot of the logistical support for the trip though – organizing visas, work permits, schooling and accommodation.

Peter is seen as a high-potential employee within Woodhouse Medical Ltd, and it was felt that not only could it trust Peter to do a good job, but also that it would be good for Peter's own career development. Whilst no formal performance review took place while Peter was on the international assignment, informal feedback suggested that he was doing an average job. The new subsidiary was up and running but the operation had not been the success that Woodhouse Medical Ltd was hoping for. There had been rumours of some problems – for example, there were a couple of incidents with local business suppliers where Peter's failure to understand Chinese culture led to some very embarrassing situations. The company was lucky that a local manager was able to sort things out before it caused any major problems. But it was clear that Peter was struggling with understanding the business context in China. Furthermore,

Peter's lack of people management skills, particularly understanding the Chinese way of managing labour, was causing some HR problems. But at this stage, Peter is focused on returning to corporate headquarters and is keen to speak to senior management to discuss what he feels will be a promotion upon his return after completing a two-year international assignment.

There have been some changes in senior management in the intervening two-year period, and it appears that Peter's return has come as a bit of a surprise to everyone at corporate headquarters. The problem is that Peter's old job has been filled by a very promising high-potential employee, and there are currently no promotions on offer at this time. Nor does the company have any replacement lined up to take over from Peter in the Chinese operation. The company does not want to lose Peter as it has invested a lot of resources into his career development, but it fears that he will leave when he realizes that there is no promotion available, nor is he likely to get his old job back.

What would you do?

1. Identify the global staffing approach of Woodhouse Medical Ltd. Compare this approach against other types of staffing approaches.
2. What advice would you give to Woodhouse Medical Ltd in relation to its recruitment and selection of people undertaking international assignments?
3. How might Woodhouse Medical Ltd have avoided the situation whereby it is likely that Peter will leave the organization upon his return?

Getty Images/Caiaimage/John Wildgoose

SUMMARY

This chapter has focused on the area of international human resource management (IHRM), the aim of which has been to introduce readers to the extant scholarship in the area of IHRM but also to keep an applied focus and explore some practical elements related to IHRM. In doing so, the chapter firstly defined and explained what IHRM is all about and considered the major debates within the IHRM literature. For example, a critical question for any IHRM scholar or practitioner is how do we understand and explain the types of HRM practices that are implemented in MNCs' foreign subsidiaries. In the section on the transfer of HRM practices, it was noted that issues like country of origin and host country impact on the type of HRM practices you will find in foreign subsidiaries. The chapter then focused on a very practical element of IHRM, namely the task of managing employees on long-term international assignments. Here the chapter detailed the process all the way, from the recruitment and selection phase, to the preparation and adjustment phase, to issues around compensation and performance management of employees on assignment, and finally to the repatriation phase. The chapter also discussed the difficulties associated with long-term assignments.

CHAPTER REVIEW QUESTIONS

1. Distinguish between parent country nationals, host country nationals and third country nationals.
2. Why do scholars suggest that we are unlikely to see a convergence of HRM practices to one best model?
3. What is meant by country of origin, host country and dominance effects?
4. Why do multinational companies send some of their employees on international assignments?
5. What types of methods can a multinational company use to prepare its employees for an international assignment?
6. Discuss the advantages and disadvantages of the balanced sheet approach to expatriate compensation.
7. What problems might employees face when they return from an international assignment?
8. Discuss the various alternative forms of international assignment.

FURTHER READING

Collings, D.G., Wood, G.T. and Caligiuri, P.M. (2015) *The Routledge Companion to International Human Resource Management*, New York: Routledge.

Dowling, P.J., Festing, M. and Engle, A.D. (2013) *International Human Resource Management*, 6th edn, London: Cengage Learning.

Edwards, T. and Rees, C. (2017) *International Human Resource Management: Globalization, National Systems and Multinational Companies*, 3rd edn, Harlow: Pearson.

Reiche, B.S., Harzing, A.W. and Tenzer, H. (2018) *International Human Resource Management*, 5th edn, London: Sage.

Tarique, I., Briscoe, D. and Schuler, R.S. (2016) *International Human Resource Management: Policies and Practices for Multinational Enterprises*, New York: Routledge.

USEFUL WEBSITES

www.bgrs.com
Brookfield Global Relocation Services produces the Global Relocation Trends Surveys, a huge source of data for issues to do with expatriation.

www.harzing.com
This is the website of Anne-Wil Harzing, a professor in international management, which provides information, online papers and resources about IHRM.

www.shrm.org/resourcesandtools/hr-topics/global-hr/pages
The website of the Society for Human Resource Management, the world's largest association devoted to HRM; this section focuses on global HRM.

www.expatfocus.com
Expat Focus provides comprehensive information and support resources for expatriates. It contains impartial information on countries and provides opinions and advice from experienced expatriates.

 For extra resources, including videos, multiple choice questions and useful weblinks, go to: **www.macmillanihe.com/carbery-cross-hrm-2e**.

iStock.com/Liuser

14: Corporate Social Responsibility and Human Resource Management

Colm McLaughlin

LEARNING OUTCOMES

By the end of this chapter you will be able to:

- Explain the concept of corporate social responsibility (CSR) and its connection to HRM
- Identify the four levels in Carroll's pyramid of CSR
- Outline some of the arguments for business adopting a CSR philosophy, including the 'business case'
- Discuss some of the arguments made by critics of CSR
- Contrast a CSR approach to a regulatory approach to addressing issues at work
- Demonstrate an understanding of some contemporary CSR labour issues

THIS CHAPTER DISCUSSES:

Introduction (274)

What is Corporate Social Responsibility? (274)

Which CSR Issues should Firms Address? (276)

The Controversy of CSR (278)

The Case against CSR (284)

A Role for Regulation? (288)

INTRODUCTION

Society expects business to adhere to certain social and ethical standards, that is, to meet its **corporate social responsibility (CSR)**. While an organization needs to make a profit in order to survive and grow, profit maximization is not the only concern of business. This is reflected in the growth of CSR as a mainstream business issue, with one analysis of FTSE 100 annual reports finding that 97% of firms included CSR-related information, while 56% included CSR in their strategic objectives (Pilot, 2011). Companies are hiring CSR managers, participating in CSR performance indices such as the FTSE4Good, joining CSR membership organizations like Business in the Community and engaging with international initiatives such as the UN's Sustainable Development Goals (SDGs), which aim to eradicate poverty, reduce inequality and injustice, and address climate change. The importance of CSR is also reflected in the fact that responsibility for it increasingly lies with a member of the board of directors and that a weblink to corporate responsibility is generally found on the home page of most large publicly listed companies. There are numerous international agreements relating to CSR, such as the United Nations Global Compact, which many multinational companies have signed up to and which commits signatories to uphold ten principles covering human rights, labour standards, the environment and anti-corruption. There has been an explosion in 'codes of conduct' used by international brands to govern the working conditions in the factories that supply their products.

This interest in CSR by corporations is partly reactive, driven by the fear of reputational damage to brand images from negative publicity. Trade unions, community groups and **nongovernmental organizations (NGOs)** can use the internet to quickly and widely circulate information about the practices used in the manufacture of a company's products, and to call for product boycotts. But part of the motivation is also proactive, with firms realizing that the public is increasingly conscious of social and environmental issues, that business has an important role to play in addressing these issues, and that there are significant business opportunities to be developed in response.

> **Corporate social responsibility (CSR)** – the duty of a business to go beyond profit maximization and act responsibly and contribute positively to society
>
> **Nongovernmental organizations (NGOs)** – organizations that are independent of government and generally run on a not-for-profit basis. Examples include Greenpeace, Friends of the Earth, Oxfam, the Fair Labor Association and the Institute for Global Labour and Human Rights

In relation to HRM, how a company treats its employees is part of its CSR agenda: many HR issues addressed in earlier chapters, such as fair payment and promotion systems, employee engagement, gender equality and diversity, work–life balance, training and development opportunities and job security, are increasingly seen as integral to CSR. Furthermore, firms are also exposed to reputational risk in relation to how contractors and workers in supplier firms are treated. For example, an item of clothing sold by a high street clothing retailer might have been manufactured by an external company, but if it is revealed that its manufacture involved child labour, unsafe working conditions or breaches of human rights then this has significant ethical and reputational implications for the high street retailer. In other words, the HR practices of a company and of its suppliers increasingly matter to the outside world. HR practitioners have an important role to play in ensuring the firm's own HRM practices are ethical, and in advising purchasing and supply chain managers on CSR and HRM issues. They also have a role to play in ensuring that employees have the skills and motivation to drive the CSR and sustainability strategy of an organization.

In this chapter, we set out what CSR is, look at some of the HRM issues that come within a firm's CSR ambit, and examine some of the ethical and financial reasons why firms engage in CSR. Next, we examine some of the controversies surrounding CSR. In particular, we assess its effectiveness in addressing employment-related CSR issues as against a greater role for government regulation.

WHAT IS CORPORATE SOCIAL RESPONSIBILITY?

So what exactly is CSR and what does society expect of business? CSR is a broad umbrella and there is no one clear definition of exactly what it entails. While there is a shared acceptance in the literature that organizations have a responsibility to a wider societal good, different definitions stress different dimensions. The Confederation of British Industry (CBI, 2001) describes CSR as: 'the acknowledgement by companies that they should be accountable not only for their financial performance, but for the impact of their activities on society and/ or the environment'. This definition suggests that business is responsible for its *own* impact on society. The European Commission (2001) defined CSR as: 'a concept whereby companies decide voluntarily to contribute to a better society and a cleaner environment'. This goes further than the CBI by implying that organizations need, more generally, to have a positive impact on societal progress. By 2011, its definition had been narrowed to: 'the responsibility of enterprises for their impact on society'. However, it expands on this by adding that firms should 'have a process in place to integrate social, environmental, ethical human rights and consumer concerns into their business operations and core strategy' (European Commission, 2011). Marks & Spencer, a leading UK retailer and an internationally recognized leader in sustainability and CSR, describes the company's social responsibility, as set out in its 'Plan A', as responding to the expectations of its stakeholders to 'have a positive impact in all that it does'. This suggests that CSR is about responding to stakeholder demands for responsible behaviour. In other words, this is what 'our customers, colleagues,

> **Stakeholders** – any individuals, groups or organizations that are affected by or can affect the actions of a company

suppliers and business partners' expect (Marks & Spencer, 2015). It uses the word **stakeholders**, a key phrase in the CSR field.

Interestingly, none of these definitions of CSR mention obeying the law. This is because while the legal framework sets minimum standards, CSR is about a higher standard. The phrase often used by CSR managers is going 'beyond compliance'. So CSR is about voluntary action and self-regulation by firms to go beyond what the law requires of them.

One of the earliest and most popular conceptual models of CSR was provided by Carroll (1979). His pyramid of CSR identified four levels of responsibility: economic, legal, ethical and discretionary (later to become philanthropic). Thus, managers have a responsibility to: produce goods and services for society and to be economically sustainable; obey all the laws and regulations of a society; act ethically, avoid harm and take account of the norms, values and expectations of different stakeholders; and make a positive contribution to society through 'giving something back' and being a good corporate citizen. Carroll (2016) acknowledges that to some it may

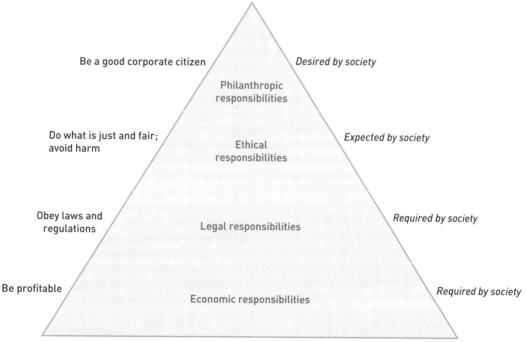

Figure 14.1 Carroll's pyramid of CSR

Source: Figure 1, Carroll's pyramid of CSR, from Carroll, A.B. (2016) 'Carroll's pyramid of CSR: taking another look', *International Journal of Corporate Social Responsibility*, 1(3). Published by SpringerOpen, DOI: doi.org/10.1186/s40991-016-0004-6. Copyright © Carroll 2016; reprinted under the CC BY 4.0 licence https://creativecommons.org/licenses/by/4.0. The Disclaimer of Warranties and Limitation of Liability can be read here: https://creativecommons.org/licenses/by/4.0/legalcode.

seem strange to have economic sustainability as a responsibility, but he argues that without profitability business cannot make a wider contribution to society. He is also adamant that the pyramid does not represent a hierarchical or sequential process, but is an integrated framework in which business addresses all four simultaneously. In contrast, Kang proposed inverting Carroll's pyramid and argued that meeting social, ethical and legal obligations should come first. That is, a firm should make a profit having met these obligations (see Wood, 2010).

Many writers in the field of CSR and firms who engage with CSR no longer use the word 'social', preferring instead to use 'corporate responsibility', 'responsible business', 'corporate citizenship' or some other broad title. This is because the CSR agenda has widened beyond social issues to include the environmental and sustainability issues of our time. When CSR initially gathered momentum in the 1970s and 80s, social issues in business were its prime focus. High-profile cases of that period included the unethical marketing of infant milk formula in Africa by Nestlé, the gas leak in 1984 at the Union Carbide factory in Bhopal, India, where thousands were killed and many suffered horrendous injuries, and the Ford Pinto car that could explode in a fireball if another vehicle crashed into it from behind. In recent decades, environmental degradation, global warming, sustainable production and other 'green' topics have become major issues of concern. Recent developments, including the United Nations Sustainable Development Goals and the Paris Agreement (on climate change), have involved significant input from the corporate sector and ensured that CSR remains high on the corporate agenda. While US President Donald Trump announced in early 2017 that the USA would withdraw from the Paris Agreement, many US states and corporations have since reaffirmed their commitment to the agreement.

WHICH CSR ISSUES SHOULD FIRMS ADDRESS?

If you were to draw up a list of social, ethical and environmental issues, you would need a fairly large canvas. The range of potential CSR issues is endless and includes: protection of the environment, sustainability, fair trade, poverty, human rights, labour standards, equality and diversity, employee engagement, health and safety, animal welfare, safe products, ethical marketing and supporting charities,

to name but a few. The suggestion is not that all firms should address all these issues, but that firms should address those that are of relevance to the nature of their business and in proportion to their size and locality. A small local business, for example, might sponsor a local charity or sports team, purchase materials from other local businesses in order to support the community, and treat its employees fairly and with respect. The expectations of society towards a large multinational corporation would be far greater. As a result, MNCs are likely to engage in a much wider range of CSR activities. Tesco, a British multinational supermarket, considers a broad range of CSR issues, such as the sustainability of fish stocks, animal welfare, global warming, fair trade, human rights and promoting healthy eating. Given its significant presence in many communities, it supports the local populations in a range of ways. As one of the largest private sector employers in the UK and one of the world's largest retail companies, its employment policies are an important area of CSR and include its approach to promoting equality and diversity, and treating its staff fairly. Tesco invests significant resources in apprenticeships, training and development. Its website claims that almost 60% of management positions are filled by internal candidates, while 32% of its senior managers are female. It has long built a positive relationship with the trade union Usdaw (Union of Shop, Distributive and Allied Workers) through the negotiation of a partnership agreement.

Tesco also has some responsibility for the working conditions of workers in its many supply chains. It was a founding member of the Ethical Trading Initiative (ETI), an alliance formed between companies, trade unions and NGOs who work together to improve conditions for vulnerable workers across the globe in a range of industries that grow or manufacture consumer goods. Member companies agree to adopt the ETI Base Code in full (Table 14.1). Thus, Tesco expects all its suppliers worldwide to comply with the ETI Base Code on labour standards, which is founded on International Labour Organization (ILO) conventions. It also provides training for suppliers on its ethical trading policy. Another consideration that might influence which issues a firm chooses to address is any negative publicity it has received. As the largest supermarket chain in the UK, Tesco has come in for criticism on a number of issues and undoubtedly this has had some effect on its CSR policy.

Issues to do with employees and labour rights are central to CSR. Stories of child labour and other forms of exploitation of workers revealed by trade unions and labour NGOs travel quickly around the

1. Employment is freely chosen
2. Freedom of association to join a trade union and the right to collective bargaining are respected
3. Working conditions are safe and hygienic
4. Child labour shall not be used
5. Living wages are paid
6. Working hours are not excessive
7. No discrimination is practised
8. Regular employment is provided
9. No harsh or inhumane treatment is allowed

As part of the ETI Principles of Implementation, corporate members also agree to:

- demonstrate a clear commitment to ethical trade
- integrate ethical trade into their core business practices
- drive year-on-year improvements to working conditions
- support suppliers to improve working conditions, for example through advice and training
- report annually on their progress, setting out how much they spend on improving working conditions, the training they have undertaken, how they monitor their suppliers/working conditions, and how they then ensure that any shortcomings identified are rectified. All reporting must be open and accurate

Table 14.1 ETI Base Code of labour standards
Sources: Ethical Trading Initiative, 2018a, 2018b. Copyright © 2018 Ethical Trading Initiative (ETI). Reprinted with permission.

globe, damaging the reputation of leading brands and high street chains. In recent years, the supply chains of many leading high street brands have been associated with underage workers. Poor working conditions have been highlighted in factories manufacturing IT products for household names, such as IBM, Hewlett-Packard, Microsoft, Lenovo and Dell (Thompson, 2009), and in leading apparel companies such as Nike (Ballinger, 2008). In the case of Nike, its own audits of factories manufacturing Nike footwear and clothing showed physical and verbal abuse of workers, restricted access to drinking water and toilets, widespread use of excessive working hours and overtime, and workers being paid below the local legal minimum wage (Teather, 2005). In the manufacture of toys for McDonald's, accusations have been made of 'appalling working conditions, slave wages and instances of child labour' (Royle, 2005: 50).

In early 2009, allegations emerged in an undercover investigation by the BBC and *The Observer* that two suppliers of knitwear to Primark (Penneys in Ireland) were employing illegal immigrants in the UK on half the minimum wage and for 12-hour shifts over seven days per week. The ETI, of which Primark was a member, '[was] horrified at allegations of abuses exposed by this investigation' (McDougall,

2009) and instructed Primark to remove all the ETI branding from its stores and website until the ETI had conducted a full investigation into Primark's adherence to its Base Code.

While these companies do not directly engage in these practices themselves, they are perceived to profit from them. Thus, society holds them responsible for rectifying such abuses and instigating fair employment practices in the companies that supply their products. In response to such accusations, many of these companies have drawn up codes of conduct setting out the labour standards their supply firms must adhere to. Internal and external auditors are then used to ensure that these standards are met, and where breaches are found, the factories are required to improve working conditions or risk losing the supply contract. Nike, for example, employs a compliance team of more than 90 staff in 21 countries, who monitor adherence by its suppliers with the Nike code of conduct. Additionally, Nike allows the Fair Labor Association to conduct independent and unannounced inspections (Locke et al., 2007). While HRM departments are not responsible directly for HR issues in supply chain factories, they are often involved in drawing up codes of conduct and have input into CSR issues (Sachdev, 2006).

HRM IN THE GLOBAL BUSINESS ENVIRONMENT

The collapse of Rana Plaza

On the morning of 24 April 2013, Rana Plaza, an eight-story commercial building in Dhaka, Bangladesh, collapsed and 1,134 people were killed and 2,500 were injured, many permanently maimed. Most of the deceased and injured were female garment workers from clothing factories within the building (Hira and Benson-Rea, 2017). The *New York Times* described it as 'the deadliest disaster in the history of the garment industry' (Yardley, 2013). Cracks in the building had been found the day before, but garment workers were ordered into work (Al-Mahmood et al., 2013). The building had been designed for offices and shops rather than industrial use, and the top four floors had been added without a permit. In the rubble were clothing labels for international brands, including Benetton, Bonmarché, Matalan, Monsoon Accessorize, Primark and Walmart. While these companies had no legal liability as they do not make the clothes, they came under mounting public pressure to provide funding for victims and their families and to take action as a sector to improve safety in their supply chain factories (Hira and Benson-Rea, 2017).

Visit the Clean Clothes Campaign to find out which companies made donations following the Rana Plaza disaster: www.cleanclothes.org/safety/ranaplaza/rana-plaza-actual-and-potential-donors-listed-by-g7-country.

THE CONTROVERSY OF CSR

While CSR has only become a mainstream business issue over the past 15 years, some companies have sought to act responsibly for as long as business has existed. The Quaker-owned companies, such as the chocolate manufacturers Cadbury, Rowntree and Fry, were well known for their enlightened employee welfare and housing schemes introduced in Victorian England in the 1800s, when working and living conditions were generally appalling. Such practices in a small number of large British companies gave birth to what became known as the 'welfare tradition', which is viewed as the early foundations of modern HRM (Gunnigle et al., 2011). The Cadbury family were also involved in wider social reforms, such as providing education to working-class adults and leading the campaign against children working as chimney sweeps (Cadbury, 2010). John D. Rockefeller, who founded the Standard Oil company in the USA in 1870, was a shining example of **philanthropy** and gave away US$550 million during his lifetime to education, science, health and the arts (Steiner and Steiner, 2012).

There are also contemporary examples of companies driven by a motive beyond just profit. In the late 1970s, scientists at Merck came up with what they thought would be a cure for onchocerciasis, or river blindness, a parasite that affects more than 18 million people, mostly in poor African countries.

> **Philanthropy** – the practice of making charitable donations to good causes

The company could develop the drug at great expense, but this would not be a profitable venture because neither the sufferers nor their governments would be able to afford it. The company decided to produce the drug anyway and to provide it free for as long as it was needed. To date, it has given away more than 1.4 billion tablets of Mectizan in 37 countries at a cost to the company of over US$2 billion. In doing so, it has prevented an estimated 40,000 cases of blindness. Merck's motivation was that it could afford to do so and, having discovered a cure for a debilitating disease, it was the humanitarian thing to do (Steiner and Steiner, 2012). The Body Shop, founded in 1976 by Anita Roddick in the UK, became a global brand based on its environmental, animal welfare and ethical trade philosophy. It has supported a range of environmental, human rights and animal welfare charities, and has led awareness-raising campaigns on a number of social issues, such as domestic violence, human trafficking, women's rights and the prevention of HIV/AIDS (Purkayastha and Fernando, 2007). The Body Shop was widely seen as being a model example of socially responsible business and has had a significant impact on embedding CSR in contemporary corporate culture (Hausman, 2007).

However, some of these exemplars of social responsibility have not been immune from criticism. Cadbury was accused in 1909 of gaining financially from slavery on cocoa plantations (Blowfield and Murray, 2011), even though the campaign against slavery had been Quaker led (Sachdev, 2006). Rockefeller was criticized for crushing his competitors through predatory pricing, underselling and other anti-competitive practices. So successful was he that Standard Oil refined more than 90% of US oil by the late 1800s. The *New York World* described Standard Oil as the 'most cruel, impudent, pitiless, and grasping monopoly that ever fastened upon a country' (Visser, 2011). The Body Shop's social responsibility has also been called into question. In an article in *Business Ethics*, Entine (1994) accused the company of hypocrisy in trading on an ethical image when much of this image was no more than public relations spin. He pointed out that the company had a reputation for supporting numerous charities, and yet official data showed that the company had made no charitable donations during its first 11 years, and over the subsequent decade, company donations were about average for large corporations (Entine, 2002; Purkayastha and Fernando, 2007). The Body Shop was also accused by London Greenpeace (an independent activist group, not to be confused with Greenpeace International) of anti-union practices, low pay, exploiting indigenous peoples, fuelling consumerism and misleading the public. The company was sold to L'Oréal in 2006, a company known to test products on animals and one which Roddick had previously criticized for its sexualization of women (Purkayastha and Fernando, 2007).

These examples raise a number of important questions about CSR that we will explore in more depth below. Can firms actually be socially responsible or will the pressure for profits trump ethical behaviour when the two come into conflict? Is CSR on the part of corporations a real attempt to grapple with important social, ethical and environmental issues, or is it just window dressing to appeal to consumer idealism and pre-empt governments from introducing regulations? If society expects business to meet higher standards of behaviour, is it not the job of the government to set these standards through legislation?

While CSR has become a mainstream corporate concern, it is not without its critics. For some, CSR is a distraction from the core concern of business, which is making a profit; this is known as the **shareholder view of the firm**. We will briefly examine this view in the next section, but it is

> **Shareholder view of the firm** – the primary objective of management should be to maximize profit for shareholders
>
> **Stakeholder view of the firm** – management should take the interests of all stakeholders into account when making decisions

no longer the mainstream view of business, having been largely replaced by the **stakeholder view of the firm**. According to this view, while firms still exist to maximize profits, they need to balance this objective against the legitimate needs of other stakeholders. Arguments in support of this position are both ethical (the 'social contract') and self-interested (the 'business case'), as set out on pages 280–284.

The real debate over CSR, however, occurs between those who think that business should *voluntarily* make a contribution to the public good, and those who think that government *regulation* is the best way to ensure that corporations adhere to the standards society expects of them. Thus, in this debate, it is not the aims of CSR that are called into question, it is the effectiveness of CSR as a method to bring about widespread change in corporate behaviour. Should working conditions be left to corporations to address voluntarily in conjunction with concerned stakeholders, such as labour rights organizations, or should governments take stronger action through regulation to set out the minimum standards that firms must adhere to? This debate is often characterized as one between the 'carrot' of the business case that incentivizes firms to do the right thing and the 'stick' of government regulation that forces firms to act in a certain way. Which is more

CONSIDER THIS

Log on to the home page of Tesco (www.tescoplc.com). What HRM-related issues of corporate responsibility does it address? Why do you think Tesco publicly makes these commitments?

Log on to www.tescopoly.org.uk, a website run by an alliance of various community groups critical of the power of all the leading UK supermarkets, not just Tesco. Click on 'Issues and Impacts' on the 'Resource Material' tab and then on the various workers links: Workers Worldwide, Garment Workers UK Workers, Homeworkers. What HRM-related criticisms of UK supermarkets do they identify?

How effective do you think NGOs and civil society organizations like Tescopoly are at making large companies act more responsibly?

effective at aligning corporate behaviour with the interests of society, the 'carrot' or the 'stick'?

The Shareholder View of the Firm

At the heart of the shareholder view of the firm is the belief that the sole aim of business is profit maximization. This was the dominant view of business for much of the twentieth century. It finds support in the theory of Adam Smith, who, in his book *The Wealth of Nations* ([1776] 2009), put forward that when individuals pursue their own interest, the invisible hand of the market delivers benefits for everyone. Through competition, resources such as capital and labour are allocated efficiently and prices are driven down. As Smith stated: 'it is not from the benevolence of the butcher, the brewer or the baker that we expect our dinner, but from their regard to their own self-interest' (p. 13). Moreover, the individual, 'by pursuing his own interest ... frequently promotes that of the society more effectually than when he really intends to promote it' (p. 264). Thus, business makes a significant contribution to society by creating jobs, contributing to taxation revenues, delivering economic growth, and providing new products and services that society wants and needs. Getting involved in solving complex social and environmental issues is a distraction best left to government, while business gets on with what it does best, which is providing goods and services in order to make profit. This view can be summed up by the economist Milton Friedman, who is widely credited with using the expression: 'the business of business is business'. As Friedman (1970) argued in an article in the *New York Times Magazine*: 'there is one and only one social responsibility of business – to use its resources and engage in activities designed to increase its profits so long as it stays within the rules of the game'. He points out that senior executives of corporations are in the service of shareholders to maximize profits. Engaging in CSR raises costs and is thus 'spending someone else's money for a general social interest'. If it results in lower profits, shareholders suffer; if it leads to higher prices, consumers suffer; and if it results in lower wages, employees suffer. Hence, he argued, managers of corporations have what is known as a 'fiduciary duty' to act in the best interests of the shareholders by maximizing shareholder value.

> **Social contract** – an implicit agreement between business and society that sets out the broad standards that business should adhere to and duties it should fulfil in order to maintain the support and legitimacy of society. These standards are partly reflected in law but are mostly contained in social norms, values and expectations

The Stakeholder View of the Firm: the 'Social Contract' Arguments

From an ethical perspective, businesses exist in a society, and although society benefits from the wealth creation, taxation revenue and job creation of successful companies, firms also benefit from the communities they operate within. For example, publicly funded universities provide educated graduates, the state provides a legal system, and the community allows a company to build plants and use local resources. A symbiotic relationship exists between business and society, resulting in the **social contract** (Steiner and Steiner, 2012). Society expects business to be guided by certain values. Even Adam Smith ([1759] 2007: 239) was a strong advocate of values underpinning the operation of business. While he advocated that individuals pursue their self-interest, he also stressed the need for the values of 'humanity, justice, generosity and public spirit'. Additionally, some social problems can only be solved with the help of business, such as unemployment or discrimination in the workplace ▶Chapter 6◀, and therefore society needs business to assist in finding solutions. Indeed, some of the problems society faces have, at least in part, been caused by business, such as environmental degradation and pollution. Finally, businesses are powerful actors in society. This power has increased since the 1980s, as western governments have increasingly liberalized and deregulated markets and undermined collective bargaining structures and trade union influence.

As Steiner and Steiner (2012: 58) note, 'business has tremendous power to change society', to change its ideas, values and institutions. Similarly, James Gross (1998: 63), professor at Cornell University, argues that corporations have:

> the power to affect people's lives, to harm or benefit them, to violate or protect their rights, to favour some over others for various reasons, to make or break their communities, and to decree many of the rules that govern who gets what in the economy and what they have to do to get it.

With great power comes great responsibility. However, the public have become increasingly disenchanted with business and its exercise of this power. From the late 1960s onwards, public opinion surveys in the USA showed a dramatic drop in the public's confidence in business to strike a fair deal between profit and public good, with little recovery in public trust in business since (Steiner and Steiner, 2012). Some of the recent issues that have undermined trust in business include:

- a raft of corporate scandals, such as the fitting of 'defeat devices' by Volkswagen to 11 million of its cars to circumvent emissions standards testing
- the 'aggressive' use of loopholes by multinational corporations to significantly reduce the amounts of corporate taxation they pay; these loopholes are legal but are not intended by regulators and are generally not available to small businesses or individual taxpayers
- an increase in job insecurity for many workers through the use of temporary and zero-hours contracts, 'bogus self-employment', the so-called 'gig economy' and other forms of temporary employment contracts ▶Chapter 5◀
- the constant flow of media stories about the use of child labour and exploitation of workers in developing countries by suppliers to brand name corporations
- astronomical bonuses for bankers and an exponentially increasing gap in pay between executives and blue-collar workers.

On the issue of pay, the influential management writer, Peter Drucker, stated that the pay of the CEO should be no more than 20 times greater than the pay of the average employee in the company. In an interview with *Wired*, Drucker said it was 'morally and socially unforgiveable' for senior executives to be rewarded exorbitantly, while making thousands of their workers redundant (Schwartz and Kelly, 1996). In the USA, the ratio of CEO pay to that of the average blue-collar worker had risen from 42:1 in 1980 to 347:1 in 2016 (AFL-CIO, 2017).

Levels of confidence in business plummeted further in the wake of the global financial meltdown, the state bailout of privately owned banks, the ensuing deep recession, soaring unemployment levels, and ongoing austerity budgets. It is no surprise that the Occupy movement, which called for capitalism to be regulated or even replaced, gained some sympathy from the public. The Occupy movement was an international protest movement against social and economic inequality, which held large-scale protests in London, New York, Santiago, Berlin, Madrid, Zagreb and many other cities around the world, beginning in September 2011. While the protests were short-lived, its activities were influential in drawing attention to the behaviour of corporations and to issues of economic inequality. Dominic Barton, the global managing director of McKinsey, went so far as to suggest that if there is not a fundamental reform of the way business is done, 'the social contract between the capitalist system and the citizenry may truly rupture, with unpredictable but severely damaging results' for the system of capitalism itself (Barton, 2011: 86). Business has lost some of its legitimacy and CSR is one method by which it seeks to regain the trust of the public.

From an HRM perspective, a number of scholars have made a strong argument for giving employees greater rights as stakeholders with a tangible 'stake' in the firm through their investment in firm-specific skills (Kochan and Rubenstein, 2000) and through the ideas they contribute. As Charles Handy (2002: 53) powerfully argues in a critique of the shareholder view of the firm, in today's knowledge economy, 'the value of a company resides largely in its intellectual property ... in the skills and experience of its workforce', and yet shareholders are paid dividends while employees are not. He claims that many shareholders 'have none of the pride or responsibility of ownership and, if truth be told, are only there for the money' (2002: 51).

The Stakeholder View of the Firm: the 'Business Case' Arguments

From a self-interest perspective, the argument for CSR is that it can improve a firm's financial performance. This is the 'business case' for CSR. It is sometimes described as 'doing well by doing good'. By acting in the best interests of society, society will, in turn, reward business for its efforts. For example, if firms support local charities, this can improve their public image and increase their customer base. By developing a new product that responds to a social or environmental need, they can increase profits. By ensuring good employment standards, they can avoid negative publicity that can lead to reputational damage to their brand. The actions of firms can thus generate positive benefits and reduce reputational risk. In this sense, CSR is, in fact, 'enlightened self-interest'. The benefits of such actions may not be immediate, however, and so CSR is seen as adding value to the firm in the long run. A long-term approach to adding value is not incompatible with the fiduciary duty of managers to act in the best interests of shareholders. In fact, in some countries such as the UK, pension funds and other institutional investors are required to disclose their social, ethical and environmental investment principles and have been encouraged to adopt a long-term view of their investments. UK company law provides another example of the compatibility of CSR with stakeholder interests: following changes in 2006, boards of directors must now take account of employee interests alongside other stakeholders when pursuing their duty to maximize financial returns. Such a longer run view is referred to as 'enlightened shareholder value' (McLaughlin and Deakin, 2012).

HRM also has a role to play in the 'business case' in ensuring that employees have the capabilities and are enabled and engaged to drive the CSR and sustainability strategy of an Organization. **Sustainable HRM** is a term that is being used increasingly to refer to the link between HRM and sustainable practices, both environmental and social. It refers to a long-term view of the firm, which emphasizes the role of HRM in balancing the delivery of financial outcomes with social and environmental outcomes. Central to this is the sustainability of human resources – the ethical treatment of people who work for an organization as well as those who do not work for the organization but are affected by it, such as contractors and workers in supply chains. In relation to environmental issues, **green HRM** refers to 'promoting a heightened sense of environmental responsibility among employees, through recruitment of people "committed to the environment"; by training, evaluating and rewarding performance based on environmental criteria; and focusing continuous improvement initiatives on environmental management activities' (Harvey et al., 2013: 153). In the case of Volkswagen, for example, questions could be asked about the training around environmental standards and targets, about the structure of the reward system or about the culture that had developed which meant that some staff felt it was permissible to fit 'cheat devices' on cars to circumvent emission tests and thus sell more cars.

According to advocates of CSR, three groups in particular will reward businesses for acting

> **Sustainable HRM** – the role of HRM in driving the social and environmental strategy and activities of an organization. It also includes the ethical treatment of people who work for an organization and who are affected by the HR practices of an organization
>
> **Green HRM** – the role of HRM in driving the environmental strategy and activities of an organization

responsibly: employees, customers and investors. These are now addressed in turn.

Employees

The ethical practices and reputation of a company are important issues for the recruitment and retention of staff ▶Chapters 3 and 4◀, as various studies show that employees want to work for companies that are ethical and make a positive contribution to social and environmental issues. In a study of MBA graduates in five business schools in the USA and Europe, over 90% reported that they would be willing to forgo some financial remuneration in order to work for a company that cared about its employees, its stakeholders and sustainability (Montgomery and Ramus, 2003). This is reflected in a growth of employee volunteering, whereby staff are encouraged to engage in socially beneficial activities during work time. This has been shown to improve employee motivation and be good for a firm's reputation at the same time (de Gilder et al., 2005). Nike is reputed to have improved the employment standards in its supply chains partly because of staff embarrassment at being associated with sweatshops. Maria Eitel, vice-president for corporate responsibility, said that staff 'were going to barbecues and people would say: "How can you work for Nike?" I don't know if we were losing employees but it sure as hell didn't help in attracting them' (Vogel, 2006: 59).

As shown in the Tesco example earlier, CSR is not restricted to issues external to the firm. How an organization looks after its own employees is also a key CSR issue. People want to work for companies that treat their own employees well, and other stakeholders want companies to treat their employees well. Thus, a reputation for good HRM practices is important in attracting the best and brightest talent and improving the reputation of the firm among various stakeholders. As a result, many employers want to be the 'employer of choice'. A range of league tables now exist to rank companies in terms of their attractiveness to work: World's Best Multinational Workplaces, UK *Sunday Times* 100 Best Companies, US *Fortune* 100 Best Companies to Work For, Where Women Want to Work Top 50, Top Employers in Asia Pacific and India, Top Employers South Africa and

Australia's Top 100 Graduate Employers are just a few of the many league tables that have proliferated in recent years. HRM policies such as flexible working, training and development, equality and diversity, fairness at work, whistleblowing, health and safety, employee engagement and so on are seen as increasingly important for HRM and CSR. The benefits of such policies for a firm's financial performance are many. Better HRM increases competitive advantage by attracting top talent, raising employee morale, and reducing costs associated with high turnover, such as recruitment and training. Policies that promote equality and diversity lead to a diverse workforce. This, in turn, reflects a diverse customer base, providing insights into customer needs and attracting new customers to the business. Good HRM policies and practices can also lead to better engagement by employees with a firm's social and environmental strategic goals (Harvey et al., 2013). It can also reduce any potential litigation risk and reputational damage associated with discrimination claims (McLaughlin and Deakin, 2012).

An example of reputational damage occurred during 2010 at the Dublin office of PricewaterhouseCoopers (PwC). Photos of the 'top 10' new female graduate recruits based on their physical appearance were collated by a few male members of PwC and circulated in an email to selected colleagues (Hickey, 2010). As is often the case with such emails, it was circulated more widely within the firm and quickly went viral around the globe to the humiliation of the women concerned and the embarrassment of the company. As a high-profile promoter of equality and diversity at work, a member of Business in the Community (a membership organization that promotes responsible and ethical business practices), and a company that goes to great lengths to recruit, develop and promote female employees, PwC was well aware of the potential reputational damage of this action. Not only might such behaviour affect recruitment and existing employee morale, it might also undermine its reputation with clients. Were PwC a publicly listed company, the negative publicity may have impacted on the share price. Thus, employee issues not only come under the HRM umbrella but they are also central to CSR.

Customers

In relation to customers, it is argued that CSR can build brand loyalty. Customers are increasingly aware of the social and environmental issues surrounding the goods they purchase, and the internet and social media provide them with easy access to information about the behaviour of corporations. Socially responsible firms will be rewarded with customer loyalty, while socially irresponsible firms will be punished through loss of sales and consumer boycotts. Evidence of socially responsible shopping is seen in the rise of ethical labelling schemes, which companies are increasingly eager to sign up to. A range of labelling schemes now exist, covering an array of products and sectors, such as the ETI (see Table 14.1), Fairtrade, GoodWeave (carpets), Make IT Fair (electronics), Marine Stewardship Council (fish sustainability), LEAF (sustainable farming) and Freedom Food (animal welfare), to name but a few. The importance that firms place on these labels can be seen in the example given earlier of Primark and the removal of the ETI label following reports in the British media. This represented significant reputational damage for the company and, in response, Primark went to great lengths to restore its reputation for CSR. For example, it has increased its auditing of suppliers and stepped up its levels of investment in community projects in the developing countries in which its products are produced. Primark has now regained the ETI label, which it clearly sees as important for its brand image and the long-term financial performance of the firm.

CONSIDER THIS

When you graduate, what sort of company do you wish to work for? Will its social, ethical and environmental record affect your decision? Are there any companies that you would not wish to work for based on their CSR reputation? As a customer, has the behaviour of a company influenced your purchasing behaviour? Ask some of your friends the same question. How much influence do you think customer buying power has over corporate behaviour?

Investors

Investors are also interested in the social responsibility of business, and engagement by shareholders with issues of social responsibility has grown significantly over the past decade. While shareholders are interested in a financial return on their investment, many do not want that return to come at any cost. Thus, they can influence the behaviour of firms through their decisions on share ownership, either individually by buying shares or institutionally through an investment or pension fund. This is known as **socially responsible investment (SRI)** and it is now a large and growing part of the investment market. It is estimated that, in 2016, €11 trillion of European investment funds had some form of SRI overlay, up from €6.8 trillion in 2012 (EUROSIF, 2016). The UN launched the United Nations Principles for Responsible Investment (UNPRI) in 2006, whereby signatory investment funds agree to integrate social, environmental and good governance principles and practices into their investment decisions and to implement them in the companies in which they invest. It is a labelling scheme for investors, similar to the labelling schemes for consumers. The aim is to provide individual investors with some certainty that their funds will be invested responsibly. At its launch, 100 institutional investment funds, representing US$6.5 trillion in assets, were signed up to the principles. By 2015, there were over 1,200 institutional signatories, representing US$59 trillion in assets (UNPRI, 2015). The FTSE4Good is another example of a labelling scheme for investors.

> **Socially responsible investment (SRI)** – investments made directly, or via a managed fund, in companies that are considered to be socially responsible

There are three ways that SRI influences firm behaviour:

- *Negative screening:* involves eliminating certain products or behaviours from funds. If someone invests in an SRI fund, they might, for example, want to know that their money is not being invested in tobacco or armaments.
- *Positive screening:* involves a fund actively investing in industries or sectors that will make a positive contribution to society, such as green energy or sustainability.
- *Engagement:* SRI funds invest in a range of firms that have not been screened in or out, and work with them to improve their CSR where issues emerge. SRI funds are likely to try and work with a company first but, failing this, might engage in what is termed 'investor activism', where they either table a motion at the company AGM or publicly embarrass the firm into changing its behaviour. An example of this is where four investment funds from the USA and the UK wrote a joint open letter to the chairman of American multinational retailer Walmart's audit committee, stating that it needed to improve its employment practices as they were damaging the share price. This followed a number of embarrassing stories in the media relating to illegal immigrant workers, a class action sex discrimination suit and cuts to employee healthcare benefits (BBC, 2005).

HRM AND ORGANIZATIONAL PERFORMANCE

Does CSR bring financial benefits?

The 'business case' for CSR is often made by those advocating socially responsible behaviour on the basis that intuitively it makes sense. But what does the evidence say about CSR and financial performance? The answer is not straightforward: it is not an easy empirical question to research, the benefits are long term and not easily measurable, and studies that have been carried out often show conflicting results. However, recent meta-analyses (combining previous studies) show that there is a positive relationship, albeit a modest one, between CSR and financial performance, but that irresponsible behaviour has a strong negative impact on share price (c.f. Wood, 2010). We can conclude that it makes financial sense to engage with CSR and it definitely makes sense not to be socially irresponsible. Of course, there is a different question to be considered: should financial performance or ethical values be the basis for taking socially responsible decisions?

THE CASE AGAINST CSR

One of the key arguments of advocates of CSR is that firms can improve their financial performance by improving their social behaviour and so it just makes good business sense to do the right thing. However, critics of CSR, such as Aneel Karnani (2010) and Robert Reich (2008), argue that this is not always the case. Yes, sometimes what is good for the firm and what is good for society will coincide, and in such cases firms can make profits by acting in the public interest. But when these two coincide, why call it corporate social responsibility? If a firm can reduce its electricity bill by investing in energy-saving technology, it makes sense to do it for financial reasons. In other words, managers should do it because it reduces costs and enhances the bottom line. If a firm can develop a new socially beneficial product that consumers want, it should do so to improve long-term value. Reducing costs, improving the bottom line, increasing long-term value and so on are what managers are paid to do. As Karnani (2010) points out, fast-food chains have not introduced healthy salads into their menus because of public health concerns, but because they realized it could increase sales. Similarly, car manufacturers are investing in fuel-efficient cars because consumers are concerned about rising energy costs and want to purchase such vehicles. Reich (2008) argues that retailer Walmart switched to using environmentally friendly packaging because it was cheaper, while coffee chain Starbucks introduced health insurance for its part-time employees to reduce staff turnover. However, 'to credit these corporations with being "socially responsible" is to stretch the term to mean anything a company might do to increase profits if, in doing so, it also happens to have some beneficent impact on the rest of society' (Reich, 2008: 171). As Karnani (2007) posits, when what is good for the firm and what is good for society coincide, then CSR is irrelevant, because firms will do it anyway. Friedman (1970) went so far as to suggest that it was 'approaching fraud' for firms to cloak self-interest in social responsibility.

BUILDING YOUR SKILLS

You have been appointed to the CSR department of a large MNC clothing company. The department is new and the firm currently has no CSR code of conduct for its supply chain, but there have been several stories in the media about poor working conditions in the factories that manufacture clothes your company sells. You have been asked to review the CSR approach of any four competitors and to come up with a list of principles and practices you think your firm should adopt so as to improve working conditions in your supply chain. What would you include on your list?

Of course, of more concern to critics is when profits and the public good do not coincide. In such cases CSR is ineffective. In many instances, doing the right thing does not lead to enhanced profit

or may run counter to the strategic goals of an organization. Research by Van Buren and colleagues (2011) among Australian HR managers found that strategic considerations were trumping employee welfare concerns and ethical considerations. They suggest that 'HRM managers are compromised and face moral dissonance ... [and are] increasingly unable to resist the pull of the organization and its demands for loyalty' (p. 211). In the area of gender inequality, Dickens (1999) has long argued that the 'business case' for gender inequality is contingent on the competitive strategy of the firm. While the 'business case' may be strong for many firms, those operating a cost-minimization strategy may benefit from discriminatory practices or the undervaluation of women's work by the market (McLaughlin and Deakin, 2012). In relation to poverty wages and poor working conditions in the supply chains of leading brands, some would suggest these issues could easily be resolved, but it would lead to lower profits and higher prices. The response to negative publicity is often a supplier code of conduct or independent audits. But critics would argue this is simply public relations spin, or corporate gloss, aimed at deflecting negative media attention, which will do little to improve working conditions. In the case of green issues, this is often referred to as 'greenwashing'. As Klein (2000: 430) notes, codes of conduct are often written by corporate public relations departments in response to negative publicity. Their aim is to 'muzzle the offshore watchdog' of NGOs and labour rights groups, not to bring about changes in working conditions. Few supplier contracts are ever terminated due to breaches of codes of conduct, and where conditions do improve following an inspection, they soon return to where they were previously. Others question the 'independence' of NGOs like the Fair Labor Association that audit big brand companies. Much of its funding comes from these same companies, and thus it is unlikely to be overly critical (Ballinger, 2008). Thus, for critics, CSR is too often about communication and public relations, not action.

Nike is a company that is sometimes held up as an example of how CSR can be effective. It came under intense public scrutiny by labour rights NGOs and trade unions throughout the 1990s for manufacturing its shoes in 'sweatshops'. Its initial response to the criticism was a public relations campaign. However, when the negative publicity did not abate and consumers began boycotting the company, it finally began to seriously address the issues. Indeed, it is now widely acknowledged as one of the CSR leaders in the apparel industry. Vogel

(2006) argues that the Nike code of conduct provides working conditions in countries like Vietnam that are well above the statutory minimum. This, he argues, is evidence that pressure from NGOs and the media is an effective mechanism for raising corporate standards. However, critics would respond that this change only came about after more than a decade of negative publicity and campaigning by NGOs. Moreover, despite significant resources being spent on auditing its supply chain companies, instances of labour rights abuses and poor working conditions continue to emerge (Locke and Romis, 2009). An analysis of more than 800 Nike audits in 51 countries found that the monitoring process has had minimal impact. As the authors of this report noted, voluntary codes of conduct are an ineffective strategy for improving working conditions (Locke et al., 2007). Ballinger (2012) cites an example where an Indonesian union won a $950,000 settlement in court for 4,500 workers who were forced to work seven-day weeks without overtime pay. This was in a factory supplying Nike that had allegedly been monitored by the Fair Labor Association for over 10 years. As Ballinger sardonically notes: 'it's easy to miss 570,000+ unpaid overtime hours, right?' LeBaron and Lister (2016) show how in the case of the collapse of Rana Plaza in 2013 (discussed in HRM and the Global Business Environment on page 278) and the slavery and human trafficking in the Thai prawn industry exposed by *The Guardian* newspaper in 2014, the supply chains had previously been audited and certified by external organizations as being compliant with relevant supply chain standards.

Reich (2008) suggests that people should not be surprised that firms say one thing to divert attention while continuing to engage in practices that drive profits. He describes the past 40 years of global capitalism as a period of 'supercapitalism', in which firms are facing relentless pressure to lower costs. This pressure comes from institutional investment funds that want increased profits and consumers who want lower prices. While there has been some growth in socially responsible investment, this is still not a large enough proportion of the investment market to make a significant impact. As for consumers, while they say they care, this is not reflected in their buying behaviour. In a 2004 EU survey, 75% of respondents said they would change their shopping behaviour in response to the social and environmental performance of firms, but in the same survey, only 3% reported ever having done so (Sachdev, 2006). And the way employees are treated will have more to do with the competitive strategy of the firm than any potential reputational risk. A high-tech company like Google will view its employees as strategic assets, but for firms competing on the basis of low price, employees may be seen as a cost to be minimized and as easily replaceable. Thus, the 'business case' pressures for CSR from employees, investors and consumers are simply not strong enough against the short-term pressure for profits. As Ballinger (2008: 95–6) points out in relation to Nike:

> My research shows that about 75 cents per pair of shoes to the worker would be needed to fix problems that workers have been complaining about since the 1980s. That is roughly 80 per cent more to workers, or $1.80 on a $70 pair of shoes at Foot Locker. If Nike, instead, paid workers 75 cents more per pair of shoes, the cost to Nike would be $210 million a year compared to the much lower CSR cost of less than $20 million.

Voluntary codes of conduct and audits are cheaper than addressing the real issues, which are a business model predicated on cheap labour, a lack of regulation, and weak collective bargaining power ▶Chapter 5◀. Tight deadlines, production quotas, price targets and other aspects of the business model set by the brand actually incentivize manufacturers to breach aspects of the code of conduct, such as long working hours or forced overtime (Steiner and Steiner, 2012).

HRM IN THE NEWS

7-Eleven Australia wages scandal

7-Eleven is one of the world's biggest operators and franchisors of convenience stores, with stores in 18 countries. In Australia it has over 600 stores with a turnover of more than A$3.9 billion, and the owners of the company are reported to be worth around A$1.5 billion. The 'Mission, Vision, Values' pages of the Australian website of 7-Eleven claim that they operate 'at the highest level of ethical standards', they 'act with fairness

iStock.com/gregory_lee

and integrity' and they 'value and respect [their] people and the relationships that define [their] business'. In August 2015 a Four Corners/Fairfax joint investigation into wage practices in 7-Eleven stores in Australia was broadcast on national television. The programme revealed widespread underpayment of wages, mostly of foreign migrant and international student workers, and fabrication of time sheets and payroll records across many of the franchised stores in the country. Many workers were only being paid half the Award (legal) rate, but to avoid detection franchisees entered half the actual hours worked into the payroll system – what came to be termed a 'half pay scam'. Many workers who complained were threatened with deportation for breaching their visa restrictions (working too many hours), and many others did not know what the going Award rate was or what their legal rights were. 7-Eleven Australia head office reacted to the ensuing media storm by claiming it did not condone the underpayment of wages, stepped up compliance checks and increased controls over payroll records, opened an online and hotline process for making claims for underpayment, and instigated an independent panel to review and authorize all claims. The panel was to be headed by Professor Allan Fels, an outspoken critic of 7-Eleven's franchise model.

Fels estimated that most of 7-Eleven's 20,000 workers over the previous ten years had been underpaid by around 50%. For Fels, the problem was not simply one of bad franchisee behaviour, but a business model that was dependent on the underpayment of wages for franchisees to make any sort of profit. It emerged that gross profits

were split such that 7-Eleven Australia took 57%, leaving franchisees only 43% to pay wages, licences, taxation and various overheads. Following the increase in compliance checks by head office, a new form of abuse of workers' pay subsequently emerged, what came to be known as the 'cash back scam'. Workers in a number of stores were paid the full amount of wages into their bank account but were being ordered to pay some of it back in cash. Workers were threatened with losing their jobs and deportation if they did not comply.

While 7-Eleven claimed it was shocked by the behaviour of some of its franchisees who were damaging the reputation of their brand, concerns about underpayment of wages had been raised with them before. A report of the Fair Work Ombudsmen's (FWO's) inquiry into 7-Eleven highlighted claims going back as far as 2008, including audits of numerous stores conducted in 2008 and 2009 showing underpayment of weekend rates and holiday pay, and concerns raised about 'many underpaid workers [being] young international students and particularly vulnerable to exploitation'. Litigation was taken in 2010 against franchisee owners of two stores in Melbourne who were paying staff for only half the hours they worked, and between 2011 and 2014 the FWO began to receive increasing numbers of complaints by individual employees about underpayment of wages. Many of these complainants had contacted 7-Eleven head office but no action had been taken. This led the FWO to conduct an inquiry in mid-2014, which included unannounced store visits to a random sample of 20 stores in some of the major cities. Significant underpayment was found to be taking place in seven stores, and in a further nine there were other violations of employment legislation. The FWO recovered over A$290,000 in unpaid wages through its inquiry. Correspondence from head office to individual complainants revealed by the FWO showed that head office notified franchisees of complaints but did not follow up with the franchisees, and stressed to complainants that head office was not the legal employer and that individuals should take up their complaints with the Fair Work Ombudsmen. The FWO inquiry concluded that there was a 'culture of complicity' at 7-Eleven and that head office 'did not adequately detect or address deliberate non-compliance and as a consequence compounded it'. This was reiterated by a 7-Eleven whistleblower who spoke to the Four Corners/Fairfax investigative team: 'Head office is not just turning a blind eye, it's a fundamental part of their business ... built on something not much different from slavery.'

Since the broadcast of the Four Corners programme, the chairman and CEO have both resigned their positions, the profit-sharing module between head office and franchisees has been modified, there has been an Australian Senate inquiry, and 7-Eleven has paid out more than A$110 million in underpaid wages. The company points to the significant payout it has made as proof of its commitment to reforming the business and repairing its reputation despite not being legally liable, though law changes are in train to increase penalties and to make franchisors responsible in certain circumstances for underpayments by franchisees.

Questions

1. To what extent do you think 7-Eleven Australia has responsibility for the employment practices of its franchisees?
2. What does this case tell you about the effectiveness of the 'business case' for CSR in low margin business models?
3. How do you think this sort of situation can be best avoided?

Sources

Chung, F. and AAP (2016) 'Panel member says "jury is out" on whether 7-Eleven can survive without underpaying staff', News.Com.Au, 13 May, www.news.com.au/finance/business/retail/panel-member-says-jury-is-out-on-whether-7eleven-can-survive-without-underpaying-staff/news-story/8f9545ba197f4b58482d05c260ba5586 (accessed 11 June 2018)

Fair Work Ombudsman (2016) *A Report of the Fair Work Ombudman's Inquiry into 7-Eleven: Identifying and Addressing the Drivers of Non-compliance in the 7-Eleven Network*, Commonwealth of Australia.

Fels, A. (2017) 'Legislation will hand higher penalties for serious contraventions of workplace laws', *The Sydney Morning Herald*, 2 Mar, www.smh.com.au/comment/legislation-will-hand-higher-penalties-for-serious-contraventions-of-workplace-laws-20170301-gunygg.html (accessed 11 June 2018)

Ferguson, A. and Danckert, S. (2015) 'How 7-Eleven is ripping off its workers', *The Sydney Morning Herald*, interactive Four Corners/Fairfax joint investigation online, July, www.smh.com.au/interactive/2015/7-eleven-revealed/ (accessed 11 June 2018)

Harrison, C. (2015) '7-Eleven workers caught in cash-back scam', BYTE, 7 September, www.thebyte.com.au/7-eleven-workers-caught-in-cash-back-scam/ (accessed 11 June 2018)

Patty, A. (2017) '7-Eleven compensation climbs over $110 million', *The Herald*, 14 June, www.theherald.com.au/story/4725373/7-eleven-compensation-climbs-over-110-million/?cs=4219 (accessed 11 June 2018)

A ROLE FOR REGULATION?

If, as critics argue, CSR is an ineffective way of bringing about real reform in working conditions, then CSR could actually be dangerous. It lulls the public into a false sense of security that the issues are being addressed and thus reduces the clamour for government regulation (Reich, 2008; Karnani, 2010). Reich (2008) goes further in arguing that CSR undermines the democratic process. In a CSR model of governance, firms decide what the minimum labour standards are in the factories in which their products are manufactured. He would argue, however, that it is the job of governments in a democratic society to decide what the appropriate standards should be and then for companies to adhere to them. As Reich stated in a debate on CSR with Vogel: 'Without regulation, CSR is whatever you want it to be. Democratic capitalism is meant to put some limits on capitalist organizations in order to deal with the social costs, externalities [a cost or benefit for a third party that is not reflected in the price of a product or service, such as pollution], and side effects of profit accumulation' (Vogel and Reich, 2008).

Given that the legal standards in many of the countries in which leading global brands operate are very low, one way of addressing the concerns of western consumers would be for western governments to pass extraterritorial legislation to make companies legally responsible for labour standards in their supply chains (Reich, 2008). An extraterritorial law passed in the USA, for example, would govern US firms in whichever countries they operated. Such a law would not be based on US minimum wage and labour laws, but would be based on the sorts of standards included in current codes of conduct, such as those in the ETI Base Code. The difference is that the standards would apply to all companies, and breaches of the standards would result in prosecution and penalties for the company concerned, a strong incentive for them to ensure that their supply chain manufacturers adhered to them. Currently, firms decide what standards they wish to apply and the only penalty for breaching these standards is negative publicity.

In an age of liberalization and free markets, the business community is generally opposed to regulation. They see it as being inflexible, bureaucratic and introducing compliance costs. Compliance costs relate to the expenditure of time or money in conforming to regulatory standards, for example keeping detailed records of employee working hours. They also argue that it brings about a 'tick box' response, where firms do the minimum to meet the legal standard, whereas what is required for addressing many CSR issues is real engagement and a change of behaviour. Thus, they see the current CSR approach of voluntary 'self-regulation' and working in cooperation with NGOs and other stakeholders to develop and monitor codes of conducts as the best way forward.

Trade union organizing at the factory level could play an important role in driving up labour standards in supply chains as an alternative to regulation. However, there have been many reports of instances where workers joined or formed trade unions to bargain for higher wages, with the end result being that the supplier contract was cancelled and a cheaper alternative was found (Ballinger, 2008). While the ETI Base Code (see Table 14.1 on page 277) includes freedom of association to join a trade union and engage in collective bargaining, research suggests that only 15% of codes include such provisions, and many western MNCs are accused of being anti-union (Sachdev, 2006).

While the critics of CSR make some valid points about its ineffectiveness, governments seem averse to introducing too much regulation. They have largely accepted the business community line that regulation distorts the market and voluntarism is a better way of bringing about change. Where regulation is introduced, it is often aimed at disclosure of information in order to facilitate pressure for corporate reform from stakeholders such as consumers, investors, employees and NGOs (Deakin et al., 2012). For example, a requirement of the UK Modern Slavery Act 2015 is that companies with an annual turnover of more than £36 million, with any part of their operation in the UK, must publish a 'slavery and human trafficking statement' setting out what steps are being taken to ensure there is no slavery or forced labour in any part of their business or supply chain. This legislation followed reports of slavery and human trafficking in a range of sectors internationally and within the UK over a long period. The ILO (2017) estimates that around 25 million people worldwide are trapped in some form of forced labour. Under the legislation, companies may indicate that no steps are being taken, but it is thought that reputational risk will deter them from this option. The legislation does not, however, make firms responsible for slavery in their supply chains – they cannot be prosecuted. Rather than regulate the behaviour of companies directly, it is trying to encourage 'ethical market forces' to drive corporate behaviour in the right direction. However, as we have seen, the evidence suggests that consumers and investors are unlikely to make a significant impact.

While NGOs and the media play an important role in embarrassing corporations about ethical, social and environmental issues, advocates of regulation argue this is not enough. An interesting development in the Rana Plaza case, following significant public outcry over the building collapse, was a legally binding agreement signed between trade unions and apparel brands called the 'Accord on Fire and Building Safety in Bangladesh'. Over 200 international companies who have clothes manufactured for them in Bangladesh, covering more than 1,600 factories and 2 million workers, have voluntarily signed up to be legally bound by the Accord (http://bangladeshaccord.org/). Finally, the proposed change of law in Australia in reaction to the 7-Eleven scandal, where companies will be held accountable for the behaviour of their subsidiaries or franchisees in certain circumstances, shows that sometimes governments will act in response to poor employment practices.

Critics of CSR are not opposed to firms taking positive action to major social issues and improving working conditions in their firms or supply chains. Most see businesses as having an important role to play. Rather, they are opposed to CSR acting as a substitute for regulation, and some see CSR as being largely about pre-empting government regulation. Handy (2002: 55), in his promotion of a stakeholder view of the firm, finishes up by imploring business to be more ethical, otherwise 'democratic pressures may force governments to shackle corporations'. For Handy, regulation is bad. Richard Locke (2013) holds a different view. He has conducted one of the most thorough studies of employment conditions in supply chains, gaining access to companies such as Nike, HP and others. He highlights the positive role that companies committed to CSR can play. However, he concludes that voluntary approaches to improving labour standards (what he calls private power) can only go so far, and that a mixture of CSR and government regulation is needed to improve working conditions.

SPOTLIGHT ON SKILLS

Integra is a digital content services company headquartered in Pondicherry, India, which works with Publishers and Corporates (Learning & Development teams) offering content and eLearning solutions, globally. The company takes great pride in being a socially responsible organization and in its treatment of employees, including initiatives for women's empowerment and health and wellness.

To address wider social issues, the founders of Integra also set up the Sriram Charitable Trust.

Visit **www.macmillanihe.com/carbery-cross-hrm-2e** to watch the founders of Integra, Sriram Subramanya and Anu Sriram, talking about corporate social responsibility and their advice on working in this field.

SUMMARY

This chapter has explored some of the HRM issues that come under the CSR umbrella. We have also looked at why CSR has become such an important business issue and examined some of the ethical and financial reasons why firms choose to engage in CSR. However, as we have seen, CSR is not universally acclaimed. While many critics of CSR share the social and environmental aims of its advocates, they have significant doubts that these aims can be achieved through a purely voluntarist approach. Relying on consumers, employees, investors and civil society organizations to change corporate behaviour is not an effective way of addressing the social and environmental issues of our time. In particular, they highlight the inevitable tension between making profits and addressing social and environmental issues, and their argument is that profits will trump CSR. For critics, it is the job of government to set the standards society expects, not corporations. Given the reluctance of governments to increase regulation, CSR will continue to be a mainstream business issue that most large businesses need to integrate into their corporate strategy.

CHAPTER REVIEW QUESTIONS

1. Explain the various definitions of CSR and find some examples on the internet of companies that illustrate the approaches. Which approach to CSR do you think is best and why?
2. Explain the difference between the shareholder and stakeholder views of the firm. Which do you think is the most appropriate in the current economic climate? Justify your decision.
3. Outline the 'business case' arguments for CSR and evaluate how effective this approach is.
4. Outline the arguments of the critics of CSR and evaluate how convincing their arguments are.
5. To what extent do you think CSR is a real attempt on the part of companies to grapple with important social, ethical and environmental issues, as opposed to window dressing designed to appeal to consumer idealism and pre-empt government regulation?
6. Which do you think will be more effective at aligning corporate behaviour with the interests of society, the 'carrot' of the business case or the 'stick' of regulation?
7. Search the internet for examples of MNCs that have been criticized by NGOs or other pressure groups about the employment practices in their supply chains. Now look at the CSR pages of the websites of these companies. Contrast what the companies say they are doing with some of the criticisms raised.

FURTHER READING

Blowfield, M. and Murray, A. (2014) *Corporate Responsibility,* 3rd edn, Oxford: Oxford University Press.

Crane, A. and Matten, D. (2015) *Business Ethics: Managing Corporate Citizenship and Sustainability in the Age of Globalization*, Oxford: Oxford University Press.

Locke, R. (2013) *The Promise and Limits of Private Power*, Cambridge: Cambridge University Press.

Reich, R. (2008) *Supercapitalism: The Battle for Democracy in an Age of Big Business,* Cambridge: Icon Books.

Steiner, J. and Steiner, G. (2012) *Business, Government, and Society: A Managerial Perspective, Text and Cases,* 13th edn, New York: McGraw-Hill.

USEFUL WEBSITES

www.fairlabor.org

The Fair Labor Association is one of the leading international organizations working with MNCs to monitor and improve working conditions in supply chain factories. It is an affiliation of NGOs, universities and CSR-minded companies. The website provides information on the companies it works with and sets out the Fair Labor Association code of conduct.

www.somo.nl/results-of-the-makeitfair-project

The makeITfair project provided information on working conditions and environmental issues in the electronics industry.

www.tescopoly.org.uk

This website is run by an alliance of various community groups critical of the power of all the leading UK supermarkets.

www.bitc.org.uk

Business in the Community is a business membership organization that promotes CSR. The website contains reports and information on a range of CSR issues. It also has case studies of best practice CSR. The Irish website is www.bitc.ie. BITC is active in campaigning on gender (gender.bitc.org.uk/about-opportunity-now/campaign-aims) and diversity (diversity.bitc.org.uk) in the workplace.

bangladeshaccord.org

This is the website of the Accord on Fire and Building Safety in Bangladesh. The Accord is a legally binding agreement signed between trade unions and international brands in the clothing sector. It is witnessed by a number of international NGOs and chaired by the ILO.

For extra resources, including videos, multiple choice questions and useful weblinks, go to: www.macmillanihe.com/carbery-cross-hrm-2e.

Glossary

Accident – an unplanned or unforeseen event that could lead to injury to people, damage to plant or machinery, or some other loss

Action planning is the stage in the human resource planning cycle where the organization makes a specific plan regarding how best to use the workforce to help meet the strategic goals of the firm

Advanced HR practices – people management practices which are strategic or progressive in nature

Agency worker – a worker with a contract of employment or an employment relationship with a temporary work agency with a view to being assigned to another organization to work under its supervision

Analytical methods – they identify characteristics of the job that are valued by the organization and assess the degree to which they are present in the job

Attitude-based approach – focuses on changing a person's feelings and inner thoughts towards safety

Authentic career – a career characterized by consistency between an individual's public and private beliefs

Base pay – hourly, weekly or monthly amount paid to an employee if they conform to the terms of their contract

Behavioural science approach – how to describe, explain and predict human behaviour in a work context

Behaviour-based approach – focuses on what people do, analyses why they do it, and then applies a research-supported intervention strategy to improve what people do

Behaviourism – semi-permanent change in behaviour resulting from the application of positive and negative reinforcements

Boundaryless career – sequences of jobs that can cross occupational, organizational and geographic boundaries

Buddy approach – an informal approach to assisting a new employee to learn about the organization and how things work around or within the organization

Bullying – inappropriate behaviour at work that repeatedly undermines an employee's right to dignity and causes that employee to become subject to high stress

Capitalist system – an economic system of private enterprise for profit

Career – a person's work experiences over the course of their life

Career capital – the skills that differentiate a person's portfolio of job, industry and networking knowledge and abilities

Career development – how a person manages their life, learning and work to achieve career goals

Causal factors are determinants. For example, education is a causal factor in employability, such that higher levels of education are determinants of greater job opportunities for individuals

Cognitivism – the process of absorbing, storing and retrieving learning in the brain through the creation, amendment and structuring of mental schemas

Collective bargaining – negotiations between an employer/group of employers and one or more workers' organizations to determine terms and conditions of employment and to regulate relations between employers and workers

Common law – law developed by judges through decisions made in courts and similar tribunals

Comparator – a person or group that someone making a claim of discrimination will compare themselves to, with the purpose of demonstrating that they have been treated differently/unfairly using that comparator as a standard

Competencies – the behavioural characteristics of an individual that are related to their effective performance in a role

Competency-based interviews – these interviews are structured around job-specific competencies that require interviewees to describe specific tasks or situations. They work on the belief that the best indication of future behaviour is past behaviour

GLOSSARY

Corporate social responsibility (CSR) – the duty of a business to go beyond profit maximization and act responsibly and contribute positively to society

Country of origin effects – the influence the country from which the MNC originates has on HRM in its foreign subsidiaries

Development – a range of activities leading to the gradual unfolding or growth of an individual and the enhancement of knowledge, skills and experiences over the long term

Devolved – the process of moving decision-making downwards, from HR to line managers

Direct discrimination – discrimination that is obviously contrary to the terms of equality legislation, such as explicitly excluding people over 50 from applying for a job

Direct pay – the financial element of the reward package received by the employee in the form of cash, cheque or direct deposit

Disciplinary procedure – a written step-by-step process that an organization uses when an employee has broken the organization's rules. Disciplinary procedures can lead to penalties, such as warnings, with the aim of changing an employee's performance/behaviour. In a severe breach of rules, an employee may be dismissed

Discrimination – treating a person or group differently and unfairly on the basis of certain traits or characteristics, such as sexuality, gender, race, religion or disability

Diversity management perspective – the diversity management perspective holds that organizations should recognize difference as a positive organizational factor and should foster, value and utilize this difference for the benefit of the organization

Dominance effects – the influence that dominant economies, like the USA, have on HRM in MNCs, regardless of where they are from or located

E-recruitment – a vacancy is advertised to potential candidates via the internet. It can target internal and/or external recruits

Education – the acquisition of knowledge, skills and experience through a period of sustained study, often leading to a qualification

Employability – being capable of getting and keeping fulfilling work

Employee burnout – this is the opposite to engagement, where the employee disengages and withdraws from work due to emotional and/or physical exhaustion

Employee engagement is a broader concept than work engagement insofar as it includes not just the relationship of the employee to their work but also their relationship with the organization itself

Employee engagement surveys – research carried out to assess the feelings of a target group of employees towards various aspects of their work, their team and their organization

Employee turnover – the number of people who leave an organization and need to be replaced in order to maintain production or service

Employee wellbeing – the overall quality of an employee's experience at work

Employer brand – an organization is recognized in its own right as a desirable place to work – positive employer brand – by the internal and external labour market

Empowerment – entrusting employees to take responsibility for their health, safety and wellbeing by giving them the right skills, and encouraging them to get involved in making decisions

Engagement – the energy, enjoyment and enthusiasm that employees exhibit towards their work

Equality – the state of being equal, especially in status, rights or opportunities

Ergonomics – the relationship between employees, physical work equipment and the environment; it focuses on matching people capabilities to their work environment and includes such things as correct working height and correct viewing distance

Evaluation – establishing the intended and unintended outcomes of learning and development activities and assessing whether the benefits justify the investment

Expatriates – also known as 'international assignees', they are employees who undertake international assignments

Expatriation – the process of transferring an employee to other international operations of the MNC to carry out a particular assignment

Experiential learning – the cyclical process of making meaning through reflection and experience

External comparison – the amount or range of pay for each job based on an examination of the pay practices of competitors

External recruitment – a vacancy is advertised to potential candidates outside the existing employee base in the organization

GLOSSARY

Feedback – information (positive and negative) on how an employee performs

Felt-fair – trust-inducing pay systems that are accepted by employees because differences in pay are based on a fair assessment of job characteristics

Flexible benefits – from a defined set of available benefits, employees select the benefits that best meet their needs

Forecasting is the stage of the human resource planning cycle where the organization must predict the demand for and supply of labour in order to meet the strategic goals of the firm

General strike – a strike by workers across many industries usually in protest against a government policy or action

'Gig' jobs – where someone is paid to complete a task, also called a 'gig', for an organization which has outsourced work and does not want to create a long-term employment relationship. An online platform acts as the intermediary between the worker and the organization

Globalization – the opening up of national markets and the creation of a global economy through the deregulation of trade, growth in foreign direct investment (FDI), movement of people and capital, and advances in information technology

Green HRM – the role of HRM in driving the environmental strategy and activities of an organization

Grievance procedure – a written step-by-step process an employee must follow to voice a complaint in an organization. The formal complaint moves from one level of authority in the organization to the next higher level if unresolved

Hazards – any source of potential damage, harm or adverse health effects on something or someone under certain conditions at work

High-commitment HRM – this approach is another way of looking at high-involvement HRM. It refers to an organization's effort to create the right conditions through which employees can be highly involved, but it also stresses the employees' role in fully engaging in this process and working hard to achieve the organization's goals

High-involvement HRM – this approach to the employment relationship encourages high levels of employee participation or 'voice' in the decisions that the organization has to make. As such, HR practice and management style seek participation and consultation through a range of formal and informal activities: weekly team meetings, project reviews, employee surveys, etc.

HIPOs/stars are those employees who are currently achieving a high level of performance and have the potential to make a key contribution to the strategic development of the firm

Horizontal integration involves strong consistency and interconnection between HRM policies and practices internally in order to achieve effective performance. This is also known as 'internal alignment' or 'internal fit'

Host country effects – the influence the country in which a foreign subsidiary is located has on HRM in that subsidiary

HR philosophy – the principles that guide how the organization leads, manages, involves, treats and views all its employees, so that it can successfully achieve its business strategy

Human capital pool – the collection of employee skill that exists within a firm at any given time

Human error – a human decision or behaviour that has undesirable effects

Human factors – how characteristics of the organization affect employee behaviour

Human resource (HR) analytics – the use of people-related data in analytical processes to address business issues

Human resource development (HRD) – the provision of learning, development and training opportunities to improve individual, team, organizational and societal effectiveness

Human resource information system (HRIS) – a software system for data entry, tracking and information needs of the HR function

Human resource management – the strategic and integrated approach taken by an organization to the management of its most valued assets, namely its people

Indirect discrimination – this occurs when a seemingly neutral provision attached to a job acts to exclude a person or group protected under equality legislation; for example, a requirement for people to be over 2m tall for a job in a shop would effectively exclude more women than men

Indirect pay or benefits – these have a financial value but are rewarded to employees in forms other than cash

Induction – the whole process whereby new employees in an organization adjust to their new roles and responsibilities within a new working environment

Industrial relations – the relationship between employers and employees, with a focus on those areas of the employment relationship where employers deal with employee representatives, such as trade unions, rather than individuals

Inferential statistics make predictions about a population (e.g. employees within an organization) based on a sample of that population (e.g. a cross-section of employees in an organization); whereas descriptive statistics provide descriptions of a population

Informational approach – this approach to induction focuses on supplying new starters with basic information regarding the working of procedures within the organization

Institutional barriers – those barriers to employment or progression within employment posed by existing structures, systems and rules, which act to exclude certain groups of people, for example a lack of childcare facilities

Internal alignment – the hierarchy of the relative value of jobs within an organization

Internal recruitment – a vacancy is advertised to potential candidates from within the existing employee base in the organization

International integration – how strongly integrated all the MNC's international operations are with each other

International recruitment – a vacancy is advertised to potential candidates who are currently residing overseas

Job analysis – the process used to gather detailed information about the various tasks and responsibilities involved in a position. Through this process, the knowledge, skills, abilities, attitudes and behaviours associated with successful performance in the role are also identified

Job description – the detailed breakdown of the purpose of the role and the various tasks and responsibilities involved in a particular job

Job evaluation – a technique used by organizations to establish the relative worth of jobs

Kaleidoscope career – a career that adjusts to changes in an individual's circumstances and motivation

Key performers are those employees who are currently achieving a high level of performance but have little potential to make a key contribution to the strategic development of the firm

Knowledge worker – an employee whose job involves developing and using knowledge rather than producing goods or services

Learning – a range of formal, informal or incidental activities leading to a semi-permanent or permanent change in behaviour which can contribute to individual, team, organizational and societal effectiveness

Line managers – managers who have employees directly reporting to them and who have a higher level of responsibility than those employees

Longitudinal study is a research study that involves repeated observations of the same variables (e.g. people) over long periods of time

Low-involvement HRM – this approach to the employment relationship is more control-based, where employees are identified as being core or peripheral in achieving the organization's goals. Peripheral employees are then managed through such HR practices as zero hours contracts, temporary contracts, vendored employment and outsourcing elements of the supply chain

Mental workload – the mental demands placed on humans at work

Mentee – the employee who is mentored by a more senior employee within the organization

Mentor – a more senior or experienced employee who acts as a role model for the employee, supporting their personal and professional development

Mentoring is the voluntary and informal exchange of career and psychosocial support

Mentoring process – a developmental process focused on the personal and professional development of the mentee

Non-analytical methods – whole jobs are compared to determine the organization's internal pay structure

Nonfinancial rewards – a wide array of HR policies and practices designed to support employees both in their lives and in their careers

Nongovernmental organizations (NGOs) – organizations that are independent of government and generally run on a not-for-profit basis. Examples include Greenpeace, Friends of the Earth, Oxfam, the Fair Labor Association and the Institute for Global Labour and Human Rights

Off-ramp career – a non-traditional career path that recognizes that individuals, usually women, will take some time out from their careers

Onboarding – the mechanism through which new employees acquire the necessary knowledge, skills and behaviours to become effective organizational members and insiders

Organizational citizenship behaviours – the behaviour of individual employees that is not directly or explicitly required by an organization as part of the role but which promotes the effective functioning of the organization

Organizational fit – the 'fit' or alignment of the personal values and work ethic of the employee with those of the organization's culture and values

GLOSSARY

Performance appraisal usually consists of an interview that takes place between employees and their managers to review the employees' performance, and set future goals which can be used to make reward, promotion and development decisions

Performance management is concerned with establishing and measuring employee goals in order to improve individual and organizational performance

Performance-related pay (PRP) – a form of direct pay linked to the performance of an individual, team or all employees when predefined objectives are achieved

Person–job fit – the extent to which the enthusiasm, knowledge, skills, abilities and motivations of the individual match those required by the job

Person–organization fit – the extent to which the values, interests and behaviours of the individual match the organizational culture

Person specification – specifies the type of person needed to do a particular job. It essentially translates the job description into human terms

Philanthropy – the practice of making charitable donations to good causes

Portfolio career – a career that involves doing two or more different jobs for different employers

Positive action – measures undertaken with the aim of achieving full and effective equality for members of groups that are socially or economically disadvantaged

Positive discrimination – preferential discriminatory treatment of a minority group over a majority group to try and counter disadvantage in the labour market

Protean career – a career defined by uniquely individual psychological success which can mean personal accomplishment, feelings of pride, achievement or family happiness

Protected grounds – those identified by national institutions as relating to areas where discrimination has or is likely to occur, such as race, sex, sexual orientation, religion, age and disability, and which are subsequently covered by equality legislation

Psychological contract – the unwritten rules and expectations that exist between the employee and employer

Pull factors – those factors beyond the control of the organization that may cause an employee to leave – such as moving to a new location/country, the arrival of children, retirement and so on

Push factors – those factors that negatively impact on an employee and may be the trigger to start them thinking about leaving an organization, such as dissatisfaction with their work, their boss or their promotional opportunities, a lack of developmental opportunities and so on

Relational approach – this approach to induction focuses on helping new starters rapidly establish a broad network of relationships with co-workers from whom they can access the information they need to be productive members of the team

Relational psychological contract – a situation where job security is provided in exchange for commitment and loyalty to the organization

Reliability – a method is identified as reliable if it consistently measures what it sets out to measure

Repatriation – the process that involves bringing the expatriate back to their home country after completing their international assignment

Retention – a strategic approach adopted by organizations to keep productive employees from seeking alternative employment

Reward package – the financial and nonfinancial elements offered to an employee in return for labour

Reward system – the combination of financial and nonfinancial elements used by an organization to compensate employees for their time, effort and commitment at work

Risk – a situation involving exposure to danger

Safety culture – the attitudes, beliefs, perceptions and values that employees share in relation to safety

Selection – a process used to find the candidate who most closely matches the specific requirements of a vacant position

Self-efficacy – self-confidence in one's ability to perform

Shareholder view of the firm – the primary objective of management should be to maximize profit for shareholders

Shortlisting – a sifting process where those candidates who most closely match the predetermined job-specific requirements are separated out from all other applicants

Shortlisting matrix – a scoring mechanism for placing the candidates who have applied for the position in a ranking order based on their suitability for the role

Social contract – an implicit agreement between business and society that sets out the broad standards that business should adhere to and duties it should fulfil in order to maintain the support and legitimacy of society. These standards are partly reflected in law but are mostly contained in social norms, values and expectations

GLOSSARY

Social inclusion – a measure of the extent to which a person or groups can participate in aspects of society to the same level as (or relative to) the average population. Key measures of social inclusion are access to work, adequate housing, education levels and access to education, healthcare and so on

Social justice approach – the social justice case for equality holds that organizations have a moral and legal obligation, regardless of profit, to recognize diversity and to develop policies and procedures to ensure that people are treated in a fair and equitable manner in all facets of the business

Socially responsible investment (SRI) – investments made directly, or via a managed fund, in companies that are considered to be socially responsible

Stakeholders – any individuals, groups or organizations that are affected by or can affect the actions of a company

Stakeholder view of the firm – management should take the interests of all stakeholders into account when making decisions

Stocktaking is the stage of the human resource planning cycle where the organization must identify a range of factors currently impacting its operations

Strategic human resource development – learning activities focused on individuals, teams and organizations and aimed at enhancing the alignment of human resources with the strategic goals of the organization

Strategic human resource management – where HR is coordinated and consistent with the overall business objectives, goals and strategy in order to increase business performance

Strategic performance management focuses on aligning individual goals with the goals of the organization to achieve a competitive advantage in the marketplace

Stress – the demands of the work environment and the ability of the employee to meet these demands

Strike – a work stoppage caused by the refusal of employees to work, in order to persuade an employer to concede to their demands

Survival curve – a model stating that new starters in an organization are more at risk of leaving in the first six weeks of commencing a new job. The likelihood of leaving decreases as the length of employment increases

Sustainable HRM – the role of HRM in driving the social and environmental strategy and activities of an organization. It also includes the ethical treatment of people who work for an organization and who are affected by the HR practices of an organization

Tangible benefits – benefits for the business that can be measured and reported on; HR must understand the business and be able to demonstrate how its work contributes to the organization's competitiveness and ultimate success.

Taylorist – a factory management system developed in the late nineteenth century to increase efficiency by breaking down production into specialized repetitive tasks

The learning organization – an organization focused on building a learning culture and integrating learning across all levels, systems and employees of the organization

Trade unions – an organized group of workers which represents members' interests in maintaining or improving the conditions of their employment by acting collectively as a way to challenge employer power

Traditional career – a direct line of career progression where seniority and length of service are rewarded with progression from one specific job to a more senior job

Training – the process of acquiring the knowledge, skills and attitudes required to perform a role effectively

Transactional psychological contract – a situation where extra money and learning and development opportunities are provided in exchange for commitment and loyalty to the organization

Underperformers are those employees who are currently not achieving a high level of performance and have little potential to make a key contribution to the strategic development of the firm

Union density – the proportion of a country's employees who are union members

Untapped potentials are those employees who are currently not achieving a high level of performance but with the necessary changes have the potential to make a key contribution to the strategic development of the firm

Validity – the extent to which a selection method measures what it purports to measure and how well it does this

GLOSSARY

Variable – a thing (a phenomenon or element) that is liable to vary, or change

Vertical integration – the matching of HRM policies and practices with business strategy – also referred to as 'external alignment' or 'external fit'

Victimizing – an act that treats someone unfairly

Work capacity – how much physical work an individual can do

Work engagement describes the level an individual is prepared to invest of themselves in their work and/or task at hand

Workforce planning is the process through which an organization ensures it has the right number of people with the right skills in the right roles both now and for the future

Working days lost – a measure of strike activity, calculated by multiplying the number of persons involved by the number of normal working days during which they were involved in the dispute

Works councils – bodies which provide employee representation in a workplace. They are not trade union bodies but trade unions can be influential in them. Works councils can mean employees have significant powers of decision-making within a workplace

Zero-hours contract – when a worker is not given any guaranteed hours of work by an employer

Bibliography

ABC News (2017) 'Oscar-winning actress Viola Davis says she struggles with "impostor" syndrome', 28 February. Available at https://abcnews.go.com/Entertainment/oscar-winning-actress-viola-davis-struggles-impostor-syndrome/story?id=45789758 (accessed 15 April 2018).

ACAS (2015) 'Bullying and harrassment'. Available at www.acas.org.uk/index.aspx?articleid=1864 (accessed 11 June 2018).

Accenture (2017) 'Getting to equal 2017'. Available at www.accenture.com/_acnmedia/PDF-45/Accenture-IWD-2017-Research-Getting-To-Equal.pdf (accessed 28 September 2018).

Adams, J.S. (1963) 'Toward an understanding of inequity', *Journal of Abnormal and Social Psychology*, 67(5), 422–36.

Adams, K., Nyuur, R.B., Ellis, F.Y. and Debrah, Y.A. (2017) 'South African MNCs' HRM systems and practices at the subsidiary level: insights from subsidiaries in Ghana', *Journal of International Management*, 23(2), 180–93.

Adler, S., Campion M., Colquitt, A. et al. (2016) 'Getting rid of performance ratings: Genius or folly? A debate', *Industrial and Organizational Psychology: Perspectives on Science and Practice*, 9(2), 219–52.

AFL-CIO (2017) 'Executive Paywatch'. Available at https://aflcio.org/paywatch (accessed 12 December 2017).

Aguinis, H. and Kraiger, K. (2009) 'Benefits of training and development for individuals and teams, organizations, and society', *Annual Review of Psychology*, 60, 451–74.

Aitkenhead, D. (2014, May 24) Lord Browne: 'I thought being gay was basically worng'. *The Guardian*. Retrieved form https://www.the gruardian.com.

Al Ariss, A., Cascio, W.F. and Paauwe, J. (2014) 'Talent management: current theories and future research directions', *Journal of World Business*, 49(2), 173-9.

Alfes, K., Shantz, A.D., Truss, C. and Soane, E.C. (2013) 'The link between perceived human resource management practices, engagement and employee behaviour: a moderated mediation model', *International Journal of Human Resource Management*, 24(2), 330–51.

Allpass v. Mooikloof Estates (Pty) Ltd t/a Mooikloof Equestrian Centre (JS178/09) [2011] ZALCJHB 7 (16 February 2011).

Al-Mahmood, S.Z., Burke, J. and Smithers, R. (2013) 'Dhaka: many dead as garment factory building that supplied west collapses', *The Guardian*, 25 April. Available at www.theguardian.com/world/2013/apr/24/bangladesh-building-collapse-shops-west (accessed 15 April 2018).

American Psychological Association (2015) *Stress in America: Paying with our Health*, Washington, DC: APA.

Anderson, L. and Wilson, S. (1997) 'Critical incident technique' in D.L. Whetzel and G.R. Wheaton (eds) *Applied Measurement Methods in Industrial Psychology*, Palo Alto, CA: Davis-Black, pp. 89–112.

Andreassen, C.S., Ursin, H. and Eriksen, H.R. (2007) 'The relationship between strong motivation to work, "workaholism", and health"', *Psychology and Health*, 22(5), 615–29.

Angrave, D., Charlwood, A., Kirkpatrick, I. et al. (2016) 'HR and analytics: why HR is set to fail the big data challenge', *Human Resource Management Journal*, 26(1), 1–11.

Anker R. (2001) 'Theories of occupational segregation by sex', in M.F. Loutfi (ed.) *Women, Gender and Work*, Geneva: ILO.

Appelbaum, E., Bailey, T., Berg, P. and Kalleberg, A. (2000) *Manufacturing Advantage: Why High-Performance Work Systems Pay Off*, London: ILR Press.

Armstrong, C., Flood, P.C., Guthrie, J.P. et al. (2010) 'The impact of diversity and equality management on firm performance: beyond high performance work systems', *Human Resource Management*, 49(6), 977–98.

Armstrong, M. (2003) *A Handbook of Human Resource Management Practice*, 9th edn, London: Kogan Page.

Armstrong, M. (2006a) *A Handbook of Human Resource Practice*, 10th edn, London: Kogan Page.

Armstrong, M. (2006b) *Performance Management: Key Strategies and Practical Guidelines*, 3rd edn, London: Kogan Page.

Armstrong, M. (2009) 'The process of performance management', in M.A. Armstrong, *Handbook of Human Resource Management Practice*, pp. 617–38.

Armstrong, M. (2015) *Armstrong's Handbook of Reward Management Practice*, 5th edn, London: Kogan Page.

Armstrong, M. and Baron, A. (2005) *Managing Performance: Performance Management in Action*, London: CIPD.

Armstrong, M. and Taylor, S. (2017) *Armstrong's Handbook of Human Resource Management Practice*, 14th edn, London: Kogan Page.

Arnold, J., Randall, R., Patterson, F. et al. (2010) *Work Psychology: Understanding Human Behaviour in the Workplace*, 5th edn, Harlow: Financial Times/Prentice Hall.

Aronsson, G., Gustafsson, K. and Mellner, C. (2011) 'Sickness presence, sickness absence, and self-reported health and symptoms', *International Journal of Workplace Health Management*, 4(3), 228–43.

Arthur, J.B. (1994) 'Effects of human resource systems on manufacturing performance and turnover', *Academy of Management Journal*, 37(3), 670–88.

300

BIBLIOGRAPHY

Arthur, M.B and Rousseau, D. (1996) *The Boundaryless Career: A New Employment Principle for a New Organizational Era*, Oxford: Oxford University Press.

Arthur, M.B., Hall, D.T. and Lawrence, B.S. (1989) *Handbook of Career Theory*, Cambridge: Cambridge University Press.

Arthur, M.B., Inkson, K. and Pringle, J.K. (1999) *The New Careers: Individual Action and Economic Change*, Thousand Oaks, CA: Sage.

Arvey R.D. (1979) 'Unfair discrimination in the employment interview: legal and psychological aspects', *Psychological Bulletin*, 86(4), 736–65.

Asante-Muhammad, D., Collins, C., Hoxie, J. and Nieves, E. (2016) *The Ever-Growing Gap: Without Change, African-American and Latino Families Won't Match White Wealth for Centuries*, Institute for Policy Studies. Available at www.ips-dc.org/report-ever-growing-gap/ (accessed 11 December 2017).

Asante-Muhammad, D., Collins, C., Hoxie, J. and Nieves, E. (2017) *The Road to Zero Wealth: How the Racial Wealth Divide is Hollowing out America's Middle Class*, Institute for Policy Studies. Available at www.ips-dc.org/wp-content/uploads/2017/09/The-Road-to-Zero-Wealth_FINAL.pdf (accessed 11 December 2017).

Aschenbrenner, K.M. and Biehl, B. (1994) 'Improved safety through improved technical measures?' Empirical studies regarding risk compensation processes in relation to anti-lock braking systems', in R.M. Trimpop and G.J. Wilde (eds) *Challenges to Accident Prevention. The Issue of Risk Compensation Behaviour*, Groningen: Styx.

Australian Bureau of Statistics. (2015) *Disability and Labour Force Participation, 2012*. http://www.abs.gov.au/ausstats/abs@.nsf/mf/4433.0.55.006.

Badgett, M.V., Durso, L.E., Kastanis A. and Mallory, C. (2013) *The Business Impact of LGBT-Supportive Workplace Policies*, Los Angeles, CA: Williams Institute.

Baker, T. and Aldrich, H.E. (1996) 'Prometheus stretches: building identity and cumulative knowledge in multiemployer careers', in M.B. Arthur and D.M. Rousseau (eds) *The Boundaryless Career: A New Employment Principle for a New Organizational Era*, Oxford: Oxford University Press, pp. 132–49.

Bakker, A.B., Demerouti, E. and Euwema, M.C. (2005) 'Job resources buffer the impact of job demands on burnout', *Journal of Occupational Health Psychology*, 10(2), 170.

Bakker, A.B., Demerouti, E. and Xanthopoulou, D. (2012) 'How do engaged employees stay engaged', *Ciencia & Trabajo*, 14, 15–21.

Ballinger, J. (2008) 'No sweat? Corporate social responsibility and the dilemma of anti-sweatshop activism', *New Labor Forum*, 17(2), 91–8.

Ballinger, J. (2012) 'State of the Apple (rotten)', *Counterpunch*, 26 January.

Bamat, J. (2017) 'French candidates divided on future of 35-hour work week', *France 24*, 14 April. Available at www.france24.com/en/20170413-french-presidential-candidates-divided-35-hour-week-economy-employment (accessed 15 April 2018).

Bamber, G.J. and Lansbury, R.D. (1998) *International and Comparative Employment Relations*, London: Sage.

Baptiste, N.R. (2008) 'Tightening the link between employee wellbeing at work and performance: a new dimension of HRM', *Management Decision*, 46(2), 284–309.

Barber, A.E. (1998) *Recruiting Employees: Individual and Organizational Perspectives*, Thousand Oaks, CA: Sage

Barney, J. (1991) 'Firm resources and sustained competitive advantage', *Journal of Management*, 17(1), 99–120.

Baron, J.D. and Cobb-Clark, D.A. (2010) 'Occupational segregation and the gender wage gap in private- and public-sector employment: a distributional analysis', *Economic Record*, 86(273), 227–46.

Barrie, D.S. and Paulson, B.C. (1991) *Professional Construction Management*, New York: McGraw-Hill.

Bartlett, C. and Ghoshal, S. (2002) 'Building competitive advantage through people', *MIT Sloan Management Review*, 43(2), 34–41.

Barton, D. (2011) 'Capitalism for the long term', *Harvard Business Review*, 89(3), 84–91.

Baruch, Y. (1999) 'Integrated career systems for the 2000s', *International Journal of Manpower*, 20(7), 432–57.

Baruch, Y. and Peiperl, M.A. (2003) 'An empirical assessment of Sonnenfeld's career systems typology', *International Journal of Human Resource Management*, 14(7), 1267–83.

Bassi, L. (2011) 'Raging debates in HR analytics', *People and Strategy*, 34(2), 14.

Battaglio, R.P. (2015) *Public Human Resource Management: Strategies and Practices in the 21st Century*, Thousand Oaks, CA: CQ Press.

Bauer, Talya & Erdogan, Berrin. (2011). 'Organizational socialization: The effective onboarding of new employees', *APA handbook of industrial and organizational psychology*. 3. 51–64. 10.1037/12171-002.

Bazerman, M.H. and Tenbrunsel, A.E. (2011) 'Ethical breakdowns', *Harvard Business Review*, 89(4), 58–65.

BBC (2005) 'Wal-Mart urged to "clean up act"', 3 June. Available at http://news.bbc.co.uk/2/hi/business/4605733.stm (accessed 12 December 2017).

BBC News (2016) 'French workers get "right to disconnect" from emails out of hours', 31 December. Available at www.bbc.com/news/world-europe-38479439 (accessed 15 April 2018).

Becker, B. and Gerhart, B. (1996) 'The impact of human resource management on organizational performance: progress and prospects', *Academy of Management Journal*, 39(4), 779–801.

Bee, F. and Bee R. (2003) *Learning Needs: Analysis and Evaluation*, 2nd edn, London: CIPD.

Beer, M., Spector, B., Lawrence, P.R. et al. (1984) *Managing Human Assets*, New York: Free Press.

Belkin, L.Y., Becker, W.J. and Conroy, S.A. (2016) 'Exhausted, but unable to disconnect: after-hours email, work-family balance and identification', *Academy of Management Proceedings*, 1, 10353.

Bell, M.P. (2007) *Diversity in Organizations*, Mason, OH: South-Western.

BIBLIOGRAPHY

Bendl, R, Bleijenjbergh, I., Henttnonen, E, and Mills A. (2016) *The Oxford Handbook of Diversity in Organizations*, Oxford: Oxford University Press.

Benko, C. and Weisberg, A. (2007) *Mass Career Customization: Aligning the Workplace with Today's Non-traditional Workforce*, Boston, MA: Harvard Business Press.

Berg, P., Bosch, G. and Charest, J. (2014) 'Working-time configurations: a framework for analyzing diversity across countries', *ILR Review*, 67(3), 805–37.

Bersin, J. (2012) 'Big data in HR: building a competitive talent analytics function – the four stages of maturity', Bersin by Deloitte. Available at www.bersin.com/Practice/Detail.aspx?docid=15430&mode=search&p=Human-Resources (accessed 28 March 2017).

Bersin, J. (2015) 'The geeks arrive in HR: people analytics is here', *Forbes Magazine*. Available at www.forbes.com/sites/joshbersin/2015/02/01/geeks-arrive-in-hr-people-analytics-is-here/ (accessed 28 March 2017).

BGRS (2016) *Global Mobility Trends 2016 Survey Report*. Available at http://globalmobilitytrends.bgrs.com/#/download (accessed December 2016).

BGRS (2017) *Brexit: Impact on Mobility*. Available at www.bgrs.com/insights-articles/brexit-wait-see/ (accessed October 2017).

Bhatnagar, J. (2007) 'Talent management strategy of employee engagement in Indian ITES employees: key to retention', *Employee Relations*, 29(6), 640–63.

Bird, F.E. (1974) *Management Guide to Loss Control*, Atlanta, GA: Institute Press.

Bird, F.E. and Germain, G.L. (1996) *Loss Control Management: Practical Loss Control Leadership, Revised Edition*, Loganville, Georgia: Det Norske Veritas.

Black, J.S. and Mendenhall, M.E. (1991) 'The U-curve adjustment hypothesis revisited: a review and theoretical framework', *Journal of International Business Studies*, 22(2), 225–47.

Black, J.S., Gregerson, H.B., Mendenhall, M.E. and Stroh, L.K. (1999) *Globalizing People through International Assignments*, Reading, M.A: Addison-Wesley.

Blau, F.D. and Kahn, L.M. (2006) 'The U.S. gender pay gap in the 1990s: slowing convergence', *Industrial and Labor Relations Review*, 60(1), 45–66.

Blau, P.M. (1964) *Exchange and Power in Social Life*, New York: John Wiley.

Block, R. (2006) 'Industrial relations in the United States and Canada', in M.J. Morley, P. Gunnigle and D.G. Collings (eds) *Global Industrial Relations*, New York: Routledge.

Bloomberg News (2017) 'Sweden abandons six-hour workday scheme because it's just too expensive', *The Telegraph*, 4 January. Available at www.telegraph.co.uk/business/2017/01/04/sweden-abandons-six-hour-workday-scheme-expensive (accessed 11 June 2018).

Blowfield, M. and Murray, A. (2011) *Corporate Responsibility*, 2nd edn, Oxford: Oxford University Press.

Bock, L. (2014) 'Google's scientific approach to work-life balance (and much more)', *Harvard Business Review*. Available at https://hbr.org/2014/03/googles-scientific-approach-to-work-life-balance-and-much-more? (accessed 15 April 2018).

Bol, J.C. (2011) 'The determinants and performance effects of manager's performance evaluation biases', *Accounting Review*, 86(5), 1549–75.

Bond, S. and Wise, S. (2003) 'Family leave policies and devolution to the line', *Personnel Review*, 32(1): 58–72.

Boon, C. and Biron, M. (2016) 'Temporal issues in person–organization fit, person–job fit and turnover: The role of leader–member exchange', *Human Relations*, 69(12), 2177–2200. First Published May 20, 2016 https://doi.org/10.1177/0018726716636945.

Boselie, P., Dietz, G. and Boon, C. (2005) 'Commonalities and contradictions in HRM and performance research', *Human Resource Management Journal*, 15(3), 67–94.

Bos-Nehles, A.C., Van Riemsdijk, M.J. and Kees Looise, J. (2013) 'Employee perceptions of line management performance: applying the AMO theory to explain the effectiveness of line managers' HRM implementation', *Human Resource Management*, 52(6), 861–77.

Boudreau, J.W. and Jesuthasan, R. (2011) *Transformative HR: How Great Companies Use Evidence-based Change for Sustainable Advantage*, Hoboken, NJ: John Wiley & Sons.

Bowen, D.E. and Ostroff, C. (2004) 'Understanding HRM-firm performance linkages: the role of the "strength" of the HRM system', *Academy of Management Review*, 29, 203–21.

Boxall, P. (2013) 'Mutuality in the management of human resources: assessing the quality of alignment in employment relationships', *Human Resource Management Journal*, 21(1), 3–17.

Boxall, P. and Macky, K. (2009) 'Research and theory on high-performance work systems: progressing the high-involvement system', *Human Resource Management Journal*, 19(1), 3–23.

Boxall, P. and Macky, K. (2014) 'High-involvement work processes, work intensification and employee well-being', *Work, Employment and Society*, 28(6), 963–84.

Boyatzis, R. (1982) *The Competent Manager: A Model for Effective Performance*, New York: Wiley.

Bradshaw, J. (2016) *The Wellbeing of Children in the UK*, Bristol: Policy Press.

Brannen, M.Y. and Lee, F. (2014) 'Bridging cultural divides: traversing organizational and psychological perspectives on multiculturalism', in V. Benet-Martínez and Y.Y. Hong (eds) *Oxford Handbook of Multicultural Identity*, pp. 417–37.

Brannen, M.Y. and Thomas, D.C. (2010) 'Bicultural individuals in organizations', *International Journal of Cross Cultural Management*, 10(1), 5–16.

Brannen, M.Y., Moore, F. and Mughan, T. (2013) 'Strategic ethnography and reinvigorating Tesco plc: leveraging inside/out bicultural bridging in multicultural teams', *Ethnographic Praxis in Industry Conference Proceedings*, 282–99.

Brazier, M. (2016) 'Will Brexit impact on global mobility?' Available at www.k2corporatemobility.com/Will-Brexit-Impact-on-Global-Mobility (accessed October 2017).

BIBLIOGRAPHY

Breevaart, K., Bakker, A.B., Demerouti, E. and Hetland, J. (2012) 'The measurement of state work engagement: a multilevel factor analytic study', *European Journal of Psychological Assessment*, 28(4), 305.

Brewster, C., Mayrhofer, W. and Morley, M. (2004) *Human Resource Management in Europe: Evidence of Convergence?*, Oxford: Butterworth-Heinemann.

Brewster, C., Sparrow, P. and Vernon, G. (2007) *International Human Resource Management,* London: CIPD.

Brewster, C., Wood, G. and Brookes, M. (2008) 'Similarity, isomorphism or duality? Recent survey evidence on the human resource management policies of multinational corporations', *British Journal of Management*, 19(4), 320–42.

Briscoe, D., Schuler, R. and Tarique, I. (2012) *International Human Resource Management. Policies and Practices for Multinational Enterprises*, London: Routledge.

Briscoe, J.P. and Hall, D.T. (2002) 'The protean orientation: creating the adaptable workforce necessary for flexibility and speed', paper presented at the annual meeting of the Academy of Management, Denver.

Briscoe, J.P., Henagan, S.C., Burton, J.P. and Murphy, W.M. (2012) 'Coping with an insecure employment environment: the differing roles of protean and boundaryless career orientations', *Journal of Vocational Behavior*, 80(2), 308–16.

Broughton, A., Green, M., Rickard, C. et al. (2016) *Precarious Employment in Europe: Patterns, Trends and Policy Strategies,* Brussels: European Parliament.

Brown, M., Kulik, C.T. and Lim, V. (2016) 'Managerial tactics for communicating negative performance feedback', *Personnel Review*, 45(5), 969–87.

Brown, W. and Rea, D. (1995) 'The changing nature of the employment contract', *Scottish Journal of Political Economy*, 42(3), 363–77.

Browne, J. (2014) *The Glass Closet: Why Coming Out is Good Business*, London: Random House.

Brunetto, Y., Teo, S.T., Shacklock, K. and Farr-Wharton, R. (2012) 'Emotional intelligence, job satisfaction, well-being and engagement: explaining organizational commitment and turnover intentions in policing', *Human Resource Management Journal*, 22(4), 428–41.

Brynin, M. and Güveli, A. (2012) 'Understanding the ethnic pay gap in Britain', *Work, Employment and Society*, 26(4), 574–87.

Buchan, J., Couper, I.D., Tangcharoensathien, V. et al. (2013) 'Early implementation of WHO recommendations for the retention of health workers in remote and rural areas', *Bulletin of the World Health Organization*, 91:834-840. Available at www.who.int/bulletin/volumes/91/11/13-119008/en/ (accessed 15 April 2018).

Busck, O., Knudsen, H. and Lind, J. (2010) 'The transformation of employee participation: consequences for the work environment', *Economic and Industrial Democracy*, 31(3), 285–305.

Cadbury, D. (2010) *Chocolate Wars: From Cadbury to Kraft: 200 Years of Sweet Success and Bitter Rivalry*, London: HarperPress.

Caligiuri, P.M. and Bucker, J.J. (2015) 'Selection for international assignments', in D.G. Collings, G. Wood and P. Caligiuri (eds) *The Routledge Companion to International Human Resource Management*, London: Routledge.

Cammett, M. and Posusney, M.P. (2010) 'Labor standards and labor market flexibility in the Middle East: free trade and freer unions?', *Studies in Comparative International Development*, 45(2), 250–79.

Cappelli, P. and Keller, J.R. (2014) 'Talent management: conceptual approaches and practical challenges', *Annual Review of Organizational Psychology and Organizational Behavior*, 1(1), 305–31.

Capventis (2017) 'How "data democratic" is your business?' Available at www.capventis.com/2017/03/27/how-data-democratic-is-your-business (accessed 12 April 2018).

Cardy, R. and Dobbins, G. (1986) 'Affect and appraisal accuracy: liking as an integral dimension in evaluating performance', *Journal of Applied Psychology*, 71(4), 672–8.

CareerBliss (2017) 'Has the time come for a shorter working day?', 15 February. Available at www.careerbliss.com/advice/has-the-time-come-for-a-shorter-working-day (accessed 15 April 2018).

Carr, J., Kelley, B. and Albrecht, C. (2011) 'Getting to grips with stress in the workplace: strategies for promoting a healthier, more productive environment', *Human Resource Management International Digest*, 19(4), 32–38.

Carroll, A. (1979) 'A three-dimensional conceptual model of corporate performance', *Academy of Management Review*, 4, 497–505.

Carroll, A. (2016) 'Carroll's pyramid of CSR: taking another look', *International Journal of Corporate Social Responsibility*, 1(3), 1–8.

Carson, K.D. and Bedeian, A.G. (1994) 'Career commitment: construction of a measure and examination of its psychometric properties', *Journal of Vocational Behavior*, 44, 237–62.

Cascio, W.F. (2005) 'Strategies for responsible restructuring', *The Academy of Management Executive*, 19(4), 39–50.

CBI (2001) *CBI Response to the European Commission Green Paper on Promoting a European Framework for Corporate Social Responsibility*, London: CBI.

Central Statistics Office (2013) *Women and Men in Ireland*, Dublin: Central Statistics Office.

Chamberlain, A. (2017) 'Why do employees stay? A clear career path and good pay, for starters', *Harvard Business Review Magazine*. Available at https://hbr.org/2017/03/why-do-employees-stay-a-clear-career-path-and-good-pay-for-starters (accessed 11 June 2018).

Cheramie, R.A., Sturman, M.C. and Walsh, K. (2007) 'Executive career management: Switching organizations and the boundaryless career', *Journal of Vocational Behavior*, 71(3), 359–74.

Cheyne, A., Cox, S., Oliver, A. and Tomas, J.M. (1998) 'Modelling safety climate in the prediction of levels of safety activity', *Work and Stress*, 12(3), 255–71.

Cheyne, A., Tomas, J.M., Cox, S., and Oliver, A. (1999) 'Modelling employee attitudes to safety: a comparison across sectors', *European Psychologist,* 4(1), 1–10.

Chiang, F.T. and Birtch, T.A. (2007) 'Examining the perceived causes of employee performance: an east-west comparison', *International Journal of Human Resource Management*, 18(2), 232–48.

Chiswick, B.R. and Miller, P.W. (2009) 'The international transferability of immigrants' human capital', *Economics of Education Review*, 28(2), 162–69.

CIPD (2005) *Bullying at Work: Beyond Policies to a Culture of Respect*, London: CIPD.

CIPD (2006) *Achieving Best Practice in Your Business: High Performance Work Practices: Linking Strategy and Skills to Performance Outcomes*, London: CIPD.

CIPD (2007) *What's Happening with Wellbeing at Work*, London: CIPD.

CIPD (2012) *Factsheet on History of HRM*. Available at www.cipd.co.uk/hr-resources/factsheets/history-hr-cipd.aspx (accessed 10 February 2012).

CIPD (2013) *Talent Analytics and Big Data: The Challenge for HR*. Available at www.cipd.co.uk/Images/talent-analytics-and-big-data_2013-challenge-for-hr_tcm18-9289.pdf (accessed 28 March 2017).

CIPD (2015) *Resourcing and Talent Planning 2015*. Available at www.cipd.co.uk/Images/resourcing-talent-planning_2015_tcm18-11303.pdf (accessed 11 June 2018).

CIPD (2016) *Growing the Health and Well-being Agenda: From First Steps to Full Potential*, London: CIPD.

CIPD (2017) *Resourcing and Talent Planning 2017*. Available at www.cipd.co.uk/Images/resourcing-talent-planning_2017_tcm18-23747.pdf (accessed 11 June 2018).

Clardy, A. (2008) 'The strategic role of human resource development in managing core competencies', *Human Resource Development International*, 11(2), 183–97.

Clarke, S. (2005) 'Post-socialist trade unions: China and Russia', *Industrial Relations Journal*, 36(1), 2–18.

Claussen, J., Grohsjean, T., Luger, J. and Probst, G. (2014) 'Talent management and career development: what it takes to get promoted', *Journal of World Business*, 49(2), 236–44.

Clegg, H. (1979) *The System of Industrial Relations in Great Britain*, Oxford: Blackwell.

Clinton, M., Totterdell, P. and Wood, S. (2006) 'A ground theory of the portfolio working: experiencing the smallest of small businesses', *International Small Business Journal*, 24(2), 179–203.

Clutterbuck, D. (2004) *Everyone Needs a Mentor: Fostering Talent in your Organization*, London: CIPD.

Coates, H. and Edwards, D. (2011) 'The graduate pathways survey: new insights on education and employment outcomes five years after bachelor degree completion', *Higher Education Quarterly*, 65(1), 74–93.

Cockayne, A. and Warburton, L. (2016) 'An investigation of Asperger Syndrome in the employment context', Conference Paper No. CIPD/ARC/2016/5, London: CIPD Applied Research Conference.

Cohen, B. (2007) 'Positive action, institutional discrimination and mainstreaming equality: a framework for discussion', keynote address, Equality & Diversity/One World Week, University of Northampton.

Cole, M.S., Walter, F., Bedeian, A.G. and O'Boyle, E.H. (2012) 'Job burnout and employee engagement: a meta-analytic examination of construct proliferation', *Journal of Management*, 38(5), 1550–81.

Collings, D.G. (2014) 'Toward mature talent management: beyond shareholder value', *Human Resource Development Quarterly*, 25(3), 301–19.

Collings, D.G. and Mellahi, K. (2009) 'Strategic talent management: a review and research agenda', *Human Resource Management Review*, 19(4), 304–13.

Collings, D.G. and Scullion, H. (2006) *Global Staffing*, London: Routledge.

Collings, D.G., Gunnigle, P. and Morley, M.J. (2008) 'Between Boston and Berlin: American MNCs and the shifting contours of industrial relations in Ireland', *International Journal of Human Resource Management*, 19(2), 242–63.

Collings, D.G., Scullion, H. and Morley, M.J. (2007) 'Changing patterns of global staffing in the multinational enterprise: challenges to the conventional expatriate assignment and emerging alternatives', *Journal of World Business*, 42(2), 198–213.

Collinson, D. and Hearn, J. (1994) 'Naming men as men: implications for work organization and management', *Gender, Work and Organization*, 1(1), 3–22.

Commission of the European Communities (2005) *Joint Report on Social Protection and Social Inclusion*, Luxembourg: Office for Official Publications of European Communities.

Compton, R., Morrissey, W. and Nankervis, A. (2009) *Effective Recruitment and Selection Practices*, 5th edn, Sydney: CCH Australia.

Cooke, F.L., Saini, D.S. and Wang, J. (2014) 'Talent management in China and India: a comparison of management perceptions and human resource practices', *Journal of World Business*, 49(2), 225–35.

Cooper-Thomas, H.D., Anderson, N. (2006) 'Organizational socialization: A new theoretical model and recommendations for future research and HRM practices in organizations', *Journal of Managerial Psychology*, 21(5), 492–516, https://doi.org/10.1108/02683940610673997.

Court of Justice of European Union, *Mahlburg* v. *Land Mecklenburg-Vorpommern*, Case C-207/98 [2000] ECR I-549, 3 February 2000.

Court of Justice of European Union, *Wolf* v. *Stadt Frankfurt am Main*, Case C-229/08 [2010] 2 CMLR 849.

Court of Justice of the European Union (2010) Press Release No 94/10, Judgment in Case C-104/09, *Roca Alvarez* v. *Sesa Start Espana ETTY SA*, Press Office, Luxemburg.

Cox, S., Tomas, J.M., Cheyne, A. and Oliver, A. (1998) 'Safety culture: the prediction of commitment to safety in the manufacturing industry', *British Journal of Management*, 9, 3–11.

Craig, E., Kimberly, J. and Bouchikhi, H. (2002) 'Can loyalty be leased?', *Harvard Business Review*, 80(9), 24.

Crawley, E. (2017) 'Brexit and the City: Will firms jump ship?' Available at www.hrmagazine.co.uk/article-details/brex-and-the-city-will-firms-jump-ship (accessed October 2017).

Cullinane, S.J., Bosak, J., Flood, P.C. and Demerouti, E. (2014) 'Job design under lean manufacturing and the quality of working life: a job demands and resources perspective', *International Journal of Human Resource Management*, 25(21), 2996–3015.

Dabos, G.E. and Rousseau, D.M. (2004) 'Mutuality and reciprocity in the psychological contracts of employee and employer', *Journal of Applied Psychology*, 89, 52–72.

Dahling, J.J. and Librizzi, U.A. (2015) 'Integrating the theory of work adjustment and attachment theory to predict job turnover intentions', *Journal of Career Development*, 42(3), 215–28.

D'Art, D. and Turner, T. (2006) 'New working arrangements: changing the nature of the employment relationship?', *International Journal of Human Resource Management*, 17(3), 523–38.

Datta, D.K., Guthrie, J.P. and Wright, P.M. (2005) 'HRM and labour productivity: Does industry matter?', *Academy of Management Journal*, 48(1), 135–45.

Davignon Group (1997) *Report of the High Level Group of Experts on European Systems of Worker's Involvement*, Brussels: European Commission.

Day, N.E. (2014) 'What the research tells us about pay secrecy', *WorldatWork Journal*, 4th Quarter, 102–10.

Day, R. and Allen, T.D. (2004) 'The relationship between career motivation and self-efficacy with protégé career success', *Journal of Vocational Behavior*, 64(1), 72–91.

Deakin, S., McLaughlin, C. and Chai, D. (2012) 'Gender inequality and reflexive law: the potential of different regulatory mechanisms', in L. Dickens and G. Morris (eds) *Fairer Workplaces: Making Employment Rights Effective*, Oxford: Hart, pp. 115–37.

De Gilder, D., Schuyt, T.N. and Breedijk, M. (2005) 'Effects of an employee volunteering program on the work force: the ABN-AMRO case', *Journal of Business Ethics*, 61, 143–52.

Dekas, K. (2013) 'Nooglers to Googlers: applying science and measurement to new hire onboarding', paper presented at the Society for Industrial and Organizational Psychology Conference, Houston, Texas.

Deloitte Development LLC (2011) 'Building a world-class workforce analytics capability. Innovations and approaches that can help take your organization to the next level'. Available at www2.deloitte.com/content/dam/Deloitte/us/Documents/process-and-operations/us-cons-build-workforce-analytics-capability-081811.pdf (accessed 28 March 2017).

Demerouti, E., Bakker, A.B., Vardakou, I. and Kantas, A. (2003) 'The convergent validity of two burnout instruments: a multi trait-multimethod analysis', *European Journal of Psychological Assessment*, 19(1), 12.

Deming, W.E. (1986) *Out of the Crisis*, Cambridge, MA: MIT Press.

Den Hartog, D.N., Boselie, P. and Paauwe, J. (2004) 'Performance management: a model and research agenda', *Applied Psychology*, 53(4), 556–69.

Desrumaux, P., de Bosscher, S. and Léoni, V. (2009) 'Effects of facial attractiveness, gender and competence of applicants on job recruitment', *Swiss Journal of Psychology*, 68(1), 33–42.

De Stefano, V. (2016) *The Rise of the 'Just-in-time Workforce': On-demand Work, Crowdwork and Labour Protection in the 'Gig-Economy'*, Geneva: ILO.

DeVoorde, K.V., Paauwe, J. and Veldhoven, M.V. (2012) 'Employee wellbeing and the HRM organizational performance relationship: a review of quantitative studies', *International Journal of Management Reviews*, 14, 391–407.

Dipboye, Robert. (1994) 'Structured and unstructured selection interviews: beyond the job-fit model'. *Research in Personnel and Human Resource Management*, 12, 79–123.

Dickens, L. (1999) 'Beyond the business case: a three-pronged approach to equality action', *Human Resource Management Journal*, 9(1), 9–19.

Dickens, L. (2007) 'The road is long: thirty years of equality legislation in Britain', *British Journal of Industrial Relations*, 45(3), 463–94.

Diehl, D. and Terlutter, R. (2003) 'The role of lifestyle and personality in explaining attitude to the ad', in F. Hansen and L.B. Christensen (eds) *Branding and Advertising*, Copenhagen: Copenhagen Business School Press.

DiMaggio, P.J. and Powell, W.W. (1991) 'Introduction', in W.W. Powell and P.J. DiMaggio (eds) *The New Institutionalism in Organizational Analysis*, Chicago: University of Chicago Press.

Dobbins, G.H., Cardy, R.L., Facteau, J.D. and Miller, J.S. (1993) 'Implications of situational constraints on performance evaluation and performance management', *Human Resource Management Review*, 3(2), 105–28.

Dowling, P.J., Festing, M. and Engle, A.D. (2008) *International Human Resource Management*, 5th edn, London: Cengage Learning.

Dowling, P.J., Festing, M. and Engle, A.D. (2013) *International Human Resource Management*, 6th edn, London: Cengage Learning.

Downey vs Coherent Scotland Ltd (2017) Case No. 4104370/2016, Employment Tribunals, Scotland.

Drescher, C. (2017) 'What US airlines can learn from the world's best', *CNN Travel*. Available at http://edition.cnn.com/travel/article/airlines-lessons-foreign-carriers/index.html (accessed 3 August 2017).

Dries, N. (2013) 'Talent management, from phenomenon to theory', *Human Resource Management Review*, 23(4), 267–71.

Dundon, T., Wilkinson, A., Marchington, M. and Ackers, P. (2004) 'The meanings and purpose of employee voice', *International Journal of Human Resource Management*, 15(6), 1149–70.

Dundon, T., Wilkinson, A., Marchington, M. and Ackers, P. (2005) 'The management of voice in non-union organizations: managers' perspectives', *Employee Relations*, 27(3), 307–19.

Ebisui, M., Cooney, S. and Fenwick, C. (2016) *Resolving Individual Labour Disputes*, Geneva: ILO.

Eby, L.T., Butts, M. and Lockwood, A. (2003) 'Predictors of success in the era of the boundaryless career', *Journal of Organizational Behavior*, 24(6), 689–708.

Edenborough, R. (1999) *Using Psychometrics A Practical Guide to Testing and Assessment*, London: Kogan Page.

Edstrom, A. and Galbraith, J. (1977) 'Alternative policies for international transfers of managers', *Management International Review*, 17(2), 11–22.

Edwards, M.R. and Edwards, K. (2016) *Predictive HR Analytics: Mastering the HR Metric*, London: Kogan Page.

Edwards, T. (2011) 'The transfer of employment practices across borders in multinational companies', in A.W. Harzing and A.H. Pinnington (eds) *International Human Resource Management*, London: Sage.

Edwards, T. and Ferner, A. (2002) 'The renewed "American challenge": a review of employment practices in US multinationals', *Industrial Relations Journal*, 33(2), 94–111.

Edwards, T., Sanchez-Mangas, R., Jalette, P. et al. (2016) 'Global standardization or national differentiation of HRM practices in multinational companies? A comparison of multinationals in five countries', *Journal of International Business Studies*, 47(8), 997–1021.

Eklund, J.A. (1998) 'Organization of assembly work: recent Swedish examples', in E.D. Megaw (ed.) *Contemporary Ergonomics*, London: Taylor & Francis, pp. 351–56.

Ellis, A., Nifadkar, S., Bauer, T. and Erdogan, B. (2017) 'Newcomer adjustment: examining the role of managers' perception of newcomer proactive behavior during organizational socialization', *Journal of Applied Psychology*, 102(6), 993–1001.

Elson, D. (1999) 'Labor markets as gendered institutions: equality, efficiency and empowerment issues', *World Development*, 27(3), 611–27.

England, P. (2005) 'Gender inequality in labor markets: the role of motherhood and segregation', *Social Politics*, 12(2), 264–88.

Entine, J. (1994) 'Shattered image: Is the Body Shop too good to be true?', *Business Ethics*, 8(5), 23–8.

Entine, J. (2002) 'Body flop', *Globe and Mail,* 31 May. Available at www.theglobeandmail.com/report-on-business/ rob-magazine/body-flop/article465059/ (accessed 12 December 2017).

Equality and Human Rights Commission (2016) *Healing a Divided Britain*, London: EHRC.

ESENER (2010) *Managing Safety and Health at Work* (European Risk Observatory Report). Available at https://osha.europa.eu/en/node/6745/file_view (accessed 11 June 2018).

Ethical Trading Initiative (2018a) 'ETI Base Code'. Available at www.ethicaltrade.org/eti-base-code (accessed 26 September 2018).

Ethical Trading Initiative (2018b) 'What members sign up to: ETI corporate membership obligations'. Available at: www.ethicaltrade.org/join-eti/what-members-sign-to (accessed 26 September 2018).

Eurofound (2014) *Social Partners and Gender Equality in Europe*, Luxembourg: Publications Office of the European Union.

Eurofound (2015) *Upgrading or Polarisation? Long-Term and Global Shifts in the Employment Structure: European Jobs Monitor 2015*, Luxembourg: Publications Office of the European Union.

Eurofound (2016) *Changes in Remuneration and Reward Systems*, Luxembourg: Publications Office of the European Union.

European Commission (2001) *Promoting a European Framework for Corporate Social Responsibility,* Green Paper 366, Commission of the European Communities.

European Commission (2005) *Joint Report on Social Protection and Social Inclusion*, SEC69, Brussels: European Commission.

European Commission (2009) *Employment in Europe 2009*, Luxembourg: Office for Official Publications of the European Communities.

European Commission (2011) 'Corporate social responsibility: a new definition, a new agenda for action', Memo 11/730, Commission of the European Communities.

European Commission (2014) *Tackling the Gender Pay Gap in the European Union,* Luxembourg: Publications Office of the European Union.

European Union Agency for Fundamental Rights (2011) *Handbook on European Non Discrimination Law*, Luxembourg: Publications Office of the European Union.

EUROSIF (2016) *European SRI Study 2016*, Brussels: EUROSIF.

Eurostat (2012) *Gender Pay Gap in Unadjusted Form, Population and Social Conditions*, Luxembourg: Eurostat.

Eurostat (2015) *Employment of Disabled People*, Luxembourg: Publications Office of the European Union.

Eurostat (2016) 'Europe 2020 indicators – education', Eurostat Statistics Explained. Available at http:// ec.europa.eu/eurostat/statistics-explained/index.php/ Europe_2020_indicators_-_education (accessed 11 June 2018).

Eurostat (2016) 'Europe 2020 indicators – poverty and social exclusion', Eurostat Statistics Explained. Available at http://ec.europa.eu/eurostat/statistics-explained/ index.php/Europe_2020_indicators_-_poverty_and_ social_exclusion (accessed 11 June 2018).

Eurostat (2016) 'People at risk of poverty', Eurostat Statistics Explained. Available at http://ec.europa.eu/ eurostat/statistics-explained/index.php/People_at_ risk_of_poverty_or_social_exclusion (accessed 11 June 2018).

Eurostat (2017a) 'Gender pay gap statistics', Eurostat Statistics Explained. Available at http://ec.europa.eu/ eurostat/statistics-explained/index.php/Gender_pay_ gap_statistics#Gender_pay_gap_levels (accessed 11 December 2017).

Eurostat (2017b) 'Structural business statistics overview', Eurostat Statistics Explained. Available at http://ec.europa.eu/eurostat/statistics-explained/index.php/Structural_business_statistics_overview#Size_class_analysis (accessed 4 April 2017).

Eurostat (2017c) 'Fatal accidents at work', Eurostat Statistics Explained. Available at http://ec.europa.eu/eurostat/statistics-explained/index.php/File:Fatal_accidents_at_work,_2013_and_2014_(incidence_rates_per_100_000_persons_employed)_YB16.png (accessed 11 June 2018).

Evans, M. (2003) 'New deal for lone parents, six years of operation and evaluation', in J. Millar and M. Evans (eds) Lone Parents and Employment, International Comparisons of What Works, Bath: Centre for the Analysis of Social Policy, University of Bath.

Expedia Group (2018a) 'Company overview'. Available at www.expediagroup.com/about (accessed 15 April 2018).

Expedia Group (2018b) 'Vision, purpose, strategy and norms'. Available at www.expediagroup.com/about/mission-vision-values (accessed 15 April 2018).

Expedia Group (2018c) 'Careers'. Available at https://lifeatexpedia.com (accessed 15 April 2018).

Farndale, E. and Kelliher, C. (2013) 'Implementing performance appraisal: exploring the employee experience', Human Resource Management, 52(6), 879–97.

Farndale, E., Biron, M., Briscoe, D. and Raghuram, S. (2015) 'A global perspective on diversity and inclusion in work organizations', International Journal of Human Resource Management, 26(6), 677–87.

Felstead, A., Gallie, D., Green, F. and Zhou, Y. (2007) Skills at Work 1986 to 2006, Oxford: ESRC Centre on Skills, Knowledge and Organizational Performance.

Ferguson, J.P. (2015) 'The control of managerial discretion: evidence from unionization's impact on employment segregation', American Journal of Sociology, 121(3), 675–721.

Ferner, A. (1997) 'Country of origin effects and hrm in multinational companies', Human Resource Management, 7(1), 19–37.

Ferner, A. and Hyman, R. (1998) 'Introduction', in A. Ferner and R. Hyman (eds) Changing Industrial Relations in Europe, Oxford: Blackwell.

Fiske, S.T. and Macrae, C.N. (2012) The Sage Handbook of Social Cognition, Los Angeles, CA: Sage.

Fitz-Enz, J. and Mattox, J. (2014) Predictive Analytics for Human Resources, Hoboken, NJ: John Wiley & Sons.

Fombrun, C.J., Tichy, N.M. and Devanna, M.A. (1984) Strategic Human Resource Management, Hoboken, NJ: John Wiley & Sons.

Forbes (2015) 'Portrait of an HR Data Analyst'. Available at www.forbes.com/sites/karenhigginbottom/2015/04/13/portrait-of-a-hr-data-analyst/#702b98946d38 (accessed 11 June 2018).

Foster, C. and Harris, L. (2005) 'Easy to say, difficult to do: diversity management in retail', Human Resource Management Journal, 15(3), 4–17.

Freeman, R.B. and Han, E. (2012) 'The war against public sector collective bargaining in the US', Journal of Industrial Relations, 54(3), 386–408.

Frey, C.B. and Osborne, M.A. (2017) 'The future of employment: How susceptible are jobs to computerisation?', Technological Forecasting and Social Change, 114(C), 254–80.

Friedman, M. (1970) 'The social responsibility of business is to increase its profits', The New York Times Magazine, 13 September.

Froud, J (2017) 'Legal lowdown: data gathering', HR Magazine. Available at www.hrmagazine.co.uk/article-details/legal-lowdown-data-gathering (accessed 30 March 2017).

Fuehrer, V. (1994) 'Total reward strategy: a prescription for organizational survival', Compensation & Benefits Review, 26(1), 44–53.

Gaines Robinson, D. and Robinson, J.C. (2005) Strategic Business Partner: Aligning People Strategies with Business Goals, San Fransisco, CA: Berrett-Koehler.

Garavan, T.N. (1991) 'Strategic human resource development', Journal of European Industrial Training, 15(1), 21–34.

Garavan, T.N. (2002) The Irish Health and Safety Handbook, 2nd edn, Dublin: Oak Tree Press.

Garavan, T.N. (2007) 'A strategic perspective on HRD', Advances in Developing Human Resources, 9(1), 11–30.

Garavan, T.N. (2012) 'Global talent management in science-based firms: an exploratory investigation of the pharmaceutical industry during the global downturn', International Journal of Human Resource Management, 23(12), 2428–49.

Garavan, T.N., Carbery, R. and Rock, A. (2012) 'Mapping talent development: definition, scope and architecture', European Journal of Training and Development, 36(1), 5–24.

Garavan, T.N., Hogan, C. and Cahir-O'Donnell A. (2003) Making Training & Development Work: A Best Practice Guide, Cork: Oak Tree Press.

Gardiner, J. (1998) 'Beyond human capital: households in the macroeconomy', New Political Economy, 3(2), 209–21.

Gardner, H.K. (2017) 'Managing organizations: getting your stars to collaborate', Harvard Business Review, February, 100–8.

Garger, E.M. (1999) 'Holding on to high performers: a strategic approach to retention', Compensation and Benefits Management, 15(4), 10–17.

Gates, G.J. (2011) How Many People are Lesbian, Gay, Bisexual and Transgender?, Los Angeles, CA: Williams Institute.

Gelens, J., Dries, N., Hofmans, J. and Pepermans, R. (2013) 'The role of perceived organizational justice in shaping the outcomes of talent management: a research agenda', Human Resource Management Review, 23(4), 341–53.

Gibb, S.J., Fergusson, D.M. and Horwood, L.J. (2012) 'Working hours and alcohol problems in early adulthood', *Addiction*, 107(1), 81–8.

Gilligan, C. (1982) *In a Different Voice: Psychological Theory and Women's Development*, Cambridge, MA: Harvard University Press.

Glassdoor (2018) 'Expedia Benefits'. Available at www.glassdoor.co.uk/Benefits/Expedia-UK-Benefits-EI_IE9876.0,7_IL.8,10_IN2.htm (accessed 15 April 2018).

Goldberg, A. (2016) 'Brexit and global mobility: what you and your employees need to know'. Available at www.lexiconrelocation.com/blog/brexit-and-global-mobility-what-you-and-your-employees-need-to-know (accessed October 2017).

Gollan, P.J. (2000) 'Nonunion forms of employee representation in the United Kingdom and Australia', in B.E. Kaufman and D.G. Taras (eds) *Nonunion Employee Representation*, Armonk, NY: M.E. Sharpe, pp. 410–52.

Gomez, R., Bryson, A., Kretschmer, T. and Willman, P. (2009) 'Employee voice and private sector workplace outcomes in Britain, 1980-2004', NIESR Discussion Paper 329, London: National Institute of Economic and Social Research.

Gooderham, P.N., Morley, M.J., Parry, E. and Stavrou, E. (2015) 'National and firm-level drivers of the devolution of HRM decision making to line managers', *Journal of International Business Studies*, 46, 715–23.

Gould, S. and Penley, L.E. (1984) 'Career strategies and salary progression: a study of their relationships in a municipal bureaucracy', *Organization Behaviour and Human Performance*, 34, 244–65.

Grant, A.M., Christianson, M.K. and Price, R.H. (2007) 'Happiness, health, or relationships? Managerial practices and employee wellbeing trade-offs', *Academy of Management Perspectives*, 21(3), 51–63.

Grawitch, M.J., Gottschalk, M. and Munz, D.C. (2006) 'The path to a healthy workplace: a critical review linking healthy workplace practices, employee wellbeing, and organizational improvements', *Consulting Psychology Journal: Research and Practice*, 58(3), 129–47.

Greasley, K. and Edwards, P. (2015) 'When do health and well-being interventions work? Managerial commitment and context', *Economic and Industrial Democracy*, 36(2), 355–77.

Griffiths, M. (2011) 'Workaholism: a 21st-century addiction', *The Psychologist*, 24(10), 740–4.

Grimland, S., Vigoda-Gadot, E. and Baruch, Y. (2012) 'Career attitudes and success of managers: the impact of chance event, protean, and traditional careers', *International Journal of Human Resource Management*, 23(6), 1074–94.

Grint, K. (1991) *The Sociology of Work*, Cambridge: Polity Press.

Gross, J. (1998) 'The common law employment contract and collective bargaining: values and views of rights and justice', *New Zealand Journal of Industrial Relations*, 23(2), 63–76.

Grote, D. (1996) *The Complete Guide to Performance Appraisal*, New York: AMA.

Groysberg, B., Nanda, A. and Nohria, N. (2004) 'The risky business of hiring stars', *Harvard Business Review*, 82(5), 92–101.

Gruman, J.A. and Saks, A.M. (2011) 'Performance management and employee engagement', *Human Resource Management Review*, 21(2), 123–36.

Guest, D. (1987) 'Human resource management and industrial relations', *Journal of Management Studies*, 24(5), 503–21.

Guest, D. (1989) 'Personnel and HRM: Can you tell the difference', *Personnel Management*, 21(1), 48–51.

Guest, D. (1997) 'Human resource management and performance: a review and research agenda', *International Journal of Human Resource Management*, 8(3), 263–76.

Guest, D. (2004) 'Flexible employment contracts, the psychological contract and employee outcomes: an analysis and review of the evidence', *International Journal of Management Reviews*, 5/6(1), 1–19.

Guest, D.E. (2004) 'The psychology of the employment relationship: an analysis based on the psychological contract', *Applied Psychology*, 53(4), 541–55.

Guest, D.E. (2017) 'Human resource management and employee wellbeing: towards a new analytical framework', *Human Resource Management Journal*, 27(1), 21–38.

Guest, D.E., Michie, J., Conway, N. and Sheehan, M. (2003) 'Human resource management and corporate performance in the UK', *British Journal of Industrial Relations*, 41(2), 291–314.

Gunnigle, P. and Flood, P. (1990) *Personnel Management in Ireland: Practice, Trends and Developments*, Dublin: Gill & Macmillan.

Gunnigle, P., Heraty, N. and Morley, M. (2011) *Human Resource Management in Ireland*, 4th edn, Dublin: Gill Education.

Gustafsson, K. and Marklund, S. (2011) 'Consequences of sickness presence and sickness absence on health and work ability: a Swedish prospective cohort study', *International Journal of Occupational Medicine and Environmental Health*, 24(2), 153–65.

Guthrie, J.P. (2001) 'High involvement work practices, turnover and productivity: evidence from New Zealand', *Academy of Management Journal*, 44(1), 180–90.

Guthrie, J.P., Flood, P.C., Liu, W. et al. (2011) 'Big hat, no cattle? High performance work systems and executives perceptions of HR capability', *International Journal of Human Resource Management*, 22(8), 1672–85.

Hackman, J.R. and Oldham, G.R. (1980) *Work Redesign*, Reading, MA: Addison-Wesley.

Halkos, G. and Bousinakis, D. (2010) 'The effect of stress and satisfaction on productivity', *International Journal of Productivity and Performance Management*, 59(5), 415–31.

Hall, D.T. (1976) *Careers in Organizations*, Glenview, IL: Scott, Foresman.

BIBLIOGRAPHY

Hall, D.T. (1996) 'Protean careers of the 21st century', *Academy of Management Executive*, 10(4), 8–16.

Hall, D.T. (2002) *Careers In and Out of Organizations*, Thousand Oaks, CA: Sage.

Hall, D.T. (2004) 'The protean career: a quarter-century journey', *Journal of Vocational Behavior*, 65(1), 1–13.

Hall, D.T. and Chandler, D. (2004) 'Psychological success: when the career is a calling', technical report, Boston University Executive Development Roundtable.

Hall, P.A. and Soskice, D. (2001) 'An introduction to varieties of capitalism', in P.A. Hall and D. Soskice (eds) *Varieties of Capitalism: The Institutional Foundations of Comparative Advantage*, Oxford: Oxford University Press.

Hamel, M.B., Julie, R., Ingelfinger, J.R. et al. (2006) 'Women in academic medicine, progress and challenges', *New England Journal of Medicine*, 355, 310–12.

Handy, C. (1989) *The Age of Unreason*, London: Random House.

Handy, C. (2002) 'What's a business for?', *Harvard Business Review*, December, 49–55.

Harbison, F. and Myers, C. (1959) *Management in the Industrialized World*, New York: McGraw-Hill.

Harding, N., Lee, H. and Ford, J. (2014) 'Who is "the middle manager"?', *Human Relations*, 67(10), 1213–37.

Harrington, D., Linehan M. and Cross, C. (2008) 'Flexible working in an Irish public sector organization: still a gender issue', *International Journal of Business and Management*, 3(9), 166–78.

Harris, H. and Brewster, C. (1999) 'The coffee-machine system: how international selection really works', *International Journal of Human Resource Management*, 10(3), 488–500.

Harrison, R. (2009) *Learning and Development*, London: CIPD.

Harrison, R. and Kessels, J. (2004) *Human Resource Development in a Knowledge Economy: An Organizational View*, Basingstoke: Palgrave Macmillan.

Harter, J.K., Schmidt, F.L. and Hayes, T.L. (2002) 'Business-unit-level relationship between employee satisfaction, employee engagement, and business outcomes: a meta-analysis', *Journal of Applied Psychology*, 87(2), 268–79.

Hartmann, E., Feisel, E. and Schober, H. (2010) 'Talent management of western MNCs in China: balancing global integration and local responsiveness', *Journal of World Business*, 45(2), 169–78.

Harvey, G., Williams, K. and Probert, J. (2013) 'Greening the airline pilot: HRM and the green performance of airlines in the UK', *International Journal of Human Resource Management*, 24(1), 152–66.

Harzing, A.W. (1995) 'The persistent myth of high expatriate failure rates', *Human Resource Management*, 6(2), 457–75.

Hausman, C. (2007) 'Who was Anita Roddick?' *Ethics Newsline*, 17 September. Available at www.globalethics.org/newsline/2007/09/17/who-was-anita-roddick/ (accessed 14 March 2012).

Health and Safety Authority (2007) *Code of Practice for Employers and Employees on the Prevention and Resolution of Bullying at Work*, Dublin: Health and Safety Authority.

Health and Safety Executive (2015) *Health and Safety Statistics: Annual Report for Great Britain*. Available at www.hse.gov.uk/statistics/overall/hssh1415.pdf (accessed 11 June 2018).

Health and Safety Executive (2016) *Health and Safety at Work: Summary Statistics for Great Britain 2016*. Available at www.hse.gov.uk/statistics/overall/hssh1516.pdf (accessed 11 June 2018).

Heimler, R., Rosenberg, S. and Morote, E.S. (2012) 'Predicting career advancement with structural equation modelling', *Education + Training*, 54(2), 85–94.

Heinrich, H.W. (1931) *Industrial Accident Prevention: A Scientific Approach*, New York: McGraw-Hill.

Hendry, C. (1995) *Human Resource Management: A Strategic Approach to Employment*, Oxford: Butterworth Heinemann.

Herring, C. (2009) 'Does diversity pay?: Race, gender, and the business case for diversity', *American Sociological Review*, 74(2), 208–24.

Herriot, P. and Pemberton, C. (1997) 'Facilitating new deals', *Human Resource Management Journal*, 7(1), 45–56.

Hewlett, S.A. (2007) *Off-ramps and On-ramps: Keeping Talented Women on the Road to Success*, Boston, MA: Harvard Business School Press.

Hewlin, P.F. (2009) 'Wearing the cloak: antecedents and consequences of creating facades of conformity', *Journal of Applied Psychology*, 94(3), 727–41.

Hickey, S. (2010) 'Women caught up in "sexist email" inquiry', *Irish Independent,* 11 November. Available at www.independent.ie/national-news/women-caught-up-in-sexist-email-inquiry-2415801.html (accessed 12 December 2017).

Higgins, M.C. and Kram, K.E. (2001) 'Reconceptualizing mentoring at work: a developmental network perspective', *Academy of Management Review*, 26(2), 264–88.

Higo, M. (2006) 'Aging workforce in Japan: an overview of three policy dilemmas', *Hallym International Journal of Aging*, 8(2), 149–73.

Hill, J. and Trist, E. (1955) Changes in accidents and other absences with length of service, *Human Relations*, 8(2), 121–52.

Hira, A. and Benson-Rea, M. (2017) *Governing Corporate Social Responsibility in the Apparel Industry after Rana Plaza*, London: Palgrave.

Hofstede, G. (1980) *Culture's Consequences: International Differences in Work-related Values*, London: Sage.

Hofstede, G. (1993) 'Cultural constraints in management theories', *Academy of Management Executive*, 7(1), 81–94.

Hofstede, G., Hofstede, G.J. and Minkov, M. (2010) *Cultures and Organizations: Software of the Mind: Intercultural Cooperation and its Importance for Survival*, New York: McGraw-Hill.

Hollis, L.P. and McCalla, S.A. (2013) 'Bullied back in the closet', *Journal of Psychological Issues in Organizational Culture*, 4(2), 6–16.

BIBLIOGRAPHY

Honey, P. and Mumford, A. (1992) *The Manual of Learning Styles*, Maidenhead: Peter Honey.

Horwitz, F. (2006) 'Industrial relations in Africa', in M.J. Morley, P. Gunnigle and D.G. Collings (eds) *Global Industrial Relations*, London: Routledge.

Howard, A. and Bray, D.W. (1981) 'Today's young managers; They can do it, but will they?', *Wharton Magazine*, 5(4), 23–28.

Huffington Post (2013) 'JC Penney exec admits its employees harbored enormous YouTube addiction', 25 February. Available at www.huffingtonpost.com/2013/02/25/jc-penney-employees-youtube_n_2759028.html (accessed 15 April 2018).

Hui, X., Pengqian. F. and Shizhen, S. (2013) 'Analysis on recognition of occupational health surveillance of workers in small and medium-sized enterprises in urban areas', *Chininse Journal of Public Health*, 29, 1054–56.

Human Resources (2017) 'DBS COO's 5 tips for setting up a human capital analytics team', 6 March. Available at www.humanresourcesonline.net/dbs-coos-5-tips-setting-human-capital-analytics-team (accessed 15 April 2018).

Hunter, J.E., Schmidt, F.L. and Judiesch, M.K. (1990) 'Individual differences in output variability as a function of job complexity', *Journal of Applied Psychology*, 75(1), 28–42.

Huselid, M.A. (1995) 'The impact of human resource management practices on turnover, productivity, and corporate financial performance', *Academy of Management Journal*, 38(3), 635–72.

Huselid, M.A., Jackson, S.E. and Schuler, R.S. (1997) 'Technical and strategic human resources management effectiveness as determinants of firm performance', *Academy of Management Journal*, 40(1), 171–88.

Huus, T. (2015) *People Data: How to Use and Apply Human Capital Metrics in your Company*, London: Palgrave.

Ibarra, II. (1999) 'Provisional selves: experimenting with image and identity in professional adaptation', *Administrative Science Quarterly*, 44(4), 764–91.

IBEC (2016) *Mental Health and Wellbeing: A Line Manager's Guide*, Dublin: IBEC.

Iles, P., Chuai, X. and Preece, D. (2010) 'Talent management and HRM in multinational companies in Beijing: definitions, differences and drivers', *Journal of World Business*, 45(2), 179–89.

Ilies, R., Wilson, K.S. and Wagner, D.T. (2009) 'The spillover of daily job satisfaction onto employees' family lives: the facilitating role of work–family integration', *Academy of Management Journal*, 52(1), 87–102.

Immervoll, H. and Barber, D. (2005) *Can Parents Afford to Work? Childcare Costs, Tax-Benefit Policies and Work Incentives*, OECD Social, Employment and Migration working papers No. 31, Geneva: OECD.

Industrial Relations News (2005) 'US Chamber leaves indelible stamp on Employee Consultation Bill', *Industrial Relations News*, 30, 2–3.

Institute for Public Policy Research (2010) *Youth Unemployment and the Recession*, London: IPPR.

Institute for Public Policy Research (2017) *Not by Degrees: Improving Student Mental Health in the UK's Universities*. Available at www.ippr.org/files/2017-09/1504645674_not-by-degrees-170905.pdf (accessed 11 June 2018).

Integrated Benefits Institute (2012) 'Poor health costs U.S. economy $576 billion'. Available at https://ibiweb.org/research-resources/detail/poor-health-costs-u.s.-economy-576-billion-infographic (accessed 11 June 2018).

International Labour Organization (ILO) (2003) *Safety in Numbers: Pointers for a Global Safety Culture at Work*, Geneva: ILO.

ILO (2007) *Discrimination at Work in the Middle East and North Africa* factsheet, Geneva: ILO.

ILO (2015) *Decent Work for People with Disabilities: Promoting Rights in the Global Development Agenda*, Geneva: ILO.

ILO (2017) *Global Estimates of Modern Slavery: Forced Labour and Forced Marriage*. Available at www.ilo.org/global/publications/books/WCMS_575479/lang--en/index.htm (accessed 4 January 2018).

Jackson, S.E., Schuler, R.S. and Jiang, K. (2014) 'An aspirational framework for strategic human resource management', *Academy of Management Annals*, 8(1), 1–56.

Janis, I.L. (1982) *Groupthink: Psychological Studies of Policy Decisions and Fiascoes*, Boston: Houghton Mifflin.

Janz, T. (1989) 'The patterned behaviour description interview: the best prophet of the future is the past', in R.W. Eder and G.R. Ferris (eds) *The Employment Interview: Theory, Research and Practice*, London: Sage.

Jaques, E. (2002) *Social Power and the CEO: Leadership and Trust in a Sustainable Free Enterprise System*, Westport, CT: Quorum Books.

Javidan, M. and Bowen, D. (2013) 'The "global mindset" of managers: what it is, why it matters, and how to develop it', *Organizational Dynamics*, 42(2), 145–55.

Jee, C. (2017) 'What it's like to work in one of the UK's happiest tech teams', *Techworld.com*, 29 May. Available at www.techworld.com/careers/what-its-like-working-in-one-of-uks-happiest-tech-teams-3659574 (accessed 15 April 2018).

Jensen, J.M. and van De Voorde, K. (2016) 'Reconciling the dark side of HPWS', in N.M. Ashkanasy, R.J. Bennett and M.J. Martinko (eds) *Understanding the High Performance Workplace: The Line Between Motivation and Abuse*, New York: Routledge, pp. 85–102.

Jensen, J.M., Patel, P.C. and Messersmith, J.G. (2013) 'High-performance work systems and job control: consequences for anxiety, role overload and turnover intentions', *Journal of Management*, 39(6), 1699–724.

Jiang, K. and Messersmith, J. (2017) 'On the shoulders of giants: a meta-review of strategic human resource management', *International Journal of Human Resource Management*, 29(1), 1–28.

Johnston, A., Hamann, K. and Kelly, J. (2016) 'Unions may be down, but they're not out: take note, governments in Western Europe!', *Social Europe*, 6 October. Available at www.socialeurope.eu/2016/10/unions-may-theyre-not-take-note-governments-western-europe/ (accessed 11 June 2018).

Joo Hun, H., Bartol, K.M. and Seongsu, K. (2015) 'Tightening up the performance-pay linkage: roles of contingent reward leadership and profit-sharing in the cross-level influence of individual pay-for-performance', *Journal of Applied Psychology*, 100(2), 417–30.

Judge, T.A., Boudreau, J.W. and Bretz, R.D. Jr. (1994) 'Job and life attitudes of male executives', *Journal of Applied Psychology*, 79(5), 767–82.

Kahn, W.A. (1990) 'Psychological conditions of personal engagement and disengagement at work', *Academy of Management Journal*, 33(4), 692–724.

Kaiser, R.B. and Overfield, D.V. (2011) 'Strengths, strengths overused, and lopsided leadership', *Consulting Psychology Journal: Practice and Research*, 63(2), 89–109.

Kandola, R. and Fullerton, J. (1998) *Diversity in Action: Managing the Mosaic*, London: CIPD.

Kang, C. (2014) 'Google data-mines its approach to promoting women', *The Washington Post*, 2 April. Available at www.washingtonpost.com/news/the-switch/wp/2014/04/02/google-data-mines-its-women-problem (accessed 15 April 2018).

Kaplan, R.S. (2008) 'Reaching your potential', *Harvard Business Review*, 86(7/8), 45–9.

Kaplan, S., Bradley-Geist, J.C., Ahmad, A. et al. (2014) 'A test of two positive psychology interventions to increase employee wellbeing', *Journal of Business Psychology*, 29(3), 367–80.

Karnani, A. (2010) 'The case against corporate social responsibility', *MIT Sloan Management Review*, 22 August.

Katz, H. and Darbishire, O. (2000) *Converging Divergences: Worldwide Changes in Employment Systems*, Ithaca, NY: ILR/Cornell University Press.

Katz, L.F. and Krueger, A.B. (2016) 'The rise and nature of alternative work arrangements in the United States, 1995-2015', National Bureau of Economic Research Working Paper No. 22667.

Kaufman, B.E. (2014) 'The historical development of American HRM broadly viewed', *Human Resource Management Review*, 24(3), 196–218.

Kell, J (2016) Majority of Nike's US employees are minorities for the first time, *Fortune*, May 12, http://fortune.com/2016/05/12/nike-staff-diversity/

Kelly, J. (1998) *Rethinking Industrial Relations: Mobilisation, Collectivism and Long Waves*, London: Routledge.

Kerr, C., Dunlop, J.T., Harbison, F.H. and Myers, C.A. (1960) *Industrialism and Industrial Man*, Cambridge, MA: Harvard University Press.

Khatri, N. and Ng, H.A. (2000) 'The role of intuition in strategic decision making', *Human Relations*, 53(1), 57–86.

Kim, S. and McLean, G.N. (2012) 'Global talent management: necessity, challenges, and the roles of HRD', *Advances in Developing Human Resources*, 14(4), 566–85.

King, K.G. (2016) 'Data analytics in human resources: a case study and critical review', *Human Resource Development Review*, 15(4), 487–95.

Kirkpatrick, D.L. and Kirkpatrick, J.D. (2006) *Evaluating Training Programs: The Four Levels*, 3rd edn, New York: Berrett-Koehler.

Kirton, G. and Greene, A.M. (2005) *The Dynamics of Managing Diversity: A Critical Approach*, 2nd edn, Oxford: Elsevier Butterworth-Heinemann.

Kirton, G. and Greene, A.M. (2016) *The Dynamics of Managing Diversity: A Critical Approach*, 4th edn, Oxford: Elsevier Butterworth-Heinemann.

Kivimäki, M., Nyberg, S.T., Batty, G.D. et al. (2012) 'Job strain as a risk factor for coronary heart disease: a collaborative meta-analysis of individual participant data', *The Lancet*, 380(9852), 1491–7.

Klein, N. (2000) *No Logo*, London: HarperCollins.

Kline, R.B. (1998) *Principles and Practice of Structural Equation Modeling*, New York: Guilford Press.

Kluger, A.N. and DeNisi, A. (1996) The effects of feedback interventions on performance: A historical review, a meta-analysis, and a preliminary feedback intervention theory. *Psychological bulletin*, 119(2), 254–284.

Knox, S. and Freeman, C. (2006) 'Measuring and managing employer brand image in the service industry', *Journal of Marketing Management*, 22(7/8), 695–716.

Kochan, T. and Rubinstein, S. (2000) 'Toward a stakeholder theory of the firm: the saturn partnership', *Organization Science*, 11(4), 367–86.

Kohn, A. (1993) 'Why incentive plans cannot work', *Harvard Business Review*, 71(6) 54–63.

Kolb, D.A. (1984) *Experiential Learning: Experience as the Source of Learning and Development*, Englewood Cliffs, NJ: Prentice-Hall.

Kramer, A. and Son, J. (2016) 'Who cares about the health of health care professionals? An 18-year longitudinal study of working time, health, and occupational turnover', *ILR Review*, 69(4), 939–60.

Kristof, A.L. (1996) 'Person-organization fit: an integrative review of its conceptualizations, measurement, and implications', *Personnel Psychology*, 49(1), 1–49.

Kuper, H. and Marmot, M. (2003) 'Job strain, job demands, decision latitude, and risk of coronary heart disease within the Whitehall II study', *Journal of Epidemiology & Community Health*, 57(2), 147–53.

Kushlev, K. and Dunn, E.W. (2015) 'Checking email less frequently reduces stress', *Computers in Human Behavior*, 43, 220–28.

Latham, G.P., Almost, J., Mann, S. and Moore, C. (2005) 'New developments in performance management', *Organizational Dynamics*, 34(1), 77–87.

BIBLIOGRAPHY

Latham, G.P., Saari, L.M., Pursell, E.D. and Campion, M.A. (1980) 'The situational interviews', *Journal of Applied Psychology*, 65(4), 422–27.

Lavelle, J., Gunnigle, P. and McDonnell, A. (2010) 'Patterning employee voice in multinational companies', *Human Relations*, 63(3), 395–418.

Lavelle, J., McDonnell, A. and Gunnigle, P. (2009) *Human Resource Practices in Multinational Companies in Ireland: A Contemporary Analysis*, Dublin: TSO.

Lawler, E.E., Levenson, A.R. and Boudreau, J.W. (2004) 'HR metrics and analytics: use and impact', *Human Resource Planning*, 27(4), 27–35.

Leatherbarrow, C., Fletcher, J. and Currie, D. (2010) *Introduction to Human Resource Management: A Guide to HR in Practice*, London: CIPD.

LeBaron, G. and Lister, J. (2016) *Ethical Audits and the Supply Chains of Global Corporations*, Sheffield: Sheffield Political Economy Research Institute.

Lee, T. and Harrison, K. (2000) 'Assessing safety culture in nuclear power stations', *Safety Science*, 30, 61–97.

Legge, K. (1995) *HRM: Rhetorics and Realities,* Basingstoke: Macmillan.

Le Grand, J. (2003) 'Individual choice and social exclusion', CASE paper 75, London: LSE.

Lengnick-Hall, C.A. and Lengnick-Hall, M.L. (1988) 'Strategic human resources management: a review of the literature and a proposed typology', *Academy of Management Review*, 13(3), 454–70.

Leopold, L. and Harris, L. (2009) *The Strategic Managing of Human Resources*, 2nd edn, Harlow: Prentice Hall.

Levinson, D. (1978) *The Seasons of a Man's Life*, New York: Knopf.

Lewin, D. (2001) 'Low-involvement work practices and business performance', proceedings of the 53rd Annual Meeting, Industrial Relations Research Association, pp. 275–92.

Lewis, P., Thornhill, A. and Saunders, M. (2003) *Employee Relations: Understanding the Employment Relationship*, Harlow: Pearson Education.

Lewis, R.E. and Heckman, R.J. (2006) 'Talent management: a critical review', *Human Resource Management Review*, 16(2), 139–154.

Lips-Wiersma, M. and Hall, D.T. (2007) 'Organizational career development is not dead: a case study on managing the new career during organizational change', *Journal of Organizational Behavior*, 28, 771–92.

Locke, E.A. and Latham, G.P. (1990) *A Theory of Goal Setting and Task Performance*, Englewood Cliffs, NJ: Prentice-Hall.

Locke, R. (2013) *The Promise and Limits of Private Power*, Cambridge: Cambridge University Press.

Locke, R. and Romis, M. (2009) 'The promise and perils of private voluntary regulation: labor standards and work organization in two Mexican garment factories', MIT Sloan Working Paper No. 4734-09.

Locke, R., Qin, F. and Brause, A. (2007) 'Does monitoring improve labour standards: lessons from Nike', *Industrial and Labour Relations Review,* 61(1), 3–31.

London, M. (1983) 'Toward a theory of career motivation', *Academy of Management Review*, 8(4), 620–30.

London, M. and Bray, D.W. (1984) 'Measuring and developing young managers' career motivation', *Journal of Management Development*, 3(3), 3–25.

London, M. and Mone, E.M. (2006) 'Career motivation', in J.H. Greenhaus and G.A. Callanan (eds) *Encyclopedia of Career Development,* Thousand Oaks, CA: Sage, pp. 130–2.

London, M. and Noe, R.A. (1997) 'London's career motivation theory: an update on measurement and research', *Journal of Career Assessment*, 5(1), 61–80.

Lopez, T.P. (2006) 'Career development of foreign-born workers: Where is the career motivation research?', *Human Resource Development Review*, 5(4), 478–93.

Lovelace, K. and Rosen, B. (1996) 'Differences in achieving person-organization fit among diverse groups of managers', *Journal of Management*, 22(5), 703–22.

Luffarelli, J., Gonçalves, D. and Stamatogiannakis, A. (2016) 'When feedback interventions backfire: why higher performance feedback may result in lower self-perceived competence and satisfaction with performance', *Human Resource Management*, 55(4), 591–614.

Lupushor, S (2017) 'The HR view on employee data gathering in HR Magazine'. Available at www.hrmagazine.co.uk/article-details/the-hr-view-on-employee-data-gathering (accessed 30 March 2017).

Luthans, F., Norman, S.M., Avolio, B.J. and Avey, J.B. (2008) 'The mediating role of psychological capital in the supportive organizational climate: employee performance relationship', *Journal of Organizational Behavior*, 29(2), 219–38.

McCarthy, J. and Heraty, N. (2017) 'Ageist attitudes', in E. Parry and J. McCarthy (eds) *The Palgrave Handbook of Age Diversity and Work*, London: Palgrave, pp. 399–422.

McCoy v. *James McGregor and Sons Ltd* (2007), Case No. 00237/07IT, Industrial Tribunals and the Fair Employment Tribunal, Northern Ireland.

McCurry, J. (2017) 'Premium Fridays: Japan gives its workers a break – to go shopping', *The Guardian*, 24 February. Available at www.theguardian.com/world/2017/feb/24/premium-fridays-japan-gives-workers-break-go-shopping (accessed 15 April 2018).

McDougall, D. (2009) 'Primark in storm over conditions at UK supplier: fashion giant acts after investigation', *The Observer*, 11 January. Available at www.guardian.co.uk/business/2009/jan/11/primark-ethical-business-living (accessed 12 December 2017).

Macey, W.H., Schneider, B., Barbera, K.M. and Young, S.A. (2009) *Employee Engagement: Tools for Analysis, Practice, and Competitive Advantage*, Malden, WA: Wiley-Blackwell.

McFadden, C. (2015) 'Lesbian, gay, bisexual, and transgender careers and human resource development: a systematic literature review', *Human Resource Development Review*, 14(2), 125–62.

McGregor, A., Magee, C.A., Caputi, P. and Iverson, D. (2016) 'A job demands resources approach to presenteeism', *Career Development International*, 21(4), 402–418.

Machlowitz, M. (1980) *Workaholics: Living with Them, Working with Them*, Reading, MA: Addison-Wesley.

McLaughlin, C. and Deakin, S. (2012) 'Equality law and the limits of the "business case" for addressing gender inequalities', in J. Scott, S. Dex and A. Plagnol (eds) *Gendered Lives: Gender Inequalities in Production and Reproduction,* Cheltenham: Edward Elgar, pp. 153–73.

Mahlburg v. *Land Mecklenburg-Vorpommern* [2000] ECR 1-549.

Mainiero, L.A. and Sullivan, S.E. (2006) *The opt-out revolt: Why people are leaving companies to create kaleidoscope careers*, Mountain View, CA: Davies-Black.

Mallon, M. (1998) 'The portfolio career: pushed or pulled to it', *Personnel Review*, 27(5), 361–77.

Manuele, F.A. (2002) *Heinrich Revisited: Truisms or Myths*, Itasca, IL: National Safety Council.

Marler, J.H. and Boudreau, J.W. (2016) 'An evidence-based review of HR analytics', *International Journal of Human Resource Management*, 28(1), 3–26.

Marsick, V.J. and Watkins, K.E. (1999) 'Envisioning new organizations of learning', in D. Boud and J. Garrick (eds) *Understanding Learning at Work*, London: Routledge.

Marsick, V.J. and Watkins, K.E. (2001) 'Informal and incidental learning', *New Directions for Adult and Continuing Education,* 89, 25–34.

Martone, D. (2003) 'A guide to developing a competency-based performance-management system', *Employee Relations Today*, 30, 23–32.

Mathieu, M. (2017) *Annual Economic Survey of Employee Share Ownership in European Countries 2016*, Brussels: European Federation of Employee Share Ownership.

Mayo, E. (1949) 'Hawthorne and the Western Electric Company', *Public Administration: Concepts and Cases*, 149–58.

Mayrhofer, W. and Brewster, C. (1996) 'In praise of ethnocentricity: expatriate policies in European multinationals', *International Executive*, 38(6), 749–78.

Meacham v. *Knolls Atomic Power Laboratory* (2008) Supreme Court of the United States, No. 06–1505. Argued April 23, 2008; decided June 19, 2008, www.supremecourt.gov.

Michalak v. *Mid Yorkshire Hospitals NHS Trust and Others*, Tribunal Decision, Case No 1810815/2008. Available at www. judiciary.gov.uk.

Miles, R.E. and Snow, C.C. (1978) *Organizational Strategy, Structure and Process*, New York: McGraw-Hill.

Milkovich, G., Newman, J. and Gerhart, B. (2011) *Compensation,* 11th edn, New York: McGraw-Hill Irwin.

Millar, J. and Evans, M. (2003) *Lone Parents and Employment: International Comparisons of What Works,* Bath: Centre for the Analysis of Social Policy, University of Bath.

Millmore, M., Lewis, P., Saunders, M. et al. (2007) *Strategic Human Resource Management: Contemporary Issues*, London: Prentice Hall.

Mondare, S., Douthitt, S. and Carson, M. (2011) 'Maximizing the impact and effectiveness of HR analytics to drive business outcomes', *People & Strategy*, 34, 20–7.

Montgomery, D. and Ramus, C. (2003) 'Corporate social responsibility: reputation effects on MBA job choice', Research Paper No. 1805, Stanford Graduate School of Business.

Mor Barak, M.E. (2000) 'The inclusive workplace: an ecosystems approach to diversity management', *Social Work*, 45(4), 339–53.

Mor Barak, M.E. (2016) *Managing Diversity: Towards a Globally Inclusive Workplace*, Thousand Oaks, CA: Sage.

Mor Barak, M.E., Lizano, E.L., Kim, A. et al. (2016) 'The promise of diversity management for climate of inclusion: a state-of-the art review and meta-analysis', *Human Service Organizations: Management, Leadership and Governance*, 40(4), 305–33.

Morgan, P. (1986) 'International human resource management: Fact or fiction?', *Personnel Administrator*, 31(9), 43–7.

Mosley, R.W. (2007) 'Customer experience, organizational culture and the employer brand', *Journal of Brand Management*, 15(2), 123–34.

Murphy, N. (2010) *HR Roles and Responsibilities: The 2010 IRS Survey, IRS Employment Review*, London: IRS.

Nair, P.K., Ke, J., Al-Emadi, M.A. et al. (2007) 'National human resource development: a multi-level perspective', paper presented at the Annual Conference of the Academy of Human Resource Development, Bowling Green, Ohio.

Neiuwoudt, H., Jones, J. and Reddy, V. (2017) 'Employment and employee benefits in South Africa: overview'. Available at https://uk.practicallaw.thomsonreuters. com/4-422-1680?transitionType=Default&contextData= (sc.Default) (accessed 14 July 2017).

Ng, E.S. and Burke, R.J. (2005) 'Person–organization fit and the war for talent: Does diversity management make a difference?', *International Journal of Human Resource Management*, 16(7), 1195–210.

Nojin v. *Commonwealth of Australia* [2012] FCAFC 192.

Noon, M. (2004) 'Managing equality and diversity', in I. Beardwell, L. Holden and T. Claydon (eds) *Human Resource Management: A Contemporary Approach*, 4th edn, London: Prentice Hall/Financial Times.

Noon, M. (2007) 'The fatal flaws of diversity and the business case for ethnic minorities', *Work, Employment and Society*, 21(4), 773–84.

Nooreyezdan, N., Abraham, A. and Singh Chandel, A. (2017) 'Employment and employee benefits in India: overview'. Available at https://uk.practicallaw.thomsonreuters. com/7-503-4567?transitionType=Default&contextData= (sc.Default)&firstPage=true&bhcp=1 (accessed 14 July 2017).

Nordlof, F. and Berterud, M. (2017) 'Employment and employee benefits in Sweden: overview'. Available at https://uk.practicallaw.thomsonreuters.com/1-503-3778?transitionType=Default&contextData=(sc.Default) (accessed 14 July 2017).

BIBLIOGRAPHY

Nyberg, A.J., Pieper, J.R. and Trevor, C.O. (2016) 'Pay-for-performance's effect on future employee performance: integrating psychological and economic principles toward a contingency perspective', *Journal of Management,* 42(7), 1753–83.

OECD (2010) LMF2.1: Usual working hours per week by gender, OECD Family database. Available at www.oecd.org/els/family/LMF2_1_Usual_working_hours_by_gender_July2013.pdf (accessed 11 June 2018).

OECD (2011) PF2.1: Key characteristics of parental leave systems, OECD Family database. Available at www.oecd.org/els/soc/PF2_1_Parental_leave_systems.pdf (accessed 11 June 2018).

OECD (2013) 'Protecting jobs, enhancing flexibility: a new look at employment protection legislation', in *OECD Employment Outlook 2013*, Paris: OECD Publishing.

OECD (2016) *Enterprise at a Glance 2016,* Paris: OECD Publishing.

OECD (2016) *Women in Public Life: Gender Law and Policy in Middle East and North Africa*, Paris: OECD Publishing.

OECD (2016) *Society at a Glance 2016: OECD Social Indicators.* Available at http://dx.doi.org/10.1787/9789264261488-en (accessed 11 June 2018).

OECD (2016) *Who Uses Childcare? Background Brief on Inequalities in the Use of Formal Early Childhood Education nnd Care* (ECEC) *Among Very Young Children*, Paris: OECD Publishing.

OECD (2017) 'Unemployment rate (indicator)'. Available at doi: 10.1787/997c8750-en (accessed 12 December 2017).

Office for National Labour Statistics (2017) *Annual Survey of Hours and Earnings: 2017 Provisional and 2016 Revised Results.* Available at www.ons.gov.uk/employmentandlabourmarket/peopleinwork/earningsandworkinghours/bulletins/annualsurveyofhoursandearnings/2017provisionaland2016revisedresults (accessed 11 November 2017).

O'Leary, J. and Sandberg, J. (2016) 'Managers' practice of managing diversity revealed: a practice-theoretical account', *Journal of Organization Behaviour*, 38(4), 512–36.

Oltermann, P. (2017) 'Sweden sees benefits of six-hour working day in trial for care workers', *The Guardian*, 4 January. Available at www.theguardian.com/world/2017/jan/04/sweden-sees-benefits-six-hour-working-day-trial-care-workers (accessed 15 April 2018).

Opray, M. (2016) 'Revealed: Rio Tinto's plan to use drones to monitor workers' private lives', *The Guardian*, 8 December. Available at www.theguardian.com/world/2016/dec/08/revealedrio-tinto-surveillance-station-plans-to-use-drones-to-monitors-staffs-private-lives (accessed 15 April 2018).

Opstrup, N. and Villadsen, A. (2015) 'The right mix? Gender diversity in top management teams and financial performance', *Public Administration Review*, 75(2), 291–301.

Østergaard, C.R., Timmermans, B. and Kristinsson, K. (2011) 'Does a different view create something new? The effect of employee diversity on innovation', *Research Policy*, 40(3), 500–9.

O'Sullivan, M., Turner, T., McMahon, J. et al. (2015) *A Study of the Prevalence of Zero Hours Contracts among Irish Employers and its Impact on Employees*, Dublin: Department of Jobs, Enterprise and Innovation.

Ozturk, M.B. and Tatli, A. (2016) 'Gender identity inclusion in the workplace: broadening diversity management research and practice through the case of transgender employees in the UK', *International Journal of Human Resource Management*, 27(8), 781–802.

Paauwe, J. and Boselie, P. (2005) 'HRM and performance: What's next?', *CAHRS Working Paper*, 5(9), 2–28.

Page, K.M. and Vella-Brodrick, D.A. (2013) 'The working for wellness program: RCT of an employee wellbeing intervention', *Journal of Happiness Studies*, 14, 1007–31.

Parry, E. and McCarthy J. (eds) (2017) *The Palgrave Handbook of Age Diversity and Work*, London: Palgrave.

Peiperl, M.A. and Baruch, Y. (1997) 'Back to square zero: the post-corporate career', *Organizational Dynamics*, 25(4), 7–22.

Peiperl, M.A., Arthur, M., Goffee, R. and Morris, T. (2000) *Career Frontiers*, Oxford: Oxford University Press.

Petrongolo, B. (2004) 'Gender segregation in employment contracts', *Journal of the European Economic Association*, 2(2/3), 331–45.

Pett, T.L. and Wolff, J.A. (2007) 'SME performance: a case for internal consistency', *Journal of Small Business Strategy,* 18(1), 1–16.

Pfeffer, J. (1998) *The Human Equation: Building Profits by Putting People First*, Boston, MA: Harvard Business School Press.

Pilbeam, S. and Corbridge, M. (2010) *People Resourcing and Talent Planning: HRM in Practice*, 4th edn, Harlow: Pearson Education.

Pilot, S. (2011) 'Companies are embracing corporate responsibility in their annual reports', *The Guardian*, 29 September. Available at www.theguardian.com/sustainable-business/blog/companies-embrace-corporate-responsibility-annual-reporting (accessed 12 December 2017).

Pink, D. (2012) 'A radical prescription for sales', *Harvard Business Review*, 90(7/8), 76–7.

Pitts, D.W., Hicklin, A.K., Hawes, D.P. and Melton, E. (2010) 'What drives the implementation of diversity management programs? Evidence from public organizations', *Journal of Public Administration, Research and Theory*, 20(4), 867–86.

Pizer, J.C., Sears, B., Mallory, C. and Hunter, N.D. (2011) 'Evidence of persistent and pervasive workplace discrimination against LGBT people: the need for federal legislation prohibiting discrimination and providing for equal employment benefits', *Loyola of Los Angeles Law Review*, 45, 715–79.

Pocha, S.K. (2016) 'Do you work for one of the UK's 25 best companies?', *Stylist*. Available at www.stylist.co.uk/life/do-you-work-for-one-of-the-uk-25-best-companies-expedia-google-best-employers-offices-happiness/62851 (accessed 15 April 2018).

Porter, M.E. (1985) *Competitive Advantage: Creating and Sustaining Superior Performance*, New York: Free Press.

Posthuma, R.A., Campion, M.C., Masimova, M. and Campion, M.A. (2013) 'A high performance work practices taxonomy: integrating the literature and directing future research', *Journal of Management*, 39(5), 1184–220.

Presser, H.B., Gornick, J.C. and Parashar, S. (2008) 'Gender and nonstandard work hours in 12 European countries', *Monthly Labor Review*, 131(2), 83–103.

Price, A. (2004) *Human Resource Management in a Business Context*, 2nd edn, London: Thomson Learning.

Priola, V., Lasio, D., De Simone, S. and Serri, F. (2014) 'The sound of silence: lesbian, gay, bisexual and transgender discrimination in "inclusive organizations"', *British Journal of Management*, 25(3), 488–502.

Proven (2017) 'What is Nitaqat?', 25 April. Available at https://proven-sa.com/2017/04/what-is-nitaqat (accessed 15 April 2018).

Pruitt, D.G. and Rubin, J.Z. (1986) *Social Conflict: Escalation, Stalemate and Settlement*, New York: Random House.

Pudelko, M. and Harzing, A.W. (2007) 'Country-of-origin, localization, or dominance effect? An empirical investigation of HRM practices in foreign subsidiaries', *Human Resource Management*, 46(4), 535–59.

Pudelko, M. and Harzing, A.W. (2008) 'The golden triangle for MNCs: standardization towards headquarters practices, standardization towards global best practices and localization', *Organizational Dynamics*, 37(4), 394–404.

Purcell, J. (2003) *Understanding the People and Performance Link: Unlocking the Black Box*, London: CIPD.

Purcell, K., Elias, P., Davies, R. and Wilton, N. (2005) *The Class of '99: A Study of the Early Labour Market Experiences of Recent Graduates*, Warwick: Department for Education and Skills, University of Warwick.

Purkayastha, D. and Fernando, R. (2007) 'The Body Shop: Social Responsibility or Sustained Greenwashing?', ICFAI Hyderabad: Oikos Sustainability Case Collection.

PWC (2015) PwC's Nextgen: a global generational study, https://www.pwc.com/gx/en/hr-management-services/pdf/pwc-nextgen-study-2013.pdf.

Pyman, A., Holland, P., Teicher, J. and Cooper, B.K. (2010) 'Industrial relations climate, employee voice and managerial attitudes to unions: an Australian study', *British Journal of Industrial Relations*, 48(2), 460–80.

Rahimnia, F. and Sharifirad, M.S. (2015) 'Authentic leaderships and employee wellbeing: the mediating role of attachment insecurity', *Journal of Business Ethics*, 132, 363–77.

Reich, R. (2008) *Supercapitalism: The Battle for Democracy in an Age of Big Business*, Cambridge: Icon Books.

Reingardė, J. (2010) 'Heteronormativity and silenced sexualities at work', *Kultūra ir visuomenė: socialinių tyrimų žurnalas*, 1(1), 83–96.

Renwick, D. (2003) 'HR managers: Guardians of employee wellbeing?', *Personnel Review*, 32(3), 341–59.

Reuters (2017) 'Factbox: Francois Fillon's presidential election policies', 14 April. Available at www.reuters.com/article/us-france-election-programme-fillon-fact/factbox-francois-fillons-presidential-election-policies-idUSKBN17G19Y (accessed 15 April 2018).

Reyneri, E. and Fullin, G. (2011) 'Labour market penalties of new immigrants in new and old receiving West European countries', *International Migration*, 49, 31–57.

Risher, H. (2005) 'Getting serious about performance management', *Compensation & Benefits Review*, 37(6), 19–26.

RNIB (2016) *People of Working Age in England*, London: RNIB.

Roberge, M.E. and van Dick, R. (2010) 'Recognizing the benefits of diversity: When and how does diversity increase group performance?', *Human Resource Management Review*, 20(4), 295–308.

Robinson, S.L. and Rousseau, D.M. (1994) 'Violating the psychological contract: not the exception but the norm', *Journal of Organizational Behaviour*, 15(3), 245–59.

Robles, B. and McGee, M. (2016) 'Exploring online and offline informal work: findings from the Enterprising and Informal Work Activities (EIWA) Survey', *Finance and Economics Discussion Series 2016-089*, Washington: Board of Governors of the Federal Reserve System. Available at https://doi.org/10.17016/FEDS.2016.089 (accessed 11 June 2018).

Roche, W.K. and Teague, P. (2014) 'Do recessions transform work and employment? Evidence from Ireland', *British Journal of Industrial Relations*, 52(2), 261–85.

Rock, D. and Jones, B. (2014a) 'Why more and more companies are ditching performance ratings', *Harvard Business Review*, 8 September. Available at https://hbr.org/2015/09/why-more-and-more-companies-are-ditching-performance-ratings (accessed 2 April 2017).

Rock, D. and Jones, B. (2014b) 'What really happens when companies nix performance ratings', *Harvard Business Digital Articles*, 6 November. Available at https://hbr.org/2015/09/why-more-and-more-companies-are-ditching-performance-ratings (accessed 2 April 2017).

Rollag, K., Parise, S. and Cross, R. (2005) 'Getting new hires up to speed quickly', *MIT Sloan Management Review*, 46(2), 35–41.

Rosenberg, S., Heimler, R. and Morote, E.S. (2012) 'Basic employability skills: a triangular design approach', *Education + Training*, 54(1), 7–20.

Rosenfeld, J. (2017) 'Don't ask or tell: pay secrecy policies in US workplaces', *Social Science Research*, 65, 1–16.

Rosenzweig, P. and Nohria, N. (1994) 'Influences on human resource management practices in multinational corporations', *Journal of International Business Studies*, 25(2), 229–52.

Roughton, J. and Mercurio, J. (2002) *Developing an Effective Safety Culture: A Leadership Approach*, Oxford: Elsevier.

Rousseau, D.M. (1990) 'New hire perceptions of their own and their employer's obligations: a study of psychological contracts', *Journal of Organizational Behavior*, 11(5), 389–400.

Rousseau, D.M. (1995) *Psychological Contracts in Organizations: Understanding Written and Unwritten Agreements*, Newbury Park, CA: Sage.

Rousseau, D.M. (2005) *I-deals: Idiosyncratic Deal Employees Bargain for Themselves*, Armonk, NY: M.E. Sharpe.

Rousseau, D.M. and Barends, E.G. (2011) 'Becoming an evidence-based HR practitioner', *Human Resource Management Journal*, 21(3), 221–35.

Rousseau, D.M. and Tijoriwala, S. (1999) 'What's a good reason to change? Motivated reasoning and social accounts in promoting organizational change', *Journal of Applied Psychology*, 84(4), 514–28.

Royle, T. (2005) 'Realism or idealism? Corporate social responsibility and the employee stakeholder in the global fast-food industry', *Business Ethics: A European Review*, 14(1), 42–55.

Rubin, A.J. (2017) 'France lets workers turn off, tune out and live life', *The New York Times*, 2 January. Available at www.nytimes.com/2017/01/02/world/europe/france-work-email.html (accessed 15 April 2018).

Rudman, L.A. and Mescher, K. (2013) 'Penalizing men who request a family leave: Is flexibility stigma a femininity stigma?', *Journal of Social Issues*, 69, 322–40.

Ruggs, E.N., Law, C., Cox, C.B. et al. (2013) 'Gone fishing: I–O psychologists' missed opportunities to understand marginalized employees' experiences with discrimination', *Industrial and Organizational Psychology*, 6(1), 39–60.

Rumar, K., Berggrund, U., Jernberg, P. and Ytterborn, U. (1976) 'Driver reaction to a technical safety measure: studded tires', *Human Factors*, 18(5), 443–54.

Russell, H., Smyth, E. and O'Connell, P.J. (2005) *Degrees of Equality: Gender Pay Differentials among Recent Graduates*, Dublin: ESRI.

Rynes, S., Gerhart, B. and Minette, K.A. (2004) 'The importance of pay in employee motivation: discrepancies between what people say and what they do', *Human Resource Management*, 43(4), 381–94.

Sachdev, S. (2006) 'International corporate social responsibility and employment relations', in T. Edwards and C. Rees (eds) *International Human Resource Management: Globalization, National Systems and Multinational Companies*, Harlow: Pearson Education.

Safe Work Australia (2015) *The Cost of Work-related Injury and Illness for Australian Employers, Workers and the Community: 2012–13*, Canberra: Safe Work Australia.

Saks, A.M. (2006) 'Antecedents and consequences of employee engagement', *Journal of Managerial Psychology*, 21(7), 600–19.

Saks, A.M. and Gruman, J. (2014) 'Making organizations more effective through organizational socialization', *Journal of Organizational Effectiveness: People and Performance*, 1(3), 261–80.

Salamon, M. (2000) *Industrial Relations: Theory and Practice*, Harlow: Pearson Education.

Sanders, M.G. and McCormick, E.J. (1993) *Research to Determine the Contributions of System Factors in the Occurrence of Underground Injury Accidents*, Pittsburgh, PA: Bureau of Mines.

Santos Angarita, C. (2017) 'Employment and employee benefits in Columbia'. Available at https://uk.practicallaw.thomsonreuters.com/7-503-1696?transitionType=Default&contextData=(sc.Default) (accessed 14 July 2017).

Sarotar-Zizek, S., Milfelner, B. and Cancer, V. (2013) 'Measurement of employee subjective wellbeing as an aim of social responsibility', *Systemic Practice and Action Research*, 26, 549–60.

Satterfield, S. (2011) 'The role of merit pay in bonuses and incentives', *Workspan*, 11(2), 42–5.

Schaufeli, W.B. (2013) 'What is engagement?', in C. Truss, K. Alfes, R. Delbridge et al. (eds) *Employee Engagement in Theory and Practice*, Oxford: Routledge.

Schaufeli, W.B., Bakker, A.B. and Salanova, M. (2006) 'The measurement of work engagement with a short questionnaire: a cross-national study', *Educational and Psychological Measurement*, 66, 701–16.

Schaufeli, W.B., Bakker, A.B. and Van Rhenen, W. (2009) 'How changes in job demands and resources predict burnout, work engagement, and sickness absenteeism', *Journal of Organizational Behavior*, 30(7), 893–917.

Schaufeli, W.B., Salanova, M., Gonzalez-Roma, V. and Bakker, A.B. (2002) 'The measurement of engagement and burnout: a two sample confirmatory factor analytic approach', *Journal of Happiness Studies*, 3(1), 71–92.

Schein, E.H., 1975. 'How career anchors hold executives to their career paths'. *Personnel*, 52(3), 11–24.

Schein, E.H. and Van Maanen, J., (2013) *Career Anchors: The Changing Nature of Careers Participant Workbook* (Vol. 1). John Wiley & Sons.

Schnabel, C. (2013) 'Union membership and density: some (not so) stylized facts and challenges', *European Journal of Industrial Relations*, 19(3), 255–72.

Schuler, R. and Jackson, S. (1987) 'Linking competitive strategies with human resource management practices', *Academy of Management Executive*, 1(3), 209–13.

Schuler, R. and Jackson, S. (2014) 'Human resource management and organizational effectiveness: yesterday and today', *Journal of Organizational Effectiveness: People and Performance*, 1(1), 35–55.

Schulten, T. and Müller, T. (2013) 'A new European interventionism? The impact of the new European economic governance on wages and collective bargaining', in D. Natali and B. Vanhercke (eds) *Social Developments in the European Union 2012*, Brussels: ETUI/OSE, pp. 181–213.

BIBLIOGRAPHY

Schur, L., Kruse, D., Blasi, J. and Blanck, P. (2009) 'Is disability disabling in all workplaces? Workplace disparities and corporate culture', *Industrial Relations: A Journal of Economy and Society*, 48, 381–410.

Schwartz, P. and Kelly, K. (1996) 'The relentless contrarian', *Wired*, 4 August. Available at www.wired.com/wired/archive/4.08/drucker.html?topic=&topic_set= (accessed 12 December 2017).

Scott, R. (1995) *Institutions and Organizations*, Thousand Oaks, CA: Sage.

Scullion, H. (1995) 'International human resource management', in J. Storey (ed.) *Human Resource Management: A Critical Text*, London: Routledge.

Sears, B. and Mallory, C. (2011) *Documented Evidence of Employment Discrimination and Its Effects on LGBT People*, Los Angeles, CA: Williams Institute.

Selmer, J. (2001) 'Expatriate selection: Back to basics?', *International Journal of Human Resource Management*, 12(8), 1219–33.

Shaw, K.N. (2004) 'Changing the goal-setting process at Microsoft', *Academy of Management Executive*, 18(4), 138–42.

Shelton, B.A., and John, D. (1996) 'The division of household labor', *Annual Review of Sociology*, 22, 299–322.

Sikora, D.M. and Ferris, G.R. (2014) 'Strategic human resource practice implementation: the critical role of line management', *Human Resource Management Review*, 24(3), 271–81.

Sisson, K. (2008) 'Putting the record straight: industrial relations and the employment relationship', Warwick Papers in Industrial Relations, No. 88, University of Warwick.

Sisson, K. and Storey, J. (2000) *The Realities of Human Resource Management*, Buckingham: Open University Press.

Skene, H., Perry, D. and Brennan, M. (2017) 'Employment and employee benefits in Australia: overview'. Available at https://uk.practicallaw.thomsonreuters.com/3-503-3758?transitionType=Default&contextData=(sc.Default) (accessed 14 July 2017).

Slay, H.S. and Taylor, M.S. (2006) 'Career systems and psychological contracts', in H. Gunz and M. Peiperl (eds) *Handbook of Career Studies*, Thousand Oaks, CA: Sage, pp. 377–98.

Sloman, M. (2010) *Learning and Development 2020: A Guide for the Next Decade*, Cambridge: Fenman.

Smith, A. ([1759]2007) *The Theory of Moral Sentiments*, Minneapolis, MN: Filiquarian.

Smith, A. ([1776]2009) *An Inquiry into the Nature and Causes of the Wealth of Nations*, Digireads.com Publishing.

Smith, C. and Meiskins, P. (1995) 'System, society, and dominance effects in cross-national organizational analysis', *Work, Employment and Society*, 9(2), 241–67.

Smith, M. and Smith, P. (2005) *Testing People at Work: Competencies in Psychometric Testing*, Oxford: BPS Blackwell.

Smith, M.J. and Sainfort, P.C. (1989) 'A balance theory of job design for stress reduction', *International Journal of Industrial Ergonomics*, 4(1), 67–79.

Snyder, M. and Swann, W.B. (1978) 'Hypothesis-testing processes in social interaction', *Journal of Personality and Social Psychology*, 36(11), 1202–12.

Sonnenfeld, J.A. and Peiperl, M.A. (1988) 'Staffing policy as a strategic response: a typology of career systems', *Academy of Management Review*, 13(4), 568–600.

Sparrow, P., Brewster, C. and Harris, H. (2004) *Globalizing Human Resource Management*, London: Routledge.

Spencer, L.M. (2001) 'The economic value of emotional intelligence competencies and EIC-based programs', in C. Cherniss and D. Goleman (eds) *The Emotionally Intelligent Workplace: How to Select for, Measure, and Improve Emotional Intelligence in Individuals, Groups and Organizations*, San Francisco, CA: Jossey-Bass/Wiley.

Steiner J. and Steiner G. (2012) *Business, Government, and Society: A Managerial Perspective, Text and Cases*, 13th edn, New York: McGraw-Hill.

Storey, J. (1989) 'Human resource management in the public sector', *Public Money and Management*, 9(3), 19–24.

Storey, J. (1992) *Developments in the Management of Human Resources*, Oxford: Blackwell.

Storey, J. (1995) *Human Resource Management: A Critical Text*, London: Routledge.

Strebler, M.T., Bevan, S. and Robinson, D. (2001) *Performance Review: Balancing Objectives and Content*, Brighton: Institute for Employment Studies.

Stumpf, S.A. (2010) 'Stakeholder competency assessments as predictors of career success', *Career Development International*, 15, 459–78.

Suchman, E. (1961) 'On accident behaviour', in E. Suchman (ed.) *Behavioural Approaches to Accident Research*, Washington DC: Association for the Aid of Crippled Children.

Sujansky, J. (2007) 'The poor performer confrontation handbook: eight rules for dealing with employees who are bringing your company down', *Cost Engineering*, 49(8), 14–15.

Suk, J.C. (2012) 'From antidiscrimination to equality: stereotypes and the lifecycle in the United States and Europe', *American Journal of Comparative Law*, 60(1), 75–98.

Sullivan, S.E. and Arthur, M.B. (2006) 'The evolution of the boundaryless career concept: examining physical and psychological mobility', *Journal of Vocational Behavior*, 69(1), 19–29.

Sun, P.Y.-T. and Scott, J.L. (2006) 'An investigation of barriers to knowledge transfer', *Journal of Knowledge Management*, 9(2), 75–90.

Super, D. (1953) 'A theory of vocational development', *American Psychologist*, 8(5), 185–90.

Super, D. (1957) *Psychology of Careers*, New York: Harper and Brothers.

BIBLIOGRAPHY

Super, D. (1980) 'A life-span, life-space approach to career development', *Journal of Vocational Behaviour*, 16(3), 282–98.

Susser, P., Weber, A. and Friedman, S. (2017) 'Employment and employee benefits in United States: overview'. Available at https://uk.practicallaw.thomsonreuters.com/1-503-3486?__lrTS=20170429215039402& transitionType=Default&contextData=(sc.Default) (accessed 14 July 2017).

Svejenova, S. (2005) '"The path with the heart": creating the authentic career', *Journal of Management Studies*, 42(5), 947–74.

Tahvanainen, M., Welch, D. and Worm, V. (2005) 'Implications of short-term international assignments', *European Management Journal*, 23(6), 663–73.

Tams, S. and Arthur, M.B. (2006) 'Boundaryless career', in J.H. Greenhaus and G.A. Callanan (eds) *Encyclopedia of Career Development*, Thousand Oaks, CA: Sage, pp. 44–9.

Taneja, S., Sewell, S.S. and Odom, R.Y. (2015) 'A culture of employee engagement: a strategic perspective for global management', *Journal of Business Strategy*, 36(3), 46–56.

Tansley, C. (2011) 'What do we mean by the term "talent" in talent management?', *Industrial and Commercial Training*, 43(5), 266–74.

Taras, D.G. and Kaufman, B.E. (2006) 'Non-union employee representation in North America: diversity, controversy and uncertain future', *Industrial Relations Journal*, 37(5), 513–42.

Taylor, F.W. (1914) *The Principles of Scientific Management*, New York: Harper.

Taylor, P. (2013) *Performance Management and the New Workplace Tyranny*, report for the Scottish Trades Union Congress, Glasgow.

Taylor, P., Baldry, C., Bain, P. and Ellis, V. (2003) 'A unique working environment: health, sickness and absence management in UK call centres', *Work, Employment and Society*, 17(3), 435–58.

Taylor, S. (2005) *People Resourcing*, 3rd edn, London: CIPD.

Teather, D. (2005) 'Nike lists abuses at Asian factories', *The Guardian*, 14 April. Available at www.theguardian.com/business/2005/apr/14/ethicalbusiness.money (accessed 12 December 2017).

Teo, S.T. and Rodwell, J.J. (2007) 'To be strategic in the new public sector, HR must remember its operational activities', *Human Resource Management*, 46(2), 265–84.

Thompson, R. (2009) '"Prison-like" conditions for workers making IBM, Dell, HP, Microsoft and Lenovo products', Computerweekly.com, 17 February. Available at www.computerweekly.com/news/2240088431/Prison-like-conditions-for-workers-making-IBM-Dell-HP-Microsoft-and-Lenovo-products (accessed 12 December 2017).

Thomson, N. (2016) *Anti-discriminatory Practice: Equality, Diversity and Social Justice*, London: Palgrave.

Thorndike, E.L. (1920) 'A constant error in psychological ratings', *Journal of Applied Psychology*, 4(1), 25–9.

Thornton, G.C. and Kedharnath, U. (2013) 'Work sample tests', in K.F. Geisinger, B.A. Bracken, J.F. Carlson et al. (eds) *APA Handbook of Testing and Assessment in Psychology*, vol. 1, *Test Theory and Testing and Assessment in Industrial and Organizational Psychology*, Washington DC: APA, pp. 533–50.

Tichy, N.M., Fombrun, C.J. and Devanna, M.A. (1982) 'Strategic human resource management', *Sloan Management Review*, 23(2), 47–61.

Tilcsik, A. (2011) 'Pride and prejudice: employment discrimination against openly gay men in the United States 1', *American Journal of Sociology*, 117(2), 586–626.

Tomlinson, F. and Schwabenland, C. (2010) 'Reconciling competing discourses of diversity? The UK non-profit sector between social justice and the business case', *Organization*, 17(1), 101–21.

Tomlinson, J., Olsen, W. and Purdam, K. (2009) 'Women returners and potential returners: employment profiles and labour market opportunities, a case study of the United Kingdom', *European Sociological Review*, 25(3), 349–63.

Trullen, J., Stirpe, L., Bonache, J. and Valverde, M. (2016) 'The HR department's contribution to line managers' effective implementation of HR practices', *Human Resource Management Journal*, 26(4), 449–70.

Truss, K. (2014) 'The future of research in employee engagement', in D. Robinson and J. Gifford (eds) *The Future of Engagement: Thought Piece Collection*, London: Engage for Success.

Turner, T. and D'Art, D. (2012) 'Public perceptions of trade unions in countries of the European Union: a causal analysis', *Labor Studies Journal*, 37(1), 33–55.

Turner, T. and Flannery, D. (2016) 'Did partnership in Ireland deliver for all workers? Unions and earnings', *Employee Relations*, 38(6), 946–60.

Turner, T. and McMahon, J. (2011) 'Women's occupational trends in the Irish economy: Moving towards high-skilled occupations or evidence of deskilling?', *Gender, Work & Organization*, 18, e222–40.

Ugwu, F.O., Onyishi, I.E. and Rodríguez-Sánchez, A.M. (2014) 'Linking organizational trust with employee engagement: the role of psychological empowerment', *Personnel Review*, 43(3), 377–400.

Ulrich, D., Younger, J. and Brockbank, W. (2008) 'The twenty-first-century HR organization', *Human Resource Management*, 47(4), 829–50.

Ulrich, D., Younger, J., Brockbank, W. and Ulrich, M. (2012) *HR from the Outside In*, New York: McGraw.

UN (2011) *The Global Social Crisis: Report on the World Situation 2011*, New York: UN.

United Nations Conference on Trade and Development (2017) *World Investment Report Investment and the Digital Economy*, New York: UN.

United States Census Bureau (2016) *Income and Poverty in the United States: 2015*. Available at www.census.gov/library/publications/2016/demo/p60-256.html (accessed 11 November 2017).

BIBLIOGRAPHY

UNPRI (2015) *Principles for Responsible Investment: PRI Report on Progress 2015*, New York: UNPRI Secretariat.

US Bureau of Labour Statistics (2016) *Quarterly Labour Statistics*. Available at www.bls.gov/cew/apps/data_views/data_views.htm#tab=Tables (accessed 8 February 2017).

US Office of Personnel Management (n.d.) *Federal Classification and Job Grading Systems*. Available at www.opm.gov/fedclass/html/gsclass.asp (accessed 6 June 2012).

Valcour, P.M. (2006) 'Customized careers', in J.H. Greenhaus and G.A. Callanan (eds) *Encyclopedia of Career Development*, Thousand Oaks, CA: Sage, pp. 220–4.

Valizade, D., Ogbonnaya, C., Tregaskis, O. and Forde, C. (2016) 'A mutual gains perspective on workplace partnership: employee outcomes and the mediating role of the employment relations climate', *Human Resource Management Journal*, 26(3), 351–68.

Van Buren, H., Greenwood, M. and Sheehan, C. (2011) 'Strategic human resource management and the decline of employee focus', *Human Resource Management Review*, 21(3), 209–19.

Van Den Heuvel, S. and Bondarouk, T. (2016) 'The rise (and fall?) of HR analytics: the future application, value, structure, and system support', *Academy of Management Proceedings*, 1, 10908.

Van Woerkom, M. and de Bruijn, M. (2016) 'Why performance appraisal does not lead to performance improvement: excellent performance as a function of uniqueness instead of uniformity', *Industrial and Organizational Psychology*, 9(2), 275–81.

Vidal-Salazar, M.D., Cordón-Pozo, E. and Ferrón-Vilchez, V. (2012) 'Human resource management and developing proactive environmental strategies: the influence of environmental training and organizational learning', *Human Resource Management*, 51(6), 905–34.

Virtanen, M., Heikkilä, K., Jokela, M. et al. (2012) 'Long working hours and coronary heart disease: a systematic review and meta-analysis', *American Journal of Epidemiology*, 176(7), 586–96.

Visser, W. (2011) *The Age of Responsibility: CSR 2.0 and the New DNA of Business*, Chichester: John Wiley & Sons.

VitalSmarts (2014) 'Does bullying provide job security?'. Available at www.vitalsmarts.com/press/2014/06/does-bullying-provide-job-security-youll-be-infuriated-by-the-answer/ (accessed 11 June 2018).

Vogel, D. (2006) *The Market for Virtue: The Potential and Limits of Corporate Social Responsibility*, Washington DC: The Brookings Institute.

Vogel, D. and Reich, R. (2008) 'Corporate social responsibility: Is it responsible', Debate, 2 September, Haas School of Business, UC Berkeley. Available at www.youtube.com/watch?v=OreAJnDuVzk (accessed 12 December 2017).

Vosko, L. (2010) *Managing the Margins: Gender, Citizenship, and the International Regulation of Precarious Employment*, Oxford: Oxford University Press.

Voydanoff, P. (2004) 'Implications of work and community demands and resources for work-to-family conflict and facilitation', *Journal of Occupational Health Psychology*, 9(4), 275–85.

Vroom, V.H. (1964) *Work and Motivation*, San Francisco, CA: Jossey-Bass.

Waber, B. (2013) *People Analytics: How Social Sensing Technology will Transform Business and What It Tells Us about the Future of Work*, Upper Saddle River, NJ: FT Press.

Wadlow, T. (2016) 'Revealed: Glassdoor's top 50 companies to work for 2017', *Business Chief Europe*, 7 December. Available at https://europe.businesschief.com/leadership/1181/Revealed:-Glassdoors-top-50-companies-to-work-for-2017 (accessed 15 April 2018).

Wall, M. (2017) 'Report outlines public hospitals' struggle to recruit consultants', *The Irish Times*, 15 May.

Wallace, J. and O'Sullivan, M. (2006) 'Contemporary strike trends since 1980: peering through the wrong end of a telescope', in M.J. Morley, P. Gunnigle and D.G. Collings (eds) *Global Industrial Relations*, London: Routledge.

Wallace, J., Gunnigle, P., McMahon, G. and O'Sullivan, M. (2013) *Industrial Relations in Ireland: Theory and Practice*, 4th edn, Dublin: Gill & Macmillan.

Walton, R. (1985) 'From control to commitment in the workplace', *Harvard Business Review*, 63, 77–84.

Wang, S. and Noe, R.A. (2010) 'Knowledge sharing: a review and directions for future research', *Human Resource Management Review*, 20(2), 115–31.

Wanous, J. P., & Colella, A. (1989). Organizational entry research: Current status and future directions. In G. Ferris & K. Rowland (Eds.), *Research in personnel and human resource management* (Vol. 7, pp. 59–120). Greenwich, CT: JAI Press.

Warburton. (2018) Autism Awareness, How Neurodiversity can Benefit your Business. https://www.csgtalent.com/blog/2018/04/autism-awareness-neurodiversity-benefit.

Wayne, S.J., Liden, R.C., Kraimer, M.L. and Graf, I.K. (1999) 'The role of human capital, motivation, and supervisor sponsorship in predicting career success', *Journal of Occupational Behavior*, 20, 577–95.

Welch, D.E. and Worm, V. (2006) 'International business travellers: a challenge for IHRM', in G.K. Stahl and I. Björkman (eds) *Handbook of Research in International Human Resource Management*, Cheltenham: Edward Elgar.

Wentworth, D. and Lombardi, M. (2014) '5 Trends for the Future of Learning and Development', *Training Magazine*. Available at https://trainingmag.com/5-trends-future-learning-and-development (accessed 15 April 2018).

Wernimont, P.F. and Campbell, J.P. (1968) 'Signs, samples and criteria', *Journal of Applied Psychology*, 52, 372–6.

Whitley, R. (2000) *Divergent Capitalism: The Social Structuring and Change of Business Systems*, Oxford: Oxford University Press.

BIBLIOGRAPHY

Whittaker, S. and Marchington, M. (2003) 'Devolving HR responsibility to the line: Threat, opportunity or partnership?', *Employee Relations*, 25(3), 245–61.

Wilensky, H. (1961) 'Work, careers and social integration', *International Social Science Journal*, 12(4), 543–74.

Wilkinson, A. and Fay, C. (2011) 'Guest editors' note: New times for employee voice?', *Human Resource Management*, 50(1), 65–74.

Willis Towers Watson (2016) 'Under pressure to remain relevant, employers look to modernize the employee value proposition. Global findings for the Global Management and Rewards and Global Workforce Studies'. Available at http://files.smart.pr/c5/32de60aca711e6ae1699296a76e296/Global-findings-report-for-the-2016-Global-Talent-Management-and-Rewards-and-Global-Workforce-Studies.pdf (accessed 17 July 2017).

Wolf v. *Stadt Frankfurt am Main* [2010] 2 CMLR 849.

Wood, D. (2010) 'Measuring corporate social performance: a review', *International Journal of Management Reviews*, 12(1), 50–84.

Wood, G. (2015) 'South African multinationals in Africa: growth and controversy', in M. Demirbag and A. Yeprak (eds) *Handbook of Emerging Market Multinational Corporations*, Cheltenham: Edward Elgar.

World Bank (2015) *Women, Business and the Law 2016: Getting to Equal*, Washington DC: World Bank.

World Economic Forum (2016) *The Global Gender Gap Report 2016*, Geneva: WEF.

Wright, T.A. and Doherty, E.M. (1998) 'Organizational behaviour "rediscovers" the role of emotional wellbeing', *Journal of Organizational Behaviour*, 19, 481–5.

Xanthopoulou, D., Bakker, A.B., Demerouti, E. and Schaufeli, W.B. (2009) 'Reciprocal relationships between job resources, personal resources, and work engagement', *Journal of Vocational Behavior*, 74(3), 235–44.

XpertHR (2015) 'Absence rates and costs: XpertHR survey 2015'. Available at www.xperthr.co.uk/survey-analysis/absence-rates-and-costs-xperthr-survey-2015/156086/ (accessed 11 June 2018).

Yardley, J. (2013) 'Justice still elusive in factory disasters in Bangladesh', *New York Times*, June 29. Available at www.nytimes.com/2013/06/30/world/asia/justice-elusive-in-a-bangladesh-factory-disaster.html (accessed 15 April 2018).

Yerkes, R.M. and Dodson, J.D. (1908) 'The relation of strength of stimulus to rapidity of habit-formation', *Journal of Comparative Neurology and Psychology*, 18, 459–82.

Zahhly, J. and Tosi, H. (1989) 'The differential effect of organizational induction process on early work role adjustment', *Journal of Organizational Behavior*, 10(1), 59–74.

Zibarras, L.D. and Woods, S.A. (2010) 'A survey of UK selection practices across different organization sizes and industry sectors', *Journal of Occupational and Organizational Psychology*, 83(2), 499–511.

Index

Page numbers in *italic* indicate figures and tables, and in **bold** indicate glossary terms.

7-Eleven stores   286–288, 289
180-degree feedback   127–128
360-degree feedback   128, 265

A

ability–motivation–opportunity (AMO) model   122, 242–243
absenteeism   241–242, 248–250
absorption   61
accidents   223–227, *224, 225, 227,* **293**
action planning   25, **293**
adaptive learning   174
ADDIE model   170, 173–181, *175*
   analysis stage   175–176, *176–177*
   design stage   177–179
   development stage   179, *180*
   evaluation stage   180–181, *181–182*
   implementation stage   179–180
adjudication services   91–92
adjustment of expatriates   263–264, *264*
advanced HR practices   9, 122, **293**
ageing populations   102–103
agency work   86, **293**
Amazon   236
AMO *see* ability–motivation–opportunity (AMO) model
analytical methods   149, 150–151, *152,* **293**
Apple   75
applicant tracking system (ATS)   43, 46
application forms   45
apps, work on demand via   87–88
arbitration services   91–92
Asperger's Syndrome   102
assessment centres   52–53, *53,* 263
assignments   179
attainment tests   52
attitude-based approach to health and safety   228–229, **293**
attributional bias   131
atypical jobs   86
austerity policies   85, 90

Australian Disability Enterprises (ADEs)   116–117
authentic careers   188, 190, 192–193, *196,* **293**
authoritarian management   81
autism   101, 102

B

balanced sheet approach to expatriate pay   265
base pay   141, *146,* **293**
behaviour-based approach to health and safety   229–230, **293**
behavioural-based interviews   50, 63
behavioural science   4
behavioural science approach to health and safety   228–230, **293**
behaviourally anchored rating scale (BARS)   126, *126*
behaviourism   168, **293**
benefits *see* employee benefits
best fit approach   16–17
best practice approach   17, 230, 235, 246, 247, 259, 260
bicultural employees   114
Big Five   52
binary variables   213
Bird, Frank   224–225
bite-sized learning strategies   178
blended learning strategies   178
Body Shop   278, 279
bonuses   143, 158–161
boundaryless careers   188, 190–191, *196,* 203, **293**
Bourdain, Anthony   203–204
BP   111
Brexit   84, 171–172, 257–258
Browne, Lord   111
buddy approach   68, **293**
building a shared vision   173
bullying   239–240, **293**
burnout, employee   65, **294**
Bush, George W.   246
business case arguments   281–282
business context   6–7
Business in the Community   274, 283
business strategy   6, 7, 8, 11–12

Business Supported Wages Assessment Tool (BSWAT)   116–117

C

Cadbury   278–279
canteens, subsidized   145
capitalist system   81, **293**
Capventis   215
career   188, **293**
career anchor theory   200–201, *201*
career capital   193, **293**
career development   147, 188–204, **293**
   authentic careers   188, 190, 192–193, *196,* **293**
   boundaryless careers   188, 190–191, *196,* 203, **293**
   career anchor theory   200–201, *201*
   career systems   202–204
   case study   203–204
   defined   188–189
   employee engagement and   203–204
   expatriates   190, 263, 267, 268
   global careers   190
   graduates   197–199
   kaleidoscope careers   188, 190, 193, *196,* **296**
   male competitive model   194
   mentoring   201, 202
   off-ramp careers   190, 193–195, *196,* **296**
   portfolio careers   188, 195–196, *196,* **297**
   protean careers   188, 190, 191–192, *196,* 203, **297**
   psychosocial support   201, *201*
   responsibility for   199–200
   scenario-based activity   202
   traditional careers   189, *189,* **298**
   women   193–195
case study learning   *180*
categorical variables   212–213
causal factors   208, **293**
central tendency bias   131
Chartered Institute of Personnel and Development (CIPD)   50, 52, 167, 209, 214, 231, *232–233*

Chernobyl nuclear power plant   223
child labour   274, 276–277
childcare   108, 145
classification systems for job
        evaluation   150, *151*
classroom courses   178
coaching   134, 178
'coffee machine' system of
        selection   263
cognitive ability tests   52
cognitivism   168, **293**
cohort analysis   76
collective bargaining   80, 81, 82, **293**
collectivism versus individualism   259
commission   143
common law   248, **293**
commuter assignments   *269*
comparators   109, **293**
compensation *see* pay and rewards
competencies
        defined   38, **293**
        of HR practitioners   12–13
        Peter Principle   74
        in recruitment and selection   38, 39
competency-based assessment   128
competency-based interviews   50, **293**
conciliation services   91–92
Confederation of British Industry
        (CBI)   212, 274–275
confirmatory bias   51, 130
conflict resolution   90–94
conflicting outcomes   242–243
conflicts   80, 81, 82, 90–91
contingency approach   16–17
continuous improvement   4
continuous variables   213
contrast error   51, 130
convergence thesis   259
coordinated market economies
        (CMEs)   259
corporate social responsibility
        (CSR)   274–290
        business case arguments   281–282
        case against   284–286, 288–290
        case study   286–288
        conceptual model   275–276, *275*
        controversy of   278–284
        customers and   283
        defined   274–275, **294**
        employees and   282–283
        investors and   282, 283–284
        issues   276–278, *277*
        regulation   279, 288–290
        social contract arguments   280–281
costs
        accidents   222, 225, *227*
        bullying   239–240

childcare   108
corporate social
        responsibility   280, 285, 286,
        288–289
employee turnover   61, 73–74
pay and rewards   141, 144, *146*,
        152–156
presenteeism   242
recruitment   42, 43
reducing working hours   245
selection methods   47
sickness absence   241, 242
country of origin effects   260, **294**
Court of Justice of the European
        Union   110, 113
courts   91, 110
crèche facilities   145
critical incident technique   127
cross-cultural adjustment   263–264, *264*
cross-cultural awareness training   263
crowdworking   86–87
CSR *see* corporate social
        responsibility (CSR)
cultural dimensions   6, 259
culture *see* national culture;
        organizational culture
CVs/résumés   45

Dana-Farber   29
Data Democratic   215
dedication   61
del Ray, Lana   192–193
Deming, W. Edwards   130
descriptive analytics   *210*
development
        defined   167, **294**
        see also career development;
                learning and development
devolved   13, **294**
digital learning   178
dignity at work policies   239
direct discrimination   109, **294**
direct pay   141–144, *141*, **294**
direct voice mechanisms   89
disability   107, 116–117
disciplinary procedures   80, 90–91,
        133, 135, 241, **294**
discrimination   54, 103–118
        defined   103, **294**
        direct   109, **294**
        disability   107, 116–117
        ethnic minorities   105, 115
        gender   105, 106, 107, 108, 109, 285
        human capital factors   105, *107*
        indirect   109–110, **295**

institutional factors   106–107, *107*,
        296
legislation   54, 91, 101, 108–114,
        112–113, 115
LGBT employees   110–112, *112–113*
older workers   106, 110, 114
positive action/discrimination
        114–115, **297**
protected grounds   108, **297**
scenario-based activity   116–118
in selection process   46, 47, 54
social justice perspective   101,
        113–114, **298**
socially constructed factors   106, *107*
victimization   110, **299**
dismissals   85, 90–91
display screens   234
disputes *see* employment disputes
distributive justice   125
divergence thesis   259
diversity   *10*, 100–103
        bicultural/multicultural
                employees   114
        case study   102–103
        defined   100
        diversity management
                perspective   101, **294**
        older workers   102–103
        recruitment   46
        social justice perspective   101,
                113–114, **298**
doctors, rural   63
dominance effects   260–261, **294**
domino theory   226
downsizing   73
due diligence   152
duty of care   248

e-recruitment   43, **294**
early school leavers   105
economic crisis   85
economies
        boom and bust   72–73, 74
        coordinated market   259
        liberal market   259
education
        defined   166, **294**
        see also learning and development
email, after-hours   241
employability   198, **294**
employee assistance programmes
        (EAP)   145
employee benefits   3, 85, 144–145
        advantages and disadvantages   *146*
        flexible   72, **295**

organization-specific *141*, 144–145
retention and 18, 72–73
statutory benefits *141*, 144, *145*
employee burnout 65, **294**
employee empowerment 223, 244, **294**
employee engagement 29, 60–61, 62, 64, 72
  career development and 203–204
  defined 62, 125, **294**
  performance management and 125–126
employee engagement surveys 72, **294**
employee handbooks 65
employee induction *see* induction
employee lifecycle 8–9, *9*
employee participation 89, 91
employee presenteeism 242
employee referrals 42
employee representation 4, 5, 81, 82–84, *83*, 88
  see also trade unions
employee retention *see* retention
employee satisfaction 62, 94–95
employee share ownership plans (ESOPs) 143–144, *146*
employee turnover 60–61, 71–76
  advantages of 73
  analysis of 76
  case study 75
  costs 61, 73–74
  defined 71, **294**
  impact of high-profile leavers 74–75
  labour market and 72–73, 74
  measuring 76
  pull factors 71, **297**
  push factors 71–72, **297**
  scenario-based activity 77
  turnover rate 76
employee voice 62, 80, 89, 91
employee wellbeing 222, 231–245, *232–233*
  bullying 239–240, **293**
  case study 236–237
  defined 231, **294**
  ergonomics 227, 228, 234–235, 246, **294**
  HRM approaches 245–247
  job characteristics 235
  job strain 238–239
  mental workload 235, **296**
  presenteeism 242
  responsibility for 243–244
  right to disconnect 241
  scenario-based activity 248–250
  sickness absence 241–242, 248–250

stress 64–65, 110, 130, 234, 237–238, *238*, **298**
theoretical considerations 242–243, *243*
work capacity 235, **299**
workaholism 240
working hours debate 245
see also health and safety
employer brand 44, **294**
employer organizations 84
employment disputes 80, 81, 82, 90–91
  resolution 90–94
employment legislation 4, 84–85
  equality 54, 91, 101, 108–114, *112–113*, 115
  exceptions to 110
  health and safety 84, 248
  LGBT employees *112–113*
  minimum wage 84, 153
  positive action 115
  right to disconnect 241
  selection process 54
employment relationship 5, 80–95
  case study 87–88
  conflict resolution 90–94
  conflicts 80, 81, 82, 90–91
  disciplinary procedures 80, 90–91, 133, 135, 241, **294**
  employee participation 89, 91
  employee representation 4, 5, 81, 82–84, *83*, 88
  employee voice 62, 80, 89, 91
  employer organizations 84
  employment rights 4, 84–85
  gig economy 86–88, **295**
  global economic crisis and 85
  grievance procedures 80, 91, **295**
  job quality 86–88
  nature of 80
  negotiation 92–94
  scenario-based activity 94–95
  theoretical perspectives 81
employment rights 4, 84–85
  abuses in supply chain 274, 277–278, *278*, 285–286
  gig economy 87–88
  LGBT employees *112–113*
  see also employment legislation
empowerment 223, 244, **294**
engagement
  defined **294**
  work 61–62, **299**
  see also employee engagement
enlightened shareholder value 282
Enron 127
environmental issues 282

equality 103–118
  defined 103, **294**
  disability 107, 116–117
  ethnic minorities 105, 115
  gender 105, 106, 107, 108, 109, 285
  human capital factors 105, *107*
  importance of 104
  institutional factors 106–107, *107*, **296**
  legislation 54, 91, 101, 108–114, *112–113*, 115
  LGBT employees 110–112, *112–113*
  older workers 106, 110, 113
  positive action/discrimination 114–115, **297**
  procedures 90–91
  scenario-based activity 116–118
  in selection process 46, 47, 54
  social justice perspective 101, 113–114, **298**
  socially constructed factors 106, *107*
  victimization 110, **299**
equity theory 124
ergonomics 227, 228, 234–235, 246, **294**
ethical labelling schemes 283
Ethical Trading Initiative (ETI) 276, 277, *277*, 283, 289
ethnic minorities 105, 114
ethnicity pay gap 147, 148
European Commission 85, 104, 275
European Federation of Employee Share Ownership 143–144
European Union 86
  Brexit 84, 171–172, 257–258
  early school leavers 105
  economic crisis and 85
  employee voice 89
  employment rights 84
  equality legislation 109
  gender pay gap 148
  labour costs 152
  unemployment 197
evaluation
  defined 181, **294**
  job evaluation 148–151, *150*, *151–152*, **296**
  learning and development 180–181, *181–182*
evidence-based approach 8
exit interviews 76
expatriates 254, 261–268, **294**
  adjustment 263–264, *264*
  career development 190, 263, 267, 268
  failure 269–270
  pay and rewards 264–265

expatriates (*cont.*)
  performance management
       265–266, *266*
  preparation 263
  recruitment and selection 262–263
  repatriation 266–267, **297**
  scenario-based activity 269–270
expatriation 254, 261–262, **294**
expectancy theory 123
Expedia 165–166
experiential learning 168–169, *169*, **294**
external comparisons 148, 154–156, *157*, **294**
external recruitment 31, 42, 44, **294**

Facebook 41, 43, 48–49
Fair Labor Association 277, 285, 286
family, expatriation and 262, 263, 267, 269–270
fatalities, workplace 223–224, *224*
feedback **295**
  180-degree 127–128
  360-degree 128, 266
  performance management 123, 125, 130
feedforward interviews 132
felt-fair concept 148–149, **295**
femininity versus masculinity 259
first impression error 51, 130
five factor model of personality 52
flexible benefits 72, **295**
flexible working arrangements 71, 107, 147, 195
forced labour 289
forced ranking 127, *127*
forecasting 24–25, **295**
foreign direct investment (FDI) 258
Fox, Alan 81
frequent flyer assignments *268*
Friedman, Milton 280, 285

gainsharing schemes 144, *146*
gender
  career development and 193–195
  inequality 105, 106, 107, 108, 109, 285
  pay gap 107, 147–148, 212
general strikes 90, **295**
gig economy 86–88, **295**
global careers 190
global economic crisis 85
global virtual teams *269*
globalization 83, 90, 152, 258–261, **295**
goal-setting theory 123

going rate approach to expatriate pay 265
Google 18, 30, 44, 61, 66, 131–132, 194, 231
graduate careers 197–199
graduate recruitment 34–35, 42
graphology 53
Great Place to Work Awards 44
Great Recession 85
green HRM 282, **295**
greenwashing 285
grievance procedures 80, 91, **295**
group discussion *180*
groupthink 73
GROW model 134
Guest model 15–16, *16*

halo effect 51, 130–131
handwriting analysis 53
Hawthorne Effect 4
hazards 230, **295**
health and safety 222–230
  accidents 223–227, *224*, *225*, *227*, **293**
  attitude-based approach 228–229, **293**
  behaviour-based approach 229–230, **293**
  behavioural science approach 228–230, **293**
  common law 248
  duty of care 248
  ergonomics 227, 228, 234–235, 246, **294**
  hazards 230, **295**
  HRM approaches 245–247
  human factors 227–230, *228*, **295**
  legislation 84, 248
  negligence 248
  reporting systems 223, 230
  risk 229, **297**
  safety culture 222–223, **297**
  safety statements 247
  workplace fatalities 223–224, *224*
Heinrich, Herbert William 224, 226, 229–230
high-commitment HRM 17, **295**
high-involvement HRM 17, **295**
high-performance work practices (HPWPs) 9, 122
high performance work system (HPWS) 9
HIPOs (high-potential employees) 29, 31, 33, 72, 73, 201, **295**
Hofstede, Geert 6, 259
holiday entitlements 144, *145*

horizontal integration 8, **295**
horns effect 51
host country effects 261, **295**
host country nationals (HCNs) *256*
HR philosophy 2, **295**
human capital 105, *107*
human capital pool 66, **295**
human error 226–227, 229–230, **295**
human factors 227–230, *228*, **295**
human resource development (HRD) 167, **295**
  strategic 170–171, **298**
  see also learning and development
human resource (HR) analytics 208–218
  capability development 211, 214, *214*
  case study 212
  data sources 210–211, *211*
  defined 208–209, **295**
  descriptive analytics *210*
  ethics 215
  evidence-based decision-making 215
  measurement and tools 212–213
  predictive analytics *210*
  prescriptive analytics *210*
  scenario-based activity 216–218
  strategic decision-making and 209–210
human resource information systems (HRIS) 208, **295**
human resource management (HRM) 2–3, **295**
  business context and 6–7
  evolution of 3–5
  features and characteristics 7–8
  green 282, **295**
  high-commitment 17, **295**
  high-involvement 17, **295**
  low-involvement 17, **296**
  philosophy 2, **295**
  strategic 6–13, *8*, *10*, 246, **298**
  structure of HR function 11–13, *13*
  sustainable 282, **298**
  theoretical basis 14–17
  who benefits from 10–11
human resource planning 22–26
  action planning 25, **293**
  forecasting 24–25, **295**
  stocktaking 23, **298**
  see also talent management
human trafficking 289

IHRM *see* international human resource management (IHRM)
IKEA 82

imposter phenomenon   197
in-tray exercises   *180*
in-tray simulations   53
income inequality   83, 86
Independent Drivers Guild   88
indirect discrimination   109–110, **295**
indirect pay   3, 85, *141*, 144–145, **295**
individualism versus collectivism   259
induction   60–61, 64–70, **295**
   buddy approach   68, **293**
   case study   70–71
   informational approach   65–66, 69,
      69, **296**
   line management involvement   65,
      70
   mentoring   68
   onboarding   66–69, *69*, **296**
   relational approach   67–69, *69*, **297**
   survival curve   64–65, **298**
industrial relations   4, 5, 81, 82–84,
   83, 90, **295**
industrial welfare   3
inequality
   disability   107, 116–117
   gender   105, 106, 107, 108, 109, 285
   income   83, 86
   see also equality
inferential statistics   208, **296**
information sharing   122
informational approach to
   induction   65–66, 69, *69*, **296**
Infosys   70–71
institutional barriers to
   employment   106–107, *107*, **296**
instrumentality   123
intelligence tests   52
interactional justice   125
internal alignment   148–151, *148*, **296**
internal recruitment   31, 41, 44, **296**
international human resource
   management (IHRM)   254–270,
   255
   adjustment of expatriates
      263–264, *264*
   alternative international
      assignments   268, *268–269*
   Brexit and   257–258
   case study   257–258
   convergence thesis   259
   country of origin effects   260, **294**
   divergence thesis   259
   dominance effects   260–261, **294**
   employee types   *256*
   expatriate assignments   261–268
   expatriate failure   267–268
   globalization and   258–261
   host country effects   261, **295**

international integration   261, **296**
   national culture and   259
   pay and rewards   264–265
   performance management
      265–266, *266*
   preparation for expatriation   263
   recruitment and selection   262–263
   repatriation   266–267, **297**
   scenario-based activity   269–270
   transfer of HRM practices
      259–261, *260*
international integration   261, **296**
International Labour Organisation
   (ILO)   86, 223, 276, 289
international recruitment   43, **296**
interviews
   behavioural-based   50, 63
   competency-based   50, **293**
   exit   76
   expatriates   262
   feedforward   132
   performance appraisal   122, 126,
      130–132, 266, **297**
   return to work   241
   selection   49–52, 262
   situational-based   50–51
   strengths-based   51, 132
intrinsic motivating factors   128

job adverts   43, 44, 109
job analysis   39, *40*, 149, **296**
job descriptions   39, *40*, 149, **296**
job evaluation   148–151, *150, 151–152*,
   296
job instruction   178–179
job quality   86–88
job redesign   134
job security   146–147, 189, 199, 200
job strain   238–239
Jobs, Steve   75

kaleidoscope careers   188, 190, 193,
   196, **296**
key performers   *29*, 30, **296**
Klopp, Jurgen   32
knowledge management
   systems   171
knowledge workers   5, **296**

labour inspectorate services   92
labour market, job quality   86–88

labour markets
   employee turnover and   72–73, 74
   graduates and   197–198
   labour costs and   152–153
   polarisation   86
   upgrading   86
   workforce planning and   24–25
labour rights abuses   274, 276–277,
   278, 285–286
language skills   105, 262
language training   263
law *see* employment legislation
leaderless group discussions   53
lean manufacturing   3–4
learning, defined   166–167, **296**
learning and development   164–184
   ADDIE model   170, 173–181, *175*
   analysis of needs   175–176, *176–177*
   behaviourism   168, **293**
   case studies   70–71, 171–172
   coaching   134, 178
   cognitivism   168, **293**
   defined   166–167, **294, 296**
   delivery methods   178–179
   designing   177–179
   developing content and
      materials   179
   evaluation   180–181, *181–182*
   expatriates   263
   experiential learning   168–169,
      169, **294**
   health and safety   229
   implementation   179–180
   job instruction   178–179
   key concepts   166–167
   key trends   174
   language training   263
   learning methods   179, *180*
   learning organization model   170,
      172–173, *173*, **298**
   learning styles   170
   mentoring   68, 178, 201, 202, **296**
   performance management
      and   122, 125–126, 134
   planned work experience   179
   scenario-based activity   183–184
   strategic HRD model   170–171
   underperformers   134
learning culture   171
learning organization model   170,
   172–173, *173*, **298**
lectures   *180*
legislation *see* employment legislation
liberal market economies (LMEs)   259
life span theory   189
line managers   8, 13, **296**
   employee induction   65, 70

line managers (*cont.*)
  employee wellbeing and   231, 244
  employment legislation   85
  sickness absence management   242
  underperformance
     management   133–135
Liverpool Football Club   32
lone parents   108
long-term sickness absence   241–242
longitudinal studies   61, **296**
L'Oréal   279
low-involvement HRM   17, **296**

manual handling   234
Marks & Spencer   275
Marx, Karl   81
Marxism   81
masculinity versus femininity   259
Maslow, Abraham   157
maternity leave   108, 144, *145*
Mayo, Elton   4
McDonald's   18
mediation services   91–92
mental models   173
mental workload   235, **296**
mentees   68, **296**
mentoring   68, 178, 201, 202, **296**
mentors   68, **296**
Merck   278
merit pay   142
Michigan model   14, *15*
Microsoft   44, 102, 134, 165
Microsoft Excel   213
migrant workers   105
minimum wage   84, 153
MNCs *see* multinational corporations
  (MNCs)
mobile learning   174
motivation
  learning and   168
  pay and rewards and   156–157
  performance management
    and   122, 123
  see also employee engagement
multi-stakeholder perspective   170
multicultural employees   114
multinational corporations (MNCs)
  defined   254
  globalization and   258
  performance management   133
  reward management   142
  talent management   30
  see also international human
    resource management (IHRM)
mutual gains   242, *243*

national competitiveness   171–172
national culture
  cultural dimensions   6, 259
  international human resource
    management (IHRM) and   259
  pay and rewards and   209
  performance management and   133
  recruitment and   55–56
  selection interviews and   50
  talent management and   30
natural wastage *see* employee turnover
needs, levels of   157
NEETs (not in education, employment
  or training)   105
negligence   248
negotiation   92–94
Netflix   18
Nike   277, 282, 285–286
Nitaqat programme, Saudi Arabia   41,
  56
nominal variables   213
non-analytical methods   149–150,
  150, *151*, **296**
non-union employee representation
  (NER)   84, 88
nonfinancial rewards   128, *141*,
  146–147, **296**
nongovernmental organizations
  (NGOs)   274, 285, 286, **296**

objectives and key results
  (OKRs)   132
Occupational Personality
  Questionnaire (OPQ)   52
Occupational Safety and Health
  Administration (OSHA), USA   246
Occupy movement   281
OECD   85, 86, 91, 105, 109, 197
off-ramp careers   190, 193–195, *196*,
  296
older workers   102–103, 106, 110, 114
onboarding   66–69, *69*, **296**
one-to-one interviews   49
online screening   43, 46
open communication   244
ordinal variables   213
organization-specific benefits   *141*,
  144–145
organizational citizenship
  behaviours   69, **296**
organizational culture   7, 8, 30
  employee satisfaction and   94–95

learning culture   171
  safety culture   222–223, **297**
organizational fit   46–47, 62–63, 64,
  188, **296**
organizational integrity   62
organizational socialization   66–69, *69*
outsourcing   261

paired comparison method of job
  evaluation   149–150, *150*, *151*
panel interviews   49
parent country nationals (PCNs)   *256*
parental leave   *145*
Paris Climate Agreement   276
part-time work   86, 195
participation, employee   89, 91
paternalistic management   81
paternity leave   23, *145*
Pavlov, Ivan   168
pay and rewards   140–161
  advantages and disadvantages   *146*
  balanced sheet approach   265
  base pay   141, *146*, **293**
  bonuses   143, 158–161
  case study   153–154
  commission   143
  costs   141, 144, *146*, 152–156
  direct pay   141–144, *141*, **294**
  employee share ownership plans
    (ESOPs)   143–144, *146*
  environmental factors   152–153
  ethnicity pay gap   147, 148
  expatriates   264–265
  external comparisons   148,
    154–156, *157*, **294**
  felt-fair concept   148–149, **295**
  flexible benefits   18, **295**
  gainsharing schemes   144, *146*
  gender pay gap   107, 147–148, 212
  going rate approach   265
  health and safety and   223, 230
  indirect pay   3, 85, *141*, 144–145, **295**
  information sources and   155–156,
    157
  internal alignment   148–151, *148*,
    296
  job evaluation   148–151, *150*,
    151–152, **296**
  living wage   153–154
  merit pay   142
  minimum wage   84, 153
  motivation and   156–157
  national culture and   209
  nonfinancial rewards   128, *141*,
    146–147

organization-specific benefits *141*, 144–145
pay secrecy policies 147
performance management and 128
performance-related pay (PRP) 128, *141*–144, *141*, *146*, 209, **297**
piecework schemes 143
premium pay 141
profit-sharing schemes 143, *146*
retention and 18, 72–73
reward packages 140–147, *141*, *146*, 265, **297**
reward systems 140, **297**
scenario-based activity 158–161
statutory benefits *141*, 144, *145*
team-based pay 143, *146*
total reward approach 128, 146–147
pensions 145
performance appraisal 122, 126, 130–132, 266, **297**
performance management 122–136, **297**
  case study 129
  competency-based assessment 128
  conceptual models 124–125
  defined 122
  employee engagement and 125–126
  expatriates 265–266, *266*
  fairness 125
  feedback 123, 125, 130
  feedforward interviews 132
  metrics and techniques 126–128, *126*, *127*
  national culture and 133
  performance appraisal 122, 126, 130–132, 266, **297**
  pitfalls 129–132
  principles 122–123
  rating 126, *126*, 130–131
  reward and 128
  scenario-based activity 135–136
  strategic 122, 124, **298**
  theoretical perspectives 123–124
  underperformance management 133–135
performance-related pay (PRP) 128, *141*–144, *141*, *146*, 209, **297**
person–job fit 46–47, **297**
person–organization fit 46–47, 62–63, 64, 188, **297**
person specifications 39, *40*, **297**
personal mastery 172–173
personality testing 46, 52
personnel management (PM) 4, 5, 10
Peter Principle 74

philanthropy 278, **297**
Piaget, Jean 168
piecework schemes 143
planned work experience 179
planning *see* workforce planning
pluralism 81
point methods of job evaluation 150–151, *152*
polarisation 86
portfolio careers 188, 195–196, *196*, **297**
positive action 114–115, **297**
positive discrimination 114, **297**
post-offer stage 54
potential/performance matrix *29*
poverty 104
power 80
power distance 6, 259
precarious employment 86
predictive analytics *210*
premium pay 141
preparation for expatriation 263
prescriptive analytics *210*
presenteeism 242
PricewaterhouseCoopers (PwC) 30, 155, 283
Primark 277, 283
privacy 231
private health insurance 144–145
procedural justice 125
profit-sharing schemes 143, *146*
projection error 51
projects 179
promotion 24, 31, 74–75
protean careers 188, 190, 191–192, *196*, 203, **297**
protected grounds 108, **297**
PRP *see* performance-related pay (PRP)
psychological contracts 86, 199–200, **297**
psychometric testing 52
pull factors 71, **297**
push factors 71–72, **297**

 Q
Quakers 3, 278, 279
quality of jobs 86–88

 R
R Project 213
Rana Plaza, Bangladesh 278, 289
ranking in performance appraisal 127, *127*
ranking method of job evaluation 148, 149, *151*
rating in performance appraisal 126, *126*, 130–131

recency effect 130
recognition policies and practices 128, 147
recruitment 39–45
  application forms 45
  case study 48–49
  CVs/résumés 45
  diversity 46
  e-recruitment 43, **294**
  employee referrals 42
  employer brand and 44
  expatriates 262–263
  external 31, 42, 44, **294**
  formal and informal methods 40–41
  graduate 34–35, 42
  internal 31, 41, 44, **296**
  international 43, **296**
  job adverts 43, 44, 109
  job analysis 39, *40*, **296**
  national culture and 55–56
  online screening 43, 46
  person specifications 39, *40*, **297**
  post-offer stage 54
  recruitment consultancies 42
  retention strategy 62–63
  scenario-based activities 34–35, 55–56
  shortlisting 43, 45–46, *45*, **297**
  strategic approach 38, *38*
  talent 31
  see also selection
recruitment consultancies 42
referrals, employee 42
relational approach to induction 67–69, *69*, **297**
relational psychological contracts 199–200, **297**
reliability **297**
  of selection methods 48
repatriation 266–267, **297**
reporting systems, health and safety 223, 230
reputational damage 274, 277–279, 283
retention 60–61, 62–63, **297**
  benefits and 18, 72–73
  rural doctors 63
  scenario-based activity 77
retirement age 102, 113
return to work interviews 241
reward packages 140–147, *141*, *146*, 265, **297**
reward systems 140, **297**
rewards *see* pay and rewards
right to disconnect 241
Rio Tinto 231
risk 229, **297**

river blindness 278
Rockefeller, John D. 278, 279
Roddick, Anita 278
role-play *180*
rotational assignments *269*
Ryanair 14

safety culture 222–223, **297**
safety statements 247
Saudi Arabia 41, 55–56
scientific management 3–4
secrecy, pay 147
segmentation 261
selection 46–55
  assessment centres 52–53, *53*, 263
  case study 48–49
  defined 38, **297**
  employment legislation 54
  equality in 46, 47, 54
  expatriates 262–263
  final decision-making 54–55
  graphology 53
  interviews 49–52, 262
  method choice 47–48
  monitoring success 55
  online screening 43, 46
  personality testing 46, 52
  post-offer stage 54
  psychometric testing 52
  retention strategy 62–63
  shortlisting 43, 45–46, *45*, **297**
  strategic approach 38, *38*
  work sample tests 52, 53
self-actualization 157
self-directedness 188
self-efficacy 123, 125, 134, **297**
self-employment 86
self-esteem 130
Senge, Peter 172–173
SHAPE framework *244*
shareholder view of the firm 279, 280, **297**
shop stewards 82
short-term international assignments *268*
shortlisting 43, 45–46, *45*, **297**
shortlisting matrix 45–46, *45*, 54, **297**
sickness absence 241–242, 248–250
sickness days 145
Silver Human Resource Centres 102–103
similar-to-me effect 131
situational-based interviews 50–51
Sixteen Personality Factor Questionnaire 52

skewing bias 131
skills
  employability 198
  language 105, 262
  negotiation 92–94
  see also learning and development
slavery 279, 289
SMART goals 123, 134
Smith, Adam 280
social attitudes and norms 106
social contract 280–281, **297**
social inclusion 104, **298**
social insurance 144, 153
social justice perspective 101, 113–114, **298**
social learning tools 174
social networking sites 41, 43, 48–49
social responsibility *see* corporate social responsibility (CSR)
socialization, organizational 66–69, *69*
socially responsible investment (SRI) 284, **298**
soft approach 7, 14–15
software packages 213
Southwest Airlines 14
SPSS package 213
stakeholder view of the firm 279, 280–282, **298**
  business case arguments 281–282
  social contract arguments 280–281
stakeholders **298**
Standard Oil 278, 279
standardization 261
star employees *see* HIPOs (high-potential employees)
Starbucks 285
statutory benefits *141*, 144, *145*
stereotyping 51, 131
stocktaking 23, **298**
strategic human resource development (SHRD) 170–171, **298**
strategic human resource management (SHRM) 6–13, *8*, *10*, 246, **298**
strategic performance management 122, 124, **298**
strength-based interviews 51, 132
stress 64–65, 110, 130, 234, 237–238, *238*, **298**
strikes 90, *90*, **298**
structured interviews 49–52
succession planning 24, 31, 74–75
survival curve 64–65, **298**
survivor guilt 73
Sustainable Development Goals (SDGs) 274, 276

sustainable HRM 282, **298**
systems thinking 172

talent management 26–33, *26*
  Brexit and 257–258
  case studies 32, 257–258
  debates *27–28*
  identifying talent 29–31, *29*
  recruiting talent 31
  scenario-based activity 34–35
  strategy 31–33, *33*
tangible benefits 60–61, **298**
taxation policy 153
Taylor, Frederick 3
Taylorism 3, **298**
team-based pay 143, *146*
team learning 173
teamwork 122
technology-delivered instruction 178
telephone interviews 49
Tesco 276, 282
third country nationals (TCNs) *256*
total reward approach 128, 146–147
trade unions 4, 5, 81, 82–83, 86, 153, **298**
  confederations of 82
  corporate social responsibility and 274, 276, 289
  declining unionization 5, 83, *83*
  density 83, *83*, **298**
  employment legislation and 84–85
traditional careers 189, *189*, **298**
train-the-trainer activities 180
training
  case studies 70–71, 171–172
  defined 166, **298**
  health and safety 229
  performance management and 122, 125–126, 134
  underperformers 134
  see also learning and development
transactional psychological contracts 199, 200, **298**
tribunals 91, 110
Troika 85
turnover *see* employee turnover

Uber 87–88
uncertainty avoidance 259
underperformance management 133–135
underperformers *29*, 30, 73, 133–135, **298**

INDEX

unemployment   5, 85, 104, 105, 197
union density   83, *83*, **298**
unions *see* trade unions
unitarism   7, 81
universal approach   14–15
universalist approach   17
unstructured interviews   49–50
untapped potentials   *29*, 30, **298**
upgrading   86
upward appraisal   127–128

valence   123
validity   **298**
   of selection methods   48
variables   212, **299**
   binary   213
   categorical   212–213
   continuous   213
   nominal   213
   ordinal   213

varieties of capitalism (VoC)
   framework   259
vertical integration   8, **299**
victimization   110, **299**
video interviews   49
video learning   *180*
vigour   61
Virgin   18, 23
Volkswagen   282
VRIO model   5

Walmart   284, 285
welfare movement   3
women
   career development   193–195
   see also gender
work capacity   235, **299**
work engagement   61–62, **299**
work–life balance policies   71,
   147, 195

work on demand via apps   87–88
work sample tests   52, 53
workaholism   240
workforce planning   22–26, **299**
   action planning   25, **293**
   forecasting   24–25, **295**
   stocktaking   23, **298**
   see also talent management
working conditions in supply
   chain 274, 276–277, 278,
   285–286
working days lost   90, *90*, **299**
working hours debate   245
works councils   84, 89, **299**

Yerkes-Dodson principle   238, *238*

zero hours contracts   86, **299**